Zondervan Illustrated Bible Backgrounds Commentary

Volume 2

Joshua, Judges, Ruth, 1 & 2 Samuel

Contributors to Volume 2

General Editor • **John H. Walton** (PhD, Hebrew Union College), Professor of Old Testament, Wheaton College and Graduate School, Wheaton, Illinois

Joshua • **Richard S. Hess** (PhD, Hebrew Union College), Earl S. Kalland Professor of Old Testament and Semitic Languages, Denver Seminary, Denver, Colorado

Judges • **Daniel I. Block** (DPhil, University of Liverpool), Gunther H. Knoedler Professor of Old Testament, Wheaton College and Graduate School, Wheaton, Illinois

Ruth • **Dale W. Manor** (PhD, University of Arizona), Professor of Archaeology and Bible, Harding University, Searcy, Arkansas

1 and 2 Samuel • **V. Philips Long** (PhD, Cambridge University), Professor of Old Testament, Regent College, Vancouver, British Columbia, Canada

Zondervan Illustrated Bible Backgrounds Commentary

Volume 2

Joshua, Judges, Ruth, 1 & 2 Samuel

John H. Walton

GENERAL EDITOR

ZONDERVAN ACADEMIC

ZONDERVAN ACADEMIC

Joshua, Judges, Ruth, 1 and 2 Samuel

Requests for information should be addressed to:
Zondervan, 3900 *Sparks Dr. SE, Grand Rapids, Michigan 49546*

Library of Congress Cataloging-in-Publication Data

Joshua, Judges, Ruth, 1 & 2 Samuel / John H. Walton, general editor.
p. cm.—(Zondervan illustrated Bible backgrounds commentary ; v. 2)
Includes index.
ISBN 978-0-310-25574-1 (hardcover, printed)
1. Bible. O.T. Joshua—Commentaries. 2. Bible. O.T. Judges—Commentaries. 3. Bible. O.T. Ruth—Commentaries. 4. Bible. O.T. Samuel—Commentaries. I. Walton, John H., 1952-
BS1295.53.J68 2009
222'.07—dc22 2009005116

Interior design: Mark Sheeres

Printed in the United States of America

---

23 24 25 26 27 28 29 30 31 32 33 /TRM/ 24 23 22 21 20 19 18 17 16 15 14 13 12 11 10 9 8 7 6

Table of Contents

Acknowledgments vi
Methodology viii
General Bibliography xv
Abbreviations. xviii

Joshua 2
Richard S. Hess

Judges 94
Daniel I. Block

Ruth 242
Dale W. Manor

1 Samuel 266
V. Philips Long

2 Samuel 412
V. Philips Long

Picture Index 493

Acknowledgments

We are grateful for so many who have provided us photographs, some at reduced prices and others free of charge, to help make this work a visual resource on the ancient world. Credits appear by each photograph, but we would especially recognize the following:

Wikimedia Commons makes photographs available through commons.wikimedia.org under a variety of licenses. We have benefited greatly from those that have been released into public domain and have sought out appropriate permission for those that have creative commons licensing (cc-by or cc-by-sa). These photographs are not copyright protected in this set but are available for use under the same terms that we used them.

In connection to Wikimedia, we have used a number of photographs from the Yorck Project, whose images are indicated as being in the public domain, but with compilation protected under the GNU Free Documentation License.

We would like especially to thank Marie-Lan Nguyen, who provided so many photos in public domain on Wikimedia, as well as Rama, who even went and took specific photos that we wanted. Others who provided numerous photographs through Wikimedia include Guillaume Blanchard and Keith Schengili-Roberts.

We are grateful to so many who posted their photographs on Flickr and made them available to us when we requested them. Lenka Peacock, Manfred Nader, and Peter White were particularly generous and gracious as they allowed us to use many of their photographs.

The Schøyen Collection supplied many photographs at no charge, and we are grateful to Elizabeth Sorenssen for her capable help.

Edward Loring, Research Fellow and Network Administrator Russian Academy of Sciences Centre for Egyptological Studies, Moscow (CESRAS), Russian Institute of Egyptology in Cairo (RIEC), provided photographs we could not have otherwise gotten.

Photography Suppliers were very helpful in our endless searches for photographs and we would especially like to acknowledge Todd Bolen (www.bibleplaces.com), Zev Radovan (www.biblelandpictures.com), Art Resource (www.artres.com, with thanks to Ann and Jennifer), Werner Forman (www.werner-forman-archive.com, with thanks to Themis), Jim Martin (see photo credits on page xxvii), Jack Hazut (www.israelimage.net), Richard Cleave (Rohr Productions), and Neal Bierling (www.phoenixdatasystems.com).

Thanks also to my colleagues who provided photographs: Fred Mabie, Steven Voth, John Monson, Jim Monson, Rami Arav, Scott Noegel, Aren Maier, Daniel Master, the Leon Levy Foundation, Alan Millard, Stephen Bourke, Constance Gane, and Randall Younker.

We are also grateful to those who supplied photographs from their personal collections: Michael Greenhalgh, Tim Bulkeley (eBibleTools.com/israel), Caryn Reeder,

Christina Beblavi, Lisa Jean Winbolt, Brian McMorrow, Kim Walton, David Hall, and the late Maurice Thompson (photographer of the Bible Scene Set), his sons Peter and Andrew, and Geoff Tucker, who scanned the slides for us.

Our gratitude also goes to Patti Ricotta, who provided helpful financing for Song of Songs pictures.

For artwork we are grateful to Susanna Vagt, Alva Steffler, and Jonathan Walton.

For help with the maps, we are most grateful to Carl Rasmussen, the author of the *Zondervan NIV Atlas of the Bible*.

Thanks also goes to Charlie Trimm for the preparation of the visuals index.

We would like to thank the always helpful staff at Zondervan whose hard work made this project possible: Katya Covrett, Verlyn Verbrugge, and Kim Zeilstra deserve special mention, as well as Jack Kuhatschek, who got the project started while he was still at Zondervan.

Finally, my entire family was involved in the project. Jill and Josh provided photos and Jonathan provided artwork. But far beyond those contributions, words cannot express the gratitude I owe to my wife, Kim, who for three years served as my research assistant in tracking down pictures with her consummate research skills. Without her perseverance, creativity, and companionship, the product here provided could not have been achieved. Through countless hours working by my side, going through the manuscript entry by entry to decide what visuals to provide and then painstakingly researching where they could be found, she became expert in iconography and art from the ancient world. But more than that, she stepped into my world as a cherished partner in my work and ministry, making every day "a day for a daydream." To her these volumes are dedicated with love, respect, and admiration.

John H. Walton
General Editor

Methodology: An Introductory Essay

John H. Walton

Comparative Studies

For over a century, studies comparing the OT and the ancient Near East have hovered on the fringe of hermeneutics and exegesis. Since these studies were at times exploited by critical scholars for polemical attacks against the biblical text, evangelicals were long inclined to avoid or even vilify them. They viewed the idea that the OT borrowed or adapted ancient Near Eastern ideas or literature as incompatible with Scripture's inspiration. Even as evangelicals in recent decades have grown more interested in tapping into the gold mine of comparative data, the results have often been considered tangential to the ultimate theological task. The influence from the ancient world has been identified with all that Israel was supposed to reject as they received the revelation from God that would purge their worldview from its pagan characteristics. Comparative studies served only as a foil to the theological interpretation of the text.

Consequently, comparative studies have been viewed as a component of historical-critical analysis at best, and more often as a threat to the uniqueness of the literature of the Bible. In contrast, today more and more biblical scholars are exploring the positive uses of comparative studies. As a result of half a century of the persistent scholarship of Assyriologists, Hittitologists, Egyptologists, and Sumerologists, we are now in a position to add significant nuances to the paradigms for studying the impact of the ancient Near East on the authors and editors of the Hebrew Bible. The end result is a more thorough and comprehensive understanding of the text.

Ever since the discovery of the Babylonian flood and creation accounts, critical scholarship has been attempting to demonstrate that the OT is derivative literature, a disadvantaged step-sister to the dominant cultures of the ancient Near East. These scholars have attempted to reduce the OT to converted mythology, whose dependency exposes its humanity. For confessing orthodoxy, however, there is no room for the conclusion that the OT is man-made theology. If the Flood is simply a human legend invented by people and borrowed into Israelite thinking, if the covenant is merely Israel's way of expressing their optimism that God has specially favored them through a treaty agreement with them, if the prophets never heard the voice of God but simply mimicked their ancient Near Eastern counterparts, then Christians are greatly to be pitied for having been duped in what would have to be considered the greatest hoax in history. It is no surprise, then, that evangelicals have often rejected the claims of these critical schools of thought.

There is, however, nothing inherently damaging to orthodox theology and beliefs about the Bible *if its authors were interacting at various levels with the literature current in the culture.* All literature is dependent on the culture in which it arises—it must be, if it intends to communicate effectively. Even when a text engages in polemic and correction of culture, it must be aware of and interact with current thinking and literature.

If we think about the example of creation texts, we realize that if God were to reveal his work of creation in our modern culture, he would have to explain how it related to the Big Bang theory or to evolution. His revelation would focus on the origins of the physical structure of the universe because that is what is important in our cultural perspective. In the ancient world, though, physical structure was relatively insignificant. People at that time were much more interested in the aspect of bringing order out of chaos and the divine exercise of jurisdiction demonstrated in giving everything a role and a purpose. In this context, any account of origins would of necessity have to be presented with these ancient ideas in mind.

The biblical text, in other words, formulated its discussion in relation to the thinking found in the ancient literature. It should be no surprise, then, if areas of similarity are found. This is far different from the contention that Israelite literature is simply derivative mythology. There is a great distance between borrowing from a particular piece of literature (as has been claimed in critical circles) and resonating with the larger culture that has itself been influenced by its literatures. When Americans speak of the philosophy of "eat, drink, and be merry, for tomorrow we die," they are resonating with an idea that has penetrated society rather than borrowing from the writings of Epicurus.

Another area where we must be sensitive to cultural issues is in the way we understand literary genres. It should be no surprise that OT genres need to be compared to genres in the larger culture. Whether we are looking at wisdom literature, hymnic literature, historical literature, or legal literature, we find generous doses of both similarities and differences. Understanding the genre of a piece of literature is necessary if we desire to perceive the author's intentions. Since perceiving such intentions is essential to our theological interpretation of a text, we recognize that understanding genre contributes to legitimate theological interpretation. Some genres will operate differently in the ancient world than they do in our own culture, so we must become familiar with the mechanics of the genres represented in the ancient Near East.

Where there are similarities, they help us to understand the genre parameters and characteristics as they existed in the ancient mind. What defined historical writing in the ancient world? How close was it to the journalistic approach of today, which relies heavily on eyewitness accounts? How did genealogies function in OT times? Were they compiled for the same purpose that we compile them for?

Occasionally comparisons within genres reveal close similarities between the biblical and ancient Near Eastern literatures on the level of content. Such similarities do not jeopardize inspiration. Even if the OT had the very same law or the very same proverb that was found in the ancient Near East, inspiration would be involved in the author choosing to incorporate that law or proverb into the canonical collection and to nuance it properly in appropriate context.

Where there are differences, it is still important to understand the ancient Near Eastern genres because the theological points will often be made by means of contrast. The theology behind the book of Job, for example, is built primarily on the distinctives of the ancient Near Eastern view (represented in the arguments of Job's friends), which was based on an appeasement mentality. The book's message is accomplished in counterpoint. If we are unaware of the contrasts, we will miss some of the nuances.

In fact, then, we must go beyond the simple identification of similarities and differences to articulate the relationships on a functional level. Similarities could exist because Israel adapted something from ancient Near Eastern culture or literature, or, as previously mentioned, because they simply resonated with the culture. Differences could reflect the Israelites' rejection of the ancient Near Eastern perspective, or they might emerge in explicit Israelite polemics against the views of their neighbors. In all such cases, the theology of the text may be nuanced by the cultural context.

In light of all of this, it may be logically concluded that without the guidance of comparative studies, we are bound to misinterpret the text at some points. A text is a complex of ideas linked by threads of writing. Each phrase and each word communicates by the ideas and thoughts that they will trigger in the reader or hearer. We can then speak of these underlying ideas as gaps that need to be filled with meaning by the audience. The writer or speaker assumes that those gaps will be filled in particular ways based on the common worldview he shares with his audience. Interpreters have the task of filling in those gaps, and when interpreting authoritative texts, it is theologically essential that we fill them appropriately.

For example, the Tower of Babel is described as being built "with its head in the heavens." Without the benefit of ancient Near Eastern backgrounds, early interpreters were inclined to provide the theological explanation that the builders were trying to build a structure that would allow them to launch an attack on the heavens. Comparative studies have allowed modern interpreters to recognize that this is an expression used to describe the ziggurats of Mesopotamia, which were intended to serve as a bridge or portal between heavens and earth. Such an understanding leads to an alternative, and arguably more accurate, interpretation of the text. In conclusion, then, as our interpretation of the text requires us to fill in the gaps, we have to be careful to consider the option of filling those gaps from the cultural context before we leap to fill them with theological significance.

As we make this transition in our thinking, we must expand the focus of our comparative studies. Too often in the past, comparative studies have been limited either to individual features (e.g., birds sent out from the ark) or to the literary preservation of traditions (e.g., creation accounts, vassal treaties) and have been conducted with either apologetics (from confessional circles) or polemics (against confessional traditions) in mind. As those interested in the interpretation of the text, we should recognize in addition the importance of comparative studies that focus on conceptual issues, conducted with illumination of the cultural dynamics behind the text in mind.

We can now create a spectrum to define the varieties of differences and similarities that can classify these nuances. The spectrum extends from differences to similarities while the matrix takes account of three categories: individual elements, worldview concepts, and literary preservation. This is represented in the following chart:

Relationships	Elements	Concepts	Literature
Totally ignores and presents different view	Sexual activity of gods	Theogony	Apotropaic rituals
Hazy familiarity leading to caricature and ridicule	Napping gods	Making of idols	Tammuz literature
Accurate knowledge resulting in rejection	Monogenesis/ polygenesis	Divine needs	Omen texts
Disagreement resulting in polemics, debate, or contention	Ziggurats	Theomachy; Flood	Cosmology texts
Awareness leading to adaptation or transformation	Circumcision	Kingship ideology; Classical prophecy	Words of the wise; Song of Songs
Conscious imitation or borrowing	Covenant-treaty format	Calf/bull image	Psalm 29
Subconscious shared heritage	Use of lots	Netherworld conditions; temple ideology	Proverbs

In conclusion, there are ten important principles that must be kept in mind when doing comparative studies:

1. Both similarities and differences must be considered.
2. Similarities may suggest a common cultural heritage rather than borrowing.
3. It is common to find similarities at the surface but differences at the conceptual level and vice versa.
4. All elements must be understood in their own context as accurately as possible before crosscultural comparisons are made.
5. Proximity in time, geography, and spheres of cultural contact all increase the possibility of interaction leading to influence.
6. A case for literary borrowing requires identification of likely channels of transmission.
7. The significance of differences between two pieces of literature is minimized if the works are not the same genre.
8. Similar functions may be performed by different genres in different cultures.
9. When literary or cultural elements are borrowed, they may in turn be transformed into something quite different.
10. A single culture will rarely be monolithic, either in a contemporary cross-section or in consideration of a passage of time.[1]

Successful interpreters must try to understand the cultural background of the ancient Near East just as successful missionaries must learn the culture, language, and worldview of the people they are trying to reach. This is the rationale for us to study the Bible in light of the ancient Near East. What we contend, then, is that comparative studies has three goals in mind:

1. We study the *history* of the ancient Near East as a means of recovering knowledge of the events that shaped the lives of people in the ancient world.
2. We study *archaeology* as a means of recovering the lifestyle reflected in the material culture of the ancient world.
3. We study the *literature* of the ancient Near East as a means of penetrating the heart and soul of the people who inhabited the ancient world that Israel shared.

These goals are at the heart of comparative studies and will help us understand the OT better.

Comparative Studies and Historical Literature

Cultural studies from the ancient Near East can provide much information to fill in the background of the second and first millennia B.C. Royal inscriptions are particularly helpful as we try to reconstruct the political events that impacted the lives of the peoples of this period. Some actually refer to Israel or to various kings of Israel.[2] Others give information about kings who interacted with Israel on various levels. Archaeological excavations help to reconstruct the daily life of the people.[3] Biblical genres such as genealogies[4] or conquest accounts[5] can be explored profitably in relation to genres in the ancient Near East. Others try to establish lines of comparison between sections of the OT and ancient Near Eastern literary works such as the Middle Assyrian Epic of Tukulti-Ninurta.[6]

Beyond the reconstruction of the events of ancient history and the study of the genres in which history is recorded, comparative studies can also help us to penetrate how people in the ancient world thought about history and what their values were in recording it.[7] Studies in ancient historiography help us to assess how to read the literature in a way that will honor the ideas, intentions, and values of the authors. Some of the conclusions from this sort of study alert us to important differences between the ancient and modern worlds. We learn that while our historians often ignore deity altogether, one of the main values of history writing in the ancient world was to clarify what the gods were doing. Modern historians often consider texts that focus on divine activity in history to be unreliable sources; ancient historians would consider modern history books that give no room for divine activity as trivial and irrelevant.

This radical difference can be explained when we understand that ancient historians were not recording events as much as they were interpreting outcomes. The truth of what "really happened" was not assessed by what the eyewitness saw but by what the final outcome was. As a result, they did not promote the role of the eyewitness as our history writing tends to do. Instead, the various subgenres of historiography promoted various people or ideas. Royal inscriptions characteristically promoted the king as they articulated what the gods were doing through his kingship. Biblical historiography often promoted the prophetic role to articulate what Yahweh was doing, particularly with regard to the covenant. This general survey indicates just a few of the ways that comparative and cultural studies will be seen to impact and illuminate our study of the historical literature in this volume.

Bibliography on Comparative Studies Methodology

Finkelstein, J. J. "Bible and Babel: A Comparative Study of the Hebrew and Babylonian Religious Spirit." Pages 355–80 in *Essential Papers on Israel and the Ancient Near East,* ed. F. E. Greenspahn. New York: New York Univ. Press, 1991.

Hallo, W. W. "New Moons and Sabbaths: A Case Study in the Contrastive Approach." *HUCA* 48 (1977): 1–18.

_____. "Biblical History in Its Near Eastern Setting: The Contextual Approach." Pages 1–26 in *Scripture in Context,* ed. C. Evans, et al. Pittsburgh: Pickwick, 1980.

_____. "Compare and Contrast: The Contextual Approach to Biblical Literature." Pages 1–19 in *The Bible In Light of Cuneiform Literature: Scripture in Context III,* ed. W. W. Hallo, B. Jones, and G. Mattingly. Lewiston, NY: Edwin Mellen, 1990.

Huffmon, H. B. "Babel und Bibel: The Encounter between Babylon and the Bible." Pages 309–20 in *The Bible and Its Traditions,* ed. M. P. O'Connor and D. N. Freedman. Ann Arbor: Univ. of Michigan Press, 1983.

Loewenstamm, S. E. "Biblical Studies in the Light of Akkadian Texts." Pages 256–67 in *From Babylon to Canaan.* Jerusalem: Magnes, 1992.

Longman, Tremper III. *Fictional Akkadian Autobiography.* Winona Lake: Eisenbrauns, 1991.

Machinist, P. "The Question of Distinctiveness in Ancient Israel." Pages 420–42 in *Essential Papers on Israel and the Ancient Near East,* ed. F. E. Greenspahn. New York: New York Univ. Press, 1991.

Malamat, A. "The Proto-History of Israel: A Study in Method." Pages 303–13 in *The Word of the Lord Shall Go Forth,* ed. C. L. Meyers and M. O'Connor. Winona Lake: Eisenbrauns: 1983.

Malul, M. *The Comparative Method in Ancient Near Eastern and Biblical Legal Studies,* AOAT 227. Kevelaer: Butzon und Bercker; Neukirchen-Vluyn: Neukirchener, 1990.

Millard, A. R. "Methods of Studying the Patriarchal Narratives As Ancient Texts." Pages 35–51 in *Essays on the Patriarchal Narratives,* ed. A. R. Millard and D. J. Wiseman. Winona Lake: Eisenbrauns, 1983.

Ringgren, H. "The Impact of the Ancient Near East on the Israelite Tradition." Pages 31–46 in *Tradition and Theology in the Old Testament,* ed. D. A. Knight. Sheffield: Sheffield Academic Press, 1977/1990.

Roberts, J. J. M. "The Ancient Near Eastern Environment." Pages 3–43 in *The Bible and the Ancient Near East.* Winona Lake: Eisenbrauns, 2002.

_____. "The Bible and the Literature of the Ancient Near East." Pages 44–58 in *The Bible and the Ancient Near East.* Winona Lake: Eisenbrauns, 2002.

_____. "Myth Versus History: Relaying the Comparative Foundations." *CBQ* 38 (1976): 1–13.

Rodriguez, A. M. "Ancient Near Eastern Parallels to the Bible and the Question of Revelation and Inspiration." *Journal of the Adventist Theological Society* 12 (2001): 43–64.

Saggs, H. W. F. *The Encounter with the Divine in Mesopotamia and Israel.* London: Athlone, 1978.

Selman, M. J. "Comparative Customs and the Patriarchal Age." Pages 93–138 in *Essays on the Patriarchal Narratives*, ed. A. R. Millard and D. J. Wiseman. Winona Lake: Eisenbrauns, 1983.

Talmon, S. "The Comparative Method in Biblical Interpretation: Principles and Problems." *VTSup* 29 (1977): 320–56.

Tigay, J. "On Evaluating Claims of Literary Borrowing." Pages 250–55 in *The Tablet and the Scroll*, ed. M. Cohen et al. Bethesda: CDL, 1993.

Toorn, K. van der. *Sin and Sanction in Israel and Mesopotamia*. Assen: Van Gorcum, 1985.

Notes

1. J. Walton, "Cultural Background of the Old Testament," in *Foundations for Biblical Interpretation*, ed. D. Dockery, K. Mathews, and R. Sloan (Nashville: Broadman & Holman, 1994), 256. See also J. Tigay, "On Evaluating Claims of Literary Borrowing," in *The Tablet and the Scroll*, ed. M. Cohen et al. (Bethesda, MD: CDL, 1993), 250–55.
2. A. R. Millard, "Israelite and Aramaean History in the Light of Inscriptions," *TynBul* 41 (1990): 261–75.
3. R. Averbeck, M. Chavalas, and D. Weisberg. *Life and Culture in the Ancient Near East* (Bethesda, MD: CDL, 2003); P. J. King and L. Stager. *Life in Biblical Israel* (Louisville: Westminster John Knox, 2002).
4. R. R. Wilson. *Genealogy and History in the Biblical World* (New Haven, CT: Yale Univ. Press, 1977).
5. K. L. Younger, *Ancient Conquest Accounts* (Sheffield: Sheffield Academic, 1990).
6. P. Machinist, "Literature As Politics: The Tukulti-Ninurta Epic and the Bible," *CBQ* 38 (1976): 455–82; H. Tadmor, "Autobiographical Apology in the Royal Assyrian Literature," in *History, Historiography and Interpretation*, ed. H. Tadmor and M. Weinfeld (Jerusalem: Magnes, 1983), 36–57.
7. T. Abusch, et al., *Historiography in the Cuneiform World* (RAI XLV, Part 1; Bethesda, MD: CDL, 2001); B. Albrektson, *History and the Gods* (Lund: Gleerup, 1967); David Damrosch, *The Narrative Covenant: Transformations of Genre in the Growth of Biblical Literature* (San Francisco: Harper and Row, 1987); J. J. Finkelstein, "Mesopotamian Historiography," *Proceedings of the American Philosophical Society* 107 (1963): 461–72; A. K. Grayson, "Assyria and Babylonia," *Or* 49 (1980): 140–94; Harry A. Hoffner, "Histories and Historians of the Ancient Near East: The Hittites," *Or* 49 (1980): 283–332; W. G. Lambert, "Destiny and Divine Intervention in Babylon and Israel," *OtSt* 17 (1972): 65–72; V. P. Long, "History and Fiction: What Is History?" in *Israel's Past in Present Research*, ed. V. P. Long (Winona Lake: Eisenbrauns, 1999), 232–54; idem, *The Art of History* (Grand Rapids: Zondervan, 1994); idem, "Historiography of the Old Testament," in *The Face of the Old Testament*, ed. D. W. Baker and B. T. Arnold (Grand Rapids: Baker, 1999), 145–75; A. Malamat, "Doctrines of Causality in Hittite and Biblical Historiography: A Parallel," *VT* 5 (1955): 1–12; P. Michalowski, "Commemoration, Writing, and Genre in Ancient Mesopotamia," in *The Limits of Historiography*, ed. C. S. Kraus (Leiden: Brill, 1999), 69–90; I. Provan, V. P. Long, and T. Longman III, *A Biblical History of Israel* (Louisville: Westminster John Knox, 2003); H. W. F. Saggs, *The Encounter with the Divine in Mesopotamia and Israel* (London: Athlone, 1978), 64–92; H. Tadmor and M. Weinfeld, *History, Historiography and Interpretation* (Jerusalem: Magnes, 1984); J. Van Seters, *In Search of History* (New Haven, CT: Yale Univ. Press, 1983; K. L. Younger, *Ancient Conquest Accounts* (Sheffield: Sheffield Academic, 1990); Z. Zevit, *The Religions of Ancient Israel* (New York: Continuum, 2001), 27–80.

General Bibliography

Reference

Anchor Bible Dictionary. Ed. D. N. Freedman. New York: Doubleday, 1992.

Ancient Near East in Pictures. Ed. J. B. Pritchard. Princeton: Princeton Univ. Press, 1954.

Cambridge Ancient History. Ed. J. Boardman et. al. Cambridge: Cambridge Univ. Press, 1970–.

Civilizations of the Ancient Near East. Ed. J. Sasson. New York: Scribners, 1995.

Companion to the Ancient Near East. Ed. Daniel Snell. Oxford: Blackwell, 2005.

Dictionary of Deities and Demons in the Bible. Ed. K. van der Toorn et al. Leiden: Brill, 1995.

Dictionary of the Ancient Near East. Ed. P. Bienkowski and A. R. Millard. Philadelphia: Univ. of Pennsylvania Press, 2000.

Handbook to Life in Ancient Mesopotamia. Ed. S. Bertman. New York: Facts on File, 2003.

IVP Dictionaries of the Old Testament. Downers Grove, Ill.: InterVarsity Press, 2003–.

New Encyclopedia of Archaeological Excavations in the Holy Land. Ed. E. Stern. New York: Simon and Schuster, 1993.

Oxford Encyclopedia of Ancient Egypt. Ed. D. B. Redford. New York: Oxford Univ. Press, 2001.

Oxford Encyclopedia of Archaeology in the Near East. Ed. E. M. Meyers. New York: Oxford Univ. Press, 1997.

Tübinger Bibelatlas. Ed. S. Mittmann and G. Schmitt. Stuttgart: Deutsche Bibelgesellschaft, 2001.

Theological Dictionary of the Old Testament. Ed. G. J. Botterweck and H. Ringgren. Trans. J. T. Willis, et al. Grand Rapids: Eerdmans, 1974–.

Views of the Biblical World. Ed. B. Mazar. Jerusalem: International, 1959.

World History of the Jewish People. Ed. B. Mazar. Jerusalem: Massada, 1963–1979.

Translations of Texts

Amarna Letters. W. L. Moran. Baltimore: Johns Hopkins Univ. Press, 1992.

Ancient Egyptian Literature. 3 vols. M. Lichtheim. Berkeley: Univ. of California Press, 1973–80.

The Ancient Near East: Historical Sources in Translation. Ed. M. Chavalas. Oxford: Blackwell, 2006.

Ancient Near Eastern Texts. Ed. J. B. Pritchard. Princeton: Princeton Univ. Press, 1969.

Babylonian Gilgamesh Epic. 2 vols. A. R. George. Oxford: Oxford Univ. Press, 2003.

Babylonian Wisdom Literature. W. G. Lambert. Oxford: Clarendon, 1960.

Before the Muses. Ed. B. Foster. 3rd ed. Bethesda, Md.: CDL, 2005.

The Context of Scripture. 3 vols. Ed. W. W. Hallo and K. L. Younger. Leiden: Brill, 1997.

Harps That Once . . . T. Jacobsen. New Haven, Conn.: Yale Univ. Press, 1987.

Literature of Ancient Sumer. J. Black et al. Oxford: Oxford Univ. Press, 2004 (see www-etcsl.orient.ox.ac.uk).

Myths of Mesopotamia. Ed. S. Dalley. New York: Oxford Univ. Press, 1991.

Near Eastern Religious Texts Relating to the Old Testament. Ed. W. Beyerlin. Philadelphia: Westminster, 1978.

Old Testament Parallels. Ed. V. Matthews and D. Benjamin. 2nd ed. New York: Paulist, 1997.

Proverbs of Ancient Sumer. 2 vols. B. Alster. Bethesda, Md.: CDL, 1997.

Readings from the Ancient Near East. Ed. B. Arnold and B. Beyer. Grand Rapids: Baker, 2002.

SBL Writings from the Ancient World Series. Ed. T. Lewis. Atlanta: SBL, 1990–.

SBLWAW 2: H. A. Hoffner. *Hittite Myths*.

SBLWAW 4: J. M. Lindenberger. *Ancient Aramaic and Hebrew Letters*.

SBLWAW 6: M. Roth. *Law Collections from Mesopotamia and Asia Minor.*

SBLWAW 7: G. Beckman. *Hittite Diplomatic Texts*.

SBLWAW 9: S. Parker. *Ugaritic Narrative Poetry*.

SBLWAW 11: I. Singer. *Hittite Prayers*.

SBLWAW 12: M. Nissinen. *Prophets and Prophecy in the Ancient Near East*.

SBLWAW 16: N. C. Strudwick. *Texts from the Pyramid Age*.

SBLWAW 19: J.-J. Glassner. *Mesopotamian Chronicles*.

SBLWAW 20: H. Vanstiphout. *Epics of Sumerian Kings: The Matter of Aratta*.

SBLWAW 23: J. P. Allen. *The Ancient Egyptian Pyramid Texts*.

Wisdom of Ancient Sumer. B. Alster. Bethesda, Md.: CDL, 2005.

Books on Bible Backgrounds

Assmann, J. *The Search for God in Ancient Egypt*. Ithaca, N.Y.: Cornell Univ. Press, 2001.

Baines, J., and J. Málek. *Atlas of Ancient Egypt*. New York: Facts on File, 1980.

Bottéro, J. *Religion in Ancient Mesopotamia*. Chicago: Univ. of Chicago Press, 2001.

_____. *Everyday Life in Ancient Mesopotamia*. Baltimore: Johns Hopkins Univ. Press, 2001.

Braun, J. *Music in Ancient Israel/Palestine*. Grand Rapids: Eerdmans, 2002.

Bryce, T. *The Kingdom of the Hittites*. New York: Oxford Univ. Press, 1998.

Coogan, M. D. *The Oxford History of the Biblical World*. New York: Oxford Univ. Press, 1998.

Day, J. *Yahweh and the Gods and Goddesses of Canaan*. Sheffield: Sheffield Academic Press, 2000.

Dearman, A. *Religion and Culture in Ancient Israel*. Peabody, Mass.: Hendrickson, 1992.

Dorsey, D. A. *The Roads and Highways of Ancient Israel*. Baltimore: Johns Hopkins Univ. Press, 1991.

Forbes, R. J. *Studies in Ancient Technology*. 9 vols. Leiden: Brill, 1964–.

Frankfort, H., et al. *The Intellectual Adventure of Ancient Man*. Chicago: Univ. of Chicago Press, 1946.

Green, A. R. W. *The Storm-God in the Ancient Near East*. Winona Lake, Ind.: Eisenbrauns, 2003.

Hoerth, A. *Archaeology and the Old Testament*. Grand Rapids: Baker, 1998.

Hoerth, A., G. Mattingly, and E. Yamauchi. *Peoples of the Old Testament World*. Grand Rapids: Baker, 1994.

Jacobsen, T. *Treasures of Darkness*. New Haven, Conn.: Yale Univ. Press, 1976.

Keel, O. *The Symbolism of the Biblical World*. New York: Seabury, 1978.

Keel, O., and C. Uehlinger. *Gods, Goddesses and Images of God in Ancient Israel*. Minneapolis: Fortress, 1998.

King, P., and L. Stager. *Life in Biblical Israel*. Louisville: Westminster John Knox, 2002.

Kitchen, K. A. *On the Reliability of the Old Testament*. Grand Rapids: Eerdmans, 2003.

Kuhrt, A. *The Ancient Near East, 3000–330 B.C.* London: Routledge, 1997.

Marsman, H. J. *Women in Ugarit and Israel.* Leiden: Brill, 2003.

Matthews, Victor. *Manners and Customs in the Bible.* Peabody, Mass.: Hendrickson, 1988.

Matthews, V., and D. Benjamin. *The Social World of the Old Testament.* Peabody, Mass.: Hendrickson, 1993.

Mazar, A. *Archaeology of the Land of the Bible.* New York: Doubleday, 1990.

Miller, J. M., and J. Hayes. *A History of Ancient Israel and Judah.* Philadelphia: Westminster, 1986.

Miller, P. D. *The Religion of Ancient Israel.* Louisville: Westminster John Knox, 2000.

Moorey, P. R. S. *Ancient Mesopotamian Materials and Industries.* Winona Lake, Ind.: Eisenbrauns, 1999.

Morenz, S. *Egyptian Religion.* Ithaca, N.Y.: Cornell Univ. Press, 1973.

Nakhai, B. A. *Archaeology and the Religions of Canaan and Israel.* Boston: ASOR, 2001.

Nemet-Nejat, K. R. *Daily Life in Ancient Mesopotamia.* Westport, Conn.: Greenwood, 1998.

Olmo Lete, G., del. *Canaanite Religion.* Winona Lake, Ind.: Eisenbrauns, 2004.

Provan, I, V. P. Long, and T. Longman. *A Biblical History of Israel.* Louisville: Westminster John Knox, 2003.

Rainey, A., and R. S. Notley. *The Sacred Bridge.* Jerusalem: Carta, 2006.

Redford, D. B. *Egypt, Canaan, and Israel in Ancient Times.* Princeton: Princeton Univ. Press, 1992.

Roaf, M. *Cultural Atlas of Mesopotamia and the Ancient Near East.* New York: Facts on File, 1990.

Saggs, H. W. F. *The Greatness That Was Babylon.* New York: Mentor, 1962.

_____. *Encounter with the Divine in Mesopotamia and Israel.* London: Athlone, 1978.

_____. *The Might That Was Assyria.* London: Sidgwick & Jackson, 1984.

Snell, D. *Life in the Ancient Near East.* New Haven, Conn.: Yale Univ. Press, 1997.

Sparks, K. L. *Ancient Texts for the Study of the Hebrew Bible.* Peabody, Mass.: Hendrickson, 2005.

Stern, E. *Archaeology of the Land of the Bible,* Vol. 2. New York: Doubleday, 2001.

Thompson, J. A. *Handbook of Life in Bible Times.* Downers Grove, Ill.: InterVarsity Press, 1986.

Toorn, K. van der. *Family Religion in Babylonia, Syria and Israel: Continuity and Change in the Forms of Religious Life.* Leiden: Brill, 1996.

Van de Mieroop, M. *The Ancient Mesopotamian City.* New York: Oxford Univ. Press, 1999.

_____. *Cuneiform Texts and the Writing of History.* London: Routledge, 1999.

_____. *A History of the Ancient Near East: ca. 3000–323 B.C.* London: Blackwell, 2003.

Walton, J. H. *Ancient Israelite Literature in Its Cultural Context.* Grand Rapids: Zondervan, 1989.

_____. *Ancient Near Eastern Thought and the Old Testament: Introducing the Conceptual World of the Hebrew Bible.* Grand Rapids: Baker, 2006.

Walton, J. H., V. Matthews, and M. Chavalas. *IVP Bible Background Commentary: Old Testament.* Downers Grove, Ill.: InterVarsity Press, 2000.

Westbrook, R. *A History of Ancient Near Eastern Law.* 2 vols. Leiden: Brill, 2003.

Wiseman, D. J. *Peoples of Old Testament Times.* Oxford: Clarendon, 1973.

Yadin, Y. *The Art of Warfare in Biblical Lands.* London: Weidenfeld & Nicolson, 1963.

Yamauchi, E. *Persia and the Bible.* Grand Rapids: Baker, 1990.

Zevit, Z. *Religions of Ancient Israel.* New York: Continuum, 2001.

Abbreviations

AAA . . . . *Annals of Archaeology and Anthropology*
AASOR . . . . Annual of the American Schools of Oriental Research
AB . . . . Anchor Bible
AB . . . . *Assyriologische Bibliothek*
ABC . . . . *Assyrian and Babylonian Chronicles*. A. K. Grayson. TCS 5. Locust Valley, New York, 1975
ABD . . . . *Anchor Bible Dictionary*. D. N. Freedman. 6 vols. New York, 1992
ABL . . . . *Assyrian and Babylonian Letters Belonging to the Kouyunjik Collections of the British Museum*. R. F. Harper. 14 vols. Chicago, 1892–1914
ABR . . . . *Australian Biblical Review*
ABRL . . . . . . Anchor Bible Reference Library
AbrN . . . . *Abr-Nahrain*
ABS . . . . Arab Background Series
ACCS . . . . . . Ancient Christian Commentary on Scripture
ACEBT . . . . . *Amsterdamse Cahiers voor Exegese en bijbelse Theologie*
ADD . . . . *Assyrian Deeds and Documents*. C. H. W. Johns. 4 vols. Cambridge, 1898–1923
AEL . . . . *Ancient Egyptian Literature*. M. Lichtheim. 3 vols. Berkeley, 1971–1980
AfO . . . . *Archiv für Orientforschung*
AfOB . . . . . . Archiv für Orientforschung: Beiheft
ÄgAbh. . . . . . Ägyptologische Abhandlungen
AHw . . . . *Akkadisches Handwörterbuch*. W. von Soden. 3 vols. Wiesbaden, 1965–81
AJA . . . . *American Journal of Archeology*
AJBA . . . . . . *Australian Journal of Biblical Archaeology*
AJSLL . . . . . . *American Journal of Semitic Languages and Literature*
AMD. . . . . . . Ancient Magic and Divination
AnBib . . . . . . Analecta biblica
ANEP . . . . . . *The Ancient Near East in Pictures Relating to the Old Testament*. J. B. Pritchard. Princeton, 1954
ANET . . . . . . *Ancient Near Eastern Texts Relating to the Old Testament*. J. B. Pritchard. 3rd ed. Princeton, 1969
ANF . . . . *Ante-Nicene Fathers*
AnOr . . . . . . Analecta orientalia
AnSt. . . . . *Anatolian Studies*
AO. . . . . Antiquités orientales
AO. . . . . *Der Alte Orient*
AOAT . . . . . . Alter Orient und Altes Testament
AOB . . . . *Altorientalische Bilder zum Alten Testament*
AOS . . . . American Oriental Series
AOTC . . . . . . Abingdon Old Testament Commentary
AOTS . . . . . . *Archaeology and Old Testament Study*. D. W. Thomas. Oxford, 1967
APOT . . . . . . *Apocrypha and Pseudepigrapha of the Old Testament*. Ed. R. H. Charles. 2 vols. Oxford: Oxford University Press, 1913
ARAB . . . . . . *Ancient Records of Assyria and Babylonia*. Daniel David Luckenbill. 2 vols. Chicago, 1926–1927
Arch . . . . *Archaeology*
ARI . . . . *Assyrian Royal Inscriptions*. A. K. Grayson. 2 vols. RANE. Wiesbaden, 1972–1976
ARM . . . . . . Archives royales de Mari
ARMT . . . . . Archives royales de Mari, transcrite et traduite
ArtH . . . . *Art History*

ARW . . . . *Archiv für Religionswissenschaft*
AS . . . . Assyriological Studies
ASJ . . . . *Acta Sumerologica (Japan)*
ASOR . . . . . . American Schools of Oriental Research
ASORDS . . . American Schools of Oriental Research Dissertation Series
ASTI . . . . *Annual of the Swedish Theological Institute*
ATJ . . . . *Ashland Theological Journal*
AThR . . . . . . *Anglican Theological Review*
ATSDS . . . . . Andrews Theological Seminary Dissertation Series
AuOr . . . . . . *Aula orientalis*
AUSDS . . . . . Andrews University Seminary Dissertation Series
AUSS. . . . . . . *Andrews University Seminary Studies*
AUU . . . . Acta Universitatis Upsaliensis
BA . . . . *Biblical Archaeologist*
BAIAS . . . . . *Bulletin of the Anglo-Israel Archeological Society*
BAR . . . . *Biblical Archaeology Review*
BARead . . . . *Biblical Archaeologist Reader*
BASOR . . . . . *Bulletin of the American Schools of Oriental Research*
BASORSup . . Bulletin of the American Schools of Oriental Research: Supplement Series
BAW . . . . Bayerischen Akademie der Wissen
BBB . . . . Bonner biblische Beiträge
BBET. . . . . . . Beiträge zur biblischen Exegese und Theologie
BBR . . . . *Bulletin for Biblical Research*
BBVO . . . . . . Berliner Beiträge zum Vorderen Orient
BCOTWP . . . Baker Commentary on the Old Testament Wisdom and Psalms
BDB. . . . . Brown, F., S. R. Driver, and C. A. Briggs. *A Hebrew and English Lexicon of the Old Testament.* Oxford, 1907
BeO . . . . *Bibbia e oriente*
BES . . . . *Bes*
BETL. . . . . . . Bibliotheca epheremeridum theologicarum lovaniensium
BETS . . . . *Bulletin of the Evangelical Society*
BHH . . . . *Biblisch-historisches Handwörterbuch.* B. Reicke and L. Rost. Göttingen, 1962-1966
Bib . . . . *Biblica*
BibOr . . . . . . Biblica et orientalia
BibSem . . . . . Biblical Seminar
BibRes . . . . . . *Biblical Research*
BiOr. . . . . *Biblioteca Orientalis*
BJRL . . . . *Bulletin of the John Rylands University Library of Manchester*
BJS . . . . Brown Judaic Studies
BM. . . . . British Museum
BN . . . . *Biblische Notizen*
BO. . . . . *Bibliotheca orientalis*
BR . . . . *Biblical Research*
BRev . . . . *Bible Review*
BRM . . . . Babylonian Religion and Mythology
BSac . . . . *Bibliotheca sacra*
BSC. . . . . Bible Student's Commentary
BSOAS . . . . . *Bulletin of the School of Oriental and African Studies*
BT . . . . *Bible Translator*
BTB . . . . *Biblical Theology Bulletin*
BWL . . . . *Babylonian Wisdom Literature.* W. G. Lambert. Oxford, 1960; reprinted Eisenbrauns, 1996
BZ . . . . *Biblische Zeitschrift*
BZABR . . . . . Beihefte zur Zeitschrift für altorientalische und biblische Rechtsgeschichte
BZAW . . . . . Beihefte zur Zeitschrift für die alttestamentliche Wissenschaft
CAD . . . . *The Assyrian Dictionary of the Oriental Institute of the University of Chicago.* Chicago, 1956–
CAH . . . . *Cambridge Ancient History*
CahRB. . . . . . Cahiers de la Revue biblique
CANE. . . . . . *Civilizations of the Ancient Near East.* J. Sasson. 4 vols. New York, 1995
CAT. . . . . Commentaire de l'Ancien Testament

CAT. . . . . . . *Cuneiform Alphabetic Texts from Ugarit, Ras Ibn Hani and Other Places*. M. Dietrich, O. Loretz, and J. Sanmartin. Munster, 1997
CBC . . . . Cambridge Bible Commentary
CBET . . . . . . Contributions to Biblical Exegesis and Theology
CBQ . . . . *Catholic Biblical Quarterly*
CBQMS . . . . Catholic Biblical Quarterly Monograph Series
CH. . . . . Code of Hammurabi
CHANE . . . . Culture and History of the Ancient Near East
CHI . . . . Cambridge History of Iran. 7 vols. 1968-91
CIS . . . . Corpus inscriptionum semiticarum
CIS . . . . *Corpus inscriptionum semiticarum*
CJ . . . . *Classical Journal*
CL . . . . Code of Lipit-Ishtar
CML . . . . *Canaanite Myths and Legends*. G. R. Driver. Edinburgh, 1956. J. C. L. Gibson, 1978[2]
CNI . . . . Carsten Niebuhr Institute
ConBOT . . . . Coniectanea biblica: Old Testament Series
COS . . . . *The Context of Scripture*. W. W. Hallo. 3 vols. Leiden, 1997–2002
CT . . . . *Cuneiform Texts from Babylonian Tablets in the British Museum*
CTA . . . . *Corpus des tablettes en cunéiformes alphabétiques découvertes à Ras Shamra-Ugarit de 1929 à 1939*. A. Herdner. Mission de Ras Shamra 10. Paris, 1963
CTH . . . . Catalogue des textes hittites
CTU . . . . *The Cuneiform Alphabetic Texts from Ugarit, Ras Ibn Hani, and Other Places*. M. Dietrich, O. Loretz, and J. Sanmartín. Münster, 1995
CU. . . . . Code of Ur-Nammu
CurTM. . . . . *Currents in Theology and Mission*
DANE . . . . . . *Dictionary of the Ancient Near East*
DBAT . . . . . . *Dielheimer Blätter zum Alten Testament*
DBI . . . . *Dictionary of Biblical Imagery*. T. Longman and L. Ryken. Downers Grove, 1998
DCH . . . . *Dictionary of Classical Hebrew*. D. J. A. Clines. Sheffield, 1993–
DDD . . . . *Dictionary of Deities and Demons in the Bible*. K. van der Toorn, B. Becking, and P. W. van der Horst. Leiden, 1995. 2nd ed., Grand Rapids, 1998
DISO . . . . . . Dictionnaire des inscriptions sémitiques de l'ouest. Ch. F. Jean and J. Hoftijzer. Leiden, 1965
DNWSI. . . . . Dictionary of the North-West Semitic Inscriptions. J. Hoftijzer and K. Jongeling. 2 vols. Leiden, 1995
DOTHB . . . . *Dictionary of the Old Testament: Historical Books*
DOTP . . . . . . *Dictionary of the Old Testament: Pentateuch*. T. D. Alexander and D. W. Baker. Downers Grove, 2003
DOTT . . . . . . *Documents from Old Testament Times*. D. W. Thomas, London, 1958
DSB . . . . Daily Study Bible
EA . . . . El-Amarna tablets. According to the edition of J. A. Knudtzon. *Die el-Amarna-Tafeln*. Leipzig, 1908–1915. Reprint, Aalen, 1964. Continued in A. F. Rainey, *El-Amarna Tablets, 359–379*. 2nd revised ed. Kevelaer, 1978
EA . . . . *Epigraphica anatolica*
EAEHL . . . . Encyclopedia of Archaeological Excavations in the Holy Land. M. Avi-Yonah. 4 vols. Jerusalem, 1975

EBC . . . . *Expositor's Bible Commentary*
ECC. . . . . Eerdmans Critical Commentary
EPRO . . . . . . Études préliminaires aux religions orientales
ErIsr . . . . *Eretz-Israel*
ET . . . . *Evangelische Theologie*
ETS . . . . Evangelical Theological Society
ETSS . . . . Evangelical Theological Society Studies
EvQ . . . . *Evangelical Quarterly*
EvTh. . . . . *Evangelische Theologie*
FAOS. . . . . . . Freiburger altorientalische Studien
FAT . . . . Forschungen zum Alten Testament
FB . . . . Forschungen zur Bibel
FCI . . . . Foundations in Contemporary Interpretation
FOTL . . . . . . Forms of the Old Testament Literature
GKC . . . . *Gesenius' Hebrew Grammar.* E. Kautzsch. Translated by A. E. Cowley. 2nd ed. Oxford, 1910
GM . . . . *Göttinger Miszellen*
GTTOT . . . . *The Geographical and Topographical Texts of the Old Testament.* J. J. Simons. Studia Francisci Scholten memoriae dicata 2. Leiden, 1959
HALOT . . . . *The Hebrew and Aramaic Lexicon of the Old Testament.* L. Koehler, W. Baumgartner, and J. J. Stamm. Translated and edited under the supervision of M. E. J. Richardson. 4 vols. Leiden, 1994–1999
HANEL. . . . . *History of Ancient Near Eastern Law.* R. Westbrook. 2 vols. Leiden, 2003
HAR . . . . *Hebrew Annual Review*
HAT . . . . Handbuch zum Alten Testament
HBD . . . . *HarperCollins Bible Dictionary*
HBS. . . . . Herders Biblische Studien
HCOT. . . . . . Historical Commentary on the Old Testament
HDR . . . . Harvard Dissertations in Religion
HKM. . . . . . . *Hethitische Keilschrifttafeln aus Masat.* Ed. Sedat Alp. Ankara: Turk Tarih Kurumu Basimevi, 1991
HL. . . . . Hittite Laws
HO . . . . Handbuch der Orientalistik
HS . . . . *Hebrew Studies*
HSM . . . . Harvard Semitic Monographs
HSS . . . . Harvard Semitic Studies
HTR . . . . *Harvard Theological Review*
HUCA . . . . . *Hebrew Union College Annual*
IB . . . . *Interpreter's Bible.* G. A. Buttrick et al. 12 vols. New York, 1951–1957
IBC . . . . Interpretation Bible Commentary
IBD . . . . *Illustrated Bible Dictionary.* J. Douglas. 3 vols. Leicester, 1980
IBHS . . . . *An Introduction to Biblical Hebrew Syntax.* B. K. Waltke and M. O'Connor. Winona Lake, 1990
ICC . . . . International Critical Commentary
IDB . . . . *The Interpreter's Dictionary of the Bible.* G. A. Buttrick. 4 vols. Nashville, 1962
IDBSup . . . . . *The Interpreter's Dictionary of the Bible: Supplementary Volume.* K. Crim. Nashville, 1976
IEJ . . . . *Israel Exploration Journal*
IOS . . . . *Israel Oriental Society*
IrAnt . . . . *Iranica Antiqua*
Iraq . . . . *Iraq*
IRT . . . . Issues in Religion and Theology
ISBE . . . . *International Standard Bible Encyclopedia.* G. W. Bromiley. 4 vols. Grand Rapids, 1979–1988
IVPBBC-OT . *IVP Bible Background Commentary on the OT.* J. H. Walton, V. H. Matthews, and M. W. Chavalas. Downers Grove, 2000

JAGNES . . . . *Journal of the Association of Graduate Near Eastern Studies* (University of Berkeley)
JANESCU . . *Journal of the Ancient Near Eastern Society of Columbia University*
JAOS . . . . . . Journal of the American Oriental Society
JB . . . . Jerusalem Bible
JBL . . . . *Journal of Biblical Literature*
JCS . . . . *Journal of Cuneiform Studies*
JDS . . . . Judean Desert Studies
JEA . . . . *Journal of Egyptian Archaeology*
JEOL . . . . . . *Jaarbericht van het Vooraziatisch-Egyptisch Gezelschap (Genootschap) Ex oriente lux*
JESHO . . . . . *Journal of the Economic and Social History of the Orient*
JETS . . . . *Journal of the Evangelical Theological Society*
JJS . . . . *Journal of Jewish Studies*
JNES . . . . *Journal of Near Eastern Studies*
JNSL . . . . *Journal of Northwest Semitic Languages*
JPS. . . . . Jewish Publication Society
JPSTC . . . . . . JPS Torah Commentary
JQR . . . . *Jewish Quarterly Review*
JR. . . . . *Journal of Religion*
JRAS . . . . *Journal of the Royal Asiatic Society*
JSem . . . . *Journal of Semitics*
JSJ . . . . *Journal for the Study of Judaism (in the Persian, Hellenistic, and Roman Periods)*
JSOT . . . . *Journal for the Study of the Old Testament*
JSOTSup . . . Journal for the Study of the Old Testament: Supplement Series
JSS . . . . *Journal of Semitic Studies*
JSSEA . . . . . . *Journal of the Society for the Study of Egyptian Antiquities*
JTS . . . . *Journal of Theological Studies*
KAH . . . . *Keilshrifttexte aus Assur historischen Inhalts*
KAI . . . . *Kanaanäische und aramäische Inschriften*. H. Donner and W. Röllig. 2nd ed. Wiesbaden, 1966–1969
KAR . . . . *Keilschrifttexte aus Assur religiösen Inhalts*. E. Ebeling. Leipzig, 1919–1923
KAT . . . . Kommentar zum Alten Testament
KBo . . . . *Keilschrifttexte aus Boghazköi*
KHC . . . . Kurzer Hand-Kommentar zum Alten Testament
KTU . . . . *Die keilalphabetischen Texte aus Ugarit*. M. Dietrich, O. Loretz, and J. Sanmartín. AOAT 24/1. Neukirchen-Vluyn, 1976. 2nd enlarged ed. of *KTU: The Cuneiform Alphabetic Texts from Ugarit, Ras Ibn Hani, and Other Places*. M. Dietrich, O. Loretz, and J. Sanmartín. Münster, 1995 (= *CTU*)
KUB . . . . *Keilschrifturkunden aus Boghazköi*
LAE. . . . . *Literature of Ancient Egypt*. W. K. Simpson. 3rd ed. New Haven, 2003
LAPO . . . . . . Litteratures anciennes du Proche-Orient
LBI. . . . . Library of Biblical Interpretation
LCL. . . . . Loeb Classical Library
LE . . . . Laws of Eshunna
Levant . . . . . . *Levant*
LH. . . . . Laws of Hammurabi
LIMC . . . . . . *Lexicon iconographicum mythologiae classicae*. Edited by H. C. Ackerman and J.-R. Gisler. 8 vols. Zurich, 1981–1997
LL . . . . Laws of Lipit-Ishtar
LU . . . . Laws of Ur-Nammu
LXX . . . . Septuagint
Maarav . . . . . *Maarav*
MAL . . . . Middle Assyrian Laws
MANE . . . . . Monographs of the Ancient Near East
MAOG . . . . . Mitteilungen der Altorientalischen Gesellschaft
MCAAS . . . . Memoires of the Connecticut Academy of Arts & Sciences

MARI . . . . . . *Mari: Annales de recherches interdisciplinaires*
MDOG . . . . Mitteilungen der Deutschen Orient-Gesellschaft
MGWJ . . . . . *Monatschrift für Geschichte und Wissenschaft des Judentums*
MOS . . . . Midden-Oosten Studies
MSJ . . . . *The Master's Seminary Journal*
Muses. . . . . . . *Before the Muses: An Anthology of Akkadian Literature.* Benjamin R. Foster. 2 vols. Bethesda, 1993
MVAG. . . . . . Mitteilungen der Vordersasiatisch-ägyptischen Gesellschaft. Vols. 1-44. 1896-1939
NAC . . . . New American Commentary
NBD . . . . *New Bible Dictionary.* J. D. Douglas and N. Hillyer. 2nd ed. Downers Grove, 1982
NBL. . . . . Neo-Babylonian Laws
NCB . . . . New Century Bible
NCBC . . . . . . New Century Bible Commentary
NEA . . . . *Near Eastern Archaeology*
NEAEHL . . . The New Encyclopedia of Archaeological Excavations in the Holy Land. E. Stern. 4 vols. Jerusalem, 1993
NEB. . . . . New English Bible
NERT . . . . . . *Near Eastern Religious Texts Relating to the Old Testament.* W. Beyerlin. OTL. London, 1978
NGTT . . . . . . *Nederduitse gereformeerde teologiese tydskrif*
NIBC. . . . . . . New International Bible Commentary
NIBCOT . . . New International Biblical Commentary on the Old Testament
NICOT . . . . . New International Commentary on the Old Testament
NIDBA . . . . . *New International Dictionary of Biblical Archaeology.* E. M. Blaiklock and R. K. Harrison. Grand Rapids, 1983
NIDOTTE . . *New International Dictionary of Old Testament Theology and Exegesis.* W. A. VanGemeren. 5 vols. Grand Rapids, 1997
NIV. . . . . New International Version
NIVAC . . . . . NIV Application Commentary
NJPS . . . . Tanakh: The Holy Scriptures: The New JPS Translation according to the Traditional Hebrew Text
NRSV . . . . New Revised Standard Version
NSBT. . . . . . . New Studies in Biblical Theology
NTOA. . . . . . Novum Testamentum et orbis antiquus
OBC . . . . Orientalia biblica et christiana
OBO . . . . Orbis biblicus et orientalis
OCD . . . . *Oxford Classical Dictionary.* S. Hornblower and A. Spawforth. 3rd ed. Oxford, 1996
OEAE . . . . . . *The Oxford Encyclopedia of Ancient Egypt.* D. Redford. 3 vols. New York, 2001
OEANE . . . . *The Oxford Encyclopedia of Archaeology in the Near East.* E. M. Meyers. 5 vols. New York, 1997
OIP . . . . Oriental Institute Publications
OLA . . . . Orientalia lovaniensia analecta
OLP . . . . Orientalia lovaniensia periodica
OLZ. . . . . *Orientalistische Literaturzeitung*
Or . . . . *Orientalia* (NS)
OrAnt . . . . . . *Oriens antiquus*
OS . . . . Oudtestamentische studiën
OTE. . . . . *Old Testament Essays*
OTG . . . . Old Testament Guides
OTL . . . . Old Testament Library
OTP. . . . . *Old Testament Pseudepigrapha.* J. H. Charlesworth. 2 vols. Garden City, 1983, 1985
OTS. . . . . Old Testament Studies

OTWSA . . . . Ou-Testamentiese Werkgemeenskap van Suid-Afrika
OtSt . . . . *Oudtestamentische Studiën*
PAPS . . . . Proceedings of the American Philosophical Society
PBS . . . . Publications of the Babylonian Section
PEQ . . . . *Palestine Exploration Quarterly*
POTT . . . . . . *Peoples of Old Testament Times*. D. J. Wiseman. Oxford, 1973
POTW. . . . . . *Peoples of the Old Testament World*. A. Hoerth, G. Mattingly and E. Yamauchi. Grand Rapids, 1994
PRU . . . . *Le palais royal d'Ugarit*
PT . . . . Pyramid Texts
RA . . . . *Revue d'assyriologie et d'archéologie orientale*
RAI . . . . Recontre assyriologique internationale
RANE . . . . . . Records of the Ancient Near East
RANE . . . . . . *Readings from the Ancient Near East*. B. Arnold and B. Beyer. Grand Rapids, 2002
RB . . . . *Revue biblique*
RevB . . . . *Revue de Qumran*
RevistB . . . . . *Revista bíblica*
RGG . . . . *Religion in Geschichte und Gegenwart*. K. Galling. 7 vols. 3rd ed. Tübingen, 1957-65
RHA . . . . *Revue hittite et asianique*
RHPR . . . . . . Revue d'Histoire et de Philosophie Religieuse
RHR . . . . *Revue de l'histoire des religions*
RIDA. . . . . . . *Revue internationale des droits de l'antiquité*
RIM . . . . The Royal Inscriptions of Mesopotamia Project. Toronto
RIMA . . . . . . The Royal Inscriptions of Mesopotamia, Assyrian Periods
RIMB . . . . . . The Royal Inscriptions of Mesopotamia, Babylonian Periods
RIME . . . . . . The Royal Inscriptions of Mesopotamia, Early Periods
RISA . . . . Royal Inscriptions of Sumer and Akkad. G. A. Barton. New Haven, 1929
RivB. . . . . *Rivista biblica italiana*
RlA . . . . *Reallexikon der Assyriologie*. Erich Ebeling et al. Berlin, 1928–
RQ. . . . . *Römische Quartalschrift für christliche Altertumskunde und Kirchengeschichte*
RS . . . . Ras Shamra
RSP . . . . *Ras Shamra Parallels*
SAA . . . . State Archives of Assyria
SAALT . . . . . State Archives of Assyria Literary Texts
SAAS . . . . . . State Archives of Assyria Studies
SAOC . . . . . . Studies in Ancient Oriental Civilizations
SBAB . . . . . . Stuttgarter biblische Aufsatzbände
SBAW . . . . . . Sitzungsberichte der bayerischen Akademie der Wissenschaften
SBB . . . . Stuttgarter biblische Beiträge
SBC . . . . Student Bible Commentary
SBFLA. . . . . . *Studii biblici Franciscani liber annus*
SBH. . . . . *Sumerische-babylonische Hymnen nach Thonafeln griechischer Zeit*. G. A. Reisner. Berlin, 1896
SBLABS . . . . Society of Biblical Literature Archaeology and Biblical Studies
SBLDS . . . . . Society of Biblical Literature Dissertation Series
SBLMS . . . . . Society of Biblical Literature Monograph Series
SBLRBS. . . . . Society of Biblical Literature Resources for Biblical Study
SBLSP . . . . . . *Society of Biblical Literature Seminar Papers*
SBLSymS . . . Society of Biblical Literature Symposium Series
SBLWAW . . . Society of Biblical Literature Writings from the Ancient World
SBONT . . . . . Sacred Books of the Old and New Testament

SBS . . . . Suttgarter Bibelstudien
SBT . . . . Studes in Biblical Theology
SBTS . . . . Sources for Biblical and Theological Study
SC . . . . Sources chrétiennes. Paris, 1943–
ScrHier . . . . . Scripta hierosolymitana
SDOAP . . . . . Studia et Documenta ad Iura Orientis Antiqui Pertinentia
SE . . . . Studies in Egyptology
SemeiaSt . . . . Semeia Studies
SHANE . . . . Studies in the History of the Ancient Near East
SHCANE . . . Studies in the History and Culture of the Ancient Near East
SHJPLI . . . . . Studies in the History of the Jewish People and the Land of Israel
SHR. . . . . Studies in the History of Religion
SJLA . . . . Studies in Judaism in Late Antiquity
SJOT . . . . *Scandinavian Journal of the Old Testament*
SNN . . . . Studia Semitica Neerlandica
SO . . . . Symbolae osloenses
SOTSMS. . . . Society for Old Testament Studies Monograph Series
SSI . . . . *Textbook of Syrian Semitic Inscriptions*. 3 vols. Oxford, 1971–82
SSN . . . . Studia semitica neerlandica
SSS . . . . Semitic Study Series
ST . . . . *Studia theologica*
StBoT. . . . . . . Studien zu den Boghazkoi Texten
StudOr . . . . . Studia orientalia
Sumer . . . . . . *Sumer: A Journal of Archaeology and History in Iraq*
SWBA . . . . . . Social World of Biblical Antiquity
Syr . . . . *Syria*
TA . . . . *Tel Avi*
TAD. . . . . *Textbook of Aramaic Documents*. B. Porten and A. Yardeni. 4 vols. Jerusalem, 1986-99
TAPS. . . . . . . Transactions of the American Philosophical Society
TB . . . . Theologische Bücherei
TBC. . . . . Texts from the Babylonian Collection (Yale)
TCL. . . . . Textes cunéiforms. Musée du Louvre
TCS . . . . Texts from Cuneiform Sources
TDOT . . . . . . *Theological Dictionary of the Old Testament*. G. J. Botterweck and H. Ringgren. Translated by J. T. Willis, G. W. Bromiley, and D. E. Green. 15 vols. Grand Rapids, 1974–
TGUOS. . . . . Transactions of the Glasgow University Oriental Society
Them . . . . *Themelios*
TJ. . . . . *Trinity Journal*
TLOT . . . . . . *Theological Lexicon of the Old Testament*. E. Jenni, with assistance from C. Westermann. Translated by M. E. Biddle. 3 vols. Peabody, Mass., 1997
TOB. . . . . *Traduction Oecuménique de la Bible*
TOTC . . . . . Tyndale Old Testament Commentaries
Transeu . . . . . *Transeuphratène*
TS . . . . *Theological Studies*
TSF Bulletin . *Theological Student's Fellowship Bulletin*
TSTT. . . . . . . Toronto Semitic Texts and Studies
TWOT . . . . . *Theological Wordbook of the Old Testament*. R. L. Harris, G. L. Archer Jr. 2 vols. Chicago, 1980
TynBul . . . . . *Tyndale Bulletin*
TZ . . . . *Theologische Zeitschrift*
UBL . . . . Ugaritisch-biblische Literatur
UCOP . . . . . . University of Cambridge Oriental Publications
UF . . . . *Ugarit-Forschungen*
UNP . . . . Ugaritic Narrative Poetry. Simon B. Parker. SBLWAW 9. Atlanta, 1997

UT . . . . *Ugaritic Textbook*. C. H. Gordon. AnOr 38. Rome, 1965
VAB. . . . . Vorderasiatische Bibliothek
VAT . . . . Vorderasiatische Abteilung Tontafel. Vorderasiatisches Museum, Berlin
VB . . . . Vorderasiatische Bibliothek
VT . . . . *Vetus Testamentum*
VTE. . . . . Vassal Treaties of Esarhaddon
VTSup . . . . . Vetus Testamentum Supplements
WBC . . . . . . Word Biblical Commentary
WHJP . . . . . . World History of the Jewish People
WO . . . . *Die Welt des Orients*
WOO . . . . . . Wiener Offene Oreintalistik
WTJ . . . . *Westminster Theological Journal*
WVDOG . . . Wissenschaftliche Veröffentlichungen der deutschen Orientgesellschaft
WZKM . . . . . *Wiener Zeitschrift für die Kunde des Morgenlandes*
YNER . . . . . . Yale New Eastern, Researches
YOS . . . . Yale Oriental Series, Texts
ZA . . . . *Zeitschrift für Assyriologie*
ZABR . . . . . . *Zeitschrift für altorientalische und biblische Rechtgeschichte*
ZÄS . . . . *Zeitschrift für ägyptische Sprache und Altertumskunde*
ZAW . . . . *Zeitschrift für die alttestamentliche Wissenschaft*
ZDMG . . . . . Zeitschrift der deutschen morgenländischen Gesellschaft
ZDPV . . . . . . *Zeitschrift des deutschen Palästina-Vereins*
ZKT. . . . . *Zeitschrift für katholische Theologie*
ZNW. . . . . . . Zeitschrift für die neutestamentliche Wissenschaft
ZPEB . . . . *Zondervan Pictorial Encyclopedia of the Bible*. M. C. Tenney. 5 vols. Grand Rapids, 1975
ZTK. . . . . *Zeitschrift für Theologie und Kirche*

Photo Credits

Credits to those providing special photographic permissions in the Martin Archive include:

Egypt

The Egyptian Ministry of Antiquities: (Cairo Museum, Elephantine Museum, Ismailiya Museum, Tombs of the Kings).

France

Musée du Louvre; Autorisation de photographer et de filmer–LOUVRE. Paris, France.

Israel

Collection of the Israel Museum, Jerusalem and courtesy of the Israel Antiquities Authority, Exhibited at the Israel Museum, Jerusalem.

Collection of the Israel Museum, Jerusalem and courtesy of the Israel Antiquities Authority, Exhibited at the Shrine of the Book, The Israel Museum, Jerusalem.

Collection of the Israel Museum, Jerusalem and courtesy of the Israel Antiquities Authority, Exhibited at the Rockefeller Museum, Jerusalem.

The Skirball Museum, Hebrew Union College–Jewish Institute of Religion. 13 King David Street. Jerusalem 94101.

Turkey

The Turkish Ministry of Antiquities: (Ankara Museum, Antalya Museum, Aphrodisias Museum, Ephesus Museum, Haytay Museum, Hierapolis Museum, Konya Museum, Manisa Museum, Istanbul Archaeological Museum).

United Kingdom

British Museum. London, England.

JOSHUA

by Richard S. Hess

River Jordan
Z. Radovan/www.BibleLandPictures.com
▲

Introduction

The book of Joshua is one of the most important books in the Bible for using historical and cultural background information in order to properly understand it. Two background areas are key for a proper understanding of the text: the historical and archaeological evidence concerning Palestine at the time of Israel's emergence in this Promised Land; and the overall literary form of the book in light of ancient Near Eastern genres of literature. Neither of these can be exhausted here, though I will attempt to cover the essential information.

Historical Background

The era of the exodus is normally dated to the Late Bronze Age, that is, between about 1550 B.C. and 1200 B.C., although many now date the end of the period a few decades into the twelfth century. It is preceded by the Middle Bronze Age (c. 2000–1550 B.C.) and followed by the Early Iron Age or Iron I, about 1200 to 1000 B.C. On the basis of most traditional analyses of biblical chronology, the Middle Bronze Age is the period of the patriarchs of Genesis 12–50 and Iron I ends about the time of David's reign. A more precise date for the events recorded in the book of Joshua depends on when one chooses to date the Exodus. Most of those scholars who accept some sort of historical exodus opt for one of two dates for the Exodus: either 1447 B.C. or during the (early) reign of Ramesses II (1279–1212 B.C.) in the first half of the thirteenth century B.C. The former is usually called the early date and the latter, the late date. Most of this commentary on Joshua will not be affected by the date chosen. But in order to fulfill the purpose of a section on historical background, some of the more salient points need to be reviewed.

The Bible may appear to settle the argument in favor of the early date in 1 Kings 6:1, where 480 years are assigned to the time between the Exodus and the dedication of the temple of Solomon. Because Egyptian

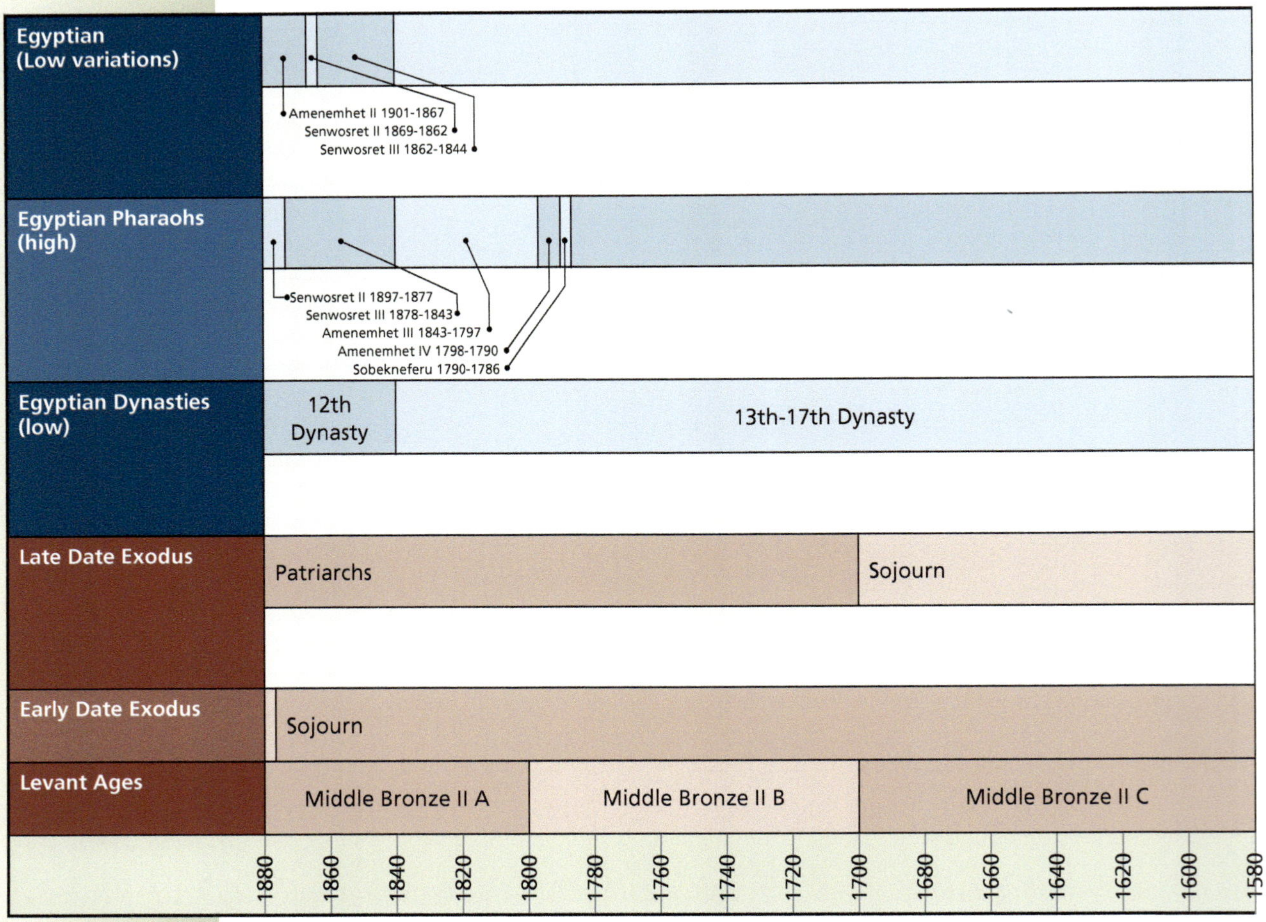

and Mesopotamian chronology schemes can be anchored to fixed astronomical events (such as an eclipse), absolute dating is possible and can be correlated with the scheme in the books of Kings. This allows for a calculation of Solomon's reign and, using the reference in 1 Kings 6:1, for the fixing of the date of the Exodus at 1447 B.C.

The chronological reference in Judges 11:26, which suggests three centuries between the desert wanderings and the time of Jephthah, may also be used.[1] However, the words of Jephthah, spoken for purposes of political expediency, need not be taken as reliable. Could 1 Kings be taken as other than a literal figure of nearly five centuries? The answer is yes. Already in Genesis 15:13–16 we see the equation of two terms, four hundred years and four generations. This alone indicates that these time statements can have different meanings than simply assigning a traditional literal interpretation. When applied to 1 Kings 6:1, it may be symbolic of twelve generations of forty years each, a complete number that could represent an equivalent distance between the Exodus and the dedication of the temple on the one hand, and between the dedication and the destruction of the temple on the other.

There are many pieces of evidence from the ancient Near Eastern records that would

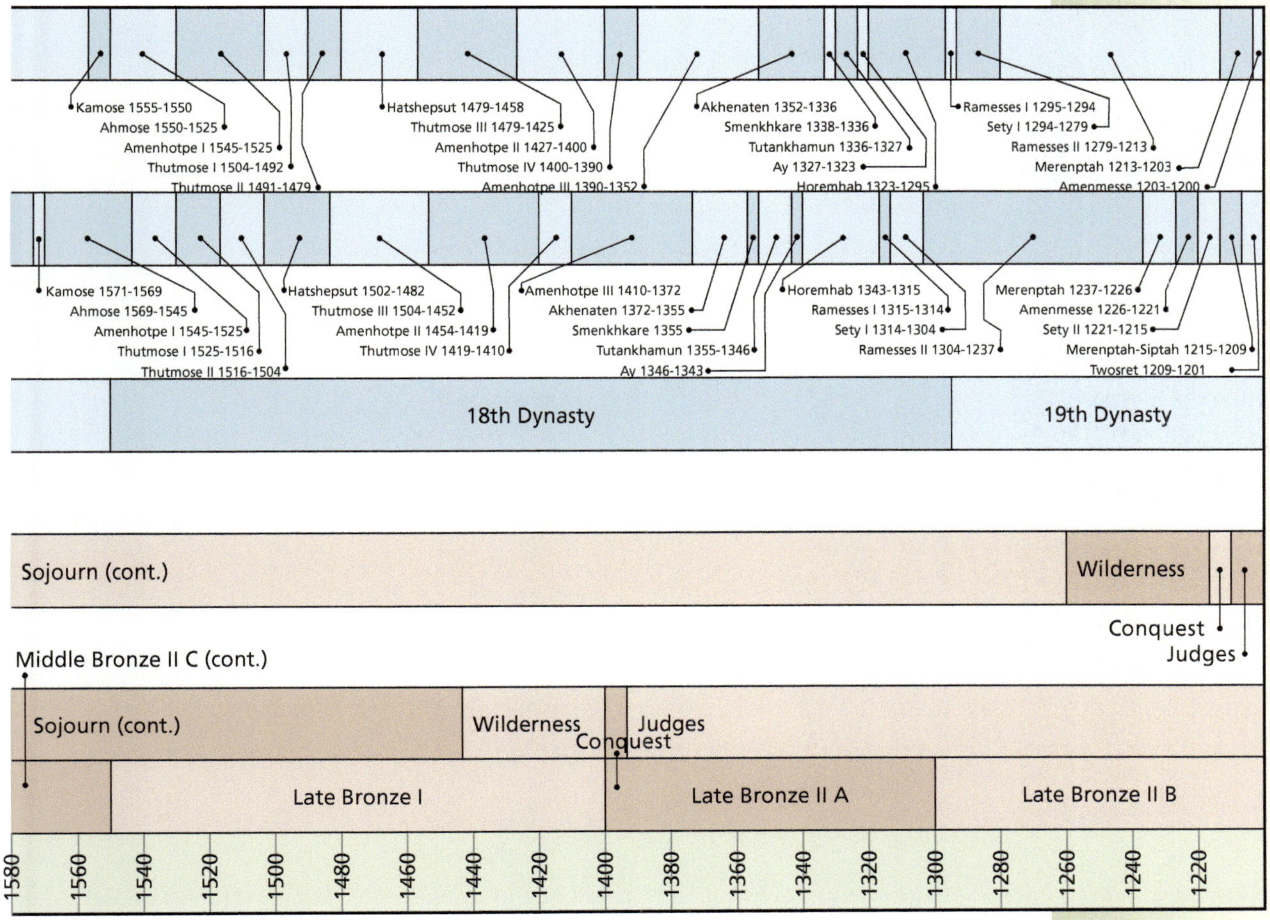

Collared-rim storage jar
Kim Walton, courtesy of the Joseph P. Free Collection and Wheaton College

Ramesses II
Z. Radovan/www.BibleLand Pictures.com

conform with a late, thirteenth-century date for the Exodus.[2] In Egypt there are the papyri Anastasi from the thirteenth century, which record daily crossings on the eastern border with the Sinai, that mention an Edomite tribe and the actual escape of two slaves and their subsequent capture. The pharaoh would be Ramesses II, who was well known as an excessively proud pharaoh, one who carved his image all over Egypt and who boasted so that military standoffs became great victories.

Further, it is known that the eldest son of Ramesses II died prematurely and did not succeed him, a hint at the account of the death of the firstborn. There is also the names of the storage cities of Pithom and Ramesses (Ex. 1:11) that fit only the thirteenth century and not earlier. In this case, Ramesses can be readily identified with Pi-Ramesses of Egyptian texts of the thirteenth century and with the archaeological site of Tell ed-Dabʾa of the same period, but not earlier in the Late Bronze Age. Egyptian names such as Moses, Phineas, Hophni, Shiphrah, and Puah have their best parallels among attested names of this period and not earlier. In the Transjordan, the identification of thirteenth-century sites such as Tall al-Umaryi and others east of the Dead Sea lends support to the Israelite itinerary of Numbers 33:42–49 (and others) as identifiable from this time, not to mention the already noted Edom and the identification of Dibon in thirteenth-century Egyptian sources.[3]

In Palestine, the thirteenth-century destruction of stratum XIII of Hazor fits well with the biblical evidence of Joshua 11.[4] The Merneptah Stele's 1209 B.C. mention of Israel as a people settled in Palestine and the complete absence of any direct correlation with Israel among the more than three hundred letters in the fourteenth century B.C. found at the royal residence in Amarna, Egypt, and written by princes and officers throughout Canaan—all this attests to the appearance of Israel in Canaan in the thirteenth century.

I could go on, but permit me to cite one final piece of evidence that will serve as a transition from this argument for a late date for the Exodus to the more pertinent question of the emergence of Israel in Palestine. In the mid-twentieth century many scholars felt that certain archaeological pieces of evidence indicated Israel's emergence in the highlands of Canaan at the end of the Late

Iron Age Hill Country Sites

vention of the loss of the extremely rich terra rosa, the Mediterranean-style topsoil that could easily be washed away by the rainstorms after the clearance of the trees and undergrowth characteristic of the region (Josh. 17:14–18). However, terraces are difficult to date. The pits or cisterns

Bronze Age. These included: the pillared-rim storage jars, the four-roomed or pillared house, the plastered pits for retaining water, and the creation of terraces. Each one of these had been identified as appearing at one or more hill country sites about 1200 B.C.

All of these possible indicators have been criticized. There are antecedents of all these phenomena in the earlier periods of Palestine. While the four-roomed house, the storage jars, and the terraces might become a much more prevalent and fixed form at this time, it is also recognized that these items were used by all peoples of the hill country, not merely by the Israelites. Thus the jar with a distinctive rim served no distinctively Israelite purpose but rather could store a large amount of grain or some other foodstuff within the house for use later in the year. This was highly desirable in all hill country villages where subsistence agriculture contributed toward the need for such storage until the next harvest and as a protection from famine. The terraces were necessary to capture the rain water, the primary source of water in the region, for watering the crops grown on the terraces. They also assisted with the pre-

provided a means for collecting rain for use as drinking water. Again, these are difficult to date, especially as it has been noticed that it was not necessary to line some of the pits with plaster in order to collect water.

At the same time that these indicators were being criticized, the survey work of the 1970s and 1980s throughout the hill country assigned to Ephraim, Manasseh, and Benjamin was leading to new conclusions. It seems that the period of c. 1200 B.C. saw a dramatic

Reconstruction of Israelite four-room house
Todd Bolen/www.BiblePlaces.com

demographic shift in this region. In place of a few larger centers that functioned as forts for the Canaanite city-state leaders, there was an explosion in the number of villages that took place at the end of the thirteenth century. Where there had been at most two or three dozen villages, there appeared as many as three hundred that have been identified so far. While there could be a variety of causes for such a change, it is difficult not to see here a sociological phenomenon that matches closely with the emergence of Israel in this same region.

Not only do at least some of the town lists and boundary descriptions in Joshua 13–21 (especially those of Ephraim and Manasseh) agree with the presence of new villages, but also the full picture of Israelite life in Judges, Ruth, and the books of Samuel before the kingship of David attest that most of Israel's daily life took place in just such villages located between the Jezreel Valley to the north and the area around Jerusalem to the south. While this has led to a review of many of the theories concerning Israel's origin and the emergence of new ones, the basic fact remains that in the late thirteenth century B.C., according to the best available pottery analysis and demographic evidence, a large group of people showed up in the highlands of Israel and lived there in villages for a generation or more.[5]

The archaeological picture of these villages suggests similar forms from village to village. The structures were largely domestic dwellings of the four-room house sort. These homes characteristically had two stories where the first was used for stables, cooking, and eating, and the second for sleeping. While serving practical domestic needs these houses were so designed to maximize the animals' natural body heat in order to provide warmth for the family in the cold winters. There is little evidence of monumental architecture or those elements, such as storehouses, that might indicate a hierarchical structure to the society. While there is some suggestion of walls around villages closer to the lowlands or to the older Canaanite towns, most of the villages do not appear to have had walls or significant defenses. This suggests the absence of an enemy who could penetrate the hills and higher areas where these population centers were situated.[6] It also implies that the inhabitants of the villages were at peace with one another and did not devote major resources to military requirements. Alternatively, it is important to realize that the absence of fortifications does not mean that the people had no threats from external enemies. It merely implies that they either were unable to build adequate defenses or used other means to combat a threat.

It is important to note that many of the elements of this Iron Age I highland culture had counterparts in the regions east of the Jordan River. Where excavations have discovered contemporary materials, it seems that similar pottery and architecture have been located. This suggests a cultural and perhaps ethnic identity between the two populations. In fact, some have argued that the movement of this continuity in culture is from east to west; that is to say, it began with a people who lived east of the Jordan River and then was brought westward across the Jordan.[7]

Finally, we should note the evidence of religious life and practice among this highland village culture that is so clearly related to Israel. Aside from a bull figurine discovered at one site east of Dothan, there is no clear evidence in these villages for the use of images. Even at the altar at Mount Ebal, if that is how it is to be understood (see comment at 8:30–35), there are no images or model furniture and figurines of the sort associated with cultic activities in the region. Further, these people appear to abstain from pork. It is not clear that any of these practices are only related to Israel and not also to other ethnic groups in the highlands. However, these are clear points of distinction from the archaeological record with the Philistines and (in terms of the absence of figurines) with other lowlanders, such as Canaanites.[8]

The historical and cultural background of these regions during the thirteenth century reveals general patterns and specific features that illuminate and relate to the picture of Israel fleeing Egypt and entering the Promised Land. Our understanding of the subsequent culture and life of Israel in the highlands of Canaan has been dramatically transformed in the last two decades by the results of the survey work done in this region, and by the excavations of villages and fortified centers in the lowlands and highlands of modern Israel as well as to the east in Jordan. The resultant picture, while it admittedly adds little to our understanding of the towns "conquered" by the forces under Joshua (with the exception of Hazor), immeasurably enhances our appreciation of the culture and lifestyle of the Iron Age settlements.

Literary Form

The book of Joshua contains numerous and widely diverse literary forms, many of which will be considered at their appropriate place in the text.[9] The search for comparisons with other ancient Near Eastern literature will take us to annals of military campaigns, suzerain/vassal treaties, itineraries of Egyptian campaigns, Egyptian scribal exercises recounting visits to Canaan, Hittite instructions for the royal bodyguard and for the border fort commanders, Hittite boundary descriptions in treaties, personal names, town lists among the West Semitic archives of Alalakh and Ugarit, cultic calendars from Emar, Old Babylonian laws, rhetorical forms in the Amarna letters from Canaan, and other literary sources. However, none of these encompasses the overall form of the book of Joshua. For that, it is necessary to look elsewhere.

The most productive source for comparison with the book of Joshua is the genre of land grants.[10] These differ from treaties and particularly from suzerain/vassal treaties, to which they have been compared.[11] Treaties tend to follow a careful and recognized form; land grants are diverse in their organization and presentation. Treaties use diplomatic language that can be recognized; land grants do not necessarily use such language but have phrases that occur in other types of literature. Treaties focus on the rights of the suzerain; land grants emphasize the rights of the vassal. The curses reflect these different emphases in the two types of documents.

Of the land grants in the Bible, the most famous is the divine grant of the Promised Land given to Abram. It first appears in Genesis 12:1–3 and is then developed over the next ten chapters. In the West Semitic world, of which Abram and later Israel were a part, there are land grants from Late Bronze Age Ugarit and from Middle Bronze Age Alalakh. Those at Ugarit function as grants of usufruct by the king for his loyal servants. The land remains within the kingdom of Ugarit and under the control of the king.

From the neighboring state to the north of Ugarit comes an important land grant. It dates centuries earlier than the Ugarit grants, back to the eighteenth century B.C. This grant is different from the ones given by the king of Ugarit to his subjects. The Alalakh grant (AT 456) describes the gift from one king to another of a city along with its villages and lands. The gift

Babylonian land grant
Michael Greenhalgh/ArtServe, courtesy of the British Museum

is thus a city-state or kingdom rather than a parcel of land. In fact, this text describes the legal deeding of the kingdom of Alalakh to the king who would begin a dynasty at the site.[12]

It is this text that provides the closest overall structure to the book of Joshua. We will take a section-by-section analysis of AT 456 and compare it with the major sections of Joshua and their function.[13] Unlike the divine grant to Abram, the text of Joshua does not focus on a promise; it only obliquely refers to this promise in its expression to Moses (1:3). Rather, Joshua resembles the royal grant of Alalakh (and others) in that the text itself functions as the actual grant from God to the tribes of Israel. Unlike the grant to Abram, it is not in any sense unconditional. Instead, both the royal grants and that of Joshua are given on the basis of continuing loyalty or faithfulness to the suzerain. In the case of Joshua, of course, God takes on the role of the suzerain (see chs. 7–8; 23–24). The gift of the land, like that of the city of Alalakh, is conditional. Israel keeps the land as long as the nation remains faithful to its suzerain.

The text of AT 456, with its seventy-six lines, divides into five major parts according to topic and form:

a town list that reviews previous exchanges of towns (lines 1–18)

a history of Yarimlim and how he assisted his suzerain, Abbael king of Aleppo, in putting down the revolt of Zitraaddu of the town of Irridi (lines 19–30)

Abbael's gift of Alalakh to Yarimlim and Abbael's additional gift of Murar (lines 31–39a)

the oath that Abbael swore to Yarimlim in making the gift (lines 39b–42)

conditions of disloyalty that would cause Yarimlim to forfeit this gift (lines 43–75 [lines 64–75 are broken with only a few words remaining]).

Sections 1 and 2 (lines 1–30) of AT 456 constitute a single concern, that of past events that lead up to the present gift by Abbael to Yarimlim. Lines 1–18 constitute a town list (see sidebar on "AT 456"). Because this is followed by a history of the recent battle that leads to the land grant, it may be assumed that the exchanges in this list refer to past history and the situation that pertained before the conflict described in the following lines. If so, then this section functions as a part of the past history that, along with lines 19–30, constitutes the story of recent history, just as that of Joshua 1–12 reviews the latest history of the events leading to the allotments in chapters 13–21. Of particular interest is Joshua 12, where there also appears a list of towns not unlike that here.

In terms of details of form, note the mention in the first line of the pasturelands that accompany the city of Emar. This compares with the fifty-seven occurrences of the expression "with their pasturelands" that appear with the Levitical towns in Joshua 21. In AT 456 the use of this term in the first line may indicate that it is intended for each town named in the following lines, just as it is explicitly stated in Joshua 21. Further, the expression "in exchange for" in lines 9 and 11 suggests that there was some sort of trade or exchange that took place. This also compares with Joshua 21, where the Israelites give back to God towns that had been given to them so that these towns can be used by the Levites who serve God. Formally, this list compares with the town lists of Joshua 12–21, but functionally the list occurs as part of the immediate background to the land grant as does Joshua 1–12.

The historical narrative of AT 456 appears in lines 19–30 (see sidebar on "AT 456"). This narrative resembles Joshua 1–12 in several ways. First, both AT 456 and Joshua 1–12 describe the necessary battles and war events that led to the allotting of the lands and towns.

AT 456

01. The city of Emar with its pasture land(s?),

02. Za[rr]at,

03. [ ]na,

04. Nashtarbe,

05. Hashnap,

06. Kazzuwe,

07. Ammakke,

08. (and) Parre,

09. in exchange for Uwiye.

10. The town Atrate

11. in exchange for the land of the towns of Zunadde,

12. which is [ ].

13. Amame,

14. Aushun,

15. Halliwe,

16. Zikirli(?),

17. Murar,

18. and Irridi–Yarimlim [ruled them(?)].

19. Zitraddu, the governor of [Irridi],

20. revolted against Yarimlim and

21. [then he sei]zed(?) robber bands(?)

22. and brought them to Irridi, his city.

23–24. He incited the whole land to rebel against Abbael [ ].

25. The mighty weapon [ ]

26. with silver, gold, lapis lazuli, crystal(?), and the great [wea]pon

27. of the weather god. (As for Abbael,) he seized Irridi and

28. destroyed the enemy bands(?).

29. To Aleppo

30. he returned in peace.

31. <He said:>"Irridi is destroyed.

32. Will I give it to my brother?

33. In exchange for Irridi

34. [that] rebelled [against] him

35. [and that I captur]ed and d[estroyed,]

36. [Alal]akh

37. [I will give to Ya]rimlim.

38. The town of Murar, in addition to [his shar]e,

39a. I will add to it."

39b–42. Abbael swore the oath to Yarimlim and cut the neck of a lamb, <saying:> "If I take back what I have given you <may I be cursed.>"

43–50a. If ever in the future Yarimlim sins against Abbael, or [if] he gives away Abbael's secret to another king, or if he lets go of the hem of Abbael's garment and grasps the hem of another king's garment, his towns and lands he shall [forfeit].

50b–57a. If a descendant of Yarimlim sins against Abbael (or a descendant of Abbael), if he rel[ease]s the h[em] of Abbael's garment, (or that of a descendant of Abbael,) and if he seizes the hem of another king's garment, his towns and lands he shall forfeit.

57b–62. If a descendant of [Y]arimlim [tries to] sell his town their older brother shall bu[y it] and give it to a descendant of Abbael. He shall not give it to another person.

Second, the suzerain, whether Abbael or God, is the main actor in the battle(s). Yarimlim, like Israel, remains loyal to his overlord. But it is the overlord who receives the credit for winning the actual battle. Yarimlim's activities in the battle are not mentioned, only those of Abbael against the disloyal enemy, Zitraddu. So Israel follows God, who acts on the nation's behalf and leads it in its battles. Again and again, God receives the credit for the major part of the battle and Israel follows and receives the land. Israel may do little more than witness God's work and then participate in the victory. But that is enough. The key issue is the loyalty of the vassal, whether Israel or Yarimlim.

Third, there are specific similarities of form. The battle accounts begin by naming the chief enemy and the town he governs. In AT 456.19 it is Zitraddu of Irridi. In Joshua it is Adoni-Zedek of Jerusalem (10:1) and Jabin of Hazor (11:1). Further, there follows an incitement by the enemy that brings his allies into the revolt and necessitates the involvement of the "good guys." Thus in AT 456.23–24 Zitraddu incited the whole land to rebellion. In Joshua 10:3–5 and 11:1–4 Adoni-Zedek and Jabin both contact the rulers in their regions and so bring them into the battle.

Finally, in AT 456.30 the conflict ends with the warrior Abbael returning to his home, with resultant peace. In Joshua 11:23, the land has rest or peace after the battles have ended. In AT 456, the actual gift of the land occurs in lines 31–39a (see sidebar on "AT 456").

Here Abbael distributes to Yarimlim the kingdom of Alalakh. He adds the town of Murar. This compares to Joshua 13–21, where God distributes to Israel the gift of the Promised Land. In Joshua there is much more detail. This is because the land grant in Joshua involves many towns and lands and multiple recipients, unlike AT 456, where only one recipient and one city is envisioned. The additional gift of Murar, which appears after the formal allotment of Alalakh, compares with the additional towns and lands given to Achsah (15:17–21), to Ephraim and Manasseh (17:14–18), and to Joshua (19:49–51). All of these additional allotments occur after the main allotments in the region are distributed, or in the case of Judah, after the boundaries of the region are described. All are given by the one who has the ownership of the land. These are also true of Abbael's gift. Abbael possesses Murar and gives it to Yarimlim. This is described after the main allotment of Alalakh.

Finally, I have elsewhere noted how this allotment is framed by a wordplay at the beginning and end.[14] In AT 456, the first word in line 31 is the town Irridi. The last word in the allotment, in line 39a, is "I shall add it" *ú-ri-id-di-šu*. Both terms sound alike, and this is no accident. It is an intentional marker designed to highlight that portion of the text that describes the actual gift from Abbael. Compare this with the marker that frames the beginning and end of the allotments in Joshua. Joshua 13:1 begins the allotment with a note of the advanced age of Joshua. After the end of the allotment, in 23:1, this is repeated as an indication that the allotment has ended. Both of these frames envelop the key sections of the texts.

Lines 39b–62 constitute the remaining unbroken text of AT 456 and describe both the oath ceremony to seal the covenant and the warning or conditions that Yarimlim must heed if he is to retain his gift (see sidebar on "AT 456").

The cutting of the animal that forms part of the oath-taking ceremony has been compared to Genesis 15, and indeed there are similar elements.[15] However, in the context of the land grant, it should also be compared with the sacrifice of animals that Israel would undertake at the altar as part of the ratification of its formal covenant agreement with God. Such an altar is made explicit in 8:30–35, but it recurs in a ceremony of much greater detail after the allotments in chapter 24. As with AT 456, Joshua 24 also includes references to confirmation of loyalty to the granter, God, and warnings of dangers for being disloyal to him (24:20). Note also that the altar described in chapter 22 also appears after the allotments in this final section. However, it is not a "true" altar for sacrifices, but only a symbol of an altar. The true act of worship toward God comes in chapter 24.

Of even greater interest is the manner in which lines 43–57a follow the ceremony with two references to the future in which conditions of disloyalty are envisioned. In both cases there follows the warning that Yarimlim or his descendants will forfeit the gift of towns and lands. The same is true in Joshua 23 and 24. In both chapters there are conditions envisioned in which Israel in the future may turn away from God and become disloyal to him (23:6–12; 24:16–19). These are both followed by the warning that Israel will then lose its divine gift of lands and towns (23:13; 24:20). In both AT 456 and in Joshua the grant is followed by two sets of warnings with the possible loss of the grant. The repetition, a key element in Semitic poetry and rhetoric, reinforces the message, making it all the more powerful to the hearers.

The final section of AT 456, lines 68–76, is largely broken, but enough can be read to note that there is a list of human witnesses to the grant followed by a final note that oaths were sworn. This compares with Joshua 24 where the people call on themselves as witnesses to the covenant (24:22). At the same time, expressions such as "far be it from us" and "surely" (24:16, 21) indicate that the people have sworn oaths before God to remain loyal to him.

Thus these two land grants share the same major parts: a narrative, including a town list, explaining the immediate martial background that resulted in the allotment; the allotment itself with specific towns named, with a few or many; the requirements for loyalty to the granter and warnings concerning disloyalty; and witnesses and oaths to seal the agreement. Structured in this manner, AT 456 provides a useful comparison to the whole book of Joshua and demonstrates how this book of the Bible functions as a West Semitic land grant from God to his people.

There is no intention here to establish a genre of land grant. Many such grants do not follow this pattern. Further, the act of granting whole towns or even a kingdom or state to either individuals or tribes is rare and not recorded in the ancient Near East beyond a few texts. However, the similarities noted here are too specific and detailed to be coincidental. They represent an authentic and ancient perspective on the necessary elements for a land grant to take place. If there was a Deuteronomist editor who later gathered together the historical books, including Joshua, and produced a final edition, then that editor did so without disturbing the basic structure of the land grant.

Furthermore, inherent within that form were theological elements fundamental to the what modern scholars sometimes designate as Deuteronomistic theology. That is, the nation of Israel as the people of God received their land as a gift from God that had long been promised; that gift formed part of a covenant with the people that called for their exclusive loyalty to the Giver; and God affirmed his sole lordship over his people in their land.

Joshua Assumes Leadership (1:1–18)

After the death of Moses (1:1). In both ancient and modern times a transition of leadership is one of the most precarious times in the security of a state. More than any other time, this can become a period of potential revolts and civil wars. Of all such transitional periods, the most dangerous are those where the transition is not dynastic but involves the enthronement of a ruler unrelated to his or her predecessor. David's acquisition of power after the deaths of Saul and Jonathan, for example, required that much of the text of 1 Samuel justify his kingship and explain how he was not disloyal to his predecessor.

This was not unique to the Bible. From Sargon I in the third millennium to Cambyses and Darius in the first millennium B.C., many rulers succeeded in place of the expected successor. In the second millennium B.C. succession was perceived to threaten the stability of the Hittite kingdom. Early on, an edict of succession was put in place in an attempt to guarantee a procedure for the next ruler of the kingdom.

Furthermore, it is clear from many of the vassal treaties that the Hittite emperor took an active role among loyal vassals to guarantee that the vassal rulers' offspring succeeded them.[16]

In Joshua 1 a major concern of the author is to describe how Joshua is the legitimate successor of Moses as leader of God's people. Although he is not biologically related, God had already established Joshua as successor with public demonstrations of his approval.[17] Joshua 1:1–9 confirms Joshua as divinely appointed. The rest of the chapter illustrates the manner in which he acts to establish authority, as well as the respect he receives from the civil authorities (1:10–11) and from the tribes least likely to follow him (1:12–18). In common with other ancient Near Eastern rulers who rose to power outside of an established dynasty, Joshua records both the divine and human approval that he gains for his leadership.

Servant of the LORD (1:1). This title is a common form of many personal names found in the ancient Near Eastern West Semitic world of the fifteenth to twelfth centuries B.C., and not as frequently earlier or later. At Ugarit, Alalakh, Emar, and Ekalte, as well as the towns of Palestine and Syria represented by the Amarna letters, the personal name formation "servant of X" (where X represents the name of a god or goddess) is found in many examples. These are often leaders of population centers. For example, there is ʿAbdi-ʾAshirta ("servant of Asherah") ruler of Amurru, and ʿAbdi-Heba ("servant of the Syrian goddess Hebat") ruler of Jerusalem.[18] The epithet "servant of the LORD" is first applied to Moses at the end of his life (Deut. 34:5) and remains reserved for a few major leaders early in Israel's history. Joshua is the second person to receive it, and he does so only at the end of his life (Josh. 24:29). While the title may reflect the faithful leader of a people who worship the Lord, it certainly contrasts with the polytheism represented by the names of the contemporary inhabitants of Canaan (see above).

Your territory (1:4). The territory of the Promised Land is defined elsewhere in Genesis 10:19; Numbers 13:17, 21–22;

Pharaoh selected by the gods for leadership
Frederick J. Mabie

and 34:3–12. Despite the protestations of a few, the usage of the name "Canaan" and the territory it defines in these early biblical texts is identical to the usage and territory that the Egyptian New Kingdom Empire (c. 1550–1150 B.C.) referred to as Canaan.[19] Only in this period do both the Bible and Egypt apply the term to this territory, and the extent of the territory for both is the same.

The territory of Canaan is defined in the south by an arc from the southeastern Mediterranean to the southern tip of the Dead Sea.[20] The eastern border traveled north along the rift valley marked by the Dead Sea, the Jordan Valley, the Sea of Kinnereth (Galilee), the Huleh basin, the Beqaʾ, and northeast to the Euphrates. The western border to Canaan was the Mediterranean Sea. The northern border did not reach as far as Ugarit or Alalakh, but lay to the south of these kingdoms. Aside from the agreement of the second millennium B.C. Egyptian sources and these texts from the Pentateuch and Joshua, there is also a theological sense in which an extension of Egyptian control is given by God to his people. Although they did not dominate the northern area of Canaan, Egypt did realize sovereignty over the southern region for most of its New Kingdom history. Not only does God defeat Pharaoh and his army, he also brings to an end the Egyptian New Kingdom empire (in the context of a thirteenth-century B.C. date for the Exodus).

All the Hittite country (1:4). Although the Hittites of the Late Bronze Age can be identified with the kingdom whose capital is at Hattusas in central Anatolia, these people did not actually refer to themselves as Hittites. Rather, the Hittite land may be identified with northern Canaan, an area controlled by the Hittite empire whose vacillating border saw clashes with Egyptian penetration to the north. If the northern border of Canaan is as defined above, then this cannot refer to the Neo-Hittite states of the first millennium B.C.

Canaan and Egyptian New Kingdom Empire

Hittite Land

that extended farther north into Anatolia. Rather, "the Hittite country" is a term applied by the Egyptians to the northern part of the region of Canaan, as for example it was in the Merneptah Stele of 1209 B.C. Thus the Hittite country was a part of Canaan that was given to the Israelites.

I will never ... forsake you (1:5). The verb "to forsake" (*ʿāzab*) describes a divine abandonment so that Joshua and the Israelites will face certain defeat at the hands of their enemies. However, the expression involves more than a casual change of sides. Elsewhere in Joshua it is used of Israel's abandonment of its God to worship other deities (24:16, 20). In military usage, it describes how the warriors abandon Ai (8:17) and how the Transjordanian tribes did not abandon their other tribal brothers in the wars west of the Jordan River (22:3). In fact, the Akkadian cognate (*ezēbu*) of this Hebrew term also describes the betrayal by someone who switches sides in a battle.[21] It is often used in the fourteenth-century B.C. Amarna letters of the manner in which Canaanites show disloyalty to the pharaoh by joining his enemies. Here its denial implies God's faithfulness toward Joshua and Israel—that he will remain on their side and fight for them.

Do not let this Book of the Law depart from your mouth (1:8). This expression describes both the importance of the covenantal document that the Israelites have received and the need for the leader to know it as well and as completely as possible. The term for "Law" is *tôrâ* ("instruction"). The formal relationship between various legal documents in the Pentateuch and Joshua has been compared to the ancient Near Eastern treaty structure. In particular, the treaties preserved by the Hittite empire provide a close correspondence with the structure of these covenants (see comments on ch. 24). Of interest here is the value placed on the writing and reading of the covenant. Deuteronomy 31 records how Moses wrote the words of the covenant (31:24) and commanded the periodic public reading of the text (31:10–12). In particular the king must copy the words of the covenant and read them at intervals (17:18–19).

The same requirement appears on some Hittite treaties. There the king is responsible for regularly copying and reading the text.[22] In the biblical texts of Deuteronomy 17 and Joshua 1 and in the Hittite vassal treaty texts, the vassal ruler is required periodically to study the treaty/covenant so as to be familiar with its words and to obey it.

Whatever you have commanded us we will do (1:16–18). Egyptian New Kingdom scholars contend that (as with rulers at other times) when a new pharaoh came to power, he required his vassals from Canaan to swear a new loyalty oath to him.[23] The pharaoh might come to Canaan, perhaps to Gaza or Gezer, and the Canaanite rulers would

Treaty between Hittites and Egyptians concluded after the battle of Kadesh
Joshua B. Miller, courtesy of the Istanbul Museum

arrive and swear an oath to him. This would assure the recognition of the pharaoh as the new ruler of the Egyptian empire, guarantee the succession of the new leader, and assist in the prevention of any revolt.

The response of the two and a half tribes in these verses represents such an oath. The oath form here could have been used by the other tribes as well. The two and a half tribes are mentioned because they have the least incentive to cross over the Jordan and fight alongside the other tribes. They have already received their land from Moses east of the Jordan and therefore can occupy it with no need for additional land acquisition or warfare (Deut. 3:12–20).

Preparations West of the Jordan River: Rahab and the Spies (2:1–24)

Sent two spies (2:1). The use of spies in military operations is attested on both sides in the thirteenth-century B.C. battle of Qadesh between the Egyptians and the Hittites.[24] In the eighteenth-century B.C. Mari letters, these West Semitic predecessors of the Israelites see the use of spies as a natural prelude to an attack on a fortified site: "Ishme-Dagan has dispatched spies to spy on the encampment of Suhum. He will attack the encampment [of] Suhum."[25]

Shittim (2:1). Possibly Tell el-Ḫammām was the site, located east of the Jordan River opposite Jericho (Tell es-Sultan).[26] The Israelites made camp there in Numbers 25:1.

Jericho (2:1). Tell es-Sultan is Jericho, a site occupied from as early as the ninth millennium B.C. Its location, ten miles north of the Dead Sea in the Jordan Valley, suggests its importance in terms of trade routes along the Jordan Valley and westward to Jerusalem, Bethel, and Ophrah. This strategic location, combined with the ideal agricultural climate of the southern Jordan Valley, made the region and this site, with its own spring, valuable.

Rahab (2:1). A form of this name occurs in a Late Bronze Age cuneiform text from nearby Taanach at the southern side of the Jezreel Valley. There a man carried the name, *e-lu-ra-ḫé-ba*, "El (or 'god') has opened (the womb)." It is a confessional name, given at the safe delivery of the child and mother at birth.[27] "Rahab" is a shortened form of this name with the omission of the divine name element. Similar forms are attested at thirteenth-century B.C. Ugarit and at eighteenth-century Mari, all among West Semitic peoples.[28]

King of Jericho (2:2). The king (Heb. *melek*) is mentioned three times in Joshua 2 and 6 (2:2, 3; 6:2) and five additional times in the book of Joshua. If this *melek* functions in the traditional understanding of the English word for king, then Jericho is the sovereign's fort and his subjects are in the surrounding area of the southern Jordan Valley. However, that is not the only explanation of *melek*, nor is it the most likely. There is no mention of other inhabitants of the area outside of Jericho in the accounts of Israel's entrance into Canaan, nor are there any south of the town of Adam east of the Jordan River.

The fourteenth-century B.C. Amarna letters, correspondence from city-state leaders of Canaan to the pharaoh in Egypt, reveal a traditional usage of the root for "king" (*mlk*) in the designation of the pharaoh as sole, ultimate sovereign. However, the *mlk* root also functions as a verb to describe one who has authority over and cares for others, without necessarily being the sole sovereign. The pharaoh "should care for his servant" uses this verbal root to describe this sense in a letter from Abimilki of Tyre.[29] Of greater significance is the description of a commissioner of the pharaoh, one who represents the royal interests but who cannot act independently. This commissioner, Piwuri, is described with the Canaanite equivalent of the Hebrew noun *melek* (i.e., *malik*).[30]

Applied to the *melek* of Jericho, this leader becomes a figure responsible for the security of Jericho and the surrounding region but is answerable to a greater authority. Given that the ancient roads from Jericho westward go toward Ophrah, Bethel, and Jerusalem, the leader of Jericho may have represented the interests of one of these leaders or, more likely (cf. Josh. 10 and 11), a coalition of hill country city-state leaders.[31]

Stalks of flax (2:6). The Gezer Calendar (c. 900 B.C.) assigns a month of harvesting flax immediately before the month of harvesting barley—that is, a flax harvest in February/March (see sidebar on "Gezer Calendar" at Ruth 1:22). Paleobotanical studies at Deir ʿAllah, north of Jericho in the Jordan Valley, have identified the growing of flax in irrigated fields from as early as c. 1200 B.C.[32] Flax seeds yielded linseed oil while the fiber produced linen yarn. To obtain the yarn the flax fibers were softened by soaking (retting), dried and bleached on the rooftops as here, crushed and beaten, and spun into yarn.

Jericho
Z. Radovan/www.BibleLandPictures.com

▸ Prostitutes and Inns

In the second millennium B.C. the West Semitic world and that of its Hittite neighbors to the north associated innkeepers with prostitutes. In the first millennium this seems to have changed, perhaps due to sociological changes brought about by developments in the brewing of alcohol.[A-1] The role of the prostitute as innkeeper is attested in the eighteenth-century Laws of Hammurabi (§109): "If there should be a woman innkeeper in whose house criminals congregate, and she does not seize those criminals and lead them off to the palace authorities, that woman innkeeper shall be put to death."[A-2]

From the Late Bronze Age Hittite empire, The Instructions to the Commander of the Border Fortress contains a prohibition of building an inn on any part of the city wall.[A-3] The text warns about bringing a torch near to the wooden fortification or the wall and, in this context, appears to forbid the building of an inn on the wall of the fort.

This instruction forms part of a context where the concern is for the safety of the city. Thus the following law forbids starting a fire near the wall, again in order to avoid breaching the defenses. That such prohibitions existed at this time indicates the concern for exactly the same sort of activity that occurred in Joshua 2.

Flax hung out to dry
Choltícha Adhakulawat

Great fear (2:9–10). For this expression and others referring to the Exodus, see comments on Ex. 15:15–16.

My family (2:12). Literally "the house of my father," this expression refers to Rahab's extended family, including the relations described in verse 13. This forms the basic sociological unit of West Semitic society (including Canaan and Israel) in the Bronze and Iron Ages. Traditionally, this family unit is led by the eldest male. Here, in a unique manner, Rahab negotiates on behalf of her extended family.[33]

Part of the city wall (2:15). John Garstang's excavations in the 1930s revealed an important fortified center at ancient Jericho with mud-brick walls. However, work two decades later by Kathleen Kenyon confirmed that these walls dated centuries earlier than any time that the Israelites could have entered Palestine. Although some have challenged this change in dating, most ceramicists who study the evidence from Tell es-Sultan affirm the absence of preserved walls in the Late Bronze Age. In itself this is not surprising. Sites such as Lachish and Megiddo have preserved no Late Bronze Age walls.[34] Yet it is clear from Egyptian accounts of the site during this period that Megiddo was fortified by a wall.[35] Perhaps the same was the case at Jericho. The walls may have eroded after their destruction in chapter 6 and before Jericho was rebuilt hundreds of years later in the ninth century B.C. (1 Kings 16:34).

The placement of a house on the city wall was not extraordinary but was known to take place at this time (see sidebar on "Prostitutes and Inns"). Casemate walls, which allowed for domestic structures "sandwiched" between

Beersheba with remains of pillared house and the wall right behind it
Kim Walton

mud-brick houses built so as to form a continuous wall around the site of Jericho.[37] The descent from Rahab's window to the ground outside Jericho could have been as small as a single story (from the second story window to the ground) or the fort could have been built beside a precipice formed by the tell and thus the descent could have been much longer.

Hide yourselves there three days (2:16, 22). The use of "three days" as a measure of time may indicate a general period of time lasting more than one or two days but not specific beyond that. The Late Bronze Age Hittite Instructions to the Commander of the Border Fortress specifies this length of

two parallel walls, could explain the presence of Rahab's "inn" on the walls, though these are not attested in Israel before the tenth century.[36] If these walls were mud brick and easily subject to erosion, a more likely possibility might be the presence of a small circle of

Jericho and the hills to the west
Copyright 1995–2009 Phoenix Data Systems

time for the pursuit of the enemy, followed by the demand that any officer who does not kill this enemy must be turned over to the king for punishment:[38]

> The troops of the posts he should count and note down. The captains of second, third, and fourth rank, he should acknowledge at each place. If the enemy strikes anywhere, let the troops follow the trace of the enemy for three days. They should hold the way for two days. Whoever has not killed the enemy, let the chief of the border guard take the second, third, or fourth rank captain. Let him send (word) to his majesty.

This provides a precedent for Rahab's advice to Jericho's enemies and a measure of her personal risk in not surrendering the spies to Jericho's leadership.

Scarlet cord (2:18, 21). This word for "cord" (*tiqwâ*) is distinct from the rope used to lower the spies (2:15). It normally describes a simple thread, such as something of low value that Abram refuses from the king of Sodom (Gen. 14:23). The term for "scarlet" (*šānî*) appears elsewhere in the Bible to describe textiles used to decorate the tabernacle (e.g., Ex. 25:4), cleansing rituals (Lev. 14:4), a bright color (Gen. 38:28), and special garments for the wealthy (Prov. 31:21).

Within the context of this story, putting out a scarlet cord seems not to have been a new act by Rahab, for it would certainly compromise her anonymity when recognized by other inhabitants of Jericho. Rather, the story suggests that this cord was already in use, perhaps as a means to denote Rahab's inn. In contrast to the usage of "red" in the contexts of holiness and purity in Israel, the origin of the Akkadian term for "Canaan" may identify the color "red-purple." This color, derived from the purple dye processed at Tyre, Dor, and other coastal cities, could have been understood as a statement of loyalty to the region by other Canaanites. However, its connection with Israel may have given it a double meaning.

Preparations East of the Jordan River: Israel, the Priests, and the Ark (3:1–17)

Early in the morning Joshua and all the Israelites set out (3:1). The crossing of the Jordan River, unlike the crossing of the Reed Sea of the previous generation (Ex. 14–15), was accomplished in an orderly fashion. Most of this chapter is taken up with the detailed procedure by which Israel was to cross the river. The ceremonial progression across the Jordan resembles the ancient West Semitic religious procession detailed at thirteenth-century Emar in northern Syria—in particular, the multiple processions of the image of Dagan Lord of the Firstborn, who proceeds from his temple to various gates and standing stones before returning.[39] However, other than the connection with a deity and his movement, there is no real parallel with the biblical texts of Joshua.

The God of Israel moves in the midst of his people in a procession that leads them into enemy territory. This forms a military procession and resembles the military marches of Egypt and the other powers of the ancient Near East. Although few descriptions remain of the procedure of such marches, there is a detailed description

Procession of priests from Medinet Habu
Manfred Näder, Gabana Studios, Germany

Jordan River
Revital Salomon, Israel

found in the second-millennium B.C. Hittite Instruction for the Royal Bodyguard.[40] This tablet describes the responsibilities of the palace guard for the protection of the king. Most of it concerns the movement of the king in a cart from his palace to the place where he gives judgment and the return at the end of the day. Although there are many differences, of special interest is the manner in which the location of the guard is specified. They surround the king and protect him on all sides. This reminds us of the Israelite camp's order of march through the desert (Num. 10:14–28).

However, the Hittite instructions also require that the guards should keep a specific distance from the king when they march. As the guards are required to stay at a certain distance from the cart carrying the king, so the Israelites are commanded to keep "a thousand yards" of distance from the ark, representing God in its movement across the Jordan River (3:4). The specific directions and the whole ceremony of Joshua 3–4 suggest a movement comparable to that of a king surrounded by his army as they march to battle.

Shittim (3:1). See 2:1.

Consecrate yourselves (3:5). At Mount Sinai Israel consecrated itself by washing clothes and abstaining from sex (Ex. 19:10–15). In the Kirta Epic from Ugarit, the god El instructs the king to prepare for his campaign by washing and rouging himself and by sacrificing animals.

Edge of the Jordan's waters (3:8). Rivers provided boundaries in sale documents for lands in thirteenth century Emar in northern Syria. They were regarded as divine in both Egypt and Mesopotamia. Later treaty

Standard of Ur war panel showing victory procession
Caryn Reeder, courtesy of the British Museum

Mitanni and Hittite Kingdoms

curses in Assyria describe how the gods can make the rivers reverse direction and cease to supply water. In Babylon, the chief god Marduk was responsible for maintaining the flow of the rivers.[41] Here God's control of the Jordan River, in contrast to that of the gods of Canaan, is asserted.

Canaanites, Hittites, Hivites, Perizzites, Girgashites, Amorites and Jebusites (3:10). Other lists of the peoples of Canaan occur in Genesis 15:19–21; Exodus 3:8, 17; 23:23; 33:2; 34:11; Deuteronomy 7:1 (same groups as here, but different order); 20:17; Joshua 9:1; 12:8. For Canaanites and Hittites, see 1:4. The Hivites, identified with the Gibeonites (9:7; 11:19), may be associated with the Hurrians (Horites) in Genesis 36:2 and 20.[42]

Perizzites also bear an association with Hurrians, insofar as they are a ethnonym that reflects the Hurrian *zzi* suffix, well known in personal names from Hurrian populations at Nuzi and elsewhere. In fact, the personal name Pirizzi occurs in a fourteenth-century

The flow of the Jordan River is much diminished today because of damming of the tributaries. This photo from the early 20th century shows the flood stage of the river prior to these controls.
Todd Bolen/www.BiblePlaces.com; Black and white: Library of Congress, LC-matpc-04342/www.LifeintheHolyLand.com

▸ The Instruction for the Royal Bodyguard

The edition and translation of Güterbock and van den Hout illustrates the details of a royal procession with the king well-guarded, not unlike Israel's procession with the ark of the covenant through the desert, across the Jordan River, and around Jericho.

There are guards and others who go in front (§15 and §16):

> Thereafter (there is) again [one IKU] be[tween: (then)...] (and) two men-of-a-field-battalion are standing. [A commander-of-a-field-battalion] and an army bailiff are standing with them. [They hold..., and they] are (to be) walking in front [of the king]. Thereafter (there is) again one IKU between: (then) [...] are standing and holding spears. [A commander-of-a-field-battalion] and an army bailiff are standing with them. They ho[ld] sticks(?). They are (to be) walking in front of the king.

There are those who travel on either side of the king (cf. the priests in Joshua; §18 and §19):

> The guard sets up the stool. The king comes out (of the palace) while the chief-of-palace-attendants is holding him by the hand. The king sits down on the (light) ca[rt]. The high ranking spear-men bow, then they run and walk in front and march with the [gold-sp]ear[-man(?)]. The gold-spear-man who stood with them [(does)...]. But the palace attendant of the spear gives the whip to the chief-of-palace-attendants, and the chief-of-palace-attendants gives it to the king. In front of the cart walks the chief-of-grooms, and he holds a staff. But when the cart begins to move out, the chief-of-palace attendants bows after it and (thus) entrusts the king to the chief-of-guards.

There are those who follow the king (as in §21, §23, §24):

> When the guards march, two guards are walking in front and hold spears; and they are lined up. [To their] left marches a palace attendant and holds a lituus; and he, too, is lined up with the two gu[ard]s (so that) the three (of them) are lined up together. The guards and the palace attendants march in three files: two files of guards and one file of palace attendants. But they march one IKU behind(?) the cart.
>
> Thereafter (there is) one IKU between: (then) a gold-spear man holds a plated spear, and a "physician" holds a sistrum. They march together, and the "physician" pronounces spells.
>
> Thereafter (there is) one IKU between: (then) two spear-men march, either officers or advanced corporals. They are wearing good festive garments (and) shoes in the manner of *ḫilammi*-men. A chief-of-spear-men and an army bailiff march with them, holding staffs.

That their function is not only ceremonial but also defensive is suggested by §27 and §28:

> The soldiers who (are) of a field-battalion keep the peaceful (population) lined up on the sides: the left ones keep (it) lined upon the left, and the right ones keep (it) lined up on the right. They march three IKU apart, but if anywhere in front of them the road is narrow, they converge. Then, if one of the first (two) lets anything in—either horses or a raging ox—then it is the first's

fault. But if one of the last (two) lets anything in, it is the lasts' fault.

God, whose presence was symbolized by the ark of the covenant, marches forward as a king among his people. As with the Hittite king, his special attendants (the biblical priests) accompany him, and his army guards the physical representation of his presence among them.

Amarna letter written from the Hurrian kingdom of Mitanni.[43]

A personal name with the same consonantal sequence as Hebrew Girgashite occurs in the alphabetic script from Ugarit.[44] The derivation of this name is unknown.

The Amorites, already mentioned in 2:10, are a general name for people east of the Jordan River. In 10:5 the Amorites are again a general name for peoples, this time those kings and populations who live west of the Jordan River in the southern hill country.

The Jebusites have no clear attestation outside the Bible. The Hittites, Hivites, and Perizzites (perhaps some of the other groups named here as well) represent populations that migrated south from the lands of the Hittites and Hurrians in modern Turkey, Syria, and Iraq. Already present in southern Canaan at the time of the fourteenth-century B.C. Amarna letters, these peoples may reflect a cultural interchange between these northern regions and the interior Beqaᶜ of Lebanon as well as the Jordan Valley and its adjacent regions in Palestine.[45]

Flood stage all during harvest (3:15). After the winter rains, the spring harvests of the grains also represent the time when the Jordan River reached maximum levels, above its average 90–100 feet of width and 3–10 feet of depth. Actually, the river narrows and becomes more turbulent as it moves farther south, where Israel would cross. A thicket (*ez-Zōr*) surrounds the river in this area and makes it more difficult to reach.[46]

Water from upstream stopped flowing ... a town called Adam in the vicinity of Zarethan (3:16). Adam is Tell ed-Damieh, almost seventeen miles north of Jericho. Zarethan lies east of the Jordan River. Either it is Tell es-Saʾidiyeh, eleven miles north of Adam, or it is Tell umm-Ḥamid, 2.8 miles north of Adam. Adam was a traditional crossing point of the Jordan River. Close to where the Jabbok River joins from the east and the Wadi el-Fara from the west, the site marks the spot where the southerly flow of the Jordan River becomes more difficult to cross. Sixteen and three-quarters miles separate Adam from the Dead Sea. This means that some 29 percent of the Jordan Valley was affected by this "amazing thing."

The high banks in the region and the tectonic nature of the Jordan Valley have contributed to periodic collapses of earthen

Tell es-Saʾidiyeh (Zarethan)
Todd Bolen/www.BiblePlaces.com

The *zukru* Festival from Thirteenth-Century B.C. Emar

Lines 174–179 describe one of the "visits" of the image of Dagan to the standing stones:

> When the sons of the land of Emar give the *zukru* festival [to] Dagan Lord of the Firstborn during the seventh year:[A-4]
>
> During the sixth year, in the month of SAG.MU, on the 15th [day], the Shaggar-day, they bring out Dagan Lord of the Offspring in procession, his face uncovered. They perform the lesser sacrificial homage before [him] at the gate of the upright stones. After they sacrifice, eat, and drink, they cover his face. The wagon of Dagan passes between the upright stones. He proceeds to [^{d}NIN.URTA]. They have ^{d}NIN.URTA mount (the wagon) with him; their faces covered.

mounds into the river, damming it temporarily. This has occurred at least three times in recent history: 1267, 1906, 1927. On the last occasion the river was blocked for some twenty-one hours.[47]

Passage and Memorial across the Jordan River (4:1–24)

When the whole nation had finished crossing the Jordan (4:1). There is no comparable description of a journey across a river and its preservation as a memorial. However, a religious procession whose goal includes the visiting of special standing stones is not unknown. In the *zukru* festival of the north Syrian city of Emar, a thirteenth-century B.C. text recalls the manner in which the image of the chief god of the city (Dagan) is taken outside the city of Emar in special procession and brought to the standing stones. This procession takes place on the fifteenth day of the first month, not unlike the date here, the tenth day of the first month.

These stones are to be a memorial to the people of Israel forever (4:7). The use of standing stones for various cultic purposes is well attested in the West Semitic world. Like Jacob at Bethel (Gen. 28) and Moses at Mount Sinai (Ex. 24), these stones could be erected as a memorial to a vow or other dedicatory purpose. More often, however, standing stones have been ascribed religious significance either in the sense of some sort of representation of a deity or as a symbol of a sacred spot for veneration. Their association with the worship of other gods is condemned in the Bible (Lev. 26:1; Deut. 7:5; 16:21–22; 1 Kings 14:22–23).

Medeba map showing twelve stones at Gilgal
Todd Bolen/www.BiblePlaces.com

In the Negev and Eastern Sinai some 142 independent sites of standing stones have been found, most with origins dating thousands of years before Israel's appearance.[48] They are generally thought to represent deities and were venerated by libations and other offerings. These were unformed stones and should be distinguished from the carved stelae found in Egypt and Hazor and mentioned in the thirteenth-century Aqhat Myth, where a son's proper respect for his dead father involves erecting a stela in the temple in his memory. Uncarved stones are also found at Shechem and at the later Iron Age sanctuary at Arad.

At thirteenth-century Emar they form part of the *zukru* ritual, a festival whose name means "remembrance." The stones lay outside the town and may have symbolized the chief god Dagan's rule before the town was constructed.[49] Here in Joshua they symbolize the unity of the people rather than gods, but they resemble the other usages insofar as they are associated with a religious center (Gilgal), with a divine act (crossing the Jordan River), and with a memorial for every generation. A close parallel may also be drawn with rock-cut crenellations, artificial piles of stones constructed in the Negev to serve as ancient billboards.[50] They pointed either to a cult site or a significant burial. The stones in Joshua 4 serve as a similar pointer.

About forty thousand armed for battle (4:13). The Hebrew word for "thousand" (*ʾelep*) can carry the sense of a group of soldiers or a squad of indeterminate number. Especially

Area between Jericho and Jordan River—tell is toward the left in the middle
Todd Bolen/www.BiblePlaces.com

Cultic site in the Golan (Rogem Hiri) marked off by concentric circles of stones
Todd Bolen/www.BiblePlaces.com

in military contexts such as this one, the idea of an organized squad is implied. The orderly march, maintaining a distance from the ark and between squads, may be compared with the instructions given to the Hittite palace guard already noted (see sidebar "The Instruction for the Royal Bodyguard" at 3:1).

On the tenth day of the first month (4:19). This expression occurs in Exodus 12:3, where it denotes the beginning of preparations for the Passover meal, which occurs on the fourteenth day. This will initiate the events of Passover and the Feast of Unleavened Bread in the following chapter. Similarities to this festival occur in the Emar *zukru* festival. However, the connection to a direct miracle as here in Joshua is not evident.

Gilgal (4:19). This name describes a "circle," perhaps of stones. If so, this may have set apart the site as a special location for worship, similar to the open air cultic sites in the Negev that were marked off by a double or triple line of stones and used for cultic purposes.[51] The location of this particular Gilgal is not certain. Several small tells in the vicinity of Jericho and the Jordan River could fulfill the requirements for identification. It is also possible, however, that there are no significant remains from this site, given its temporary nature as a camp.

Hand of the LORD is powerful (4:24). The reference here to "the hand of the LORD" matches other usages in contexts where God opposes his enemies (Ex. 9:3; 16:3; Num. 11:23; Deut. 2:15; Josh. 23:31). In the fourteenth-century B.C. Amarna correspondence from the ruler of Jerusalem, that leader appeals to the "arm of the pharaoh" as the source of his own authority and as the only means for continued protection of the city. In one place (EA 287.27), the reference to "arm" is glossed with the term for "hand."[52] The hand of Pharaoh, like the hand of the Lord, becomes an image of his power and might to act on behalf of his subjects.

Preparations West of the Jordan River (5:1–6:5).

All the Amorite kings west of the Jordan and all the Canaanite kings along the coast (5:1). Although war accounts are replete with sacrifices given to appease the gods before a battle, there is little in other ancient literature to compare with the circumcision and celebration of the Passover (with no mention of a lamb or any other animal; 5:1–12). Although Egyptian and Mesopotamian sources speak of the accompaniment of the king by the god, there is little that describes a conversation with the divine or the sort of specific instructions that are found in 5:13–6:5. The role of Israel's God in encouraging Joshua and the role of Israel in preparing and enacting the battle ceremonies are unique.

No longer had the courage (5:1). The fear of enemy leaders is a common motif in ancient Near Eastern battle accounts. As in many such accounts, it forms a prelude to victory over the enemy.

Flint knives and circumcise (5:2). Better understood as obsidian, the use of such smooth and sharp stones for cutting is attested long after the introduction of bronze and iron. The sharpness of the stones would be on a par with anything the metalsmiths might produce. Obsidian knives are

Relief in the tomb of Ankhmahor at Saqqara depicting a priest performing ritual circumcision
Werner Forman Archive

mentioned and portrayed in Egyptian scenes from as early as the Sixth Dynasty in circumcision. One text from nearly a thousand years earlier describes the circumcision of 120 males at one time.[53]

Land flowing with milk and honey (5:6). Having already occurred fifteen times in the Pentateuch as a common epithet for the Promised Land of Canaan, this picture of agricultural and pastoral abundance envisions life in the highlands of Canaan, where Israel would initially settle and grow in numbers. In particular, date honey and goat milk may be anticipated. In the early second millennium, the Egyptian Sinuhe visited this area and described it as follows: "Plentiful was its honey.... There was no limit to any (kind of) cattle."[54]

The day after the Passover ... they ate some of the produce of the land: unleavened bread and roasted grain (5:11). The Passover celebration culminates the crossing of the Jordan River and the entrance into the Promised Land. The Passover occurs on the fourteenth day of the first month at the time of the barley harvest. Therefore the "elevation offering" of the barley sheaf takes place at this time (Lev. 23:10–14). It is the presentation of the firstfruits of the barley, a grain that matures around this time and forms the most important staple for the inhabitants of Canaan. The Passover and Feast of Unleavened Bread constitute both a memory of the Exodus and a celebration of gratitude for the firstfruits of barley. The unleavened bread would require time to make; as a complement the roasted grain could be made more quickly (1 Sam. 17:17).[55]

The change in diet, from manna to grain, provides one more signal that the time in the desert has ended and a new age is dawning. The literary connection of this Passover with the crossing of the Jordan River and the beginning of the occupation of the Promised Land adds to the connection with the crossing of the Red Sea. An additional significance for two similar or identical festivals occurring at the same time of the year may already be indicated by a similar connection of the Feast of Tabernacles with the Feast of Yahweh in Leviticus 23:33–36 and 39–44. These are usually taken to describe the same feast although the details differ.

Such a phenomenon also occurs in the multimonth ritual calendar from Emar (#446). In this calendar two festivals,

Cylinder seal impression showing presentation of grain sheaf
Kim Walton, courtesy of the Oriental Institute Museum

perhaps two parts of the same festival, are described as beginning on the fifteenth day of the first month (cf. the beginning of the Feast of Unleavened Bread).[56] There are many similarities although the two separate descriptions focus on two different deities in the text. The point of connection with the Passover and subsequent feast in Joshua 5 is that its significance can take on multiple meanings and that this can occur early in the development of the festival(s).

Then the LORD said to Joshua, "See, I have delivered Jericho into your hands" (6:2). This statement is a continuation of the words of the commander of Yahweh's army in 5:13–15. Like the patriarchal accounts of divine visitations (Gen. 18 and 22) and like Moses (Ex. 3), distinctions between the messenger and the Lord are not clearly maintained.

On the seventh day (6:4). The number seven in these seven days has a twofold significance. First, as the note on 5:11 indicates, the Passover takes on a special and new significance with the crossing of the Jordan River. The seven days of marching around Jericho are identical to the seven days of Feast of Unleavened Bread. They thus continue to invest this annual event with new significance. See comments on 5:11 for the comparisons with Emar calendar.

Second, the use of "seven" in a temporal context is known in Egyptian sources where an attack may occur on the seventh day or a besieged town may fall on the seventh month. Thus the seventh day could have ominous implications for Jericho.[57] Further, the Legend of Kirta from Ugarit records how King Kirta waits outside the city of Udum for seven days before the king of Udum appeals for peace.[58]

Orthostat from Tell Halaf with relief of man carrying what may be a shofar, though some identify it as a throwing stick
Z. Radovan/www.BibleLandPictures.com

Trumpets (6:4–5). The use of the *šôpār* or "ram's horn" was the most common wind instrument in the Israelite repertoire of musical performance. If we continue the comparison of the procession with the ark with the Hittite Instructions for the Royal Bodyguard (see the introduction to ch. 3), then the blowing on the horns by the priests corresponds to the cries of welcome given to the king when he arrives at his destination.

Jericho Captured (6:6–27)

Joshua son of Nun called the priests (6:6). The account of verses 6–15 and 20 repeats all the phrases found in verses 3–5 of the preceding section. The emphasis is on obedience, carrying out the word of Joshua given to him by God. The movement as a ceremonial procession continues the ongoing purpose of God and his people begun in the Exodus and at Mount Sinai and culminating in the deposit of the ark in Jerusalem (2 Sam. 6) and the temple. Seen in this manner and compared to the material already noted in the Hittite Instruction for the Royal Bodyguard and, to a lesser extent, in the procession of the divine image in the Emar *zukru* festival, the emphasis is on the movement of the ark and its escort. Thus the collapse of the walls and the destruction of Jericho are a consequence rather than the focus of the main action. Unlike modern storytellers, the text emphasizes the obedience of Joshua and the Israelite army.

Devoted to the LORD (6:17). "Devote" (*ḥērem*) was already used by Rahab to describe Israel's treatment of Sihon and Og (2:10). However, its most significant and controversial usage is as applied to Jericho and the subsequent battles in Joshua. It is commanded in the law of Moses as something that must be done to every Canaanite population center in the Promised Land (Deut. 20:6–8). The same term is used in the ninth-century B.C. Moabite Inscription of King Mesha concerning his treatment of the men of Gad in the land of Ataroth. The text describes how he killed all the people and "devoted them to the ban." Thus, the practice was not limited to Israel. Indeed, similar customs occurred among the Egyptian and Mesopotamian civilizations.[59]

The Aramaic inscription on the funerary stele of Sin zir Ibni curses anyone who might try to harm it and blesses anyone who protects it. The gods invoked are Mesopotamian: Sin, Shamash, Nergal, and Nusku.
Marie-Lan Nguyen/ Wikimedia Commons, courtesy of the Louvre

In every case, there is some sense in which the destruction of a people and their possessions relates to a dedication to the deity of the conquering army. In Israel, this was understood as returning to God what belonged to him but had departed from his sovereignty through accumulated sin (cf. Gen. 15:16). The description of "men and women, young and old, cattle, sheep and donkeys" as "devoted to the LORD" when they were killed by Israel may be stereotypical and synonymous with "all, everyone," rather than an indication of the killing of noncombatants.[60]

Wall collapsed (6:20). Like the miraculous crossing of the Jordan River, this sign indicates God's presence with his people and the futility of resistance. A Hittite text attributes a similar act to the deity Shaushga: "Shaushga of Shamuha, my lady, revealed also then her divine justice: in the very moment I reached him, the wooden fortifications fell down to the length of one *gippešar*."[61] This text indicates that those who heard of the destruction of this site would have understood the significance of Israel's mission and the power of its God.

Cursed before the LORD is the man who undertakes to rebuild this city, Jericho (6:26). The first millennium B.C. Phoenician kings left sarcophagi with inscriptions on them that curse anyone who would disturb their burials. Kings such as Ahiram and Eshmunezer mention the offspring of the perpetrator and warn of their loss.[62]

Achan and the Defeat at Ai (7:1–26)

Achan son of Carmi, the son of Zimri, the son of Zerah, of the tribe of Judah (7:1). This genealogy, the longest one in the book of Joshua, ties the perpetrator with the tribes of Israel and thus implicates the whole nation. The names of Achan's line are all West Semitic names, with parallels elsewhere among the ancient Israelites and West Semitic peoples. Achan's name is not Israelite and has a possible parallel from early second millennium B.C. Alalakh in northern Syria. This name may be Hurrian in origin and would not have been understood to later Israelite scribes. Perhaps for this reason, the Chronicler (1 Chron. 2:7) and the Septuagint (in both Joshua and Chronicles) change the last consonant and read Achar, a nickname that connects the figure with the Valley of Achor (7:26). The Hebrew root behind Achar/Achor means "disaster" (7:26).[63]

Ai, which is near Beth Aven to the east of Bethel (7:2). Although there have been attempts to reassign these sites, the traditional identifications place Ai at et-Tell, Beth-Aven at Tell Maryam, and Bethel

The Fall of Jericho

The question arises as to what was the Jericho that the Israelites were conquering. Given the absence of much, though not all, archaeological evidence for settlement in the Late Bronze Age period (1550–1200 B.C.), the picture of a small settlement surrounded by mudbrick walls (see comment on 2:15) seems reasonable. Indeed, the term translated "city" (*ʿîr*) can describe a citadel (2 Sam. 12:26) or a fort (5:7, 9), perhaps within a city. This seems a more reasonable understanding of Jericho. It was primarily a military compound designed to guard strategic passes east and west, as well as the north-south road, and to do so on behalf of towns in the hill country, such as Bethel and Jerusalem. This would be an ideal location for an inn or hostel, such as Rahab operated with her family (cf. the story of the good Samaritan in Jesus' time).

The "king" of Jericho would then have been a military commander under the authority of hill country leaders. From about the same time period the Amarna letters reveal the West Semitic root for "king" (*mlk*), used in Joshua, to apply as well to commissioners and others under a higher authority (see comment on 2:2).[A-5]

The Amarna letters also provide examples of the size of armies in Canaan in the fourteenth century B.C., textual evidence that is closer than any other to the period in which the Bible places the story of Joshua. Here many princes of Canaan request forces from the pharaoh to supplement their own in order to fight their enemies. The numbers requested are never higher than a few hundred and sometimes as low as twenty—this being the number requested by the king of the important coastal city of Tyre (EA 151.14–16). The evidence from the town closest to Jericho is that of the leader of Jerusalem, who requests fifty reinforcements (EA 289.42). These are reinforcements, not the whole number of defenders.

Remains of the earlier Middle Bronze walls
Jack Hazut

Nevertheless, it would not make sense to request reinforcements unless they significantly enhanced the strength of the existing force, increasing it by at least a fourth, or more likely something on the order of doubling the force. Jericho, a smaller site than Jerusalem, could have a hundred soldiers or less guarding it.[A-6]

If this is so, then why does the book of Joshua make so much of the attack on Jericho? One may balance this observation with the note that the actual Hebrew text of Jericho's attack (6:16–25) contains 86 words devoted to the salvation of Rahab and her family and 102 devoted to the destruction of Jericho. Thus the author of Joshua regarded Rahab's deliverance almost as important as Jericho's destruction. From a comparative perspective, the importance of Jericho is that of the important victory of the first battle by a new leader. Thus a Hittite king wrote to a newly crowned Assyrian monarch with this advice: "On whatever campaign he goes for the first time, where he is three or four times superior, or which is some overpowered place, let him go for the first time against such a place."[A-7]

Whatever the actual size of Jericho, this victory will serve to confirm Joshua as the true leader and successor of Moses in the eyes of Israel (3:7) and will further demoralize the Canaanite opponents (5:1).[A-8]

The lengthy nature of initial battles should also be noted. This occurs, for example, in the campaign of Tuthmosis III for years 22–42 (c. 1458–1438 B.C.), where his initial battle at Megiddo receives the fullest account. So in Joshua the first battles at Jericho and Ai receive more detailed discussion than the later ones.[A-9]

at Beitin.[64] Ai is then a mile southeast of Bethel and Beth-Aven is three and a third miles south of Ai. There were three main routes in the Iron Age that led from Jericho westward into the hill country.[65] The best known was the southerly road to Jerusalem. The northernmost road led to Ophrah. In between there was a road that led to Beitin, with Ai functioning as a fort (like Jericho) to guard the approach.

Et-Tell
Todd Bolen/www.BiblePlaces.com

Hittite plague prayer of Murshili II
Istanbul Archaeological Museum; © Dr. James C. Martin

Ai means "ruin," and this may point to an explanation for the problem of the absence of Late Bronze Age occupation. It functioned as a fort to guard the eastern flank of Ai at this time. As such there was no need for permanent occupation and so the warriors assigned to the site created a makeshift construction by reusing some of the already existing Early Bronze Age walls.

Tell Miryam
Todd Bolen/www.BiblePlaces.com

Stone quarries (7:5). The Hebrew word *š^ebārîm* describes the steep slopes of the Wadi el-Makkuk, about three and a half miles east-southeast from Ai along the road to Jericho.[66]

Tore his clothes and fell facedown ... sprinkled dust on their heads (7:6). These are common symbols of mourning in the Bible and the ancient Near East.[67] Compare the plague prayers of Murshili II (see next comment) for similar penitence of the leader(s) before a deity at the time of a national catastrophe.

Consecrate the people (7:13). The story of Joshua 7 is one of an attempt by the Israelites to pursue a military campaign against Ai apart from God, its failure, confession before God, and the subsequent identification and eradication of the sin of Achan. Ancient Near Eastern literature does not often address failed military campaigns. Most of this literature served royal interests of propaganda and thus did not emphasize such campaigns.

The Hittite rituals, however, do include one notation about an army that is defeated by the enemy.[68] In this ritual a human corpse and several animals are divided into two pieces. The army marches between them and between two fires as they pass through a gate constructed for the ritual. They come to a river where they sprinkle water on themselves and perform the ritual again in the steppe. The significance of these actions does not receive explanation. It is very different from the events of Joshua 7. However, the sprinkling with water may suggest some sort of purification, which may be compared to the search of Joshua and the elders for forgiveness and reconciliation with Israel's God.

Perhaps related to the subject of divine punishment are the plague prayers of Murshili II, which come from the latter part of the fourteenth century B.C. These prayers assume that the plague that Mushili's father, Shuppiluliuma, brought from Egypt and that killed him and continued to ravage among the Hittites forms a divine judgment. Thus Murshili confesses the sin of his father, pleads innocence for himself, and requests divine advice through oracles, dreams, or prophets.[69] Like Joshua 7, the leader of the people confesses sin and waits on God for divine guidance through whatever means possible.

Burial cairn at Rogem Hiri in the Golan
Todd Bolen/www.BiblePlaces.com

Tribes ... clans ... families (7:17–18). These are the building blocks of Israelite tribal society. The family was the "house of a father" (Heb. *bêt-ʾāb*). It was the basic societal unit, an extended family headed by the senior living male. Its physical manifestation remains in the architectural forms of early Israel. Clusters of houses in villages and towns may reflect the architectural reality of this social group in the Iron Age. Clans might be represented at times by villages or groups of villages.[70]

Beautiful robe from Babylonia ... a wedge of gold weighing fifty shekels (7:21). Inventory lists contemporary with early Israel are found in Babylonia and Egypt, as well as the culturally closer city-states of Ugarit and Alalakh. Descriptions of garments as well as precious metals occur on such texts in similar constructions. The Hebrew text indicates the origin of the robe in Shinar. This term for Babylon occurs primarily in second-millennium B.C. texts. The same is true of the term for "wedge" of gold (lit., "tongue" of gold). The term in identical word order (tongue–gold–number–shekels–weight) occurs only one other place in the ancient Near East, on a fourteenth-century B.C. list of gifts from the Hurrian king of Mitanni to the pharaoh.[71] Two hundred shekels of silver would amount to about six pounds, while fifty shekels of gold calculate to about one and a quarter pounds. The note of a garment followed by its place of origin

Beersheba residential complex
Kim Walton

(Babylon) is found repeatedly on inventories from thirteenth-century B.C. Ugarit.[72]

Spread them out before the Lord ... they burned them (7:23, 25). The items that Achan had taken belonged to the Lord and had to be returned to the deity. The expression here may suggest a formal display of these items before the ark of the covenant as part of the ceremony to appease the divine wrath directed against Israel. In the Old Babylonian period, the theft of temple property was a serious offense. It is among the first of the laws in Hammurabi's collection (CH §6). The punishment for theft of property dedicated to a deity (*asakku*) was death by burning.[73] The Israelite approach appears more merciful, with death by stoning preceding the incineration.

Over Achan they heaped up a large pile of rocks, which remains to this day.... Therefore that place has been called the Valley of Achor ever since (7:26). It is well known that many cairns or mounds of stones throughout the Middle East mark the burial site of a revered sheikh. Insofar as Achan comes to be known as Achor (see comment on 7:2), this resembles the manner in which many sheikhs' names are identical with the place names of their burial sites.[74] Dating back thousands of years in the Negev, artificial piles of stone mark the burial sites of special people, just as with Achan.[75]

Region of Beitin and et-Tell

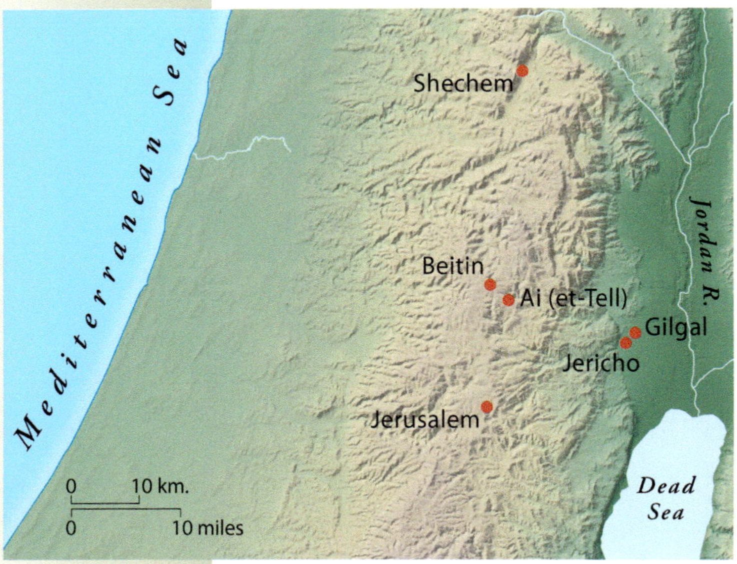

Assault on Ai (8:1–29)

Attack Ai (8:1). With the sin of Achan repented of and atoned for, the narrative turns to the attack against the leader of Ai, his forces, and his stronghold. The particulars of the plan used here are not unusual, as will be seen. However, the comprehensive description of this battle has no parallel in the writings of the ancient Near East.

This is not to say that battles were not described. They were. Rather, the emphasis on the Israelite forces remains surprising. Most of the detailed contemporary battle accounts emphasize the role of the commander and hardly mention that of the soldiers. Here Joshua also leads; there is no doubt about that. However, the soldiers with him receive full credit for their work in the military expedition. Thus the story is not of a sole king or leader, such as the Egyptian accounts of campaigns where the pharaoh reigns triumphant. Instead, the unity of the army of Israel is emphasized, in contrast to the partial force of Joshua 7. In this manner success is assured and the victory belongs to the nation and its God rather than to the individual leader.

Set an ambush behind the city (8:2, 4). The use of an ambush in warfare has great antiquity. It occurs in Canaan in the thirteenth century B.C. where Egyptians record it in the Papyrus Anastasi I.[76] It appears again in the strategy of a tenth-century B.C. Assyrian king, where it resembles the tactic used by Israel in this chapter: "While I remained in front of (the city of) Parsindi I set the cavalry (and) pioneers in ambush (behind the city). I killed fifty troops, the fighting men of Ameka, in the open country."[77]

Also comparable is the ambush by the Israelites against the Benjamites at Gibeah in Judges 20. There as well the topography allowed for a hiding place near the target. Further examples occur in the ancient literature well into classical times.[78]

Beitin
Todd Bolen/www.BiblePlaces.com

Sent them out at night (8:3). Maneuvers and whole battles might be fought at night. There are examples centuries earlier at Mari of night warfare. Night marches and attacks were used by the fourteenth-century B.C. Hittite king Murshili II and by the opponents of a military commander from thirteenth-century Ugarit.[79]

Bethel (8:9, 12, 17). Located perhaps one mile west of Ai (according to the traditional designations of the sites), Bethel represents the main population center of the immediate area. If Ai is indeed a fort intended to guard Bethel, then it was probably staffed by soldiers from Bethel so that the two armies were parts of one and the same military force. For this reason, Joshua took Bethel into account in his strategy, and, as expected, the army of Bethel joined Ai in the apparent rout of the Israelites—now a much larger force than in chapter 7, where the army of Ai could handle things by itself. That a major center should be surrounded by forts may be suggested by Iron Age Jerusalem and what are best understood as contemporary forts guarding it located in the modern suburbs of Giloh and French Hill.

Javelin (8:18, 26). The Hebrew *kîdôn* was actually a curved sword, either a sickle sword or a scimitar (in the Philistine version

Sickle sword
Guillaume Blanchard/Wikimedia Commons, courtesy of the Louvre

Egyptian deity holding out sickle sword
William Benson

of 1 Sam. 17). In Egyptian it was called the *khopesh*, the foreleg of an animal.[80]

Israel did carry off for themselves the livestock and plunder of this city (8:27; cf. 2). This verse demonstrates the flexibility of the *ḥērem*. God changed the rules in comparison with what he had commanded at Jericho. At Ai the Israelites could and did carry off the plunder for themselves. This would be crucial for the people. The manna had stopped before they attacked Jericho. While in the fertile Jordan Valley, they might enjoy both cultivated and wild barley that was ready for harvest. Now that they were in the less fertile highland and the rather arid region of Ai, they might have found less available food growing naturally. Thus the livestock and other supplies provided essential support for the continued success of the army.

Permanent heap of ruins ... king of Ai ... his body ... raised a large pile of rocks over it (8:28–29). Compare this treatment of Ai and its leader to that of Achan in 7:26 and see the note there for memorial cairns.

He hung the king of Ai on a tree and left him there until evening (8:29). This treatment of Ai's commander resembles that of the five Amorite kings in 10:26–27 and is characteristic of the method of execution for enemy leaders, especially those whom the victor wishes to use for an example. Compare the fate of the rebel leaders of Ekron whom the Assyrian king Sennacherib defeated in 701 B.C.: "... the governors (and) nobles who had sinned I put to death; and I hung their corpses on poles around the city" (Col. III.8–10).[81]

Mount Ebal Altar (8:30–35)

Altar of uncut stones, on which no iron tool had been used (8:31). This is the type of altar commanded in Exodus 20:22–26 and specifically for Mount Ebal in Deuteronomy 27:5. A parallel occurs in the Iron Age II sanctuary at Tel Arad in southern Judah. There Y. Aharoni discovered an Israelite-period altar made of field stones. Otherwise, altars (and other cultic objects) within Canaan were constructed of carefully cut stones. The use of uncut stones in constructions of religious significance can be compared with the standing stones and other cultic items from the Negev desert.[82]

Joshua copied on stones the law of Moses, which he had written (8:32). Here Joshua fulfills the law of Moses regarding the king who must copy and read the law (Deut. 17:18–19). He also fulfills the command to

Impaling of prisoners by Assyrians from palace of Tiglath-pileser III
Werner Forman Archive/The British Museum

Altar on Mount Ebal

Joshua 8:30–31 clearly states that Joshua built "an altar of uncut stones" on Mount Ebal in accordance with divine instructions to Moses (Deut. 27:2–8). Israeli archeologist Adam Zertal surveyed Mount Ebal, north of Shechem. He found no evidence from the Late Bronze or Early Iron Ages with the exception of one site. That site was located on the third highest peak near (though not on) the ridge facing an open area where a large number of people could easily gather and reasonably expect to hear what was said from the site. Zertal identified the site as an open air altar with two levels of occupation. Based on scarab and pottery evidence found at the site, he suggested that a rather simple pit was built and used for sacrifices in the second half of the thirteenth century B.C. This was followed peacefully by a more elaborate structure built of field stones, surrounded by a veranda, and accessed by a ramp. Its occupation occurred in the first half of the twelfth century B.C.

Zertal found that the main animals killed there (for sacrifice) were cattle, sheep, and a local species of deer. No pigs were slaughtered at the site. Suggestions that the site was a watchtower raise the question of its isolated structure with no sign of human occupation nearby and its location away from the ridge itself. Theories that it was a single farm house create an anomaly in a region otherwise comprised of villages and the absence of what one might expect to see at a domestic dwelling of the Early Iron Age.

Is this the altar described in Joshua 8:30–35 and perhaps suggested again in chapter 24? It is not possible to say with certainty. However, after reading the excavator's report and conducting a visual tour of the site, it certainly looks like an early Israelite altar such as is described in this text in Joshua. Despite strong opposition by others, there remains no better explanation than that this represents an anomalous Early Iron Age cultic site that has no clear cultural antecedents anywhere in the region.[A-10]

Altar on Mount Ebal (in foreground)
Z. Radovan/www.BibleLandPictures.com

Arad altar of fieldstones
Kim Walton

the ninth century from the sites of Kuntillet ʿAjrud in the northern Sinai and at Tell Deir ʿAlla in the Jordan Valley. In both cases this occurs in cultic contexts. Writing in alphabetic (proto-) Hebrew script is known in the second millennium B.C., and examples have been found in the land of Israel from the thirteenth and twelfth centuries onward through every subsequent century in all major areas of the land; these reflect a variety of writers. Leaders such as Joshua would have known how to write and likely many of the Israelites had some measure of literacy.[83]

coat the stones with plaster and to write on them the words of the law at Mount Ebal (Deut. 27:4, 8). Writing on plaster is known in

Gibeonite Ruse (9:1–27).

Hittites, Amorites, Canaanites, Perizzites, Hivites and Jebusites (9:1). See comments on 3:10 for these groups.

Now when all the kings west of the Jordan heard ... they came together to make war against Joshua and Israel (9:1–2). These introductory remarks, which preface chapters 9–12, are followed by a story of the ruse of the Gibeonites. This account has no precise parallels in the ancient Near East. That may be because victors were reluctant to admit being tricked and because the nature of deceptions means that many of them may never have been revealed to the party deceived. Nevertheless, major parts of the text do have their correspondent in the annals of the great powers of the ancient world: Hittites, Egyptians, Assyrians, and Babylonians.

Of special interest is the overall sense of the chapter in which the general hostility of the nations "west of the Jordan" corresponds to the specific concerns of a people in the immediate vicinity of the Israelites. The association of the Gibeonites with the Hivites (9:3) and of

Deir 'Alla inscription concerning Balaam written on plaster
Todd Bolen/www.BiblePlaces.com

Region of Gibeon

together for war has a long tradition in the annals of the ancient Near East. Compare the seventh-century Neo-Assyrian account of the background to the war against the Egyptian pharaoh Taharqa: "Taharaqa, the king of Egypt and Nubia, in Memphis heard of the coming of my expeditionary force; and in order to make armed resistance and to make battle with me he mustered his warriors."[84]

The people of Gibeon (9:3). The identification of Gibeon with el-Jib seems assured on the basis of the Iron Age jar handles found there. Although Middle Bronze and Iron Age settlements and walls have been identified, no occupation of the Late Bronze Age has yet been uncovered. This would have been the period during which the Bible's chronology places the events of Joshua 9. However, Kitchen estimates that only 5 percent (or less)

the Hivites with the Hurrians (see comment on 3:10), a second-millennium B.C. people of northern Syria and southern Turkey, invites comparisons with the materials of the Hittite archives. The Hittite culture was influenced by the Hurrians, and similar customs often prevailed there (see sidebar, "They Resorted to a Ruse"). However, the aspects of this ruse have similarities in the war and conquest annals of the other cultures.

The sense in which potential hostility begins with the enemy "hearing" and coming

Gibeon (el-Jib)
Bible Scene Multimedia/Maurice Thompson

▸ They Resorted to a Ruse

Despite the absence of an exact parallel, the Hittite annals of Murshili II do record examples of willing capitulation of a region that leads to servitude instead of annihilation, of the use of vulnerable "emissaries" instead of the leader to negotiate, and of elders of a town coming and subjugating themselves. Two examples are cited by Younger.[A-11] The first comes from the land of the Seha River:

> But as I came back out of the land of the Seha River, I would have had to fight in the heart of Seha River(-land) Manapa-Datta who was the ruler (of that region). (However), when Manapa-Datta heard concerning me: "The king of Hatti comes!" He was afraid, and did not come forth to meet me. He sent forth his mother, the old men, (and) the old women to meet me. They came to me. They bowed down at (my) feet. Now because women bowed down at my feet I gave to the women as they wished. And so I did not go to the Seha River(-land). The fugitives of Hattusha, who were in the Seha River(-land), they handed over to me (freely). The fugitives which they handed over to me were 4,000 people. And I sent them forth to Hattusha. And they brought them forth. But Manapa-Datta and the land of the Seha River I took into servitude.[A-12]

The handing over of fugitives is a common treaty provision for vassal states and suggests a defined treaty relationship was created. The second example deals with a town and region apparently ruled by elders:

> When the people of the city of Azzi saw that fighting (their) strong cities I subjugated them: the people of Azzi, who have strong cities, rocky mountains, (and) high difficult terrain—they were afraid! And the elders of the land came before me, and they bowed themselves down at (my) feet. And they spoke:
>
> "Our lord! Do not destroy us! Lord, take us into servitude, and we will begin to provide your lordship troops and charioteers. The Hittite fugitives which (are) with us, we will provide these."
>
> Then, I, my sun, did not destroy them. I took them into servitude; and I made them slaves.[A-13]

of the site has been dug.[85] Furthermore, the presence of at least eight Late Bronze Age tombs at el-Jib suggests that occupation may have occurred there.

Nevertheless, the identification remains a problem. The use of the expression "the people of Gibeon" rather than "king of Gibeon," as is customary at the other places named, suggests a different form of government. No king of Gibeon is ever designated. Given the identification with the Hivites/Hurrians and their influence on the Hittites, it is interesting to note that the local government by councils of elders seems to have been known among the Hittite provinces and surrounding peoples.[86]

Gilgal (9:6). If this is the Gilgal of 4:19–20 and 5:9–10, then the story would appear out of sequence, for the Israelites at the end of chapter 8 are based in the central hill country near Shechem. However, as noted at 4:19, Gilgal may be a description of any oval-shaped site. El-ʾUnuq, east of Shechem, could qualify.[87]

Treaty (9:11, 16). The suzerain/vassal treaty has many examples preserved from the Hittite archives. It was used by that empire for making official agreements with neighboring states of lesser strength. This would have been the type of treaty made with the Gibeonites. An element of such a

Kiriath Jearim: Tell el-Azhar
Daniel Frese/www.BiblePlaces.com

treaty is the list of gods of each side who are called upon to uphold the treaty. This recognition of foreign deities is one reason why the Israelites were forbidden to make such treaties with their neighbors in the land (Ex. 34:12, 15; Deut. 7:2; 23:6).

Kephirah, Beeroth and Kiriath Jearim (9:17). Mentioned along with Gibeon, this suggests that there was a league of four cities of Hivites in what would become the heart of the territory of Benjamin. Kephirah may be identified with Khirbet el-Kefireh, five miles west-southwest of Gibeon. Kiriath Jearim is perhaps Tell el-Azhar, about eight miles north of Jerusalem. Is Beeroth el-Bireh at Khirbet Raddana? If so, then all these towns lay close to one another. The region should not take three days to reach from the area of Mount Ebal (8:30–35). Either the Israelites were interrupted on their journey, perhaps by unrecorded battles, or the term "three days" signifies a general period of time rather than a specific number of days.

He made the Gibeonites woodcutters and water carriers for the community and for the altar of the LORD (9:27). Assuming that the Gibeonites remained in their cities (as the next chapter suggests), it seems reasonable that part of the community and at least one sanctuary were located in the region of Gibeon. This may refer to the high place at Gibeon that Solomon later visited (1 Kings 3:4–5). An Israelite sanctuary, like those of their neighbors, would require wood to burn the incense and sacrifices and water to keep the altar and sanctuary clean from the blood and gore of the animal sacrifices.

Southern Coalition (10:1–43)

Now Adoni-Zedek king of Jerusalem heard (10:1). Perhaps more than any other chapter of Joshua, chapter 10 is filled with material that possesses parallels in ancient Near Eastern literature and can be further illuminated by comparisons with aspects of contemporary

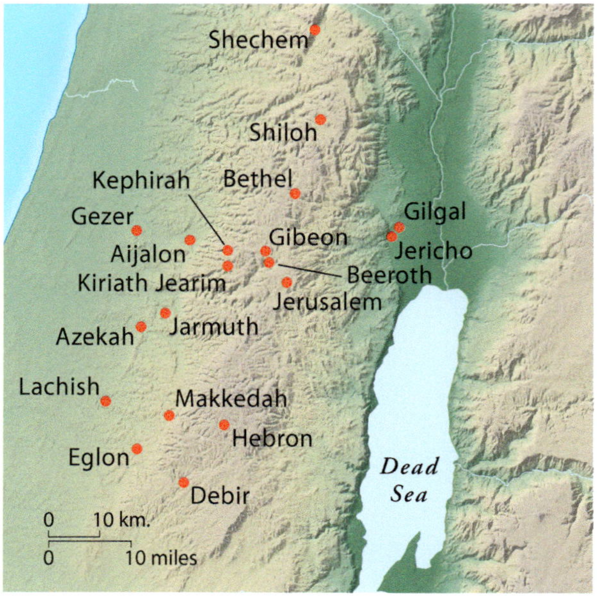

Southern Coalition Sites

Amarna letter 287 referring to Abdi-Heba of Jerusalem
Bildarchiv Preussischer Kulturbesitz/ Art Resource, NY, courtesy of Vorderasiatisches Museum, Staatliche Museen zu Berlin, Berlin, Germany

culture. In its totality it resembles the annalistic accounts of the ancient Near East. Kitchen has noted the manner in which Egyptian and Hittite annalistic accounts of the Late Bronze Age preserve an overall structure similar to Joshua 10.[88]

Thus, the Ten Year Annals of Murshili II include near their beginning a description of hostilities taken against Murshili and his response in the destruction of two cities. This is followed by the Kashka enemy all gathering together against him for war and his defeat of them. Then in subsequent years, there is an iterative construction in which the same phrases are used repeatedly to describe the assault and defeat of enemy city after enemy city. This bears a surprising resemblance to Joshua, where the Israelites first defeat two "cities," Jericho and Ai. This is followed by a coalition coming together to oppose them (10:1–5). There follows a description of town after town being attacked and destroyed in an iterative fashion (10:28–42).

Also of interest are the annals of Tuthmosis III, covering years 22–42 of his reign (c. 1458–1438 B.C.). Here as well is the threat of the enemy consolidating diverse forces and coming together at Megiddo to battle the pharaoh. The first battle at Megiddo and its immediate background receive the greatest detail of coverage. This resembles Joshua's initial battle from Gibeon to Makkedah (10:9–27). In both cases the far greater detail of the initial battle contrasts with the briefer, more repetitious descriptions of the following battles in the campaign, whether the sixteen of Tuthmosis or the five or six of Joshua 10. The similarities in style argue that this chapter is patterned according to royal annals and followed forms used in the Late Bronze Age.

Adoni-Zedek king of Jerusalem (10:1). The king's name may well be interpreted as "my lord is the (god) Tsaduq/Tsedeq." Both elements occur in personal names of West Semites in the fourteenth century.[89] Jerusalem was an important center in the fourteenth century B.C. Its leader, Abdi-Heba, wrote at least six letters that suggest a regional administrative center overseen by a court possessing some literary sophistication.[90] Whether or not the Middle Bronze Age walls remained in use through this period and the stepped structure can be dated to the end of the period, it is clear that the large amount of Late Bronze Age pottery found supports occupation at this site.[91]

Hoham king of Hebron, Piram king of Jarmuth, Japhia king of Lachish and Debir king of Eglon (10:3). Hoham and Piram are names with Hurrian or Anatolian elements attested elsewhere in personal names of the Late Bronze Age. Japhia and Debir are West Semitic names, both of whose roots have personal names also attested in the late second millennium B.C. Japhia is the name of the leader of nearby Gezer in the Amarna letters.[92] Hebron is identi-

The Annals of Tuthmosis III from Karnak

This excerpted text contains a similar structure as that of Joshua 10 with its observation of all the armies gathered against the pharaoh:

> Year 23, 1st month of the third season, day 16–as far as the town of Yehem. [His majesty] ordered a conference with his victorious army, speaking as follows: "That [wretched] enemy of Kadesh has come and has entered into Megiddo. He is [there] at this moment. He has gathered to him the princes of [every] foreign country [which had been] loyal to Egypt, as well as (those) as far as Naharin and M[itanni], them of Hurru, them of Kode, their horses, their armies, [and their people], for he says–so it is reported–"I shall wait [here] in Megiddo [to fight against his majesty]."[A-14]

This is followed by a lengthy description of the defeat of Megiddo and then abbreviated descriptions of the remaining cities taken.

Annals of Tuthmosis III from Karnak
Dr. James C. Martin

Victories of Thutmose III are portrayed on the wall of the seventh pylon at the temple at Karnak.
Markh/Wikimedia Commons

fied with Tell er-Rumeideh, Lachish with Tell ed-Duweir, Jarmuth with Tel Yarmut, and Debir with Khirbet Rabud. Jarmuth would then lie sixteen miles west-southwest of Jerusalem, guarding the Sorek and Elah valleys. The other sites form an arc sweeping southeast, providing key strategic centers through the area.[93] Although Late

Bronze Age occupation has been disputed at Hebron, a thirteenth-century B.C. itinerary of Ramesses II seems to name it.[94]

"Come up and help me attack Gibeon," he said, "because it has made peace with Joshua and the Israelites" (10:4). This is the only biblical example of a reported message from one Canaanite king to another. Although most likely a summary of what was sent, it preserves rhetorical forms not unlike the Amarna letters from Canaan in the fourteenth century B.C. The use of threefold repetition in the verbs (come up, help me, attack) and in the identification of the king's enemy (Gibeon, Joshua, the Israelites) all have their parallels in letters from Canaanite kings of Jerusalem and Shechem. Even the manner in which "peace" becomes a pretext for war has a parallel. Thus the message reflects authentic style of this period.[95]

Jarmuth as seen from Azekah
Todd Bolen/www.BiblePlaces.com

After an all-night march from Gilgal, Joshua took them by surprise (10:9). Of the many such events that took place in ancient warfare, one finds the following example in the Ten Year Annals of Murshili II: "But when night fell, I turned about and advanced against Pitaggatalli. I marched the whole night through, and daybreak found me on the outskirts of Sapidduwa. And as soon as the sun rose I advanced to battle against him."[96]

Beth Horon ... Azekah and Makkedah (10:10). Beth Horon is situated at the major pass from the hill country of Gibeon to the coastal plain. Fleeing westward and then

Beth Horon ridge
Bible Scene Multimedia/Maurice Thompson

Azekah
Todd Bolen/www.BiblePlaces.com

southward to Azekah, the coalition would be close to Jarmuth, but apparently the majority did not seek refuge there. Makkedah should be identified with Khirbet el-Qom further east and south in the Shephelah. At this point the remaining forces would be equidistant from Lachish, Eglon, and Hebron and thus able to seek refuge there.[97] This forms a summary of the more detailed account of verses 28–42.

The LORD hurled large hailstones down on them from the sky (10:11). Again, there are parallels to such divine intervention in the annals of ancient kings and their battles. Close in type is that of the eighth-century Assyrian Sargon, who writes concerning one campaign:

> The rest of the people, who had fled to save their lives, whom he had abandoned that the glorious might of Ashur, my lord, might be magnified, Adad, the violent, the son of Anu, the valiant, uttered his loud cry against them; and with the flood cloud and hailstones, he totally annihilated the remainder.[98]

"O sun, stand still over Gibeon, O moon, over the Valley of Aijalon" (10:12). This event has motivated interpreters to seek a variety of solutions, and it remains among the most widely contested of events in the Bible. Did the sun actually cease to move? The verb allows for other interpretations. Why would Joshua request this in the morning (when the moon would be visible) as the battle was still young and there would be many hours of daylight remaining? Is it a solar eclipse?[99] If so, there is no apparent benefit for Israel. Is it a celestial omen?[100] But then why would it remain "until the nation avenged itself on its enemies?" An omen need be present only briefly to have its effect.

Perhaps in addressing the sun Joshua originally addressed a deity.[101] However, both the sun and moon are addressed, so are both deities addressed? If so, then why would the monotheistic author of Joshua retain this

Tell-Bornat (Libnah)
Todd Bolen/www.BiblePlaces.com

fragment when the remainder of the text reads perfectly well without it? Perhaps this is an ancient fragment of a poem following theophanies such as Habakkuk 3, Judges 5, and Exodus 15.[102] But if so, then why quote this part of the poem with such extraordinary polytheistic overtones?

Two factors within the biblical context are important. First, as in 10:4, 6, and 8, this also is a message with a request to render military aid. None of these messages mention the addressee in their actual message text, but all identify the addressee in the introduction. So the sun and moon are not the primary addressees, but God is identified in the first part of verse 12.

Second, in the larger context of Deuteronomy and the related history books of the Old Testament, all references to the sun and the moon are idolatrous. Thus the reference here may indeed suggest a celestial omen or some sort of deified sun and moon, as are known in comparative West Semitic religion. Certainty about the specific interpretation remains obscure, in part because only six Hebrew words describe Joshua's request. Whatever the original meaning, the clear intent of the text is to establish the Lord's authority over these objects and thereby to aid and enhance Israel's victory.[103]

Killed the kings and hung them on five trees (10:26). Compare the fate of the king of Ai and the comparative note at 8:29.

Libnah (10:29). This is identified with Tel Burna, at the northwest corner of the arc through Lachish, Eglon, and Hebron that the Israelite army traveled before turning south to Debir.[104]

Horam king of Gezer (10:33). The personal name of this leader derives from a West Semitic root that is found in names of the second and first millennia B.C.[105] The site of Gezer occupies a key place in the list of seven sites attacked by Israel. It is the fourth site named (the middle one), and it occupies a distinctive place in this list. Of all the sites described, Gezer is the only one that Israel does not destroy. They defeat the army of Gezer.

Of interest is the role of Gezer in the Merneptah Stele, a text from c. 1209 B.C. that provides the first extrabiblical mention of Israel as a people in Canaan. The text describes three major population centers that the Egyptian pharaoh conquered, including Ashkelon, Gezer, and Yenoam. Of these, Gezer is the only one mentioned in Joshua 10. Its importance to Egyptian security is established from this source as well as other records, such as the Amarna texts from Gezer. If Gezer functioned as an Egyptian military base at this time, it might explain why the Israelites did not attack

Merneptah Stele
Todd Bolen/www.BiblePlaces.com

Gezer
Todd Bolen/www.BiblePlaces.com

Gezer itself.[106] The archaeology supports a picture of Gezer stratum XV that was not taken by Israel in the thirteenth century but was destroyed by Pharaoh Merneptah in the final decade of that century.[107]

Debir (10:38). Khirbet Rabud is ancient Debir, perhaps the most important Late Bronze Age site in the region south of Hebron.[108]

The hill country, the Negev, the western foothills and the mountain slopes (10:40). This summarizes the whole region south of Gibeon. The hill country includes the region immediately south and dominated by sites such as Jerusalem and Hebron, with Arad and Beersheba at the southern tip. The Negev in the Bible refers to the region around the Beersheba Valley at the southern end of the region of Judah. The western foothills and mountain slopes seem to describe the same area, that which is located between the coastal plain and the hill country. It is called the Shephelah (Heb. for "foothills").

Kadesh Barnea (10:41). This is ʿEin el-Qudeirât, the place where the previous generation reached the southern border of the Promised Land but was unable to enter (Num. 11).

Gaza (10:41). The traditional southwestern corner of the land of Canaan and the first Canaanite city that the Egyptians reached when traveling from their country across the northern Sinai.

Region of Goshen (10:41). Mentioned as a southern boundary of Canaan in 11:16 and as an otherwise unattested Judean hill country town in 15:51, this is not the region of Egypt where the Israelites lived before the Exodus. Rather, it may refer to a region at the south-central or southeastern edge of Canaan (and Judah).

Northern Coalition (11:1–23)

Jabin king of Hazor … (Hazor had been the head of all these kingdoms.) (11:1, 10). The

Debir (Khirbet Rabud)
Todd Bolen/www.BiblePlaces.com

name of Jabin, as vocalized in the Masoretic text and the Septuagint (A), is derived from the West Semitic and Hebrew root *byn*, which is productive of personal names in the second millennium but not in the first millennium B.C. From the time of the Middle Bronze Age Mari letters, the leader at Hazor was a Yabni-Addu, where the first part of the name sounds like Jabin but is not identical to it and in fact is derived from a different root.[109] The form *ib-ni* also occurs in a Middle Bronze letter from Hazor as part of a personal name.[110] It is not impossible that this was a dynastic name at Hazor that was preserved in the Bible, both in Joshua 11 and in Judges 4–5, but with a different vocalization added later.

The site of Hazor, including its lower tel, covers some 175 acres. This makes it the largest city in ancient Israel. Stratum XIII was destroyed by violent conflagration in the thirteenth century B.C. This may relate to the events of Joshua 11, as the excavator Yigael Yadin thought.[111]

Jobab king of Madon (11:1). The name Jobab may be understood as South Semitic, where a similar tribal name occurs (*yhybb*). However, its actual root may be attested in West Semitic Amorite names from the early second millennium B.C.[112] Like Jabin, this name fits well in the time and place described by Joshua 11. Madon, which occurs elsewhere only in 12:19, should probably be identified with Merom. The *d* and *r* resemble one another in biblical Hebrew, so this could be a copyist error. Alternatively, there could be two slightly different names for the same place, perhaps dialectical variants. The battle "at the Waters of Merom" (11:5–7) would then have been near a site that itself would be close to Hazor, Tel Qarnei Hittin, on the heights west of the Sea of Galilee.[113]

Shimron and Acshaph (11:1). Shimron is Tel Shimron, five miles west of Nazareth at the western end of the Jezreel Valley.[114] Acshaph may be Tell Keisan, four and a half miles south of Acco on the plain, or it may be Tel Regev, at the foot of Mount Carmel and at the entrance to the Jokneam Pass to the Jezreel Valley.[115] Both sites are mentioned in the fifteenth-century itinerary of Tuthmosis III and in the fourteenth-century Amarna letters.[116]

Northern kings who were in the mountains (11:2). Like the summary of the south-

Hazor Acropolis
Todd Bolen/www.BiblePlaces.com

Tel Kinrot, Kinnereth
Todd Bolen/www.BiblePlaces.com

Hivites below Hermon in the region of Mizpah (11:3). For the Hivites located around Gibeon, see 9:7 and 11:19. In Genesis 34:2 there are Hivites living in Shechem. Here the description takes the reader farther north. If Hermon is equated with Sirion and Senir in Deuteronomy 3:9 and identified with the Ante-Lebanon range in Egyptian sources early in the second millennium B.C., then Mizpah could refer to the eastern part of the Litani River, which flows south from the Beqaᶜ and turns westward toward Tyre at a point close to the northern end of the Huleh Basin.[117] This would be the region of Dan and the northern limits of the Israelite settlement.

Waters of Merom (11:5). Perhaps these are to be located north of Tel Qarnei Hittin at Wadi el-Hamam.[118] This site lay on the ancient road north to Hazor and would provide a staging point for the coalition.

ern coalition region in 10:40, the description here divides the north into four areas. The description begins in the north and proceeds in a clockwise direction. This term includes the towns in the Galilean highlands north of the Jezreel Valley.

In the Arabah south of Kinnereth (11:2). Kinnereth is Tel Kinrot, overlooking the northwest shore of the Sea of Galilee. The Arabah is the whole region of the Sea of Galilee and the northern half of the Jordan Valley.

In the western foothills (11:2). In Hebrew, the Shephelah; see comment on 10:40.

In Naphoth Dor on the west (11:2). There is no certain translation of Naphoth. Dor lies on the Mediterranean coast, south of Mount Carmel. This expression could refer to the coastal plain in that region.

Jebusites in the hill country (11:3). While the southern coalition is designated simply as Amorite, the northern assembly is composed of diverse groups (see comment on 3:10), perhaps reflecting the international cultural and commercial importance of the north, as seen in the later history of the northern kingdom of Israel. The Jebusites are encountered around Jerusalem (15:8, 63; 18:16). The hill country may be the central hill country and reflect their presence north of Jerusalem.

Horns of Hattin
Todd Bolen/www.BiblePlaces.com

Hamstring their horses and burn their chariots (11:6, 9). The presence of chariots among the northern coalition suggests a sophistication not found in the south. Here in the north the leaders had more wealth and power so that they could afford to field the most advanced weaponry of the era. Horses were not used for transportation by themselves but rather to pull chariots.[119] The chariots functioned as mobile fighting platforms, particularly to move archers quickly across the battlefield and to aid in their effectiveness. Hamstringing the horses would render them useless for battle. Chariots needed to be light and were often built of wood. Hence they could be burned. Bronze or iron could be used as linchpins for the wheels and perhaps to protect the wood—hence the description of iron chariots in 17:16, 18.

To Greater Sidon, to Misrephoth Maim, and to the Valley of Mizpah on the east (11:8). Following a clockwise route around the Galilee, it begins with the northwestern border of the tribal allotments around Sidon. Misrephoth Maim moves eastward along the Litani River, which then forms the Valley of Mizpah. At the southeastern bend of the river the route southward reaches to the Huleh Basin and Hazor. This would appear to be part of the itinerary of the pursuers.

Israel did not burn any of the cities built on their mounds—except Hazor (11:13). In the thirteenth century B.C. Hazor stratum XIII came to a fiery end. The book of Joshua records that Jericho and Ai were also burned (6:24; 8:28). However, there is no record of other towns of either the southern or northern coalition as being burnt. For this reason archaeologists have not found burned destruction layers at the many other sites listed in chapters 10 and 11.

Whole region of Goshen (11:16). See comment on 10:41.

From Mount Halak, which rises toward Seir, to Baal Gad in the Valley of Lebanon below Mount Hermon (11:17). In 12:7 Mount Halak lies between Israel and Edom. Jebel Halaq is located midway between Kadesh Barnea and the southern end of the Dead Sea. If it marks the southern end of Israel's activity, Baal Gad marks the northern end. If Mount Hermon is indeed the Ante-Lebanon range (see comment on 11:3), then the Valley of Lebanon could be the Beqa or the Valley of Mizpah to its south.[120]

Destroyed the Anakites from the hill country: from Hebron, Debir and Anab, from all the hill country of Judah, and from all the hill country of Israel ... only in Gaza, Gath and Ashdod did any survive (11:21–22). The Bible associates the sons of Anak with the Nephilim (Num. 13:33), and they are in turn connected to the Rephaim (Deut. 2:11).[121] These as a whole are best understood as mighty warriors who fell in battle, often slain by Israel. They are not a race but an ethnic group. The thirteenth-century Egyptian Papyrus Anastasi I notes that

Northern Coalition Sites

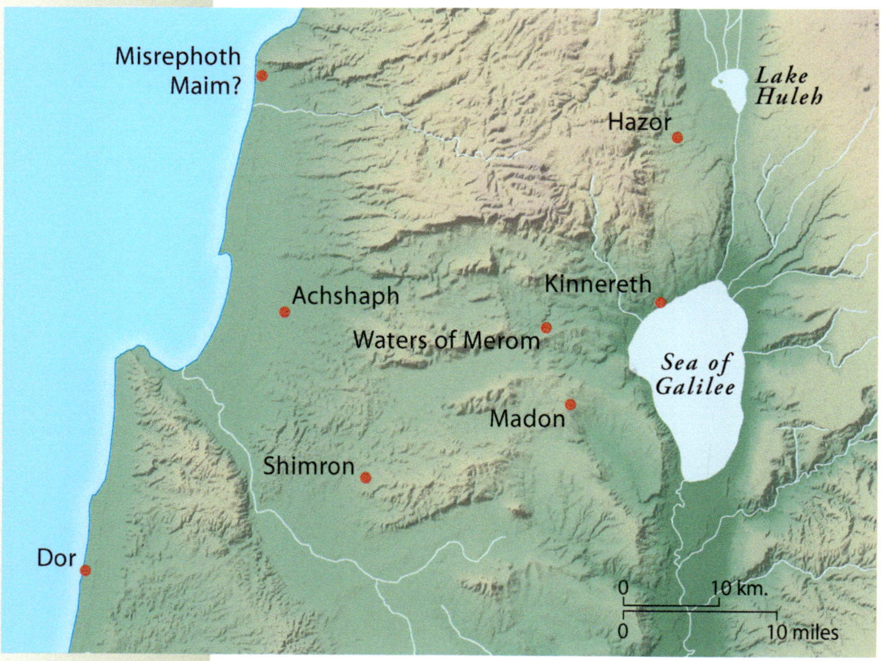

among the Canaanites are "some of whom are four cubits or five cubits (from) their nose to foot and have fierce faces."[122] Five Egyptian cubits would be a few inches short of nine feet. The Egyptian Execration Texts of the first half of the second millennium B.C. identify three rulers in Palestine who are each a ruler of *Iy-ʾAnaq*.[123]

For Hebron and Debir see notes on 10:3 and 38. Anab may be associated with Khirbet ʿUnnab eṣ-Ṣeghîr, some fifteen miles southwest of Hebron.[124] Hebron and Debir anticipate later individual conquests of Caleb and Othniel (14:6–15; 15:13–19). The towns where Anakites remained—Gaza, Gath, and Ashdod—all lay on or near the southwestern Palestinian coast. Og of Bashan (12:4) and Goliath of Gath are examples of this type of warrior (1 Sam. 17).

Summary of the Battles to Date (12 :1–24)

These are the kings of the land (12:1). This chapter reviews all the battles to this point where Israel acquired land. Thus, it begins with a review of the land east of the Jordan River acquired through the defeat of Sihon of Heshbon and Og of Bashan (Num. 21). This review lists their territories by regions and natural landmarks, such as mountains and rivers (12:1–6). This is followed by a list of the leaders and their towns west of the Jordan River that Israel defeated.

There are three comparative features of note: summarizing texts, selectivity in lists, and the use of itinerary lists. (1) Summarizing texts such as 12:1–6 occur in annalistic inscriptions. Younger cites an example of a summarizing statement from two Neo-Assyrian inscriptions that begin with the same wording.[125] The texts go on to provide a list of towns conquered. The two lists, although often overlapping, are different.

(2) Each list is selective in its identification of different cities. The same is true in 12:7–24. Some of these towns do not occur in the campaign accounts of chapters 1–11.

(3) Joshua 12:7–24 forms a verbal counterpart to the lists of conquests made by kings of the New Kingdom Egyptian empire, which they left on the pylons and outside temple walls from Tuthmosis III (c. 1479–1425 B.C.) to Ramesses III (c. 1184–1153 B.C.), and the post-New Kingdom pharaoh Shishak (c. 945–924 B.C.). The list of conquests is a series of ovals that Kitchen likens to forts.[126] These have a single head on top that reflects the general ethnicity of the region and may suggest the leader.

Joshua 12 Sites

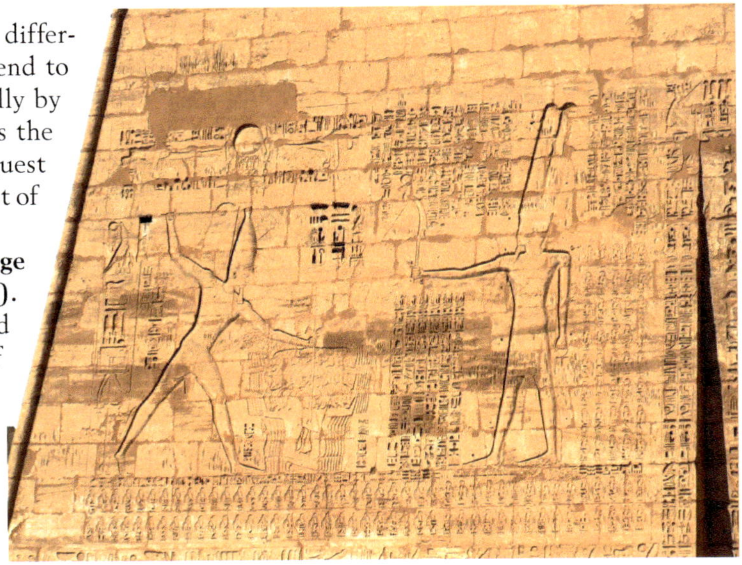

Ramesses III summary list of enemies shown under his feet
Janice Watson-Bernard, Ph.D.

The ovals each contain a different place name. They tend to be grouped geographically by region. In all these ways the Egyptian summary conquest lists correspond to the list of 12:9–24.

From the Arnon Gorge to Mount Hermon (12:1). The southernmost and northernmost extent of Sihon's kingdom and of Israel's possessions. The Arnon Gorge lay between Moab to the south and the tribal territories of Reuben and Gad to the north. The Arnon River (Wadi el-Mujib) flows into the Dead Sea at a point across the Dead Sea from the location of En-Gedi. On Mount Hermon see comment on 11:3.

Heshbon (12:2). This town has been identified with Tell Hesban, but excavations have not identified a Late Bronze occupation. It may be that the second-millennium B.C. site should be sought elsewhere and that the name shifted from the other site to Tell Hesban in the Iron Age.[127] Candidates from other sites include Tall Jalul and Tall al-Umayri, both of which possess the necessary occupation levels.[128] Aroer is Tell

Bashan
Peter White

▸ The Summary of the Seventh Campaign of Sennacherib

Joshua 12 records a list of defeated cities that includes some names not found in chapters 1–11. It is not a unique document in this respect. The Assyrian king Sennacherib's seventh campaign is recorded in the Annals (Chicago–Taylor Prism) and in what Younger refers to as the Walters Art Gallery inscription. Both begin this campaign with the same wording:[A-15]

> I conquered in the course of my campaign (the cities of) Bit-Ha'iri (and) Raza, cities on the border of Assyria, which during the time of my father, the Elamite had seized by force; and I carried off their spoil. I caused soldiers, my garrison, to enter into their midst. I returned them to the border of Assyria. I assigned (them) into the hands of the commander of the fort of Der.

Chicago–Sennacherib Prism
Kim Walton, courtesy of the Oriental Institute Museum ◂

Then follows the actual cities captured. The difference can be seen by citing only the first five of each inscription:

> Annals: Bube, Dunni-Shamash, Bit-Risia, Bit-Ahlame, Duru
> Walters: Bit-arrabi, Alum-qasti, Bube, Dunni-Shamash, Eka-Ishalla.

ʿAraʿir (228097).[129] The Jabbok River is the Wadi ez-Zerqa (see comment on 3:16). Thus Gilead has as its southern border the Arnon Gorge. Its western border is the Jordan River and its eastern border is the desert. Its northern border is perhaps the Yarmuk River, as the Jabbok River divides the area in half.

Eastern Arabah (12:3). This constitutes the Jordan Valley east of the Jordan River. The Sea of Kinnereth is the Sea of Galilee, while the Sea of the Arabah (the Salt Sea) is the Dead Sea. Beth Jeshimoth is possibly Tell ʿAzeimeh (208132). Whether or not Pisgah is Ras es-Siyagha (218130), the slopes of Pisgah are found at the northwestern edge of the Moabite tableland, where it descends into the Jordan Valley.

Bashan (12:4). This is the area ruled by Og. It lay in the southern Hauran, an area on the western part of the border between Syria and Jordan. The association of the towns of Ashtaroth (Tell ʿAshtarah 243244) and Edrei (Derʿa 253244) with the Rephaites (or Rephaim, see note on 11:21–22) raises questions about the sacred and ancient nature of these sites. Late Bronze Age remains have been found at both towns. When Derʿa was excavated about 150 years ago, the excavator found underground tombs interconnected and with connecting spouts at each tomb room that reached to the fresh air above. There are some similarities with the tomb structures in urban Ugarit, including drainage pipes from the ground level to the tombs.

A Ugaritic ritual text connects the deity Rapiʾu with both these sites. The text at this point (RS 24.252.2–3) may be translated:

"The god who dwells in Athtartu; the god who rules in Hadraᶜyi."[130] Rapiᵓu has associations with the deceased members of the royal family at Ugarit. Many accept the identification of Athtartu with Astaroth and that of Hadraᶜyi with Edrei.[131] If so, then the origins of the Ugaritic dynasty may come from Bashan, and Og himself may have been related to that royal family. The cult of burial and the dead may also have had a prominent role in this region.

Salecah (12:5). This town is possibly Salkhad (311212). "The people of Geshur and Maacah" would constitute a region east and north of the Sea of Galilee, and west of Bashan.[132]

These are the kings (12:7). This phrase is followed by a list of place names most of which have occurred previously in Joshua 1–11. Joshua 12:10–16 includes southern sites, many of which are mentioned in chapter 10. Joshua 12:17–24 includes northern places, many of which are mentioned in chapter 11. Below are names introduced into the book for the first time that reflect sites where evidence of occupation is not found lacking in the Late Bronze Age.[133]

Geder (12:13). It is possibly Arabic Khirbet Jedûr (158115).[134]

Hormah (12:14). It is possibly Arabic Khirbet el-Meshâsh or Hebrew Tel Masos (146069).

Arad (12:14). It is possibly Arabic Tell el-Milḥ or Hebrew Tel Malḥata (152069). The traditional site, Tel Arad, has no evidence of occupation in the Late Bronze Age.

Adullam (12:15). It is possibly Arabic Tell esh-Sheikh Madhkûr or Hebrew Ḥirbet ᶜAdullam (150117).

Tappuah (12:17). It is possibly Arabic Sheikh Abû Zarad (172168).

Hepher (12:17). It has been identified as Arabic Tell el-Muḥafar (171205).[135]

Aphek (12:18). It is possibly Râs el-ᵓAin or Hebrew Tel ᵓAfeq (143168).

Lasharon (12:18). It should be identified with the Plain of Sharon.

Taanach (12:21). It is Arabic Tell Tiᶜinnik or Hebrew Tel Taᶜanakh (171214).

Megiddo (12:21). It is Arabic Tell el-Mutesellim or Hebrew Tel Megiddo (167221).

Kedesh (12:22). It is possibly Arabic Tell Abu Qudeis or Hebrew Tel Qedesh (170218).

Jokneam in Carmel (12:22). It is Arabic Tell Qeimûn or Hebrew Tel Yoqneam (160230).

Taanach
Todd Bolen/www.BiblePlaces.com

Goyim in Gilgal (12:23). It is Goyim in Galilee according to the Septuagint. As with Dor and Jokneam before it, this has the same construction of two place names in which the first is a town and the second should be a region. Galilee is a region; Gilgal is usually thought of as a town or cult site (see comment on 4:19).[136] However, both Gilgal and Galilee come from the same root *gll*. Therefore, these could be variants of the same place name. It is probably related to Harosheth Haggoyim in or near the Galilee (Judg. 4:13, 16). If so, it may come from a

Megiddo
Z. Radovan/www.BibleLandPictures.com

region of pharaonic royal estates known from the Amarna letters in this area.[137] An Arabic site possibly preserving the name is Jiljuliyey (145173), a few miles north of Aphek.[138]

Tirzah (12:24). It is Arabic Khirbet Tell el-Fârḥah north (182188).

Land Where No Battle Was Fought (13:1–7)

All the regions of the Philistines and Geshurites (13:2). Before the allotment can go ahead, there is a list of regions and towns within Canaan that have not been defeated by Israel. The allotments will include these areas, however, so that the picture created is one in which the document that follows remains in use through the period of the monarchy for various legal and royal purposes.

Although Geshur has been previously mentioned (12:5), this is the first and only occurrence of the Philistines in the book of Joshua. Three traditional Philistine cities connected with the Anakites had appeared in 11:22, but there was no explicit association with the Philistines. The Philistines,

Jokneam from Mount Carmel
Todd Bolen/www.BiblePlaces.com

▸ Literary Background and Forms of the Allotments

In general, the allotments follow the battles and procurement of the land. Although the land may not have been conquered in the sense that it was now entirely to be occupied, it is a normal expectation that the "trophy" of land won in battle should now be distributed to the victors. M. Weinfeld has shown how this follows the sequence of Mediterranean and especially Greek and Roman stories of conquest and settlement.[A-16]

The order of the allotments approximates the biblical sequence of the battles: Transjordan followed by Benjamin, Judah, and Simeon, which are then followed by the northern tribes. This sequence is interrupted by special accounts of Caleb's family and the daughters of Zelophehad, which either relate to the previous generation of Moses or derive specifically from the lawgiver. No other period in Israel's history matches this sequence.[A-17] In addition, the demographic settlement patterns of the Early Iron Age allow for a time when boundary definitions became a desirable goal.[A-18] Therefore, it should not be surprising to find comparative forms for this complex of geographic data in those administrative practices and traditions that would have been active in the Early Iron Age and indeed may have reached back into the Late Bronze Age West Semitic archives of Alalakh (Level IV), Ugarit, and Emar, and the related archive of Hittite texts from Hattusas.

Research into treaty, property, ration, and corvée texts from the fifteenth to the early twelfth centuries B.C. reveals two types of collections of place names: boundary descriptions and place name lists. This distinction was first made by Alt, before the discovery of the many cuneiform texts that now assist in confirming it.[A-19] It has long been noted that, except for the Transjordanian tribal allotments of chapter 13, the tribal boundaries match the borders of Canaan as defined in the Bible and in Egyptian texts of the second millennium B.C. The boundaries between tribes create a contiguous whole with no gaps. Thus it is reasonable to assume that the boundaries were created at the same time.[A-20]

Boundary descriptions occur for most but not all of the tribes. Neither Simeon nor Levi have such descriptions. The former is concentrated within the southern area of the much larger allotment of Judah while the latter receives towns but is specifically denied territories. Such boundary descriptions have a direct parallel in treaty documents from Hattusas.[A-21] Like the context of the tribal allotments that lie between two covenant/treaty events (8:30–35 and chs. 23–24), so the Hittite boundary lists form part of treaties with vassal states. The parties involved are always those on both sides of the boundary,

remembered in the Bible as the challengers to such Israelites as Samson, Saul, and David, occur as a general term for the Sea Peoples who came to the shores of Palestine in the twelfth century B.C. The group known as the *plst* (i.e., Philistines) are mentioned by Ramesses III (c. 1180/1177 B.C.) and at that time began settlement in southwest Canaan. There the excavated sites of Ashdod, Ashkelon, and Ekron reveal violent destructions followed by new settlements with distinctive Philistine bichrome pottery. This culture remains different from the nearby Canaanite sites of Lachish Stratum VI and Tel Sera Stratum IX.

In the following generation these latter two sites were subject to destruction by the Philistines, who were expanding throughout

List of the Land That Remains (Jos. 13:1–7)

whether Israelite tribes or such vassals of the Hittites as Ugarit and its neighbors. There are formal similarities of an introduction and conclusion naming the parties, historical notes interspersed within the boundary descriptions, and variations in the spellings and selection of place names where the same boundary is described in multiple editions of a treaty and boundary description.

The town lists occur in administrative texts from Alalakh and Ugarit.[A-22] They form census lists from towns and villages within the kingdom. The towns listed always occur as part of a list of people or objects associated with those towns. There is usually an introduction and a conclusion, where the total number of persons or objects is given. Longer lists are subdivided into smaller units, each with its own introduction and summary conclusion. The simple form, without the attached lists of persons or objects, can be found in the town lists of Benjamin (18:21–28), Dan (19:41–46), Simeon (19:2–7), Issachar (19:18–21), and Naphtali (19:35–38). The more complex form with subdivisions, usually according to region, appear in the town lists of Judah (15:21–62) and the Levitical town list (ch. 21). The lists for Manasseh (13:31; 17:2–3, 11) have a different form, discussed where they occur.

this region.[139] The mention of the Philistines in Joshua occurs in connection with the final years of Joshua's life (13:1) and suggests a tradition that connects these people with the southwestern coast at the end of this generation. Israel's mention in the Merneptah stele of 1209 B.C. suggests that they had already been in the land some thirty years before the Philistines appear. Thus, whether a later gloss or something more contemporary, this appearance of the Philistines betrays an ancient memory of their appearance in Canaan several decades into the twelfth century.

Shihor River (13:3). This has been identified either as the easternmost branch of the Nile (Pelusiac) or as the Wadi el-Arîsh in northeastern Sinai. The latter would fit

Boundary Description in the Hittite Treaty between Tudhaliya IV of Hatti and Kurunta of Tarhuntassa

The boundary descriptions of Joshua 13–19 have their closest parallel with those found in Hittite treaties and edicts. These texts demonstrate that boundaries, like those of the Israelite tribes, did exist in written form and were implemented generation after generation, with changes made according to the political realities of the age. Following his father's earlier treaty, the Hittite king Tudhaliya confirms the arrangement with the king of Tarhuntassa. He notes changes to the old boundary, and these can be checked by comparison with the treaty between Tudhaliya's father Hattusili III of Hatti and Ulmi-Teshup of Tarhuntassa. The first several paragraphs of Tudhaliya's treaty are provided here:

Bronze tablet recording land agreement between Tudhaliya IV and Karunta
Ankara Archaeological Museum; © Dr. James C. Martin

> §3b The treaty which my father made with him, and how he established the frontiers for him—concerning this my father made a written treaty with him, and it is in Kurunta's possession. His frontiers were established as follows: In the direction of the land of Pitassa, his(!) frontier is Mount Hawa, the *kantanna* of the city of Zarniya, and the city of Sanantarwa, but the *kantanna* of Zarniya belongs to the land of the Hulaya River, while Sanantarwa belongs to the land of Pitassa.
>
> §4 Previously, in the direction of the land of Pitassa, his frontier was the city of Nahhanta. My father pushed back his frontier, and on my father's treaty tablet the sinkholes of the city of Arimmatta are made the frontier. Now I, My Majesty, have reestablished the earlier frontier for him. In the direction of the land of Pitassa, in the direction of the border district of the city of Arimmatta, his frontier is the cities of Nahhanta and Hautassa, but Nahhanta and Hautassa belong to the land of the Hulaya River.[A-23]

better as a border for the known sites of the Philistines.

Ekron (13:3). At Arabic Khirbet el-Muqannaʾ and Hebrew Tel Miqne (136131), this is the most northeastern of the five cities of the Philistines. Thus the region between the Shihor River and Ekron would be the home of the Philistine newcomers.

Philistine rulers (13:3). The term for "ruler" (*seren*) is unique to the Philistines in the Bible. It is generally regarded as a Philistine term brought from their Aegean and

Ekron: Tel Miqne
Bible Scene Multimedia/Maurice Thompson

Mycenaean homeland and possibly reflected in the later Greek word for a type of leader, *tyrannos* (from which English derives "tyrant").[140]

Gaza, Ashdod, Ashkelon, Gath and Ekron (13:3). These comprise the traditional pentapolis of the Philistines and are here so associated for the first time. Ashkelon (107118) and Ekron are mentioned here for the first time in Joshua.

Avvites (13:3). Also called the Avvim, these are the pre-Philistine inhabitants of this region (Deut. 2:23).

All the land of the Canaanites, from Arah of the Sidonians as far as Aphek ... the Amorites, the Gebalites; and all Lebanon to the east, from Baal Gad below Mount Hermon to Lebo Hamath (13:4–5). This constitutes the coastal area and the entire northern region of Canaan. Arah is not identified. The Septuagint translates this word as "Gaza," but this is doubtful as the Philistine region was already discussed. The coastal region of the Sidonians includes the region north of the area of the Philistines (which here may include other Sea People settlements, such as the Sikil at Dor) to Aphek, which is Tell Afqâ (231382) near the sources of the Nahr Ibrahim and southeast of Byblos. The Amorites refer here to the ancient kingdom of Amurru that flourished from only in the Late Bronze Age. This could include the Lebanon mountain range and some of the Beqaᶜ to the east.

Gebal is the ancient name for Byblos (210391) and constitutes the third major coastal division, after that of the Philistines and the Sidonians. Baal Gad was the northern limit of Israel's activity in 11:17, located somewhere north of Galilee in the Beqaᶜ. Lebo Hamath is the northern limit of Canaan, perhaps as Lebweh (277397). Thus the entire region north of the Galilee remained as did the coast.

Misrephoth Maim (13:6). The site is located just north of Galilee (see comment on 11:7) and formed the northern boundary of Israel's control before the united monarchy.

Lebanon and Coastal Regions

Land Allocated East of the Jordan River (13:8–33)

Verses 8–13 define the major topography of the Transjordanian allotments. Then, moving from south to north, the allotments include those given to Reuben (13:15–23), Gad (13:24–28), and the half tribe of Manasseh (13:29–31).

Town in the middle of the gorge ... Dibon (13:9). Of the places named, some have appeared before (Aroer and Arnon Gorge, 12:2) and another is probably located at the site of modern towns (Medeba). The town in the middle of the gorge may have been a temporary unnamed outpost. Alternatively, Miller has suggested the Khirbet el-Medeineh (240092) at the junction of Wadi Sālīyeh and the Wadi Saʿīdeh.[141] Although Tell Dhibân may be the Iron Age site of Dibon, there is a lack of evidence of Late Bronze Age occupation there. Nevertheless, Egyptian scribes of the thirteenth century B.C. knew of the existence of a Dibon in this area.[142]

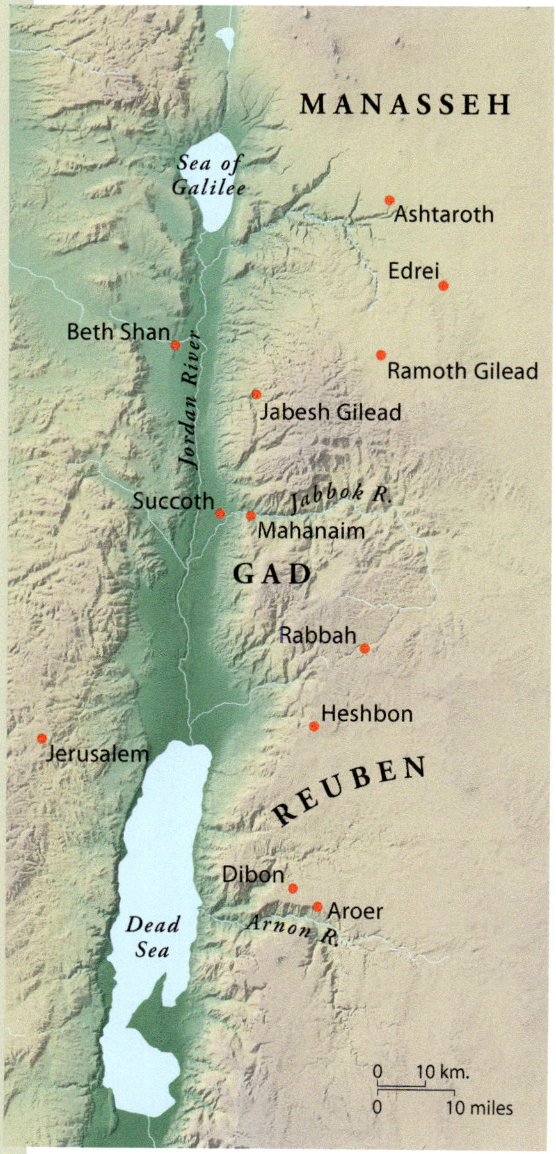

Transjordan Tribes of Reuben, Gad, and Manasseh

Given to the tribe of Reuben (13:15). All the sites of 13:10–13 are discussed at 12:2–5. The allotment for Reuben includes the following sites not previously mentioned: Bamoth Baal may possibly be Khirbet el-Quweiqiyeh (220126) or Khirbet Libb (222113),[143] Beth Baal Meon may be Māʿîn (219120), Jahaz may be Khirbet el-Medeineh (236111),[144] Kedemoth may be ʿAleiyân or Saliyah (233104), Mephaath is probably Umm er-Raṣaṣ (237101),[145] Kiriathaim may possibly be Qaryat el-Mekhaiyeṭ (220128) or Khirbet el-Qereiyât (216124), Sibmah may be an undetermined site not far from Beth Baal Maon, Zereth Shahar may possibly be ez-Zārât (203111), the hill in the valley has been identified with Mt. ʿAṭṭarus, Beth Peor has no obvious identification.

Given to the tribe of Gad (13:24). The allotments for Gad (13:24–28) not already mentioned include: Jazer perhaps as Khirbet Jazzir (219156), Rabbah may be at the Amman acropolis (238151), Ramath Mizpah may be at Khirbet Jelʿad (223169), Betonim may be Khirbet Baṭneh (217154), Mahanaim may be Khirbet ed-Dhahab el-Garbi (214177) on the north side of the Zerqa Valley,[146] Debir as Lo-debar may be Tell Dober (209232) on the southwestern tip of the Golan Heights and north of the Yarmuk Valley,[147] Beth Haram may be Tell Iktanu (214136), Beth Nimrah may possibly be Tell el-Bleibil (210146), Succoth may be Tell Deir ʿAllā (208178), Zaphon may possibly be Tell el-Qôs (208182).[148]

Yarmuk Valley
Todd Bolen/www.BiblePlaces.com

Settlements of Jair (13:30). This is the only place name in the description of Manasseh not mentioned earlier. Jair, a son of Manasseh, occupied a territory east of the Sea of Galilee containing sixty settlements (Num. 32:41; Deut. 3:13–14; 1 Kings 4:13; but twenty-three settlements in 1 Chron. 2:22–23), where thirty sons ruled (Judg. 10:4). If Geshur is to be identified in a single occurrence in Amarna letter 256 (see comment and note on 12:5), then the nine towns named as part of the land of Geshur may constitute some of what becomes the settlements of Jair.

Introduction to the Allotment West of the Jordan River (14:1–5)

Eleazar the priest (14:1). He is the son and successor to Aaron the high priest, who will oversee the allotment of the land (17:4; 19:51), the assignment of the priestly towns (21:1), and the mediation with the Transjordanian tribes (22:13, 31–32).

Assigned by lot (14:2). Divination was widely practiced in the ancient Near East. There were a variety of techniques, including the observation of signs in the sky, the observation of unusual births and other aberrations in nature, prophets, and necromancy. However, in Israel the only approved instruments for determining God's will were the Urim and Thummim.[149] Otherwise, dreams and prophets might instruct (1 Sam. 28:6). The Urim and Thummim fit into the breastpiece of the high priest (Ex. 28:30; Lev. 8:8) and were used only by the priest (Num. 27:21; Deut. 33:8; Ezra 2:63 = Neh. 7:65). They may well have been the lots used in the division of the land.[150] Note the association of division with the high priest in 14:1, although Joshua does the lot in 18:6–10. Behind the casting of lots is the principle that the ownership of the land, and therefore the right to give it according to his wishes, belongs to God. As with the land grant of the king of Alalakh (see Introduction), the suzerain has the right to assign the land to whomever he wills.

Pasturelands for their flocks and herds (14:4). In addition to the towns for the Levites, they received pasturelands for their flocks and herds. The Hebrew term *migrāš* describes

Area around Hebron
Z. Radovan/www.BibleLandPictures.com

districts or regions that were allotted to the Levites who otherwise did not receive land for farming. See the Introduction and comparison with ancient Near Eastern land grants, as well as Joshua 21. It seems that in the West Semitic world, towns normally had specific areas set aside for use by the townspeople for grazing and perhaps some gardening.

Allotment for Judah (14:6–15:63)

Now the men of Judah (14:6). The most lengthy of the town lists is that of Judah. It is itself subdivided and has an introduction and conclusion, as noted among other long town lists of the West Semitic world. However, this list also includes stories of the acquisition of Hebron and associated lands by the family of Caleb, the most illustrious of the Judahites among the generation entering the land. The purpose of this construction is not clear nor found in comparable town lists; although it may serve to suggest the theological significance of Caleb's faithfulness as a root cause for the favorable treatment of Judah in receiving so much land and so many towns.

Furthermore, the first part of Caleb's story (14:6–15) parallels the first part of the town list (15:1–12) as it deals with the general areas acquired and allotted. The second part of Caleb's story (15:13–19) parallels the second half of the allotment of Judah (15:20–63) as they both deal with specific towns acquired and allotted. Thus, the four parts appear in a kind of A-B-A'-B' parallelism, a structure known in the poetics and rhetorics of the ancient Near East, even in the fourteenth-century B.C. Amarna letters from Jerusalem.[151]

Caleb's Allotment, Part I (14:6–14)

Caleb son of Jephunneh the Kenizzite (14:6, 14). Caleb explored the land with the other eleven spies in Numbers 13–14. Only Caleb and Joshua returned a positive report and were rewarded with living to see the Promised Land and their inheritance. This complete designation of Caleb, with patronym and ethnic origin, occurs only in this chapter (14:6, 14) and at Numbers 32:12. The names Caleb and Jephunneh are both West Semitic and Hebrew. However, Kenizzite is not necessarily Hebrew or even West Semitic. It may be related to Hurrian name formations such as *ki-in-zi* found at Late Bronze Age Nuzi.[152] However, the more common Hurrian element is *kizzi-* rather than *kinzi-*.[153] *Kinzi* may be related to the place name of Qedesh, written in the Amarna letters as *qí-in-sà*.[154] Alternatively, this name could be connected to South Arabian and related to the son of Esau, Kenaz, an Edomite clan chief.[155] Related occurrences of the same personal names at Ugarit demonstrate its existence in the Late Bronze Age.[156]

Hebron used to be called Kiriath Arba after Arba, who was the greatest man among the Anakites (14:15). On Anakites as renowned warriors of old, see note on 11:21–22. Kiriath Arba may be translated as "city of Arba." In West Semitic, Arba would mean "four." This could be connected with the three sons of Anak (15:14; Judg. 1:20) plus a fourth figure such as their father or even Caleb. Such an interpretation could relate to the West Semitic meaning of Hebron itself as "a place of alliance." Non-Semitic etymologies are not as clear.[157] Arba as the number four in Hebrew is otherwise unattested in personal names, except as a verbal root without its initial prosthetic consonant. It has been read as the first element of a Mari personal name of the early second millennium B.C.: *ra-ba(?)-aḫ-du-ud-mu*.[158]

The Boundaries of Judah (15:1–12)

Extended down to the territory of Edom, to the Desert of Zin in the extreme south (15:1). The southern boundary appears in 15:1–4. Edom's territory lay east of the Arabah during the period of the settlement. Unless this represents an otherwise unattested incursion to the west, Judah's land would have "touched" only south of the Dead Sea. The Desert of Zin is first mentioned in Numbers 13:21 and last mentioned in Joshua 15:3. It describes the desert area around Kadesh Barnea on the edge of Judah's settlement. "The extreme south" may be transliterated as Teiman, a desert region in the south whose name is attested in the ninth century inscriptions from Kuntillet ʿAjrud, south of Kadesh Barnea in the northeastern Sinai.

Salt Sea (15:2). This is the Dead Sea. The bay is the southern extension, the Lisan.

Scorpion Pass (15:3–4). This is probably Naqb eṣ-Ṣafā. Zin (15:1) and Kadesh Barnea (10:41) are followed by Hezron (Addar) at ʿAin Qedeis and Karka at ʿAin Qoṣeimeh (089007). Proceeding farther westward (10:5) the border passes Azmon (ʿAin Muweiliḥ, 085010) and reaches the Wadi of Egypt (Wadi el-ʿArîsh).

Salt Sea (15:5). The eastern boundary is defined by the Salt Sea (the Dead Sea) and the mouth of the Jordan River (15:5a).

Scorpion Pass (Ascent of Akkrabim)
Z. Radovan/www.BibleLandPictures.com

Northern boundary (15:5). The northern boundary proceeds from the mouth of the Jordan River westwards (15:5b–11).[159] It is the most detailed, reflecting the use of this list throughout the monarchy to determine boundary disputes between Judah and its northern tribal neighbors. Beth Hoglah may be Deir Ḥajlah (197136). Beth Arabah may be ʿAin el-Gharabeh (197139). The Stone of Bohan has not been identified. West of the Valley of Achor (7:24) lies Debir, perhaps Khan et Ḥatrur (184136).[160] This Gilgal may be Talʿat ed-Dam (178132). If so, then the Pass of Adummim may be Arabic Talʿat ed-Damm or Hebrew Maʿalê ʾAdummîm (178132). The gorge could be Wadi el-Havd (178133), the Waters of En Shemesh southwest of the gorge at ʿAin el-Hôd (175131), and En Rogel at Arabic Bir Ayyûb or Hebrew En Rogel (1731330).

The Valley of Ben Hinnom lay west of the Old City of Jerusalem, whereas the City of David lay mostly to the south of the Old City. The Valley of Rephaim is Wadi el-Ward and the Waters of Nephtoah is Arabic Liftā or Mê Neftoaḥ (168133), often thought to have been named after the pharaoh Merneptah, whose campaign against Israel is recorded on his 1209 B.C. stele. Mount Ephron may be Arabic el-Qastel or Hebrew Mevasseret Ṣiyyon, 165134). Baalah (Kiriath Jearim) (9:17) is followed by Mount Seir, perhaps Arabic Sārîs or Hebrew Śōeš Beth-Meir (157134). Mount Jearim may by Hebrew Kesalon (154132). Beth Shemesh is probably Arabic Tell er-Rumeileh or Hebrew Tel Bet Shemesh (147128); Timnah Tell Baṭashi or Tel Baṭash (141132); Ekron Khirbet el-Muqanna or Tel Miqne (136131); Shikkeron Tell el-Fûl (132137); Mount Baalah Mughâr (130139); Jabneel Yebnā or Yavne (126141).

Great Sea (15:12). The Mediterranean Sea forms the western boundary.

Caleb's Allotment, Part II (15:13–19)[161]

Sheshai, Ahiman and Talmai (15:14). These appear here for the first time in Joshua. As three sons of Anak they remind us of the three rulers of Iy-Ạnaq in Palestine mentioned in the Egyptian Execration texts of the first half of the second millennium B.C. The names Sheshai and Talmai are both Hurrian (or possibly Talmai is Anatolian); their elements have parallels in north Syrian cuneiform cultures of the Late Bronze Age. Ahiman is a West Semitic name whose elements are also known at this time.[162]

Debir (formerly called Kiriath Sepher) (15:15). Debir is discussed in comments on 10:3 and 38. Kiriath Sepher is literally "city of (the) scroll." There is no obvious reason for this name as it stands. The closest second-millennium B.C. evidence of extrabiblical texts is the Middle Bronze Age tablet from Tell er-Rumeideh (Hebron).

She urged him to ask her father for a field (15:18). Following the Hebrew text here, this understanding suggests that the women in this society retained some right over their dowry although it became part of their husband's property. So Acsah requests her

Valley of Rephaim (Wadi el-Ward)
Bible Scene Multimedia/Maurice Thompson

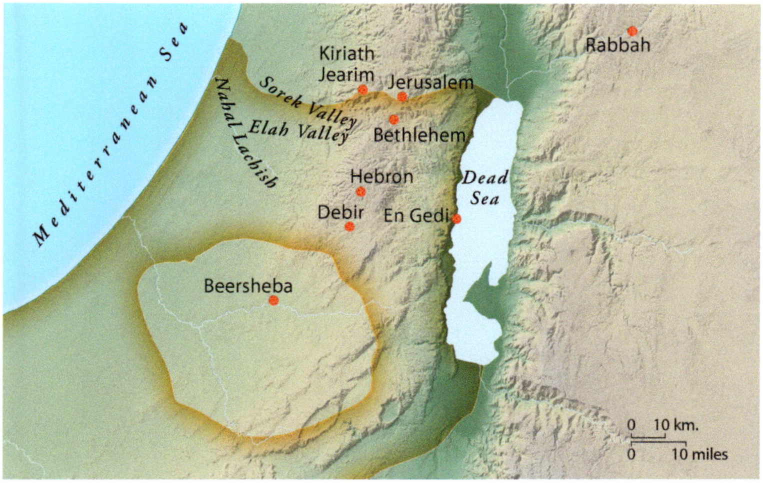

52–54, 55–57). A region to the north appears in verses 58–59. The Hebrew text of verse 60 preserves only two towns, Kiriath Jearim and Rabbah. However, the Septuagint adds eleven additional towns immediately before these two. This includes Ephrathah (Bethlehem), otherwise not found in

husband to request her dowry from her father, Caleb. However, she then requests additional water sources directly from her father.[163]

Judah's Town List (15:20–63)

This is the inheritance of the tribe of Judah, clan by clan (15:20). The town list forms the longest and most complex for any tribe. Many of the sites are not otherwise known, although some can be identified.[164] The lists are divided according to regions that are identified at the beginning of each section. Each section and subsection concludes with a summary statement of the total number of towns and villages.

Verses 21–32 begin the lists in the southern Negev. The western foothills or Shephelah (vv. 33–47) include towns divided into three districts (vv. 33–36, 37–41, 41–44). Rainey finds each district organized between the east-west valleys from north to south: from the Soreq Valley to the Elah Valley, from the Elah Valley to Naḥal Lachish, and from Naḥal Lachish to the Negev.[165] A fourth district in this region is the towns on the coastal plain (15:45–47) that were not occupied (13:2–3) until the united monarchy.

The hill country includes five districts in the region. The first three are in the south and include Debir and Hebron (15:48–51, 52–54, 55–57). A region to the north appears in verses 58–59. The Hebrew text of verse 60 preserves only two towns, Kiriath Jearim and Rabbah. However, the Septuagint adds eleven additional towns immediately before these two. This includes Ephrathah (Bethlehem), otherwise not found in the Hebrew list of Judah. The final list of six towns in the desert (15:61–62) includes En Gedi and other towns that lay along the western coast of the Dead Sea. Survey work and excavations have not identified any habitation that predates the eighth century B.C.[166] This form parallels that of various administrative lists that are found in the Late Bronze Age cuneiform archives of the Syrian cities of Alalakh and Ugarit.[167]

Jebusites (15:63). A customary note ends many of the tribal allotments, as it does here, indicating areas within the allotments that were not captured by the Israelites. The Jebusites previously appeared in lists as in Joshua 9:1 (see comment there); 11:3; and 12:8. Here for the first time in Joshua they are associated with Jerusalem. Although the king of Jerusalem was killed and his army was defeated in chapter 10, Jerusalem itself was apparently not captured.

The Allotment for Ephraim and Manasseh (16:1–17:18)

Bethel (that is, Luz) ... the Arkites in Ataroth (16:2). The southeastern boundary of Ephraim begins at the Jordan River and passes through Jericho (2:1) and Bethel (7:2). The association of the name of Bethel with Luz occurs three times in Genesis (Gen. 28:19; 35:6; 48:3), twice in Joshua

Towns Belonging to Another Tribe or State

As with Ephraim and Manasseh (16:9; 17:9, 11), some towns belonging to one tribe lay within the boundaries of another tribe. The same is true in the Hittite treaties where towns belonging to the Hittite sovereign lay within the borders of another kingdom. As in the Bible, so in the already mentioned treaty between Tudhaliya IV of Hatti and Kurunta of Tarhuntassa, these towns appear at the end of the boundary description:

> §9 The cities and population groups within the land of Tarhuntassa which belonged to the King of Hatti were: Anta and its deserted settlements, the cities of Lahhwiyassi, Wastissa, Hadduwassa, Handawa, Daganza, Simmuwa, Sahita, the men of Kammama under service obligation.[A-24]

Ephraim and Manasseh Territories

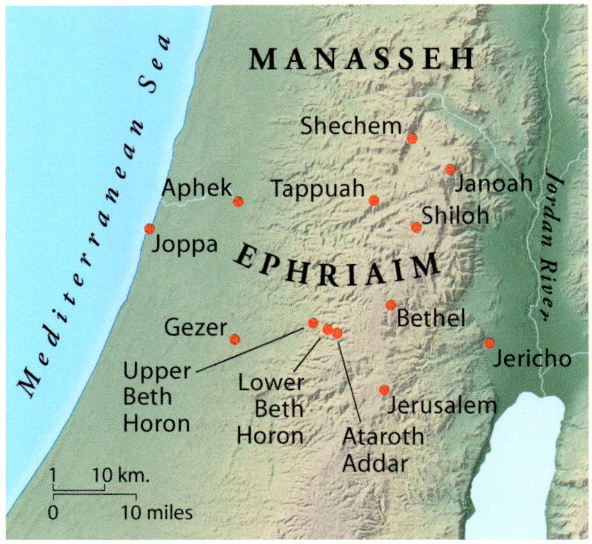

(here and Josh. 18:13), and twice in Judges (Judg. 1:23, 26). The last occurrence in Judges suggests that a survivor of the Israelite destruction of Bethel/Luz there went to the land of the Hittites and built a city called Luz.

Among the proposed connections with Luz is the kingdom of Lydia in Iron Age southwestern Anatolia, and a Hebrew version of a known Hittite city such as Lahhuwiyassi.[168] Arkites are unattested outside this reference (Gen. 10:17 is a different spelling and so a different group), except for David's diplomat Hushai, who was one (2 Sam. 16:16 et passim). Like other more frequently mentioned people groups these may also have come from the north (see comment on 3:10). Ataroth may be Tell el Mazar (eṣ-Ṣimadi; 196171).

Territory of the Japhletites (16:3). This group is unattested other than perhaps a son of Heber who carries the name Japhlet in 1 Chronicles 7:32–33. Lower Beth Horon and Gezer have already been mentioned (10:10, 33).

Micmethath ... Taanath Shiloh ... Janoah ... Naarah (16:6–7). These previously unattested sites move from west to east along the northern border of Ephraim and the southern border of Manasseh. Naʾaman suggests that this follows water courses, the Wadi Qanah in the west and the Wadi Farʿah in the east.[169] Thus he identifies Micmethath with the mountain Jebel el-Kabîr (181183). The other three sites may be Khirbet Taʿna el-Fôqā (185175); either Khirbet Marāḥ el-ʿInab (193179), Bab en-Naqb (190182), or Tell Miske (187183); and Khirbet el-Mifğir (193193).[170]

Required to do forced labor (16:10). This reference, part of the customary note at the end of a tribal allotment regarding unconquered land, refers to the *mas* or corvée that was extracted from subject towns by a more powerful ruler. It was a form of taxation known in Late Bronze Age and Iron Age Palestine. Thus the term appears in a fourteenth-century B.C. Amarna letter from the leader of Megiddo who is using a corvée to cultivate the pharaoh's land near Shunem.[171] Solomon also uses this type of labor (1 Kings 4:6). Here it may have come as a result of the battles of either Joshua 11 or Judges 4–5.

Makir (17:1). This represents that part of the tribe of Manasseh that settled east of the Jordan River and north of Reuben and Gad (13:31).

Abiezer, Helek, Asriel, Shechem, Hepher and Shemida (17:2). These are the remaining clans other than Makir. In the Samaria ostraca of the first half of the eighth century B.C., these clan names appear as regions and towns neighboring Samaria. In relation to the city of Samaria, Abiezer lies to the south; Helek is immediately southeast; Asriel is farther south than Abiezer; Shechem (Tell Balâṭah, 176179) is farther southeast than Helek; Hepher is northeast; Shemida is west.[172]

Daughters, whose names were Mahlah, Noah, Hoglah, Milcah and Tirzah (17:3). Zelophehad's daughters were the granddaughters of Hepher and thus the names of their towns are located northeast and east of Samaria by the beginning of the eighth century B.C. (see comment on 17:2). Despite the practice of giving inheritance to the sons, inheritance by daughters is known in the Bronze Age archives. There are examples in texts where a daughter is legally declared to be a son and thereby given the inheritance.[173]

Samaria ostraca
Todd Bolen/www.BiblePlaces.com

Beth Shan, Ibleam ... Endor (17:11). These are the only towns among those belonging to Manasseh that did not appear earlier in Joshua. Beth Shan is Hebrew Tel Bet Shean (197212). Ibleam is possibly Arabic Tell Belʿameh (177205). Endor is Hebrew Ḥirbet Ṣafṣafot (187227).

Canaanites were determined to live in that region (17:12). These towns are better known because they are larger and

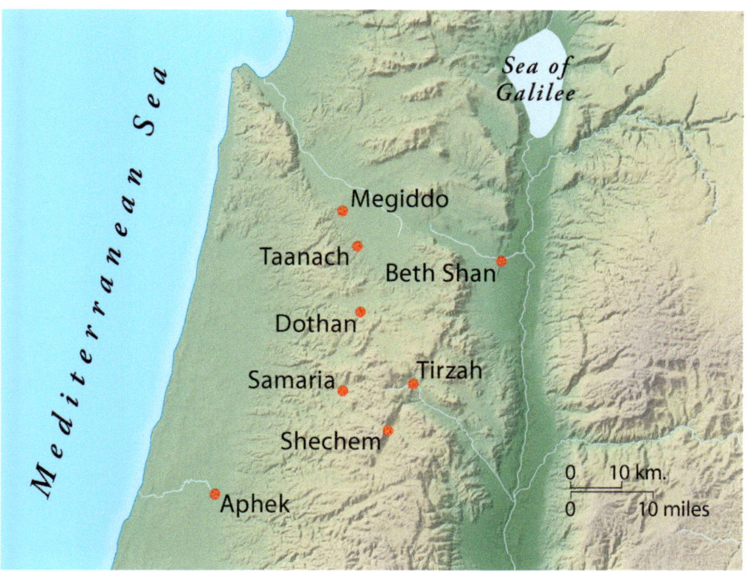

Regions of Samaria

Terraces
Z. Radovan/www.BibleLandPictures.com

ance of some three hundred villages dating to the first half of the twelfth century B.C. and situated in the hill country occupied by Manasseh and, to a lesser extent, Ephraim attests to the presence of Israel and its expansion in the region suggested in this verse. There is no greater concurrence between the biblical evidence (assuming a thirteenth-century date for the Exodus),

more prominent centers in and around the Jezreel Valley. Many of these names appear in Egyptian sources and in Amarna letters from the Late Bronze Age. The wealth of such towns in terms of agriculture in the fertile valley and, above all, in terms of trade made them highly desirable prizes that the Canaanites held on to, in some cases until the united monarchy.

Forced labor (17:13). See note on 16:10.

"If you are so numerous," Joshua answered, "and if the hill country of Ephraim is too small for you, go up into the forest and clear land for yourselves there" (17:15). The sudden appear-

both here and in the sociological descriptions of village life in Judges, Ruth, and 1 Samuel, and in the archaeological evidence for these villages for the early period of Israel's history.[174] The clearing of the forest and the consequent construction of terraces to retain the topsoil is well attested throughout the region. Although terraces are difficult to date, there was apparently a considerable development of these in the early Iron Age (1200–1000 B.C.).[175]

Perizzites and Rephaites (17:15). See comments on 10:3 and 12:4.

Iron chariots (17:16, 18). See comment on 11:6, 9.

Shiloh
Bible Scene Multimedia/Maurice Thompson

Remaining Tribal Allotments (18:1–19:51)

Israelites gathered at Shiloh and set up the Tent of Meeting there (18:1). The location of Shiloh is probably Khirbet Seilûn, where excavations have uncovered a shrine in the Middle Bronze Age and a population center in the Late Bronze Age. Occupation continued into the Iron Age until it was destroyed in the eleventh century, perhaps by Philistines.[176] The Tent of Meeting is mentioned only here and in 19:51 in Joshua. The absence of evidence for the Tent of Meeting at Shiloh may result from the temporary

Benjamin and Dan

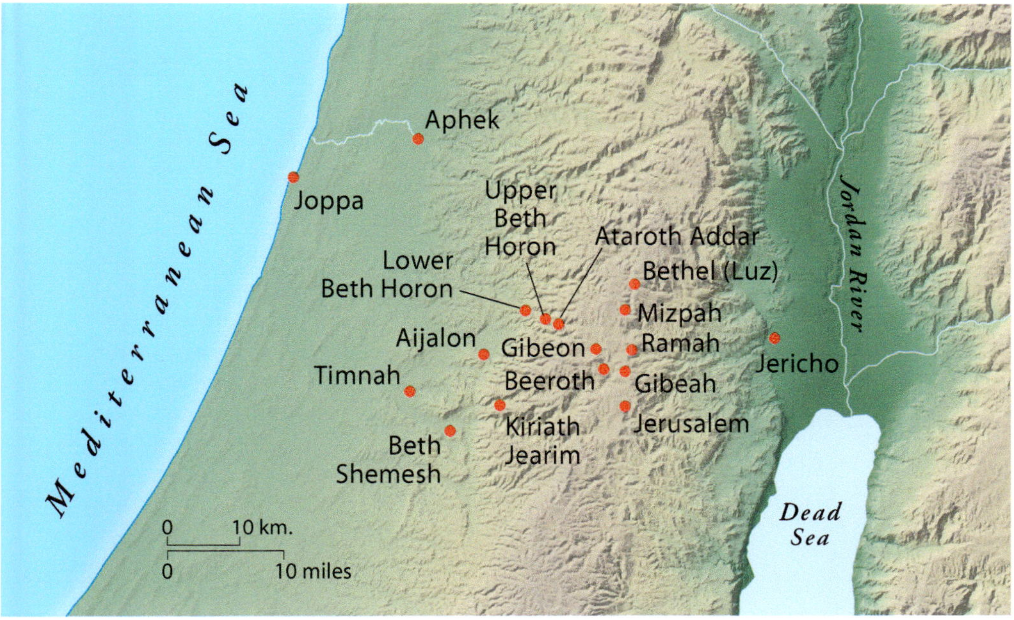

nature of its structure and from the absence of any early remains at the top of the site. This area was reused later and has left no earlier remains although something was there. Does this note indicate a transfer of the ark and center of worship at this time, from Gilgal and Ebal to Shiloh? If so, it seems to have returned to Shechem at the end of the book and then appears again at Shiloh at the beginning of 1 Samuel.

There were still seven Israelite tribes who had not yet received their inheritance (18:2). Seven tribes remain who receive allotments. This section begins with a review of the tribes that have received allotments and the sending forth of mapmakers to ascertain the boundaries for the remaining tribes (18:1–10). There is a lengthy description of the allotment of Benjamin, consisting of borders and two regions of town lists (18:11–28). Simeon's allotment consists entirely of two regions of town lists (19:1–9). Zebulun's allotment consists of border descriptions (19:10–16). Issachar's allotment is defined by a town list (19:17–23). Asher's tribal allotment is given in terms of a boundary description (19:24–31). Naphtali's allotment consists of both a southern boundary description and a town list (19:32–39). Finally, Dan's allotment consists of two town lists followed by a note on the city of Dan (19:40–48). A note on Joshua's inheritance concludes the allotments (19:49–51).

As with the earlier tribes, many of the sites named are unknown or speculative.[177] There is overlap where two borders are identical, such as the southern border of Benjamin and the northern border of Judah. The boundary descriptions contain both towns and natural phenomena. This description of the northern half of the settlement regions may be compared to the thirteenth-century B.C. Papyrus Anastasi I, which includes a description of the region.

Cast lots (18:6, 8). See comment on 14:2.

Make a survey of the land and write a description of it (18:8). For an Egyptian example of a thirteenth-century description of the land, see the sidebar "Papyrus Anastasi I".

The allotments for Benjamin include the largest number of towns of any in these two chapters and second only to the allotments of Judah. Whatever the significance

Descriptions of Regions in Canaan in the Papyrus Anastasi I

The following description of Canaan provides a picture of the region outlined in Joshua 18–19 from the Egyptian point of view, dating from the thirteenth century B.C. and the time of Ramesses II. It seems to describe a chariot journey from Lebanon to the south along major routes:

> I will mention to you another difficulty: "The Pass of the Hornets" (the Ladder of Tyre). You will say that it burns more than a (hornet's) sting. How miserable he is, a Maher-warrior! Come and put [me] on the road heading south to the region of Acco. Where does the route to Acshaph originate? Next to which city? Please inform me about the mountain of User. What is its summit like? Where does the mountain of Shechem rise? Who can conquer it? The Maher-warrior, where does he march to get to Hazor? What is its river like? Put me [on] the highway to Hamath, Dagal, and Dagal-El, the promenade of every Maher-warrior. Please instruct me about his route and let me visit Yan. If someone is traveling to Adumim, in which direction should he head? Do not falter from your teaching. Guide us to know them (the places)!
>
> Come and I will tell you of other cities which lie above these. You have not gone to the land of Takhsy, to Kur-Marruna, Taminta, Kadesh, Dapur, Azaya, or Hermon. You have not visited Kiriath-Anab and Beth-Sopher. You are not acquainted with Adurun or Sidiputu either. You do not know the name of Khalsu, which is in the land of Upe, a bull on its frontier and the battle scene of all sorts of champions. Please instruct me about the topography of Kina, acquaint me with Rehob, and explain Bethshan and Tirek-El. As for the river Jordan, how can it be crossed? Inform me of the pass to Megiddo, which lies above it.
>
> You are a Maher-warrior who is experienced in heroic deeds. A Maher-warrior such as yourself should be found qualified to advance at the head of an army. O Maryan-warrior, forward to shoot! See, the declivity(?) is a ravine 2,000 cubits deep, filled with boulders and small stones, so you make a detour. You pick up the bow and draw to your left so that you might let them see,

of these lists, the number of sites is out of proportion to those of other tribes. Like the towns of Judah and Simeon, this suggests the ongoing use of these documents for administrative purposes right to the end of the Judean monarchy, when the population of the region was much larger and the towns far more numerous. The boundaries of Benjamin (18:12–20) match those of their surrounding tribes. The following town lists are divided into the eastern (18:21–24) and western (18:25–28) lists. The Simeon allotment is also divided into eastern (19:2–6) and western (19:7–8) lists.

The allotment for Zebulun lies in the western part of Lower Galilee, north of the Jezreel Valley and reaching north to include the fertile Beit Netofa Valley. The southern boundary (19:10–11) proceeds to the east (19:12–13) and then turns north (19:14–15).

but their vision is perfect and weakness is discerned(?) in your hands. "You wander about like a sheep, dear Maher-soldier!" Thus you celebrate the name of every Maher-warrior, Egypt's chariot officers. Your name has become like that of Kezardy, the prince of Asher, when the bear found him in the balsam tree.

The narrow pass is dangerous, having Shasu-Bedouin concealed beneath the bushes, some of whom are of four cubits or five cubits (from) their nose to foot and have fierce faces. They are unfriendly and do not take to cajolery while you are alone having no aide with you nor soldiery backing you up. You find no scout to prepare safe passage for you. You reach a decision by forging ahead ignorant of the road. Such bristling fright grips you that (the hair of) your head is ruffled. Your *Ba* lies in your hands. Your path is filled with boulders and small stones without a toe hold for passage as it is overgrown with reeds and thorns, brambles, and "wolf's paw." The declivities lie to one side of you, and the mountain rises on the other side of you. With your chariot lying on its side, you move along swaying to and fro too afraid to pursue your horses. If you are thrown toward the abyss, your horse collar is left exposed and your harness(?) falls. You unharness the team in order to repair the horse collar in the middle of the narrow pass, but you are unexperienced in how to lash it and cannot tie it fast. The clamp(?) is left where it is, for the team is too overburdened to support it. You are disgusted and get set to trot off. The sky is now clear, but you imagine that the enemy is behind you, and trembling grips you. If only you had a hedge of shrubbery to put on the other side! The team is exhausted by the time you locate the camping spot. You have undergone a miserable experience.

You have now entered Joppa and find the meadowland verdant in its season.[A-25]

From this description and its inclusion in what was probably a school exercise text, the reader learns of the fascination that northern Palestine held for the Egyptian scribes at about the same time as the events recorded in Joshua. It was a dangerous place because of both the inhabitants and its difficult and varying terrain. Israel would have difficulties dispossessing these inhabitants, and some Canaanite enclaves remained untouched for generations.

Beit Netofa Valley
Todd Bolen/www.BiblePlaces.com

Issachar's inheritance (19:17–23) includes only a town list, the southern part of which overlaps with towns belonging to Manasseh. Issachar reaches the Beth Shan Valley in the south and the Valley of Yiptahel in the north with towns on the edge of cliffs, on the basalt heights, and in the Jezreel Valley. The name Issachar refers to "hireling," a term that suggests the *mas* or corvée to which both Israelites and Canaanites in this region were subject (see comment on 16:10).

Northern Tribal Areas

Asher (19:24–31) includes the territories from Carmel to the south along the Acco Plain to the north as far as Tyre and greater Sidon. Cabul (Ḥirbet Roʾsh Zayit, 172254) and the eastern region was given to Hiram by Solomon (1 Kings 9:11–13). The name Asher may appear in Papyrus Anastasi I, but this is not certain.

The territory of Naphtali (19:32–39) includes the rest of Galilee (other than the southwestern part occupied by Zebulun), the area west of the Sea of Galilee, Hazor, and the Huleh basin. The absence of Ijon and Abel Beth Maacah suggests that this list predates their incorporation into Israel during the period of the united monarchy.

Like the other major town lists in these chapters, the town list of Dan is divided into eastern (19:41–44) and western sections (19:45–47). It is coordinated with the conquest of the town of Leshem/Dan in Judges 18:11.

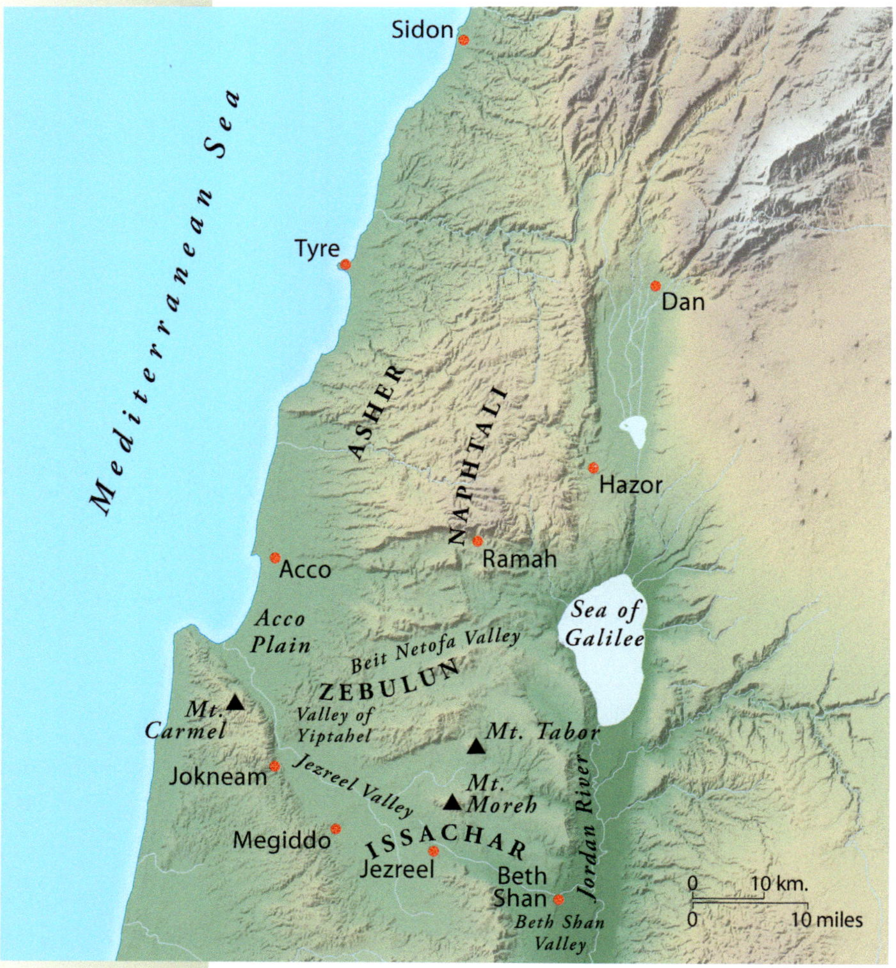

Timnath Serah (19:50). This inheritance of Joshua is probably Khirbet Tibnah (160157), sixteen miles southwest of Shechem.

Eleazar the priest (19:51). See comment on 14:1.

Towns of Refuge (20:1–9)

Tell the Israelites to designate the cities of refuge (20:2). At the end of the formal allotments are two chapters in which towns within the allotted territory are set aside for other purposes. The towns of refuge were so designated in the Pentateuch (Ex. 21:12–14; Num. 35:9–15, 22–28; Deut. 4:41–43; 19:1–10) and occur here again. Although comparisons have been made with treaty clauses regarding refugees, these normally have to do with those fleeing from another state and concern individuals wanted by the king, not nonstate issues of murder and family blood vengeance.

Laws such as the Hittite Laws and the Laws of Hammurabi provide lesser penalties for inadvertent homicide, but there is no mention of setting aside places of asylum.[178]

It is therefore interesting that this provision occurs at the beginning of the laws concerning homicide in the earliest civil law collection of Israel's book of the covenant (Ex. 20:22–23:33). This suggests that such provision formed a part of Israel's legal understanding of jurisprudence from its earliest times.

Cities of refuge ... avenger of blood (20:2–3, 9). Its unique presence only in Israelite laws may reflect the background of a tribal society with strong traditions of blood vengeance in clans and tribes. Thus the kinsman-redeemer or blood avenger (Heb. *goʾēl*; Lev. 25:26) would also appear to come from similar origins.

Stand in the entrance of the city gate and state his case before the elders of that city (20:4). The city gate functioned as the town square in a fortified city of ancient Israel. Here all the major activities of the city took place, including sales and contracts as well as legal decisions. At Tel Dan the excavations from the period of the monarchy have revealed a large and complex city gate with plazas for business. At one side are benches that may have been used by the elders who represent the city and render judgment in cases over which the local authority has sovereignty. Beside the benches a special structure could be provision for a chair or throne where the leader or king of the region might sit and render judgment. The elders of the city are a kinship-based institution that was already operating in some form in Israel's tribal origins.

Kedesh in Galilee in the hill country of Naphtali, Shechem in the hill country of Ephraim, and Kiriath Arba (that is, Hebron) in the hill country of Judah (20:7). These are

Jezreel Valley
Bible Scene Multimedia/Maurice Thompson

Gate at Dan with ruler's seat and bench along wall for elders
© William D. Mounce

Shechem have revealed a remarkably strong wall and gate system built of cyclopean stones and dating from the Middle Bronze Age.

Bezer in the desert on the plateau in the tribe of Reuben, Ramoth in Gilead in the tribe of Gad, and Golan in Bashan in the tribe of Manasseh (20:8). These are the three towns of asylum east of the Jordan River. They are spread throughout the country from south to north. Bezer may possibly be Umm el-ʾAmad (235132), Ramoth may be Tell Ramith (244210). Golan may be Sahem el-Joulan (238243), although the identifications east of the Jordan are not as clear as those west of the river.[180]

the three towns of asylum west of the Jordan River. They are spread throughout the country from north to south. Although the name of a clan of Manasseh (12:33), Shechem is a recognized town elsewhere (17:7). It is identified with Tell Balâtah (176179). Kedesh, distinct from the town in 12:22, should be identified with Arabic Tell Qades or Hebrew Tel Qedesh (199279). For Hebron and Kiriath Arba see comments on 10:3 and 14:15.

Although Deuteronomy 19:1–10 suggests an additional three towns west of the Jordan River, they are not allocated. Perhaps this is due to a failure to achieve a complete conquest.[179] These towns would have been fortified and provided a safe refuge from the blood avenger. In particular, excavations at

Levitical Towns (21:1–45)

Now the family heads of the Levites approached Eleazar the priest ... "The LORD commanded through Moses that you give us towns to live in, with pasturelands for our livestock" (21:1–2). The principle of providing for the Levites assumes that the Israelites will return to God something of the gift he has given to them. Just as with the Sabbath and the tithes and firstfruit offerings, so with the gift of the land there is a sense that returning to God a token of what he has given to the people is an appropriate way of honoring him. Of course, the Levites need a place to live, and God has directed that this is also the means to satisfy that need (Num. 35:1–8). The instructions there require that not only the town but also the surrounding pastures for up to three thousand feet away be given to the Levites.

That priests and priestly assistants should receive provision certainly has support throughout the ancient Near East. In particular the Egyptian temples were endowed with lands and settlements to provide food and income for the priests. The famous temple of

Shechem wall with gate visible at far left
Copyright 1995–2009 Phoenix Data Systems

Amun Re in Thebes owned fifty-six towns in Egypt during the time of Ramesses III, not to mention nine additional estates in Palestine and Nubia. The Levitical town system is a simplification of this. There was no central temple to which these towns and their lands were given. Further, the Levites lived in the towns and worked the lands themselves. The complex and almost certainly oppressive Egyptian system was alien to the Israelite system.[181]

Temple of Amun at Thebes
Frederick J. Mabie

Perhaps closer in similarity is the Middle Bronze Age Alalakh Level VII text 56, wherein there is a list of place names and territories. The text transfers the ownership of these lands in exchange for an initial payment and an annual payment during the life of the seller. It also specifies that the towns are given *qa-du-um pa-ṭì-šu-nu* ("with their districts"), not unlike the regular town list comment on Joshua 21, *w^{e}ʾet-migrāšêhen* ("with their pasturelands"). Thus this type of note affixed to towns and other geographical entities was known in the West Semitic world centuries before the allotments of Joshua.[182]

As in many texts with town lists from Alalakh, Ugarit, and elsewhere, the Levitical list is subdivided into smaller groups. The Levitical towns were divided into four groups: thirteen towns in the south (Judah, Simeon, and Benjamin) for the Kohathites, who were descendants of Aaron (10:4); ten towns in the middle hill country (Ephraim, Dan, and Manasseh) for the rest of the Kohathites (21:5); thirteen towns in the north (Issachar, Asher, Naphtali, and Manasseh in Bashan) for the descendants of Gershon (21:6); twelve towns in Transjordan and

Levitical Towns

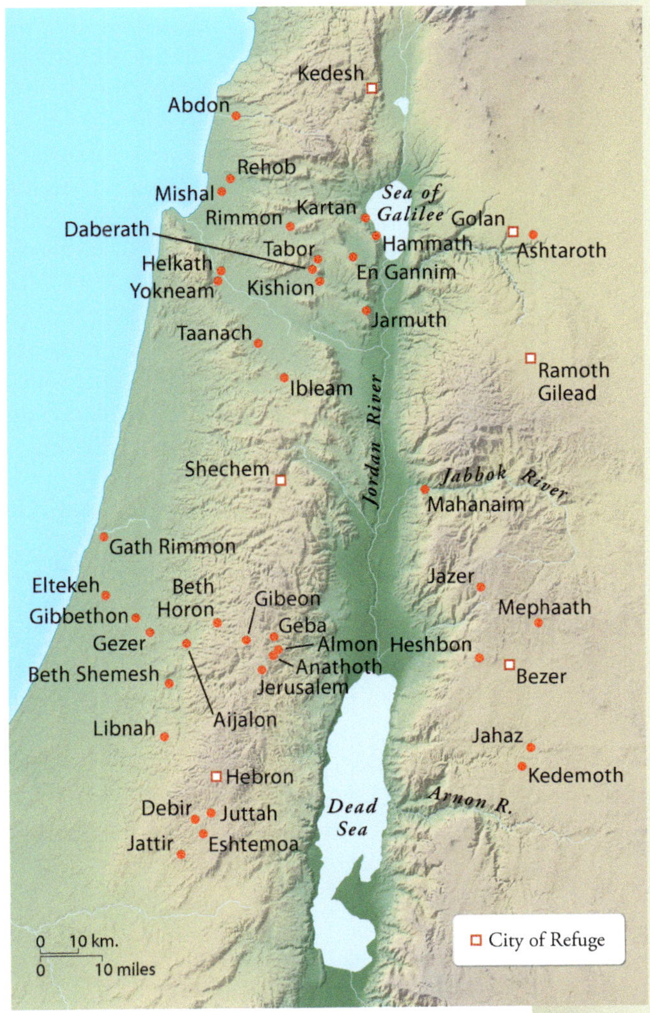

Zebulun (Reuben, Gad, and Zebulun) for the descendants of Merari (21:7). Gershon, Kohath, and Merari are the three sons of Levi in Genesis 46:11.

Many of the Levitical towns are well known and represent many significant fortified centers scattered throughout the land of Israel. The responsibility for the priests to teach and proclaim the Torah (cf. Lev. 10:10–11), one that is not well attested in other ancient Near Eastern cultures, could indeed suggest that these towns served the purpose of centers for the dissemination of the Torah of Israel and understanding of the God of Israel.[183]

Descendants of Aaron (21:10–19). The following towns include possible identifications only where none have been given previously: Hebron (10:3–5; 10:36–39; 10:39; 14:13–15; 15:13), Libnah (10:29–32), Jattir (also at 15:48; Arabic Khirbet ʿAttîr, Hebrew Ḥirbet Yatir, 151084), Eshtemoa (also at 15:50; es-Semûʿ, 156089), Holon (also at 15:51; Khirbet ʿAfîn, 152118), Debir (10:38–39), Ain (also at 15:32; not certain), Juttah (also at 15:55; Yaṭṭā, 158095), Beth Shemesh (also at 15:10; Arabic Tell er-Rumeileh, Hebrew Tel Bet Shemesh, 147128), Gibeon (9:3, 17), Geba (Jabaʿ, 175140), Anathoth (Ras el-Karrubeh, 175135), and Almon (Kh ʿAlmit, 176136);

Rest of the Kohathite clans (21:20–26). Possible identifications here include: Shechem (17:7), Gezer (10:33; 16:3, 10), Kibzaim (not certain), Beth Horon (10:10–11), Eltekeh (also at 19:44; Arabic Tell esh-Shallaf, Hebrew Tel Shalaf, 128144), Gibbethon (also at 19:44; Tell Melât, 137140), Aijalon (also at 19:42; Yâlō, 152138), Gath Rimmon (also at 19:45; Arabic Tell el-Jerîsheh or Tell Abu Zeitun, Hebrew Tel Gerisa, 132166 or 134167), Taanach (12:21; 17:11) and Ibleam (also at 17:11; Tell Belʿameh, 177205).

Gershonites (21:27–33). Again, possible identifications where none have been previously given include: Golan in Bashan (also at 20:8; Sahem el-Joulan? 238243), Be Eshtarah (= Ashtaroth, 12:4; 13:31), Kishion (also at 19:20; Arabic Khirbet Qasyûn, Hebrew Tel Qishyon, 187229), Daberath (19:12; Dabûriyeh, 185233), Jarmuth (10:3, 5, 23), En Gannim (also at 19:21; Arabic el-Ḥadetheh, Hebrew Tel ʿEn Ḥadda, 195232), Mishal (also at 19:26; Tell el-Naḥal? 157245), Abdon (also at 19:28; Arabic Khirbet ʿAbdeh, Hebrew Tel ʿAvdon, 165272), Helkath (also at 19:25; Tel ʿAmar, 159237), Rehob (also at 19:28, 30; Arabic Tell el-Gharbī, Hebrew Tell Bira, 166256), Kedesh in Galilee (20:7), Hammoth Dor (= Hammath, also at 19:35; Arabic Ḥammâm Ṭabarîyeh, Hebrew Ḥame Ṭeveriya, 201241) and Kartan (Khirbet el-Qureiyeh, 194280).

Merarites (21:34–40). Possible identifications, where none have appeared previously, include: Jokneam (12:22; 19:11), Kartah[184] (cf. [Kisloth] Tabor of 1 Chron. 6:77, also at Josh. 19:12; Iksâl, 180232), Dimnah (= Rimmon of 1 Chron. 6:77, also at Josh. 19:13; Arabic Qarn Ḥaṭṭîn, Hebrew Ḥirbet Qarnei Hiṭṭin, 193245), Nahalal (also at 19:15; Maʿlul,[185] 173234), Bezer (20:8), Jahaz (13:18), Kedemoth (13:18), Mephaath (13:18), Ramoth in Gilead (20:8), Mahanaim (13:26, 30), Heshbon (9:10; 12:2, 5; 13:10–27), and Jazer (13:25).

Altar of the Transjordanian Tribes (22:1–34)

Then Joshua summoned the Reubenites, the Gadites and the half-tribe of Manasseh and said to them, "You have done all that Moses the servant of the LORD commanded, and you have obeyed me in everything I commanded (22:1–2). This story, while set in the time of Joshua, seems out of place. However, it has a literary context within the book. Our interest concerns the background in the ancient world. There is no clear example of a story like this. This is a story about the building of an altar and thus might be related to 8:30–35. However, there are no examples of an altar built purely as a memorial. The erection

▸ An Old Babylonian Town List from Alalakh

Alalakh text 56 preserves the sale of a list of towns and territories that are mentioned with their districts, similar to the notes on the Levitical town lists. Note also the distinction between the towns themselves and adjacent territories—a distinction made in the boundary descriptions of Joshua 14–19. This is the opening half of this text (lines 1–17, 19–25):

> The town of Shallum,
> the town of Tarmanne,
> the town of Amakwan,
> with their districts;
> the territory of Igar,
> the territory of Shipte,
> the territory of Aleppo,
> the territory of Ure,
> the territory of Erib-ambi,
> with its territory wherever it is,
> he shall transfer and take from Labbina for 3,080 shekels of silver,
> [ ]00 parisi-measures of barley,
> 50 parisi-measures of fodder, 7 vessels of oil, 24 vessels of wine, 3 lengths of cloth… as the full price Irpaʾaddu has bought. Moreover, as long as Labbina is living 100 iku of land in the area of Lakka, when Irpaʾaddu has been given them, he shall retain unmolested. In the future.…

of standing stones of special significance seems to have served that purpose elsewhere (see comment on 4:7). Further, none of the six or seven likely altars so far discovered within the territory of ancient Israel fulfills the requirements for the location of this altar, visible on both sides of the Jordan. The closest may be the recently discovered four-horned altar, located a mile from Shiloh. However, this remains much too far from the Jordan River; nor is its dating assured.[186]

Another approach views Joshua 22 in the context of the boundary descriptions and considers it in terms of the formalization of religious, cultural, and political boundaries between groups. From the perspective of the ancient Near East, comparative background sources occur in terms of the essential function of this chapter. It occurs at the conclusion of the allotments, before moving on to the final chapters of covenant-making. The account provides a dramatic visual and verbal means to affirm the ongoing unity of Israel and affirmation of the boundaries. The Transjordanian tribes affirm their unity with the rest of the nation, and by doing so and by extracting a confession from the other tribes, they also seek to guarantee that their own lands and borders will be respected. There will not come some future time

High place with standing stones outside the gate at Dan
Kim Walton
◂

when the tribes west of the Jordan will see them as non-Israelites who worship other deities and thus may be attacked and killed and their land seized.

Both Joshua the commander and Phinehas the priest confirm the loyalty and faithfulness of the Transjordanian tribes (22:1–8, 31). The future is guaranteed in the other texts we have compared. Thus in the Tudhaliya and Kurunta treaty, with its boundary clauses, there are the customary divine witnesses, curses, and blessings that appear at the end of a treaty and serve to ensure the perpetuity of the treaty. In the context of Joshua the altar serves as a witness because there are no other deities than the God of Israel that can be recognized. For this reason the altar is named "A Witness between Us that the LORD Is God." In the Tudhaliya and Kurunta treaty, divine witnesses are used:

> And in regard to the fact that I have made this treaty for you, the Thousand Gods are now summoned to assembly in this matter. They shall observe and be witnesses: The Sun-god of Heaven, the Sun-goddess of Arinna, the Storm-god of Heaven, the Storm-god of the Army. . . .[187]

In Joshua 22, Phinehas the priest and the leaders of the community also serve as human witnesses to the discussion that takes place. The Tudhaliya and Kurunta treaty also includes human witnesses who are of high status in leadership in the Hittite empire, many of whom would be affected by the boundaries drawn:

> Halwa-ziti, the scribe, son of Lupakki, man of the city of Ukkiya, wrote this tablet in the city of Tawa in the presence of Prince Nerikkaili; Huzziya, chief of the royal bodyguard; Prince Kurakura; Ini-Teshshup, king of the land of Carchemish; Masturi, king of the land of the Seha River; Shaushga-muwa, brother-in-law of the King; Uppara-muwa, Antuwasalli; Tattamaru, commander of the troops of the left. . . .[188]

This treaty that establishes boundaries, among other things, concludes with a substantial deposition clause, just as the boundary descriptions and town lists of Joshua 13–21 conclude with a chapter that describes at length the large stone altar that serves as a permanent reminder. The Hittite act of depositing a treaty in temples corresponds here to the Israelite act of building a permanent witness. In both cases the security of the agreement is guaranteed by the security of the object that attests to it. The Hittite treaty is further secured by the fact that it is written on a bronze metal tablet weighing some five kilograms. The deposition clause is as follows:

> This document is made in seven copies and is sealed with the seal of the Sun-goddess of Arinna and the seal of the Storm-god of Hatti. One tablet is deposited in the presence of the Sun-goddess of Arinna, one tablet in the presence of the Storm-god of Hatti, one tablet in the presence of Lelwani, one tablet in the presence of Hebat of Kizzuwatna, one tablet in the presence of the Storm-god of Lightning, and one tablet in the presence of Zithariya. And Kurunta, king of the land of Tarhuntassa, has one tablet in his residence.[189]

Geliloth near the Jordan in the land of Canaan (22:10). This is possibly Araq ed-Deir (180133), a site on the border with Benjamin in 18:17.[190]

Gilead (22:15). See comment on 12:2.

The sin of Peor (22:17). This was stopped by Phineas at Baal Peor in Transjordan (Num. 25:6–18).

Joshua's Farewell Sermon (23:1–16)

Joshua, by then old and well advanced in years, summoned all Israel ... and said to them (23:1–2). This is the final sermon of Joshua. It is followed by a covenant renewal. But even here aspects of ancient Near Eastern treaties appear. The first part (23:2–14) reviews Israel's experience in the Promised

Land and the manner in which God enabled the nation to have success against all of its enemies. It concludes with observations about the manner in which God has blessed the people. Thus verse 10 ("one of you routs a thousand, because the LORD your God fights for you") sounds similar to the blessings of ancient Near Eastern treaties of the second millennium B.C., although the latter are more general, as in the blessing of the treaty between Suppiluliumas and Kirtiwaza:

> May these gods protect you, Kurtiwaza, together with your wife, the daughter of the Hatti land, her children, and her children's children, and also (you), the Hurrians, together with your wives, your children, and your children's children and together with your country. May the Mitanni country return to the place which it occupied before, may it thrive and expand. May you, Kurtiwaza, your sons and your sons' sons (descended) from the daughter of the Great King of the Hatti land, and (you), the Hurrians, exercise kingship forever. May the throne of your father persist, may the Mitanni country persist.[191]

Canaanite deity

The same is true of 23:15–16, which resembles curses such as may be found on many treaties, with an emphasis on divine judgment. Note these words from the same treaty of Suppiluliumas and Kirtiwaza:

> May the gods, the lords of the oath, blot you out, (you) Kurtiwaza and (you) the Hurri men together with your country, your wives and all that you have. May they draw you like malt from its hull. Just as one does not obtain a plant from bubuwahi, even so may you Kurtiwaza with a second wife that you may take, and (you) the Hurri men with your wives, your sons and your country have no seed. These gods of the contracting parties may bring misery and poverty over you. May they overturn your throne, (yours) of Kurtiwaza....[192]

All Israel—their elders, leaders, judges and officials (23:2). This is a good example of the use of the expression "all Israel" in a context where it is immediately qualified by the leadership that represents the nation. Thus, neither here nor elsewhere in the book does "all Israel" imply every man, woman, and child in the nation. This type of rhetorical expression has parallels in the ancient Near Eastern annals. Thus Younger, in making the same point about "all Israel" in chapters 10 and 11, compares the annals of Mursilis and the annals of Tiglath-pileser I:

> Mursilis: The entire land of the Kasdaeans came together to help.... The whole country of Arzawa fled.... And because the whole land of Arzawa ... had gone over to the area of Puranda ... the whole country withdrew to the fortress towns.[193]

In the ancient Near Eastern contexts, the historical context denies that truly every man, woman, and child was involved in these expressions. The same is true where "all Israel" is used in the book of Joshua.

Do not associate with these nations that remain among you; do not invoke the names of their gods or swear by them. You must not serve them or bow down to them (23:7). The equation of invoking the names of the deities with service and worship of them recalls the use of their names in the treaties. Every treaty that has not had its latter section destroyed preserves a listing of divine witnesses. This places the gods of both parties side by side. Thus, this statement includes an implicit warning against joining with other nations in treaties and thereby implicitly recognizing their deities on a par with the God of Israel. These elements occur in the same sequence in the structure of Joshua 24, although only a small trace of the blessing is preserved.

Joshua's Covenant Renewal (24:1–28)

Joshua assembled all the tribes of Israel at Shechem (24:1). The earlier covenant ceremony of 8:30–35 was at Mount Ebal, just north of Shechem. Shechem (17:2), a site with occupation in the Middle Bronze Age, Late Bronze Age, and Iron Age, and its defenses and *migdol*-type fortified sanctuary are associated with the story of Abimelech in Judges 9 but may also have been used earlier by the Israelites. Because this chapter does not mention Mount Ebal, whereas chapter 8 does not mention Shechem, it is possible that the location of this covenant renewal was not at the same place as that of chapter 8 (which itself is portrayed as a fulfillment of Deut. 27:2–8). However, no attack or conquest of Shechem is ever mentioned.

This has raised the question of how Israel came to occupy this city. Perhaps there was a battle that, like the one mentioned on the Merneptah Stele, was simply not recorded. Or it may be that Israel peacefully occupied the region and did not fight against the inhabitants of Shechem. Although this latter suggestion seems to contradict 11:19, it is possible that some other accommodation was made at Shechem. We cannot be certain.

The assembly point at Shechem suggests that, despite the important role Shiloh was taking on, it did not replace Shechem (and Mount Ebal?) as a center for other national meetings, for covenant renewal, and for religious acts such as the erection of a sacred memorial stone (24:26). Furthermore, Shechem was the first place where Abram built an altar when he first came to Canaan (Gen. 12:6) and the first place where Jacob came when he returned from Aram, and where he also built an altar (33:18–20). Furthermore, land nearby is associated with one of the early patriarchal plots purchased by Jacob (33:19), where Joseph would be buried (Josh. 24:32).

Shechem
Bible Scene Multimedia/Maurice Thompson

Elders, leaders, judges and officials of Israel (24:1). See comment on 23:2.

Terah the father of Abraham and Nahor, lived beyond the River and worshiped other gods (24:2). The references are to Terah as the father of Abram and Nahor (Gen. 11:26). The region "beyond the River" is that of the area north and east of Canaan across the Euphrates River. The area discussed here lay in the Balikh flood plain and those of other rivers that flow into and form the Euphrates River in north-

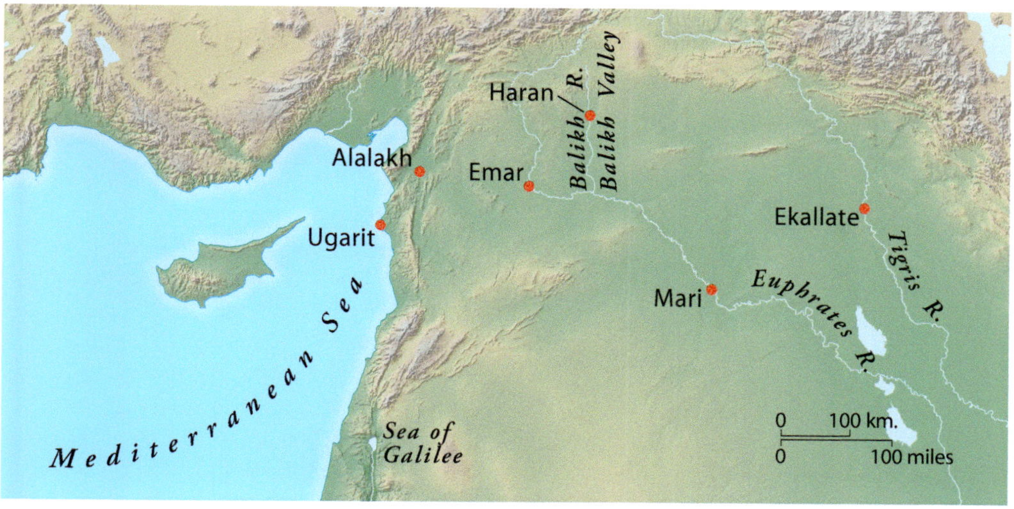

Upper Euphrates ◄

ern Syria. If the patriarchal times refer to the Middle Bronze Age, the nearby sites of Mari and Alalakh (Stratum VII) have yielded archives of cuneiform tablets from this period that attest to many deities worshiped by peoples of the region and same linguistic background as the patriarchs. Compare also the Late Bronze Age archives at Alalakh (Stratum IV), Ugarit, Emar, and Ekalte, where archives attest to a wide variety of deities recognized and worshiped.

The treaty that Jacob and Laban concluded in Genesis 31:53, where each swears by the god(s) of their fathers, follows a standard form of treaties in the ancient Near East where the gods are invoked to enforce treaty obligations (see comment on ch. 23). Both Nahor and Terah have personal names that occur elsewhere in the early second millennium B.C. Both names can also be associated with places near Haran in the Balikh River Valley.[194]

I brought you out (24:5). Here and in many of the following phrases, note the switch to the second person as this report of a covenant renewal follows treaty language where a significant part of the historical reminiscence is directed to the actual recipient(s) of the treaty/covenant rather than previous generations. The emphasis is on what God did for that generation and what they witnessed with their own eyes. While Rahab (2:9–11) mentions the drying up of the Red Sea as part of her confession, no mention of that is made here. More than the miracles, this covenant renewal review emphasizes God's acts of deliverance of his people from their enemies.

Citizens of Jericho (24:11). As the first enemies in the Promised Land, these symbolize the rest. The term is used of a group or assembly that makes decisions for the towns of Shechem (Judg. 9:2), Keilah (1 Sam. 23:11–12), and at Late Bronze Age Ampi and Aleppo.[195] At Ampi in the Amarna letters (EA 102.20–28) they appear as a council who make decisions along with the governor:

> Now Ampi is at war with me. Know t<hat> the magnate and the lords of the city are at peace with the sons of ʿAbdi-Aširta, and accordingly I am unable to go. Know that all are traitors, and you must not inquire about me from my enemies. Now, because of the situation, I am afraid.[196]

I sent the hornet ahead of you (24:12). Although some have suggested that the hornet is Egypt, this seems unlikely because this identification is nowhere made in the Bible. The use of insects in warfare is attested but not found in the war chronicles of Israel unlike, for example, the use of (hail)stones that God also sends. The hornet may be a symbol of terror, or perhaps the word for "hornet" should be read as "terror." This

Hittite vassal treaty between Shuppiluliuma and Hakkuana
Istanbul Archaeological Museum; © Dr. James C. Martin

A Comparison of Joshua 24:2b–20, 22, 27 and a Hittite Treaty

Although this text is not itself a covenant, through the charge of Joshua and the interaction between Joshua and the people, we see the emergence of a covenant form that in many ways resembles that of an ancient Near Eastern treaty. There are two types of treaties in the ancient Near East—parity and suzerain/vassal treaties. The latter define a relationship between a sovereign overlord and vassal. In the preserved treaties of the second millennium, which are almost exclusively found in the Hittite archives, there are inevitably six parts that occur in sequence: titulary, historical prologue, stipulations, witnesses, curses, and blessings. These also occur in Joshua 24[A-26] (see chart below). Although only the slightest trace of a blessing exists, the other elements are all present. The Hittite treaty here is between Mursilis and Duppi-Teshub.[A-27]

Titulary	24:2b: This is what the LORD, the God of Israel, says:	These are the words of the Sun Mursilis, the Great King, the king of Hatti land, the valiant, the favorite of the storm-god, the son of Suppiluliumas, the Great King, the king of Hatti land, the valiant.
Historical prologue	24:2c–13: Long ago your forefathers, including Terah the father of Abraham and Nahor, lived beyond the River and worshiped other gods. But I took your father Abraham from the land beyond the River and led him throughout Canaan and gave him many descendants. I gave him Isaac, and to Isaac I gave Jacob and Esau. I assigned the hill country of Seir to Esau, but Jacob and his sons went down to Egypt …	Aziras was the grandfather of you, Duppi-Teshub. He rebelled against my father, but submitted again to my father. When the kings of Nuhasse land and the kings of Kinza rebelled against my father, Aziras did not rebel. As he was bound by treaty, he remained bound by treaty. As my father fought against his enemies, in the same manner fought Aziras. Aziras remained loyal toward my father …

would exemplify the terror that is elsewhere attributed to the battles of Israel as in Exodus 15:14–16; Joshua 2:9–11; 5:1; 6:27.[197]

Eat from vineyards and olive groves (24:13). These constitute important nutritional and food sources for Israel. Mentioned some 185 times in the Old Testament, wine was the most commonly consumed beverage. Wine culture in the region was known from the third millennium B.C. Water could be contaminated and other beverages were not available. Olive trees grow well in the

Stipulations	24:14–21: Now fear the LORD and serve him with all faithfulness. Throw away the gods your forefathers worshiped beyond the River and in Egypt, and serve the LORD. But if serving the LORD seems undesirable to you, then choose for yourselves this day whom you will serve, whether the gods your forefathers served beyond the River, or the gods of the Amorites, in whose land you are living. But as for me and my household, we will serve the LORD ...	With my friend you shall be friend, and with my enemy you shall be enemy. If the king of Hatti land is either in the Hurri land or in the land of Egypt, or in the country of Astata, or in the country of Alse—any country coming in contact with the territory of your country that is friendly with the king of Hatti land—*or in* any country coming in contact with the territory of your country that is friendly with the king of Hatti land—*as* the country of Mukis, or the country of Halba ...
Witnesses	24:22, 27: Then Joshua said, "You are witnesses against yourselves that you have chosen to serve the LORD." "Yes, we are witnesses," they replied.... "See!" he said to all the people. "This stone will be a witness against us. It has heard all the words the LORD has said to us. It will be a witness against you if you are untrue to your God."	The sun-god of heaven, the sun-goddess of Arinna, the storm-god of heaven, the Hattian storm-god, Seris and Hurris, Mount Nanni and Mount Hazzi ... the storm-god of Halab, the storm-god of Zippalanda, the storm-god of Nerik, the storm-god of Lihzina, the storm-god of Hissashapa ...
Curses	24:20a: If you forsake the LORD and serve foreign gods, he will turn and bring disaster on you and make an end of you.	Should Duppi-Teshub not honor the words of the treaty and the oath, may these gods of the oath destroy Duppi-Teshub together with his person, his wife, his son, his grandson, his house, his land, and together with everything that he owns.
Blessings	24:20b: after he has been good to you.	If Duppi-Teshub honors these words of the treaty and the oath that are inscribed on this tablet, may these gods of the oath protect him together with his person, his wife, his son, his grandson, his house, and his country.

There are also many treaties in Akkadian and Aramaic texts of the first millennium B.C. during the Neo-Assyrian empire. These regularly possess in sequence: titulary, stipulations, witnesses, and curses. They do not, however, contain a historical prologue or blessings. Thus, the closest comparison remains the Hittite treaties of the second millennium B.C.[A-28]

climate and soil of the hill country of Palestine. They do not compete with the staple diet grains that grow in different soil. Because it can take many years for olive trees to mature and yield fruit, the presence of these groves, as well as vineyards, suggests the replacement of one civilization by the other without the destruction of the natural resources.

At seventh-century Ekron, the city processed a thousand tons of olive oil annually, most of which was exported. Olive oil was used for food, medicine, and lamp fuel, and as a base for cosmetics. It was used in anointing kings and in ritual contexts.[198]

You are witnesses.... Yes, we are witnesses (24:22). The people agree with the covenant stipulations just as the vassal in a suzerain/vassal treaty had to accept the treaty stipulations. Of course, in treaties the witnesses are customarily the gods of the parties involved. Therefore, it is of greatest interest that the reference to "witnesses" is followed immediately by a charge from

Olive grove
Gabriella Bottka

of the Covenant (Ex. 20:22–23:33). On the role of writing and the significance of God's covenant for Joshua, see comment on 1:8.

He took a large stone and set it up there under the oak near the holy place of the LORD (24:26). On the role of standing stones as memorials, see the comment on 4:7. Although the oak or great tree at Shechem had a long history of association with Israel's ancestors and their worship of God (Gen. 12:6; 35:4; cf. Judg. 9:6), there is no known preservation of this tree. There is, however, a standing stone that is visible in the cult center of the ancient site. Whatever association it may have with the account here is not known.

Joshua that the people should throw away their divine images of other gods and goddesses. The context is the town of Shechem and the manner in which Jacob's family responded to his charge to do away with their divine images by handing them over to Jacob so that he could bury them under the oak at Shechem (Gen. 35:2–4).

In the context of a treaty/covenant and the reference to witnesses, Joshua's exhortation denies to the images any validity to function as witnesses to this covenant. The response of the people is, "We will serve the LORD our God and obey him" (22:24). This sounds fine, but an ominous indicator is that no mention is made of any Israelite relinquishing their images to Joshua; unlike the earlier "Israel" who relinquished their images to Jacob.

On that day Joshua made a covenant for the people, and there at Shechem he drew up for them decrees and laws (24:25). The text provides no further information although such a treaty/covenant would likely include the sorts of statements that Joshua charged the people with in 24:14–24. It may even be larger, along the lines of the Book

The End of Joshua's Generation (24:29–33)

Joshua son of Nun, the servant of the LORD, died at the age of a hundred and ten (24:29). This age matches that of Joseph, who also appears here. In addition, both the age of Joseph and that of Joshua are mentioned twice in the Bible (Gen. 50:22, 26; Judg. 2:8).

They buried him ... north of Mount Gaash (24:30). This site is otherwise unknown, although the ravine of Gaash occurs in the duplicate texts of 2 Samuel 23:30 and 1 Chronicles 11:32. The Hebrew root behind Gaash means "to belch forth, rise and fall," and may suggest that this describes a kind of topographical feature rather than a proper name.

Bibliography

For current annotated bibliography, see sections on "Histories of Israel," "Archaeology," "Joshua," etc., in *Denver Journal: An Online Review of Current Biblical and Theological Studies*, accessible at www.denverseminary.edu/article/annotated-old-testament-bibliography-2009/.

Boling, R., and G. E. Wright. *Joshua: A New Translation with Introduction and Commentary.* AB. Garden City, N.Y.: Doubleday, 1982. Good discussion of the archaeology, although now dated.

Butler, T. *Joshua.* WBC 7. Waco, Tex.: Word, 1983. Emphasis on literary-critical aspects of the text as a Deuteronomistic work.

Fritz, V. *Das Buch Josua.* HAT I/7. Tübingen: J. C. B. Mohr, 1994. An archaeologist looks at Joshua as a first millennium B.C. work.

Hess, R. S. *Joshua: An Introduction and Commentary.* TOTC 5. Downers Grove, Ill.: InterVarsity Press, 1996. Integrates recent archaeological discoveries and literary analysis.

_____. "West Semitic Texts and the Book of Joshua." *BBR* 7 (1997): 63–76. Broad overview of major points of comparison between the literature of Joshua and that of its immediate cultural milieu.

_____. "Early Israel in Canaan: A Survey of Recent Evidence and Interpretations." Pp. 492–518 in *Israel's Past in Present Research: Essays on Ancient Israelite Historiography.* Edited V. Philips Long. Sources for Biblical and Theological Study 7. Winona Lake, Ind.: Eisenbrauns, 1999. Reprint of same article in *PEQ* 126 (1993): 125–42. Comprehensive survey and evaluation of the major historical models for the emergence of Israel in the Palestinian highlands c. 1200 B.C.

_____. "The Book of Joshua as a Land Grant." *Bib* 83 (2002): 493–506. Comparative study of the structure of the book as a whole.

Howard, D. M., Jr. *Joshua.* NAC 5. Nashville: Broadman, 1998. Appreciation of the history, with useful word studies.

Kallai, Z. *Historical Geography of the Bible: The Tribal Territories of Israel.* Jerusalem: Magnes; Leiden: Brill, 1986. An integrated overview of the sites of Joshua and their location.

Merling, D., Sr. *The Book of Joshua: Its Theme and Role in Archaeological Discussions.* AUSDS 23. Berrien Springs, Mich.: Andrews Univ. Press, 1997. Useful summary of the archaeological background and debate.

Nelson, R. D. *Joshua.* OTL. Louisville: Westminster John Knox, 1997. Joshua as the product of Deuteronomistic redaction.

Ottosson, M. *Josuaboken: En programskrift for davidisk restauration.* Acta Universitatis upsaliensis, Studia biblica pusaliensia 1. Stockholm: Almqvist & Wiksell, 1991. Detailed comments on history and sites.

Weinfeld, M. *The Promise of the Land: The Inheritance of the Land of Canaan by the Israelites.* The Taubman Lectures in Jewish Studies. Berkeley: Univ. of California Press, 1993. Comparative explorations into ancient Near Eastern and classical literature.

Woudstra, M. *The Book of Joshua.* NICOT. Grand Rapids: Eerdmans, 1981. Regards the narrative as historical.

Younger, K. L., Jr. *Ancient Conquest Accounts: A Study in Ancient Near Eastern and Biblical History Writing.* JSOTSup 98. Sheffield: Sheffield Academic Press, 1990. Comparisons between Joshua 9–11 and ancient Near Eastern annals and rhetorical forms.

CHAPTER NOTES

Main Text Notes

1. Further discussion and defense of the early date for the Exodus may be found in D. Merling Sr., *The Book of Joshua: Its Theme and Role in Archaeological Discussions* (AUSDDS 23; Berrien Springs, Mich.: Andrews Univ. Press, 1997); M. W. Chavalas and M. R. Adamthwaite, "Archaeological Light on the Old Testament," in *The Face of Old Testament Studies: A Survey of Contemporary Approaches*, ed. D. W. Baker and B. T. Arnold (Grand Rapids: Baker, 1999), 78–90.
2. See further discussion of this evidence and more in B. Halpern, "The Exodus from Egypt? Myth or Reality," in *The Rise of Ancient Israel*, ed. H. Shanks et al. (Washington, D.C.: Biblical Archaeology Society, 1992), 87–113; F. I. Yurco, "Merneptah's Canaanite Campaign and Israel's Origins," in *Exodus: The Egyptian Evidence*, ed. E. S. Frerichs and L. H. Lesko, eds (Winona Lake, Ind.: Eisenbrauns, 1997), 27–55; J. K. Hoffmeier, *Israel in Egypt: The Evidence for the Authenticity of the Exodus Tradition* (Oxford: Oxford Univ. Press, 1997).
3. L. G. Herr, "Tall Al-ʾUmayri and the Reubenite Hypothesis," *ErIsr* 26 (1999): 64*–77*; R. S. Hess, "Fallacies in the Study of Early Israel: An Onomastic Perspective," *TynBul* 45 (1994): 339–54; C. R. Krahmalkov, "Exodus Itinerary Confirmed by Egyptian Evidence," *BAR* 20/5 (September/October 1994): 54–62, 79.
4. A. Ben-Tor and M. T. Rubiato, "Excavating Hazor: Part Two: Did the Israelites Destroy the Canaanite City?" *BAR* 25/3 (May/June 1999): 22–39; A. Ben-Tor, "Tel Hazor, 1996," *IEJ* 46 (1996): 262–68; idem, "Tel Hazor, 1997," *IEJ* 47 (1997): 261–68.
5. For more on the theories of Israelite settlement and the evidence discussed here, see R. S. Hess, "Early Israel in Canaan: A Survey of Recent Evidence and Interpretations," in *Israel's Past in Present Research: Essays on Ancient Israelite Historiography*, ed. V. P. Long (Sources for Biblical and Theological Study 7; Winona Lake, Ind.: Eisenbrauns, 1999), 492–518; reprint of same article in *PEQ* 126 (1993): 125–42.
6. E. Bloch-Smith and B. A. Nakhai, "A Landscape Come to Life: The Iron Age I," *NEA* 62 (1999): 62–92, 101–27; E. Bloch-Smith, "Israelite Ethnicity in Iron I: Archaeology Preserves What Is Remembered and What Is Forgotten in Israel's History," *JBL* 122 (2003): 401–25.
7. A. Zertal, "Israel Enters Canaan—Following the Pottery Trail," *BAR* 17/5 (September/October 1991): 28–47; idem, "The Trek of the Tribes as They Settled in Canaan," *BAR* 17/5 (September/October 1991): 48–49, 75; idem, "The Iron Age I Culture in the Hill-Country of Canaan—a Manassite Perspective," in *Mediterranean Peoples in Transition: Thirteenth to Tenth Centuries B.C.E.*, ed. S. Gitin, A. Mazar, and E. Stern (Jerusalem: Israel Exploration Society, 1998), 238–50.
8. See Bloch-Smith, "Israelite Ethnicity."
9. For an earlier survey of these, see R. S. Hess, "West Semitic Texts and the Book of Joshua," *BBR* 7 (1997): 63–76.
10. R. S. Hess, "The Book of Joshua as a Land Grant," *Bib* 83 (2002): 493–506. The following discussion is adapted from this article.
11. G. N. Knoppers, "Ancient Near Eastern Royal Grants and the Davidic Covenant: A Parallel?" *JAOS* 116 (1996): 670–97.
12. AT 456 was discovered by Sir Leonard Woolley at Tell Atchana in modern Turkey. The cuneiform tablet, written in Old Babylonian, is housed in the Hatay Museum in Turkey. The text is nearly completely preserved.
13. The translation followed here is that of Hess, "The Book of Joshua as a Land Grant." For earlier translations of the text, see R. S. Hess in COS, 2:137. The editio princeps is that of D. J. Wiseman, "Abban and Alalaḫ?," *JCS* 12 (1958): 124–29. See also A. Draffkorn, "Was King Abba-An of Yamḫad a Vizier for the King of Ḫattuša?" *JCS* 13 (1959): 94–97.
14. Hess, "The Book of Joshua as a Land Grant."
15. R. S. Hess, "The Slaughter of the Animals in Genesis 15:18–21 and Its Ancient Near Eastern Context," in *He Swore an Oath: Biblical Themes from Genesis 12–50*, ed. R. S. Hess, P. E. Satterthwaite, and G. J. Wenham (Cambridge: Tyndale, 1993; 2nd ed; Grand Rapids: Baker, 1994), 55–65.
16. Cf. paragraphs 2–7 in the Treaty of Murshili and Duppi-Teshub, in *ANET*, 202–3.
17. See Num. 27; 32; Deut. 1:38; 3:21–28, 31–32; 34:9.
18. R. S. Hess, *Amarna Personal Names* (ASORDS 9; Winona Lake, Ind.: Eisenbrauns, 1993), 7–9, 176–77.
19. Despite the numerous occurrences of "Canaan" in Egyptian sources that conform to this understanding, the single disputed occurrence (in an Amarna letter from the ruler of Tyre, EA 151.49–51) is subject to various interpretations. See the discussions of the borders in R. S. Hess, "Occurrences of Canaan in Late Bronze Age Archives of the West Semitic World," in *Israel Oriental Studies 18: Past Links: Studies in the Languages and Cultures of the Ancient Near East*, ed. Sh. Izreʾel, I. Singer, and R. Zadok (Winona Lake, Ind.: Eisenbrauns, 1998), 365–72.
20. Both Gen. 10:19 and Num. 34:3–5 define the southern boundary with the Wadi of Egypt on the west. This is identified with the Wadi el-ʿArish, whose mouth lies not far from Gaza. See N. Naʾaman, "The Brook of Egypt and Assyrian Policy on the Border of Egypt," *TA* 6 (1979): 68–90; A. F. Rainey, "Toponymic Problems (cont.): The Brook of Egypt," *TA* 9 (1982): 131–32.
21. In a fourteenth-century B.C. Amarna letter from the leader of Jerusalem to the pharaoh, the former says, "I am not able to abandon the lands of

Jerusalem" (EA 287.62–63; cf. EA 288.5–7). He uses the cognate verb in the form *e-za-bi-aš*.

22. Cf. the treaty fragment between Suppiluliuma and Kurtiwaza in *ANET*, 205.
23. W. Helck, *Die Beziehungen Ägyptens zu Vorderasien im 3. und 2. Jahrtausend v. Chr.* (2nd ed; Wiesbaden: Harrassowitz, 1971), 246–47.
24. K. A. Kitchen, *On the Reliability of the Old Testament* (Grand Rapids: Eerdmans, 2003), 167.
25. Mari text, ARM 26.420, trans. by W. Heimpel, *Letters to the King of Mari: A New Translation with Historical Introduction, Notes, and Commentary* (Mesopotamian Civilizations 12; Winona Lake, Ind.: Eisenbrauns, 2003), 359.
26. N. Glueck, "Some Ancient Towns in the Plains of Moab," *BASOR* 91 (1943): 7–26.
27. Taanach text 4.9. See A. Gustavs, "Die Personenamen in den Tontafeln von Tell Taʿannek," *ZDPV* 51 (1928): 189; D. Sivan, *Grammatical Analysis and Glossary of the Northwest Semitic Vocables in Akkadian Texts of the 15th–13th C. B.C. from Canaan and Syria* (AOAT 214; Kevelaer: Butzon & Bercker; Neukirchen-Vluyn: Neukirchener, 1984), 264.
28. See R. S. Hess, "Non-Israelite Personal Names in the Book of Joshua," *CBQ* 58 (1996): 205–14.
29. EA 149.8.
30. EA 131.21.
31. R. S. Hess, "The Jericho and Ai of the Book of Joshua," in R. S. Hess, G. A. Klingbeil, and P. J. Ray Jr., eds., *Critical Issues in Early Israelite History* (CBBR Sup 3; Winona Lake, Ind.: Eisenbrauns, 2008), 33–46.
32. King and Stager, *Life in Biblical Israel*, 149–50.
33. J. D. Schloen, *The House of the Father as Fact and Symbol: Patrimonialism in Ugarit and the Ancient Near East* (Studies in the Archaeology and History of the Levant 2; Winona Lake, Ind.: Eisenbrauns, 2001).
34. R. Gonen, "Urban Canaan in the Late Bronze Period," *BASOR* 253 (1984): 69–70.
35. I. Finkelstein and D. Ussishkin, "Back to Megiddo," *BAR* 20/1 (January/February 1994): 32.
36. King and Stager, *Life in Biblical Israel*, 232.
37. Merling, *The Book of Joshua*, 251; Kitchen, *On the Reliability*, 188.
38. The text is *KUB* XIII.2.13–19. The trans. is my own, previously unpublished. See also COS, 1:84.
39. This is part of the *zukru* festival. See D. E. Fleming, *Time at Emar: The Cultic Calendar and the Rituals from the Diviner's Archive* (Winona Lake, Ind.: Eisenbrauns, 2000), 248–51, 336–39.
40. H. G. Güterbock and Th. P. J. van den Hout, *The Hittite Instruction for the Royal Bodyguard* (Assyriological Studies 24; Chicago: The Oriental Institute of the Univ. of Chicago, 1991).
41. *CAD* N1 (vol. 11), 375.
42. H. A. Hoffner, "Hittites and Hurrians," *POTT*, 225.
43. Hess, *Amarna*, 124–25. M. Görg, "Ḥiwwiter im 13. Jahrhundert v. Chr.," *UF* 8 (1976): 53–55, suggests identification with the land of *pi-ri-in-du* in Cilicia. R. F. Schnell, "Perizzite," *IDB*, 3:735, attempts a sociological definition, as a people who dwell in unwalled villages and in the highland countryside. The former is phonologically less likely than the proposal here, while the latter is speculative.
44. See F. Gröndahl, *Die Personennamen der Texte aus Ugarit* (Studia Pohl 1; Rome: Pontifical Bible Institute, 1967), 23, 31, 129. She suggests a West Semitic etymology, but this is not at all certain.
45. R. S. Hess, "Cultural Aspects of Onomastic Distribution in the Amarna Texts," *UF* 21 (1989): 209–21; idem, "Hurrians and Other Inhabitants of Late Bronze Age Palestine," *Levant* 29 (1997): 153–56.
46. In ancient times wild animals roamed the area. See R. de Vaux, *The Early History of Israel* (Philadelphia: Westminster, 1978), 12–13.
47. Kitchen, *On the Reliability*, 167.
48. U. Avner, "Sacred Stones in the Desert," *BAR* 27/3 (May/June 2003): 30–41.
49. COS, 2:431–36.
50. R. S. Hess, "The Southern Desert," *Archaeology and the Biblical World* 2/2 (Spring 1994): 22–33.
51. Hess, "The Southern Desert," 29.
52. R. S. Hess, "Hebrew Psalms and Amarna Correspondence from Jerusalem: Some Comparisons and Implications," *ZAW* 101 (1989): 249–65.
53. A. R. Millard, "Back to the Iron Bed: Og's or Procrustes?" *Congress Volume Paris 1992* (VTSup 61; Leiden: Brill, 1995), 195–97; *ANET*, 206.
54. *ANET*, 19.
55. King and Stager, *Life in Biblical Israel*, 93.
56. R. S. Hess, "Multi-Month Ritual Calendars in the West Semitic World," in *The Future of Biblical Archaeology: Reassessing Methodologies and Assumptions*, ed. J. K. Hoffmeier and A. R. Millard (Grand Rapids: Eerdmans, 2004), 233–53.
57. M. Liverani, *Prestige and Interest: International Relations in the Near East ca. 1600–1100 B.C.* (History of the Ancient Near East/Studies 1; Padova: Sargon, 1990), 174.
58. *KTU* 1.14. III 4–49; IV 47–V 45. Cf. S. B. Parker, *Ugaritic Narrative Poetry* (SBLWAW 9; Atlanta: Scholars, 1997), 16–23.
59. Examples from Tuthmosis III, Merneptah, and Ashurnasirpal are cited in K. L. Younger Jr., *Ancient Conquest Accounts: A Study in Ancient Near Eastern and Biblical History Writing* (JSOTSup 98; Sheffield: Sheffield Academic Press, 1990), 227, 236.
60. Hess, "The Jericho and Ai of the Book of Joshua." No noncombatants are specifically mentioned.
61. Liverani, *Prestige and Interest*, 155. The Hittite text is *KUB* VI.2.29–33.
62. *ANET*, 661–62.
63. See further on the names and references, R. S. Hess, "Achan and Achor: Names and Wordplay in Joshua 7," *HAR* 14 (1994): 89–98.
64. A. F. Rainey, "Bethel is Still Beitin," *WTJ* 33 (1971): 175–78.
65. D. A. Dorsey, *The Roads and Highways of Ancient Israel* (Baltimore: Johns Hopkins Univ. Press, 1991), 201–6.
66. B. P. Irwin, "Shebarim," *ABD*, 5:1171–72.

67. Job 1:20; 2:12–13; and El's and Anat's mourning for Baal in the Baal cycle from Ugarit (*KTU*, 1.5.VI 14–25; 1.6.I 2–10). See further biblical material in P. S. Johnston, *Shades of Sheol: Death and Afterlife in the Old Testament* (Downers Grove, Ill.: InterVarsity Press, 2002), 46–47.
68. *COS*, 1:160–61.
69. Ibid., 1:156–60.
70. J. D. Schloen, *The House of the Father*, 150–55.
71. EA 29.34, 39; Hess, *Joshua*, 28–29.
72. Millard, "Back to the Iron Bed," 197–200, citing Ugaritic text *KTU*, 4.132.4. See further texts in W. van Soldt, "Fabrics and Dyes at Ugarit," *UF* 22 (1990): 321–57, esp. 331 and 337.
73. M. Anbar, "Le châtiment du crime de sacrilège d'après la Bible et un texte hépatoscopique paléo-babylonien," *Revue d'Assyriologique et d'archéologie orientale* 68 (1974): 172–73.
74. A. F. Rainey, "The Toponymics of Eretz-Israel," *BASOR* 231 (1978): 10.
75. Hess, "The Southern Desert," 29.
76. E. Wente, *Letters from Ancient Egypt* (SBLWAW 1; Atlanta: Scholars, 1990), 108.
77. A. K. Grayson, "Ambush and Animal Pit in Akkadian," in *Studies Presented to A. Leo Oppenheim June 7, 1964*, ed. R. D. Biggs and J. A. Brinkman (Chicago: Oriental Institute of the Univ. of Chicago, 1964), 91.
78. A. Malamat, "Israelite Conduct of War in the Conquest of Canaan according to the Biblical Tradition," in *Symposia Celebrating the Seventy-Fifth Anniversary of the Founding of the ASOR (1900–1975)*, ed. F. M. Cross (Cambridge: ASOR, 1979), 49–51.
79. See Kitchen, *On the Reliability*, 168, for references.
80. King and Stager, *Life in Biblical Israel*, 224, 228. Cf. O. Keel, *Wirkmächtige Siegeszeichen im Alten Testament* (Freiburg: Universitätsverlag, 1974), 11–83, esp. 34, 51–76.
81. Younger, *Ancient Conquest Accounts*, 223.
82. Cf. 4:7; Hess, "The Southern Desert."
83. See R. S. Hess, "Literacy in Iron Age Israel, " in *Windows into Old Testament History: Evidence, Argument, and the Crisis of "Biblical Israel,"* ed. V. P. Long, D. W. Baker, and G. J. Wenham (Grand Rapids: Eerdmans, 2002), 82–102. This needs to be supplemented in light of additional evidence that has come to light since the article was written.
84. Younger, *Ancient Conquest Accounts*, 200; Ashurbanipal Prism A (Rassam) I.78–80.
85. Kitchen, *On the Reliability*, 189.
86. O. R. Gurney, *The Hittites* (Harmondsworth: Penguin, 1952), 72.
87. A. Zertal, "Israel Enters Canaan: Following the Pottery Trail," *BAR* 17/5 (September/October 1991): 28–47.
88. Kitchen, *On the Reliability*, 170.
89. Hess, "Non-Israelite Personal Names," 207–8.
90. R. S. Hess, "Rhetorical Forms in the Amarna Correspondence from Jerusalem," *Maarav* 10 (2003): 221–44.
91. J. M. Cahill, "Jerusalem at the Time of the United Monarchy: The Archaeological Evidence," in *Jerusalem in Bible and Archaeology: The First Temple Period*, ed. A. G. Vaughn and A. E. Killebrew (SBLSymS 18; Atlanta: Society of Biblical Literature, 2003), 13–80. Other essays in this volume take alternative positions.
92. See summary in Hess, "Non-Israelite Personal Names," 206–10.
93. Hess, *Joshua*, 188–89.
94. C. R. Krahmalkov, "Exodus Itinerary Confirmed by Egyptian Evidence," *BAR* 20/5 (September/October 1994): 60–61.
95. R. S. Hess, "Rhetorical Forms in Joshua 10:4," in *"Und Moses schrieb dieses Lied auf": Studien zum Alten Testament und zum Alten Orient: Festschrift für Oswald Loretz zur Vollendung seines 70. Lebensjahres mit Beiträgen von Freunden, Schülern und Kollegen*, ed. M. Dietrich and I. Kottsieper (Münster: Ugarit-Verlag, 1998), 363–67; idem, "Rhetorical Forms in the Amarna Correspondence from Jerusalem," idem, "Smitten Ant Bites Back: Rhetorical Forms in the Amarna Correspondence from Shechem," in *Verse in Ancient Near Eastern Prose*, ed. J. C. de Moor and W. G. E. Watson (AOAT 42, Kevelaer: Butzon & Bercker; Neukirchen-Vluyn: Neukirchener, 1993), 95–111.
96. Younger, *Ancient Conquest Accounts*, 207.
97. D. A. Dorsey, "The Location of Biblical Makkedah," *TA* 7 (1980): 185–93; idem, *The Roads and Highways*, 152–53; Hess, *Joshua*, 195.
98. Younger, *Ancient Conquest Accounts*, 210.
99. W. Phythian-Adams, "A Meteorite of the Fourteenth Century B.C.," *PEQ* 78 (1946): 116–24; R. Scott, "Meteorological Phenomena and Terminology in the Old Testament," *ZAW* 64 (1952): 19–20; J. F. A. Sawyer, "Joshua 10:12–14 and the Solar Eclipse of 30 September 1131 B.C.," *PEQ* 104 (1972): 139–46.
100. J. Heller, "Die schweigende Sonne," *Communio Viatorum* 9 (1966): 73–78; J. Holladay, "The Day(s) the Moon Stood Still," *JBL* 87 (1968): 166–78; J. Walton, "Joshua 10:12–15 and Mesopotamian Celestial Omen Texts," in *Faith, Tradition, and History: Old Testament Historiography in Its Ancient Near Eastern Context*, ed. A. R. Millard, J. K. Hoffmeier, and D. W. Baker (Winona Lake, Ind.: Eisenbrauns, 1994), 181–90.
101. J. G. Taylor, *Yahweh and the Sun: Biblical and Archaeological Evidence for Sun Worship in Ancient Israel* (JSOTSup 111; Sheffield: Sheffield Academic Press, 1993), 114–18.
102. R. D. Nelson, *Joshua* (OTL; Louisville: Westminster John Knox, 1997), 141–45.
103. For further on this, see R. S. Hess, "Joshua 10 and the Sun that Stood Still," *Buried History* 35/1 (1999): 26–33.
104. W. F. Albright, "Researches of the School in Western Judaea," *BASOR* 15 (1924): 9.
105. Hess, "Non-Israelite Personal Names," 207.
106. Hess, *Joshua*, 204.
107. W. G. Dever, "Gezer," *ABD*, 2:1001.
108. A. F. Rainey, "Debir," *ISBE*, 1:901–4.
109. Hess, "Non-Israelite Personal Names," 206–7.

110. W. Horowitz and A. Shaffer, "A Fragment of a Letter from Hazor," *IEJ* 42 (1992): 165–66.
111. Kitchen, *On the Reliability*, 184–85.
112. Hess, "Non-Israelite Personal Names," 208–9.
113. Hess, *Joshua*, 208, 227.
114. A. F. Rainey, "Toponymic Problems: Shim'on–Shimron," *TA* 3 (1976): 57–69.
115. Y. Aharoni, *The Land of the Bible: A Historical Geography*, rev. and trans. A. F. Rainey (Westminster: Philadelphia, 1979), 429.
116. See ibid., 160, for the Egyptian reference; and Amarna letters 225 and 367.
117. B. Mazar, *The Early Biblical Period: Historical Essays*, ed. S. Ahituv and B. A. Levine (Jerusalem: Israel Exploration Society, 1986), 194–95 n. 27; N. Naʾaman, *Borders and Districts in Biblical Historiography* (Jerusalem Biblical Studies 4; Jerusalem: Simor, 1986), 43.
118. Naʾaman, *Borders*, 211.
119. King and Stager, *Life in Biblical Israel*, 114–16.
120. Hess, *Joshua*, 216.
121. R. S. Hess, "Nephilim," *ABD*, 4:1072–73.
122. Wente, *Letters from Ancient Egypt*, 108.
123. E. Lipinski, " ʾAnaq-Kiryat 'Arba'—Hébron et ses sanctuaires tribaux," *VT* 24 (1974): 41–48.
124. D. B. Redford, *Egypt, Canaan, and Israel in Ancient Times* (Princeton: Princeton Univ. Press, 1992), 90–91.
125. Younger, *Ancient Conquest Accounts*, 230.
126. Kitchen, *On the Reliability*, 178–79.
127. On this phenomenon, see A. F. Rainey, "Historical Geography," in *Benchmarks in Time and Culture: Essays in Honor of Jospeh A. Callaway*, ed. J. F. Drinkard Jr., G. L. Mattingly, and J. M. Miller (Archaeology and Biblical Studies 1; Atlanta: Scholars, 1988), 362; Aharoni, *Land of the Bible*, 123–24.
128. Hess, *Joshua*, 225.
129. The six-digit number that will follow most sites identified in this and the following chapters is a recognized grid number. The first three numbers indicate how far east the site is (the higher the number, the farther east it is located). The last three numbers indicate how far north the site is (the higher the number, the farther north it is located).
130. D. Pardee, *Ritual and Cult at Ugarit* (SBLWAW 10; Atlanta: Society of Biblical Literature, 2002), 194, 205.
131. First proposed by B. Margulis, "A Ugaritic Psalm (RS 24.252)," *JBL* 89 (1970): 292–304. For further bibliography and discussion of the archaeological and textual evidence, see D. Pardee, *Les textes para-mythologiques de la 24ᵉ campagne (1961)* (Ras Shamra-Ougarit IV; Paris: Éditions recherche sur les civilisations, 1988), 94–96; H. Niehr, "Herkunft, Geschichte und Wirkungsgeschichte eines Unterweltsgottes in Ugarit, Phönizien und Israel," *UF* 30 (1998): 570–74, 584–85; M. S. Smith, *The Early History of God: Yahweh and the Other Deities in Ancient Israel* (2nd ed.; Grand Rapids: Eerdmans, 2002), 166 n. 16, 179 n. 69. Smith notes a possible deity from an Emar property text that may be translated as "Nergal of Idri (Edrei?)." Nergal is the East Semitic name for an underworld god.
132. For possible mention of Geshur in Amarna letter 256, see R. S. Hess, "Geshurite Onomastica of the Bronze and Iron Ages," in *Bethsaida Volume 3*, ed. R. Arav and R. Freund (Kirksville, Mo.: Truman State Univ. Press, 2004), 49–64.
133. See Hess, *Joshua*, 227–28.
134. S. Ben-Arieh, "Tell Jedur," *ErIsr* 15 (1981): 115–28 (Hebrew).
135. A. Zertal, *Arruboth, Hepher, and the Third Solomonic District* (Tel Aviv: Hakibutz Hmeuchad, 1984), 70–72, 98–99 (Hebrew).
136. Aharoni, *Land of the Bible*, 223.
137. A. F. Rainey, "The Military Camp Ground at Taanach by the Waters of Megiddo," *ErIsr* 15 (1981): 61*–66*; idem, "Toponymic Problems (cont.)," *TA* 10 (1983): 46–48.
138. F. M. Abel, *Géographie de la Palestine* (2 vols.; Paris, 1933), 327; W. R. Kotter, "Gilgal, 4," *ABD*, 2:1023.
139. Kitchen, *On the Reliability*, 138–43.
140. A. Lemaire, "The United Monarchy: Saul, David and Solomon," in *Ancient Israel: From Abraham to the Roman Destruction of the Temple*, ed. H. Shanks, 2nd ed. (Washington, D.C.: Biblical Archaeological Society, 1999), 93–94.
141. J. M. Miller, "Six Khirbet el-Medeinehs in the Region East of the Dead Sea," *BASOR* 276 (1989): 25–28.
142. R. S. Hess, "Fallacies in the Study of Early Israel," *TynBul* 45 (1994): 342–44.
143. J. A. Dearman, "Historical Reconstruction and the Mesha Inscription," in *Studies in the Mesha Inscription and in Moab*, ed. J. A. Dearman (Archaeology and Biblical Studies 2; Atlanta: Scholars, 1989), 185–86; J. M. Miller, "The Israelite Journey through (around) Moab and Moabite Toponymy," *JBL* 108 (1989): 589–90.
144. Miller, "Six Khirbet el-Medeinehs," 25; J. A. Dearman, "The Location of Jahaz," *ZDPV* 100 (1984): 122–26.
145. A. Niccacci, "Scoperto l'antico nome di Um Er-Rasas: Mefaa," *RivB* 35 (1987): 83–84; Y. Elitzur, "The Identification of Mefaʿat in View of the Discoveries from Kh. Umm er-Raṣāṣ," *IEJ* 39 (1989): 267–77; R. W. Younker and P. M. Daviau, "Is Mefaʾat to be Found at Tell Jawa (South)?" *IEJ* 43 (1993): 23–28.
146. D. V. Edelman, "Mahaniam," *ABD*, 4:472–73.
147. Idem, "Lo-debar," *ABD*, 4:345–46.
148. P. N. Franklyn, "Zaphon," *ABD*, 6:1040.
149. C. Van Dam, *The Urim and Thummim: A Means of Revelation in Ancient Israel* (Winona Lake, Ind.: Eisenbrauns, 1997).
150. For a comparison with Sumerian lot casting as recorded in inheritance texts of the Old Babylonian period, see A. M. Kitz, "Undivided Inheritance and Lot Casting in the Book of Joshua," *JBL* 119 (2000): 601–18.
151. Hess, "Rhetorical Forms," 228–31.
152. I. J. Gelb et al., *Nuzi Personal Names* (Chicago: Oriental Institute Press of the Univ. of Chicago, 1943), 227.

153. R. Pruzsinszky, *Die Personennamen der Texte aus Emar* (Studies on the Civilization and Culture of Nuzi and the Hurrians 13; Bethesda, Md.: CDL, 2003), 243–44, and bibliography there.
154. Gelb et al., *Nuzi Personal Names*, 227; R. S. Hess, *Amarna Proper Names* (Ann Arbor, Mich.: Univ. Microfilms International, 1984), 532.
155. Gen. 36:11, 15, 42; 1 Chron. 1:36, 53; J. K. Kuntz, "Kenaz," *ABD*, 4:17.
156. Gröndahl, *Die Personennamen*, 176, lists both syllabic *qa-na-zi* and alphabetic *bn qnd* spellings.
157. See Hess, *Joshua*, 241, and references there.
158. I. J. Gelb et al., *Computer-Aided Analysis of Amorite* (Assyriological Studies 21; Chicago: Oriental Institute of the Univ. of Chicago, 1980), 345.
159. Hess, *Joshua*, 242–44.
160. R. Boling, "Where Were Debir 2 and Gilgal 3?" *ASOR Newsletter* (July/August 1976): 7–8.
161. The various persons, places, and people groups already mentioned in Part I (14:6–15) are discussed there.
162. Hess, "Non-Israelite Personal Names," 210–13.
163. R. Westbrook, *Property and the Family in Biblical Law* (JSOTSup 113; Sheffield: Sheffield Academic Press, 1991), 152–53.
164. Hess, *Joshua*, 249–55.
165. A. F. Rainey, "The Biblical Shephelah of Judah," *BASOR* 251 (1983): 7.
166. Z. Greenhut, "The City of Salt," *BAR* 19/4 (July/August 1993): 32–35, 38–43.
167. Hess, "A Typology"; see also idem, "The Form and Structure of the Solomonic District List in 1 Kings 4: 7–19," in *Crossing Boundaries and Linking Horizons: Studies in Honor of Michael C. Astour*, ed. G. D. Young, M. W. Chavalas, and R. E. Averbeck (Bethesda, Md.: CDL, 1997), 279–92.
168. For the former see A. Kempinski, "Hittites in the Bible: What Does Archaeology Say?" *BAR* 5/5 (September/October 1979):20–45.
169. Naʾaman, *Borders*, 145–66.
170. For the identification of Khirbet el-Mifǧir with Naarah, see Z. Kallai, *Historical Geography of the Bible: The Tribal Territories of Israel* (Jerusalem: Magnes, Leiden: Brill, 1986), 164.
171. EA 365.8–14. A. F. Rainey, *El Amarna Tablets 359–379: Supplement to J. A. Knudtzon; Die El-Amarna-Tafeln* (2nd ed.; AOAT 8; Butzon & Bercker: Kevelaer; Neukirchen-Vluyn: Neukirchener, 1978), 29; idem, "Compulsory Labor Gangs in Ancient Israel," *IEJ* 20 (1970): 194–95.
172. J. Renz, *Die Althebräischen Inschriften: Teil 1: Text und Kommentar* (Handbuch der Althebräischen Epigraphik Band 1; Darmstadt: Wissenschaftliche Buchgesellschaft, 1995), 87.
173. J. Paradise, "Daughters as 'Sons' at Nuzi," in *Studies on the Civilization and Culture of Nuzi and the Hurrians, Volume 2*, ed. D. I. Owen and M. A. Morrison (Winona Lake, Ind.: Eisenbrauns, 1987), 203–13. See further bibliography in Hess, *Joshua*, 258.
174. For a recent review and evaluation of this evidence see W. G. Dever, *Who Were the Early Israelites and Where Did They Come From?* (Grand Rapids: Eerdmans, 2003).
175. D. G. Hopkins, *The Highlands of Canaan* (Sheffield: Sheffield Academic Press, 1985), 64–65, 79.
176. I. Finkelstein, "Excavations at Shiloh: 1981–1984: Preliminary Report," *TA* 12 (1985): 131–38, 169–70.
177. For lists of many possible identifications, see Hess, *Joshua*, 265–76; Z. Gal, *Lower Galilee during the Iron Age* (ASORDS 8; Winona Lake, Ind.: Eisenbrauns, 1992).
178. Cf. Hammurabi Laws 206–207 and Hittite Laws 1–6 in M. E. J. Richardson, *Hammurabi's Laws: Text, Translation and Glossary* (The Biblical Seminar 73; Semitic Texts and Studies 2; Sheffield: Sheffield Academic Press, 2000); H. A. Hoffner Jr., *The Laws of the Hittites: A Critical Edition* (Documenta et Monumenta Orientis Antiqui 23; Leiden: Brill, 1997). For comparative discussions of these laws with the biblical legal collections, see recently D. P. Wright, "The Laws of Hammurabi as a Source for the Covenant Collection (Exodus 20:23–23:19)," *Maarav* 10 (2003): 11–87, esp. 17–18; R. S. Hess, "Review of H. A. Hoffner Jr., *The Laws of the Hittites*," in *JBL* 118 (1999): 171–72.
179. R. Polzin, *Moses and the Deuteronomist: A Literary Study of the Deuteronomistic History. Part One. Deuteronomy, Joshua, Judges* (New York: Seabury, 1980), 129–30.
180. Hess, *Joshua*, 279.
181. Kitchen, *On the Reliability*, 182; Hess, "A Typology," 162.
182. Hess, "A Typology," 163. See also the use of this expression in the first line of Alalakh text 456 as discussed in the Introduction.
183. J. Peterson, *A Topographical Surface Survey of the Levitical "Cities" of Joshua 21 and 1 Chronicles 6* (Ph.D. diss.; Chicago: Chicago Institute of Advanced Theological Studies and Seabury-Western, 1977).
184. The parallel 1 Chron. 6:76–77 [Heb. 61–62] has no such name but does include Tabor.
185. So Gal, *Lower Galilee*, 102.
186. Y. Elitzur and D. Nir-Zevi, "Four-Horned Altar Discovered in Judean Hills," *BAR* 30/3 (May/June 2004): 34–39.
187. Beckman, *Hittite Diplomatic Texts*, 115–16.
188. Ibid., 117.
189. Ibid.
190. W. R. Kotter, "Gilgal," *ABD*, 2:1022–24.
191. *ANET*, 206.
192. Ibid.
193. Younger, *Ancient Conquest Accounts*, 247–49.
194. R. S. Hess, "Nahor," *ABD*, 4:986–87; idem, "Terah," *ABD*, 6:387–88; idem, *Studies in the Personal Names of Genesis 1–11* (AOAT 234; Kevelaer: Butzon & Bercker; Neukirchen-Vluyn: Neukirchener, 1993).
195. W. L. Moran, *The Amarna Letters* (Baltimore: Johns Hopkins Univ. Press, 1992), 175–76 n. 5.
196. Ibid.
197. See further discussion and bibliography in Hess, *Joshua*, 303–4.
198. King and Stager, *Life in Biblical Israel*, 95–102.

Sidebar and Chart Notes

A-1. As suggested by Kitchen, *On the Reliability*, 167.
A-2. M. T. Roth, *Law Collections from Mesopotamia and Asia Minor*, ed. P. Michalowski (SBLWAW 6; Atlanta: Scholars, 1995), 101.
A-3. See the translation in COS, 1:84, paragraph 24; M. Weinfeld, *The Promise of the Land: The Inheritance of the Land of Canaan by the Israelites* (The Taubman Lectures in Jewish Studies; Berkeley: Univ. of California Press, 1993), 141–43.
A-4. Fleming, *Time at Emar*, 249.
A-5. EA 131.21–24. See further on the whole matter of Jericho as a fort, Hess, "The Jericho and Ai of the Book of Joshua."
A-6. Ibid.
A-7. Liverani, *Prestige and Interest*, 133, and notes there. The text quoted is from *KUB*, XXIII.103.Rs 12–18.
A-8. See R. S. Hess, *Joshua: An Introduction and Commentary* (TOTC 6; Downers Grove, Ill.: InterVarsity Press, 1996), 132–38.
A-9. Kitchen, *On the Reliability*, 170; J. K. Hoffmeier, "The Structure of Joshua 1–11 and the Annals of Thutmose III," in *Faith, Tradition, History: Old Testament Historiography in Its Near Eastern Context*, ed. A. R. Millard, J. K. Hoffmeier, and D. W. Baker (Winona Lake, Ind.: Eisenbrauns, 1994): 172–74.
A-10. A. Zertal, "Has Joshua's Altar Been Found on Mt. Ebal?" *BAR* 11/1 (1985): 26–43; idem, "How Can Kempinski Be So Wrong!" *BAR* 12/1 (1986): 43, 47, 49–53; idem, "An Early Iron Age Cult Site on Mount Ebal: Excavation Seasons 1982–1987," *TA* 13–14 (1986–1987): 105–65.
A-11. Younger, *Ancient Conquest Accounts*, 202–3. His translation is followed here.
A-12. *KBo* III.4.Rs III.10–22.
A-13. The Detailed Annals of Murshili IV.28–37.
A-14. *ANET*, 235.
A-15. Younger, *Ancient Conquest Accounts*, 230–31.
A-16. Weinfeld, *The Promise of the Land*, 22–51.
A-17. Z. Kallai, "Organizational and Administrative Frameworks in the Kingdom of David and Solomon," in *Proceedings of the Sixth World Congress of Jewish Studies, Volume 1* (Jerusalem: World Congress of Jewish Studies, 1977), 213–20; Hess, *Joshua*, 55–60.
A-18. R. S. Hess, "Asking Historical Questions of Joshua 13–19: Recent Discussion Concerning the Date of the Boundary Lists," in *Faith, Tradition, History: Old Testament Historiography in Its Near Eastern Context*, ed. A. R. Millard, J. K. Hoffmeier, and D. W. Baker (Winona Lake, Ind.: Eisenbrauns, 1994), 191–205.
A-19. A. Alt, "Judas Gaue unter Josia," *Palästinajahrbuch* 21 (1925): 100–16.
A-20. F. M. Cross and G. E. Wright, "The Boundary and Province Lists of the Kingdom of Judah," *JBL* 75 (1956): 207.
A-21. R. S. Hess, "Late Bronze Age and Biblical Boundary Descriptions of the West Semitic World," in *Ugarit and the Bible: Proceedings of the International Symposium on Ugarit and the Bible. Manchester, September 1992*, ed. G. Brooke, A. Curtis, and J. Healey (Ugaritisch-Biblische Literatur Band 11; Münster: Ugarit-Verlag, 1994), 123–38. Boundary descriptions also occur in property deeds from the city of Emar.
A-22. R. S. Hess, "A Typology of West Semitic Place Name Lists with Special Reference to Joshua 13–21," *BA* 59/3 (September 1996): 160–70; idem, "Typology of a Late Bronze Age Administrative Tablet from Hazor," *UF* 33 (2001): 237–43.
A-23. G. Beckman, *Hittite Diplomatic Texts*, ed. H. A. Hoffner Jr. (SBLWAW 7; Atlanta: Scholars, 1996), 109. Ths may be compared to the parallel clauses in the treaty of Hattusili, ibid., 104–5.
A-24. Beckman, *Hittite Diplomatic Texts*, 111.
A-25. Wente, *Letters from Egypt*, 107–8. See also the translation in COS, 3.2.12–14.
A-26. See Kitchen, *On the Reliability*, 244.
A-27. *ANET*, 203–5.
A-28. K. A. Kitchen, "The Fall and Rise of Covenant, Law and Treaty," *TynBul* 40 (1989): 124–35; idem, "The Patriarchal Age: Myth or History?" *BAR* 21/2 (March/April 1995): 52–56.

JUDGES

by Daniel I. Block

Jezreel Valley with Mt. Tabor on horizon
Z. Radovan/www.BibleLandPictures.com

Introduction

The book of Ruth opens with "in the days when the judges judged," suggesting that ancient Israelites regarded the events described in the book of Judges as occurring in an identifiable historical period. In one sense, the purpose of Judges is to explain how the Israelites made the transition from being a nomadic people wandering in the desert to the settled agriculturalists that provided the basis for the monarchies of Saul and David. One might have expected their conquest of Canaan, as described in Joshua, to have been followed quickly by the development of sophisticated monarchic political institutions, but this process took from three to four hundred years (depending on the date of the Exodus).[1]

Much of what is described in Judges and the literary forms incorporated in the book find counterparts in extrabiblical writings from the second and first millennia B.C. The book contains annalistic summaries of conquests, a victory hymn, prayers, prophecies, political speeches, a fable, geographic equations (Bethel = Luz), and so on, all of which are attested outside the Bible. However, while the literary style represented by Judges resembles other biblical compositions (Joshua, Samuel–Kings), it is unlike anything found outside the Bible in the ancient Near East. Whereas the archaeologists' spades have unearthed inscriptions with literary links to virtually every type of writing found in Judges, nowhere do we find a coherent portrayal of history incorporating the forms and contents of these documents as we find in Judges.

The nearest analogues are the historiographic writings of Herodotus and Thucydides, but these are far removed from the composition of Judges—in time (fifth century B.C.), space (Greece), and language (Greek). Whereas other ancient Near Eastern societies managed to preserve literary artifacts that contain snippets of historical and cultural information, these remain isolated and unintegrated; they provide the raw materials necessary for historical composition, but none represents the kind of intentional historiography as found in Judges. The biblical author has taken the raw materials and crafted a document that is not only compelling, but also represents a remarkable literary achievement. By deliberately selecting, arranging, and shaping these materials, he presents a picture of the Canaanization of Israelite culture between the Conquest and the establishment of the monarchy.

Tribes of Israel ▶

Historical Background

For the most part, the events described in Judges take place in Canaan, the small strip of land on the eastern Mediterranean sandwiched between Egypt to the south and the territories occupied by Phoenicians and Arameans in the north. Most of its narratives involved Israelites living west of the Jordan, though occasionally the effects spilled over into the Transjordan (e.g., Gideon's pursuit of the Midianites, ch. 8). The account of Jephthah (10:6–12:7), located in the region of Gilead east of the Jordan, represents a significant exception.

According to chronologies established by archaeologists, the events described in this book transpired in the Late Bronze Age and Early Iron (Iron A and B) Ages. These labels are based on cultural features, specifically the technological transition from bronze to iron as the primary metal of choice. The significance of this shift, and the cultural lag experienced by the Israelites vis-à-vis the Canaanites, is reflected in 1:19 and 4:3, 13, where the narrator acknowledges the latter's military superiority because they possessed iron chariots.

Establishing the chronological sequence of the events described in Judges poses special problems. While many of the places named in the book can be firmly identified geographically, not a single character is named in any contemporary ancient Near Eastern literature. Consequently, attempts to establish chronological relationships depend on internal biblical evidence of the book on the one hand, and extrabiblical evidence for contemporary developments on the other. We will deal with these separately.

Internal evidence for the chronology of the period of the Judges. Temporal notices appear regularly in this book, declaring the duration of the oppressions and the lengths

Table 1: The Pattern of Chronological Notices in the Book of Judges

Text	Oppressor	Years	Period of peace	Years	Judgeship	Years	Total years
3:8	Cushan-Rishathaim	8					8
3:11			After Othniel (Judah)	40			40[A-1]
3:14	Moab	18					18
3:30			After Ehud (Benjamin)	80			80
4:3	Jabin	20					20
5:31			After Barak (Naphtali)	40			40
6:1	Midian	7					7
8:28			After/During Gideon (Manasseh)	40			40
9:22					Abimelech	3	3
10:2					Tola (Issachar)	23	23
10:3					Jair (Gilead)	22	22
10:8	Ammonites	18					18
12:7					Jephthah (Gilead)	6	6
12:9					Ibzan (Zebulun or Judah?)	7	7
12:11					Elon (Zebulun)	10	10
12:14					Abdon (Ephraim?)	8	8
13:1	Philistines	40					40
15:20					Samson (Dan)	20	20
16:31							–
Totals		111		200		99	410[A-2]

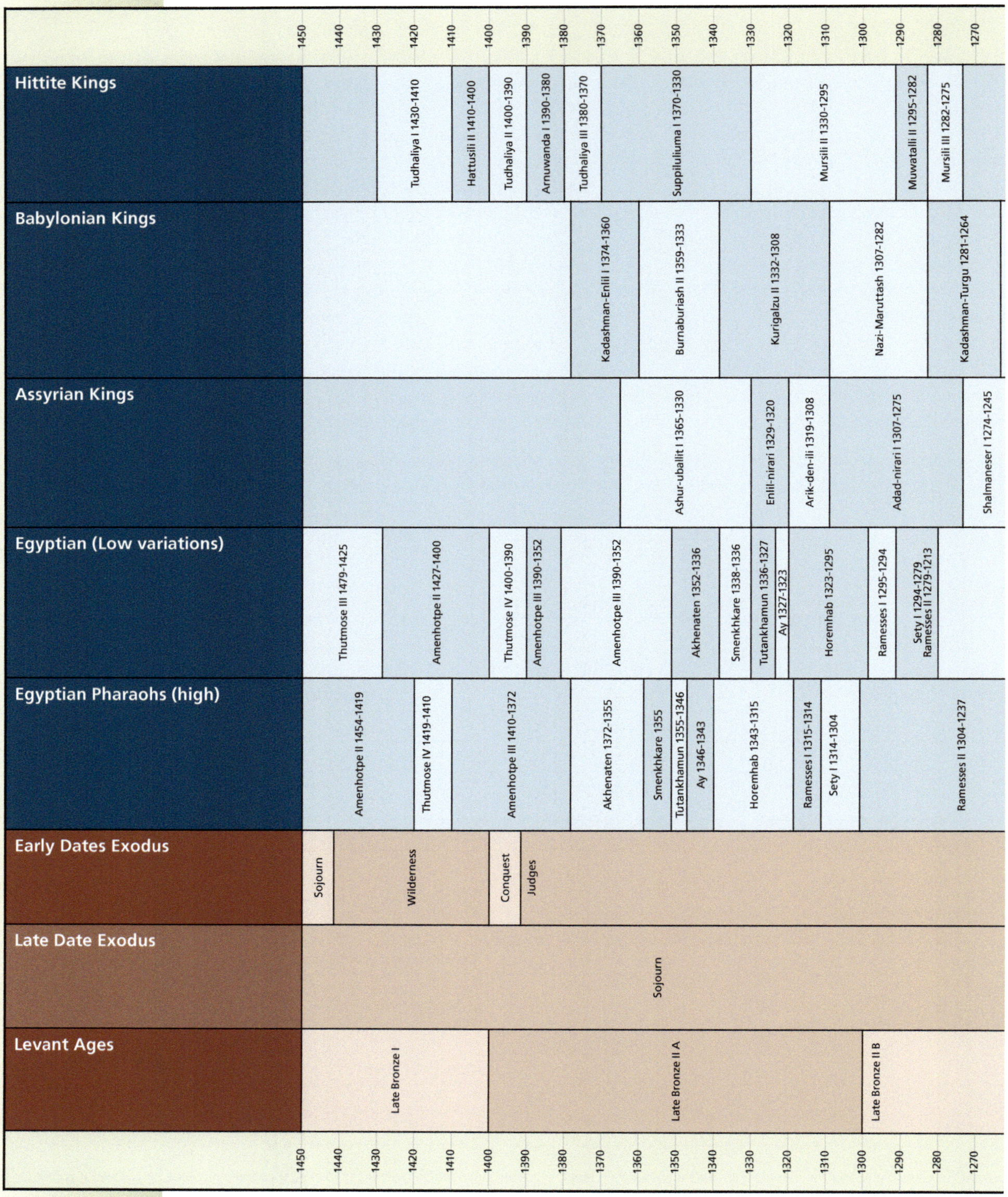
1450
1440
1430
1420
1410
1400
1390
1380
1370
1360
1350
1340
1330
1320
1310
1300
1290
1280
1270
Hittite Kings
Tudhaliya I 1430-1410
Hattusili II 1410-1400
Tudhaliya II 1400-1390
Arnuwanda I 1390-1380
Tudhaliya III 1380-1370
Suppiluliuma I 1370-1330
Mursili II 1330-1295
Muwatalli II 1295-1282
Mursili III 1282-1275
Babylonian Kings
Kadashman-Enlil I 1374-1360
Burnaburiash II 1359-1333
Kurigalzu II 1332-1308
Nazi-Maruttash 1307-1282
Kadashman-Turgu 1281-1264
Assyrian Kings
Ashur-uballit I 1365-1330
Enlil-nirari 1329-1320
Arik-den-ili 1319-1308
Adad-nirari I 1307-1275
Shalmaneser I 1274-1245
Egyptian (Low variations)
Thutmose III 1479-1425
Amenhotpe II 1427-1400
Thutmose IV 1400-1390
Amenhotpe III 1390-1352
Amenhotpe III 1390-1352
Akhenaten 1352-1336
Smenkhkare 1338-1336
Tutankhamun 1336-1327
Ay 1327-1323
Horemhab 1323-1295
Ramesses I 1295-1294
Sety I 1294-1279
Ramesses II 1279-1213
Egyptian Pharaohs (high)
Amenhotpe II 1454-1419
Thutmose IV 1419-1410
Amenhotpe III 1410-1372
Akhenaten 1372-1355
Smenkhkare 1355
Tutankhamun 1355-1346
Ay 1346-1343
Horemhab 1343-1315
Ramesses I 1315-1314
Sety I 1314-1304
Ramesses II 1304-1237
Early Dates Exodus
Sojourn
Wilderness
Conquest
Judges
Late Date Exodus
Sojourn
Levant Ages
Late Bronze I
Late Bronze II A
Late Bronze II B
1450
1440
1430
1420
1410
1400
1390
1380
1370
1360
1350
1340
1330
1320
1310
1300
1290
1280
1270

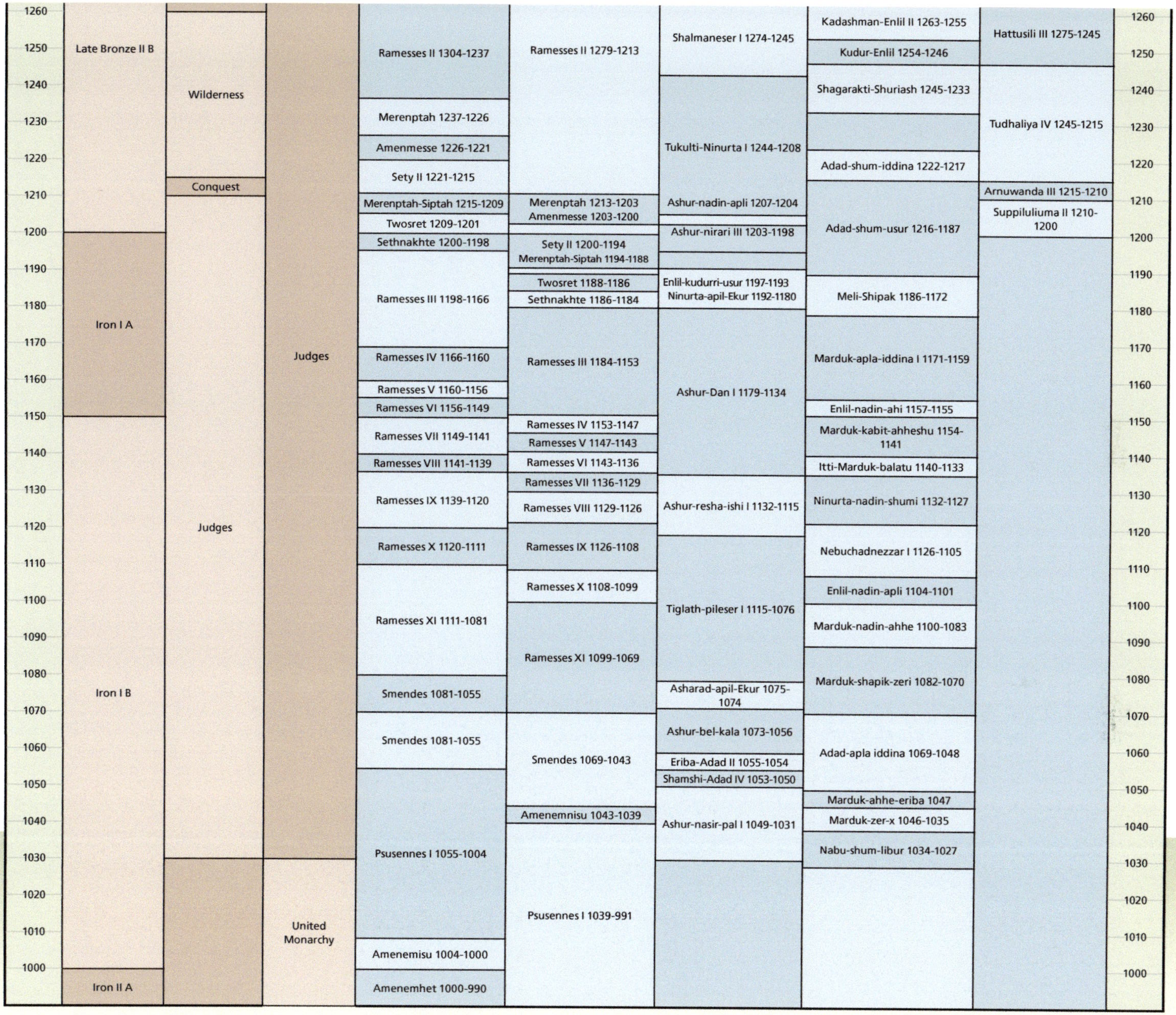
1260
1250
1240
1230
1220
1210
1200
1190
1180
1170
1160
1150
1140
1130
1120
1110
1100
1090
1080
1070
1060
1050
1040
1030
1020
1010
1000
Late Bronze II B
Iron I A
Iron I B
Iron II A
Wilderness
Conquest
Judges
Judges
United Monarchy
Ramesses II 1304-1237
Merenptah 1237-1226
Amenmesse 1226-1221
Sety II 1221-1215
Merenptah-Siptah 1215-1209
Twosret 1209-1201
Sethnakhte 1200-1198
Ramesses III 1198-1166
Ramesses IV 1166-1160
Ramesses V 1160-1156
Ramesses VI 1156-1149
Ramesses VII 1149-1141
Ramesses VIII 1141-1139
Ramesses IX 1139-1120
Ramesses X 1120-1111
Ramesses XI 1111-1081
Smendes 1081-1055
Smendes 1081-1055
Psusennes I 1055-1004
Amenemisu 1004-1000
Amenemhet 1000-990
Ramesses II 1279-1213
Merenptah 1213-1203
Amenmesse 1203-1200
Sety II 1200-1194
Merenptah-Siptah 1194-1188
Twosret 1188-1186
Sethnakhte 1186-1184
Ramesses III 1184-1153
Ramesses IV 1153-1147
Ramesses V 1147-1143
Ramesses VI 1143-1136
Ramesses VII 1136-1129
Ramesses VIII 1129-1126
Ramesses IX 1126-1108
Ramesses X 1108-1099
Ramesses XI 1099-1069
Smendes 1069-1043
Amenemnisu 1043-1039
Psusennes I 1039-991
Shalmaneser I 1274-1245
Tukulti-Ninurta I 1244-1208
Ashur-nadin-apli 1207-1204
Ashur-nirari III 1203-1198
Enlil-kudurri-usur 1197-1193
Ninurta-apil-Ekur 1192-1180
Ashur-Dan I 1179-1134
Ashur-resha-ishi I 1132-1115
Tiglath-pileser I 1115-1076
Asharad-apil-Ekur 1075-1074
Ashur-bel-kala 1073-1056
Eriba-Adad II 1055-1054
Shamshi-Adad IV 1053-1050
Ashur-nasir-pal I 1049-1031
Kadashman-Enlil II 1263-1255
Kudur-Enlil 1254-1246
Shagarakti-Shuriash 1245-1233
Adad-shum-iddina 1222-1217
Adad-shum-usur 1216-1187
Meli-Shipak 1186-1172
Marduk-apla-iddina I 1171-1159
Enlil-nadin-ahi 1157-1155
Marduk-kabit-ahheshu 1154-1141
Itti-Marduk-balatu 1140-1133
Ninurta-nadin-shumi 1132-1127
Nebuchadnezzar I 1126-1105
Enlil-nadin-apli 1104-1101
Marduk-nadin-ahhe 1100-1083
Marduk-shapik-zeri 1082-1070
Adad-apla iddina 1069-1048
Marduk-ahhe-eriba 1047
Marduk-zer-x 1046-1035
Nabu-shum-libur 1034-1027
Hattusili III 1275-1245
Tudhaliya IV 1245-1215
Arnuwanda III 1215-1210
Suppiluliuma II 1210-1200

Table 2: Chronological Notices between the Exodus and the Temple

Text	Event	Ruler	Years	
			Taking the texts at face value	Allowing for overlapping tenures
Num. 14:33; Deut. 2:7	Desert Wandering	Moses	40	40
Josh. 14:7, 10[A-3]	Conquest	Joshua & elders	7	7
Judges	Settlement	Judges	410	375[A-4]
1 Sam. 4:18	Settlement	Eli	40	
Josephus, *Ant.* 6.13.5	Settlement	Samuel	12[A-5]	
Acts 13:21; 1 Sam. 13:1	Monarchy	Saul	40[A-6]	20[A-7]
1 Kings 2:11	Monarchy	David	40	40
1 Kings 6:1	Monarchy	Solomon	4	4
Totals			593[A-8]	486

of the respective rulers' terms in office. The internal data may be summarized in tabular form.

But this scheme is difficult to reconcile with 1 Kings 6:1, which declares that Solomon commenced constructing the temple 480 years after the Exodus. Taken together, the times given in the Bible for the significant events between the Exodus and the building of the temple yield the following scheme (see Table 2).

The problem is obvious: 591 years exceeds the 480 cited in 1 Kings 6:1 by more than a century.[2] The difficulty may be partially resolved by allowing for chronological overlapping among the various judges. It is evident that many of the judgeships were tribally based, and the oppressions affected only portions of the Israelite population, as the following chart suggests (see Table 3).

It appears from 5:6 that the judgeships of Barak and Shamgar overlapped, and from 10:6 that the Ammonite and Philistine oppressions overlapped, which suggests concurrency between several of the judges' terms in office, cutting at least eighteen years from the total. Since Samson, Eli, and Samuel all had to deal with the Philistines, their tenures in office may also have run concurrently during the forty years of Philistine oppression cited in 1 Samuel 4:18, allowing a deduction of thirty-two additional years

Table 3: Points of Pressure on Israel

Enemy	Deliverer	Tribal supporters	Locus of pressure
Moabites	Ehud	Benjamin	Heartland
Philistines	Shamgar		Southwest
Canaanites	Barak	Ephraim, Zebulun, Naphtali, Issachar	North
Midianites	Gideon	Manasseh, Ephraim	Heartland
Ammonites	Jephthah	Gileadites	Transjordan
Philistines	Samson	Dan	Southwest

from the total in Table 1. Abimelech's three years should perhaps be deleted from the computation, since he was not an actual judge.

The biblical evidence for the duration of Samuel's and Saul's terms in office is uncertain. The reference to forty years for the latter in Acts 13:21 may include Samuel's tenure. Even so, the number forty for Saul seems high and may be intended as a round figure for one generation.[3] If Samuel's tenure is included in the forty years of Philistine oppression, as suggested above, and Saul functioned as king for twenty, which seems reasonable,[4] then the figures total 486 years—very close to the 480 years cited in 1 Kings 6:1.

The use of the number 480 raises the question whether this entire scheme is perhaps artificially constructed. The figure, representing twelve generations of forty years, seems to reflect a theology of history more than a precise chronology of historical events. The inconsistencies with which the author uses numbers may suggest that we should not try to force the calculations into a coherent scheme. Figures included in the formula "PN judged Israel *x* years,"[5] and those identifying lengths of oppressions[6] tend to be precise, whereas periods of peace are announced as multiples of forty, presumably because this was considered a generational lifespan.

This impression of literary structuring is strengthened by the fact that the number of judges/rulers in/over Israel is exactly twelve, matching the number of tribes.[7] The differences in the types of numbers used in the book probably derive from the sources used by the author, who made no effort to synchronize them with external chronological data or make them conform to any predetermined quota.

This conclusion is reinforced by Jephthah's claim in 11:26 that the Israelites have occupied Heshbon for three hundred years. If the Ammonite and Philistine oppressions coincided, this speech must have been delivered within forty to fifty years of David's tenure (ca. 1050 B.C.), which fixes the date of Conquest at 1350 and the Exodus at 1390 B.C. But this does not square with 1 Kings 6:1 either, according to which, if taken literally, the Exodus occurred in 1446 B.C. However, the reader should note that, unlike the 480 years in 1 Kings 6:1, this figure is not given by the narrator, but by a character in direct speech.

Furthermore, since it is a round figure, uttered in a political speech, it may have been fabricated for polemical reasons.[8] The fact that Jephthah erroneously refers to Chemosh as the god of the Ammonites (11:24)[9] shows that he was not above misrepresenting historical reality in other details. One might also find support for this skeptical interpretation of Jephthah's number from the character of the man himself. Appearing second last in the narrator's parade of deliverers, only Samson is given a more negative character evaluation than Jephthah.

External evidence for the period of the Judges. Efforts to gain a contextual ancient Near Eastern perspective on events described in Judges are aided greatly by extrabiblical textual and material evidence. Here I will summarize their significance for understanding the period of the judges. With respect to literary evidence, the Merneptah Stela, erected in ca. 1209/08 B.C. to commemorate the Egyptian Pharaoh's Libyan victories, concludes with a stanza celebrating his conquests in Canaan.[10] This document provides the earliest extrabiblical attestation of an entity known as "Israel," confirming that by the end of the thirteenth century B.C., the nation was a significant force in Canaan.

The so-called Amarna letters, discovered at Tel el-Amarna in Egypt in 1888–89, provide the clearest window into the Canaanite political situation at the beginning of the period of the Judges.[11] This cache of more than three hundred clay tablets inscribed in Akkadian, the language of trade and

Repeatedly in Judges the Israelites cry out to the Lord when conquered by their enemies. Here the inhabitants of Ashkelon cry out to their God as they are under attack by the Egyptians. Merneptah relief at Karnak.
Todd Bolen/www.BiblePlaces.com

diplomacy in the fourteenth century B.C., contains the written correspondence between the Egyptian king Amenhotep IV (also called Akhenaten, ca. 1352–1336 B.C.) and his vassal kingdoms in Canaan and Syria. These letters describe a political landscape dominated by a small city-states often at odds with each other and harassed by a troublesome group of landless people known as *ʿapiru*. In the past, this designation has been associated with biblical *ʿibrîm* ("Hebrews"), but this equation is no longer widely held (see comment on 11:3).[12]

The religious situation in Canaan during this period has been illuminated by the discovery of several collections of clay tablets from twelfth-century B.C. Ugarit on the Mediterranean coast in northern Syria. Discovered in palace and temple libraries, these texts were written in alphabetic and syllabic Akkadian cuneiform and have yielded a host of invaluable ritual and mythological texts, clarifying the relationships among the Canaanite deities mentioned in Judges and the nature of Canaanite religion found so repugnant by the author of Judges.[13] Ugarit was destroyed at the beginning of the twelfth century B.C., presumably by the Sea Peoples, with whom the Philistines are associated.

Great Inscription of Merneptah at Karnak
Manfred Näder, Gabana Studios, Germany

Antiquity of Judges 1

Judges 1 contains two types of materials: annalistic chronicles focusing on the military achievements (or lack thereof) of the tribes of Israel, and anecdotal reports of personal affairs at three literarily critical junctures (1:5–7, 11–15, 23–26). Most scholars recognize the former as from ancient sources.[A-9] Evidences of antiquity include:

- There is no hint of Philistine presence.
- Judah wrests the Shephelah (v. 9) and Gaza, Ashkelon, and Ekron (v. 18) from Canaanites, and the Danites are hard-pressed by Amorites (vv. 34–36) rather than by Philistines as in the Samson stories.
- Dan is still in the southwest (v. 34); there is no hint of the later migration to Laish.
- Simeon is still relatively independent (vv. 3, 17), whereas by the time of Saul that tribe has been absorbed into Judah (1 Sam. 30:26–30).
- Iron war chariots feature as a decisive factor (v. 19), a reality that changed by the time of Sisera (4:3, 13, 15; 5:28).
- The tribes are still fighting for themselves rather than on behalf of the kingdom of Israel.
- The Canaanite city-states are autonomous.

Whereas Joshua presents a holistic and "pan-Israelite" view of the Conquest, the present account is piecemeal, incomplete, and tribal in perspective,[A-10] leading some to conclude that this account preserves a more genuine memory of the period.[A-11]

Speaking of the Sea Peoples, this expression occurs only once in extrabiblical texts, in the Great Karnak Inscription of Merneptah, dated to the late thirteenth century B.C., where the Egyptian boasts of having defeated an invasion of allied forces referred to as "the foreign countries [or 'peoples'] of the sea."[14] This was a general designation for a group that included Peleset ("Philistines," from which Palestine gets its name), Tjeker (Sikils), Shekelesh, Denyen, Weshesh, and Shardana.[15] Our knowledge of Philistine culture has been greatly enhanced by archaeological excavations at Ashdod, Ekron, Ashkelon, and Tell Qasile.[16] As we will see, archaeological excavations have illuminated many critical elements in the narratives of Judges, including the accounts of the demise of Abimelech in Judges 9, especially the fortifications of Shechem, the conquest of the northern city of Dan (Laish) in Judges 18, and many others.

Although somewhat removed from Judges both with respect to time and space, the royal correspondence that archaeologists have recovered from eighteenth-century B.C. Mari offers another helpful window into ancient societies making the transition from seminomadic to settled forms of existence. These letters depict a world in which settled urban communities are coming to terms with seminomads and in which political and military institutions bear striking resemblances to those portrayed in Judges.[17]

Introduction to the Book of Judges (1:1–36)

Liver model used for divination
Marie-Lan Nguyen/ Wikimedia Commons, courtesy of the Louvre

Asked the LORD (1:1). In Old Testament times military leaders generally consulted their gods before embarking on military campaigns. To determine the will of the gods they resorted to a variety of oracular means, such as

▸ Genre: Judges 1 as Annalistic Military Reporting

Although Judges 1 is dependent on the account of the conquest of Canaan found in Joshua 13–19, the literary form adopted here resembles that of Assyrian summary inscriptions of military campaigns.[A-12] Two episodes from the annalistic account of Tiglath-pileser I of Assyria (1114–1076 B.C.), who spread his terror in Mesopotamia precisely during the time of the judges in Palestine, illustrate the character of summary inscriptions:

> (v 64–6.6) Tiglath-pileser, who treads upon dangerous people, who lays low the insubmissive, pacifier of all the rebellious:
> (v 67–81) The god Aššur, the lord, commanded me to conquer the land Muṣri and I took the way between Mounts Elamuni, Tala, and Ḫarusa. I conquered all the land of Muṣri (and) laid low their warriors. I burnt, razed, (and) destroyed their cities. The troops of the Qumanu came to the aid of the land Muṣri. I fought with them in the mountains, (and) brought about their defeat. I confined them to one city, the city Arinu which is at the foot of Mount Aisa. They submitted to me (and) I spared that city. I imposed upon them hostages, tribute, (and) impost.
> . . . .
> (v 99—vi 21) I overwhelmed the city Ḫunusu, their fortified city, (so that it looked) like a ruin hill (created by) the deluge. Violently I fought with their mighty army in city and mountain (and) brought about their defeat. I laid low their men-at-arms in the mountains like sheep. Like lambs I cut off their

Annals of Tiglath-Pileser I from Nimrud
Michael Greenhalgh/ArtServe, courtesy of the British Museum
▸

examining the liver of a slaughtered sheep for special markings or observing astrological phenomena. Sometimes the reception of an oracle was preceded by sacrificial rituals, as in the following report of an oracle favoring Zimri-Lim from the eighteenth-century B.C. site of Mari:

> Speak to my lord: "Thus Mukannišum, your servant, 'I have made the offerings for Dagan for the sake of the life of my lord. A prophet of Dagan of Tutt[ul] arose and spoke as follows: "Babylon, what are you constantly doing? I will gather you into a net and. . . . The dwellings of the seven accomplices and all their wealth I give into the hand of Zimri-L[im]." ' "[18]

The present text is silent on the method used by the Israelites to determine the will of Yahweh. The fact that later the Israelites went to Bethel, where the ark of the covenant was located and where Phinehas, son of Eleazar, the son of Aaron, served as high priest (20:27–28), suggests the divine will was ascertained by manipulating the Urim

heads (and) made their blood flow into the hollows and plains of the mountains. (Thus) I conquered that city. I took their gods (and) brought out their booty, possessions, (and) property. I burnt the city. The three walls which were constructed with baked brick and the entire city I razed, destroyed, turned into a ruin hill and strewed *ṣīpu*-stones over it. I made bronze lightning bolts (and) inscribed on them (a description of) the conquest of the lands which with the god Aššur, my lord, I conquered (and a warning) not to occupy that city and not to rebuild its wall. On that (site) I built a house of baked brick and put inside those bronze lightning bolts.[A-13]

Although these accounts often begin with a chronological note, they generally arrange events geographically. The descriptions tend to be short, telescoping relatively long periods of time into brief spans of reading time. Summary inscriptions tend to describe a static world in general terms, rather than dynamic scenes of action developing a narrative plot. They are often characterized by iterative schemes, they regularly resort to hyperbole and other forms of rhetorical flourish, and they often refer to the involvement of deity.[A-14]

Judges 1 does indeed begin with a chronological note, but after that it is impossible to construct a chronology of the Conquest from this chapter. Except for the anecdotal notes (which represent insertions from other sources interested less in tribal achievements than personal fates/fortunes), the accounts of individual campaigns are brief, static, and without characterization or plot. Accordingly, the present document serves as a summary of Israel's fortunes after the death of Joshua.

Even so, since Judges 1 recounts more failures than success, a summary inscription of military conquests is transformed ironically into an *anti-conquest account*. Unlike most ancient military reports, the aim of this document is not to celebrate the achievements of the generation of Israelites that survived Joshua, but to lament their sorry response to the divine mandate to occupy the land and to eliminate the Canaanites. Although the author delays sermonizing on the subject (cf. 2:1–5; 2:6–3:6), the structure of the chapter declares that this military failure accounts for the disastrous history of the nation in the next two or three centuries.

and Thummim, as prescribed for Joshua in Numbers 27:21 (cf. 1 Sam. 28:6).

Who will be the first to go up? (1:1). The verb "go up" reflects the mountainous terrain of much of Palestine and the common Canaanite practice of fortifying settlements on hilltops or mounds. Since campaigns of conquest often involved sieges of fortified towns rather than pitched battles between two armies in the open field, this verb became idiomatic for "to attack."

Canaanites (1:1). Like the terms for other ethnic groups in this chapter (Perizzites, v. 5; Jebusites, v. 21; Hittites, v. 26; Amorites, vv. 34–36), "the Canaanites" is a collective gentilic expression. The cumulative evidence of second millennium B.C. references in extrabiblical texts from Alalakh, Ugarit, Mitanni, Babylon, and Egypt suggests that, although no specific boundaries are given, the peoples who lived in this region had a clear geographic and social understanding of the term "Canaan," and that the boundaries of this region accord with Late Bronze Age realities.[19] The word probably derives from the root *kānāʿ* ("to bend, to bow low"). Specifically the name seems to have identified the coastal and river valley lowlands, in contrast to the hill country. But it was generalized to encompass most of Palestine west of the Jordan, modern Lebanon, and parts of southwestern Syria.[20]

I have given the land into their hands (1:2). As reflected in the oracle from Dagan (see 1:1), this *committal formula* reflects the ancient belief that the outcome of battles was always determined by the gods. This statement portrays Yahweh as a divine warrior who marches before his people, defeats the enemy, and hands their territory over to those on whose behalf he was fighting. Note also a seventh-century B.C. oracle in support of Esarhaddon, king of Assyria: "Bel (Marduk) has said, 'Like Marduk-šapik-zeri, may Esarhaddon, king of Assyria, And I will deliver all the countries into his hands!"[21]

Judah's Upland Campaign (1:3–8)

Judah said to the Simeonites their brothers (1:3). In ancient tribal contexts, tribes were often named after their "eponymous" ancestor. Although originally Judah and Simeon were full brothers, the sons of Jacob and his first wife Leah (Gen. 29:33, 35), political and military allies were frequently referred to as brothers. According to Joshua 19:1–9, the territorial allotment of Simeon consisted of scattered towns within the grant of Judah. Within a century or two Simeon ceased to exist as a separate tribe.[22]

Perizzites (1:4). The Perizzites were a minor branch of the pre-Israelite population of Canaan residing in the territory allotted to Judah. They are frequently identified as targets of Israel's holy war, hence under the *ḥerem* law (Gen. 15:20; Deut. 7:1; Josh. 3:10; 9:1). The etymology of "Perizzite" is uncertain, but the personal name Perizzi occurs in a fourteenth-century Amarna letter written from the Hurrian kingdom of Mitanni.[23]

Bezek (1:4). The location of Bezek is unknown, but it cannot have been far from Jerusalem. Boling suggests an identification with Khirbet Bizqa, near Gezer.[24]

Ten thousand men (1:4). This is obviously a rounded figure, perhaps a conventional generic number for "innumerable." Although this figure correlates well with the figures given for the registration of Israel's men of military age in Numbers 2 and 26 and with the song composed to celebrate David's victory over Goliath (1 Sam. 18:7), in the light of archaeological evidence for population levels in Canaan at this time it seems inordinately high.

Based on a comparison of these numbers with those found in Assyrian records, some conclude that the numbers should not be interpreted literally but as intentionally and conventionally hyperbolic.[25] A more likely option is to reinterpret the expression *ʾelep*, usually rendered "thousand." Since the consonantal form of this word (*ʾlp*) can also mean "clan, head of a clan," the word may either refer to the leader of a contingent of troops a clan could muster[26] or function as a collective for the troop itself.[27]

Adoni-Bezek (1:5). The NIV follows an ancient tradition in interpreting *ʾădōnî bezeq* as a personal name, Adoni-Bezek (like Adoni-Zedek, king of Jerusalem, in Josh. 10:1–3), but this is improbable, since, unlike *ṣedeq*, *bezeq* never appears in the Old Testament or elsewhere as a name of a divinity. This expression is probably intended as a title, "Lord of Bezek," a reference to the governor or mayor of the city.[28]

They ... cut off his thumbs and his big toes (1:6). As we will learn from the Philistines' gouging out Samson's eyes in 16:21, the mutilation of captives was common in the ancient world. See sidebar on "Inhumane Treatment of Captives."

Seventy kings (1:7). The number "seventy" is probably intended as a round and/or hyperbolic number, meaning "all the chieftains in the area." In Canaanite mythology the high god El and his wife Asherah are portrayed as the parents of the seventy gods, including Baal (the male fertility deity, El's opposite), Mot (the god of death and the netherworld), and Yam (the god of the sea). The reference to seventy offspring suggests all the gods derive from these two.[29]

"God has paid me back for what I did to them" (1:7). As any ancient person would have done, the governor of Bezek interprets his fate theologically: Adoni-Bezek's reference to God is ambiguous. In ascribing responsibility for his punishment to deity he uses the generic designation *ʾelōhîm*, which could refer either to Yahweh by the generic title or his own pagan god. As a Canaanite we would not expect him to refer to Yahweh, the God of Israel.

The Judahite treatment of Adoni-Bezek is likely an application of the law of *lex talionis*, "an eye for an eye and a tooth for a tooth," but it is striking that the newly arrived Israelites have actually adopted a Canaanite ethic. Instead of looking to Yahweh for ethical guidance (cf. Samson in 15:12–13), the Judahites find their models on treatment of captives in their predecessors in this land.

Jerusalem (1:7). The name "Jerusalem" means something like "establishment of [the god] Shalem." Although archaeological evidence suggests the site was occupied during Early Bronze Age I, the earliest extrabiblical attestation of the name derives from the nineteenth to eighteenth century B.C. Execration texts from Egypt, where it is spelled *Rusalimum*. According to the Amarna correspondence, in the fourteenth century the city (spelled *Urusalim*) was ruled by Abdi-Hiba, a vassal of the Egyptian Pharaoh Amenophis IV (Akhenaten). The common biblical name for this place, Jebus (cf. v. 21), is unattested outside the Old Testament.[30] See also comment on 18:10.

The association of Judah with Jerusalem at this early date is problematic. (1) Second Samuel 5:6–9 reports that David wrested Jerusalem out of Jebusite hands. (2) Judges 1:21 and Joshua 15:8 testify that Jerusalem was occupied by Jebusites (not Canaanites or Perizzites). (3) According to Joshua 18:16, 28, the city was located within the territory allotted to Benjamin.

The most likely explanation recognizes Jerusalem as a border city, located on the boundary between Judah and Benjamin. The city burned in verse 8 probably refers to the Jebusite fortress on the southern hill of the city, between the Kidron and Hinnom Valleys, which David eventually captured and made his capital. Accordingly, the unsuccessful Benjamite effort in verse 21 seems directed against a citadel on the north end of the city.

The fact that David had to reconquer Jerusalem suggests that the Judahite hold on the city was weak and short-lived. Shortly after the Judahites sacked it, the Jebusites probably moved in from the north and took control, which they then held for several centuries.

Egyptian Execration texts from around 1900 B.C. mentioning Jerusalem (*Rusalimum*)
Z. Radovan/www.BibleLandPictures.com

Judah's Lowland Campaign (1:9–20)

Hill country, the Negev and the western foothills (1:9). The Canaanites targeted by this campaign are identified generally according to three topographic areas: "the hill country" (the Judaean uplands south of Jerusalem), "the Negev" (the southern part of Judah, largely desert), and the "western foothills" (the transitional region of Judah between "the hill country" and the coastal plain).[31]

Debir (formerly called Kiriath Sepher) (1:11). Like Hebron (v. 10), Debir is also identified by its ancient

Inhuman Treatment of Captives

Although we have no ancient records of the torturous cutting off of toes and thumbs (cf. Judg. 1:6), the Assyrian king Ashurnasirpal II (883–859 B.C.) boasted of his treatment of captives from Tela:

> In strife and conflict I besieged (and) conquered the city. I felled 3,000 of their fighting men with the sword. I carried off prisoners, possessions, oxen, (and) cattle from them. I burnt many captives from them. I captured many troops alive: from some I cut off of some their arms (and) hands; from others I cut off their noses, ears, (and) extremities. I gouged out the eyes of many troops. I made one pile of the living (and) one of heads. I hung their heads on trees around the city.[A-15]

Such inhumane treatment of captives is attested visually in the bronze bands decorating the doors of one of Shalmaneser III's (858–824 B.C.) buildings at Balawat, near Nimrud (ancient Calah). The images on the bands show an Assyrian soldier seizing the hand and arm of a captive, who has already lost his other hand and both feet. Dismembered feet and hands punctuate the scene, while the severed heads of enemies dangle from the walls of the conquered city.[A-16]

The purpose of this kind of torture is not merely to incapacitate an enemy or to cause pain, but also to humiliate. By cutting off fingers and toes, Adoni-Bezek has treated his enemies like dogs and reduced them to scavenging scraps under his table.[A-17]

Mutilation portrayed on Balawat gate
Werner Forman Archive/The British Museum

name, Kiriath Sepher. The latter name translates literally "city of the letter/document," which suggests this site may have originally housed an official library or archive.[32] However, one major Old Greek text tradition (LXX[B]) reads *Kariassōpar,* which seems to point to an original Kiriat Sopher, "city of the [muster-]officer,"[33] in which case Debir may have been an important army or government post. The location of ancient Debir is still uncertain, but it most likely links with Khirbet Rabud, southwest of Hebron.[34]

Caleb (1:12). The name means "dog." Although ancient Israelites considered dogs to be unclean scavengers, their value in Mesopotamia and Egypt is reflected in personal names with the form "dog of DN" (DN being the name of a deity).[35] Not only his name, but also his identification elsewhere by patronymic and gentilic as "Caleb son of Jephunneh, the Kenizzite" (Num. 32:12; Josh. 14:6, 14) suggests he was not a native Israelite. "Kenizzite" suggests a link with Kenaz, an Edomite clan chief in Genesis 36:11, 15, 42.

I will give my daughter Achsah in marriage (1:12). Some modern readers find Caleb's treatment of his daughter offensive, as if she is mere property, an object to be awarded by one man to another for a job well done. However, in this world, where clan loyalties are high and the well-being of the extended family takes precendence over personal and individual interests, Achsah probably felt honored to be given in marriage to a military hero like Othniel. As in the patricentric and patrilocal world around Israel, where fathers regularly gave their daughters in marriage to their husbands, Caleb's actions would be viewed as perfectly normal, securing his own daughter's well-being and honoring a worthy suitor.[36]

Do me a special favor (1:15). Two issues may be at stake: the paternal blessing on a daughter as she is given away in marriage (considered to be a key to her own and probably her husband's future; cf. Gen. 24:60), or the dowry, a portion of the patrimonial estate given to a daughter at the time of marriage to ensure her a measure of security. In the ancient world the dowry could be in the form of slaves (Gen. 24:59, 61; 29:24, 29), movable property, and in exceptional endogamous cases (as here), land.[37]

Descendants of Moses' father-in-law, the Kenite (1:16). Judging from the name *qênî* ("smith"), the Kenites may have represented an itinerant band of coppersmiths. The area south of the Dead Sea and north of the Gulf of Aqaba around Timna was an important source of copper in ancient times.[38] Since Moses' father-in-law is referred to elsewhere as a Midianite priest (Ex. 3:1; 18:1), Moses may have had more than one wife, or the Israelites were imprecise in their identification of the nomadic groups that migrated back and forth in the desert regions south of Judah, or the gentilic Kenite refers to a Midianite clan or subgroup.[39]

Negev near Arad (1:16). This expression (lit., "Negev of Arad") compares with "Negev of the Kenites" in 1 Samuel 27:10. The traditional site, Tel Arad, is located eighteen miles northeast of Beersheba, on a hill rising forty meters above the surrounding landscape. Since the archaeological record of Late Bronze Age (the time of the Judges) gives no evidence of occupation of the site identified today as Tel Arad, the site referred to by this name seems to have shifted.[40]

City of Palms (1:16). Unlike 3:13, where the same expression refers to Jericho,[41] here it functions as a generic designation for a fortified oasis settlement, most likely Tamar on the western edge of the Arabah south of the Dead Sea.[42]

Zephath ... Hormah (1:17). The location of this site is unknown. The treatment of the city appears on the surface to be according to the law of *ḥērem* as reflected not only in Deuteronomy 7:1–5, but also according to

Timna copper mine (Tel Batash)
Christine Thompson

the ninth-century B.C. Mesha Inscription, in which he describes his sacking of Nebo, an Israelite town:

> I went in the night, and I fought against it [Nebo] from the break of dawn until noon, and I took it, and I killed [its] population, seven thousand male citizens(?) and aliens(?), and female citizens(?) and aliens(?), and servant girls; for I had put it to the ban [*ḥrm*] for Ashtar Kemosh.[43]

The renaming of a site accords with common ancient Near Eastern practice of conquerors renaming conquered territories (cf. the Danites' renaming of Laish as Dan in 18:29). The town of Til Barsip (modern Tell Ahmar) on the upper Euphrates, twelve miles downstream from Carchemish, provides an interesting example of this kind of renaming. The Luwian name of the site was Masuwari, but when the Arameans gained control of the region and made it the capital of their state (referred to in Neo-Assyrian texts as Bit-Adini), they renamed it Til Barsip. Later, when Shalmaneser III of Assyria (858–824 B.C.) conquered the region, he renamed the town after himself, Kār-Shalmaneser. He also changed the names of Nappigu, Alligu, and Rugultu as Līta-Aššur, Aṣbat-lā-kunu, and Qibīt-[Aššur], respectively.[44] In the present case, Hormah (*ḥormâ*), which means "destruction," plays on the term *ḥērem*, "devoted [to God] for destruction," the technical expression for Israel's mandate to destroy the Canaanites utterly.

Gaza, Ashkelon and Ekron (1:18). These are the names of three cities near the Mediterranean coast straight west of the Dead Sea. Gaza is identified as Tell ʿAzza, on Israel's southern coastal plain, three miles from the Mediterranean. Strategically located on a caravan route between Egypt and Syria, Gaza was often caught in wars between Egypt and Palestine, Syria, and Mesopotamia. The name first appears in a fifteenth-century B.C. list of cities conquered by Thutmose III. Its significance is reflected in the epithet for the city, "That which the Ruler Captured."[45] In the El Amarna letters the town appears as Azzatu (EA 297:32).

The importance of Ashkelon as early as the nineteenth century is reflected in its appear-

Middle Bronze ramparts at Ashkelon
Kim Walton

ance in Egyptian Execration texts from this period.[46] The city also figures prominently in the fourteenth-century B.C. Amarna correspondence between Canaanite city rulers and their Egyptian overlord[47] and is listed among a series of Canaanite cities conquered by Merneptah in the thirteenth century.[48] If any historical value is to be ascribed to the tradition that Ashkelon was founded by Mopsus, a seer and hero of the Trojan War in the twelfth-century B.C., it probably relates to the establishment of Ashkelon as a Philistine city.[49] Recent archaeological excavations have dramatically demonstrated the prominence of Ashkelon as a Philistine city.[50]

Located twenty-two miles southwest of Jerusalem, Ekron (modern Tell Miqne) is one of the largest Iron Age sites in Israel, encompassing more than forty acres. Archaeological excavations indicate that the site was occupied as early as the fifteenth century B.C.[51]

At the beginning of the period of the judges these three towns were occupied by Canaanites. However, in the twelfth century the Philistines, a group representing the Sea Peoples, took over all three. Eventually, together with Ashdod and Gath, they formed the Philistine Pentapolis. Since the present text seems unaware of these events, they must have transpired soon after the arrival of the Israelites and before the appearance of Shamgar (3:31) and Samson (13:1–16:31).

Iron chariots (1:19). Judah's failure to dislodge the inhabitants of the lowland regions is a result of the Canaanites' technological superiority with iron chariots. See sidebar on "Iron Chariots."

The Failures of the Remaining Tribes (1:21–36)

Bethel (1:22). Scholars dispute the exact location of Bethel. Based on the geographical information provided by biblical texts such as Genesis 12:8 and Judges 21:19 on the one hand, and the correlation of the name "Bethel" with Beitin, the Arabic name of the modern village, on the other, most scholars identify the city with Tell Beitin, about eight miles north of Jerusalem. However, others have located Bethel at el-Bireh, a mile or so farther west for several reasons. (1) There is no archaeological evidence for Beitin being occupied in the Late Bronze Age. (2) Beitin is not on the main north-south road between Jerusalem and Nablus.[52] (3) There is no evidence for Ai east of Bethel (cf. Josh. 7–8) if Bethel is Beitin. (4) The etymological link between Bethel and Beitin is suspect.[53] Consensus on the issue depends on further exploration and discovery.

They sent men to spy out Bethel (1:23). The common rendering of this verse as "they spied out" (v. 23) and as "spies" (v. 24) are both doubtful. The context and especially the use of latter word (*haššōmᵉrîm*), which normally means "guards, watchmen," suggest that here the verb *wayyātîrû* (hiphil of *twr*, "to spy") denotes the erection of an observation post,[54] presumably to watch the movements of the local population in preparation

Beitin
Z. Radovan/www.BibleLand Pictures.com

Iron Chariots

Chariots were useless in the highlands of Judah, but in the valleys and river plains they proved a great advantage.[A-18] The author's note that these were "iron" chariots is extremely significant, not only because it expresses the impressive nature of the Canaanites' military hardware, but also because it announces the beginning of the Iron Age in Palestine.

Textual and archaeological evidence shows that iron was known in the ancient Near East prior to the Iron Age (ca. 1200–586 B.C.), but because of the difficulty in refining it (the ore had to be heated to 1530° C), the refined metal was rare and precious. However, the discovery of the process of carburization at the beginning of this period ushered in a new technological age,[A-19] which the Canaanites exploited to full advantage.

Many dismiss the present reference to iron chariots as an anachronistic retrojection of a later age when iron was abundant and reflective of eighth-century B.C. Assyrian or even later Persian models.[A-20] However, this interpretation is unnecessary in the light of the widespread use of iron by the Hittites and the extension of their power as far south as northern Lebanon and Damascus in the thirteenth century. Their new technology could easily have found its way into the Egyptian province of Canaan. How much iron was used in the chariots is an open question. The chariots were obviously not made entirely of iron, but the metal could have been used on the hubs or rims of wheels, as reinforcement of other features, or as decoration.[A-21]

Chariot of Pharaoh Tutankhamun
The Yorck Project/ Wikimedia Commons

for an attack.[55] An eighteenth-century B.C. text from Mari on the Euphrates reflects a similar blurring of the boundaries between spies (*sakbum*) and guards (*maṣṣartum*).[56]

Show us how to get into the city (1:24). If Bethel were a walled town like some of the major cities of Canaan in the Middle Bronze Age and Israel's fortified towns of the Iron Age, the request to be shown the entrance to the city sounds ridiculous, since any passerby could have observed the nature of the walls and the location of the gates. However, the archaeological record suggests that in Late Bronze I the defenses of many towns involved a perimeter of houses constructed close together.[57] Presumably the spies wanted to know the best route of access into Bethel. Their appeal to a local citizen for aid is illuminated by second millennium B.C. Mesopotamian correspondence

Hatti-Land

between Zimri-Lim and his officials, who report the use of local people as scouts and guides when their army entered unfamiliar territory.[58]

Land of the Hittites (1:26). Contrary to the *ḥerem* law, the house of Joseph not only spared the life of the "traitor" (from the Canaanite point of view) but also allowed him to leave, build his own city, and continue his life as a Hittite. In these texts the Hittites are presented as one of the Canaanite ethnic groups (presumably the "descendants of Heth," Heb. of Gen. 23).

It is doubtful the territory in question is to be identified with the Hittites (Akkadian derived from *ḫatti*), whose capital was in Ḫattusas in Anatolia and who vied with Egypt for hegemony over Canaan in the Late Bronze Age. Rather, the Merneptah Stele of 1209 B.C. confirms that the "land of the Hittites" refers to a region of Hatti in the northern part of the territory assigned by Yahweh to the Israelites.[59] Perhaps the pockets of Hittite settlement in Palestine represented remnants of the Hittites after the decline of the Hittite empire. Technically Luz/Bethel was conquered, but in reality the city was simply transferred to a new site and continued to function as a sanctioned symbol of "the Canaanites in their midst."

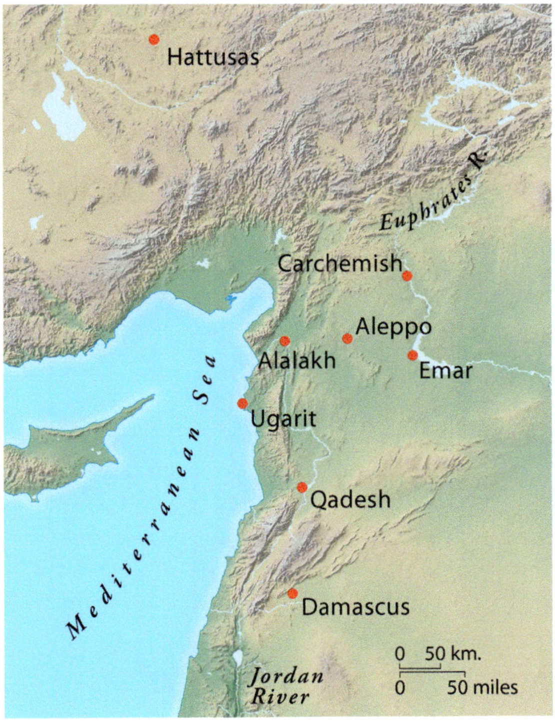

Beth Shan or Taanach or Dor or Ibleam or Megiddo (1:27). The Manassite failure to fulfill the divine mandate is summarized by listing a series of unconquered cities and their respective dependent territories in a narrow strip of land extending from the Jordan in the east to the Mediterranean in the west. Beth Shean was an important city at the junction of the Jordan and Jezreel valleys. In the twelfth century the site was under Egyptian control (under Ramesses III [1184–53 B.C.]), though later it was occupied by Philistines (1 Sam. 31:10).[60]

Taanach was five miles southeast of Megiddo, with which it is often linked (Josh. 12:21; 17:11; Judg. 5:19; 1 Kings 4:12).[61]

Dor was an important coastal town just south of the Carmel ridge.[62]

Ibleam is probably to be identified with Khirbet Belʿameh, guarding the easternmost pass from the Ephraimite highlands into the Valley of Jezreel.[63]

Megiddo was a major fortress in the Valley of Jezreel. In the Late Bronze Age, when urban development declined elsewhere, Megiddo (and Hazor) retained their character as major fortified urban sites. The city was occupied by Egyptians until the middle of the twelfth century, when it was destroyed, presumably by the Sea Peoples (Philistines). Solomon recognized its strategic location, for he rebuilt the city as a major Israelite military fortress.[64]

The order in which these towns are named does not follow a normal east-west itinerary. Rather the narrator moves in a straight line from the eastern extremity (Beth Shean) to the center (Taanach) to the western extremity (Dor), and then from the southernmost (Ibleam) to the northernmost site (Megiddo). The effect is not only to highlight Canaanite control of the fertile Jezreel Valley, but also the geographic wedge this created between the northern tribes and Ephraim to the south.

Settlements (1:27). The villages surrounding the captured sites are referred to as (lit.) "her daughters." This expression refers to the satellite villages and settlements within the economic and political orbit of the town named. Since most of the villages were unfortified, in time of war their inhabitants sought protection in the "mother" town. Some have estimated that in the Late Bronze Age the radius of the areas of influence of these small-scale city-states may have averaged twelve miles—the distance one could travel in a one-day round trip.[65] In the Old Testament the expression usually translated "city" or "town" refers by definition to a settlement fortified with walls and defensive gate structures.

Forced labor (1:28). This expression refers to the common ancient Near Eastern practice of conquerors subjecting conquered populations into virtual slavery, though evidence for lifetime servitude is scanty. In Mesopotamia captives could be ransomed, but until the money was raised they were put to work.[66] Note how the Gibeonites were treated in Joshua 9:21 and the remnant of the original population in 1 Kings 9:20–21. This practice is distinguished from the corvée service Solomon imposed on his own people (1 Kings 9:22).

Gezer (1:29). Gezer was located on the southwest corner of the Ephraimite allotment, due west of Jerusalem, on the last of the foothills where the Judean range meets the Shephelah. Located at the western end of the Valley of Aijalon, Gezer guarded an important crossroad of Palestine, where the east-west and north-south roads intersected, which was undoubtedly one of the reasons why Solomon invested so heavily in its fortification (1 Kings 9:15–17).[67]

The Amarna correspondence and the archaeological evidence suggest that Gezer flourished as an economic and political center in the fourteenth century B.C. Although the town seems to have declined in significance in the Late Bronze II period, by ca. 1210 B.C. it was important enough to be listed among Merneptah's conquests in Syria-Canaan.[68] Culturally Gezer has yielded one of the most significant inscriptions from ancient Israel, the so-called Gezer Calendar, dated to the tenth century. The text is significant not only for our understanding of the history of the Hebrew alphabet, but also of the agricultural cycle one century after the end of the period of the judges (see sidebar on "Gezer Calendar" at Ruth 1:22).

Acco or Sidon or Ahlab or Aczib or Helbah or Aphik or Rehob (1:31).

Major Cities of Israel

Though named only here in the Old Testament, Acco (later known as Ptolemais)[69] was one of the most important seaports in Canaan.

Sidon was a major Phoenician city that competed with Tyre to the south for economic hegemony for centuries. The inclusion of Sidon meant that most of Phoenicia was originally included in Asher's allotment (cf. Josh. 19:24–31). But the major Phoenician cities were never brought under Israelite control.[70]

Ahlab appears to be textually suspect and may be a corruption of a Canaanite counterpart to *Maḥalliba* (a site near Sidon) in an Assyrian inscription of Sennacherib.[71]

Aczib was a coastal town north of Acco.[72]

The location of Helbah is unknown. Some have proposed an identification with in Joshua 19:29.[73]

The Asherite Aphek has been identified with both Tel Kurdana, five plus miles southeast of Acco, and Tel Kabri, a large site east of Nahariya.[74]

Rehob was a Levitical city in Asher (Josh. 21:31; 1 Chron. 6:75), usually identified with Tell el-Bi el-Gharbi.[75]

Beth Shemesh or Beth Anath (1:33). Beth Shemesh, located in the Sorek Valley in the northeastern Shephelah, was 12.5 miles west of Jerusalem. The name means "House of the Sun [God]," suggesting this was the site of a temple to the solar deity. In Joshua 19:41, the place goes by the name Ir Shemesh ("City of the Sun"). While archaeological excavations have not uncovered this temple, Late Bronze II remains include some significant buildings, evidence of copper smelting, and a couple of inscribed sherds indicating some literacy among the population.[76]

The location of Beth Anath is unknown.[77] Similar to Beth Shemesh, Beth Anat means "House of Anath," suggesting a cult center devoted to this deity. In the mythology of the Canaanites, Anath, a prominent female goddess, is often portrayed as the consort and lover of Baal.[78]

Amorites (1:34). The name "Amorite" is related to Akkadian Amurru ("the west"), which could designate a direction, region, or people. The heartland of the Amorites described in Mesopotamian texts was located in northern Syria, between the western Euphrates and the Khabur and Balikh rivers. From here elements of the population apparently migrated to lower Mesopotamia, eventually achieving political control in such major cities as Larsa, Babylon (Hammurabi), and Mari.

When the Amurru/Amorites migrated west and south into the region of Palestine is not clear. It seems, however, that by the seventeenth century B.C., the term "Amurru" was increasingly used to designate central and

Beth Shemesh
Todd Bolen/www.BiblePlaces.com

southern Syria, and by the fifteenth century "the kingdom of Amurru" denoted a realm in the mountains of northern Lebanon. In time the expression could be used of the mountainous region farther south as well.

In the biblical texts "Amorite" is sometimes limited to a specific subgroup of the pre-Israelite populations of Palestine (Deut. 7:1, etc.). Sometimes narrators use "Amorite" where "Canaanite" would be inappropriate, particularly when speaking of the Transjordanian kingdoms of Sihon and Og and the hill country of the Cisjordan. "Canaanite" cities were generally located in the valleys and coastal regions; "Amorite" cities tended to be in the highlands. Yet the present preference for "Amorite" may have an historical base, in which case verse 36 declares the southern extent of Amorite settlement.[79]

Mount Heres, Aijalon and Shaalbim (1:35). This grant of land assigned to the tribe of Dan consisted of a small strip of land along the Aijalon Valley extending from the Mediterranean Sea to the Judean hills west of Jerusalem, sandwiched between Judah and Ephraim. Mount Heres is identified with Yalo, twelve miles west-northwest of Jerusalem, which guarded the most important trade route through the Shephelah.[80] Shaalbim is probably to be identified with Selbit, three miles northwest of Aijalon.[81]

The geographic designation *har ḥeres* (lit., "Sun Mountain") involves an archaic term for "sun."[82] The mountain may be associated with the town Beth Shemesh ("House of the Sun"; cf. v. 33). This suggestion seems to be supported by 1 Kings 4:9, which associates Shaalbim not with Har Heres but with Beth Shemesh, which is also known as Ir Shemesh, "City of the Sun" (Josh. 19:41).[83]

From Scorpion Pass to Sela (1:36). The "ascent of scorpions" is presumably so named because of the problem these creatures posed for travelers through this region. Southwest of the Dead Sea,[84] Akkrabim represented the farthest point on the border of Judah extending through Sela (site unknown) and up into the hills.

The Theological Interpretation of Israel's Failures (2:1–23)

Angel of the LORD (2:1). The person who confronts the Israelites is identified as the *malʾak yhwh*, usually rendered "angel of Yahweh/the LORD." Because of the popular modern view of angels as feathery, winged creatures, the translation "angel" is best avoided and replaced with either "messenger" or "envoy," for this is precisely what *malʾak* means.[85] Although the moral and spiritual scolding of an entire nation by this messenger is exceptional within the ancient Near Eastern context, the notion of human beings sent out as messengers of the gods is common. In The Report of Wenamun, an Egyptian text from the period of the

Tell Yalo, Aijalon
Todd Bolen/www.BiblePlaces.com

judges, Wenamun advises the prince of Byblos in Phoenicia to erect a stele and inscribe on it the following message:

> Amun-Re, King of the Gods, sent me, Amun-of-the-Road, his envoy, together with Wenamun, his human envoy, in quest of timber for the great noble bark of Amun-Re, King of the Gods. . . .[86]

Gilgal (2:1). Although Joshua 4:19 locates Gilgal "on the eastern border of Jericho," its precise location is unknown. Tell en-Nitla, two miles east of Jericho, and Khirbet el-Mefjir have been proposed.[87]

My covenant (2:1). In the Old Testament the word *bᵉrît* ("covenant, treaty") is used of a pact of friendship between individuals (e.g., David and Jonathan, 1 Sam. 18:3; 20:8; 23:18), or a treaty/alliance between rulers (Gen. 14:13; 21:27, 32; 1 Kings 5:12; 20:34) or nations (1 Kings 15:19; Amos 1:9). If it is a treaty between equals, it is called a parity treaty; where it involves a superior king and an inferior ruler, it is called a suzerainty treaty (e.g., Nebuchadnezzar and Zedekiah, Ezek. 17:13–19; Egypt and the nations, Ezek. 30:5; Assyria and Ephraim, Hos. 12:1).

Some argue that the word *bᵉrît* and the notion of covenant entered biblical tradition late, but the root *brt* is attested in twelfth-century Egyptian, fourteenth- to thirteenth-century Ugaritic, and fourteenth-century Qatna texts.[88] The covenant spoken of is the one ratified by Yahweh and Israel at Mount Sinai. Here and elsewhere it is referred to as Yahweh's covenant—never Israel's. This accords with the pattern of suzerainty treaties contracted between Hittite overlords and their vassal kings of the late second millennium B.C., as well as the neo-Assyrian vassal treaties from the first millennium B.C.[89]

Megiddo incense altar
Kim Walton, courtesy of the Oriental Institute Museum

Altars (2:2). Like Israel's religious rites, Canaanite rituals involved altars, which came in a variety of shapes and sizes, depending on function. The excavations at Megiddo have unearthed a small horned altar about one foot square and slightly more than two feet high, undoubtedly used for offering incense, libations of wine, or grain offerings. Also unearthed was a massive circular altar from the Early Bronze Age, more than thirty feet in diameter, on which many animals could have been slaughtered at once. The fact that Gideon uses oxen to tear down the altar of Baal on his father's property (6:25–27) suggests a large structure.

Joshua son of Nun, the servant of the Lord (2:7). The notion of human beings as servants of deities was common in the ancient Near East. Many theophoric names (names with a reference to a god) use the root *ʿebed* not only in Hebrew (Obadiah, "one who serves Yahweh"), but also in the Semitic world around Israel.[90] Palestinian rulers and officials named in the Amarna Letters include ʿAbdi-Aširta ("servant of Ashirtu"), Abdi-Aštarti ("servant of Aštartu"), and ʿAbdi-Ḫeba ("servant of Ḫeba").[91] Phoenician names include *ʿabdʾmn* ("servant of Amun") and *ʿbdʾšmn* ("servant of Eshmun").[92]

Although "servant" is often understood as a menial role, the

The broken-off horn of an altar found at Dan is reminiscent of tearing down altars as instructed in Judges.
Z. Radovan/www.BibleLandPictures.com

Seal of "Shema servant of Jeroboam"
Z. Radovan/www.BibleLandPictures.com

Baal
Z. Radovan/www.BibleLandPictures.com

fact that court officials in the ancient world were called "a servant of the king" (*ʿebed hammelek*) demonstrates that in contexts like this it actually bears honorific significance (2 Kings 25:8). This interpretation is reinforced by the discovery of dozens of seals from ancient Palestine referring to the bearer of the seal either generally as "servant of the king" or "servant of a specific king."

Elders (2:7). The book of Judges has elders governing both tribes on the move (as here) and settled communities, villages, and towns (8:14, 16). Later the elders of Gilead contract with Jephthah to lead their forces against the Ammonites (11:5–11). It is unclear how fixed the body of elders in Israel was or how men attained this status. Nevertheless, the title clearly designated "senior leadership" with "collective authority" in judicial and administrative matters that affected the whole village or tribe. Once the Israelites had settled down, elders conducted their business in the gates of the towns, and their deliberations were open to the public (Ruth 4:1–12).[93] Such ruling councils of elders are attested widely in the ancient Near East. The eighteenth-century B.C. correspondence at Mari is particularly helpful in illuminating how elders represented villages and tribes with outsiders and before kings.[94]

Timnath Heres ... north of Mount Gaash (2:9). Like Beth Shemesh in 1:33 and Mount Heres in 1:34, this name may reflect the presence of a Canaanite sanctuary devoted to the sun god. The site is probably to be identified with Khirbet Tibnah, ten miles northwest of Bethel and sixteen miles southwest of Shechem.[95]

Gathered to their fathers (2:10). This expression functions euphemistically for "they died and were buried." The idiom derives from the Israelite custom of burying the deceased in family/ancestral tombs (see comment on 16:31).[96]

Baals (2:11). When applied to a god, the name Baal (*baʿal*) functions as a title, "divine lord, master," rather than a personal name and is used as an appellative for many gods in the ancient world, such as the Babylonian god Marduk, also known as Bel (the Akkadian form of *baʿal*). Occurring as a divine title more than seventy times in the Old Testament, *baʿal* usually refers to the storm/weather god, who in the Canaanite mythological literature goes by the name Hadad, and several other titles: *ʾalʾayn baʿal* ("the victor Baal"), *rkb ʿrpt* ("Rider of the Clouds"), and *bʿl ṣpn* ("Baal of Zaphan").

Like Mount Olympus in Greek mythology, Zaphan (biblical Zaphon), meaning "north," was the mythical mountain on which Baal resided. It is generally identified with Jebel ʿel-Aqraʿ, located twenty-five miles north of Ugarit, near the mouth of the Orontes River in northern Syria. In Canaanite mythology Baal was one of the seventy sons of El and Asherah.[97]

The plural form "the Baals" does not refer to a multiplicity of gods, but to numerous manifestations of the one weather god, on whose blessing the fertility of the land was thought to depend. These manifestations are reflected in the biblical place names bearing Baal, such as Baal Peor, Baal Hazor, Baal Gad, and Baal Shalisha.

Ashtoreths (2:13). The NIV's rendering is a mistransliteration of the divine name *ʿaštārôt*, presumably under the influence of 1 Kings 11:5, 33 and 2 Kings 23:13, where the form appears to represent a deliberate distortion of the original name (Ashtaroth) by vocalizing the name with the vowels of *bōšet* ("shame"). The present form represents a plural form of *ʿaštart*, commonly known as Astarte, who was worshiped widely as the goddess of love and war. This deity was identified in Ebla as Ashtar and in Mesopotamia as Ishtar, from which is derived the biblical name Esther[98] (see sidebar on "Baal and Astarte").

Anger [of the LORD] against Israel (2:14–23). The notion of divine anger with the people over whom the deity served as patron/matron is common in the ancient Near East. Where records give reasons for the divine fury, the cause tends to be for a failure to satisfy the god with proper rituals. Here the cause is failure to be devoted exclusively to Yahweh.

In this regard Israel's religion is unique. Among the peoples around Israel the gods were much more tolerant than Yahweh. Other patron deities did not mind if their devotees worshiped other gods. Indeed, it was commonly assumed that responsibilities for the welfare of the people were distributed among the deities, which meant that in addition to a weather god, the Canaanites also recognized a god of grain, a god of wine, and so on. For example, although Marduk was the supreme deity of Babylon, the city had at least nine other temples dedicated to other divinities. One could enter the city through any one of nine gates, each named after a different deity.[99] Yahweh, by contrast, tolerated no rivals (Ex. 20:3–6; Deut. 5:7–10; 6:14–15).

While Yahweh's intolerance of the worship of other deities was unique, his expression of anger would have been familiar to many outside Israel. In the ancient world divine fury was typically expressed by the deity leaving the city and allowing enemy forces to move in to wreak havoc on the place. Yahweh's softening toward his people and restoring peace would also have been familiar, though the pattern of rescue and restoration is different here than in most ancient accounts. Esarhaddon's account of Marduk's return to Babylon after a lengthy absence has Marduk himself restoring the city, and when the people have returned, he appoints a new king to shepherd them. In the book of Judges Yahweh raises up judges, who, empowered by Yahweh, lead the Israelite forces in their own rescue.[100]

The LORD raised up judges (2:16, 18–19). Unlike the English word "judge," which is usually associated with judicial activity, the meaning of *šōpᵉṭîm* in the book of Judges is established here: Each one functioned as a "deliverer, liberator," who rescued the Israelites from outside oppressors. Although the verb "judge" is applied to several individuals in this book,[101] none of these persons is portrayed as exercising judicial function. The expression should therefore be interpreted more broadly as "to govern, administer, exercise leadership,"[102] either in internal or in external affairs.[103] Note how in the Mari texts, the Akkadian *šapāṭum* applied to "administrative heads of districts" accountable to the king.[104] Ugaritic texts employ *ṯpṭ* similarly, as in the following citation:

> Surely he will remove the support of your throne,
> Surely he will overturn the seat of your kingship;
> Surely he will break the scepter of your rule [*mṯpṭk*].[105]

There may be some merit in G. W. Ahlström's suggestion that these "judges" should be perceived like all other Canaanite princes and petty kings of the presettlement time.[106]

To test Israel (2:22). The Old Testament uses three words for testing: *nsh* (here and in

Ivory of unknown goddess often identified as Asherah
beat69 Flickr, courtesy of the Louvre

Baal and Astarte

Although in the Ugaritic mythological literature Anath usually functions as Baal's consort (see comment on 3:31), Astarte also appears as his spouse, which agrees with the broader ancient Near Eastern world reflected in the Old Testament. Like "the Baals" (see comment on 2:11), the plural form refers to the local manifestations of the deity.

In the fertility cult of Canaan, Baal was represented by an upright stone (*maṣṣēbâ*); Astarte was portrayed by carved female figurines, with exaggerated breasts and prominent genitals.[A-22] Together these two gods formed a powerful force in ancient Near Eastern spirituality. Israel's abandonment of Yahweh may be attributable to an inability to conceive of Yahweh as the God of this land, where Baal and Astarte ruled with apparent effectiveness. The newcomers had experienced Yahweh's power in Egypt, at Mount Sinai, and in the desert, but once they crossed the Jordan, they found it easier to change allegiance to the gods of this new land than to transfer to Yahweh the fertility functions of a territorial god.

3:1, 4; 6:39), *bḥn*, and *ṣrp* (Judg. 7:4; 17:4). When used metaphorically, the notion of testing is closely linked to the metallurgical process of producing precious metals from ore. In most instances the test is performed either for *quality control* (a superior's check on the loyalty of the inferior) or *quality enhancement* (a superior's effort to improve the loyalty of the inferior).[107] According to verse 20, the nations do not represent the actual test; rather, in accordance with Exodus 19:5, the test consists in whether or not the Israelites will listen to Yahweh's voice.

The Testing of Israel (3:1–6)

These are the nations (3:1). The following list of nations (v. 3) does not follow the stereotypical list (e.g., Deut. 7:1). Instead, the given names function as general designations covering the entire population of the land of Canaan.

To test all those Israelites (3:1, 4). See comment on 2:22.

Five rulers of the Philistines (3:3). Remarkably, although unlike the rest of the peoples listed here the Philistines were not native to Canaan, the memory of their involvement in the region is reflected in the modern name Palestine. The Hebrew word *p^elištîm* (represented in ancient Egyptian texts as *P-r-š-t-w*) identifies one of several groups of Sea Peoples[108] who swept into Palestine from Anatolia and the Mediterranean in the twelfth to eleventh centuries B.C., leaving in their wake a trail of ruins.

▸ Following the Will of One's Lord

In the correspondence between political superiors and vassals from the ancient Near East, the motif of doing what one's superior instructs shows up repeatedly. Here are a few examples from a wide range of sources:

Mari

They (said), "Besides Nahur before Haya-Sume, there is no second lord and father. We will do what our lord Zimri-Lim says."[A-23]

Assyria

Whatever the king (my lord) says (I will do).[A-24]

El-Amarna

So may the king take cognizance of his servant and of Tyre, the city of Mayati, for whatever command has issued from the mouth of the king to his servant, that he has done. The word of the king [g]oes before him.[A-25]

Lachish

And now, your servant has done everything my lord sent (word to do). I have posted everything my lord has written me.[A-26]

The effect on the eastern Mediterranean is reflected in an inscription by Ramesses III (1184–1153 B.C.):

> The foreign countries [Sea Peoples] made a conspiracy in their islands. All at once the lands were removed and scattered in the fray. No land could stand before their arms, from Hatti, Kode [Cilicia], Carchemish, Arzawa, and Alashiya [Cyprus] on, being cut off [at one time]. A camp [was set up] in one place in Amor [Amurru]. They desolated its people, and its land was like that which has never come into being. They were coming forward to Egypt, while the flame was prepared before them. Their confederation [of Sea Peoples] was the Philistines, Tjeker [Sikils], Shekelesh, Denye(n) and Weshesh, lands united.[109]

Biblical tradition, which traces their origins to Crete,[110] accords with the archaeological record, which suggests they came from the Aegean. But how they arrived in Palestine is the subject of some debate: Some argue they came by sea, others that they came overland via Anatolia and down through Syria.[111] It seems their original goal was to settle in Egypt, but Ramesses III was able to defeat them. He settled the vanquished forces in the coastal towns of southern Canaan, but in the mid-twelfth century, the Philistines succeeded in driving out their Egyptian overlords, forming the Philistine Pentapolis, a federation of five major city-states: Ashdod, Ashkelon, Ekron, Gath, and Gaza.[112]

The only Philistine ruler named in the Old Testament is Achish, identified as *melek* ("king") of Gath (1 Sam. 21:10).[113] Faced with a numerically overwhelming native

Sea Peoples with distinctive headdress
Z. Radovan/www.BibleLand Pictures.com ◂

population, the ethnically distinct Philistines appear to have valued cooperation over competition.

All the Canaanites (3:3). Extrabiblical sources from the second half of the second millennium B.C. agree with the biblical terminology in their definition of the region called "Canaan."[114] The southern border was defined by an arc from the southern tip of the Dead Sea to the southeastern shore of the Mediterranean; the Mediterranean seashore represented the western border as far north as just south of the kingdom of Ugarit; the northern border ran south of Ugarit and Alalakh almost to the Euphrates; the eastern border ran south down the Beqaᶜ, through the Huleh Valley, across Lake Kinnereth (Galilee), and down the Jordan Valley to the southern end of the Dead Sea.

Here, however, the gentilic "Canaanites" appears to be used in a more limited sense, as a general designation for the inhabitants of the hill country between the territories occupied by Philistines and Sidonians on the one hand and the Jordan Rift Valley on the other.

Canaan

Sidonians (3:3). The Sidonians (cf. 1:31) do not figure in the stereotypical lists of Canaanite nations whom the Israelites will displace (e.g., Deut. 7:1). Here "Sidonians" stands generally for all the Phoenicians living along the Mediterranean coast north of the area occupied by the Philistines. The frequency with which the name Sidon surfaces in extrabiblical writings reflects the city's importance in the last half of the second millennium B.C.

Three important sources derive from the fourteenth century B.C. A Hittite incantation mentions Sidon ahead of Tyre in a list of geographic names;[115] in the Ugaritic Kirta Epic, on the third day of his trek the hero makes a vow "at the shrine of the Asherah of Tyre, at the shrine of the Goddess of Sidon";[116] in the Amarna correspondence Sidon is mentioned repeatedly as one of the leaders in an anti-Egyptian coalition.[117] Sidon was part of a mercantile corporation employing fifty vessels to carry trade between Egypt and Phoenicia.[118]

Hivites ... Mount Baal Hermon to Lebo Hamath (3:3). Some have associated the Hivites with the Hurrians (Horites) of Genesis 36:2 and 20.[119] Although Joshua 9:7 and 11:19 link the Gibeonites to the Hivites, our text seems to use the expression generally for the peoples occupying the regions north of the Sea of Galilee, in the Lebanon mountains, west of a line running from Mount Baal Hermon to Lebo Hamath. This is in line with Joshua 11:3, which has the Hivites living in the shadow of Mount Hermon. Mount Baal Hermon abbreviates "Baal Gad in the Valley of Lebanon below Mount Hermon" in Joshua 11:17.

As often occurs, different people call the same place by different names. According to a geographic note in Deuteronomy 3:9, the Sidonians called Hermon Sirion, and the Amorites called it Senir, which accords with the reference to the mountain as *śryn* in a Ugaritic text from the period of the Judges.[120] This memory is preserved in several later biblical texts as well. Song of Songs 4:8 speaks of "the top of Senir, the summit

Sidon region
Brian J. McMorrow

of Hermon" (cf. also 1 Chron. 5:23). Psalm 29:6 and Ezekiel 27:5–6 associate the name with Lebanon and recognize it as a source of timber. The annals of Shalmaneser III identify Senir (Akk. *saniru*), "facing Lebanon," as the location of this Assyrian's decisive defeat of Hazael of Damascus.[121] These texts suggest Mount Hermon was considered part of the Anti-Lebanon Range.

Some interpret *l^e^bô^ḥ^a^māt* as "the Pass of Hamath,"[122] but it is more likely a specific place, modern Lebweh, near the spring of Nabaᶜ Labweh, one of the principal sources of the Orontes River in the Beqaᶜ.[123] The name appears as Labʾu in the Egyptian texts and Labaʾû in Assyrian inscriptions.[124] Later Lebo Hamath constituted the northern border of Solomon's kingdom (1 Kings 8:65), and of Jeroboam II's northern kingdom of Israel (2 Kings 14:25).

Canaanites, Hittites, Amorites, Perizzites, Hivites and Jebusites (3:5). For discussion of these names see comment on Joshua 3:10.

Mount Hermon
Bible Scene Multimedia/Maurice Thompson

The Aram Naharaim and Othniel Cycle (3:7–11)

The Baals and the Asherahs (3:7). On "the Baals" see comments on 2:11. Whereas in 2:13 the female counterpart to the Baals is identified as the Ashtaroth, here the text speaks of Asherahs. Since the Asherahs are known from other biblical contexts to have been made of wood and their demolition involved chopping them down (Deut. 7:5), the KJV rendered *hāʾᵃšērôt* as "groves," that is, sacred cult trees. However, in the light of the Ugaritic evidence that has surfaced, Asherah (also identified Athirat [*ʾatrt*]) is now known to have been a prominent goddess in Canaanite mythology, the wife of the high god El (*ʾil*) and mother of seventy gods. Her titles in the Ugaritic myths include "Lady Athirat of the Sea" and "Creatress of the Gods,"[125] which reflects her role as mother of the gods (who are referred to elsewhere as "the seventy sons of Athirat").[126]

The seductive power of the Canaanite Asherah cult to the Israelites is attested by several Hebrew inscriptions in the form of blessings from the eighth century B.C. that speak of "Yahweh and his Asherah":

- Kintillet ʿAjrud pithos 1 (northeastern Sinai): "I have blessed you by Yahweh of Samaria and his Asherah."
- Khirbet el-Qom inscriptions (near Hebron): "Uriyahu the rich wrote it / Blessed be Uriyahu by Yahweh / For from his enemies by his Asherah he has saved him / by Oniyahu / and by his Asherah / his A(she)rah."[127]

Even with this new information, the mention of Asherah alongside Baal in our text (presumably as his consort) is surprising, especially since 2:13 associated the Baals with the Ashtartes. Either the author confuses the two deities, or he recognizes both as consorts of Baal in this fertility religion. In either case, in worshiping these Canaanite deities the Israelites exchange the worship of the living God for the service of wood and stone. The lofty theology, austere morality, and abstract cult of Yahwism were replaced with the tangible and exciting fertility religion.

Cushan-Rishathaim king of Aram Naharaim (3:8). This title appears straightforward. Aram, rendered *Syria* in the LXX, is the name given to

Portion of a storage jar from Kuntillet Ajrud that mentions Asherah in inscription across the top
Z. Radovan/www.BibleLand Pictures.com ▸

the area populated primarily by Arameans, one of the most important ethnic groups in the late second and early first millennia. Their territory extended from northeast of the Sea of Galilee to the Taurus Mountains in the north and eastward beyond the Habur tributary of the upper Euphrates River. While his capital is not identified, the addition of Naharaim ("of the two rivers"; cf. Mesopotamia, meaning "between the rivers") fixes his home somewhere near or east of the great bend of the Euphrates.[128]

During the fourteenth to thirteenth centuries B.C., this region was politically subservient to the empire of the Hittites with their capital at Ḫattuša, serving as a buffer to the Assyrians to the east and the Egyptians to the south. However, during the last half of the thirteenth century, under Tukulti-Ninurta I (1245–1208 B.C.), the region east of the great bend in the Euphrates was controlled by the Assyrians. By the end of Tukulti-Ninurta's reign Akhlamu Arameans were infiltrating the western part of the empire. Their influence is reflected in the first appearance of Aram as the name of a region in the fourteenth-century B.C. Egyptian inscription of Amenophis III.[129] On Cushan-Rishathaim, see sidebar on "Who Is Cushan-Rishathaim?"

The LORD gave Cushan-Rishathaim ... into the hands of Othniel (3:10). The attribution of Othniel's successes over such a formidable foe as Cushan-Rishathaim to Yahweh would have been understood by all ancient Near Easterners. It was universally acknowledged that rulers governed by the will of the gods and especially that the outcomes of battles depended ultimately on the intervention of the gods. The annals of Tiglath-pileser I (1114–1076 B.C.), an Assyrian contemporary of the later deliverers, are laced with references to the involvement of Asshur, the patron divinity of Assyria. Centuries later, a neo-Assyrian successor to Tiglath-pileser, Shalmaneser III (854–24 B.C.) credited Asshur with his victory over a western alliance of kings that included Hadadezer of Damascus and Ahab the Israelite as follows:

> They marched against me [to do] war and battle. With the supreme forces which Aššur, my lord, had given me (and) with the mighty weapons which the divine standard, which goes before me, had granted me, I fought with them.[130]

The Moab and Ehud Cycle (3:8–30)

Eglon king of Moab (3:12). The name *ʿeglôn*, a diminutive form of *ʿēgel* ("bull, calf"), also recalls the term *ʿāgōl* ("round, rotund").[131] Moab designates the nation state that emerged on the plateau east and northeast of the Dead Sea in the late second millennium B.C. The heartland of this nation during the period of the judges was the region between the Wadi Zered, which flows into the southeastern corner of the Dead Sea, and the Arnon Gorge, which

Balu'a stele
Todd Bolen/www.BiblePlaces.com

▸ Who Is Cushan-Rishathaim?

Who is Cushan-Rishathaim? The man's name is even more problematic than his title. Formally, it looks like "Cushan of Double Wickedness," in which case it probably functions as a mocking and parodic pseudonym.[A-27] There is no consensus on who Cushan-Rishathaim may have been, though a variety of identifications have been proposed: a leader of the Kassites, who controlled Babylonia from 1600–1150 B.C. (Gen. 10:8); a Nubian (= Cush); an Asiatic usurper in Egypt, known in Egyptian sources as Arsu or Irsu;[A-28] a Midianite chieftain (cf. Num. 12:1; Hab. 3:7); a surviving chieftain of southern Judah.[A-29] Josephus (*Ant* 5.180) proposes an identification with Chusarsathus, king of the Assyrians, which might suggest Tiglath-pileser I of Assyria (1114–1076 B.C.), but this is too late for Othniel.

At this point it seems best to see in Cushan-Rishathaim of Aram Naharaim one of the Akhlamu Aramean adventurers who established a base of power in the Aramean heartland, claimed the title of "king," and embarked on a southward campaign of terror that eventually brought him into conflict with the newly arrived Israelites. Since he extended his tentacles as far south as Judah, he appears to have been a world-class emperor, who held Canaan in his grip for at least eight years. Some suggest that Cushan-Rishathaim's activities in southern Canaan were not undertaken simply to subjugate a small tribe (Judah) but were directed at Egypt.[A-30] In the end it is impossible to link Cushan-Rishathaim with any known historical figure.

splits the Moabite plateau into two halves. However, both the biblical record and the ninth-century B.C. Mesha Inscription suggest that for much of this time the northern half, which had been assigned to the tribe of Reuben, was under Moabite control.

Genesis 19:30–38 suggests the Moabites were relatives to the Israelites, having descended from an eponymous ancestor named Moab, son of Abraham's nephew Lot; the name probably means "from [my] father." The archaeological evidence for Moab in the Late Bronze and Early Iron Ages is incomplete and inconclusive, largely because of insufficient attention by archaeologists. However, this lacuna is filled in somewhat from the Balua Stele, which shows two Moabite rulers standing before an Egyptian deity, and a thirteenth-century B.C. topographical list of Ramesses II, which refers to his warring in Moab and capturing five forts. Apparently at this time Moab was a significant political and military force in the mind of the Egyptians.[132]

Whether Eglon was the king of a highly developed sedentary population or the foremost ruler over a group of tribes each led by an elder or sheikh is not clear, though his present residence in Jericho shows his preference for the town over tents. Eglon's capital has not yet been discovered, nor has any other Moabite capital from the time of the judges. One may expect that further excavations and the carbon-dating of organic material already discovered may push back the dates of some of the evidence for an early Moabite kingdom in the Transjordan, even as they are doing for Edom to the south.[133]

City of Palms (3:13). "The City of Palms" is Jericho (Deut. 34:3; 2 Chron. 28:15), modern Tell es-Sultan, whose occupation dates back more than seven thousand years before the event described here. Located by an oasis in the Jordan Valley ten miles north of the Dead Sea, the site was an important stopping place on trade routes along the Jordan Valley and westward to Jerusalem, Bethel, and Ophrah. Eglon probably selected

Jericho, the City of Palms
Kim Walton

Jericho as the base of his Cisjordanian rule because of its desirable location and its longstanding history as a major Canaanite city. He is oblivious to the curse Joshua had invoked on the city in Joshua 6:26.

Ammonites (3:13). According to Genesis 19:37–38, the Ammonites were cousins to the Moabites, the descendants of the eponymous ancestor Ben-ammi (also a son of Lot with his daughter), which means "son of my paternal grandfather." As almost everywhere in the Old Testament, the national name is *bᵉnê ʿammôn* ("sons of Ammon") rather than the gentilic form "Ammonites." This accords with extrabiblical references to this nation, which display a remarkable preference for the compound form of the name. The most remarkable is a seventh-century B.C. Ammonite inscription on a bronze bottle, which not only gives the names of a series of Ammonite kings, but remarkably refers to the kingdom by the compound form of the name, *bn ʿmn*.[134]

> The accomplishment of Amminadab, king of Banē ʿAmmōn,
> the son of Hiṣṣalʾel, King of Banē ʿAmmōn,
> the son of Amminadab, king of Banē ʿAmmōn:
> a vineyard and the gardens and the ʾtḥr and cisterns.
> May he rejoice and be glad
> for many days and distant years.

The Ammonites occupied an ill-defined territory northeast of Moab, separated from the Jordan first by the Amorite kingdoms of Sihon of Heshbon and Og of Bashan, and then their Israelite successors (Deut. 2:24–3:22). According to 2:20–21 the Ammonites had displaced an ancient people known to the Israelites as Rephaim but to the Ammonites as Zamzummim.

Amalekites (3:13). In the absence of any firm archaeological evidence for the Amalekites,[135] the Old Testament remains our only source of information. Genesis 36:16 suggests the Amalekites were linked ethnically with the Edomites, though they seem to have remained a migratory people throughout their history.

Ehud, a left-handed man, the son of Gera the Benjamite (3:15). Israel's second deliverer is identified by name and patronymic. Ehud consists of two elements, *ʾê* and *hûd*, which together denote "Where is the splendor, majesty?"[136] Although in a

Bronze dagger from Megiddo
Kim Walton, courtesy of the Oriental Institute Museum

troop of right-handed men a left-handed person would have been difficult to accommodate, if all the men were left-handed (as a troop of Benjamites are in 20:16), in line combat, trained left-handers actually have a decided advantage over right-handers, who are taught to fight sword against shield.[137] Even so, in interpreting the expression translated "a left-handed man," it seems best to follow the lead of the LXX's *amphoterodexios*, and interpret Ehud's condition and that of the Benjaminites in 20:16 as "ambidextrous," that is, skilled in the use of both hands. The meaning is fleshed out in 1 Chronicles 12:2, which describes a group of Benjamites, relatives of Saul who defected to David, as "armed with bows" and "able to shoot arrows or to sling stones right-handed or left-handed."

Black Obelisk of Shalmaneser III with tribute bearers
Todd Bolen/www.BiblePlaces.com

Ehud had made a double-edged sword (3:16). This sword was double-edged to facilitate a straight stab rather than a hacking stroke and to slice cleanly into the king's flesh. Because the present text uses the term *gōmed*, which occurs only here, it is not clear whether this dagger was a full cubit in length or a fraction thereof. If *gōmed* is the length of the *ʾammâ* ("cubit"), then the weapon was approximately eighteen inches long. The length of a cubit is generally thought to be the distance between the elbow and the finger tips in an adult male. Since this distance varies from person to person, it is not surprising that scholars have had difficulty establishing precise definitions of the cubit.

Elsewhere in the ancient Near East the length of the cubit was determined either on the basis of fingers (a twenty-four-finger cubit is common, but a thirty-finger cubit was also used in Babylon) or palms (the standard cubit being five handbreadths and the royal cubit being six (cf. Ezek. 40:5).[138] Since most men were right-handed, the weapon would have been worn on one's left side. Being ambidextrous Ehud fastened the dagger under his garment to his right hip, where no one would suspect it.

Tribute (3:17). In the Old Testament this term is used most often of gift offerings made to God as an expression of gratitude and reverence, but it is also used for a voluntary gift of homage (Gen. 32:14, 19, 21) or political friendship (2 Kings 20:12). Here it applies to the tribute required of a vassal by a superior.[139] The present text does not describe the nature of the tribute. The most valued items were precious metals, silver and gold,[140] but other items were often included. The following excerpts from the Black Obelisk of Shalmaneser III of Assyria illustrate this fact:

> I received the tribute of Sûs, the Gilzânean: silver, gold, tin, bronze vessels, the staffs of the king's hand, horses, (and) two-humped camels.
>
> I received the tribute of Jehu (the mans) of Bīt Humrî: silver, gold, a golden bowl, a golden goblet, golden cups, golden buckets, tin, a staff of the king's hand, (and) javelins(?).
>
> I received the tribute of Egypt: two-humped camels, a water buffalo (lit. "river ox"), a rhinoceros, an antelope, female elephants, female monkeys, (and) apes.[141]

Seti Stele from Beth Shean
Stephen Voth

The fact that Ehud was accompanied by an unspecified number of other men who carried the tribute suggests a payment in kind, as in Mesha's tribute to Ahab in 2 Kings 3:4, rather than only silver and gold.

Idols near Gilgal (3:19). Elsewhere in the Old Testament, the word *p*^{e}*sālîm* always denotes sculpted pagan cult images, but this ill-suits the present context. By itself the word means simply "carved images [of stone]." Here it seems best to interpret these objects as stelae either marking the boundary of the territory claimed by Eglon or as a monument to a battle by which Eglon achieved control over this region, perhaps analogous to the rock of Ebenezer commemorating the Israelites' victory over the Philistines in 1 Samuel 7:12[142] or the Mesha Stele commemorating Mesha's victory over the Israelites.[143]

Outside Israel such markers often contained the following features:

- They were made of stone.
- They were inscribed with text.
- They often contained sculpted imagery that complemented the text.
- The inscription closed with curses on any who would damage or deface the monument.
- The monument was erected in a public place for public observation.
- Royal monuments commemorated achievements emblematic of the king's role, such as military victories or building projects.
- Royal monuments were treasured as trophies by victorious opponents.
- After the death of the king the monuments served as his memorial.[144]

It is easy to imagine that these *p*^{e}*sālîm* were intended for some such function.

Attendants (3:19). This is a technical expression for courtiers of the king, those who have official access to his presence. These could include his ministers, advisors, and bodyguards, charged with securing the safety of the monarch. Ancient Near Eastern kings seem to have employed such guards as a matter of course.

Assyrian bodyguard
Marie-Lan Nguyen/Wikimedia Commons, courtesy of the Louvre

Upper room (3:20). This phrase is generally interpreted something like "cool roof chamber," based on the obvious meaning of the first word ("upper") and a derivation of the second from the root *qrr* ("to be cold").[145] In ancient Israel and undoubtedly among the neighbors the house of the wealthy houses often included upper stories to which the family would retreat for the sake of comfort.[146] However, Halpern has rightly noted that not only is "cool" not an architectural term; to escape the heat in the southern Jordan Valley near the Dead Sea one does not build upward, but burrows down into the ground. Appealing to Psalm 104:3, which conjoins *ʿaliyyôt* ("upper chambers") with *hamqāreh*, a participle form of a denominative verb derived from *qôraʿ* ("rafter, beam") rather than from *qrr*, he suggests plausibly that the present phrase means "the room over the beams,"[147] that is, the raised throne room.

Porch (3:23). As intimated, the NIV's "porch" probably involves the pillared portico of the king's summer residence. In the modest homes of ordinary citizens the pillars held up the ceilings and supported the second floor.[148] The statelier the building, the more substantial and decorative were the pillars. Temples and palaces and other stately structures were often designed with porticoes lined by pillars or entryways held up by pillars.

They took a key and unlocked them [the doors] (3:25). The logistics of Ehud's actions are difficult: How would Ehud escape the throne room if the door were locked from the inside? The answer lies in the nature of locks and keys in the ancient world. See sidebar on "Locks and Keys in the Ancient World."

Seirah (3:26). The location of Seirah is unknown, but apparently it was in the vicinity of Gilgal.

Trumpet (3:27). The translation of *šôpār* as "trumpet" conjures up wrong images for the modern reader. This instrument was not made of brass, but consisted simply of a goat or ram's horn with the cut-off tip serving as the mouthpiece. In Joshua 6:5 this word is interchanged with *qeren* ("[ram's] horn").

The word *šôpār* seems to be cognate to Akkadian *šappāru*, which is itself a loanword from Sumerian *šegbar* ("ibex, wild goat").[149]

▸ Locks and Keys in the Ancient World

Replica of "pin tumbler" Egyptian lock
Lenka Peacock, courtesy of the Science Museum, Kensington

The Song of Songs provides a clue to ancient locks and keys in noting that the character thrusts his hand through the hole in the door and unlocks the bolt (Song 5:4–6). If the door can be unlocked from the outside, it can also be locked from the outside. King and Stager have logically proposed that the locks in both instances involve "tumbler (or Egyptian) locks." They write:

> In ancient Israel the doors of palaces, temples, granaries, and domestic dwellings were locked with a wooden bolt and a tumbler lock mounted on the inside of the door.... A wooden box containing loose pins was attached to the inside of the door above the wooden bolt, oarlock case, into which the pins drop when the bar is moved into the locked position. To unlock the door the key is inserted into a lot in the bolt until the matching teeth of the key push up the moveable pins so that the sliding bolt can be drawn. When the key is withdrawn, the bolt can be secured by sliding it horizontally into a position in which the pins drop from the box into the slots of the bolt. To make the tumbler locks more difficult to pick, they were mounted on the inside of the door and reached by passing one's hand and key through a hole in the door.[A-31]

As for the keys themselves,[A-32] they came in various sizes, from ten to twenty inches long, with some so large they were carried on the shoulders (Isa. 22:22). Some resembled large toothbrushes with handles bent near the end. Doors could be locked without the key simply by sliding the bolt in place and waiting for the pins to drop, but they could not be unlocked without the key.

In the present instance, after Ehud had stabbed Eglon, he went out through the door of the throne room and closed it behind him. Reaching his hand through the keyhole, he would have slid the bolt back into place. When he heard the pins drop, he turned around and fled through the pillared portico. However, to enter the king's room his servants needed to retrieve the key to unlock the door—by which time Eglon was long dead.[A-33]

Shofar
Kim Walton

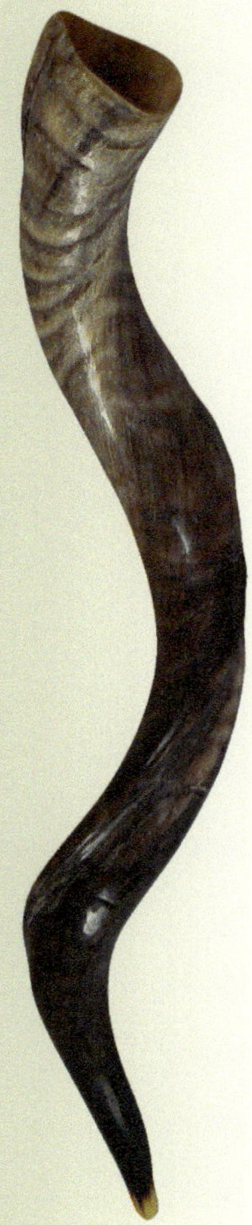

The *šôpār* was always used as a solo instrument. Although its range of sounds was limited, the particular character of the sounds it could produce made it an especially important instrument of communication.[150]

The fords of the Jordan (3:28). Although the Jordan Rift Valley averages six miles wide and at Jericho fifteen miles wide, the river itself is modest in size. The Romans were the first to build bridges across the river. Until then

Jordan near Jericho
Todd Bolen/www.BiblePlaces.com

people had to wade across. Except in the rainy season there were many places where this was possible—which is probably why the narrator does not specify where the present fords are.

Struck down about ten thousand Moabites (3:29). On the interpretation of seemingly inordinately high numbers in Judges, see comment on 1:4.

The Governorship of Shamgar (3:31)

Shamgar son of Anath (3:31). The name of this deliverer is a riddle. Since the Hebrew vocabulary (like that of most Semitic languages) is based on triliteral roots, the presence of four strong consonants *š-m-g-r* suggests he was not an Israelite.[151] The presence of analogous forms of the name in Nuzi texts suggests he may have been a Hurrian mercenary.[152] Equally puzzling is his characterization as ben ʿAnat ("son of Anath").[153] In the past interpreters have assumed this meant Shamgar was a resident of Beth-Anath in Galilee.[154] Now it seems more likely this is a dedicatory expression: Shamgar was devoted to the service of Anath.[155]

What this means can be learned from extrabiblical sources. In Canaanite mythology Anath was at the same time the consort

Model of cattle drivers holding ox goads
Werner Forman Archive/The Egyptian Museum, Cairo

of Baal and Canaanite goddess of war.[156] But the fame of Anath extended far beyond Palestine. At the beginning of the Nineteenth Dynasty, she was accepted into the Egyptian pantheon, functioning particularly as the goddess of war and personal protectress of the pharaoh.[157]

Of special interest is an inscription from the Wadi Hammâmaât dated in the third year of Ramesses IV (1166–60 B.C.), which reads, "ʿprw of the troop of ʿAn[ath] eight hundred men."[158] On the assumption that the same Egyptian troop had fought against the Sea Peoples during the reign of Ramesses III (1198–1166 B.C.), Shupak suggests that Shamgar may have been one of these ʿprw (*ḫabiru*), among whom were found a variety of ethnic elements, including Hurrians. As a member of an ʿApiru troop of mercenaries in Pharaoh's army named after the Canaanite goddess of war and as a man of valor, Shamgar bore the widely used military cognomen, ben ʿAnath.[159] Since at first the Sea Peoples' base of land operations in Palestine was located in northern Lebanon and the Song of Deborah associates Shamgar with problems in northern Israel, the latter's confrontation with the Philistines probably occurred in the north at the beginning of the twelfth century B.C. As an officer under the command of the Egyptian pharaoh, Shamgar ben ʿAnath was not intentionally serving Israelite interests.[160]

Six hundred Philistines (3:31). On the Philistines see comment on 3:3.

Oxgoad (3:31). This word occurs only here in the Old Testament, but in postbiblical Hebrew it identifies a guiding instrument, a pointer (*m. Sanh.* 10:28a). The present instrument, normally used to train and control livestock, was made of hard wood and probably tipped with metal.

The Canaanites and Barak Cycle: The Narrative Version (4:1–24)

Jabin, a king of Canaan, who reigned in Hazor (4:2). This Jabin should not be confused with the Jabin who ruled Hazor at least thirty or forty years earlier and who headed an alliance of Canaanite forces against Joshua (Josh. 11:1–15). In the ancient Near East royal names were commonly repeated and even took on the form of dynastic names (e.g., Ramesses I-XI).[161] The name Jabin is based on a root *byn*, which occurs in personal names of the second millennium but not later. Remarkably the first part of the name has surfaced in a fragment of a royal letter found at Hazor from the eighteenth to seventeenth centuries addressed to Ibni (= Yabin).[162] From Egypt, the topographical list of Ramesses II at Karnak includes the intriguing entry, Qishon of Jabin (*ybn*).[163] The present text identifies Jabin as "the king of Canaan," suggesting he had recaptured for Hazor the dominant position among Canaanite cities that had not fallen into Israelite control. See sidebar on "Hazor."

Sisera (4:2). Sisera is unknown as a Canaanite name. The name seems not to be Semitic, suggesting he may have been a

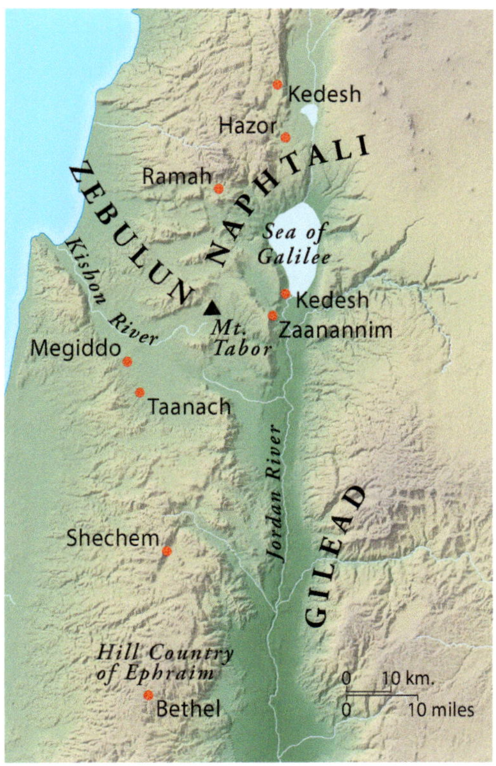

Locations and movements mentioned in Judges 4

Hazor

Covering 175 acres, the archaeological site of Hazor is the largest city in ancient Israel. As "the head of all these kingdoms" (Josh. 11:10) in the Late Bronze Age, Hazor dominated the valley north of the Sea of Galilee. Except for Laish (Dan), Hazor is the only settlement within the territory allotted to Israel mentioned among the 25,000 cuneiform tablets found at Mari. One of the tablets (dated to the eighteenth century B.C.) reveals that Canaanite Hazor was so important that King Hammurabi of Babylon placed two ambassadors there.

Other tablets associate Hazor with trading in tin, essential for the manufacture of bronze weapons. We also know that Hazor continued to thrive into the Late Bronze Age (1550–1200 B.C.), because it is also mentioned in three letters found among the archives at Tel el-Amarna. Of all the Canaanite rulers whose letters are included in this archive, he alone is called "king."

According to Joshua 11:10–15, Hazor received more severe treatment at the hands of the Israelites than any other northern city.[A-34] Archaeological evidence points to the destruction of the lower city of Hazor in the thirteenth century. Several Israeli scholars attribute this to the Israelites. It seems that elements of the Hazor dynasty escaped the destruction of Joshua. But with the Israelite failure to consolidate control over all the conquered territory in the wake of the Conquest, a member of the royal house returned to the ruins, reasserted the rule of the royal house, and restored Hazor to her status of the dominant Canaanite city in the twelfth century.

Hazor: The lower city dominates the upper central portion of the picture with the upper city ruins visible on the left. Todd Bolen/www.BiblePlaces.com

The Megiddo Ivory, dated to the same period as Deborah, is from the same geographic region as the setting of Judges 4. The king on the ivory, like Jabin of Hazor, has subjugated the people and here is celebrating victory over defeated leaders. It is even possible that the captives portrayed are Israelite (note the circumcision).
Z. Radovan/www.BibleLandPictures.com

Hittite or Hurrian mercenary like Shamgar in 3:31 or a member of the Sea Peoples.[164] Mercenaries were opportunists, offering their services to anyone who would hire them.

Harosheth Haggoyim (4:2). While prevailing opinion understands the word *ḥ^{a}rōšet* to mean "forested area,"[165] the fact that Sisera's forces included 900 chariots, which could be deployed only in coastal and alluvial plains (1:19), renders this interpretation problematic.[166] A more logical solution relates the expression to the Akkadian cognate *erištu* ("cultivated land")[167] and explains the vocalization as another example of "pejorative pointing," presumably because of some pagan association (cf. comment on 2:13). Accordingly, Harosheth Haggoyim probably means "cultivated field of the Gentiles," an explanation that not only suits the fertile alluvial plain between Taanach and Megiddo but also accords with the present linkage with chariots, the reference to the Canaanite chariot bases in the river plains in 1:19,[168] and the location of the battle in 5:19.

Nine hundred iron chariots (4:3). In view of the claim of Thutmose III in the fifteenth century B.C. to have captured 924 chariots at Megiddo, including the ruler of Megiddo's chariot decorated with gold,[169] this reference is feasible.[170] Whether the number is interpreted literally or as epic exaggeration, in the light of 1:19, this superior technology rendered the Canaanites invincible to Israelite armies marching out in their own strength.

Deborah, a prophetess, the wife of Lappidoth (4:4). Like Caleb ("dog") and Jael ("ibex"), Deborah, which means "bee," derives the name from the animal world. The epithet, "a woman, a prophet," thrusts her profession and her gender into sharp relief.[171] While the Old Testament refers to prophets by several designations (seer, visionary, servant of Yahweh, messenger of Yahweh, man of God), *nābîʾ* is the most common designation. The etymology of this word remains uncertain, though a link with Akkadian *nabū* ("to call, name") is certain.[172]

A prophet serves as a spokesperson for deity to the people. In the patricentric world of the Old Testament, few if any standing leadership offices were open to women.[173] By contrast, there seems to have been no hesitation in Israel or elsewhere to engage women as prophets. Not only was prophecy widespread in the ancient Near East,[174] but Mesopotamian prophecy in particular involved an unusually large proportion of female prophets.[175]

In Israel the prophetic office had an ad hoc character. Whereas elsewhere, especially in the Neo-Assyrian courts, prophets tended to function as part of the courts of kings, in Israel they were engaged directly by Yahweh, and in monarchic times often worked in opposition to kings.[176]

Deborah is identified as the wife of Lappidoth.[177] The use of a feminine plural form for a man's name seems odd at first, but *lappîdôt* (lit., "torches, flashes") should probably be interpreted as an abstract plural. Traditionally torches were made either of a long pole with rags soaked in oil wrapped around one end, or reeds tightly tied together and often attached to a pole. The association of the wife of Lappidoth with Barak, which means "lightning," evokes associations with

Cylinder seal impression of emissaries coming to king seated by palm trees
Z. Radovan/www.BibleLandPictures.com

Baal, the storm god, whose titles in the mythological texts include "Mightiest of Warriors" and "Rider of the Clouds,"[178] and is portrayed iconographically as a strident deity with right arm raised and holding a stylized thunderbolt.

She held court under the Palm of Deborah (4:5). This reading reflects too legal an interpretation of the verb *yāšab*, which means simply "to sit." Deborah functions here as the agent through whom the people expect a divine word regarding their present crisis. The context is analogous to that represented in autobiographic style on the eighth-century B.C. stela of Zakkur, the usurper of the throne of Luash and Hamath:

> Bir-Hadad the son of Hazael, the king of Aram, formed an alliance against me of sev[en]teen king[s]: .... All these kings set up a siege against Hazr[ak]. They raised a wall higher than the wall of Hazr[ak]. They dug a moat deeper than [its] moat. But I lifted my hands to Baalshamayn, and Baalshamay[n] answered me, [and] Baalshamayn [spoke] to me [thr]ough seers (*ḥzyn*) and visionaries (*ʿddn*), [and] Baalshamayn [said], "F[ea]r not, for I have made [you] king, [and I will st]and with [you], and I will deliver (*ḥṣl*) you from all [these kings who] have forced a siege against you."[179]

Deborah's role is precisely that of the seers and visionaries in this text. Seated beneath the palm,[180] like Zakkur, the people come to her for a divine judgment on the crisis created by the Canaanites. The divine response is to call Barak to rescue the people.

Ramah and Bethel (4:5). Ramah is usually identified with modern er-Ram, a little more than five miles north of Jerusalem. On Bethel, see comment on 1:22.

Kedesh in Naphtali (4:6). In the ancient Semitic world Kedesh ("sanctuary") was an element in many place names.[181] The present Kedesh is to be identified with Tell Qades in upper Galilee about nine miles north of Safed.[182] Joshua had conquered this city earlier (Josh. 12:22) and set it aside as a Levitical city (21:32) and city of refuge (20:7). This was the first Naphtalite city to fall to Tiglath-pileser III when he invaded northern Israel in 734–732 B.C. (2 Kings 15:29).

Mount Tabor (4:6). This mountain rises steeply 1,843 feet above sea level at the northeast corner of the Jezreel Valley, controlling one of the most important crossroads in the region.

Kishon (4:7). This name is usually identified with Wadi al Muqatta that drains the Jezreel (Esdraelon) Valley from southeast to northwest, beginning its course in the hills of northern Samaria near Megiddo,[183]

Kishon River (follows the tree line across middle of photo)
Todd Bolen/www.BiblePlaces.com

flowing northwestward through the plain of Acre, and finally emptying into the Mediterranean at the foot of Mount Carmel.[184]

Ten thousand men (4:6, 10). On this seemingly high number, see comment on 1:4.

The LORD will hand Sisera over to a woman (4:9). This stronger version of the committal formula (cf. v. 7) shares with many war oracles a notorious ambiguity, similar to the ambiguity in the Levite's supposed oracle to the Danites (18:6) and the oracle concerning the outcome of Ahab's battle with the Arameans (1 Kings 22:6). See sidebar on "War Oracles."

By the great tree in Zaanannim near Kedesh (4:11). Heber seems to have moved as far away from his clan as possible. The noun *ʾēlôn* may denote any large tree, but it often refers to a specific tree, a terebinth or oak that marks a

Mount Tabor
Bible Scene Multimedia/Maurice Thompson

War Oracles

In the ancient world before kings embarked on a military campaign, they consulted with the deity regarding the wisdom of the campaign and the chances for success, to which the deity responded with an oracle. Though certain elements of the procedure may be missing in the narrative, we will encounter examples of such oracles later in Judges 7:13; 18:5; 20:27–28.

Many examples can be adduced from outside the Old Testament.[A-35] Although Deborah's charge to Barak in 4:6–7 functions primarily as a commissioning charge, it has the form of a modified war oracle. Note the comparisons with 1 Kings 22:5–6, an eighteenth-century B.C. oracle given in response to Zimri-Lim's inquiry before Dagon, and an oracle of reassurance for Esarhaddon of Assyria in the seventh century B.C.[A-36] The presence of the committal formula is a striking common denominator.

The Oracular Element	Deborah's Oracle to Barak Judges 4:6–7	Ahab's Prophets' Oracle for Ahab 1 Kings 22:5–6	Dagon's Oracle for Zimri-Lim *ARM* 26 209 = *ARM* 13 23	Bel-ušezib's Oracle for Esarhaddon *ABL* 1237 = SAA 10
The Citation Formula	Yahweh, the God of Israel, commands you:			Bel has said,
The Challenge/ Charge	"Go, take with you ten thousand men of Naphtali and Zebulun and lead the way to Mount Tabor.	"Go up	"Babylon, what are you constantly doing?	"Like Marduk-šapik-zeri may Esarhaddon, king of Assyria, be seated on his throne!
The Committal Formula	I will lure Sisera, the commander of Jabin's army, with his chariots and his troops to the Kishon River **and give him into your hands."**	for **the Lord will give into the king's hand."**	I will gather you into a net and.... The dwellings of the seven accomplices and all their wealth **I give in the hand of Zimri-L[im]."**	And **I will deliver all the countries into his hands!"**

sacred spot.[185] Heber may have viewed this tree as a symbol of divine protection and blessing.

Zaanannim seems to derive from *ṣāʿan* ("to pack up"), which is cognate to Arabic *ṣʿn* ("to wander about as a nomad, roam"), suggesting a place where caravaneers stop or transfer goods.[186] Assuming Heber's camp must be located near Mount Tabor, most understand Heber to have pitched his tent at Khirbet Qedish, near the southern end of the Sea of Galilee.[187]

While this identification may answer one geographic question, it creates several of its own, and identification with the northern Kedesh remains the best solution for several reasons.[188] (1) It avoids the need to identify Kedesh with two different locations in a single literary context. (2) It takes seriously the preposition *ʿad* ("unto, as far as"), which suggests an extreme northerly location. (3) A seminomad allied with the king of Hazor (v. 17) is better located near Hazor than at the southern end of the Sea of Galilee. (4) Since Sisera is portrayed as Jabin's commander, with his forces in shambles (v. 15) he would naturally seek protection

War oracles were notoriously ambiguous. Note the oracle reported by Herodotus of the Greek oracle at Delphi concerning the fate of the Lydian King Croesus in his conflict with the Persians. After lavish offerings to the temple at Delphi to secure the favor of the gods, Croesus sends his agents to the oracles with the question: "Shall Croesus send an army against the Persians, and shall he strengthen himself with a military alliance?" Both oracles respond with the same message: If Croesus attacks the Persians, he will destroy a great empire. The oracles also counsel him to determine which are the strongest Greek states and to make them his friends.[A-37] Delighted with the answer and convinced that he will destroy the Persians, Croesus follows the first inquiry with a second, seeking to know whether his reign will endure for a long time. The priestess of Delphi answers this request with the following oracular pronouncement:

> When comes the day that a mule shall sit on the Median throne,
> Then, tender-footed Lydian, by pebbly Hermus
> Run and abide not, nor think it shame to be a coward.[A-38]

Since a mule will never become king of the Medes, the Lydian king concludes that he and his descendants will remain in power forever. Croesus then begins the war. When the outcome proves to be a total disaster, Croesus sends a delegation back to Delphi, charging the Greek gods with thanklessness and the oracle with deceit for telling him that he would destroy Cyrus's power (1.90). Herodotus explains the oracle's response to the latter charge as follows:

> As to the oracle, Croesus had no right to find fault with it: the god had declared that if he attacked the Persians he would bring down a mighty empire. After an answer like that, the wise thing would have been to send again to inquire which empire was meant, Cyrus's or his own. But as he misinterpreted what was said and made no second inquiry, he must admit the fault to have been his own. Moreover, the last time he consulted the oracle he failed also to understand what Apollo said about the mule. The mule was Cyrus, who was the child of parents of different races—a nobler mother and a baser father. His mother was a Mede and daughter of Astyages, king of Media; but his father was a Persian, subject to the Medes, and had married his queen to whom he was in every way inferior.[A-39]

from his superior and head for the vicinity of Hazor. Heber's tent nearby would not be suspected by his pursuers. (5) If Heber's camp were near Barak's Kedesh, he may be the informer who reported to Jabin (and by extension to Sisera) that Barak's troops had left Kedesh and were headed for Mount Tabor (v. 12).[189]

When they told Sisera (4:12). The informer is not identified. One may surmise that Heber passed on the word that Barak had assembled his troops, or that Jabin had observed them move from Kedesh to Mount Tabor and had relayed orders to Sisera to mobilize. Alternatively, Sisera may have sent out scouts to watch the enemy's movements or perhaps informers to infiltrate the enemy camp. On the use of scouts in ancient warfare see comment on 1:23.

Nine hundred iron chariots (4:13). On these chariots see comment on 4:3. The account that follows represents the only geographically detailed story we have from northern Israel.[190]

The LORD routed Sisera (4:15). This verb, which means "to bring into motion

The god Ashur as winged sun disk with bow accompanying the king into battle
Caryn Reeder, courtesy of the British Museum

and confusion,"[191] recalls several other texts, most notably Yahweh's action against the Egyptians in Exodus 14:24, in which natural phenomena are marshalled to effect the rout.[192] The description of his involvement is reminiscent of Assyrian accounts that speak of the awe-inspiring terror of Asshur going before the Assyrian king. The following excerpts from the annals of Tiglath-pileser I (1114–1076 B.C.) and Ashurnasirpal II (883–859 B.C.) respectively are typical:

> (The people of) the land Adauš were frightened by my belligerent attack and abandoned their territory. They flew like birds to ledges on high mountains. (But) the splendour of the god Aššur, my lord, overwhelmed them and they came back down and submitted to me.[193]

> While I was in Mount Kirriru the radiance of Aššur, my lord, overwhelmed the Gilzānu and the Ḫubušku (and) they brought to me as their tribute horses, silver, gold, tin, bronze, (and) bronze casseroles.[194]

In other respects, however, the contrast could scarcely be more stark. Whereas the Assyrian accounts, cast in bombastic autobiographical style, are written intentionally to magnify the victorious human king, in our account the role of Barak is deliberately diminished, not only by retaining Yahweh as the subject of the verb, but also by taking the sword out of Barak's hand[195] and emphasizing that all the action occurs "before" him.[196] Yahweh is the divine warrior who goes before his hosts.

Sisera, however, fled on foot (4:17). Sensing the hopelessness of his army's situation, Sisera leaps from his chariot and flees on foot. He logically heads northeast along the Grand Trunk Highway that ran from Megiddo to Hazor, the seat of his suzerain Jabin. This road ran diagonally through the Jezreel Valley, between the hills of Nazareth on the west and Mount Tabor on the east, past the "Horns of Hattin," through the Arbel pass, into the plain north of the Sea of Galilee, where Hazor is situated.[197] As the crow flies, these cities are less than forty-five miles apart, considerably less than half the distance Elijah ran from Jezebel in 1 Kings 19:3.

The picture of a defeated general fleeing for his life from a battle is found in many Assyrian annals. Ashurnasirpal II recounts how Nūr-Adad, the rebel sheikh of Dagara, "to save his life, climbed up a rugged mountain" in the face of his overwhelming defeat by the Assyrian.[198] Recognizing that with Jabin's main forces decimated no protection can be found in the capital (cf. v. 23), the general continued running north until he comes to the tent of Heber the Kenite, a recognized ally of Jabin.

Jael (4:17). Biblical variations of the name *yāʿēl*, which means "mountain goat," are found in the names Jaalah in Ezra 2:56 and Jaala in Nehemiah 7:58. Extrabiblical analogues include Ugaritic *yʿl*, Phoenician *yʿl*, and earlier similar Amorite forms. The etymology of the name is confirmed by the Phoenician version, which appears on a seal and is accompanied by a representation of a mountain goat.[199]

Friendly relations (4:17). This phrase translates the Hebrew word *šālôm* ("peace"). In contexts like this it functions as a covenant term. The fact that Heber's clan is directly linked by treaty to Jabin, "king of Hazor" and "king of Canaan" (v. 2), suggests that Heber is a significant political force.

Tent of Jael (4:17). In ancient Israel households often consisted of several branches of an extended family under the headship of the "father," hence the designation *bêt ʾāb* ("house of the father") for "family, clan."[200] Accordingly, the homes of a family were often more like a compound, consisting of several houses. Since Heber is a Kenite, making the transition from a nomadic to a sedentary lifestyle, it is not surprising to read that his household lives in tents (vv. 11, 17–22), and since his clan represents a significant political force in this context, it is not surprising to read that his compound in Zaanannim consists of more than one tent. Apparently Jael has her own tent. It is unclear whether Heber has other wives who have their own tents, but presumably as the head of this household he has his own.

In the actions that follow Jael violates a series of fundamental social norms. (1) In offering hospitality to Sisera, she usurps her husband's exclusive right as a male to offer hospitality to a male. (2) In killing Sisera, she violates the covenant between Heber and Sisera's superior. (3) In killing Sisera, who sought hospitality and protection in her house, she violates the fundamental rights of guests in dramatic fashion.[201] As in the Middle East today, hospitality toward strangers represents one of the highest social values. This value could even supersede a man's responsibility for the well-being of his children (see 19:22–26).

Covering (4:18). The covering is probably a thick sheep or goatskin rug, which would be extremely warm, to be sure, but this is no time to worry about comfort. In addition to Sisera's concern for concealment, Jael may have been taking intentional steps to stifle the noise involved in her subsequent actions.

Skin of milk (4:19). Milk was a staple in the ancient Near East, being consumed as a liquid, as yogurt, as curds, or as cheese. Goats were the main source of milk. Their milk is richer in fat and protein than cow's or sheep's milk. The curds were probably produced by churning fresh milk, either by shaking a skin containing the liquid or by beating a skin of milk with a stick. See comment on 5:25.[202]

A tent peg and a hammer (4:21). The tent peg and hammer/mallet were standard equipment for those who lived in tents. Since Jael lives in a tent and the clan has recently pitched their tents in

Wooden mallet from roughly the time period of the Judges
Kim Walton, courtesy of the Oriental Institute Museum

Wooden stakes
Kim Walton, courtesy of the Oriental Institute Museum

warrior and seducer, alluring and dangerous, nurturing and bloodthirsty" bear a striking resemblance to the portrayal of Anath in Ugaritic myths.[206]

Bronze stake
Kim Walton, courtesy of the Oriental Institute Museum

Zaanannim, handling these objects is no problem for her. The word for "hammer" occurs with this meaning only three times elsewhere in the Old Testament, but cognate expressions are found in Ugaritic *mqb* and Akkadian *maqqabu*.[203]

There lay Sisera with the tent peg through his temple—dead (4:22). Like Ehud's assassination of Eglon in the previous chapter, the account of Jael's behavior seems to have been lifted from a Canaanite notebook. Her actions were not only deviant and violent; they were socially revolutionary, challenging prevailing views of female roles in general and the relationship of husband and wife in particular.[204] Some have argued that the picture of Jael derives from ancient Near Eastern goddesses.[205] While this interpretation is rightly rejected, the similarities between her character as "a

The Poetic Celebration of Victory over the Canaanites (5:1–31)

When princes in Israel take the lead (5:2). Rendering of p^{e}*rāʿôt* as "princes" assumes an etymological link with Arabic *faraʿa* ("to excel, be eminent"). The more likely translation of NRSV, "When locks are long in Israel," is based on comparison with an Akkadian cognate *pirtu* ("hair"), which occurs in a context similar to this.[207] Linking the present usage with Numbers 5:18 and 6:5, where *prʿ* speaks of loosing the hair, one may imagine either some routine act of preparation for battle or a ritual act of dedication. The context requires a correlative for *hitnaddēb* ("to present oneself, volunteer") in the next line. This suggests a derived meaning something like "to let go, to abandon everything" [for the battle], referring to "the spontaneity and enthusiasm of the citizens in arms in their spirited response to the call to battle."[208]

Seir (5:4). In Genesis 36:20–21 and 1 Chronicles 1:38, Seir (which means "hairy") functions as a personal name, identifying the ancestor of an ethnic group asso-

Shasu being trampled by Pharaoh's chariot
Lenka Peacock

Triumph Hymns in the Ancient Near East

After the dramatic narrative of the victory over the Canaanites, we encounter one of the oldest poems in the Old Testament. Intrigued by its textual riddles, emotional intensity, psychological energy, and theological profundity, scholars have tried to resolve the interpretive issues raised by this song from many different angles. Since this literary piece was "sung" (5:1), it is distinguished formally from the surrounding narrative. From the perspective of comparative literature, Judges 5 represents a genre of writing known as triumph hymns, often composed to celebrate a victory over an enemy. Egyptian literature of this type is attested from the mid-thirteenth century B.C. Uni, an officer of Pepi I (ca. 2350 B.C.), inscribed his recollections in poetic format on his cenotaph in Abydos:

> This army returned in safety,
> After it had hacked up the land of the [Sand]-Dwellers.
> This army returned in safety,
> After it had crushed the land of the Sand-Dwellers.
> This army returned in safety,
> After it had thrown down its enclosures.
> This army returned in safety,
> After it had cut down its fig trees and its vines.
> This army returned in safety,
> After it had cast fire into all its dwellings.
> This army returned in safety,
> After it had killed troops in it by many ten thousands.
> This army returned in safety,
> [After it had taken troops] in it, a great multitude as living captives.[A-40]

Hymns of a similar genre celebrate the triumphs of Sesostris I and III (early second millennium B.C.), Thutmosis III, Amenophis III, and Ramesses II (mid to late second millennium B.C.).[A-41] The most famous of these is the victory hymn of Thutmosis III, found in the temple at Karnak. This hymn is much more theological than historical, being cast in autobiographical form intent on glorifying the deity, Amun-Re, the supposed composer:

> I came to let you tread on Djahi's chiefs,
> I spread them under your feet throughout their lands.
> I let them see your majesty as lord of light,
> so that you shone before them in my likeness.
> I came to let you tread on those of Asia,
> to smite the Asians' heads in Reljenu;
> I let them see your majesty clad in your panoply,
> when you displayed your weapons on your chariot.
> (15) I came to let you tread on eastern lands,
> to crush the dwellers in the realm of god's land;
> I let them see your majesty as shooting star,
> that scatters fire as it sheds its flame....
> I let them see your majesty as southern jacka1,
> the racer, runner, roving the Two Lands.
> I came to let you tread on Nubians;
> as far as Shat you hold them in your grasp;
> I let them see your majesty as your Two Brothers,
> whose hands I joined for you in victory.[A-42]

Perhaps historically more significant is the "Israel Stele" of Merneptah (1208 B.C.), the last part of which celebrates Merneptah's triumphant campaign in Palestine, and called thus because the final stanza contains the earliest extra-biblical reference to Israel.[A-43]

Poetic commemorations of military victories are also attested in Mesopotamian literature, most notably the lengthy Tukulti-Ninurta Epic, celebrating the Assyrian's triumph over Kaštiliaš.[A-44]

P. C. Craigie has observed that the Song of Deborah and Barak shares several significant features with the Tukulti-Ninurta ode. In both (1) people invoke divine aid on the basis of a previous relationship and covenant with the deity; (2) they use the war cry to conjure up the drama of the battle; (3) they mock the pathetic flight of the enemy leader with sarcastic taunts; and (4) they invoke females (human or divine) in inspiring the victorious warriors.[A-45]

Even so, the present song bears the closest resemblance to another biblical hymn of triumph, the Song of the Sea in Exodus 15:1–18.[A-46] Whereas the extrabiblical odes tend to represent hyperbolic celebrations of superhuman achievements, Exodus 15 and Judges 5 overflow with praise to God. But our text is not exclusively so. The last two stanzas focus on individual human activity—Jael's brutal murder of Sisera and the portrait of Sisera's anxious mother, waiting for her son. Because this seems odd in a victory hymn, some have preferred to identify this poem as a ballad.[A-47] Yet the poet's inclusion of this unrestrained praise of the woman not only assumes her participation in the divine work; it also functions as a taunt of Sisera, and with him the Canaanites, who stand in the way of Yahweh's agenda.

Merneptah Stele showing the reference to Israel
Matt Floreen/www.BiblePlaces.com

ciated with the Horites, who lived in the hill country of Seir (Gen. 14:6). Elsewhere Seir is always a geographic designation for the mountainous region south of the Dead Sea occupied by the Edomites. Most agree that these mountains are to be located to the east of the Arabah, south of Moab. However, perhaps because of the encroachment of the Seir-based Edomites into the territory adjoining Judah, sometimes the name is applied to the region west of the Arabah (Deut. 1:2, 44).

The place name is well attested in both Egyptian and Neo-Assyrian sources. It occurs in Amarna Letter 288:23–27.[209] It also appears in several Ramesside inscriptions, including the Tanis Obelisk where Ramesses II boasts of having plundered Mount Seir.[210] In Papyrus Harris I (Ramesses III, 1184–1153 B.C.), the Seirites are pre-

▸ Edom

Apart from two enigmatic references to Shamash-Edom,[A-48] the earliest clear reference to Edom occurs in the letter of a frontier official to his superior preserved in Papyris Anastasi IV from the reign of Merneptah (1224–1214 B.C.):

> We have finished letting the Bedouin tribes (Shasu) of Edom (ʾ-*d-w-m*) pass the Fortress [of] Mer-ne-ptah Hotep-hir-Maat—life, prosperity, health! which is in Tjeku, to the pools of per-Atum ... to keep them alive and to keep their cattle alive.[A-49]

The earliest neo-Assyrian references to Edom date from the eighth century B.C., when the expansion of the Assyrian empire had reached southern Syria. In most instances, Edom (*U-du-mu*) is depicted as one member among a series of western lands conquered by successive Assyrian emperors.[A-50] Even so, the nature of Edomite society at the end of the Late Bronze Age still remains largely a mystery, though recent excavations at Khirbet en-Nahas reveal an active copper-smelting industry here as early as the twelfth century B.C.[A-51]

Edom at Bozrah
Todd Bolen/www.BiblePlaces.com

sented as a segment of the Shosu tribes, a group that apparently had not yet become sedentary.[211] In a Neo-Assyrian reference to Seir from a later time, Ashurbanipal boasts of having won a battle in Saʾarri in his Arabian campaign.[212]

O Lord, when you went out from Seir, when you marched from the land of Edom (5:4). This song portrays Yahweh as a divine warrior marching forth from Seir/Edom to the aid of his people. In terms reminiscent of his descent on Mount Sinai (Ex. 19), the song celebrates the arrival of Yahweh.

Scholars have long been intrigued by the association of Yahweh not only with Sinai, but also with Seir/Edom in this text, as well as in several other ancient and/or archaizing poems.[213] Many find in these allusions support for what is commonly known as the Kenite/Midianite hypothesis, according to which Yahweh was originally a Kenite or Midianite deity, whose homeland was in the south but who was adopted by clans that eventually became a part of Israel.[214] This portrayal of Yahweh marching forth from Sinai/Seir/Edom represents a deliberate polemic against the perspectives cherished by the kings whom the poet has summoned to listen (v. 3). They were Canaanites, whose god Baal resided in the north, on Mount Zaphon. But the Israelite triumph over Sisera and Jabin represented more than an earthly victory of an oppressed people over the oppressor; Yahweh had triumphed over Baal.

Edom (5:4). Edom is the name of the nation-state that occupied the region east of the Arabah and south of Moab. According to Genesis 25:30; 36:1–43, the Edomites were distant cousins of the Israelites, being descendants of Esau, the twin brother of Jacob. The name is derived from a root *ʾdm*, meaning "red," presumably because of the redness of the rocks in the region the Edomites occupied—though the account of his birth notes that Esau was red all over when he was born (25:25). See sidebar on "Edom."

The One of Sinai (5:5). The epithet "the One of Sinai" occurs only here and in Psalm 68:8 and is presumably an archaic title of Yahweh.[215] Yahweh's status as the singular God of Israel is reinforced by the storm imagery, which the Canaanite religion generally associates with Baal. But the poet hereby claims that Yahweh, not Baal, rides the clouds to the aid of his people (cf. Deut. 33:26–29; Ps. 68:4, 33–34; 104:3). At the same time the storm imagery anticipates the cosmic aspects of the victory later in the poem (Judg. 5:19–21).[216]

Days of Shamgar ... days of Jael (5:6). By identifying Shamgar by patronymic "son of Anath," the song heightens the irony of the situation (cf. comment on 3:31). Yahweh, who has discredited Baal with this victory over the Canaanites, is not above employing Shamgar, a member of a military guild dedicated to Anath, the consort of Baal in Canaanite mythology.

Village life (5:7). The word *pᵉrāzôn* functions as a collective designation for residents of rural unwalled settlements, in contrast to *ʿārîm* ("towns"), which were fortified with protective walls. This interpretation is confirmed by the cognate Akkadian expression *ālani pu-ru-zi*, which occurs several times in the Amarna correspondence. Since it occurs nowhere else in cuneiform texts, it is best understood as a Canaanite loanword.[217] Unlike the walled Canaanite towns of the valleys and plains, Israelite villages in the hill country were unfortified and vulnerable to outside harassment (cf. Ezek. 38:11). Defense was based on their elevated hilltop locations and the arrangement of houses on the village perimeters. This situation undoubtedly derives from the economic and military superiority of the Canaanites living in the fertile valleys, but it may also be a leftover effect of Merneptah's campaign in Palestine in 1207 B.C.[218]

City gates (5:8). Since the Israelites lived in unwalled villages, "gates" probably refers to the fortified Canaanite towns in the valleys.

Willing volunteers (5:9). This expression highlights the contrast between the way this army was raised and the typical ancient Near Eastern pattern of conscripted and professional armies.[219] Note Samuel's warning to the elders of Israel in 1 Samuel 8:11–12, where military forces consisted largely of conscripts forced into military duty.

White donkeys (5:10). While donkeys were used primarily as pack and draft animals, they were also ridden by the upper classes. The NIV's "white" translates a word used only here in the Old Testament meaning "tawny," that is, light-colored animals, brownish orange to light brown. Because female donkeys of this color would have been rare, as symbols of status the rich preferred them over the generic gray animals. Among the Canaanites the economically powerful advertised their social standing further by dressing the donkeys with luxurious (saddle) blankets. In a time of trouble for Israel, Canaanite merchants rode up and down the public roads in confidence, on their equivalents to luxury limousines.[220]

Voice of the singers at the watering places (5:11). Like the post office in many small towns of the prairies, the watering holes served as community gathering places, where people exchanged gossip and celebrated significant events.

People of the LORD (5:11, 13). This is the only occurrence of the expression *ʿam yhwh* ("people of Yahweh") in Judges. It expresses the obverse of the phrase "Yahweh, the God of Israel" in verse 3; the Israelites are the people of their divine patron. In the surrounding territories, divine patrons related to specific people only secondarily, as a consequence of their being in his territory. Marduk, for example, was first of all the god of the city Babylon. In Israel's case, Yahweh's relationship was primarily with his covenant people and secondarily with the land.[221]

Terra cotta flute player from Horvat Qitmit
Z. Radovan/www.BibleLand Pictures.com

Whistling for the flocks (5:16). This expression occurs elsewhere only in Jeremiah 18:16, where it speaks of derisive hissing. In Daniel 3:5, 7, 10, 15, an Aramaic word from the same root refers to pipes used in Nebuchadnezzar's orchestra. The Old Greek renders the present expression *syrinx*, which in the Seleucid period referred to a large, double-bound instrument. The instrument in question here was probably a flute made of a reed or of the bone of a bird or goat, like the third-millennium B.C. two-tone flute found at Megiddo or the seventh- to sixth-century instrument found at En-Gedi.[222]

Why did he linger by the ships? (5:17). According to this song, the Danites were too busy in the shipping industry—presumably as clients of the Phoenicians or perhaps the Sea Peoples.[223] The association of Dan with the northern tribe of Asher suggests that the battle with the Canaanites occurred later than the events described in chapters 17–18, and that the Danites had already arrived in the Hulah Valley north of the Sea of Galilee. When they took over the territory around Laish, they also gained control of the east-west trade from Banias along the Litani River to Tyre. Those who gained control of the trade route inevitably came into contact with Phoenician merchants, and some Danites may even have taken positions on board their ships.[224] The nature of the shipping industry in the eastern Mediterranean during this period has been spectacularly illuminated by the discovery of a merchant vessel loaded with goods at Uluburun, off the coast of Turkey.[225]

The kings ... fought at Taanach by the waters of Megiddo (5:19). Since Megiddo is not located on the Kishon (Wadi el-Muqatta[c]), the phrase "the waters of

Bands of the Balawat Gate showing boats carrying off plunder
Werner Forman Archive/The British Museum

Megiddo" anticipates the course of the battle.[226] For most of the year the Kishon is little more than a brook, which would have posed no problem for infantry or chariotry. But the last line of verse 19 hints at how badly the battle went for the Canaanites, in that they failed to make off with any loot.

Thutmose III Gebel Barkal Stele referring to fighting star
Photograph © 2009 Museum of Fine Arts, Boston

From the heavens the stars fought, from their courses they fought against Sisera (5:20). While most interpret "from their courses," to mean that the stars functioned like an army, each in its place, it is preferable to see here the heavenly bodies leaving their normal orbits to fight against Israel's enemy.[227] In this imagery, Deborah draws on a common ancient Near Eastern mythological motif, according to which the gods intervene on their devotees' behalf by engaging the heavenly hosts. Especially illuminating is the following excerpt from the Gebel Barkal Stele of Thutmose III of Egypt (1479–1425 B.C.):

> Pay attention, O people of the south land, who are in the pure mountain, which is called "Thrones of the Two Lands" among people, (yet) it is unknown; then you will know the miracle of [Amun-Re] in the presence of the Two Lands. [...] not [... sentr]ies) were in the very act of being posted at night in order to do their regular watch. There were two astronomers (present). A star approached, coming to the south of them. The like had not happened before. It shot toward them (the enemy), not one of them could stand [...] falling headlong. Now then [...] was behind them with fire in their faces. Not one of them even retaliated; no one looked back. Their chariotry is gone, they (the horses?) having bolted in [...] in order that all foreigners might see the awe of my majesty.[228]

However, the link between the stars and divinity portrayed in our text is quite different from the common Mesopotamian portrayal. Whereas in the latter the stars are deified or viewed as representatives of the deities, here the stars are nothing more nor less than agents of Yahweh, without personality or independent power.

The river Kishon swept them away (5:21). The sudden flooding of the Kishon and the crippling of Sisera's chariotry echo what had happened to Pharaoh's armies at the Reed Sea,[229] suddenly transforming an advantage into a death trap. This association of the stars fighting from heaven and the flooding of the Kishon seems odd to the modern reader, but both may be understood as evidences of the arrival of Yahweh (cf. vv. 4–5), who usurps the signs of theophanic advent that Canaanites had associated with Baal. Indeed, in some Ugaritic texts the stars are declared to be the source of rain.[230]

Curse Meroz (5:23). Meroz is mentioned only here in the Old Testament and cannot be located. It must have been within a triangle whose apexes are marked by Mount Tabor on the east, where Barak assembled his troops (4:6, 12, 14), the Kishon in the west, and Megiddo or Taanach in the south, perhaps near Sarid.[231]

Angel of the LORD (5:23). On the role of the divine envoys, see comment on 2:4.

He asked ... she gave (5:25). The poetic description of Jael's treatment of Sisera highlights the trap she set for Sisera by going beyond his expectations and probably beyond custom. See comment on 4:19.

Bowl fit for nobles (5:25). This expression, "a stately dish," links the quality of the bowl with the quality of the Canaanite forces in verse 13. Perhaps the poet has in mind the kind of golden chalice found in the fourteenth-century shipwreck at Uluburun.[232]

Fluted gold jar from the tomb of Pharaoh Psusennes I
Werner Forman Archive/The Egyptian Museum, Cairo

At her feet he sank (5:27). The rhetorical force of this verse rests both on the pattern of repetition (ABCD/ABC/EBFCG) and on the visual impression created by beginning the cola with the prepositional phrase, "Between her feet...." Such staircase parallelism is common in extrabiblical texts as well, especially in the mytho-poetic texts from Ugarit, as in this example:

> Weeping, she leads the donkey,
> Weeping, ropes up the ass,
> Weeping, she lifts up her father,
> Onto the back of the donkey,
> The shapely back of the ass.[233]

Through the window peered Sisera's mother (5:28). Assuming the posture of an outside observer, the poet describes Sisera's mother gazing out her window and wringing her hands. The picture of this noble woman in her palace with royal retainers presents a sharp contrast to Jael, the rustic wife of Heber the Kenite living in her tent. She too is a victim of war. This image is preserved in exceptional visual form in several ivory carvings from the ancient world. The celebration Sisera's mother expects is illustrated beautifully on an ivory plaque from Megiddo, found near the sight of this battle with Sisera, up the Wadi Kishon.

Dividing the spoils (5:30). Although ancient Near Easterners justified warfare as having been commanded by the gods or as serving the king's/nation's honor, its real attraction was a hunger for plunder. The items Sisera's mother lists represent the highest prizes of war: women and luxury garments.

A girl or two for each man (5:30). This phrase literally translates "a womb, a pair of wombs for every man," thus highlighting the realities of war. To victorious soldiers the women of vanquished foes represented primarily objects for their sexual gratification—one more realm to conquer—or as potential wives to bear their children. Deuteronomy 21:10–14 aims to rein in the abuse of captive women by Israelite warriors.

Colorful garments ... highly embroidered garments (5:30). Two expressions describe the second treasured prize of war. The meaning of the root *ṣeba*^{c} and its biform *ṣ*^{e}*bā*^{c}*îm* (which occur only here in the Old Testament) is established by reference to the Akkadian cognates *ṣubātum* ("fabric, dyed

Nimrud ivory carving with "Lady at the Window" motif
Z. Radovan/www.BibleLand Pictures.com

Embroidered garment
Z. Radovan/www.BibleLandPictures.com

material")[234] and *ṣīp/bu* ("dyed fabric").[235] In addition to colorful dyes, the luxury clothes were also decorated with fine needlework and embroidered with geometric patterns and images. Such garments were considered luxuries worn by priests (Ex. 28:15) and royalty (Ps. 45:14; Ezek. 16:10). Ezekiel 27:7 and 16 single out Egypt and Edom as producers of embroidered goods. The needles used in embroidery were made of bronze, bone, or ivory.

The description of the loot for which Sisera's mother is waiting is realistic and functions as shorthand for many more items often taken by conquerors, as reflected in this excerpt of a tribute list from Ashurnasirpal of Assyria (883–859 B.C.):

> I received tribute from Sangara, king of the land of Ḫatti, 20 talents of silver, a gold ring, a gold bracelet, gold daggers, 100 talents of bronze, 250 talents of iron, bronze (tubs), bronze pails, bronze bathtubs, a bronze oven, many ornaments from his palace the weight of which could not be determined, beds of boxwood, thrones of boxwood, dishes of boxwood decorated with ivory, 200 adolescent girls, linen garments with multi-coloured trim, purple wool, red-purple wool, *gišnugallu*-alabaster, elephants' tusks, a chariot of polished (gold), a gold couch with trimming—objects befitting his royalty.[236]

The Call of Gideon (6:1–40)

Midianites (6:1). We know the Midianites by name only from biblical texts, which portray them as a seminomadic bedouin people of the Sinai peninsula and western Arabia, who relied on the camel for transportation (cf. v. 5).[237] Recent archaeological investigations of the northern Hejaz region east of the Gulf of Aqaba suggest that the Midianites were not entirely nomadic. The archaeological site of Qurayya has yielded evidence of walls, a citadel, and distinctive pottery, known as "Qurayya ware" or "Midianite ware." This pottery has been dated to the thirteenth and twelfth centuries B.C., contemporary with the Ramesside pharaohs Sethos I and Ramesses V (1295–1143 B.C.),[238] which fits the context of Judges 6–8.

Amalekites (6:3). See comment on 3:13.

Eastern peoples (6:3). Literally "sons of the east." This is a vague gentilic label used by westerners to denote the nomadic groups that migrated about the Arabian desert, often raiding the settled communities of the Trans-

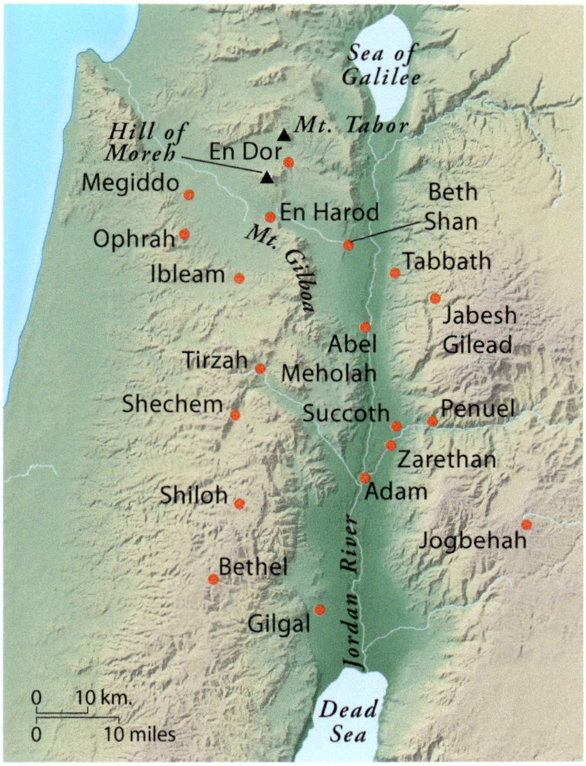

jordan and sometimes of Cisjordan.[239] The use of *qdm* ("east") as a geographic designation is also attested in the twentieth-century B.C. Egyptian Tale of Sinuhe, where it denotes the region east of the coastal Phoenician cities.[240] This expression is the opposite of *amurru* ("west"), from which comes "Amorite," an Akkadian designation for the territory to the northwest of Mesopotamia.

Locusts (6:5). These is the *schistocerca gregaria*, a species of desert locust that is normally solitary, but under certain conditions undergoes morphological and behavioral changes, resulting in migratory swarms capable of devastating regions on an international scale. The swarm of locusts that invaded Somaliland in 1957 is estimated to have numbered 16,000,000,000 and to have weighed 50,000 tons. Since each insect eats its own weight in green food every day, the devastation from a swarm of locusts is almost unimaginable.[241]

Camels (6:5). Archaeological evidence suggests that camels were domesticated as early as the third millennium B.C.; by the middle of the second millennium they were widely used as pack animals in southern Arabia. A sherd depicting a camel was found at Qurayya,[242] and considerable quantities of camel bones have been found at the thirteenth- to twelfth-century site of the Timna copper mines and smelters, where camels were used as pack animals.[243]

Here the Midianites appear not as caravaneers but as camel-riding warriors, who were probably driven by the need to supplement the food being produced in their own territory. In any case, the camels served as pack animals to carry off the loot collected in the Midianites' forays into Israelite and Canaanite territory.[244]

From the power of Egypt (6:9). This Hebrew expression (lit., "from the hand of Egypt") is especially apt, given the dominance of the motif of the hand and the raised arm in Egyptian textual and iconographic

Gideon's Activity

Camel raiders being pursued by Assyrian troops
Werner Forman Archive/The British Museum

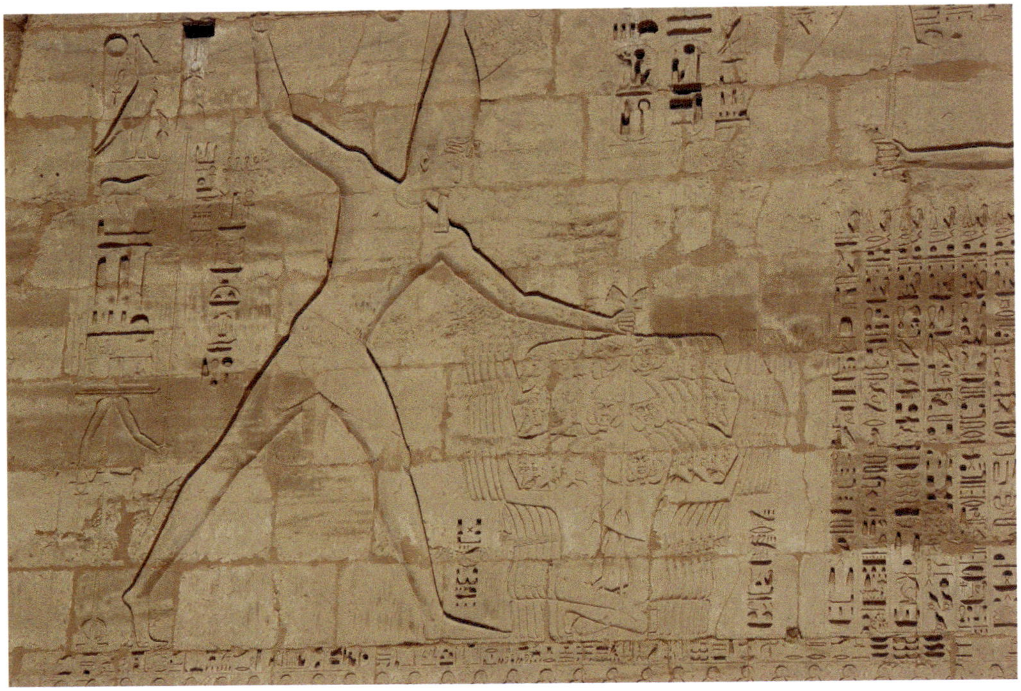

Pharaoh Ramesses III raising arm over enemies grasped by hair
Frederick J. Mabie

portrayals of the pharaoh wielding control over his enemies.[245]

I am the LORD your God (6:10). This is the only occurrence in Judges of the divine self-introduction formula, which occurs dozens of times elsewhere. The use of this formula in the context of references to Yahweh's defeat of his vassal's enemies recalls a Neo-Assyrian prophecy communicated by the prophet Issar-la-tašiyaṭ to Esarhaddon to reassure him of Ishtar's support:

> I am the great Lady, I am Ištar of Arbela who throws your enemies before your feet.
> Have I spoken to you any words that you could not rely upon?
> I am Ištar of Arbela, I will flay your enemies and deliver them up to you.
> I am Ištar of Arbela, I go before you and behind you.
> Fear not! You have got cramps, but I, in the midst of wailing, will get up and sit down.[246]

Obviously the timing of the divine actions on behalf of the vassal differ; whereas the prophet here speaks of Yahweh's past acts of deliverance of Israel, Issar-la-tašiyaṭ promises Esarhaddon future deliverances. Apart from this difference, the parallels are remarkable.

Angel of the LORD (6:11). On divine envoys, see comment on 2:1.

The oak in Ophrah (6:11). While trees were often associated with sacred shrines or oracles (cf. 4:5), Gideon is probably using this oak simply for cover. Many identify Ophrah, the site of Joash's estate, with ʿAfulleh in the Jezreel Valley.[247] Joshua 17:2 and 1 Chronicles 7:18 suggest that the Abiezrites are a clan of Manasseh, a tribe granted land on both sides of the Jordan. However, verse 35 states that this Abiezrite allotment is located west of the Jordan.

Joash the Abiezrite (6:11). In the ancient world, names often represented statements of faith. Joash is an abbreviated version of Jehoash, which means "Yahweh is strong," and in form resembles Hammurabi, "[Divine] Kinsman is great,"[248] or Ashur-nirari, "Ashur is my help."[249] Like Micah in 17:1 (see comment), "Joash" suggests

Detail of an Egyptian painting from the tomb of Nakht depicting the treading of the grapes
Werner Forman Archive

that his parents had a memory of Yahweh, though Joash's possession of an altar of Baal and an image of Asherah (6:25), symbols of the Canaanite religion, suggest that his own faith has been compromised.

Threshing wheat in a winepress (6:11). Ancient people threshed their grain by beating the heads of the cut stalks with a flail, discarding the straw, and then tossing the mixture of chaff and grain in the air, allowing the wind to blow away the chaff while the heavier kernels of grain fall to the floor. This is normally done on hilltops to take advantage of the wind.[250] Because this would have aroused the attention of the marauding Midianites, Gideon resorts to beating the grain under an oak in a sheltered vat used for pressing grapes.

Generally winepresses involved two excavated depressions in the rock, one above the other. The grapes were gathered and trampled in the upper, while a conduit drained the juices to the lower.[251] The present location was probably satisfactory for beating out the grain, but separating the grain from the chaff in these circumstances would have been more difficult. Gideon either had to wait for a windy day, or the grain and chaff mixture was carried quickly to an exposed area and tossed in the air, and the grain quickly whisked away.

If the LORD is with us, why has all this happened to us? (6:13). Gideon's reference to Yahweh as the God of the Exodus here suggests he and his clan have trouble perceiving him as the Deity who will take care of them in the land of Canaan. Judging by Gideon's cynical questions, Yahweh has been either apathetic or impotent to intervene in Israel's present crisis or in securing this clan's well-being in general.

This impression is reinforced later by the need to tear down the cult installation dedicated to Baal in his father's yard. The theological world of ancient Near Easterners was complex, often recognizing divinities to be operative at four levels: cosmic deities, national/state deities, clan deities,

Altar in front of palace at Hazor
Kim Walton

and ancestral deities (deceased ancestors elevated to semi-divine status).[252] While Yahweh had demonstrated his cosmic sovereignty through the wonders he had performed in Egypt (Deut. 4:32–40), and his role as Israel's national God by entering into relationship with them at Sinai (cf. Judg. 6:8–10), during the period of the judges the Israelites apparently had difficulty conceiving of him as a personal and family deity.

Thus, they turned to local gods of the Canaanites to take care of them at this level. These are the gods on whom one depended for the fertility of livestock, the soil, and their own wives. They have forgotten Yahweh's explicit declarations and covenant promises to satisfy their needs at *every* level, including securing the well-being of individuals and clans (Deut. 7:6–16).

My clan is the weakest in Manasseh, and I am the least in my family (6:15). The expressions *ʾelep* ("clan") and *bêt ʾābî* ("house of my father") reflect two levels in Israel's tribal structure, which may be illustrated as in the graphic below.

I will be with you, and you will strike down all the Midianites together (6:16). Typical of ancient Near Eastern official messenger style, speaking on behalf of Yahweh, the divine envoy uses the first person. Yahweh presents himself as the divine warrior who will go out and fight with the person whom he calls.

Ephah of flour (6:19). An ephah of flour is about six gallons, which points either to a single huge loaf or up to a dozen flat cakes—an extremely generous meal in these hard times.

Broth in a pot (6:19). Hebrew *pārûr* refers to some type of boiling pot, but its precise nature is unknown (cf. Num. 11:8; 1 Sam. 2:14). The term is related to Akkadian *pūru* ("stone basin") for oil or fat.[253] The word for "broth" occurs elsewhere only in Isaiah 65:4[254] and refers to the liquid that results when meat is boiled in water.

Your father's altar to Baal (6:25). Altars were at the heart of ancient Near Eastern reli-

The social structure of ancient Israel

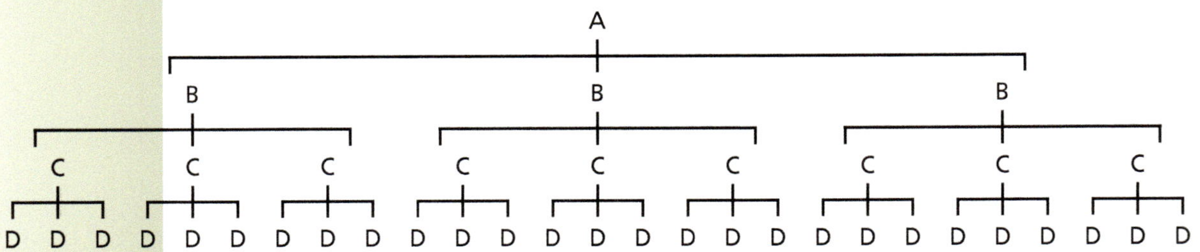

A = *ʾam*, "people" (Israel); B = *šebet*, "tribe" (e.g., Manasseh);
C = *ʾelep, mišpāḥâ*, "clan" (Abiezrites); D = *bêt ʾāb*, "father's household" (Joash)

gion. Canaanite altars ranged in shape and size from small square horned altars less than two feet high to the large circular altar more than thirty feet in diameter found at Megiddo.[255] Since this altar was a clan rather than city cultic installation, it was likely moderate in size. The smaller altars were generally built of specially cut stone, hence the command to tear it down rather than to "cut it down," as would have been the case with the wooden Asherah image/symbol. This Baal of Ophrah represents one of many local manifestations of the storm god Baal (see comment on 2:11).

Asherah pole (6:25). On the significance of Asherah see comment on 3:7.

On the top of this height (6:26). The NRSV's rendering of *māʿōz* as "stronghold" is preferable to the NIV's "height." Canaanite temple sanctuaries were often fortified with walls and towers. By commanding Gideon to build the altar on this pagan site, Yahweh is ordering him to reclaim this paganized land for himself.

If Baal really is a God, he can defend himself (6:31). Ancient Near Easterners perceived deities as present in the images that represented them. By an elaborate process, an object made with human hands was transformed into a representative of the god, indwelt by his spirit/breath.[256] Once an object was transformed into a god, it should have been able to defend itself. Furthermore, people worshiped them precisely to defend and take care of their devotees.

But there is more to Joash's comment. The NIV's insertion of "really" leads the reader astray into thinking that Gideon's actions have tested Baal's divinity and that Joash's rhetorical question anticipates a negative answer—"No, Baal is not a god."[257] However, it seems unlikely that the sponsor of the Baal installation at Ophrah would have conceded this so quickly. Joash is not challenging Baal to defend his divinity, but to defend his altar and his cult.

The quasi-legal form of the question confirms this interpretation. Here and elsewhere (cf. Ex. 1:16; 21:3; 22:14; Lev. 27:8; Josh. 17:15; Hos. 4:15) the syntactical structure involving the sequence, conditional conjunction *ʾim* ("if") + noun + pronoun, serves as a functional rather than ontological challenge. Joash's point is that Baal does not need anyone to defend him. Given his status as divinity, he can defend himself. After all, his altar has been torn down, which means that he has lost the means whereby his needs are met; through sacrifices the gods were nourished. Given the tolerance of ancient Near Eastern gods toward their devotees worshiping other gods, Baal would not have been that upset if an altar to Yahweh was erected next to his own. But when his source of food is cut off, Joash expects him to stand up for his own interests.

Jerub-Baal (6:32). The form of the name is difficult. Joash's explanation puts a positive spin on it, as if by "hacking" down Baal's altar and the Asherah, Gideon contended against Baal, and Baal was challenged to defend himself against Gideon.[258] Although the name *yᵉrubbaʿal* has been traditionally interpreted as a jussive, "Let Baal contend [against him]," it is preferable to interpret the form as a verbal sentence name following the prevalent predicate-subject order with "Baal" functioning as the subject of the verb, hence "Baal will contend for him." Normally names of this sort lauded the deity for action on behalf of the one who gave or bore the name.

Then the Spirit of the LORD came upon Gideon (6:34). According to the normal use of the Qal of *lābaš* ("to clothe"), the Hebrew reads "The Spirit of Yahweh put on Gideon," suggesting that the Spirit "wears" Gideon; that is, the Spirit is inside him, rather than that Gideon "wears" the Spirit as an external force. This raises the question

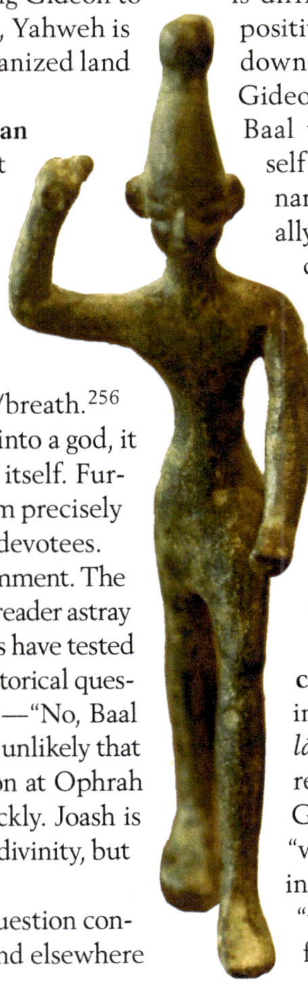

Baal
Marie-Lan Nguyen/Wikimedia Commons, courtesy of the Louvre

▸ The Spirit of God and the Individual

A statement in an Akkadian wisdom text raises the issue of how the spirit relates to an individual: "The *alû*-demon has clothed himself in my body as with a garment; sleep covers me like a net,"[A-52] which some translate as "The *alû*-demon has wrapped my body as with a garment."[A-53] However, the exceptional interpretation of the verb reflected in the NIV and most English translations in 6:34 assumes the present idiom represents a stronger version of the divine empowerment formula than "The Spirit came [*hāyâ*] upon X" in 3:10 and 11:29, and a more colorful version than "The Spirit rushed [*ṣālaḥ*] upon X" (14:6, 19; 15:14).[A-54]

This interpretation finds some support in Job 29:14, but especially in extrabiblical texts, which often use clothing imagery to describe a person as covered or overwhelmed by divine or demonic forces. One Akkadian text reads, "He [the *asakku*-demon] enveloped the miserable man like a garment."[A-55] Given the pervasive fear of demons in the ancient Near East and their prevalence in the New Testament, the paucity of references to demonic spirit forces in the Old Testament is remarkable. Powers that others attribute to other gods and to evil spirits Yahweh claims for himself. Not that Yahweh hereby acts demonically. Rather, the narrator attributes the supernatural empowerment later demonstrated by Gideon to Yahweh.

We should not interpret the present idiom as a contrast to later statements regarding the regenerating indwelling of the Spirit. Not only does the Spirit of Yahweh perform many different functions in the Old Testament,[A-56] but variations of the present clothing idiom also occur in the New Testament.[A-57] The present use of the idiom speaks of the supernatural empowerment of a person who is fearful and resistant to the call of God. Yahweh hereby seizes control of Gideon and energizes him for feats that would otherwise be impossible.

whether the Spirit functions as an internal or external force. See sidebar on "The Spirit of God and the Individual."

I will place a wool fleece (6:36). In our day "to put out the fleece" has become idiomatic for expecting a sign from God by which he reveals to us the course of action one should take. At the outset, we should recognize that Gideon's putting out the fleece does not represent an act of faith by which he seeks knowledge of God's will. He already knows it—he is to lead the Israelites in throwing off the Midianite hordes (6:14). Instead, the fleece turns out to be an act of unbelief, an effort to get out of doing that will. The method adopted represents not only a clear violation of Yahweh's prohibition on testing him (Deut. 6:16), but also an effort to get Yahweh to change his mind through a means that comes extremely close to the forms of pagan divination forbidden in Deut. 18:20–22. See sidebar on "Testing the Deity."

Fleece
Jill Walton
▸

Sheep intestines used for divination
Marie-Lan Nguyen/ Wikimedia Commons, courtesy of the Louvre

▸ Testing the Deity

Gideon's demands have much in common with divination.

- As in many extra-biblical contexts, a military crisis precipitates the present ritual performances.
- Even more so than in the reading of omens, like the liver of a sheep (extispicy), Gideon's demand that Yahweh treat his fleece different from the environment around it operates on simple binary principles—it can only yield a yes or no answer.[A-58]
- In keeping with a common purpose of Mesopotamian divination, Gideon's aim is to reassure himself of divine support for the venture against the Midianites.
- Like many ancient diviners, Gideon is not confident in the verdict of a single sign; he needs reinforcement through a second performance of the test. Indeed, the results of his first test could be explained as a purely natural phenomenon: When soft and absorbent material is left overnight on the hard ground or the rocky surface of a threshing floor, in the morning it will feel wetter than the ground around it. So Gideon demands reiteration through a reversal of the phenomena: wet fleece, dry ground followed by dry fleece, wet ground. His request that Yahweh do something that will be regarded as abnormal[A-59] is analogous to diviners seeking reinforcement through signs of a different genre and involving a different realm. Hepatoscopic messages (based on marks on a liver) could be reinforced by rhabdomantic (observing the pattern arrows create when they are tossed or dropped) or hydromantic (observing the patterns of substances dropped in water) signs.[A-60]

But the relationship between Gideon's test of Yahweh and ancient Near Eastern divination may be explored in several additional aspects.

- As was often the case in the Mari prophecies, Gideon sought to verify a divine oracle through another mechanism. The will of God was clear, but he appears to have hoped that Yahweh's intentions would change.
- As in the case of extaspicic divination following a prophetic or celestial omen, the form of divination here is provoked rather than passive. Whereas most forms of divination involve the observance of phenomena over which the observer has no control, Gideon prescribes for Yahweh both the method and the meaning of the results. In this respect, the present case differs significantly from the Urim and the Thummim, which were inaccessible to Gideon. In the Urim and Thummim Yahweh both provided the instruments and prescribed the method whereby the high priest could establish his will in such contexts (Num. 27:21).
- Unlike prevailing custom, according to which kings or generals engaged professional diviners to determine the will of the gods, Gideon takes matters into his own hands. The fact

that Gideon, an ordinary citizen from a minor clan of Israel, even thinks about demanding signs suggests that common people may have had their own ad hoc divinatory practices by which they sought to determine the will of the gods in their own domestic affairs. However, since Yahweh is calling on him to deliver the nation from the Midianites, the stakes are much higher here.

The outcome of Gideon's testing of Yahweh is most remarkable. Despite previous prohibitions on testing Yahweh, despite Gideon's faithless disposition, and despite the questionable strategy, Yahweh responds favorably and reassures Gideon of his support.[A-61]

Gideon's Victory over the Midianites (7:1–25)

Spring of Harod (7:1). The spring of Harod is traditionally identified with Ain Jalud, nine miles west-northwest of Beth Shan.[259]

Hill of Moreh (7:1). This expression means literally "hill of the teacher."[260] The topography of the Harod Valley satisfies the geographical requirements of this passage.[261]

Leave Mount Gilead (7:3). The traditional reading reflected in the NIV's "Mount Gilead" creates impossible problems, because the only Gilead known in the Old Testament is the mountainous region east of the Jordan (cf. comment on 10:3). It seems best to associate *gilʿād* with the modern name of the spring Ain Galud.

Harod Spring
Ken Schenck

Twenty-two thousand men left, while ten thousand remained (7:3). On the seemingly inordinately high numbers, see comment on 1:4.

Those who lap the water with their tongues like a dog ... and all who kneel down to drink (7:5). The NIV's insertion of "from those" between these clauses is textually unwarranted and creates serious logistical problems. It is best to interpret the *waw* conjunction that introduces the second clauses epexegetically, that is, the second clause clarifies the first statement. In order to lap water with one's tongue like a dog, it is necessary for human beings to kneel down.[262]

Here all but three hundred kneel down and lap like dogs; the remaining ones chose to dip water with their hands and drink it out of their hands. It is commonly thought that these were retained because they could keep their eyes on the enemy while they drank; hence, they were better prepared for battle. However, not only is this interpretation contradicted by the choice of the general himself (Gideon), the folly of using three hundred men against this innumerable host of Midianites, the weapons chosen for the battle, and the strategy for engagement (7:19–22); it also annuls the point of the text—the victory is entirely a divine act. The criteria for paring the troops down to three hundred men appear to be arbitrary.

Trumpets (7:8). As noted in 3:27, *šôpār* refers to a ram's horn used to sound alarms or marshal troops.

Hill of Moreh
Z. Radovan/www.BibleLandPictures.com

Locusts (7:12). On locusts as a metaphor for invading armies, see comment on 6:5.

I had a dream (7:13). As if to complete the reassurance of Gideon with a third sign (after the two involving the fleece), Yahweh volunteers a word of assurance for the man. In the Old Testament most dreams involve non-Israelites.[263] This should not surprise us, since portentous dreams were a common feature of ancient Near Eastern life (see sidebar on "Dreams in the Ancient World"). The present text is exceptional in that, although for the dreamer and the interpreter the dream communicated a disastrous message, for Gideon, who overhears the telling and the interpretation, it offers a welcome word of assurance.

Trumpets ... empty jars ... torches (7:16). By ancient Near Eastern standards (as by our own), the weapons with which Gideon attacks the Midianites are ridiculous. The trumpets involve a ram's horn (see comment on 3:27). The word "jars" identifies a small to medium-sized storage jar. The torches probably involve a stick with rags soaked in oil and wrapped around the end, or, since it is harvest time, reeds or stalks of grain tightly bound and attached to a short stick. So long as the lit torches are covered by the jars, they smolder, but once the jars are removed they burst into flame.

Storage jars
Todd Bolen/www.BiblePlaces.com

While the sound of smashing pottery undoubtedly awakens the Midianites, they probably interpret the sight of three hundred torches lighting up the night sky as the awesome glory of the God of the Israelites, analogous to the *melammu* referred to so often in Neo-Assyrian sources. The Akkadian word refers to the brilliant visible splendor exuded by gods, which in the context of battle terrifies and overwhelms the enemy.[264]

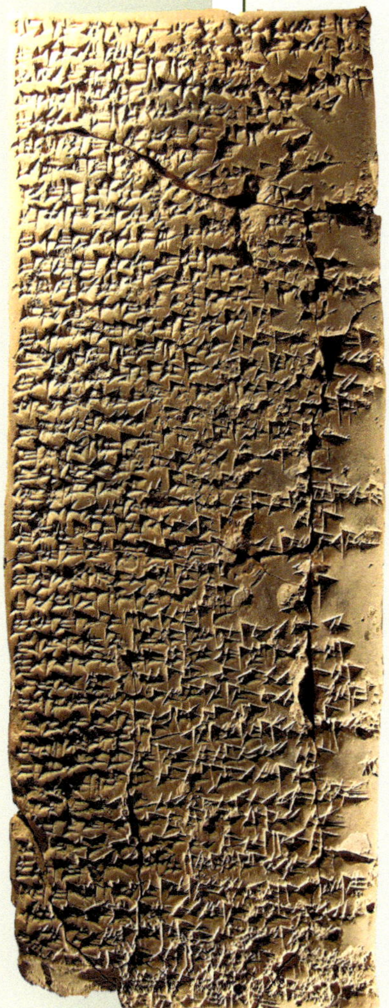

Tablet contains the first two of Gilgamesh's nightmares during the expedition to the cedar forest. Also includes Enkidu's explanations of them.
The Schøyen Collection MS 3025, Oslo and London

Dreams in the Ancient World

Dreams recorded in the ancient world tended to be of one of two types. *Message dreams* often involved theophanies that communicated a clear and simple message. They required no outside interpreter. The accounts available to us usually involve monarchs and serve one or more of four purposes: (1) to assure the recipient of the deity's presence and care; (2) to warn or offer counsel; (3) to foretell events in the future; and (4) to command the recipient to particular action.

The present account involves a *symbolic dream*, which occurs less frequently than message dreams. Symbolic dreams involve little if any dialogue; instead, the recipient witnesses a symbolic event that typically requires interpretation by an outsider after the person wakes up. In keeping with common human experience, the content of the dream in Judges 7:13 is quite absurd: a griddle cake (cf. Ezek. 4:12) of barley bread tumbles into the camp of the Midianites, smashing into the tent with such force that it overturns and collapses. This dream bears striking resemblances in form and content to the accounts of Gilgamesh's dreams in the Mesopotamian epic. The account of the first dream is preserved as follows:

> Gilgamesh rose to relate a dream, saying to his mother:
> "O mother, this is the dream I had in the night—
> "The stars of the heavens appeared above me,
> like a rock from the sky one fell down before me.
> I lifted it up, but it weighed too much for me,
> I tried to roll it, but I could not dislodge it.
> "The land of Uruk was standing around it,
> [the land was gathered] about it.
> A crowd [was milling about] before it,
> [the menfolk were] thronging around it.
> "[Like a babe-in]-arms they were kissing its feet,
> like a wife [I loved it,] caressed and embraced it.
> [I lifted it up,] set it down at your feet,
> [and you, O mother, you] made it my equal."
> [The mother of Gilgamesh] was clever and wise,
> well versed in everything, she said to her son;
> [Wild-Cow] Ninsun was clever and wise,
> well versed in everything, she said to Gilgamesh:
> "The stars of heaven [appeared] above you,
> [like a] rock from the sky one fell down before you.
> You lifted it up, but it weighed too much for you,
> you tried to roll it, but you could not dislodge it.
> "You lifted it up, set it down at my feet,
> and I, Ninsun, I made it your equal.
> Like a wife you loved it, caressed and embraced it:
> a mighty comrade will come to you,
> and be his friend's saviour.
> "Mightiest in the land, strength he possesses,
> his strength is as mighty as a rock from the sky.
> Like a wife you'll love him, caress and embrace him,
> he will be mighty, and often will save you."[A-62]

Hittite musician playing ram's horn in basalt bas-relief from Carchemish
Erich Lessing/Art Resource, NY

For the LORD and for Gideon (7:18). The truncated construction expresses the excitement of the moment[265] and contrasts with David's fuller comment as he faced Goliath, "It is not by sword or spear that the LORD saves; for the battle is the LORD's, and he will give all of you into our hands" (1 Sam. 17:47; cf. 2 Chron. 20:15). Interpreted positively, Gideon recognizes that the battle belongs to Yahweh, the Commander-in-Chief, and with the addition of his own name he may have recognized his role as Yahweh's deputy.[266]

The identical form has surfaced on a seventh-century B.C. inscription found in a side room of the sanctuary in Ekron: *lbʿl wlpdy* ("for Baal and for Padi").[267] Although Gideon's statement seems innocent, his conduct following this may suggest that the narrator understands this as an adaptation of a stock phrase, subtly hinting at Gideon's royal pretensions.[268]

Beth Shittah ... Zerarah ... Abel Meholah ... Tabbah (7:22). Beth Shittah means "house of acacia [wood]." The place has been identified with Shatta, 2.5 miles east of Harod (west of Beth Shan) and Tell Sleihat, east of the Jordan. Zererah is probably a variant spelling of Zeredah (1 Kings 11:26) and Zarethan (Josh. 3:16; 1 Kings 4:12), and is to be identified with Tell es-Saʿidiyah in the Jordan Valley. Abel Meholah, in the Jordan Valley west of the river, twelve miles south of Beth Shan, was the hometown of Elisha (1 Kings 19:16). Tabbath has been linked with Ras Abu Ṭabat on the Wadi Kufrinjeh, halfway between Succoth and Jabesh Gilead.[269]

Midianite leaders, Oreb and Zeeb (7:25). These animal names (Oreb means "raven"; Zeeb means "wolf") contribute to the image of the enemy's character and conduct in war.[270] The status of the men is represented by the term used earlier of Sisera, the captain of the forces of Jabin, king of Canaan (4:2). Following an ancient Near Eastern custom, the Ephraimites memorialize the victory over Midian by renaming the sites where they killed the commanders "the rock of Oreb" and "the winepress of Zeeb," respectively.

The Rise and Demise of Gideon (8:1–35)

Succoth (8:5). Succoth (meaning "booths") should not be confused with the first stopping place of the Israelites when they came out of Egypt (Ex. 12:37; Num. 33:5). This place is generally identified with Tell Deir ʿAllah in the Transjordan.[271] Archaeological evidence suggests that around 1200 B.C. the Late Bronze Age sacred place was destroyed in a massive fire. Thereafter the population appears to have been seminomadic, as evidenced by the redigging of old silo pits.[272]

Succoth was under Israelite control, having been taken from Sihon, king of Heshbon, and was allotted by Moses to the tribe of Gad (Josh. 13:27). But the ensuing dialogue indicates that the residents of this town were obviously suspicious of Gideon, indicating the tribal tensions within Israel in the late second millennium B.C.

Tell Deir Alla (Succoth)
Kim Walton

Zebah and Zalmunna (8:5). Zebah means "sacrifice," but Zalumma may be interpreted either as "shade withheld/shelter refused"[273] or "May [the god] Ṣalm protect."

Kings of Midian (8:5). Whereas in 7:24–25 Oreb and Zeeb were identified as "commanders," these men are identified as "kings." Since the Midianites are commonly thought to have been a seminomadic migratory desert tribe, we might have expected the narrator to identify them either as a *nāśî*ʾ ("chief") or *nāgîd* ("prince, ruler"). However, as noted in the comment on 6:1, the archaeological evidence of Qurayya in the Sinai points to a more sedentary community. Furthermore, the boundaries between the office of chieftain and king were often blurred, the critical factor apparently being the number and levels of bureaucratic officials involved in the administration of the society, that is, how far removed the ruler was from the common people.[274]

Do you already have the hands of Zebah and Zalmunna in your possession? (8:6).

Pile of hands given as evidence of defeated enemies. Medinet Habu
Manfred Näder, Gabana Studios, Germany

Penuel
Todd Bolen/www.BiblePlaces.com

The Hebrew translates literally, "Are the palms of Zeba and Zalmunna now in your hand?" which alludes to the ancient Near Eastern practice of cutting off the hands of captives,[275] taking these back to the base, and using them to tally the number of casualties in battle.

Desert thorns and briers (8:7). The first word, *qôṣîm*, is cognate to Akkadian *giṣṣu(m)* and seems to be a generic expression for thorny bushes.[276] The second, which occurs only here and in verse 16, is thought to identify a large bramble or thistle.[277] In 1 Chronicles 21:20 the verb *dûš* is used of Araunah beating grain on a threshing floor. Elsewhere it denotes "to thresh" in general (Deut. 25:4; Jer. 50:11; Amos 1:3; Mic. 4:13), a meaning consistent with cognates in other Semitic languages.[278] Presumably Gideon threatens to beat the "pulp" out of the people of Succoth the way one beats grain out of a sheaf of grain.

Peniel (8:8). Peniel/Penuel is identified with modern Tell edh-Dhahab esh-Shirqiyeh, five miles up the Wadi Jabbok from Succoth. This may be Pernoual in Shishak's list of conquered cities.[279] In Assyrian sources the site is called Panili.[280]

I will tear down this tower (8:9). Although no evidence of fortifications in Peniel have been found, the reference to a "tower" suggests that Succoth was a fortified town, a notion reinforced by the designation of her leaders as "officials, military commanders" (8:6).

Karkor (8:10). The article on this word suggests the Massoretes understood it as a common noun and should perhaps be translated "at the watering hole."[281] While the site cannot be located with certainty, it is likely on the Wadi Sirḥān, one hundred miles east of the Dead Sea, approaching the Midianite homeland.[282]

Fifteen thousand men ... a hundred and twenty thousand swordsmen (8:10). On these seemingly inordinately high numbers, see comment on 1:4.

The eastern peoples (8:10). On "sons of the east," see comment on 6:3.

Route of the nomads east of Nobah and Jogbehah (8:11). Although the exact location of Nobah is unknown, an identification with Kenath, which the Manassite Nobah renamed after himself (Num. 32:42), is

A model of the reconstructed mud-brick gate and towers of the Canaanite city of Laish (Dan)
Z. Radovan/www.BibleLandPictures.com

possible. Jogbehah is commonly identified with *Ruğm ʿal Gubēḥah* on an ancient caravan route northwest of Amman, where an Ammonite military tower has been discovered.[283] These were probably stopping places on a caravan route away from the main north-south trade routes.

Pass of Heres (8:13). Since Heres has the article, this may not be a specific mountain. Hebrew *ḥeres* means "sun." The location is unknown, but the Pass of Heres should not be confused with "Mount Heres" (1:35) and "Timnath Heres" (2:9).

The young man wrote down for him the names of the seventy-seven officials of Succoth (8:14). This statement is critical for our understanding of literacy in the ancient world. The young man probably wrote in the "Canaanite" alphabetic linear script, which had developed and diffused in the Levant during the previous four or five centuries. While many questions of the origins of the alphabet remain, the earliest known written records of communication with alphabetic pictographic script derive from Wadi el-Hol in Egypt. Scholars have dated these inscriptions to about 1850–1700 B.C.[284]

Tenth-century abecedary from Tel Zayit
Z. Radovan/www.BibleLandPictures.com

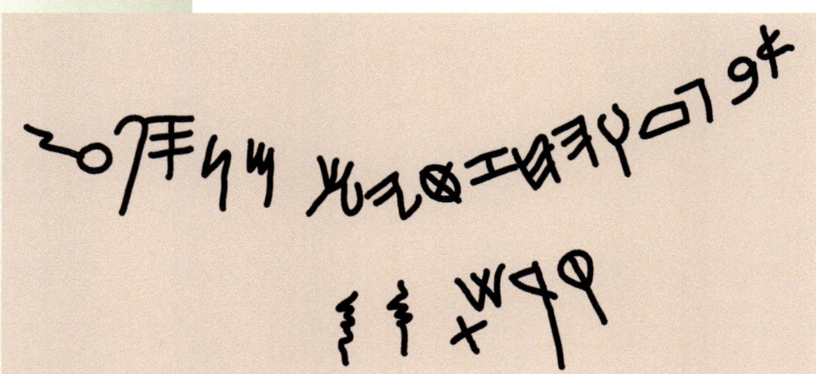

Among the most significant extrabiblical evidences for literacy in ancient Israel we may cite the tenth-century B.C. Gezer Calendar (see comment on 1:29), containing a summary list of the agricultural months,[285] the recently discovered tenth-century B.C. abecedary from Tel Zayit,[286] and the ostracon from Izbet Sarta, on which is inscribed an alphabet in Proto-Canaanite characters from the period of the judges.[287] In contrast to Egyptian hieroglyphics and Mesopotamian cuneiform, which took a lifetime to learn and guaranteed literacy for only a privileged few,[288] the reduction of the sounds of a culture to two dozen symbols opened up the possibility of widespread literacy. The person whom this text assumes to be literate is identified as a *naʿar,* which refers to a young man being trained for service as an elder.[289] The text

Pictured here is a Late Bronze crescent-shaped silver pendant from Tell el-Ajjul, though there is no indication this was for a camel.
Erich Lessing/ Art Resource, NY, courtesy of the Israel Museum (IDAM)

does not inform us on what he may have written their names. Presumably he used either ostraca (broken pieces of pottery) or tanned skins.[290]

Elders of the town (8:14). On the administration of tribes and towns by elders, see comment on 2:7.[291]

Tabor (8:18). On the location of Tabor see comment on 4:6. Because Tabor is totally out of the picture in the preceding narrative and because of its distance from Ophrah, the seat of the Abiezrite clan, some doubt the authenticity of this statement. However, since Tabor was not far from the camp of the Midianites on the northern side of the Valley of Harod (7:1), forays by their leaders to Tabor are not out of the question. Indeed, given its location, where the borders of Naphtali, Zebulun, and Issachar meet, atrocities like this may have galvanized these tribes behind Gideon (cf. 6:35). From verse 19 it seems that Gideon had stationed his own brothers at a strategic location to block the Midianites' retreat after their defeat.

He took the ornaments off the camels' necks (8:21). This scene closes with an image of a conqueror claiming the customary trophies of victory—the crescent ornaments, worn on the necks of "royal" camels. The significance of the crescent ornaments was linked with the moon god worshiped as Shahr in Old South Arabia.[292]

I will not rule over you (8:23). Although Gideon appears to reject the invitation to rule as king and establish a hereditary dynasty, by ancient Near Eastern standards all his actions hereafter are typical of kings. (1) He claims the lion's share of the booty from battle for himself (vv. 24, 26); (2) he claims the purple garments of the Midianite kings (v. 26); (3) he establishes a national cult center complete with divine image; (4) he is identified by patronymic (Jerub-Baal son of Joash) and "sits" on a throne in his house; (5) he establishes a large harem and fathers seventy sons; (6) he names his son Abimelech, which means "my father is king."[293]

Earrings (8:24). In the ancient Near East both men and women wore earrings. It is doubtful that the earrings in question here functioned simply as ornaments. Based on the study of earrings in the Old Testament and in the ancient Near East, Nili Fox has argued that the earrings involved in the accounts of Jacob's family gods (Gen. 35:1–7), the golden calf (Ex. 32:1–6), and the present story were not simply arbitrary items of jewelry.[294] Rather, they symbolized the relationship between the deity and the worshiper at several levels.

(1) Since deities are often portrayed with holes in their ears or as wearing earrings, they represented precious gifts from devotee to deity. (2) Analogous to piercing the ear of a slave who chose not to leave his master (Ex. 21:5–6; Deut. 15:16–17),

Statue of deity (El) with earring
Kim Walton, courtesy of the Oriental Institute Museum

the pierced ear symbolized the worshiper's devotion to the deity. (3) Attached to the organ of listening, the earrings reminded the devotee to be ever attentive to the voice of the deity. Like Aaron in Exodus 32, Gideon melts down the gold and uses this "sacred" metal to create new religious symbols.

Ishmaelites (8:24). In the ancient Near East ethnic designations were not always used with precision. According to Genesis 25:12, Ishmael was the (elder) son of Abraham by Hagar. However, this identification of Midianites as Ishmaelites (cf. also Gen. 37:27–28, 36) suggests that either the latter term could also be used of desert people [bedouins?] in general or the Midianite alliance extended beyond the Amalekites and the "sons of the east" mentioned earlier. If so, Zebah and Zalmunna may actually have belonged to the Ishmaelite branch of this alliance.

Weight of the gold rings he asked for came to seventeen hundred shekels (8:26). Calculated at .4046 ounces (11.33 grams) per shekel,[295] 1,700 shekels of gold amounts to 43 pounds. This is indeed a treasure fit for a king!

Ephod (8:27). The nature of this object is not clear. Elsewhere in the Old Testament "ephod" denotes the priest's special breastpiece (Ex. 28:15–30). In Judges 17:5 and 18:14–20 the same word refers to the priestly vestments of Micah. However, because this object was erected in Gideon's city and became an object of pagan worship, this meaning seems unlikely here.

The solution to this problem may be suggested by the Akkadian cognate *epattu*, which, in several old Assyrian texts, apparently refers to the costly garments that were worn by high officials and/or were draped over images of the gods.[296] The Old Assyrian word *epattu* is also to be associated with Hittite *ipantu*, the latter of which in at least one instance is construed with the preceding genitive of silver.[297] This suggests minimally that precious metals were used for the ephod's ornamentation, and maximally that the garment itself was made of precious metal fiber.

In the present context, the part stands for the whole; that is, the word "ephod" represents not only the garment that clothed a sacred image, but also the image over which the garment was draped and which became the object of worship. The narrator does not reveal the nature of the image, but most likely he has reconstructed the shrine to Baal, which he had earlier torn down at Yahweh's command (6:25–32).

Seventy sons (8:30). Seventy sounds like an idealized number, perhaps the number of a complete royal household. This number occurs not only in the Old Testament[298] but also in extrabiblical texts. In the eighth-century B.C. Aramaic inscription from Samal (Zincirli), Bar-rakib reports that Panamuwa had assassinated his father Barṣūr and seventy of his own brothers (see comment on 9:5).[299]

The author of Judges may also have seen Gideon's family as a reflection of the Canaanite pantheon. According to mythological texts discovered at Ras Shamra/Ugarit, the high god El and his wife Asherah had seventy sons.[300]

Abimelech (8:31). Three other characters—all non-Israelites—in the Old Testament bear the name Abimelech,[301] which is remarkable, especially in light of the repeated appearance of Abi-Milku, the mayor of Tyre, in the fourteenth-century B.C. El-Amarna correspondence between rulers in Canaan and the Egyptian pharaoh.[302]

Like many Semitic names, Abimelech is a sentence name, but Gideon's intentions in naming his son are not clear; several interpretations of the name are possible. (1) "Melek is my father." By this interpretation *mlk* is a proper divine name, related to Malik, a deity worshiped at Ebla (third millennium B.C.), Ugarit (second millennium B.C.), Phoenicia (first millennium B.C.),[303] and among the Ammonites (first millennium B.C.).[304] (2) "The [divine] king is my father."[305] By this interpretation, the divine king is Yahweh, which accords well with Gideon's statement

Ophrah, Tell Afula
Todd Bolen/www.BiblePlaces.com

in verse 23, but it flies in the face of Gideon's conduct. (3) "The king [Gideon] is my father." Under normal circumstances, a name like Abimelech would have reflected the faith of the person giving the name, and many who heard the name and knew Gideon would have seen in "Abimelech" evidence for Gideon's perception of his status in Israel.

His concubine, who lived in Shechem (8:31). Gideon's marriage to a concubine (see sidebar on "Concubines") reinforces the impression that he is behaving like a typical oriental king on two counts: She is added to an already large harem, and she is a Canaanite. The note that the woman lived in Shechem is significant on two counts. (1) Since marriages in the ancient Semitic world were generally patrilocal, it breaks the normal pattern of wives leaving their "father's houses" and joining the clan of their husbands. (2) By marrying a Shechemite Gideon seems either to be establishing a claim to this town or entering into a marriage alliance with the rulers of the town.[306]

Ancient Shechem is identified with modern Tell Balâtah, near Nablus, between Mounts Gerizim and Ebal. If Ophrah is identified with ʿAfulleh in the Jezreel valley (see comment on 6:11), then Gideon and his concubine lived between twenty-five and thirty miles apart. Shechem's significance in the second millennium is reflected not only by the role this place plays in the patriarchal narratives, but also by extrabiblical sources and in archaeological excavations.[307] The Amarna letters suggest that when Egyptian influence over Canaan waned, Labaʾyu, the ruler of Shechem (Shakmu in the letters), established control over a large area from Jezreel in the north almost to Jerusalem in the south.[308] By the time of Gideon, a power vacuum existed in Shechem, enabling Abimelech to rule the city for a short while.

Baal-Berith (8:33). This name, which occurs only here and in 9:4, translates literally as "Lord/Baal of the Covenant." But who is this divinity? To answer the question we must resolve two issues: the identity of Baal and the nature of the covenant. In view of the prominence of Baal in this book, this Baal is probably the Canaanite storm and warrior deity (see comment on 2:11).[309]

However, the issue is complicated by the reference to the Shechemite temple of El-Berith in 9:46. It is possible that Baal-Berith and El-Berith represent two separate deities, both of whom were worshiped in Shechem, but it is more likely that Baal and El were interchangeable designations for the same god. In Canaanite mythology El was the name of the supreme god, the husband of Asherah and father of seventy offspring, including Baal.[310] However, the word *baʿal* is not primarily a proper name but a title meaning "lord, master," and the

Amarna letter 252 from Labayu of Shechem
Todd Bolen/www.BiblePlaces.com

Wood statuette of Lady Touy, head of the harem of Min at Thebes
Réunion des Musées Nationaux/Art Resource, NY, courtesy of the Louvre

Concubines

In most contexts in the Old Testament, the concubine was considered a legal if second-ranked wife, subordinate to full-status wives (Gen. 16:2–3; 29:24, 29), and were more easily divorced (21:10–14). Concubines generally began as servants or slaves and were legally elevated to their status with the consent of the husband's full-status wife or wives, without bringing with them a dowry. Their purpose was either to provide offspring for the husband or simply to serve him as a contracted sexual partner.

The institution of concubinage is widely attested in the ancient Near East. Mesopotamian law permitted men to have sexual relations with slaves, but they could also acquire freeborn concubines, who were nevertheless subordinate to the primary wife. According to the Law Code of Hammurabi (CH §§146–147), if a slave-concubine causes stress in the home by making herself equal to the wife who had given her to her husband, the mistress could sell her into slavery to someone else. But an exception was provided for concubines who had borne a child to their husbands, in which case they could be reduced to the status of slave but could not be sold.[A-63]

Nineteenth-century B.C. texts from Cappadocia and mid-second millennium B.C. documents from Alalakh permit a man to marry a second wife if the first has not borne him a son within a specified time (three to seven years). The fourteenth-century B.C. texts from Ugarit refer to a man who had a concubine as "the owner of one who completes [the family]."[A-64]

In the ancient Near Eastern context, kings amassed large harems for several reasons. (1) Most obviously, a harem provided the king with unlimited opportunity to satisfy his sexual cravings with the most beautiful women in the kingdom. (2) Since marriages were often arranged to strengthen alliances with other states,[A-65] the harem enabled a king to be allied simultaneously with many outside rulers (cf. 1 Kings 11:1). (3) Just as the male members of a royal court served to reflect the glory and majesty of a king,[A-66] so the larger the harem and the more beautiful its members, the more impressed foreign visitors would be when they visited the king. In short, one main function of the harem was to enhance the status of the king among his international peers.

phrase *baʿal bᵉrît* could mean "lord of the covenant" rather than Baal-Berith.

Many understand El as the patron deity of Canaanite Shechem. This theory may be supported by the second part of the phrase, *berît* ("covenant, treaty"). In the expression some see an allusion to a political treaty between Shechem and some other Canaanite state, perhaps even Israel, in which El\Baal-Berith was invoked as the divine guardian and guarantor.[311] However, it is preferable to see in El/Baal-Berith an allusion to a treaty between Shechem and El that knit the deity and the population of the city in a special relationship, analogous to (but certainly different in many ways

Temple ruins at Shechem with ancient standing stone in front
Todd Bolen/www.BiblePlaces.com

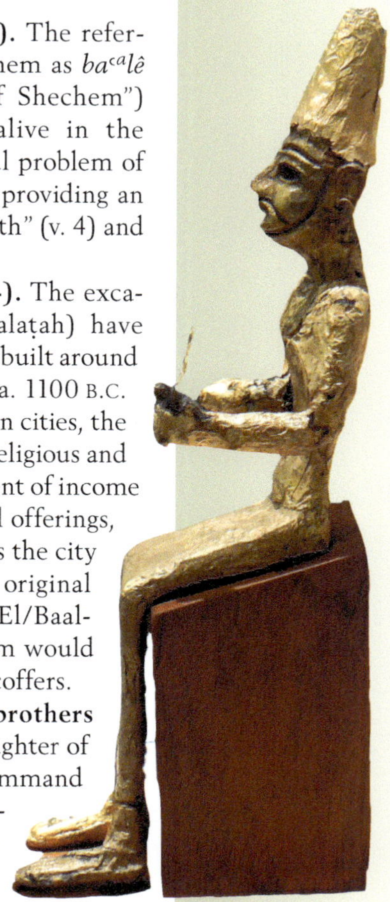

Image found at Megiddo, from the same time period, depicts El, and may be the same deity worshipped at Shechem.
Kim Walton, courtesy of the Oriental Institute Museum

from) Yahweh's covenant with Israel.[312] This probably explains why the residents of Shechem retreated to the temple of El-Berith for protection when they were in mortal danger (9:46).[313]

The Legacy of Gideon (9:1–57)

Abimelech son of Jerub-Baal (9:1). With its preoccupation with the machinations and violence of Abimelech and the Shechemites, this chapter reads like a page out of a Canaanite history notebook. In the Amarna correspondence (see comment on 8:31), the petty kings of the city-states in Canaan complain of the aggressive conduct of Labaʾyu of Shechem and his sons. If Abimelech's mother is from the ruling clan, his violent actions to regain control of the city become understandable.[314] However, since Abimelech also represents the new Israelite population, some may have considered him one of the SA.GAZ/ʿApiru, a designation found in the Amarna letters for troublesome segments of society accused of disloyalty, taking over cities, looting, and robbery.[315]

Citizens of Shechem (9:2). The reference to these leaders of Shechem as *baʿalê šekem* (lit., "lords/masters of Shechem") seems deliberate, keeping alive in the reader's mind the fundamental problem of Baalism on the one hand, and providing an assonantal link with "Baal-Berith" (v. 4) and "Jerub-Baal" on the other.

Temple of Baal-Berith (9:4). The excavations at Shechem (Tell Balaṭah) have revealed a large fortress temple built around 1600 B.C. that operated until ca. 1100 B.C. As in other ancient Near Eastern cities, the temple was the center of both religious and economic life, being the recipient of income of many kinds: vows, sacrificial offerings, gifts, penalties, and the like. As the city aristocracy (and heirs of the original makers of the covenant with El/Baal-Berith), the *baʿalîm* of Shechem would have had access to the temple coffers.

Murdered his seventy brothers (9:5). In contrast to Jehu's slaughter of Ahab's seventy sons at the command of Yahweh in 2 Kings 10, Abimelech's violent acts express

▸ Fables in the Ancient World

Judges 9:8–15 contains one of the finest examples of fables from the ancient world. By definition a fable is a short narrative in poetry or prose that teaches a moral lesson and involves creatures, plants, and/or inanimate objects speaking or behaving like human characters.[A-67] The best-known examples of ancient fables are found in the Greek collection associated with Aesop, but the ancient Semitic world has also produced several impressive examples.

The text bearing the closest resemblance to Jotham's fable is an entertaining ancient Babylonian text, The Dispute between the Tamarisk and the Date Palm, in which these two trees debate who is greater. Although this and several other texts bear some of the features of fables, they are better classified as debate literature.[A-68] Since the plot in Jotham's fable moves to a proper climax without any dispute, it seems to function as an antidispute parody of kingship, providing an ancient version of the adage that in politics the scum rises to the top.

raw personal ambition and bear a closer resemblance to Panamuwa's brutal seizure of power in the Cilician kingdom of Samal (Zincirli) as cited in the eighth-century B.C. Aramaic inscription of his son Bar-rakib: "And(?) he [Pananmuwa] destroyed(?) [ ] in the house of his father. And he killed his father Barṣūr; and he killed seventy brothers of his father."[316]

Shechem
RØHR Productions Ltd. Rohr Productions 'Holy Land Satellite Atlas'

All the citizens of Shechem and Beth Millo (9:6). The meaning of *bêt millôʾ* is uncertain. The most likely interpretation understands this as a massive platform made of earthen fill on which large urban structures such as temples or defensive towers (v. 46) were built.[317] In this case, since Beth Millo follows a reference to the "lords of Shechem," it may refer to the site where such decisions were made.[318] The role of the nobles of Shechem in the installation of Abimelech and in their independence of him later in the chapter suggests a level of democracy in the pre-Israelite town that seems exceptional in the broader context.[319]

The great tree at the pillar (9:6). Trees often marked sacred sites (see comments on 4:5 and 6:11). While the nature and significance of this "oak of the pillar" is unclear, the association of the tree with a "pil-

"Jotham's Pulpit" on Mount Gerizim facing Mount Ebal
Bible Scene Multimedia/Maurice Thompson

lar" suggests the tree shaded a propped up stone representing Baal in Canaanite cult installations. In Late Bronze Age Emar in Syria upright stones (*šikkānu*) functioned like figurines or statues of deities and symbolized the god's presence. Like the Hittite *ḫuwaši* stones, these were identified with a specific deity and could be erected either inside or outside the shrine.[320] The present shrine may have been located at a spring, perhaps the spring of Askar, just northeast of Tell Balata.[321] The location heightens the religious significance of the installation of Abimelech as king.[322]

Mount Gerizim (9:7). Mount Gerizim is identified with modern Jebel et-Tor on the south side of the Nablus Valley, which overlooked the city of Shechem from the south. Jotham issued his speech from the acoustically advantageous top of the mountain.[323]

Anoint a king for themselves (9:8). Through anointing with oil individuals were ritually consecrated[324] and conferred special power, authority, honor, and glory. There is no evidence for the anointing of kings in ancient Mesopotamia or in Egypt, but the ritual was practiced by the Hittites.[325]

Oil (9:9). The product of the olive is identified as *dešen* (lit., "fatness"), which serves as a synonym for *šemen*, the usual term for olive "oil." Olive oil was probably the most valuable agricultural product in the ancient world, used every day as cooking oil, medicine, a laxative, a lubricant, leather softener, fuel in lamps, and an ingredient in perfumes, as well as in sacred rituals as a sacrificial offering and in anointing ceremonies.

Wine (9:13). The vine highlights the value of its product by referring to its wine as *tîrôš* rather than the common word *yayin* (cf. 13:14). *Tîrôš* denotes the drink of grapes incompletely fermented and is cognate to the name of the god Tirshu/Tirash, attested in the El-Amarna letters and in Ugaritic (as *trt*).[326]

Thornbush (9:14). The word *ʾāṭād* denotes a species of buckthorn, usually equated with *lycium europaeum*.[327] However, not only is the word cognate to Akkadian *ed-de-tu*, which refers to a thorn-tree,

Christ thorn
Kim Walton, courtesy of the Eretz Israel Museum

but the present context also requires something larger—it gives a significant amount of shade and when it burns, it provides fuel for a great conflagration (vv. 15, 20). It is preferable, therefore, to equate this with Christ Thorn (*ziziphus spina-Christi*), a stately evergreen that grows to a height of thirty feet[328] and whose branches are armed with spines.[329]

Beth Millo (9:20). See comment on 9:6.

Beer (9:21). The site cannot be identified, and the word *b^{e}ʾēr* ("well") may be intended as a generic designation for an empty well where Jotham hid out for a long time, perhaps even until after Abimelech's death.[330]

Evil spirit (9:23). To understand the meaning of the phrase *rûaḥ rāʿâ*, two considerations must be borne in mind. First, the Hebrew word *rāʿâ* can have two meanings: moral malignancy and experiential misfortune. In this and other similar contexts,[331] the word is not to be interpreted in a moral sense, as if the Spirit of God were morally defective, but in the profane sense of "bad, unfavorable" as opposed to "good, favorable."

The activity attributed to the *rûaḥ* here comes dangerously close to the role played by demons in ancient Near Eastern thought. In general demons were perceived as agents of the gods, whose role was to execute divinely decreed blessings and punishments for sin, the latter usually by inflicting their victims with illnesses. In the first millennium B.C., however, demons came to be increasingly associated with the netherworld, which was thought to be populated by them.[332] This extrabiblical preoccupation with demons contrasts sharply with the picture in the Old Testament, which fails to develop a sophisticated demonology. Although in later Jewish magical texts *rûaḥ* came to be understood as "demon,"[333] in our passages its identity remains vague, but it is clearly subservient to Yahweh.

Gaal son of Ebed (9:26). The name Gaal (from *gāʿal*, "to loathe") looks suspiciously like a nickname, but it bears a striking assonantal resemblance to *gōʾēl* ("kinsman redeemer").[334] His patronymic, "son of Ebed," is an abbreviation for a common type of name in the Semitic world, *ʿebed*-DN, "servant of god X."[335] The behavior of this disenfranchised band of brothers is reminiscent of the the Ḫabiru, a class of disenfranchised social renegades in Palestine in the Late Bronze Age, who are portrayed in the Amarna letters as bandits in the hills, creating political instability for the rulers of the city-states.

Zebul (9:28). The name Zebul, which means "prince," recalls *zbl bʿl ʾrṣ* ("prince, lord of the netherworld"), an epithet of Baal in the Ugaritic mythological texts.[336]

Center of the land (9:37). This expression (*ṭabbûr hāʾāreṣ*), which occurs elsewhere in the Bible only in Ezekiel 38:12, has traditionally been interpreted as "navel of the earth."[337] The NIV's "center of the land" reflects a common modern interpretation, by which the reference must be to Mount Gerizim overlooking Shechem, which some contend was considered by the Canaanites as the navel, viz., center of the land of Canaan.[338] However, although *ṭabbûr* is used of the umbilical cord in Mishnaic Hebrew and later Aramaic, biblical Hebrew

Mount Gerizim
Z. Radovan/www.BibleLandPictures.com

refers to the "navel" or "umbilical cord" with *šōr* (Prov. 3:8; Song 7:3; Ezek. 16:4).

Furthermore, the needs of the present context are met perfectly if *ṭabbûr* is interpreted simply as "elevated ground."[339] This interpretation also suits Ezekiel 38:12, where its juxtaposition with "unwalled villages" points to some safe and secure location. Thus, the phrase *ṭabbûr hāʾāreṣ* is best interpreted as an elevated plateau without external fortifications.

Soothsayers' tree (9:37). This tree (see comment on 4:11) seems to have marked a sacred spot, perhaps to which the Canaanites of the region resorted for a decision from the gods. Its precise location cannot be determined.

Arumah (9:41). Arumah is generally identified with Jebel el-ʿUrmah, five miles southeast of Shechem.[340]

Entrance to the city gate (9:44). Normally we think of gates as entrances to a town. However in ancient Israel gates were complex structures, often involving defensive towers and two or three guardrooms on each side.

He destroyed the city and scattered salt over it (9:45). The significance of salting the conquered site is not clear. See sidebar on "The Scattering of Salt on Shechem."

Stronghold of the temple of El-Berith (9:46). Although there are many questions about the "tower of Shechem" and the "stronghold of the temple of El-Berith," excavations at Shechem may have yielded the foundations of what was probably the temple fortress referred to here.[341] This two-story structure was huge by Canaanite standards, measuring 70 feet wide and 86 feet long, easily large enough for 1,000 people to huddle inside. It is evident from the ruins that a massive fire destroyed the temple. Although the original excavators dated this destruction to the Middle Bronze Age,[342] recent analyses of the data suggest it was razed in the period of the judges and should be identified with the temple fortress involved in what is described here.[343]

Mount Zalmon (9:48). The identity and location of this "mountain of deep darkness" remains a mystery. This could be another designation for Ebal or Gerizim.

Thebez (9:50). The location of Thebez is uncertain, though it was probably a satellite town near Shechem.[344] It is possibly Tubas, thirteen miles northeast of Shechem.[345]

Upper millstone (9:53). Most likely this does not refer to the large upper stone of a rotary quern at the mill, which came into general use in the Iron Age. Rather, we should imagine the smaller round muller used to grind grain spread out on a larger slightly concaved bottom stone. Kneeling in front of the quern, the grinder poured some grain into the bottom stone and then pulverized it by moving the upper stone back and forth over the grain.

Millstones were usually made of basalt.[346] Within the household grinding grain usually fell to women, which added to the insult of forcing prisoners to grind grain (cf. 16:21). In the present instance, this resourceful woman transformed an ordinary utensil into a lethal weapon.

The Scattering of Salt on Shechem

Deeds of Anitta
Istanbul Archaeological Museum; © Dr. James C. Martin

Some have suggested that since salt renders a land infertile, by spreading salt on a city a conqueror may be guaranteeing that it would never rise again. But this gesture is also perhaps illuminated by extrabiblical texts.[A-69] Several Assyrian conquest reports follow announcements of the destruction of a city with declarations that the conqueror strewed a substance over the ruins. In the description of Tiglath-pileser I's capture of Ḫanusa he boasts, "The entire city I razed, destroyed, turned into a ruin hill and strewed *ṣipu*-stones over it."[A-70] After this statement Tiglath-pileser I declares that he constructed a monument inscribed with a warning never to occupy the city again or to rebuild its walls.

In several records of his campaigns against Elam, Ashurbanipal speaks of laying waste the land and scattering salt (*tabtu*) and cress (*saḫlu*) over it.[A-71]

An eighth-century B.C. Aramaic inscription that records the treaty between Bar-gaʾyah, king of KTK, and Matiʿel, king of Arpad, explicitly links scattering salt over a destroyed city with curses for violating an agreement:

> Just as wax is burned by fire, so may Arpad be burned and [her gr]eat [daughter-cities] May Hadad [the storm god] sow in them salt [*mlḥ*, the same word as in our text] and weeds(?), and may it not be mentioned (again)![A-72]

This also occurs in a Hittite annalistic text from about 1300 B.C., which summarizes the conquest of Ḫattuša by Anitta, king of Kuššara, as follows: "I took it by storm. On its site I so[wed] cress." This notice is followed by a curse: "Whoever shall become king after me and shall settle Ḫattuša again [may] the Storm-god of heaven strike him!"[A-73] The curses of a Hittite treaty text between Shattiwaza of Mittani and Suppiluliuma I of Hatti also associate salt with barrenness:

> As salt has no seed, let me, Shattiwaza, together with any other wife whom I might take, and the Hurrians, together with our lands, our wives, and our sons, like salt indeed have no progeny. Like a (dissolved) lump of salt let us not return to our place.[A-74]

It seems best, therefore, to interpret Abimelech's scattering salt over Shechem as a nonverbal gesture, equivalent to the curse Yahweh pronounced on Jericho through Joshua.[A-75]

Baal Berith temple at Shechem
Todd Bolen/www.BiblePlaces.com

Parenthesis 2: The Governorships of Tola and Jair (10:1–5)

Shamir (10:2). The location of Shamir is unknown. An identification with Samaria is tempting but unlikely.[347]

Jair of Gilead (10:3). The exact location of Jair's territory is unknown. As a geographic designation, "Gilead" refers to the rugged mountain range east of the Jordan River, bounded to the north by the Yarmuk River and to the south by Wadi Hesban.

Thirty sons, who rode on thirty donkeys (10:4). Thirty sons suggest a multiplicity of wives, which suggests Jair may have functioned as a major chieftain or a minor monarch.[348] This interpretation is reinforced by the observation that each son owned one of the thirty villages that made up the "villages of Jair" (Havvoth Jair). Interpreted sociopolitically, the territory governed by Jair seems to have consisted of a confederacy of thirty cities.

The significance of the donkeys is not clear, though the narrator's designation of these as *ʿayir* rather than *ḥ^{a}môr* highlights their function as riding rather than pack animals. The prestige associated with owning asses is reflected in the Song of Deborah (5:10) and in extrabiblical writings. Several centuries earlier a palace official had written King Zimri-Lim of Mari:

Millstones
Z. Radovan/www.BibleLandPictures.com

> [If] you are the king of the Ḫaneans, you are, moreover, a "king of the Akkadians." [My lord] should not ride horses (that is, in tribal fashion). May my lord drive in a wagon and mules (that is, in a "civilized manner"), and may he (thus) honor his royalty.[349]

Beem suggests that to describe each son as riding on his own donkey is like saying each son was given his own Porsche.[350]

Kamon (10:5). Kamon is probably to be identified with Qamm/Qumeim, halfway between the Sea of Galilee and Ramoth Gilead.[351]

The Ammonite and Jephthah Cycle (10:6–12:7)

The Baals and the Ashtoreths, and the gods of Aram ... Sidon ... Moab ... the Ammonites ... the Philistines (10:6). Interpreted within the ancient Near Eastern context the sevenfold catalogue of foreign divinities reflects the intensity of Israel's degradation. The first two entries in the list may be viewed as a general heading for the list or a specific reference to the gods of the Canaanites. In either case the plurals, "Baals" and "Ashtoreths," represent local manifestations of the male and female fertility divinities.

Philistines (10:7). See comments on 3:3, 31.

We have sinned against you, forsaking our God and serving the Baals (10:10). This confession of sin arises out of the distress caused by the Israelites' defeat at the hands of the Ammonites (v. 9). The conviction of this distress as representing divine punishment for sin would be at home among most ancient Near Eastern peoples.

But the cause of the anger is distinctively Israelite. Whereas orthodox Yahwism demanded exclusive devotion to Yahweh (Deut. 6:4–5), pagan divinities did not take great offense at their devotees worshiping other gods. Indeed, in one of his plague prayers, Mursili II pleads with the Storm God and expressly declares his attention to all the gods: "When I celebrated the festivals, I busied myself for all the gods. I did not pick out any single temple."[352] The "plague prayers" of Mursili II, who reigned over the Hittites at the end of the fourteenth century B.C., contain the most moving confessions of sin known

Shamash-res-usur, governor of Mari, and Suhi worshiping before the gods
Todd Bolen/www.BiblePlaces.com

from the ancient world outside the Old Testament.[353]

Mizpah (10:17). This Mizpah, located in Gilead, is not to be confused with the Benjamite town of the same name in chapters 19–21. The location is unknown.

Prostitute (11:1). In the ancient world, women often resorted to prostitution if they had no other means of economic support, especially if they were widows or orphans.[354] Many prostitutes offered their services at cult centers.[355] However, Jephthah also illustrates the plight of the children of prostitutes in the ancient Near East. Without legal attachment to the head of a household, they were generally denied inheritance of property and social standing within the community and thus forced into a life of brigandage simply to survive.

Land of Tob (11:3). The location of Tob is uncertain, though the present context suggests a sparsely populated district north of the Jabbok.

Group of adventurers (11:3). This rendering of a Hebrew phrase (lit., "empty men") misses the narrator's intentionally negative evaluation of these men. We can compare these men with the SA.GAZ/ʿApiru mentioned frequently in the Amarna letters[356] and found throughout the ancient world. According to Carol Redmount:

> The Apiru had no common ethnic affiliations, they spoke no common language, and they normally led a marginal and sometimes lawless existence on the fringes of settled society. The Apiru constituted, in effect, a loosely defined, inferior social class composed of shifting and shifty population elements without secure ties to settled communities. Apiru are frequently encountered in the texts as outlaws, mercenaries, and slaves.[357]

He repeated all his words before the LORD in Mizpah (11:11). In solemnizing the agreement between Jephthah and the leaders of Gilead at the sanctuary in the presence of Yahweh, the parties to this contract follow regular ancient Near Eastern custom. Deities were invoked as witnesses to agreements and as guarantors of the fidelity of the parties.

Jephthah sent messengers to the Ammonite king (11:12). Jephthah acts remarkably king-like, dispatching envoys negotiating directly with the king of the Ammonites, dealing with the conflicting issues as if they were personal between him and the Ammonite king, and claiming the land as his own. With reference to style and form, Jephthah's speech (delivered by the envoys) is formal and conventional, incorporating many features of the ancient Near Eastesrn *rîb* or lawsuit genre. R. O'Connell has recognized the following conventional features:[358]

(1) A declaration of obligations/rhetorical interrogation (by Jepththah, vv. 12b, 23, 25–26);
(2) A declaration of violations (by the Ammonite king, v. 13a);
(3) A declaration of culpability (by Jephthah, v. 27a);
(4) A declaration of covenant innocence by Jephthah in two parts:
  (a) Initiation of the covenant/status quo (vv. 15b–16a, 21);
  (b) Loyalty to the covenant/status quo (vv. 16b–21a);
(5) A declaration of the right to vindication (by Jephthah, v. 24);
(6) An ultimatum consisting of a summons to trial by combat (by Jephthah, v. 27b);
(7) An appeal, declaring the terms of reinstatement/reparations (by the Ammonite king, v. 13b).

Ammonite king (11:12). The identity of the king is unknown. This may have been the predecessor to Nahash (ca. 1030–1000 B.C.), the first Ammonite king identifiable by name, who appears in 1 Samuel 11:1–13; 12:12; 2 Samuel 10:2. Based on the biblical and extrabiblical evidence, eleven Ammonite kings can now be identified.[359]

Wadi es_Sir between Arnon and Jabbok Rivers
Todd Bolen/www.BiblePlaces.com

They took away my land from the Arnon to the Jabbok (11:13). The Ammonite king accuses the Israelites of robbing him of the territory between the Arnon and Jabbok tributaries of the Jordan (modern Wadi Mugîb and Wadi Ez-Zarqa respectively). Their territorial claims are understandable when we recognize that the Ammonite heartland consisted of an amorphous region, without distinct geographic boundaries between the desert to the east and the hills of Gilead in the west.[360]

Arnon to Jabbok Region

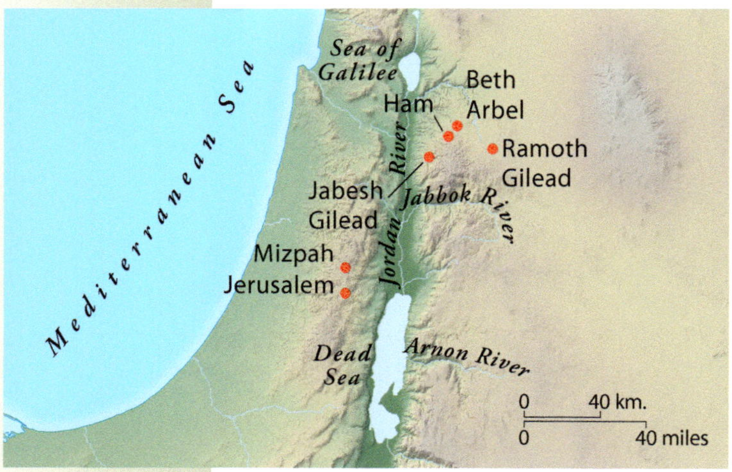

This is what Jephthah says (11:15). Typical of ancient Near Eastern style, Jephthah's envoys begin their speech to the Ammonite king with the "citation formula": *kōh ʾāmar* PN ("Thus has PN declared"), in which PN identifies the source of the speech (v. 15a). This formula highlights the speaker's heraldic role, and the first person style of the speech that follows casts the address as the very words of the one who sent him, that is, Jephthah.[361]

Kadesh (11:16). The site is Ein el-Qudeirât, the place from which the Israelite scouts were originally sent on their reconnaissance mission of the Promised Land, but the nation refused to enter (Num. 11–14).

The lands of Edom and Moab ... the territory of Moab (11:18). Whereas the former expression uses "the land of Moab," the latter speaks of "the boundary of Moab." Although the eastern border of Moab was ill-defined, the southern and northern borders were marked by Wadi Zered (Wadi al-Ḥesa) and the Wadi Hasban respectively. The deep Arnon Gorge/River, leading to the Dead Sea, divided this territory into two halves.

Moab

Numbers 21:13 and Deuteronomy 2:24 suggest the Arnon River (Wadi al-Mujib) separated Moab from the territory of Sihon the Amorite king who ruled in Heshbon, but before long the demographic, economic, and political power was concentrated in the northern segment (Mishor).[362]

Sihon king of the Amorites, who ruled in Heshbon (11:19). Heshbon is identified with modern Tell Hesban in Jordan, about thirteen miles southwest of Amman.[363]

Jahaz (11:20). According to Joshua 13:18, Jahaz was allocated to Reuben, which suggests it was within Sihon's, rather than Moabite, territory (cf. Num. 21:13; Deut. 2:24).[364] Although Mishor was probably in Moabite hands for most of the following four or five centuries, according to the ninth-century B.C. inscription of Mesha, king of Moab, the Israelites had fortified Jahaz (*yhṣ*) as an outpost against Mesha, but Mesha captured the site and annexed it to the region associated with Dibon. The location of Jahaz is not known. However, it was likely near Dibon (modern Dhiban), forty miles south of Amman, Jordan, and two miles north of the Arnon River.[365]

Will you not take what your god Chemosh gives you? (11:24). The ninth-century B.C. Mesha Inscription illuminates this comment on two counts. First, Mesha's perspective on the role of deities in determining who rules over specific territories is much like that of Jephthah, who claims in verse 21 that Yahweh, the God of Israel, gave Sihon into Israel's hands. In lines 14–15, Mesha's scribe writes (on his behalf): "Kemosh said to me: 'Go take Nebo from Israel!' And I went in the night, and I fought against it from the break of dawn until noon."[366]

Second, Jephthah refers to the deity involved in the present territorial debate as Chemosh. Chemosh is well attested in extrabiblical texts, not only in the Mesha Inscription but also in documents as early as the third millennium

Heshbon (Hesban) ruins
Bible Scene Multimedia/Maurice Thompson

Stele found at Shihan portrays a warrior deity that some believe is a depiction of Chemosh.
Marie-Lan Nguyen/Wikimedia Commons, courtesy of the Louvre

tablets from Ebla, in northern Syria (^{d}*Kà-mi-iš*), in the twelfth-century B.C. texts from Ugarit (*kmt*), and in the first millennium Neo-Assyrian texts (^{d}*Ka-am-muš*). The problem with Jephthah's comment is that as a national deity, Chemosh was not the god of the Ammonites but the patron deity of Moab. This is confirmed not only by the Mesha Inscription, but also by a series of personal names that scholars generally recognize to be Moabite.[367] The patron status of Milcom is reflected also in a recently discovered seal from Tell El ʿUmeiri, bearing the inscription *lmlkm-ʾwr ʿbd bʿl-yšʿ* ("belonging to Milkom-ʿur, servant of Baal-yashaʿ").[368] The name Milkom-ʿur means "Milkom is light."

Three hundred years (11:26). Scholars who defend an early (fifteenth century B.C.) date for the Exodus generally treat the number literally, claiming this figure and 1 Kings 6:1 as the primary evidence for their position.[369] However, since Jephthah is mistaken in other details (Chemosh for Milkom) and since this is a political speech, one should perhaps not take him seriously on this point. A figure such as three hundred years was intended to make an impression on the Ammonites. However it is interpreted, it finds an approximate analogue in the Mesha Inscription referred to earlier. Line 10 asserts, "And the men of Gad lived in the land of Ataroth from ancient times."[370]

Jephthah made a vow to the LORD (11:30). Analogues to Jephthah's vow are found in both biblical[371] and extrabiblical texts. People uttered such vows when they were anxious about issues like a safe return from a journey, a need for a military victory, or a desire for children. Roughly contemporary texts from Ugarit recount Kirta's votive expression of his anxiety regarding his long journey to procure Huraya as his wife. Arriving at the shrine of Asherah of Tyre, also identified as the goddess of Sidon,

Four-room house at Tell Qasile
Kim Walton, courtesy of the Eretz Israel Museum

Ugaritic Vow	Hittite Vow	Jephthah's Vow
As Asherah of Tyrians lives, The Goddess of the Sidonians	Lelwanis, my lady,	[O Yahweh]
If I take Huraya into my palace, And have the girl enter my court,	If you relay the good (word) to the gods, grant life to your servant Hattusilis, (and) give him long years, months (and) days,	If you give the Ammonites into my hands,
Her two parts I'll make silver, Her third part I'll make gold.[A-76]	then I will go (and) make for Lelwanis, my lady, a silver statue of Hattusilis— as tall as Hattusilis himself, with its head, its hands (and) its feet of gold— moreover I will hang it (with ornaments).[A-77]	whatever comes out of the door of my house to meet me when I return in triumph from the Ammonites will be Yahweh's, and I will sacrifice it as a burnt offering.

Kirta the Noble makes a vow (*ndr*). From approximately the same time we also have a vow by a Hittite queen Puduhepas, anxious about the health of her husband. The resemblance between the form of these vows and that of Jephthah is striking, as the following synopsis illustrates (see chart).

Jephthah's vow is as vague as Kirta's, and undoubtedly for him this vow was an expression of piety adding force to a prayer by making a contract with God.[372]

Whatever comes out of the door of my house (11:31). Although we might find it strange for Jephthah to speak of a sheep or calf coming out of his house, the word "house" refers to a complex domestic structure known as the four-room house, which included rooms for the animals. However, since livestock do not usually greet a person returning from a journey, Jephthah's promise expresses a readiness to sacrifice a member of his own family.

Twenty towns from Aroer to the vicinity of Minnith, as far as Abel Keramim (11:33). Aroer is best linked with "Aroer, near Rabbah" (Josh. 13:25); it is located southwest of modern Amman.[373] Minnith has not been identified with certainty, but a location between Amman and Heshbon is reasonable.[374] Abel Keramim ("pasture of vineyards") should probably be equated with Abila, located by Eusebius (*Onomastica* 32.14–25) six Roman leagues from Amman.[375] Since the territory of the Ammonites lacked clear geographical boundaries, these three sites, together with the rest of the twenty "towns," performed an important function in defining the border between Israelite and Ammonite land.

Tambourines (11:34). This word refers to a variety of hand-held percussion instruments often associated with dancing; the musicians were usually female.[376] Unlike modern tambourines, the instruments did not have metal jingles on the sides, but consisted of a circular wood frame about ten inches in diameter, over which was stretched a piece of goatskin leather. In contrast to the *šôpār*, tambourines were used in combination with other instruments (2 Sam. 6:5), though it is never mentioned in connection with music in the temple.[377]

She was an only child (11:34). This emphatic statement heightens the crisis that the appearance of Jephthah's daughter creates for him, for he realizes that if he does with her as he has vowed, he not only sacrifices his daughter but also himself. In the ancient world people were thought to live on through their children. Accordingly, the worst fate one could experience was to have one's "seed" cut off and "name" destroyed from one's father's household.[378]

Terra cotta figure with tambourine
Z. Radovan/www.BibleLand Pictures.com

Musical procession of women and rows of soldiers from tomb at Saqqara
Werner Forman Archive/Egyptian Museum, Cairo

This conviction is also expressed in extrabiblical texts, such as in Esarhaddon's treaty with his vassals. While this document makes frequent reference to destroying the enemies' seed,[379] the repetition of this motif in the covenant curses is especially striking:

> May Zarpanitu, who grants name and seed, destroy your name and your seed from the land (§45; l. 435).
> May Girra, who gives food to small and great, burn up your name and your seed (§62; l. 524).
> Just as a mule has not offspring, may your name, your seed, and the seed of your sons and daughters disappear from the land (§66; l. 537).
> May Nabu, bearer of the tablet of fates of the gods, erase your name, and destroy your seed from the land (§105; l. 660).[380]

He did to her as he had vowed (11:39). The statement should be interpreted in the light of the Canaanized Israelite society and culture to which Jephthah belonged. In 10:6 the narrator testifies that at this time the Israelites worshiped Milkom, the Ammonite god, and Chemosh, the god of the Moabites, whose leaders are known to have sacrificed children on occasion (2 Kings 3:27).[381] Jephthah's motives and the form of his vow bear a striking resemblance to many vows inscribed in funerary monuments in Carthage by Punic descendants of the Canaanites/Phoenicians in northern Africa. The following votive inscription is typical:

> To our lady, to Tanit, the face of Baᶜal and to our lord, to Baᶜal Hammon that which was vowed (by) PN son of PN, son of PN because he [the deity] heard his [the dedicant's] voice and blessed him.[382]

For these people vows to sacrifice children were not rash or impulsive, but deadly serious expressions of devotion.

The symbol shown here represents Tanit and urns are usually found buried under stela.
BishkekRocks/Wikimedia Commons

Scholars have long noted the thematic links between this short episode and several stories from ancient writings. Idomenaeus, a king of Crete, was caught in a shipwreck and made a vow to sacrifice to Neptune the first person to come out to meet him should he return safely.[383] Cited more often is the Greek legend of the daughter of Agamemnon, Iphegenia, which appears in many variations. Particularly tantalizing is a Euripidean version that has Agamemnon vowing to sacrifice to Artemis the most beautiful creature born that year within his kingdom. When that creature turns out to be his daughter he wavers, until the prophet Calchas declares to him that a fleet of ships that has been grounded for weeks in Aulis will be released by a favorable wind only if and when he complies. The speech of Calchas reads as follows:

> Agamemnon, Captain of Hellas, there can be no way of setting your ships free, till the offering you promised Artemis is given to her. You had vowed to render her in sacrifice the loveliest thing each year should bear. You have owed long since the loveliness which Clytemnestra had borne to you, your daughter, Iphegenia. Summon your daughter now and keep your word.[384]

However, at the last moment Artemis provides a hind as a substitute and carries the young girl off to the region of the Taurians in the Crimea and makes her a priestess.[385]

Zaphon (12:1). The site is probably to be identified with Tell es-Saᶜidiye, seventeen miles south-southeast of Beth Shan, just across the Jordan River.[386]

Fords of the Jordan (12:5). See comment on 3:28.

Shibboleth ... sibboleth (12:6). The Gileadites plan to identify Ephraimites involves a dialectical *shin/samek* contrast. The origin of the variation is not clear, though the issue seems to be phonetic rather than phonemic. This is probably not a case of divergent development of sibilants in Gileadite and Ephraimite dialects of Hebrew,[387] but simply a case of differentiation in the pronunciation of the same sibilant in these regions.[388] To the Gileadites, the Ephraimite pronunciation of *shin* sounded exactly like a *samek*. Accordingly, whenever the Gileadites demanded an Ephraimite to say "Shibboleth," he would have betrayed his origin by saying "Sibboleth."

Tell es-Saidiyeh (Zaphon)
Todd Bolen/www.BiblePlaces.com

Extrabiblical evidence for the persistence of this phenomenon is provided by a sixth-century B.C. Ammonite seal found at Tell el-ᶜUmeiri bearing the inscription, "[belonging] to Milkom-ᶜûr, servant of Baᶜalyšaᶜ." Scholars are agreed that the Baᶜalyšaᶜ named here is to be identified with Baᶜalis referred to in Jeremiah 40:14. As in our text, the latter spelling reflects the way a Cisjordanian speaker would have heard and reproduced the Transjordanian *shin*.

Forty-two thousand Ephraimites were killed (12:6). On the seemingly inordinately high numbers, see comment on 1:4. This event reflects and reinforces the significance of the Jordan River as a geographical and psychological barrier between eastern and western Israelites.

Parenthesis 3: The Governorships of Ibzan, Elon, and Abdon (12:8–15)

Thirty sons and thirty daughters (12:9). On the number of children, see comment on 10:4. Ibzan gave his daughters away in marriage to those outside his clan, and for his sons he brought in thirty young women as wives from outside his clan (12:9). Sending his daughters away reflects the patrilocal pattern of marriage. These marriages probably cemented clan alliances and extended the scope of his political influence. At the same time, Ibzan's initiative in all of these marriages arose out of a concern to build a community with sound foundations.

A parallel to this kind of family is recounted in a second millennium B.C. Hittite text, in which the Queen of Kanish gives birth to thirty sons in a single year. Overwhelmed with this horde, she places them in baskets and sends them down the river to the land of Zalpuwa. The gods rescue them and raise them to adulthood. Later the queen gives birth to thirty daughters, but these she keeps. In time the sons return "driving a donkey," and, except for divine intervention and quick thinking,

Fords at Adam with Jordan running across lower part of picture just above the road
Todd Bolen/www.BiblePlaces.com

In this aerial of the Sorek Valley, Eshtaol is located in the bare patch among the trees at the far right side of the forested hill. Zorah is at the left end of the same hill.
Todd Bolen/www.BiblePlaces.com

they would have married their own sisters.[389]

Abdon son of Hillel, from Pirathon (12:13–15). Pirathon is probably modern Farata, six miles west-southwest of Shechem.[390] The location of this town in Ephraim is problematic, since the brook Kanah several miles south of Pirathon formed the boundary between the territories allotted to Manasseh and Ephraim (Josh. 17:7–9). Either the boundaries were not firmly fixed at this time, or the term Ephraim is being used loosely for the hill country south of the Wadi Fariʿa.

Seventy donkeys (12:14). On the significance of this comment, see comment on 10:4.

The Birth of Samson (13:1–25)

Philistines (13:1). On the Philistines, see comments on 3:3, 31.

Zorah (13:2). Zorah is to be identified with modern Sarʿa (Tel Zorʿa), a small Israelite town on the north side of the fertile Sorek Valley, a couple of miles north of Beth Shemesh. The Amarna letters (EA 273) name Zorah (Ṣarha) as one of the towns belonging to the king of Gezer being attacked by the ʿApiru.[391] According to the tribal allotments described in Joshua, Zorah fell within the territories of both Judah (15:33) and Dan (19:41), probably because

Sorek Valley

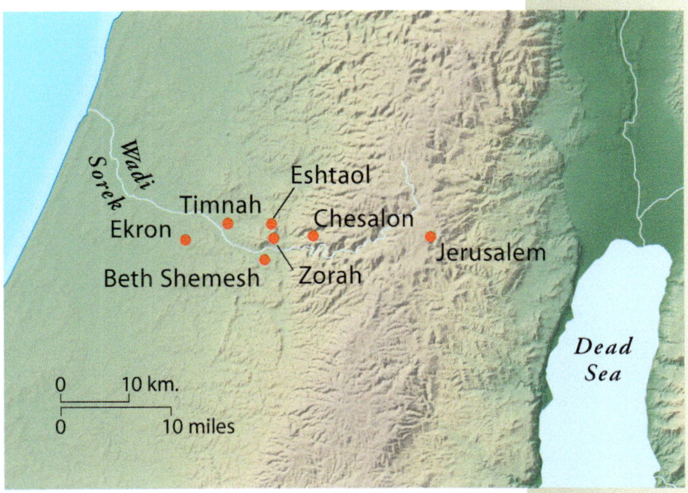

This fertility figurine shows two children reaching toward the breasts. On the thighs are the fertility images of caprids by trees. The presumed goddess pictured holds open her vulva for delivery. In Israel God is the one who opens the womb and gives children to the barren.
Dr. James C. Martin, courtesy of the Israel Museum

the town was located on the Wadi Sorek, the boundary between Judah and Dan. Accordingly, territory associated with the town would have been located on both sides of the wadi (cf. Josh. 15:10–11; 19:40–48). The Hebrew construction, "a certain man from Zorah" rather than "a certain man of Zorah," may suggest that Manoah had moved out of the town and settled in a more felicitous location up the valley toward Eshtaol.[392]

[He] had a wife who was sterile and remained childless (13:2). As Jephthah's future was cut off at the back end because he sacrificed his daughter, Manoah's and his wife's future was cut off at the front end because she was barren. The problem of childlessness and divine involvement in overcoming it plays an important role, not only in biblical narratives[393] but also in extrabiblical texts.

Whereas the present account involves an ordinary man and his wife, in the Ugaritic Legend of Kirta, the death of the hero's wife and all his children by her creates a serious crisis for the royal line, requiring the intervention of El.[394] In ancient Mesopotamia infertility was considered a serious problem. According to the Law Code of Hammurabi, barrenness was considered valid grounds for divorce (CH §138). If infertility was linked with a physical disease, her husband could opt to marry another woman, though he could not divorce her for this reason and had to support her all her life (CH §148).[395]

We do not know what steps Manoah and his wife may have taken to overcome her barrenness. A magical text from Mesopotamia prescribes a remedy for this malady: "Total: 21 stones to help a barren woman become pregnant; you string them on a linen thread and put them around your neck."[396] However, the ancients recognized that failure to have children was not only a female problem. A Middle Hittite text suggests that the cure for male impotence and sexual arousal was incantations, eating ritual meals, and sleeping in front of a table laden with offerings for a goddess.[397]

Angel of the LORD (13:3). On *mal'ak yhwh* as an authorized messenger from the court of heaven, see comment on 2:1.

You are going to conceive and have a son (13:3). Whereas in this case a messenger announces to Manoah's barren wife that she will bear a son (see sidebar on "The Importance of a Son"), in the Kirta Epic. El announces to Kirta in a dream that he must first get a new wife. To King Pabuli Kirta says:

> You must give me Lady Huraya,
> The Fair One, your firstborn child!
> . . . .
> Whom El has given in my dream,
> The Father of Man in my vision;
> Who will bear a child for Kirta,
> A lad for the Servant of El.[398]

Do not eat anything unclean (13:4). The Israelite regulations concerning clean and unclean food are found in Leviticus 11 and Deuteronomy 14. The notion of food taboos is not unique to Israel. In the Akkadian Prayer to Every God, the supplicant complains:

> The sin which I have done, indeed I do not know.
> The forbidden thing which I have eaten, indeed I do not know.
> The prohibited (place) on which I have set foot, indeed I do not know.[399]

Drink no wine or other fermented drink (13:4). The narrator uses the common word for wine, *yayin*. The term *šēkār* is a general designation for any intoxicating drink. The most common alcoholic drinks of the day were made of grains (beer), dates, or honey.[400]

No razor may be used on his head (13:5). Presumably the razor was a sharpened bronze or copper instrument. Egyptians shaved with a stone blade at first, later with a copper blade, and during the Middle Kingdom with a bronze razor.

Nazirite (13:5). The noun *nāzîr* derives from a root meaning (in Niphal) "to dedicate, consecrate oneself."[401] According to Numbers 6:1–8, a person under the Nazirite vow committed himself to three abstentions: (1) from wine or any other intoxicating drink; (2) from having his hair cut; (3) from contact with a corpse. Unlike Hannah's voluntary dedication of her son Samuel to divine service in the sanctuary (1 Sam. 1–2), Samson is claimed by God himself for divine service, not in the sanctuary but in driving out the Philistines. These dedications to divine service contrast with the dedication of daughters to the service of the goddess as *nadu*-priestesses in the temple.[402]

Neither Samson nor Samuel after him was cloistered away in a sanctuary; both were dedicated for public service.

Sumerian statue of man with goat for sacrifice
Z. Radovan/www.BibleLand Pictures.com

Rule for the boy's life and work (13:12). The phrase *mišpaṭ hannaʿar* refers to the oracle concerning the boy first announced in verses 3b–5.[403] Interpreted this way, our verse finds a remarkable parallel in a Ugaritic text. While the fragmentary nature of the text precludes a clear understanding of the entire passage, the reading of line 3 is quite secure:

> When he arrives at the lord of the great gods with a gift,
> he must ask for a decision [mtpṭ] about the child.

A few lines later the text reads:

> And your messenger will arrive with a gift;
> he will receive a decision [mtpṭ].[404]

As Cazelles has observed, at Ugarit, as at Babylon, people's destinies (in this case a child's) were determined by the gods.[405]

We would like you to stay until we prepare a young goat for you (13:15). Like Gideon's response in 6:18, Manoah's invitation to the envoy to stay for a meal represents typical ancient Near Eastern hospitality.[406] As in 6:18, the expression refers to a specially selected young goat.

It is beyond understanding (13:18). Instead of acceding to Manoah's request and giving his name, the divine envoy

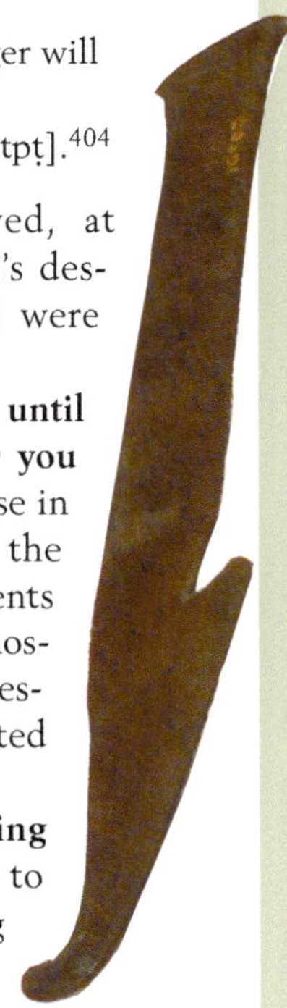

Razor
Kim Walton, courtesy of the Oriental Institute Museum

▶ The Importance of a Son

Epic of Aqhat
Rama/Wikimedia Commons, courtesy of the Louvre

Given the androcentric social structures of ancient Israel, the announcement to Manoah's wife that she will bear a son is especially welcome.[A-78] A son not only carries on the family name but also provides leadership in the home and community. In the world outside Israel, a son was also the key to a person's well-being here and now, as well as in the afterlife. Danʾel's plea to the gods in the Ugaritic Epic of Aqhat eloquently expresses the importance of a son:

> Will he have no son like his siblings,
> No offspring like that of his fellows,
> Who, girded, gives food to the gods,
> Girded, gives drink to the deities?
> Bless him, Bull, El my father,
> Prosper him, Creator of Creatures.
> Let him have a son in his house,
> Offspring within his palace,
> To set up his Ancestor's stela,
> The sign of his Sib in the sanctuary;
> To rescue his smoke from the Underworld,
> To protect his steps from the Dust;
> To stop his abusers' spite,
> To drive his troublers away;
> To grasp his arm when he's drunk,
> To support him when sated with wine;
> To eat his portion in Baal's house,
> His share in the house of El;
> To daub his roof when there's [mu]d,
> To wash his stuff when there's dirt.[A-79]

describes it: His name is extraordinary. The Hebrew word reflects the awe-inspiring numinosity of divinity, here perceived by Manoah to be fatal to a human observer (v. 22). The present notion may be compared to the *melammu*, the divine brilliance of deities in Mesopotamia. While the *melammu* would strike terror in the hearts of those who saw it, it was not deemed fatal.[407]

[She] named him Samson (13:24). In ancient Israel, either parent could name a child, though the Old Testament reports mothers naming their children more often than fathers.[408] Names were chosen for a variety of reasons in biblical times, and names fell into several categories: (1) status-names, (2) occasion-names, (3) event-names, (4) circumstance-names, (5) transformation/alteration-names, (6) predictive/admonitory-names, (7) precative/theophoric names.[409] The name Samson seems to fall into the last category.

With respect to its form, Samson consists of the Hebrew word for sun (*šemeš*), with the diminutive ending *-ôn*, hence *šimšôn* ("little sun, sunny-boy!"). It is tempting to give the name a positive spin as a celebration of the ray of light, which the boy's birth represented in the dark days of the judges. Some have suggested it anticipates his "sun-like" strength.[410]

Samson's extraordinary strength has also led to comparisons with the Greek legends of Heracles/Hercules.[411] A more common view links the name with the solar cult, which provides the background for the Samson narratives. The fact that Samson's name incorporates the same element as Beth Shemesh (lit., "house of Shemesh")—the name of an important town just a few miles from Zorah and Eshtaol down the Sorek Valley (see comment on 1:35), once the focal point of sun worship—offers strong support for this interpretation.[412] While interpreting the Samson narratives as a whole as an adaptation of a solar myth seems forced, it does seem best to find in the name a memory of the sun god, Shemesh[413] (cf. also Shimsai in Ezra 4:8).

The LORD blessed him (13:24). The verb *brk* means fundamentally "to endue someone with special power to achieve what is desirable in life."[414] How people outside Israel may have interpreted the statement is expressed concretely in an eighth-century B.C. Phoenician inscription of Azatiwada from Kartatepe in Anatolia:

> Now may Baᶜal KRNTRYŠ bless Azatiwada with life and health (*šlm*) and mighty strength over every king; may Baᶜal KRNTRYŠ and all the gods of the city give Azatiwada length of days and multitude of years and good prosperity, and mighty strength over every king.[415]

The obvious reference here is to Azatiwada's success in life, health, and good prosperity. These seem to have been lavished on Samson, so that he emerges in the next chapter as a man of exceptional health and extraordinary strength. Ironically, after this opening statement, in Samson's personal life he seems more plagued by curses than sustained by blessings.

Shamash
Jill Walton, courtesy of the Louvre

Mahaneh Dan, between Zorah and Eshtaol (13:25). Mahaneh Dan, which means "the camp of Dan," suggests this may have been the site of the first camp of the Danite tribe after the Israelites had been disbursed by Joshua (Josh. 24:28), and/or the headquarters from which the tribe set out later in search for new territory. Judges 18:12 refers to a Mahaneh Dan west of Kiriath Jearim, suggesting there might have been two places by this name. However, it is possible either or neither of these was an actual place name, and that the Hebrew expression means simply "the military camp of Dan."[416]

For the location of Zorah, see comment on 13:2. Like Eshtemoa in Joshua 21:14, the place name Eshtaol derives from a root meaning "to ask." The name suggests this was "a place of inquiry [before a deity]," presumably because in pre-Israelite times people came here to ask for an oracle from the gods.[417] Some identify the place with Khirbet Deir Shubeib, near Ishwa.[418] In any case, "Mahaneh Dan between Zorah and Eshtaol" represents the core area of early Danite settlement.

Samson's Marriage to the Philistine Woman of Timnah (14:1–20)

Timnah (14:1). Timnah, identified with modern Tell el-Batash in the Sorek Valley,[419] lay six miles straight west of Zorah.

Eshtaol
Todd Bolen/www.BiblePlaces.com

The description of Samson going down to Timnah is geographically accurate inasmuch as Timnah was located downstream from Zorah and Beth Shemesh on the south side of the Wadi Sorek. According to Joshua 19:43, Timnah was originally allotted to the tribe of Dan, though 15:10 suggests it was located on Judah's northern border. At this time the town was obviously still in the hands of the Philistines, but because it was located in the border region between Israelite and Philistine populations, a clash was almost inevitable.

Uncircumcised Philistines (14:3). This is an intentionally pejorative slur. Although the origins of circumcision are unknown, the practice was widespread in the ancient world, being attested not only in Israel, but also among Egyptians, Ammonites, Moabites, Edomites, and perhaps

Samson's hometown of Zorah is just off the picture on the top right. Timnah is at the west end of the Sorek Valley just to the right of the road as it fades out at the top of the picture. The site visible at right middle is Beth Shemesh.
Todd Bolen/www.BiblePlaces.com

Midianites (Ex. 4:24–26), but not among the eastern Semites of Mesopotamia. It is unknown whether ancient Canaanites practiced circumcision, though the account of Jacob's sons and the Shechemites in Genesis 34 suggests they did not.[420]

Whatever the significance of the ritual elsewhere, in Israel circumcision was the sign and seal of covenant relationship with Yahweh.[421] Because the Philistines did not adhere to this practice, culturally they were considered at the bottom rung of the social ladder. According to Israelite perceptions of life after death, the uncircumcised are consigned to the farthest recesses and least desirable parts of the netherworld, together with other unclean and vile persons.[422]

Israelite marriages were generally endogamous, that is, within the clan or tribe, though there were no laws against marrying someone from another tribe. But for an Israelite to marry a Philistine posed a special problem. After all, marriage not only brought an Israelite into direct physical contact with an uncircumcised heathen—a shocking thought to orthodox Yahwists—but also reflected a commitment to peaceful coexistence and mutual acceptance (Gen. 34:14–17).

This is precisely what Deuteronomy 7:1–8 forbids on spiritual and theological grounds: Israel is Yahweh's holy people. Since the Philistines are not listed in verse 1, technically one might argue that they are excluded from the prohibition. To Samson's parents his proposition to marry this Philistine appears simply a cultural and ethnic issue—they say nothing of Yahweh's prohibition on intermarriage with non-Israelites, Samson's call to special Nazirite status within Israel, or Yahweh's agenda for him to deliver Israel from Philistine oppression.

Get her for me (14:2). Though parentally arranged marriages are nowhere mandated in the Old Testament, this tended to be the practice, a fact reflected in expressions like "to give one's sons or daughters in marriage" (Deut. 7:3).[423] In contrast to modern Western marriages, where marriage tends to be an individual matter and driven by personal desire for companionship and romance, arranged marriages in the ancient world often represented alliances intended to ensure the continuation of the families through progeny.[424] Though practice and law were often quite different, a clause from the Mesopotamian Law of Eshnunna (ca. 2000 B.C.) declares:

> If a man marries the daughter of another man without the consent of her father and mother, and moreover does not conclude the nuptial feast and contract for(?) her father and mother, should she reside in his house for even one full year, she is not his wife.[425]

Young lion (14:5). Although lions are found in Israel only in captivity today, in ancient times Asiatic lions were common throughout the fertile crescent.[426] Indeed, in ancient Assyria the lion, termed "ferocious creature of the wilderness,"[427] symbolized chaos and the untamed world in all its forms. Through their successes as lion hunters Neo-Assyrian kings demonstrated their authority over evil forces, both cosmic and human, and proved that they deserved the title "Master of the Beasts."[428] In Judges 14–15 Samson proves himself "Master of the Beasts," first by overpowering a lion effortlessly as if it were nothing more than a

Hero defeating lion
Werner Forman Archive/The British Museum

kid, and later by capturing and manipulating three hundred foxes (15:4–5).

Swarm of bees and some honey (14:8). What Samson found inside the carcass of the lion caught him by surprise—and rightly so. Bees do not normally inhabit cadavers; flies and maggots do. Apparently this carcass dehydrated quickly, eliminating putrification, and in no time at all provided a hospitable environment for bees not only to live but also to produce their honey.

Samson made a feast there, as was customary for bridegrooms (14:10). The word *mišteh* ("feast") in this context refers to a seven-day feast at the home of the bride's parents, climaxing in the consummation of the marriage. The picture of drunken revelry at a Philistine event is realistic. Among the most common types of pottery found in Philistine settlements is the strainer-spout, often thought to be "beer jugs."[429] However, since the ecology of Philistia is more conducive to producing grapes than barley, some have recently argued that these vessels served as carafes for wine.[430] By this interpretation, the seriousness of the issue for Samson is heightened, inasmuch as his Nazirite status specifically prohibited him from consuming products derived from grapes.

The account offers some interesting information on Philistine wedding customs. The narrator notes that such parties were a regular part of the wedding festivities. While it is possible that the banquet included the families of the bride and groom, the focus is on the select young men of the town (NIV "bridegrooms"). Elsewhere "choice [young men]" refers to select warriors (20:15–16), which hints that the narrator recognizes the military implications of this event.

Thirty companions (14:11). The role of these thirty companions is uncertain. Traditionally the response of the Philistines has been interpreted as arising out of a concern to maintain Philistine custom. Apparently grooms did not host such feasts without attendants.[431] However, by this understanding the attention to custom given by these "uncivilized" Philistines stands in sharp contrast to Samson's own disregard for both Israelite custom and the Nazirite vow. On the surface the Philistines' action appears to be a gesture of goodwill—they are providing companions for him. However, since Samson is a stranger and "friendship" implies a measure of intimacy, it is doubtful the narrator looks upon these as Samson's friends. Either the expression is used ironically, or these thirty men are "friends" of the Philistine guests.

Even so, the manner in which these thirty men were engaged is odd. The choice of verb (*lāqaḥ*, "to take") suggests these youths were conscripted for this role. On the analogy of David's thirty military men (2 Sam. 23:13), this may be intended as a conventional figure for a body of public officers.[432] Yet there is no suggestion that this context involves a military escort.

Let me tell you a riddle (14:12). Instead of worrying about the thirty guards, Samson makes sport of the situation and proposes a riddle for them. In the ancient world people often spoke in riddles, simultaneously hiding information from some while divulging it to others, who were able to break the code. As in modern contexts, the ancients also delighted in spicing up conversations at festive occasions or intellectual gatherings with riddles. The key to a good riddle is to create as much ambiguity

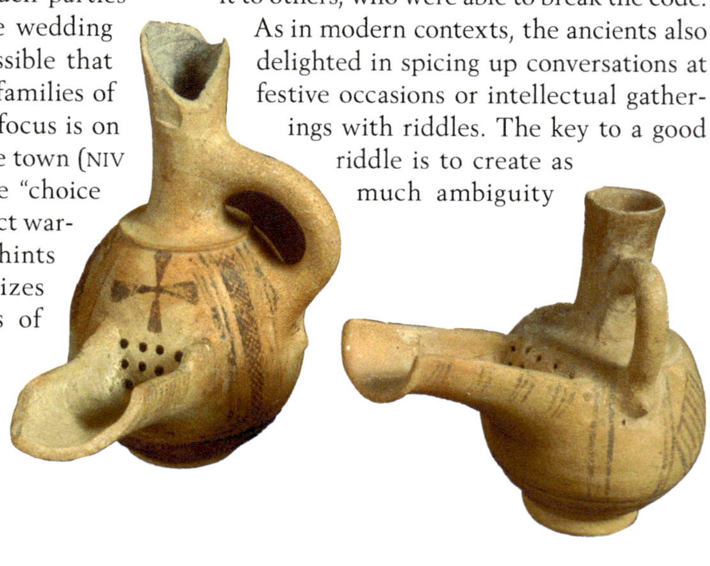

Philistine beer jug
Z. Radovan/www.BibleLandPictures.com

as possible by using words and idioms that functioned at more than one level. The code is broken when the persons to whom the riddle is posed discover the meaning of the elements. The following represent two sets of riddles from Sumerian sources of the second millennium B.C.:

> A house with a foundation like heaven,
> A house which, like a tablet-box, has been covered with linen,
> A house which, like a goose, stands on a (firm) base.
> One with open eyes has come out of it.
> (Solution: the school)
> When I was small, I was the child of a plant.
> When I grew big, I was the body of a god.
> When I became old, I was the country's physician.
> (Solution: linen)[433]

From a later time Strabo (*Geography* 14.1.27) reports a legend according to which the Greeks left Troy and headed south under the leadership of two seers, Amphilochus and Calchas. At Clarus they encountered a man named Mopsus (who is supposed to have founded Ashkelon!), who engaged Calchas in a riddle contest. Some have seen a riddle like this in the following quotation:

> [Another] question propounded by Calchas was in regard to a pregnant sow, how many pigs she carried, and Mopsus said, "Three, one of which is a female" ... When Mopsus proved to have spoken the truth, Calchas died of grief.[434]

Thirty linen garments and thirty sets of clothes (14:13). The first expression, *s^edînîm*, is cognate to Akkadian *š/saddinu*, which refers to an item of clothing.[435] Traditionally the former has been understood as a luxurious cape and the latter as festal clothing.[436]

Out of the eater, something to eat; out of the strong, something sweet (14:14). Like many riddles, Samson's riddle is short and cryptic. According to the rules of parallelism, the first line functions as a general statement, and the second line builds on

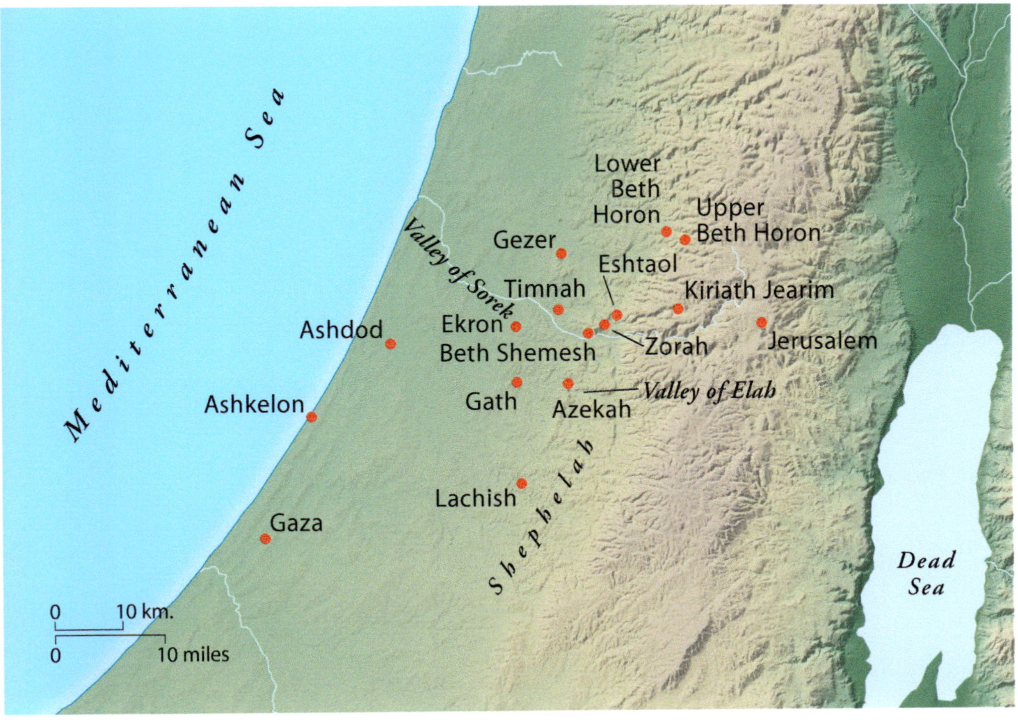

Philistia and the Shephelah

the first. This suggests an identification of the "eater" with the "strong" and food with the "sweet." The Philistines would probably regard the present festivities as the most likely clues to its solution, guessing that the first line refers to the disgorging of food by drunken revelers, perhaps Samson. The second is more difficult. The "strong" could be either a flattering reference to the guests or the thirty guards, or to Samson himself. But given Samson's weakness for Philistine women, the "strong" could refer more specifically to his sex organ. Either way the last word is the crux. The present wedding context supports a common interpretation that this refers to Samson's sperm.

Samson's wife (14:15). In Hebrew the word *ʾiššâ* denotes both "woman" and "wife." If the Philistines followed the custom reflected in Genesis 29:23, 27, the marriage would not have been consummated until the seventh day of the feast, but in this cultural context the status of a betrothed woman was not sharply distinguished from that of a wife.

What is sweeter than honey? What is stronger than a lion? (14:18). Like the riddle itself, the Philistines' answer is cast as two parallel lines. The echo of the riddle is heard in the concentration on the two key words: "honey," which is sweetness par excellence, and "lion," which is strength par excellence. The answer itself is a riddle, which Samson immediately solves, interpreting it to mean they have pressured his wife to entice him. In the end, the enticement of a woman is indeed sweeter than honey and stronger than a lion. Since the word for lion sounds the same as an Arabic word for "honey" (*ʿary*),[437] there may be an intentional wordplay. Of course, this works only if the Philistines and Samson spoke a common language, either Hebrew or

Ashkelon
Todd Bolen/www.BiblePlaces.com

Canaanite, of which Hebrew seems to be a dialectical variation.[438]

If you had not plowed with my heifer (14:18). Furious that he has lost his wager, Samson reacts to the Philistines' answer to his riddle with another "two liner," which has its own riddle-like quality: "If you had not plowed with my heifer, you would not have solved my riddle." Samson's reference to his new bride as "his heifer" (*ʿeglâ*)[439] is as disparaging in the Hebrew as it is in English.

Ashkelon (14:19). Located on the Mediterranean coast some twenty miles southwest of Timnah, Ashkelon was one of the five Philistine cities that constituted the Philistine Pentapolis. For more on this city, see comments on 1:18; 3:3.

Belongings (14:19). This expression occurs elsewhere only in 2 Samuel 2:21, denoting the equipment stripped from a slain man, particularly the belt from which weapons and tools were hung.[440] Carrying these items twenty miles back to Timnah, in a mocking gesture Samson presents them to the Philistine guards as their promised change of clothes.

He went up to his father's house (14:19). This entire story offers a fascinating cultural study on ancient "courtship" and weddings. Whether these were Philistine or Israelite customs is not clear. See sidebar on "Ancient Courtship and Weddings."

Samson's Vengeance on the Philistines (15:1–20)

Wheat harvest (15:1). The word refers to naked wheat of the durum variety, *triticum durum*.[441] Judging from its frequent occurrence in Ugaritic and other Northwest Semitic texts from the first millennium B.C.,[442] this grain was obviously common throughout the ancient Near East (see the "Gezer Calendar" at Ruth 1:22).

I'm going to my wife's room (15:1). This refers to an inner chamber of her father's house. In 3:24 the same word identified the inner room where Eglon's servants thought he was relieving himself. It is unclear what Samson's purpose was in "going in to her." Was it simply to visit her, or does he intend to consummate the marriage with sexual intercourse? In either case, he seeks to soften his wife's heart with a gift of a young goat, which serves as an ancient counterpart to a box of chocolates today.[443] Although Samson had left her home in a huff in the wake of the wedding fiasco (14:19–20), apparently he never meant to break off the marriage.

Caution is advised in drawing links between Philistine and Israelite marriage practices of the thirteenth to eleventh centuries B.C. with Mesopotamian customs from a half millennium earlier[444] or a half millennium later.[445] Nevertheless, chronologically and culturally the links between these societies and Israel/Philistia are much closer than the links between marriage practices in modern Western society and ancient Israel. See sidebar on "Ancient Courtship and Weddings" at 15:2.

I was so sure you thoroughly hated her (15:2). At the climax of the wedding festivities, Samson had left his wife in anger, and her family understandably assumed that he had repudiated the marriage and rejected his wife. The bride's father's assessment of the situation is expressed emphatically with the infinitive absolute and finite verb and may be interpreted as "you have surely divorced her,"[446] with no intention of returning to claim her. This Hebrew verb is analogous to the use of *zᵉrum* in Old Babylonian marriage settings. See, for example, the following law from Hammurabi's Code:

> If a woman repudiates [*zᵉrum*] her husband and declares, "You will not have marital relations with me"—her circumstances shall be investigated by the authorities of her city quarter. (LH §142)

Wheat (triticum durum)
Markus Hagenlocher/Wikimedia Commons, GNU 1.2

Ancient Courtship and Weddings

It seems odd at first that Samson's wedding feast was held in the home of the bride rather than the groom. This may reflect a Philistine convention.[A-80] But it would probably have seemed incongruous for Samson's parents, who did not sanction this marriage, to have hosted the wedding. Accordingly, having decided to marry a Philistine and having to arrange this wedding with Philistine parents of the bride, the wedding therefore presumably followed Philistine custom, which involved a seven-day festival of eating, drinking, and games. In this event, the father of the bride would have the last word in this marriage.

Old Babylonian laws show that in ancient Mesopotamia a considerable space of time often separated the betrothal and the consummation of a marriage. In connection with the betrothal, the groom presented a gift to the parents of the bride, which founded the groom's right to take the woman as his wife and functioned as the marriage contract. The step remaining involved the groom's claiming his wife.[A-81] During the intervening period the marriage was considered inchoate, though the woman was considered by all to be the man's wife. Such marriages were considered true marriages, but without permanent cohabitation.

Thus, within the context of ancient Near Eastern marriage customs, the fact that Samson went home after the wedding was probably not unusual. His new father-in-law could have interpreted his action as a return home to get the house in order. Such periods of separation often lasted several months. Meanwhile, the wife continued to live at home, and the husband would visit her at more or less regular intervals, bringing gifts and enjoying a night of love. According to 15:1, Samson seems to think he can return to his wife at any time.

Given the patricentric and often patriarchal social structures of the time, it is probably not surprising that later the author gives us only the father-in-law's interpretation of Samson's departure. Not a word is said about the feelings of his wife. Did she have any say in whether her father would give her to another man? Did she love Samson? Did she want him back? In the ancient world most women in this situation would probably have longed for their husbands to return. A Babylonian prayer to Ishtar reflects the disposition of a woman whose husband has left her by leaving in anger:

> Goddess of goddesses, Ishtar of men,
> who gives a blush of pleasure to experienced women,
> and makes [women] who are despis[ed] experience love yet;
> who brings back the irritated youth to the house of his in-laws:
> I call upon you, O Ishtar, again and again I call on you,
> O Ishtar, in the midst of the heavens.
> Because he no longer says a cordial word to me,
> because he is angry and no longer speaks with me—
> Give him (back) to me and...
> On my word and on the word that the Wise Lady speaks:
> make me live again!
> This incantation does not originate with me,
> it is the incantation of Ishtar (and) Nanaya.
> Ishtar spoke to me and I repeat (her words).[A-82]

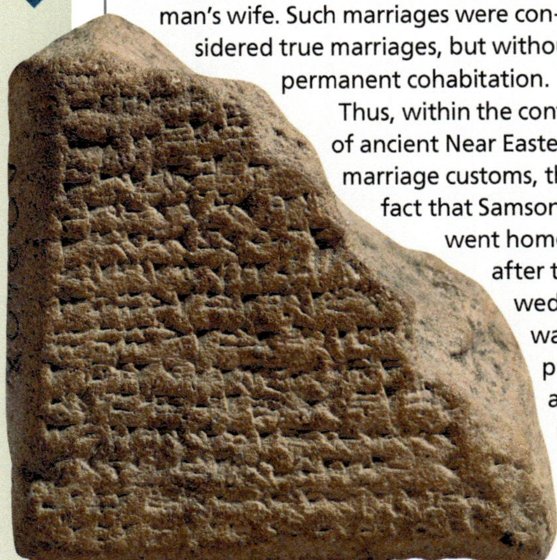

This letter is from Pharaoh Ramsses II to the Hittite king Hattusili III concerning the marriage of one of the daughters of Hattusili to the Pharaoh and the presents sent by the Egyptian court.
Erich Lessing/Art Resource, NY, courtesy of the Louvre

Obviously Samson's father-in-law had no greater affection for his son-in-law than Samson's parents had for their daughter-in-law. As a dutiful father, he found a felicitous solution for his daughter by giving her to one of the men who had accompanied him at the wedding. This action cannot be reversed; the father-in-law's actions find an analogue in Old Babylonian law:

> If a man deserts his city and flees, and after his departure his wife enters another's house—if that man should then return and seize his wife, because he repudiated [*z^e^rum*] his city and fled, the wife of the deserted will not return to her husband (LH §136).

Although both cases result in the dissolution of the marriage, here the issue is the husband's repudiation of his own city rather than his wife. Samson's father-in-law's refusal to give his daughter to him to fulfill the marriage contract recalls another Old Babylonian law:

> If a man comes to claim his bride at the house of his father-in-law, but his father-in-law wrongs(?) him and then gives his daughter to [another], the father of the daughter shall return two-fold the bride-wealth which he received (LE §25).

Three hundred foxes (15:4). The Hebrew word used here applies to both foxes and jackals. Since the latter were more common in Palestine and since foxes are solitary animals, Samson is probably dealing with jackals, which live in packs (cf. Ps. 63:10; Lam. 5:18; Ezek. 13:4, where the same word is used).[447] The rapid succession of verbs here creates the impression that his actions take no effort at all.

Religious Year	Civil Year	Hebrew Month	Western Correlation	Farm Seasons	Climate	Special Days
1	7	Nisan	March-April	Barley harvest	Latter Rains (*Malqosh*)	14: Passover 21: First Fruits
2	8	Iyyar	April-May	General harvest		
3	9	Sivan	May-June	Wheat harvest Vine tending	Dry Season	6: Pentecost
4	10	Tammuz	June-July	First grapes		
5	11	Ab	July-August	Grapes, figs, olives		9: Destruction of Temple
6	12	Elul	August-September	Vintage		
7	1	Tishri	Setember-October	Ploughing		1: New Year 10: Day of Atonement 15–21: Feast of Tabernacles
8	2	Marchesvan	October-November	Grain planting	Early Rains (*Yoreh*)	
9	3	Kislev	November-December		Rain Season	25: Dedication
10	4	Tebet	December-January	Spring growth		
11	5	Shebat	January-February	Winter figs		
12	6	Adar	February-March	Pulling flax Almonds bloom		13–14: Purim
		Adar Sheni	Intercalary Month			

Jackal
SoopySue/www.istockphoto.com

Standing grain of the Philistines (15:5). Philistia was grain country, and with his actions Samson strikes at the heart of the Philistine economy. But in the narrator's mind the action may also contain a veiled polemic against idolatry, especially if Dagon, the primary god of the Philistines, is understood as the god of grain (*dāgān*), as has been traditionally thought.[448] However, recent research has shown the fallacy of these etymological explanations of Dagon/Dagon's functions and established that in the Bronze Age the cult of Dagon was centered in the mid-Euphrates region from Emar to Suḫum.

In the eighteenth century B.C., this included the significant cities of Terqa, Tuttul, and Mari, where Dagon was the head of the pantheon and the favored deity of kings. The cult of Dagon also flourished in Ugarit, farther to the west, in the Late Bronze Age, where he is identified as the father of Baal. The fact that El was also considered the father of Baal and sixty-nine other gods suggests a blurring of the boundaries between these two deities. However, two references to Dagon of Tuttul in Ugaritic texts suggest he was always perceived as a foreign deity.[449] How Dagon came to be the patron deity of the Philistines we may only speculate.

Rock of Etam (15:8). The location of Etam is uncertain, and in any case may carry more meaning symbolically than geographically. Samson seeks refuge from his enemies in a fissure of a rock as an animal hides from its predator.

Lehi (15:9). The name means "jawbone," anticipating the outcome of this crisis. If Lehi is intended as place name, then the best candidate seems to be Khirbet eṣ Ṣiyyāgh, between four and five miles east of Timnah. However, since the Akkadian cognate *lītu* ("cheek, jawbone") was also employed in the sense of "border, circumference," here the word may be intended as a common noun for the border region between Judah and Philistia.[450]

New ropes (15:13). The reference to charred flax (lit., "flax burned with fire") in verse 15 suggests that the "new ropes" were made of flax fibers. Whereas people would use the finer fibers to make linen cloth, ropes were made of the tougher fibers from more mature plants. Although Egypt was the most important producer of flax in ancient times, the Gezer Calendar confirms that in Gezer (see sidebar at Ruth 1:22), less than five miles north of Timnah, this crop was grown regularly in the region where the stories of Samson take place.

It normally takes about one hundred days to grow a flax plant from seed to a mature plant, which grows to a height of between two and three feet. The Gezer Calendar also confirms that the flax harvest preceded the harvests of grain. Flax fibers are among the strongest and longest natural fibers in use by human beings, and they gain in strength when they are wet. In the present instance, the "new ropes" were undoubtedly ropes made of fresh fibers harvested from this year's crop.[451]

Fresh jawbone of a donkey (15:15). Reminiscent of Shamgar's victory over the Philistines using an oxgoad, Samson used a fresh jawbone to slaughter a thou-

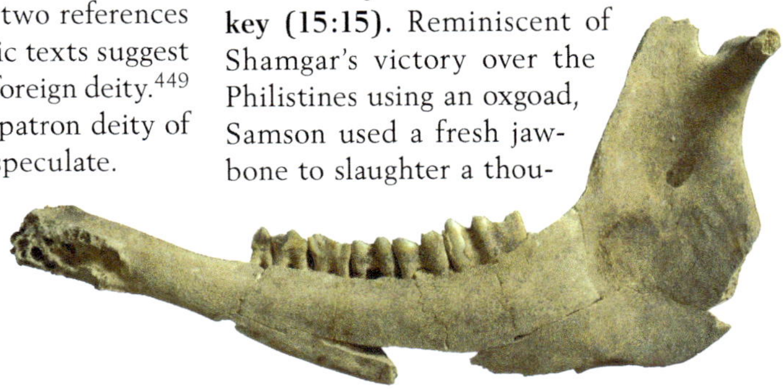

Donkey's jawbone
Z. Radovan/www.BibleLandPictures.com

sand men. The image is intended to be comical. Being only about nine inches long, a donkey's jawbone is an unlikely weapon.

En Hakkore (15:19). The name is ambiguous and impossible to locate. It may be interpreted either as "the spring of the one who calls" or "the spring of the one who names."

Gaza
Copyright 1995–2009 Phoenix Data Systems

Samson's Demise (16:1–31)

Gaza (16:1). Whereas Samson's previous experiences had happened at Timnah, on the northern edge of territory occupied by the Philistines, in 16:1 he is in Gaza, more than thirty miles southwest of Timnah. Gaza was the southernmost city of the Philistine Pentapolis, situated near the Mediterranean coast. While the fifteenth-century B.C. list of conquests by Thutmose III refers to Gaza as "a prize city of the governor," in the twelfth century the Philistines took over the city.

Prostitute (16:1). On prostitution in ancient Israel and the surrounding peoples, see comment on 11:1.

City gate (16:2). By definition, the Hebrew word "city" (*ʿîr*) refers to a settlement with a wall surrounding it. People entered the city through elaborate gatehouses that were often two or three stories high, with guardrooms flanking the tunnel-like opening. The Philistine city of Ashdod had a four-room gate house in the eleventh century B.C., two on each side of the entryway; in the tenth century their number was increased to six, three on each side.[452] In Iron Age I the fortifications of Gaza were built of unbaked brick.[453] To get to the gate of the city Samson would have had to get past four or six groups of guards stationed in the guardrooms.

Doors of the city gate (16:3). The gates of major fortifications had to be wide enough for chariots to drive through. They consisted of double doors made of wood; to prevent easy entry by an enemy they had to be made of thick boards. They were barred on the side by means of a heavy horizontal beam slid

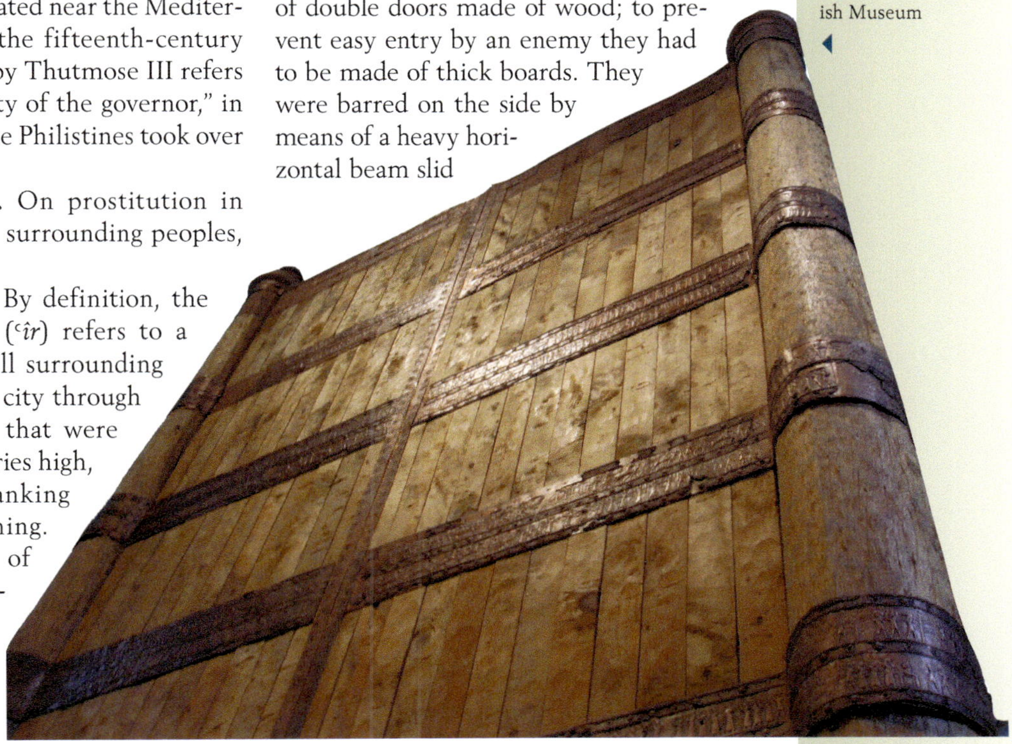

City gate from Balawat
Timoni M. Grone, courtesy of the British Museum

Gate socket
Kim Walton, courtesy of the Oriental Institute Museum

through slots in the doorposts. The doors were braced by wooden posts, the outside of which pivoted in stone sockets. The gates of Gaza that Samson pulled out of their sockets and hoisted onto his shoulders must have weighed at least four or five hundred pounds. How he could have accomplished this without waking the guards is difficult to imagine.

Carried them to the top of the hill that faces Hebron (16:3). According to 1:10, early in the Conquest Hebron (formerly known as Kiriath Arba) fell under Judahite control. This city, situated on a low spur of Jebel Rumeida, rose 3,350 feet above sea level at the junction of the north-south road from Jerusalem to Beersheba and two routes coming in from the Shephelah. As the crow flies, the distance from Gaza to Hebron is forty miles. But if Samson followed the route along the Wadi Guvrin, as is most likely, the distance would have been even greater.

It is not clear how far Samson carried the gates. Since the idiom *ʿal pᵉnê* + GN (geographic name) often means "in the direction of" (see, e.g., Gen. 18:16; 19:28; 23:19; Josh. 13:3), it seems most likely that Samson headed off in the direction of Hebron, and when he reached the top of the hill—probably overlooking Gaza—he deposited the gates.

Valley of Sorek (16:4). Sorek was the name of a valley that ran from the hill country of Judah and Dan down to the Mediterranean coast, through the northern part of Philistia (see comment on 13:2).

Five-mina weight in shape of a duck
Marie-Lan Nguyen/Wikimedia Commons, courtesy of the Louvre

Delilah (16:4). Like many other elements in the Samson narrative, the name Delilah is a riddle. The most likely explanation associates it with an Akkadian word *dalālum* ("to worship, honor, praise"), as in some Akkadian personal names (e.g., Dalīl-Ishtar, Dalīlūša).[454] However, ancient Israelites could have interpreted the name as an artificial punning construct consisting of *d* + *lylh* ("of the night").

Eleven hundred shekels of silver (16:5). These shekels should not be confused with coinage that was invented much later; rather, in the Old Testament the shekel was the primary unit of weight, used especially to measure commodities in a business transaction. The reward the Philistine lords offer Delilah for betraying Samson is exorbitant: 5,500 shekels of silver, more than three times the weight of the gold retained by Gideon after the victory over the Midianite kings (8:26). These figures present a sharp contrast to the four hundred shekels of silver paid by Abraham to purchase a burial plot for his wife (Gen. 23:15, 19), the fifty shekels David paid Araunah for his oxen and threshing floor (2 Sam. 24:24), the seventeen shekels Jeremiah paid to purchase a field (Jer. 32:9), and the thirty shekels set as a price for a slave in Exodus 21:32.

Although the value of a unit of silver fluctuated in biblical times, if we figure that a shekel weighed about 2/5 of an ounce (11.5 grams), at 40 shekels a pound the promised payoff is approximately 140 pounds of silver. Calculated according to the standard of ancient wages, if the average wage of a day laborer was ten shekels a year (cf. 17:10), this amount is equivalent to 550 years' wages.[455]

Seven fresh thongs (16:7). The meaning of this noun is uncertain, but the word is used elsewhere of bowstrings (Ps. 11:2; Job

Hero with six locks of hair
Rama/Wikimedia Commons, courtesy of the Louvre

30:11) and tent cords (Job 4:21), made from the tendons of a sheep or a cow.[456] Normally these would have been laid out to dry, but in specifying these to be "fresh" and "undried," Samson again trivializes his Nazirite vow not to touch a corpse. He assumes the Philistines will understand these unprocessed sinews to have magical powers, an interpretation reinforced by his specification that they use seven bowstrings.

New ropes (16:11). See comment on 15:13.

Seven braids of my head (16:13). In the ancient world, long hair was considered a mark of beauty on both men and women.[457] The reference to "seven" locks hints at a perceived magical understanding of the relationship between the hair and Samson's strength. Hebrew "braids" occurs only in this context (vv. 13–19) in the Old Testament, but it is attested in an ancient Phoenician inscription.[458] Some have linked Samson's seven-locked hair and his extraordinary strength to ancient Near Eastern literature and sculptured portrayal of heroes.[459]

Weave ... into the fabric [on the loom] and tighten it with a pin (16:13). In ancient times weaving involved two types of looms. Vertical looms consisted of a horizontal beam fastened at the top of two vertical beams, which were often leaned up against a wall. The threads that made up the warp were tied to the horizontal beam and were kept taut by fastening clay loom weights to the bottom.[460] The weaver would thread the woof back and forth through the warp with a shuttle.

Horizontal looms consisted of two pairs of pegs driven into the ground, with two parallel beams fastened to the respective pairs of pegs. The warp was stretched

Wooden model depicts a weavers' workshop. Two women weave on horizontal looms while others spin thread or wind skeins for weaving. Pegs used for warping can be seen on the wall.
Werner Forman Archive/Egyptian Museum, Cairo

between these two beams. As in the vertical looms, the weaver would thread the woof back and forth between the threads of the warp with a shuttle. A loom pin pushed the latest woof tight against the previous one.

Vertical loom with loom weights
Todd Bolen/www.BiblePlaces.com

It is not clear what kind of loom people would have used here. If Samson was sleeping with his head on the ground, the latter seems more likely.[461] However, if Samson was seated on the ground and sleeping with his head in Delilah's lap (cf. v. 19), then a vertical loom was possible.[462] The discovery of large numbers of loom weights at Iron Age Timnah (Tel Batash) and other Philistine sites confirms that weaving was an important industry in this region.[463]

If my head were shaved, my strength would leave me (16:17). The association of long hair with invincibility is reminiscent of two stories reported by Apollodorus. See sidebar on "Stories of Long, Invincible Hair."

Gouged out his eyes (16:21). In subjecting Samson to this kind of punishment, the Philistines follow a common ancient Near Eastern custom. In Mesopotamia defeated enemies were often blinded by gouging out their eyes and then humiliated by being forced to perform the most menial of tasks, customarily assigned to slaves and women.[464] Hittite sources report that captors blinded particularly dangerous captives to prevent them from taking up arms or trying to flee. Some, like the following letter from Kikarša to Taḫazzili, report that blinded hostages were forced to grind grain in the mill houses:

> I hope all is well with my dear brother and that the gods are lovingly protecting you. Concerning the matter of the blind men that you wrote me about: they have conducted all of the blind men up to the city of Šapinuwa. They have left behind here ten men (to work) in the mill houses. I have inquired about them, and there is no one here by the name you wrote me. You should write to Mr. Šarpa in Šapinuwa. All the (other) blind men are there.[465]

Obviously sight is not needed to grind grain. As in 9:52, the mill involved here would have been a smaller handmill, in contrast to larger mills turned by livestock.[466]

Women using handmills
Art Resource, NY, courtesy of the British Museum

Sacrifices to Dagon their god (16:23). One may assume from the presentation of sacrifices that the festivities described here took place in the temple of Dagon, the patron deity of the Philistines (see comment on 15:5). Although the Philistines were non-Semitic peoples (see comment on 13:5), they adapted quickly to prevailing religious ideologies in Canaan. While the deity goes back to the third millennium B.C. (Ebla, Mari, and Ugarit), in the Old Testament Dagon is always associated with the Philistines (cf. 1 Sam. 5), which demonstrates that the Israelites were not the only newcomers attracted by Canaanite religion.[467]

Our God has delivered Samson, our enemy, into our hands (16:23). This is a Philistine version of the divine committal formula, variations of which occur in many extrabiblical texts (see comment on 2:14). This quotation, which may have been chanted by the governors, captures the theme of the celebration

Stories of Long, Invincible Hair

The second-century B.C. Greek author Apollodorus reports two stories on long hair associated with invincibility. In the first one he writes of king Nisus of Megara, who was distinguished for his purple hair on the middle of his head. An oracle had declared that if it should ever be pulled out, that very day he would die. Meanwhile his daughter Scylla had fallen in love with the enemy Minos, who ruled Crete as king in the seventeenth century B.C. In a dreadfully treacherous act, Scylla pulled out her father's purple hair and he died.[A-83]

A similar fate happened to King Ptrerlaos of Teleboea. His daughter Comaetho fell in love with the enemy Amphitryon, who was terrorizing the Aegean islands. When she pulled out his golden hair, he died and Amphitryon subjugated all the islands.[A-84] Tragically, in both tales the treacherous daughter died at the hands of the man with whom each had fallen in love.

These stories bear striking resemblances to what Robert Alter calls a "type scene."[A-85] Since the Philistines came originally from the Aegean, they may have brought these and other similar stories with them. Whether or not the biblical author was aware of these stories, perhaps in the providence of God, Samson's demise appears to be an adaptation of this type scene. Like these two Aegean kings, the cause of Samson's death ultimately goes back to the treacherous actions of a woman.

Isometric reconstruction of temple of Dagon at Beth Shean
From the *Illustrated Bible Dictionary*, published by Inter-Varsity Press, UK

and in so doing reflects several important features of common ancient Near Eastern theology. First, even though Dagon has been out of the picture in the preceding episodes, the narrator presents the captivity of Samson, not as the result of human decision and machinations but as a divine accomplishment. Second, although Dagon may have been primarily associated with grain and harvest,[468] this chant portrays him in a military role.

Pillars that support the temple (16:26). While no Philistine temple to Dagon has been discovered in Gaza, excavations at Tell Qasile (located inside modern Tel Aviv) have revealed a building in Stratum X that illuminates this text. The temple used in Iron Age I was a complex structure forty feet long and twenty-five feet wide. Two cedar pillars slightly less than ten feet apart set on round stone bases supported the roof and upper story of this large temple.[469]

On the roof were about three thousand men and women (16:27). The scene is difficult to visualize. Here the word *gāg*, which usually means "roof," may refer to a balcony

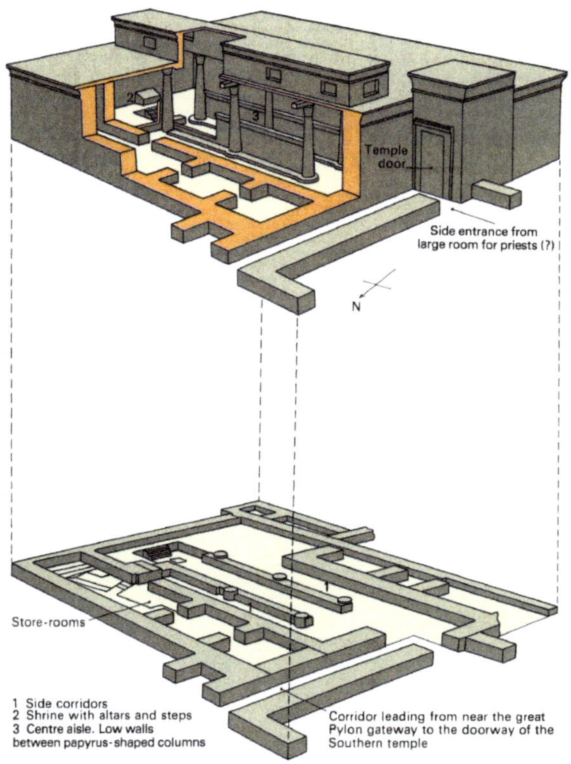

Remains of Philistine temple at Tell Qasile showing column bases
Kim Walton, courtesy of the Eretz Israel Museum

and some translations (e.g., NASB) interpret *lāpat* as "to grasp," but this reading assumes the pillars are close enough together that Samson can put his arms around them simultaneously. If this temple was designed like the Tell Qasile temple, where the two main pillars were approximately ten feet apart, it seems more likely that Samson pushed them off their stone bases, causing

or terrace surrounding the central courtyard where Samson was standing. Ancient public buildings, including temples, often included central courtyards, surrounded by rooms and balconies on the second floor. Presumably all the rulers and the temple functionaries were on the ground floor, where Samson was entertaining them, while three thousand spectators looked on from above. The number seems inordinately high, but it should be interpreted along the lines of other high figures in the book (cf. comment on 1:4).

Samson reached toward the two central pillars (16:29). Many popular presentations

the house to collapse above and around him. The semantic range of cognates of *lpt* in other languages is too broad to determine the nature of the action here (it occurs elsewhere only in Ruth 3:8; Job 6:18).

Zorah and Eshtaol (16:31). On these places, see comment on 13:25.

In the tomb of Manoah his father (16:31). In ancient Israel when people died, their bodies were deposited in family tombs, often in natural caves or in tombs cut into the rock. Although this text says nothing about how Samson was buried, the ritual seems to have involved his brothers and all the members of his father's household.

Typically in ancient Israel the clothed bodies of the deceased were laid out on a bench or the floor of the tomb, along with their favorite ornaments and jewelry. After decomposition the skeletal remains were piled up or deposited in a pit dug out for this purpose. Family tombs often consisted of a main front room, with elevated rock benches where the corpses lay until they were decomposed and the bench was needed for the body of another family member. Longstanding tombs of more significant families often included more than one side chamber where the bones were deposited. This design of family tombs explains why

Family tomb
Z. Radovan/www.BibleLandPictures.com

biblical authors speak euphemistically of death and burial as "to sleep with the ancestors" or "to be gathered to one's fathers."[470]

The Religious Degeneration of Israel (17:1–18:31)

Micah (17:1). Like many names in the ancient Near East, *mîkāyᵉhû* (in vv. 1, 4) and the abbreviated form *mîkâ* (in the rest of the story) is a sentence name.[471] Consisting of the elements *mî-kā-yāhû*, it translates "Who is like Yahweh?" a rhetorical question anticipating the answer, "No one!" In the ancient world, theophoric names (names with a reference to a god) of this type generally reflected the faith of the one who named the person. Accordingly one might surmise that the parent who named Micah was a devotee of Yahweh and considered Yahweh to be in a class all his own, distinct from all the Canaanite gods. However, the actions of this man hardly conform to the covenant standards expected of those devoted to Yahweh.

Hill country of Ephraim (17:1). The territory of Ephraim extended from the Jordan almost forty miles to the west. Encountered earlier in 3:27, it refers to the highland region between Bethel and Shechem.

Eleven hundred shekels of silver (17:2). On this amount of silver, see comment on 16:5.

Curse (17:2). This verb for "cursing" (*ʾālâ*) is relatively rare[472] and serves as an abbreviated version of the curse formula, which more often involves the verb *ʾrr*. In general *ʾālâ* signifies a conditional curse, in this case the invocation of some horrendous fate on someone who commits a crime. An analogue to this case is found in a contemporary Bedouin custom; if a Bedouin loses something he declares publicly, "I hold the person who finds this thing responsible for it. If he keeps it may Allah cut him off from his property and his family."[473] In such cases no one would dare to keep the article if found.

The LORD bless you, my son (17:2). By exchanging the curse for a blessing, Micah's mother seeks to prevent the disaster threatened by the previous curse. Her blessing is cast in typical form, *bārûk bᵉnî layhwh*, "May my son be blessed by Yahweh." This bears a close resemblance to the syncretistic blessings

Hill country of Ephraim
Z. Radovan/www.BibleLandPictures.com

Bull figurine from Ashkelon
Z. Radovan/www.BibleLand Pictures.com

on two Hebrew inscriptions from southern Judah: (from Kuntillet ʿAjrud) "May you be blessed by Yahweh of Samaria and by his Asherah," and (from Khirbet el-Qom) "May Uriyahu be blessed by Yahweh."[474]

A hint of what was expected from a blessing like this is provided by a recently discovered late eighth- to early seventh-century B.C. inscription from the Philistine town of Ekron:

> The temple that ʿAkish, son of Padi, son of Yasid, son of Ada, son of Yaʾir, ruler of Ekron, built for Ptgyh, his [divine] lady. May she bless him, and protect him, and prolong his days, and bless his land.[475]

Utterances like this characteristically express the speaker's grateful response to a good deed done for him or her by the third party on whose behalf the blessing is invoked.

But the utterance in 17:2 is more than an expression of thanksgiving because the woman has recovered her lost goods. The fact that Micah's mother commends Micah to Yahweh rather than Baal or some other Canaanite deity suggests she is devoted to the covenant God of Israel—though this devotion is not firm, as the sequel demonstrates.

I solemnly consecrate my silver to the LORD (17:3). In the ancient world, the manufacture of images of gods was a complex process that began with the consecration of the materials out of which the images were to be made. But Micah's mother only gives him two hundred shekels of silver (ca. five pounds), which would actually not have yielded a very impressive cult statue if it were made of solid silver.

A recently discovered metal calf, discovered inside what was apparently a model clay shrine in the remains of Middle Bronze IIC (1700–1550 B.C.) Ashkelon, may offer perspective on this order. The bull calf, apparently associated with the worship of El or Baal, is 4.1 inches high and 4.3 inches long and weighs just under a pound. Its body was made of solid cast bronze and still retains some of the thick overleaf of pure silver that once covered the entire body.[476] If this is the process used in the image here, then two hundred shekels of silver should yield an image about five times the size—that is, if the image were cast entirely of silver. But this is unlikely. Divine images were often carved out of wood and then plated with precious metals. Five pounds of silver could plate an image much more impressive than this calf.[477]

Carved image and a cast idol (17:3). The NIV creates the impression that Micah's mother desired two objects. The phrase is translated literally, "a sculpture and something poured"; this is a hendiadys reflecting the process of idol manufacture, namely, "a carved image overlaid with molten metal." The first word (*pāsal*, "to hew, cut") speaks of the carving activity of the craftsman as he sculpts a stone or piece of wood into the desired shape. The second word (from *nāsak*, "to pour") alludes to the melting down of precious metal with which the sculpture

Mold for casting images
Z. Radovan/www.BibleLand Pictures.com

will then be overlaid. Archaeologists have found molds of bronze and stone used to cast images.

Shrine (17:5). The expression "house of god" (used here) reflects the primary function of temples/shrines in the ancient world—a residence for deity. Being a family shrine or chapel, the present structure must have been modest in size, perhaps consisting of a small building in which the image was housed. This shrine was intended to serve the needs of the family, providing a means of securing divine assistance in conception and childbirth, fertility of flocks and fields, and protection from natural calamities and enemies.

Ephod and some idols (17:5). On the ephod, see comment on 8:27. On the word "idols," see sidebar on "The Teraphim."

[He] installed one of his sons as the priest (17:5). In most instances the idiom for "install" (lit., "to fill the hands") is used of the consecration of priests.[478] The nature of the ceremony of dedication is unclear, but the occurrence in Akkadian of an exact cognate suggests it involved the placement of some symbol of authority into the hands of the person being installed. This action posed a direct challenge to the officially authorized Aaronic priesthood.

In those days Israel had no king (17:6). As noted earlier, during the settlement period Israel had a decentralized government, each tribe being governed by its own chieftains, which left local communities with a lot of freedom to govern their own lives. This

The Teraphim

The word "idols" in 17:5 is the word *t^erāpîm*. In Genesis 31:9 this word seems to refer to miniature household gods.[A-86] But the form and function of *t^erāpîm* in the ancient Near East remains unclear. Scholars have proposed no fewer than six different etymologies for the word. The most likely explanation recognizes in the expression a Hittite loanword from *tarpi(š)*, which refers to "a spirit which can on some occasions be regarded as protective and on others as malevolent."[A-87]

Zechariah 10:2 links *t^erāpîm* with diviners (*qôs^emîm*) who prophesy through visions and dreams, suggesting these objects may have had a divinatory function, comparable to oracular alabaster and hematite stones known from Akkadian sources.[A-88] Contextually, this finds support in 18:5, where the Danite agents request an oracular word from Micah.[A-89]

The fact that in 1 Samuel 19:11–17 Michal's *t^erāpîm* were mistaken for a sick man suggests these images were anthropomorphic, lending support to the view that they were figurines representing deceased ancestors.[A-90]

also meant there was no centralized control over religious matters, so that Micah and his household had complete independence in shaping the cult in their own household.[479]

This episode is critical for illustrating the distinction between state religion and family or clan religion. State religion required a central political authority and a major temple of the patron deity in the capital, which served as symbols of the people's political and spiritual unity. Even in contexts of centralized political power and centralized worship, the people in the villages would often have felt that the great gods were inaccessible or disinterested in their domestic concerns. Consequently, they would rely on ancestral and family gods to ensure their material prosperity, the continuation of their families through progeny, and social success.[480]

Travels of Danite Scouts and Tribe in Judges 18

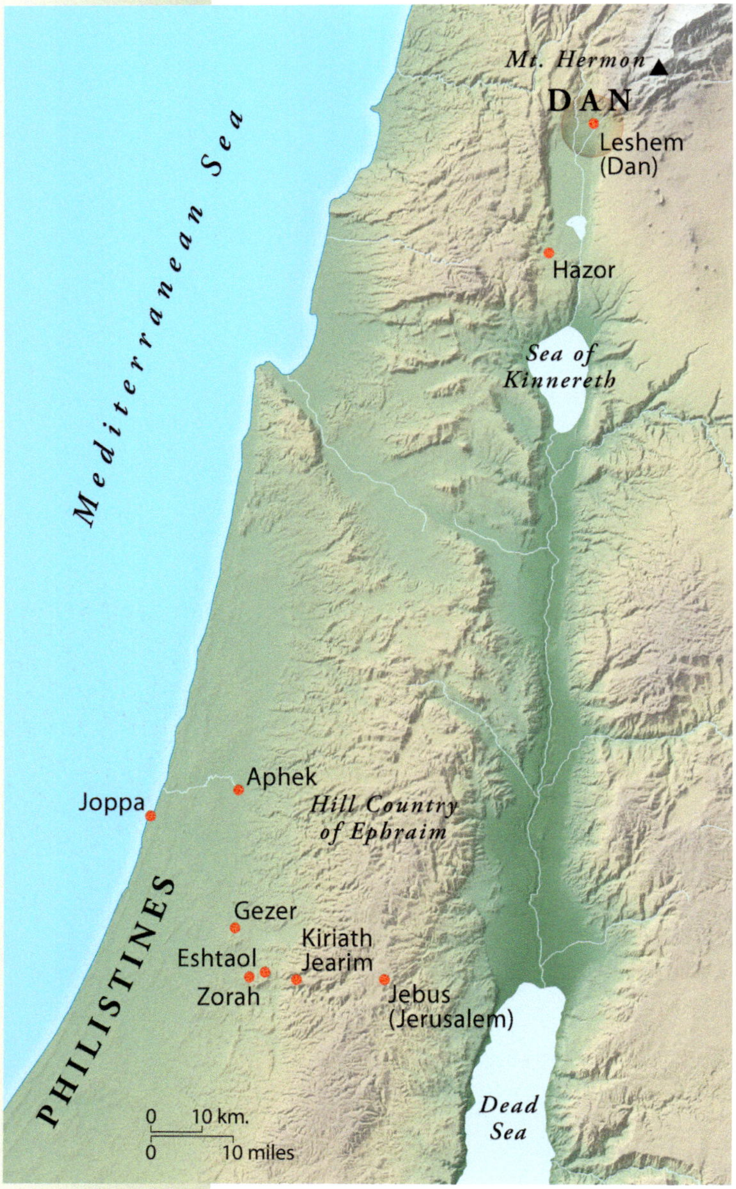

A young Levite from Bethlehem in Judah (17:7). The tribal reference intentionally distinguishes this site five miles south of Jerusalem from a Zebulunite place of the same name near Nazareth mentioned in Joshua 19:15.

Ten shekels of silver a year (17:10). This was the typical annual salary for laborers. The Pentateuch never stipulates the salary for priests or Levites.

The Danites (18:1). According to Joshua 19:40–48, the original Danite territorial allotment was located west of the Benjamite land, between the territories of Ephraim and Judah. This territory included productive agricultural land in the valleys and the coastal plain, most of which was drained by the wadis Sorek and Aijalon. The present events must have happened soon after Joshua's death and prior to the events described in chapters 13–16. First, the Levitical priest is identified in 18:30 as Jonathan, the son of Gershom, the son of Moses, which would locate these events within two generations of the conquest. Second, the Philistines claimed a large part of the territory allotted to the Danites. But there is no hint of Philistine involvement here—unless of course they were the reason the Danites could not occupy the land assigned to them.

Inheritance (18:1). Although most English versions translate the word *naḥ^{a}lâ* with inheritance terminology, this is a feudal expression, referring primarily to land given by a superior to his vassals as a reward for past services—fundamentally military service is involved—and in anticipation of future service.[481] This designation is appropriate for the territory originally given to Israel by Yahweh and distributed by Joshua by lot among the tribes, but it does not suit territory seized by force, particularly when it is at another Israelite tribe's expense. The *naḥ^alâ* expresses solidarity between a donor and recipient. Of course, since the land was given to each of the tribes and clans as an entitlement passed on from one generation to another, subsequent owners could refer to it as their "inheritance."

Zorah and Eshtaol (18:2). See comment on 13:25. These place names link the present events geographically with the Samson stories.

To spy out the land and explore it (18:2). The way this story is told invites comparison with Moses' sending of the scouts in Numbers 12:16–14:15,[482] but the strategy follows common ancient Near Eastern practice. Centuries earlier, kings of Mari sent scouts out on reconnaissance missions to the enemy camp or fortress prior to an attack. An eighteenth-century B.C. letter reports, "Ishme-Dagan has dispatched spies to spy on the encampment of Suhum. He will attack the encampment [of] Suhum. He has set sight on doing harm."[483] Closer in time and location to our text, spies and counterspies played a critical role in the outcome of the battle between the Egyptians and the Hittites at Qadesh on the Orontes in the thirteenth century B.C.[484]

Please inquire of God (18:5). Within the ancient Near Eastern context what the scouts lacked was divine authorization or guarantee of success in this adventure. Before embarking on an adventure like this, which had military implications, leaders would consult their deities to determine their disposition toward the mission. To the Danites the Levitical priest was the equivalent of a Mesopotamian *baru* priest. Sometimes the intermediary would attempt to curry the favor of the deity through sacrifices, as in the following letter from Mari on behalf of Zimri-Lim: "Speak to my lord: Thus Mukannišum, your servant: I have made the offerings for Dagon for the sake of the life of my lord."[485] The present context gives no indication how—or even if—the Levitical priest sought his oracle from Yahweh. Presumably he used the teraphim or ephod mentioned in 17:5.

Go in peace. Your journey has the LORD's approval (18:6). The first part of the answer is stereotypical, involving the word *šālôm* ("peace, well-being").[486] Most translations (including the NIV) interpret the second part positively, but in fact it is ambiguous. Translated literally the Hebrew reads, "Before Yahweh is your course on which you are going." This could mean that it has the approval of Yahweh's watchful eye, but it could also mean the opposite,[487] that is, that the conduct of the scouts and the Danites as a tribe is under critical scrutiny by Yahweh. As we noted in the sidebar on "War Oracles" at 4:9, such ambiguity was characteristic of many ancient prophecies.[488] In this instance, the Danite scouts should have come back and asked the Levite what he meant by his oracle.

Laish (18:7). This site was located at the northern extremity of the Promised Land.

Dan, ancient Laish, Middle Bronze mud-brick gate (see Judg. 8:9 for reconstruction)
Todd Bolen/www.BiblePlaces.com

Late Bronze dancer from Dan
Z. Radovan/www.BibleLandPictures.com

Laish ("lion") had a long history even before the arrival of the Israelites. The name appears in the nineteenth-century Execration texts from Egypt,[489] in the eighteenth-century Mari texts from Mesopotamia (*La-yi-iš*),[490] and in the early fifteenth-century list of Asiatic cities conquered by Thutmose III.[491] With its pleasant climate and watered by copious springs that fed into the Jordan River, this site at the foot of Mount Hermon was the most productive region of the country. Its political power in the second millennium was exceeded only by Hazor, eighteen miles to the south down the Huleh Valley (see sidebar on "Hazor" at 4:2).

Like the Sidonians, unsuspecting and secure (18:7). The first phrase is literally "according to the rule of the Sidonians." The idiom suggests that Laish was located within the sphere of Sidon, a major Phoenician coastal city.[492] This accords with what we know of Sidon's status at the end of the second millennium B.C. Although Sidon existed in the shadow of Tyre from the time of Solomon, prior to this she had been the premiere Phoenician city.[493] In the Old Testament the gentilic "Sidonians" stands for "the Phoenicians."[494] A delightful fourteenth- to thirteenth-century B.C. sculpture of a dancer illustrates the carefree character of the city of Laish.

A long way from the Sidonians (18:7). Separated from Laish by the Lebanon mountains and preoccupied with their maritime interests, the Sidonians apparently had no time or interest in exerting political control in the interior.

[They] had no relationship with anyone else (18:7). Nestled in the shadow of Mount Hermon, between the Lebanon and Anti-Lebanon mountain ranges, the people of Laish lived in splendid isolation from the Arameans to the east and north and in independence from Sidon to the west. Recent archaeological excavations of Dan may have unearthed one more reason for the Laishite smugness: the massive defensive ramparts. Like most Canaanite cities of the time, Laish was not defended by stone walls but by huge ramparts consisting of alternating layers of soil from the surrounding region and debris from previous settlements.[495]

Land that God has put into your hands (18:10). On this divine committal formula, see comment on 1:2 and the sidebar "War Oracles" at 4:8.

Kiriath Jearim (18:12). Many identify the place with modern Tell el-Achar, eight miles northwest of Jerusalem, though this is uncertain. Since it is associated with Mahaneh Dan here and with the Gibeonites in Joshua 9, it should perhaps be located farther west.

Huleh Basin, a lush area north of the Sea of Galilee
Todd Bolen/www.BiblePlaces.com

An ephod, other household gods, a carved image and a cast idol (18:14; cf. v. 17). See comment on 17:4–5. When the Danites seized the idol and the articles associated with this cult center, they were following normal ancient customs. In the conquest of cities the invaders normally aimed for the temple, seized the images, and took them out of the city, thereby asserting their dominance over the place and demonstrating the deity's inability to defend his worshipers. Furthermore, temples were storehouses for valuable objects and metals as well as for grain. The narrator casts this account as a scathing polemic against idolatry and idolaters.

[They] burned down their city (18:27). Technically the slaughter of the population and the torching of the city looks like the application of the *ḥērem* policy (Deut. 7:1–5). But this was common practice in ancient Near Eastern warfare. A Mesopotamian contemporary of the events in the book of Judges, Tukulti-Ninurta I (ca. 1243–1207) boasts: "180 of their fortified cities I destroyed, ravaged, burnt, (and) turned into ruin hills."[496] Archaeological excavations of Stratum V at Laish indicate the city was destroyed by a massive conflagration in the mid-eleventh century B.C., leaving a layer of ash and rubble two to four feet thick in some places.[497] Whether those remains point to the events described here is uncertain.

Beth Rehob (18:28). The exact location of the site (lit., "house of Rehob") remains unknown, but the phrase "Rehob near the entrance of Hamath" in Numbers 13:21 suggests a site at the northern extremity of the officially recognized Promised Land. An Aramean composition of the population is suggested by 2 Samuel 8:3–8, which notes that David defeated the Aramean king of Zobah, identified as Hadadezer, "the son of Rehob."[498]

The territory claimed by Beth Rehob may be understood broadly as the Beka Valley. Although Arameans claimed control of the entire valley, apparently their jurisdiction was effective primarily in the part drained by the northward-flowing Litani River. Living beyond the height of land that separated the Litani drainage basin from the southward-sloping Huleh basin, the Canaanite population of Laish managed to live independently of the Arameans.

Danites rebuilt the city (18:28). This statement accords with the archaeological evidence, which suggests that despite the total destruction of the city people continued to occupy it. The walls of the previous occupation continued in use and the material culture continued without appreciable change.[499]

They named it Dan after their forefather Dan (18:29). Formerly identified as Tell el Qadi, the tell has been confirmed archaeologically as the ancient city of Laish/Dan by the discovery of a bilingual inscription (Aramaic and Greek) from the second century B.C., which translates "to the god who is among the Danites, Zoilos made a vow."[500]

Until the time of the captivity of the land (18:30). The word for captivity refers to the common ancient Near Eastern practice of deporting the populations of conquered territories. Although the present reference to the exile of a land is exceptional, this comment refers to the population of Dan by Tiglath-pileser III to Assyria in 734 B.C. (2 Kings 15:29). This provides a helpful clue for determining the earliest date of composition of the book.

House of God was in Shiloh (18:31). According to 21:19 and 1 Samuel 1:3, for

Zoilos inscription with "To the god who is at Dan"
Z. Radovan/www.BibleLand Pictures.com

Shiloh

some time prior to the establishment of the monarchy Shiloh functioned as the cultic center for the nation, being home to the tabernacle that housed the ark of the covenant (cf. also Ps. 78:60; Jer. 7:12; 26:6–9). Located midway between Bethel and Shechem in the Ephraimite heartland near a reliable water source, Shiloh (modern Khirbet Seilun) offered a convenient place in the middle of the land of Israel to base religious operations.

While the nature of the sanctuary at Shiloh is unknown, the seven and one-half acre site suggests that by the time the Philistines captured the ark, a more permanent structure than the tabernacle used in the desert wanderings had been erected.[501] Archaeological excavations at Seilun show that the fortunes of Shiloh reached their peak in the eleventh century B.C. The ruins dated to middle of that century are to be associated with the Philistine victory reported in 1 Samuel 4:10.[502]

The Moral Degeneration of Israel (19:1–21:25)

In those days Israel had no king (19:1). On the significance of this sentence, see comment on 17:6.

Concubine from Bethlehem in Judah (19:1). On Bethlehem in Judah, see comment on 17:5. On concubines, see sidebar on "Concubines" at 8:31.

He remained with him three days, eating and drinking, and sleeping there (19:4). This account is all about hospitality, an extremely important ancient Near Eastern value. The fact that the man feasted with his father-in-law for three days indicates that whatever the cause of the tension between the man and his concubine, unlike Samson's case, the relationship between husband and father-in-law appears not to have been strained. On the contrary, the latter is portrayed as a model of hospitality, exceeding even the oriental standards honored by Abraham in Genesis 18.

The man left and went toward Jebus (that is, Jerusalem) (19:10). Having departed in the afternoon (cf. v. 8), this company traveled less than six miles (the distance from Bethlehem to Jerusalem) when they realized they would need to look for a place to spend the night. On the name Jerusalem, see comment on 1:7.

The present author departs from convention and applies the ethnic name of the inhabitants of the region to the city. Jebus occurs as a place name only four times in the Old Testament.[503] The gentilic "Jebusites" appears twenty-two times in the twenty-seven occurrences of the list of pre-Israelite inhabitants of Canaan. Although the relationship of the Jebusites to the other Canaanite nations is not clear, most agree that like the Hittites and Hivites, the Jebusites were a non-Semitic people.[504]

Gibeah (19:12). It is not clear whether Gibeah of Benjamin should be identified with modern Tell el-Fûl,[505] a northern part of the ridge that includes the Mount of Olives and Mount Scopus north of Jeru-

Gibeah
Z. Radovan/www.BibleLandPictures.com

salem, or Jabaʿ,[506] some 5.6 miles north of Jerusalem. In either case, having left too late in the afternoon to reach home in one day, this party of travelers is forced to seek a place to spend the night. In order to avoid contact with the Jebusites, they probably took the road around the west of Jerusalem, then through Anathoth and on to Gibeah.

Ramah (19:13). Ramah is identified with modern er-Ram, four miles north of Jerusalem.[507]

City square (19:15). The presence of a city square in Gibeah assumes some town planning, if not a defensive wall and a gate entrance. The town square was typically located just inside the city gates. It provided space for events that involved the whole community: a market place for merchants, a rallying place for political leaders, a gathering place for religious festivities. On a normal day, all the residents would pass through the square and through the gate in the morning to work out in the fields, and return through the gate and square in the evening. In times of crisis the gates were closed to traffic at night and everyone should be safe. The present travelers assume that as the residents returned and passed by them, surely someone would invite them to their home for the night. Ancient Near Eastern hospitality would expect that.

House of the Lord (19:18). The expression "house of Yahweh" reflects the primary function of temples in the ancient Near East—a place for the deity to reside. The reference is probably to Bethel, where later

Beersheba town square with gate chamber visible at upper left corner
Kim Walton

Sexual Deviation in the Ancient Near East

In Mesopotamia, the disposition toward male homosexuals ranged from toleration to contempt to outright prohibition. It seems the cultic community was most tolerant toward homosexuality, especially the cult of Ishtar.[A-91] The attitude of Assyrians of the second millennium B.C. is reflected in MAL §§19 and 20:

> If a man furtively spreads rumors about his comrade, saying, "Everyone sodomizes him," or in a quarrel in public says to him, "I can prove the charges against you," but he is unable to prove the charges, they shall strike that man 50 blows with rods; he shall perform the king's service for one full month; they shall cut off his hair; moreover, he shall pay 3,600 shekels of lead.
>
> If a man sodomizes his comrade and they prove the charges against him and find him guilty, they shall sodomize him and they shall turn him into a eunuch.[A-92]

Apparently, people viewed homosexuality with contempt because such acts "did not serve the purpose of having children" and thus contributed nothing to the community.[A-93]

Hittite laws call illegal sexual couplings *ḫurkel*. Actions classified as *ḫurkel* include bestiality (HL §§187–88, §§199–200A), intercourse with one's mother, daughter, or son (§189), with one's stepmother while one's father is living (§190), with one's sister-in-law while one's brother is living (§195), and with a free woman and her mother (§195) or her sister (§195). Apparently the man who sodomizes his son is guilty of *ḫurkel*, not because they are the same sex but because he is his son.[A-94]

the Israelites inquired of Yahweh through Phinehas the priest concerning the prosecution of the battle against Benjamin (20:18, 26–28), though 21:19 notes that a religious festival was held annually at Shiloh.

After they had washed their feet, they had something to eat and drink (19:21). These are all important elements of ancient hospitality (cf. Gen. 18:4; 19:2). Like their neighbors, ancient Israelites either went barefoot or wore leather sandals. In either case, to wash a guest's feet was a welcoming convention of hospitality, intended not only to remove the dust but also to refresh the visitor after a hot and dusty trip. The meal served two purposes: to nourish the guests and to express solidarity with them.[508]

Bring out the man … so we can have sex with him (19:22). Information on homosexuality in the ancient world outside the Old Testament is sketchy. See sidebar on "Sexual Deviation in the Ancient Near East." In demanding to have sexual intercourse with the Levite, the "wicked [worthless] men" of Gibeah violate three fundamental social/moral laws: the law of hospitality, the proscription on intercourse outside of marriage, and proscription on homosexual intercourse.

In the doorway of the house, with her hands on the threshold (19:27). The man's house was probably built of stone or mud brick—which was cheaper to use—though here in central Israel we should not rule out timber. Certainly the doors would have been made of wood, designed so that they opened inward and pivoted on sockets carved into the threshold below and the lintel above.[509]

He took a knife and cut up his concubine, limb by limb, into twelve parts and sent them into all the areas of Israel (19:29). The clos-

Four-room house at Hazor taken from threshhold into house
Kim Walton

est biblical analogue to this horrific scene is found in 1 Samuel 11:7, where Saul cuts up his team of oxen and sends the bits throughout the land of Israel as a symbolic act to coerce people to enlist in his army. There the messengers who delivered the pieces to their intended destinations expressly declare the significance of the action: "This is what will be done to the oxen of anyone who does not follow Saul and Samuel." Its effect is to strike divine terror on all the people, causing them to turn out in full force. Our text offers no such interpretation, expressing only the shocking effect of the Levite's action on the population of Israel.

A Mari document from several centuries earlier illuminates this incident with a striking parallel. In a letter to his king Zimri-Lim, Baḫdi-Lim writes:

> To my lord, speak! Your servant Baḫdi -Lim [says] as follows: For five full days I have waited for the Hanaeans but the people do not assemble. The Hanaeans have arrived from the steppe and established themselves among the settlements. Once, twice, I have sent [word] to the settlements and the appeal has been made. But they have not assembled, and for the third day they have not assembled. Now, it is the desire of my lord, a criminal in jail should be killed, beheaded, and [his body] be carried transported around throughout the area between the villages as far as Hudnim and Appan to cause the people to be fearful and assemble quickly. And in keeping with the charge that my lord has given me, I could embark on an expedition and quickly carry out the campaign.[510]

From Dan to Beersheba (20:1). This is the first occurrence of this merismic geographic definition of territory of Israel spanning a distance of about 160 miles. This stereotypical phrase reflects the narrator's own perspective of the nation of Israel as an ideal state consisting of all twelve/thirteen tribes[511] and occupying all the land promised to the ancestors. The book was written long after the events described in chapters 17–18 made Dan a major northern outpost of Israelite settlement, and after the political division of the nation in 931

Beersheba well
Dr. Tim Bulkeley, eBibleTools.com

Mizpah (Tell en-Nasbeh)
Todd Bolen/www.BiblePlaces.com

B.C. and Jeroboam's establishment of Dan as a major cult center.[512]

The ancient site of Beersheba (modern Tel es Saba[c]) is located just northeast of modern-day Beersheba. Despite limited rainfall, located in a region of rich soils and freshwater springs, Beersheba has a long history going back to the patriarchs (Gen. 21:31–33; 26:23–33) and beyond. It is situated at the intersection of the main north-south road from Hebron to Kadesh Barnea and the east-west road from Gaza to Arad and on to the Dead Sea. The name Beersheba may be explained either as "well of seven" or "well of the oath" (cf. Gen. 21:31). In either case the name associates the place with a well. The well after which the city is named is probably to be associated with the ancient well 130 feet deep located outside the city walls.

From the land of Gilead (20:1). The geographic name Gilead serves as shorthand for the Israelites living east of the Jordan. The events described in Joshua 22 demonstrate how critical the Jordan was as a geographical and psychological barrier between those tribes who lived within the boundaries of the Promised Land and those who lived outside. With the exception of Jabesh Gilead (21:9), in the civil war that follows, those east of the Jordan still felt solidarity with those to the west of the river.

Before the LORD in Mizpah (20:1). The assembly "before Yahweh" suggests Mizpah was recognized as a sacred site—perhaps even the temporary location of the tabernacle. According to 21:1 the commitment expressed in 20:8–11 is recognized as a pact sworn presumably with Yahweh as a witness. In the ancient Near East, agreements were concluded before the gods of the parties involved, who served as guarantors of the pact.

Mizpah derives from a root meaning "to watch," which suggests the site was originally built as a military lookout post. This

Mizpah should not be confused with the Transjordanian site where Jephthah sealed his pact with the Gileadites in 11:11. The present site is generally identified with modern Tell en-Nasbeh, seven miles north of Jerusalem about three miles northwest of Gibeah, on the boundary between Benjamin and Ephraim.[513]

Assembly of the people of God (20:2). The expression "people of God" points to the nation of Israel as a community of people united in their religious allegiance to Yahweh; they are a vassal community covenantally committed to Yahweh. The proceedings that follow include the presentation of evidence by a witness (the Levite, vv. 4–6), the call for a verdict (v. 7),[514] the announcement of the sentence (vv. 8–10), the preparations for the execution of the sentence (v. 11), and the effort to arrive at a negotiation resolution with the community to which the offenders belonged (vv. 12–13). These represent essential elements of an ancient legal process.

Four hundred thousand soldiers armed with swords (20:2). The Hebrew specifies these troops as *ʾîš raglî* ("foot men"), in contrast to cavalry or charioteers, like Sisera's forces in 4:3, 15. The Israelites' economy and organizational structures had not developed enough to produce a more sophisticated military force. Since this is only the beginning of the Iron Age, the swords they wielded were probably made of bronze.

Like many other numbers in the book, 400,000 seems inordinately high,[515] presupposing a population of at least 2,000,000. But based on the archaeological evidence for population (primarily the number and sizes of villages), it is doubtful the entire population of the region, including the native Canaanites, was much more than 200,000. Whether the key word *ʾelep* is interpreted as "thousand" or the contingents mustered by individual clans, in comparison with the numbers in Numbers 1 and 26 the population of Israel had fallen by one-third. Any explanation for this decrease in the population is speculative, but famine and a reduced birth rate (cf. 13:2–3; Ruth 1:1–5; 1 Sam. 1:2) caused by the stress of threats from outside may have been interpreted as fulfillments of the covenant curses in Leviticus 26 and Deuteronomy 28.

As the lot directs (20:9). Whereas in chapter 1 the narrator intimates that the tribes had inquired of Yahweh directly to see who was to lead the attack against the Canaanites, here there is no reference to Yahweh, only the method by which his reply will be determined: the lot. The use of the lot is required in the absence of a leader, who would normally have chosen his troops. This kind of divination, which assumed that the gods determined the way the lots fell (Prov. 16:33), was widespread in the ancient Near East (see sidebar on "Testing the Deity" at 6:36).

We'll take ten men out of every hundred from all the tribes of Israel, and a hundred from a thousand, and a thousand from ten thousand, to get provisions for the army (20:10). Although all the numbers in the present account seem inflated (see comment on v. 2), the present proportion of one-tenth of the force being assigned supply duty finds a close parallel in a report from Mari that notes that in a force of 12,000 troops, 1,000 were appointed to transport food.[516]

Twenty-six thousand swordsmen (20:15). On the large number, see comments on 1:4 and 20:2. The decline in Benjamin's military force since the Exodus (cf. Num. 1:37 [35,400]; 26:41 [45,600]) is proportional to the drop in Israel as a whole.

Seven hundred chosen men who were left-handed (20:16). In an ordinary troop where the majority of the men were right-handed, left-handed men were a liability. However, if an entire troop of left-handed men can be mustered, they become a formidable independent troop, often with a decided physical and psychological advantage. But as was the case with the individual Benjamite Ehud (see comment on 3:15), these men were probably ambidextrous.

Slingstones found in the excavations at Lachish
Todd Bolen/www.BiblePlaces.com

[They] could sling a stone at a hair and not miss (20:16). In Israel slings were used mainly by shepherds to ward off marauding animals, but they were used in Egypt and Assyria as weapons of war. These slings consisted of a patch of leather or cloth, with leather straps or rope cords tied to opposite ends. Holding the ends of the cords firmly in his hand the warrior would swing the loaded sling around above his head and then when it had reached maximum speed release one of the cords. The sling stones could reach speeds of 100 to 150 miles per hour. The stones used by the Assyrians at Lachish in the eighth century were 2 ½ to 3 inches in diameter and weighed about 250 grams.[517]

Bethel (20:18). On the location of Bethel (meaning "house of God"), see comment on 1:22–23. Bethel had a longstanding history as a sacred site in Israelite tradition (Gen. 28), and its place in Israel's cultic life was secured by Jeroboam when the united kingdom was divided in 932 B.C. (1 Kings 12:25–33).

Twenty-two thousand Israelites (20:21). On the seemingly high number, see comments on 1:4 and 20:2. So also verse 25.

They fasted that day (20:26). The practice of fasting outside Israel is reflected in Daniel 6:18, which Darius fasts from food and refuses all diversions because his decision has apparently sent Daniel to his doom at the mouths of lions. Fasting is not widely attested in extrabiblical texts,[518] but the following excerpt from a seventh-century B.C. letter from a court official to the Neo-Assyrian king seems to involve the practice:

> The king, our lord, will pardon us. Is one day not enough for the king to mope and to eat nothing? For how long (still)? This is already the third day (when the king does not eat anything). The king, a beggar! (Surely) when, in the beginning of the month, the moon appears, he says: "I will not fast (any more)! It is the beginning of the month! I want bread to eat and wine to drink! Now Jupiter is the moon. The king can ask for food for even the whole of the year! We became worried and were afraid, and that is why we are (now) writing to the king."[519]

Ark of the covenant of God (20:27). This is the only reference to the "ark of the covenant" in Judges. Under normal circumstances, the ark was supposed to be in the inner sanctum, the Most Holy Place of the tabernacle, where it functioned as the receptacle of the tablets of the Decalogue, the symbol of Yahweh's covenant with Israel, and as a throne for the invisible Yahweh. For Israel's neighbors the image of the deity seated on a throne in the sanctuary was the most important religious artifact. But orthodox Yahwism was aniconic—prohibiting any images of deity. The closest the Israelites came to possessing an image of Yahweh was the ark of the covenant in the tabernacle.

The ark was a beautifully crafted object with a solid gold cover that included two carved cherubim guarding it (Ex. 25:10–22). It seems that the Israelites had brought the ark to Bethel from Shiloh, presumably to function as a palladium,[520] a symbol of God's presence and "good luck charm" in the battle against the Benjamites. They might have claimed precedents for this manipulation of the ark in the Israelites' crossing of the Jordan (Josh. 3) and the circling of Jericho (Josh. 6), except that in those instances they had explicit instructions from Yahweh, the nation's Commander in Chief.

A more likely analogue is found in 1 Samuel 4, where the ark is brought up to secure victory for the Israelites after a disastrous defeat at the hands of the Philistines. If this comparison is sound, the Israelites treated the ark as their neighbors treated the images of their deities—as a physical and magical symbol of Yahweh's protective presence as they engaged the enemy in battle.

Phinehas son of Elazar, the son of Aaron (20:28). The name Phinehas is Egyptian in origin, being derived from *pꜣ nḥśy* ("the dark-skinned, the Negro").

Then Israel set an ambush around Gibeah (20:29). While the sequence of the events in verses 29–40 is not entirely clear, the strategy of setting an ambush against one's target is attested not only in biblical texts,[521] but also in extrabiblical battle accounts, as in the account of Ramesses II's defeat at the hands of the Hittites at Kadesh on the Orontes in 1274 B.C.[522]

Baal Tamar (20:33). The site was obviously near Gibeah, but its precise location is unknown. Possibilities include modern Khirbet Atarah, Ras et-Tavil, and Ṣahre al Gibiyeh, 500 meters east of Tel el-Ful.[523]

Struck down 25,100 Benjamites (20:35). On the seemingly high numbers, see comments on 1:4 and 20:2. This was obviously a total rout. Of the twenty-six divisions plus seven hundred select troops with which the Benjamites had started (20:15), eighteen were wiped out on the battlefield (v. 44), five during their flight (v. 45), and two more in the mopping-up operations (v. 45). Of the seven hundred select troops, one hundred were killed; the remaining six hundred sought refuge at the rock of Rimmon.

Rock of Rimmon (20:47). The name means "Pomegranate Rock," probably the el-Jaia cave in the Wadi es-Swenit, less than a mile east of Gibeah (modern Jabaᶜ). This hundred-foot high cave, pitted on the inside with hundreds of smaller caves and holes, not only resembled a split pomegranate but also offered an ideal refuge for beleaguered warriors.[524]

All the towns they came across they set on fire (20:48). This extreme policy toward conquered peoples involved the *ḥērem*-style slaughter of the entire population of Benjamin—human and animal alike—and the torching of all their cities as a ritual sacrifice to God. On this policy in ancient warfare and in Israel, see comment on 1:17.

Oath at Mizpah (21:1). This is the first reference to an oath in the book. In the ancient world oaths and curses were thought to derive their potency through people's appeals to the gods to guarantee by divine sanction that promises made in agreements would be fulfilled. Accordingly, although breaking an agreement could pose a legal problem to be resolved by the courts, through their own agents the gods meted out punishment for perjury.

Oaths typically spelled out the consequences to be experienced by the person who swore the oath. The deities appealed to in oaths were those of one's own city or country. Since the Israelites had gathered "before Yahweh" at Mizpah (20:1) and "before Yahweh" (21:5), we may assume that Yahweh was invoked as the guarantor of the present agreement (cf. v. 7). The commitment to which they bound themselves is stated in the next clause.

They sat before God (21:2). On sitting as a posture of grief and lamentation, compare Psalm 132:1. On the custom of loud weeping to express intense lamentation, see comment on 2:4.

O LORD, the God of Israel (21:3). In the ancient world, nations were often identified on the basis of their relationship to their divine patron. Thus, just as the Israelites may be called "the people of Yahweh" (5:11, 13), Moabites were called "the people of Chemosh" (Num. 21:29; Jer. 48:46).

Jabesh-Gilead region
Todd Bolen/www.BiblePlaces.com

Conversely, deities could be identified on the basis of their special relationship to a people. First Kings 11:33 speaks of "Ashtoreth the goddess of the Sidonians, Chemosh the god of the Moabites, and Molech the god of the Ammonites." Here Yahweh is identified as "the God of Israel."

Jabesh Gilead (21:8). This is the first mention of Jabesh Gilead in the Old Testament.

The name means "well-drained soil of Gilead." It is preserved in modern Wadi el-Yabis, one of the main east-west tributaries of the Jordan cutting through the hills of Gilead. The precise location of the town along this wadi is uncertain, but the most likely candidate is Tell Maqlub, seven miles east of the Jordan and thirteen miles southeast of Beth Shan. Some time later Saul rescued this town from oppression by the Ammonites (1 Sam. 11:1–11), for which they remained grateful until Saul's death (31:11–13). Since he was a descendant of one of the six hundred Benjamites, Saul's interest in Jabesh Gilead was based on his sense of kinship with the people of this region.

Twelve thousand fighting men (21:10). On the seemingly high number, see comments on 1:4 and 20:2.

Elders of the assembly (21:16). In premonarchic times the administration of justice was in the hands of a counsel of elders, drawn from the heads of households and clans in each village (see comment on 2:7).

Annual festival of the LORD in Shiloh (21:19). Hebrew *ḥag* is a generic term for any periodic pilgrimage festival, but which specific festival is in mind is not clear. According to Deuteronomy 16:1–17 (cf. also Ex. 23:14–17; 34:18–23), all Israelite males were required to appear three times a year before Yahweh at the place he approved and established as his authorized cult site: the Feast of Passover and Unleavened Bread, the Feast of Weeks (also known as the Feast of Harvest), and the Feast of Firstfruits. Deuteronomy 16:16 and Exodus 23:17 obligate only adult males to attend, although from Deuteronomy 16:11, 14 it is clear that women and children were welcome.

East of the road that goes from Bethel to Shechem, and to the south of Lebonah (21:19). This detailed geographic note highlights the Israelites' concern that the Benjamites succeed in their quest for wives. The road from Bethel to Shechem is a thirteen-mile segment of the regional north-south thoroughfare that ran from Hazor in the north to Beersheba in the south. The location of Lebonah is uncertain; El-Lubban and Lubban Sherqujeh have been proposed.

When the girls of Shiloh come out to join in the dancing (21:21). The expression "daughters of Shiloh" suggests a special professional class of female dancers associated with the cult of Shiloh. The inspiration for such cultic personnel and activity may well have come from Canaanite religious customs, which often involved women. In the Late Bronze Age at Emar in Syria, the great festivals were headed by the high priestess and involved several additional classes of priestesses.

While the regulations concerning worship in Israel freely admitted women and children to participate (Deut. 12:12; 31:10–12) and the narratives occasionally highlight the role of women in celebrative dance (Ex. 15:20), the ritual of Yahweh at the tabernacle and later the temple never involved women in priestly roles. This annual festival may have simply involved cultic dance in joyful celebration of Yahweh.

The instructions to the Benjamites to hide in the vineyards may suggest a festival of thanksgiving for the grape harvest, which would be characterized by revelry, music, and dance. However, the reference to the dancers as "daughters of Shiloh" rather than the more common "daughters of Israel" may still point to a class of women professionally linked to the cult.

In those days Israel had no king (21:25). See comment on 17:6.

Vineyards at Shiloh
Yakov Ben-Avraham of ePublicist.ca

Bibliography

Block, Daniel I. *Judges, Ruth*. NAC 6. Nashville: Broadman & Holman, 1999. Thorough exegetical commentary combining an emphasis on the theological and literary features and attention to extrabiblical information that illumines the text.

Boling, Robert G. *Judges*. AB 6A. Garden City, N.Y.: Doubleday, 1975. Somewhat dated, but still provides helpful geographic and archaeological background information on Judges.

Crenshaw, J. L. *Samson: A Secret Betrayed, a Vow Ignored*. Atlanta: John Knox, 1978. Somewhat dated, but still valuable for background information.

Marcus, D. *Jephthah and His Vow*. Lubbock, Tex.: Texas Tech Press, 1986. A detailed interpretation of Jephthah's vow within its ancient Near Eastern context.

Soggin, J. A. *Judges*. OTL. Philadelphia: Westminster, 1981. A classic European source and redaction-critical approach to exegesis. Each section is preceded by a short bibliography, often citing essays offering helpful background information.

CHAPTER NOTES

Main Text Notes

1. See the discussion in Joshua introduction.
2. The problem is not resolved by positing a shorter reign for Saul, as, for example, the 22 years proposed by D. V. Edelman, "Saul," *ABD*, 5:993.
3. Compare the Exodus generation, which took thrity-eight years to be eliminated.
4. Cf. I. Provan, V. P. Long, and T. Longman III, *A Biblical History of Israel* (Louisville: Westminster John Knox, 2003), 199–201.
5. Judg. 9:22; 10:2, 3; 12:7, 9, 11, 14.
6. Judg. 3:8, 14; 6:1; 10:8.
7. This probably accounts for the Abimelech note in 9:22, which completes the quota.
8. So also K. L. Younger Jr., *Judges* (NIVAC; Grand Rapids: Zondervan, 2002), 258. Contra D. L. Washburn, "The Chronology of Judges: Another Look," *BibSac* 147 (1990): 425; E. Merrill, *Kingdom of Priests* (Grand Rapids: Baker, 1987), 68.
9. The patron deity of the Ammonites was Milcom (1 Kings 11:5, 33); Chemosh was the patron deity of Moab.
10. COS, 2.6; *ANET*, 376–78. For discussion of the text see J. K. Hoffmeier, *Israel in Egypt: The Evidence for the Authenticity of the Exodus Traditions* (Oxford: Oxford Univ. Press, 1997), 27–31.
11. Translations of the texts are provided by W. Moran, *The Amarna Letters* (Baltimore: Johns Hopkins Univ. Press, 1992).
12. See Provan, Long, and Longman, *Biblical History of Israel*, 170–72.
13. For translations of the texts, see D. Pardee, ed., *Ugaritic Narrative Poetry* (SBLWAW 9; Atlanta: Scholars Press, 1997).
14. Line 52. For a study of the text, see C. Manassa, *The Great Karnak Inscription of Merneptah: Grand Strategy in the Thirteenth Century* B.C. (New Haven, Conn.: Yale Egyptological Seminar, 2004).
15. Ramesses III also refers to some of these in his Medinet Habu Inscription (see *ANET*, 262).
16. See T. Dothan and M. Dothan, *People of the Sea: The Search for the Philistines* (New York: Macmillan, 1992); L. E. Stager, "The Impact of the Sea Peoples in Canaan (1185–1050 B.C.E.)," in *The Archaeology of Society in the Holy Land*, ed. T. Levy (New York: Facts on File, 1995), 332–48.
17. For a helpful collection of many Mari texts in translation, see W. Heimpel, *Letters to the King of Mari: A New Translation with Historical Introduction, Notes, and Commentary* (Mesopotamian Civlizations 12; Winona Lake, Ind.: Eisenbrauns, 2003). For a discussion of social and political institutions in the region of Mari in the eighteenth century B.C., see D. Fleming, *Democracy's Ancient Ancestors: Mari and Early Collective Governance* (Cambridge: Cambridge Univ. Press, 2004).
18. For citation and discussion of this text, see D. I. Block, "What has Delphi to do with Samaria? Ambiguity and Delusion in Israelite Prophecy," in *Writing and Ancient Near Eastern Society: Papers in Honour of Alan R. Millard*, ed. P. Bienkowski (British Academy Monographs in Archaeology Series; Oxford: Oxford Univ. Press, 2005), 196–97.
19. See further A. Rainey, "Who is a Canaanite? A Review of the Textual Evidence," *BASOR* 304 (1996): 1–15; R. S. Hess, "Occurrences of Canaan in Late Bronze Age Archives of the West Semitic World," in *Israel Oriental Studies 18: Past Links: Studies in the Languages and Cultures of the Ancient Near East*, ed. Sh. Izreʾel, I. Singer, and R. Zadok (Winona Lake, Ind.: Eisenbrauns, 1998), 365–72.
20. For discussions of the land and the people, see K. N. Schoville, "Canaanites and Amorites," *POTW*, 157–82; P. C. Schmitz, "Canaan (Place)," *ABD*, 1:828–31.
21. As translated by M. Nissinen, *Prophets and Prophecy in the Ancient Near East* (SBLWAW 12; Atlanta: SBL, 2003), 44.

22. Simeon is missing in Moses' blessing of the tribes (Deut. 33) and in the Song of Deborah (Judg. 5).
23. For discussion of the name and the identity of this people see comment of R. Hess on Josh. 3:10 (R. Hess, *Joshua* [TOTC; Downers Grove, Ill: Inter-Varsity Press, 1996]). Some associate the expression with *p^e^rāzî* (Deut. 3:5; 1 Sam. 6:18), *p^e^rāzôn*, (Jdg. 5:7, 11), and *p^e^rāzôt*, "unwalled cities" (Ezek. 38:11; Zech. 2:8), hence "inhabitants of unwalled settlements." Cf. S. A. Reed, "Perizzite," *ABD*, 5:231.
24. R. G. Boling, *Judges* (AB 6A; Garden City, N.Y.: Doubleday, 1975), 55. Based on 1 Sam 11:8, A. Zertal locates Bezek near Shechem, "Bezek," *ABD*, 1:717–18. However, that Bezek is too far north for the present context.
25. See D. M. Fouts, "A Defense of the Hyperbolic Interpretation of Large Numbers in the Old Testament," *JETS* 40 (1997): 377–88. J. Milgrom argues that biblical authors intended that such numbers be interpreted literally, but this tendency to inflate numbers is characteristic of ancient epic literature. See *Numbers* (JPS Torah Commentary; Philadelphia: Jewish Publication Society, 1990), 339. Compare the legendary Canaanite account of King Keret, who calls for a mighty army, "three hundred myriads, peasant levies without number, regular levies beyond counting, marching in thousands like storm clouds, and in myriads as autumn rains" (*ANET*, 143).
26. In Gen. 36:15–43, where the same root (pointed by the Masoretes as *ʾallûp*) refers to Edomite "chieftains," suggesting to J. W. Wenham ("Large Numbers in the Old Testament," *TynBul* 18 [1967]: 19–53) that in such contexts *ʾlpym* should perhaps be repointed to *ʾallûpîm*, and understood as "heads" or "clan leader," that is, a professional military officer. On the numbers in Numbers see Milgrom, *Numbers*, 339.
27. Thus C. Humphries, working with the numbers in Numbers, "The Number of People in the Exodus from Egypt: Decoding Mathematically the very Large Numbers in Numbers I and XXVI," *VT* 49 (1999): 196–211; idem, "The Numbers in the Exodus from Egypt: A Reappraisal," *VT* 50 (2000): 323–28. With reference to Num. 3:43, for example, he interprets the expression usually interpreted numerically as 22,273 men as 22 troops consisting of 273 men.
28. So also S. Layton, *Archaic Features of Canaanite Personal Names in the Hebrew Bible* (HSM 47; Atlanta: Scholars Press, 1990), 117.
29. *ANET*, 129–42. For further discussion of this Canaanite divinity, see J. Day, "Baal," *ABD*, 1:545–49; W. Herrmann, "Baal," *DDD*, 132–39.
30. On the pre-Israelite history of Jerusalem, see Y. Shiloh, "Jerusalem," *NEAEHL*, 2:701.
31. On this region, see H. Brodsky, "Shephelah," *ABD*, 5:1204.
32. Cf. H. Wolf, "Judges," *EBC*, 3:388. Boling (*Judges*, 56) proposes "Town of the Treaty-Stele."
33. Similarly Targum's *qiryat ʾarkî*, "city of the officer."
34. See M. Kochavi, "Rabud, Khirbet," in *NEAEHL*, 4:1252; idem, "Khirbet Rabud = Debir," *TA* 1 (1974): 2–33; A. F. Rainey, "Debir," *ISBE*², 1:901–4.
35. For discussion, see J. Crawford, "Caleb the Dog: How a Biblical Good Guy Got a Bad Name," *BRev* 20/2 (2004): 20–27, 45.
36. For further discussion of the role of women in the patricentric biblical world see D. I. Block, "Marriage and Family in Ancient Israel," in *Marriage and Family in the Biblical World*, ed. K. Campbell (Downers Grove, Ill.: InterVarsity Press, 2003), 33–102.
37. Cf. R. Westbrook, *Property and the Family in Biblical Law* (JSOTSup 113; Sheffield: Sheffield Academic Press, 1991), 152–53. According to P. S. Hiebert, "the dowry was property owned by the woman, her share of the family inheritance" ("'Whence Shall Help Come to Me?': The Biblical Widow," in *Gender and Difference in Ancient Israel*, ed. P. L. Day [Minneapolis: Fortress, 1989], 136).
38. See D. W. Manor, "Timnaʿ," *ABD*, 6:553–54.
39. Both Midianites and Kenites are associated with the Amalekites, another migratory southern tribe (Judg. 6:3–5, 33; 1 Sam. 15:4–9). In Gen. 15:19 the Kenites are associated with the Kenizzites, Caleb's clan. Another Kenite, Heber, appears in Judg. 4:17.
40. On this site, see D. W. Manor and G. A. Herions, "Arad," *ABD*, 1:331–36; M. Aharoni, *NEAEHL*, 1:75–87.
41. So also Deut. 34:3 and 2 Chr. 28:15.
42. S. Mittmann identifies it with ʿAin el-ʿAruš. See "Ri. 1, 16f und das Siedlungsgebiet der kenitischen Sippe Hobab," *ZDPV* 93 (1977): 213–35.
43. As translated by K. A. D. Smelik, in *COS*, 2.23.
44. The Kurkh Monolith, *COS*, 2.113A (p. 263).
45. *COS*, 2.2A, p. 9.
46. *COS*, 1.32.
47. Vocalized *Ašqaluna* in these Akkadian texts: §§287, 320–26, 370.
48. *COS*, 2.6.
49. On the origins of the Philistines and the link to Troy, see Assaf Yasur-Landau, "One if by Sea ... Two if by Land: How Did the Philistines Get to Canaan?" *BAR* 29/2 (March-April 2003): 35–39, 66.
50. See L. E. Stager, "Askelon," *NEAEHL*, 1:103–12.
51. See T. Dothan and S. Gitin, "Ekron," *ABD*, 2:415–19 for its early history and the excavations.
52. Cf. Eusebius, *Onomasticon* 40.20–21.
53. See esp. D. Livingston, "The Location of Biblical Bethel and Ai Reconsidered," *WTJ* 33 (1970): 20–44; 34 (1971): 39–50; idem, "One Last Word on Bethel and Ai—Fairness Requires No More," *BAR* 15/1 (1989): 11. For a response and defense of the traditional scholarly view see A. F. Rainey, "Bethel is Still Beitin," *WTJ* 33 (1971): 175–88; idem, "Rainey on the Location of Bethel and Ai," *BAR* 14/5 (1988): 67–68. See also W. J. Dever, "Beitin," *ABD*, 1:651–52; J. L. Kelso, "Bethel," *NEAEHL*, 1:192–94. For discussion of the

options see Provan, Long, and Longman, *Biblical History of Israel*, 176–78.

54. So also Lindars, *Judges 1–5*, 53. Cf. 18:2 (and Josh. 2:1), where completely different vocabulary is used of scouts sent to explore the land.
55. See comments on 1:24.
56. Heimpel, *Letters to the King of Mari*, §26 247.
57. See further Z. Herzog, *Archaeology of the City: Urban Planning in Ancient Israel and its Social Implications* (Tel Aviv: Emery and Claire Yass Archaeology Press, 1997), 164–89; and more briefly A. Mazar, *Archaeology of the Land of the Bible* (New York: Doubleday, 1990), 231; P. J. King and L. E. Stager, *Life in Biblical Israel* (Louisville: Westminster John Knox, 2001), 231.
58. Heimpel, *Letters to the King of Mari*, §§26 498, 514, 169. Cf. Hamblin, *Warfare*, 204.
59. In the Merneptah Stele Hatti occurs in the second place in a series of regions subjugated by the pharaoh: Tehenu, Hatti, Canaan, Ashkelon, Gezer, Yanoam, Israel (with people determinative), Hurru. See *ANET*, 378; *COS*, 2.41.
60. On Beth Shean in the Late Bronze Age, see further P. E. McGovern, "Beth-Shan," *ABD*, 1:693–96; A. Mazar, "Beth-Shean," *NEAEHL*, 1.214–23; Herzog, *Archaeology of the City*, 172 (LB I), 175–78 (LB IIA), 184–87 (LB IIB).
61. See further A. E. Glock, "Taanach," *ABD*, 6:287–90; idem, "Taanach," *NEAEHL*, 4:1428–33.
62. Cf. E. Stern, "Dor," *ABD*, 2:223–25; idem, "Dor," *NEAEHL*, 1:357–68.
63. Cf. M. Hunt, "Ibleam," *ABD*, 3:355.
64. On the history and archaeology of the site, see D. Ussishkin, "Megiddo," *ABD*, 4:666–79; G. I. Davies, "Megiddo in the Period of the Judges," in *Crises and Perspectives: Studies in Ancient Near Eastern Polytheism, Biblical Theology, Palestinian Archaeology and Intertestamental Literature* (OTS 24; Leiden: Brill, 1986), 34–53; Y. Shiloh, "Megiddo," *NEAEHL*, 3:1003–24; Herzog, *Archaeology of the City*, 165–69.
65. Thus S. Bunimovitz, "On the Edge of Empires—Late Bronze Age (1500–1200 B.C.E.)," in *The Archaeology of Society in the Holy Land*, ed. T. Levy (New York: Facts on File, 1995), 326. Bunimovitz provides a helpful discussion of socio-political realities in Palestine in the Late Bronze Age, 320–31.
66. See S. Dalley, "Ancient Mesopotamian Military Organization," *CANE*, 415–16. For a fuller discussion of slavery in the ancient Near East, see I. Mendelsohn, *Slavery in the Ancient Near East* (New York: Oxford Univ. Press, 1949); M. A. Dandamayev, "Slavery, Ancient Near East," *ABD*, 6:58–62.
67. On Gezer see Herzog, *Archaeology of the City*, 178–79; W. G. Dever, "Gezer," *ABD*, 2:998–1003; idem, "Gezer," *NEAEHL*, 2:496–506. For a map of roadways in ancient Israel, see J. B. Pritchard, ed., *The Harper Atlas of the Bible* (New York: Harper & Row, 1987), 58.
68. *COS*, 2.6.
69. M. Dothan, "Acco," *ABD*, 1:50–53; idem, "Tel Acco," *NEAEHL*, 1:17–24.
70. Cf. P. C. Schmitz, "Sidon," *ABD*, 6:17–18.
71. Cf. *ANET*, 287. Cf. M. J. Fretz, "Ahlab," *ABD*, 1:123.
72. M. W. Prausnitz, "Achzib," *ABD*, 1:57–58; idem, "Achzib," *NEAEHL*, 1:32–35.
73. Cf. M. Hunt, "Helbah," *ABD*, 3:117.
74. See R. Frankel, "Aphek," *ABD*, 1:276–77; P. Beck and M. Kochavi, "Aphek," *NEAEHL*, 1:62–72.
75. Cf. J. L. Petersen and R. Arav, "Rehob," *ABD*, 5:661; F. Vitto, "Rehob," *NEAEHL*, 3:1272–74.
76. Cf. Herzog, *Archaeology of the City*, 162 (MB IIB); F. Brandfon, "Beth-Shemesh," *ABD*, 1:696–98; S. Bunimovitz and Z. Lederman, "Beth-Shemesh," *NEAEHL*, 1:249–53.
77. On the possible locations of the site see M. Lubetski, "Beth-Anath," *ABD*, 1:680–81.
78. Cf. *ANET*, 129–49. See also the identification of Shamgar as "son of Anath," in 3:31. For further discussion of Anath, see W. A. Meier III, "Anath," *ABD*, 1:225–27; on Canaanite religion see P. D. Miller Jr., "Aspects of the Religion of Ugarit," in *Ancient Israelite Religion: Essays in Honor of Frank Moore Cross*, ed. P. D. Miller et al. (Philadelphia: Fortress, 1987), 53–66.
79. Thus R. O'Connell, *Rhetoric of the Book of Judges* (Leiden: Brill, 1996), 452. On the Amorites and their relation to the Canaanites, see Schoville, "Canaanites and Amorites," 164–67; M. Liverani, "The Amorites," *POTT*, 100–133; G. Mendenhall, "Amorites," *ABD*, 1:199–202.
80. Cf. J. L. Petersen, "Aijalon," *ABD*, 1:131.
81. Cf. W. J. Toews, "Shaalbim," *ABD*, 5:1147; A. Segal and Y. Naor, "Shaalbim," *NEAEHL*, 4:1339–40.
82. Cf. Job 9:7, which pairs *ḥeres* ("sun") with *kôkābîm* ("stars"). Judg. 8:13 refers to *maʿălēh heḥāres* ("the ascent of the sun") and Isa. 19:18 mentions *ʿir haḥeres* ("city of the sun"; thus NRSV; cf. NIV "City of Destruction"). The root is also preserved in the place name Timnath-Heres (*timnat ḥeres*) in Judg. 2:9.
83. Alternatively, some translate "scurfy mountain" and associate this name with Khirbet Khirsha two miles southeast of Yalo, or Khirbet Kharsis nearby (K.-D. Schunk, "Har-Heres," *ABD*, 3:56). Z. Kallai identifies *har ḥeres* with Timnath-Ḥeres, Joshua's town in the Aijalon Valley (Judg. 2:9). See "The Settlement Traditions of Ephraim," *ZDPV* 102 (1986): 68–74.
84. Cf. M. Görg, "Akrabbim," *ABD*, 1:141.
85. The same word is used in 6:35 of the "messengers" Gideon sends throughout the northern tribes to muster an army to take on the Midianites, as well as the envoys that Jephthah sends to the Ammonites in 11:12–19.
86. As translated by M. Lichtheim, *COS*, 1.41 (p. 92).
87. Cf. W. R. Kotter, "Gilgal (Place)," *ABD*, 2:1022–23; T. Noy, "Gilgal," *NEAEHL*, 2:517–18.
88. For discussion, see K. A. Kitchen, "Egypt, Ugarit, Qatna and Covenant," *UF* 11 (1979): 453–64.
89. For a collection of the former, see G. Beckman, *Hittite Diplomatic Texts*, 2nd ed. (SBLWAW 7; Atlanta: Scholars Press, 1999); for the latter see

S. Parpola and K. Watanabe, *Neo-Assyrian Treaties and Loyalty Oaths* (SAA 2; Helsinki: Helsinki Univ. Press, 1988).

90. For Mari, see H. B. Huffmon, *Amorite Personal Names in the Mari Texts: A Structural and Lexical Study* (Baltimore: John Hopkins Univ. Press, 1965), 118–19, 189; for Canaanite names in the Amarna tablets, see R. S. Hess, *Amarna Personal Names* (ASORDS 9; Winona Lake, Ind.: Eisenbrauns, 1996), 7–13, 244; for Phoenicia, see F. L. Benz, *Personal Names in the Phoenician and Punic Inscriptions* (Studia Pohl 8; Rome: Pontifical Biblical Institute, 1972), 371; for Ugarit, F. Gröndahl, *Die Personnenamender Texte aus Ugarit* (Studia Pohl 1; Rome: Pontifical Biblical Institute, 1967), 80, 105; for Aramaic, M. Maraqten, *Die semitischen Personennamen in den alt und reischsaramäischen Inschriften aus Vorderasien* (Hildesheim: Olms Verlag, 1988), 94, 192.
91. Moran, *Amarna Letters,* 379.
92. See *SSI* 2, p. 166, for more.
93. For discussion of the Israelite institution, see T. M. Willis, *The Elders of the City: A Study of the Elders-Laws in Deuteronomy* (SBLMS 55; Atlanta: Scholars Press, 2001).
94. See the fine study on the role of elders at Mari by Fleming, *Democracy's Ancient Ancestors,* 190–200.
95. For a full study, see E. Noort, "Josua 24,28–31, Richter 2,6–9 und das Josuagrab; Gedanken zu einem Strassenbild," in *Biblische Welten: Festschrift für Metin Metzger zu seinem 65. Geburtstag,* ed. W. Zwickel (OBO 123; Fribourg: Edition universitaires/Göttingen: Vandenhoeck & Ruprecht, 1993), 109–23; cf. more briefly H. R. Weeks, "Timnath-heres," *ABD,* 6:557–58.
96. Cf. E. Bloch-Smith, *Judahite Burial Practices and Beliefs about the Dead* (JSOTSup 123; Sheffield: JSOT Press, 1992), 87–88.
97. These myths are conveniently translated in *ANET,* 129–42. For further discussion of this Canaanite divinity, see J. Day, "Baal," *ABD,* 1:545–49; W. Herrmann, "Baal," *DDD,* 132–39.
98. In classical times Astarte was identified with Aphrodite and Venus.
99. For a helpful map, see D. J. Wiseman, "Babylon," *IBD,* 1:159.
100. For studies of ancient Near Eastern accounts of divine fury, abandonment, and return, see D. I. Block, "Divine Abandonment: Ezekiel's Adaptation of an Ancient Near Eastern Motif," in *Perspectives on Ezekiel: Theology and Anthropology,* ed. M. S. Odell and J. T. Strong (SBL Symposium Series 9; Atlanta: Scholars Press, 2000), 15–42; idem, *The Gods of the Nations: Studies in Ancient Near Eastern National Theology,* 2nd ed. (ETSS 2; Grand Rapids: Baker, 2000), 113–48.
101. To three primary "judges": Othniel (3:10), Jephthah (12:7), Samson (15:20; 16:30); to Deborah (4:4); and to five secondary judges: Tola (10:2), Jair (10:3), Ibzan (12:8, 9), Elon (12:11), Abdon (12:13–14).
102. T. L. J. Mafico notes that the role of judges was "to restore *shalom,* harmonious relations." See "Judge, Judging," *ABD,* 3:1104–5.
103. The nonjudicial sense of the verb is evident elsewhere in 2 Kings 15:5; Ps. 2:10; 94:2; 96:13; 148:11; Isa. 40:23; Amos 2:3.
104. Heimpel, *Letters to the King of Mari,* 582; Fleming, *Democracy's Ancient Ancestors,* 76. For a study of the root in Akkadian, see T. J. Mafico, "The Term *šapīṭum* in Akkadian Documents," *JNSL* 13 (1987): 69–87.
105. As translated by M. S. Smith in *Ugaritic Narrative,* ed. S. B. Parker (SBLWAWS 9; Atlanta: Scholars Press, 1997), 163. See further F. C. Fensham, "The Ugaritic Root *ṯpṭ* *JNSL* 12 (1984): 63–69; H. Cazelles, "*Mṯpṭ* à Ugarit," *Or* 53 (1984): 177–82.
106. G. W. Ahlström, *The History of Ancient Palestine from the Paleolithic Period to Alexander's Conquest* (JSOTSup 146; Sheffield: Sheffield Academic Press, 1993), 372.
107. For further study on the nature and purpose of testing, see G. S. Smith, "The Testing of Our Faith: A Pentateuchal Theology of Testing," unpublished dissertation, The Southern Baptist Theological Seminary, Louisville, Ky., 2005.
108. The groups generally recognized as belonging to the Sea Peoples include, among others, the Peleset, Tjeker (Sikils), Shekelesh, Denyen, Weshesh, and Shardana. See I. Singer, "Sea Peoples," *ABD,* 5:1059–61; Dothan and Dothan, *People of the Sea,* 23, 210, *et passim.*
109. As translated by J. Wilson, *ANET,* 262.
110. Biblical Caphtor. See Gen. 10:13–14; Jer. 47:4; Amos 9:7. Num. 24:24 may allude to the first waves of Sea Peoples arriving from Kittim (Cyprus).
111. See the discussions by Barako and Yasur-Landau, "One if by Sea ... Two if by Land," 24–39, 64, 66, who represent the former and latter respectively. For defense of the former see also L. E. Stager, "Forging an Identity: The Emergence of Ancient Israel," in *The Oxford History of the Biblical World,* ed. M. D. Coogan (Oxford: Oxford Univ. Press, 1998), 152–66.
112. For further studies of the Philistines, see K. A. Kitchen, "The Philistines," *POTT,* 53–78; D. M. Howard Jr., "Philistines," *Peoples of the Old Testament World,* ed. A. J. Hoerth, et al. (Grand Rapids: Baker, 1994), 231–50; T. Dothan and M. Dothan, *People of the Sea: The Search for the Philistines* (New York: Macmillan, 1992); T. Dothan, "Philistines," *ABD,* 5:326–33; idem, *The Philistines and Their Material Culture* (New Haven, Conn.: Yale Univ. Press, 1982).
113. The name has surfaced in the following recently discovered inscription: "The temple which he built, *ʾkys* [Achish, Ikausu] son of Padi, son of *Ysd,* son of Ada, son of Ya'ir, ruler of Ekron, for *Ptgyh* his lady. May she bless him, and protect him, and prolong his days, and bless his land. See S. Gitin, Trude Dothan, and Joseph Naveh, "A Royal Dedicatory Inscription from Ekron," *IEJ* 48 (1997): 1–18; idem, "Special Report: Ekron Identity Confirmed," *Archaeology* 51/1 (January/February 1998): 30–31.
114. See Hess, "Occurrences of Canaan," 365–72.
115. *ANET,* 352.
116. *UNP* 1.IV.34–43 (pp. 19–20).

117. EA 85.71, *et passim*. For additional references, see Moran, *Amarna Letters*, 391.
118. *COS*, 1.41 (p. 91).
119. H. A. Hoffner, "The Hittites and Hurrians," *POTT*, 225.
120. *KTU* 4.6:18–21; for the Ugaritic text in transliteration and translation, see *UNP*, 133; for the translation alone, *COS*, 1.86.
121. *ANET*, 280.
122. JB; cf. J. Gray, *I & II Kings*, rev. ed. (OTL; Philadelphia: Westminster, 1970), 615.
123. Cf. B. Mazar, *Cities and Districts in Eretz Israel* (Jerusalem: Mosad Bialik, 1975), 167–81.
124. Cf. S. Ahituv, *Canaanite Toponyms in Ancient Egyptian Documents* (Jerusalem: Magnes, 1984), 131; Y. Aharoni, *The Land of the Bible* (Philadelphia: Westminster, 1979), 72–73.
125. *UNP*, 120–21.
126. *KTU* 1.4.VI.46 = *CTA* 4.VI.46; *UNP*, p. 134). For discussions and sources, see J. Day, "Asherah," *ABD*, 1:483–87; idem, "Asherah in the Hebrew Bible and Northwest Semitic Literature," *JBL* 31 (1980): 385–408; N. Wyatt, "Asherah," *DDD*, 99–105.
127. Cf. the translation by Day, "Asherah," 1:484–85.
128. Unless, of course, *ʾrm* is a corruption of *ʾdm* (Edom). J. Gray (*Joshua, Judges, Ruth* [NCB; Grand Rapids: Eerdmans, 1986], 260–61) suggests Naharaim was added to clarify Aram, once the error had entered the text. The names Aram (ארם) and Edom (אדם) are confused elsewhere in 2 Sam. 8:12–13; 1 Chron. 18:11; 2 Chron. 20:2.
129. K. A. Kitchen, *On the Reliability of the Old Testament* (Grand Rapids: Eerdmans, 2003), 212.
130. From the Kurkh Monolith, as translated by K. L. Younger, *COS*, 2.113A, 264.
131. On the mocking character of the name "Eglon," see M. Garsiel, *Biblical Names: A Literary Study of Midrashic Derivations and Puns*, trans. P. Hackett (Ramat-Gan: Bar-Ilan Univ., 1991), 215.
132. So also Kitchen, *Reliability of the Old Testament*, 195; Udo Worschech, "Egypt and Moab," *BA* 60 (1997): 229–36.
133. On which see T. E. Levy and M. Najjar, "Edom & Copper: The Emergence of Israel's Rival," *BAR* 32 (July/August 2006): 24–35, 70.
134. See W. E. Aufrecht, *A Corpus of Ammonite Inscriptions* (Ancient Near Eastern Texts and Studies 4; Lewiston, N.Y.: Mellen, 1990), 203–11; idem, *COS*, 2.25. Our transliteration of *bny ʿmwn* follows K. Beyer, "The Ammonite Tell Siran Bottle Inscription Reconsidered," in *Solving Riddles and Untying Knots: Biblical, Epigraphic, and Semitic Studies in Honor of Jonas C. Greenfield*, ed. Z. Zevit, S. Gitin, and M. Sokoloff (Winona Lake, Ind.: Eisenbrauns, 1995), 389–91.
135. Though S. A. Rosen suggests some of the remains of eleventh- to tenth-century fortresses in the Negev may be Amalekite. See Rosen, "Finding Evidence of Ancient Nomads," *BAR* 14/5 (1988): 46–53, 58–59.
136. Like Ichabod (*ʾî kābôd*, "Where is the glory?") in 1 Sam. 4:21, this name reflects the despondency of the times.
137. See more fully, B. Halpern, "A Message for Eglon: The Case of Ehud ben-Gera," in *The First Historians: The Hebrew Bible and History* (San Francisco: Harper & Row, 1988), 40–43.
138. See further M. A. Powell, "Weights and Measures," *ABD*, 6:899–900.
139. The Neo-Assyrians used different words for objects presented by a vassal to a superior. *Madattu* refers to tribute and other objects usually given under compulsion and in fulfillment of a demand by the superior. "Gifts" are usually expressed by *nidintu* (*nidittu*). On the range of meanings of *madattu*, see *CAD* M/1, 13.
140. According to 2 Kings 23:33, Pharaoh Neco demanded from Judah tribute of 7,500 pounds of silver and 75 pounds of gold.
141. RIMA §§87, 88, 89, as translated by K. L. Younger, *COS*, 269–70.
142. The statement "Till here Yahweh has helped us" may represent an oral reading of a statement inscribed on the stele. Compare also the references to analogous monuments set up by Saul (1 Sam. 15:12) and David (2 Sam. 8:3 = 1 Chr. 18:3).
143. *COS*, 2.23. For discussion of this text see J. A. Dearman and G. L. Mattingly, "Mesha Stele," *ABD*, 4:708–9.
144. For further discussion, see K. E. Slanski, *The Babylonian Entitlement* narûs (kudurrus)*: A Study of their Form and Function* (ASOR Books 9; Boston: American Schools of Oriental Research, 2003), 266–70.
145. *HALOT*, 1149.
146. Thus Lindars, *Judges 1–5*, 144; Halpern, *First Historians*, 45. Cf. 2 Sam. 9:25; 1 Kings 17:19; 2 Kings 1:2; 4:10.
147. Halpern, *First Historians*, 45–46; for a popular version of this discussion see idem, "The Assassination of Eglon—The First Locked-Room Murder Mystery," *BR* 4 (1988): 32–41, 44, esp. 38. This interpretation finds support in v. 24, which uses *ḥᵃdar hammᵉqērâ* ("upper dark inner room," *HALOT*, 293) as a variant of the present expression.
148. Cf. King and Stager, *Life in Biblical Israel*, 28–35.
149. See J. Braun, *Music in Ancient Israel/Palestine: Archaeological, Written, and Comparative Sources*, trans. D. W. Scott (Grand Rapids: Eerdmans, 2002), 26.
150. As such it was employed in a variety of situations: (1) to call people to worship (Lev. 25:9; Joel 2:15); (2) to lead in procession (Josh. 6:5; 2 Sam. 6:15); (3) to signal the arrival of the king or other important figure (Ex. 19:16–18; cf. the use of *yôbel* in v. 13); (4) to alert the people to the arrival of an enemy (Jer. 4:19; Joel 2:1); (5) to create panic (Judg. 7:18); (6) to rally troops (Judg. 3:27; 6:34; 1 Sam. 13:3); (7) to signal various instructions (2 Sam. 18:16).
151. Though Soggin argues the name could be West Semitic, based on the Shapel stem of the root *mgr* ("to submit"); see J. A. Soggin, *Judges: A Commentary* (OTL; Philadelphia: Westminster, 1981), 57.
152. See B. Maisler (Mazar), "Shamgar ben ʿAnat," *PEQ* 66 (1934): 192–94; W. Feiler, "Hurritische Namen im Alten Testament," *ZA* 45 (1939): 219. This

Hurrian solution is preferable to a proposed conflation of the transliterated and translated Hebrew forms of Egyptian *sʾm*, meaning "wanderer, stranger," viz., Sham-gēr. Cf. N. Shupak, "New Light on Shamgar ben ʿAnath," *Bib* 70 (1980): 518; E. Danelius, "Judge Shamgar," *JNES* 22 (1963): 191–93. P. C. Craigie adduces Ugaritic, Mari, and Egyptian evidence for foreign mercenaries in "A Reconsideration of Shamgar ben Anath (Exod. 3:31 and 5:6)," *JBL* 91 (1972): 239–80.

153. Compare the name of Jeremiah's hometown, Anathoth, Jer. 1:1.
154. Cf. 1:33; Josh. 19:32–39. Thus Gray, *Joshua, Judges, and Ruth*, 216.
155. Compare Mal. 2:11, which refers to non-Israelite women as daughters "of a foreign God." Note also names like Ben-Hadad, "Son of Hadad."
156. On Anath, see Walter A. Meier III, "Anath (Deity)," *ABD*, 1:225–26; P. L. Day, "Anat," *DDD*, 62–77.
157. For the evidence, see Shupak, "New Light," 518–19.
158. As read by W. Helck, *Die Beziehungen Aegyptens zu Vorderasien im 3. und 2. Jahr. V. Chr.* (Wiessbaden: Harrassowitz, 1971), 487.
159. Further evidence of the use of *bn ʿnt* as a military cognomen appears on an El-Khadr arrowhead dated ca. 1100 B.C., bearing the incised inscription, *ʿbdlbʾt bn ʿnt*, on which see F. M. Cross, "Newly Found Inscriptions in Old Canaanite and Early Phoenician Scripts," *BASOR* 238 (1980): 4, 6–7. Cf. also an eleventh- or tenth-century bronze arrowhead discussed by J. T. Milik and F. M. Cross, "Inscribed Javelin-Heads from the Period of the Judges: A Recent Discovery in Palestine," *BASOR* 134 (1954): 5–15.
160. See Shupak, "New Light," 524.
161. For additional examples from Ugarit, the Hittites, and Egypt, see Kitchen, *On the Reliability of the Old Testament*, 184–85.
162. W. Horowitz and A. Schaffer, "A Fragment of a Letter from Hazor," *IEJ* 42 (1992): 165–67.
163. C. R. Krahmalkov, "Exodus Itinerary Confirmed by Egyptian Evidence," *BAR* 20/5 (September-October 1994): 61.
164. Soggin follows Albright in accepting Sisera as a Luvian name. Soggin, *Judges*, 63; cf. W. F. Albright, "Prolegomenon" to C. F. Burney, *Book of Judges: With Introduction and Notes* (New York: Ktav, 1970), 15. See also R. de Vaux, trans. D. Smith (London: Darton, Longman, & Todd, 1978), *The Early History of Israel*, 792.
165. *HALOT*, 1:358.
166. As does an association with the supposed Akkadian cognate *ḫušānu* ("mountain"). So also A. F. Rainey, "Toponymic Problems," *TA* 10 (1983): 46.
167. *CAD* E, 300b.
168. See further Rainey, "Toponymic Problems," 46–48; idem, "The Military Camp Ground at Taanach by the Waters of Megiddo," *ErIsr* 15 (1981): 61*–66*.
169. *ANET*, 237.
170. On the nature and significance of iron chariots, see comment on 1:19.
171. Cf. (lit.) "a man, a prophet" in 6:8.
172. *AHw*, 697b, 699b. The verb occurs in the Old Testament only in the reflexive stems (Niphal, Hithpael). *HALOT*, 659. On the etymology of the word, see J. Huehnergard, "On the Etymology and Meaning of Hebrew *nābîʾ*," *EI* 26 (1999): 88*–93; D. E. Fleming, "The Etymological Origins of the Hebrew *nābîʾ*, The One Who Invokes God," *CBQ* 55 (1993): 217–24, who argues for an active meaning, "one who invokes the gods."
173. Persons explicitly identified as female prophets include Miriam (Ex. 15:20), Deborah (Judg. 4:4), Huldah (2 Kings 22:14), Noadiah (Neh. 6:14), and the unnamed wife of Isaiah (Isa. 8:3). To this list the Targums rightly add Hannah, whose poem in 1 Sam. 2:1–10 bears all the marks of a prophetic pronouncement. Cf. also Anna in Luke 2:36.
174. For a convenient collection of ancient Near Eastern prophetic texts, see Nissinen et al., *Prophets and Prophecy in the Ancient Near East.*
175. A. Malamat has recognized an unusually high proportion of women among the lay prophets at Mari. See "A Forerunner of Biblical Prophecy: The Mari Documents," in *Ancient Israelite Religion*, ed. P. D. Miller, P. D. Hanson, and S. D. McBride (Philadelphia: Fortress, 1987), 43–44.
176. This pattern is evident in the cases of the prophets of Baal, "who eat at Jezebel's table" (1 Kings 18:19), and Ahab's prophets in 1 Kings 22:22; (note the reference to "his prophets"). Because kings were deemed to be tools in the hands of the gods, prophetic declarations against the king's interests were by definition false, regardless of the source of the inspiration. Thus M. Nissinen, *References to Prophecy in Neo-Assyrian Sources* (SAA 7; Helsinki: Neo-Assyrian Text Corpus Project, 1999), 166–67.
177. Compare Miriam, who is introduced as "Miriam, the prophetess, the sister of Aaron" (Ex. 15:20); Huldah, who is "Huldah, the prophetess, the wife of Shallum ben Tikvah" (2 Kings 22:14). In the New Testament Anna is identified as "the prophetess, the daughter of Phanuel" (Luke 2:36).
178. See *UNP*, 112.
179. For the text and translation, see Seow in Nissinen, *Prophets and Prophecy*, 204–6.
180. On the palm as a sacred symbol in the ancient Near East, see U. Magen, *Assyrische Königsdarstellungen—Aspekte der Herrschaft* (Baghdader Forschungen 9; Mainz am Rhein: Philipp von Zabern, 1986), 79–81.
181. As in Kadesh Barnea, Kedesh in Issachar (1 Chron. 6:57), and Kadesh-on-the-Orontes, the site of the great battle between Ramesses II of Egypt and the Hittite king Muwatallis.
182. D. J. Wiseman, "Kedesh, Kedesh in Naphtali," *IBD*, 2:847; Halpern, *First Historians*, 92–93. On this site see A. Ovadiah et al., "Kedesh (In Upper Galilee)," *NEAEHL*, 3:855–59. Assuming this Kedesh must be relatively near to Mount Tabor and that it is the same Kedesh mentioned in v. 11, some identify this site with modern Khirbet Qedish, one mile west of the southern end of the

Sea of Galilee (e.g., Ovadiah et al., "Kedesh [In Upper Galilee]," 3:855); N. Naʿaman, "Literary and Topographical Notes on the Battle of Kishon (Judges IV-V)," *VT* 40 (1990): 429; C. Rasmussen, *NIV Atlas of the Bible* (Grand Rapids: Zondervan, 1989), 241.

183. Cf. the Song of Deborah (5:19), which calls the Kishon "the waters of Megiddo."
184. Though some link it with Wadi el-Bira that flows east from Tabor into the Jordan. See R. Frankel, "Kishon," *ABD*, 4:89. The topographical names in Song 5 support the former view.
185. Cf. the compound place names such as Elon Tabor (1 Sam. 10:3) and Elon Moreh (Gen. 12:6). Note also the variant Allon Bacuth in Gen. 35:8.
186. Soggin rightly rejects an identification with the similar-sounding place name referred to in Josh. 19:33 (*Judges*, 66).
187. In addition to the sources cited above on v. 6, see B. Margalit, "Observations on the Jael-Sisera Story (Judges 4–5)," in *Pomegranates and Golden Bells: Studies in Biblical, Jewish, and Near Eastern Ritual, Law, and Literature in Honor of Jacob Milgrom*, ed. D. P. Wright et al. (Winona Lake, Ind.: Eisenbrauns, 1995), 629–31.
188. Some identify the site with Tel Kedesh (Tell Abu Qedesh) in the Jezreel Valley, midway between Taanach and Megiddo. So E. Stern, "Kedesh, Tel [In Jezreel Valley]," *NEAEHL*, 2:860; Soggin, *Judges*, 66; J. Hofbauer, in a review of W. Richter, *Traditionsgeschichtliche Untersuchungen zum Richterbuch*, *ZKT* 87 (1965): 319. However, one wonders why Heber would settle here if allied with and counting on the protection of Jabin.
189. Especially if he were a nomadic mercenary charged by the king of Hazor to police the area around Kedesh. Thus Margalit, "Observations on the Jael-Sisera Story," 640, though he locates Kedesh southwest of Galilee.
190. Naʿaman, "Literary and Topographical Notes," 427. For a reconstruction of the events involved in this battle, see Rainey, "The Military Camp Ground at Taanach," 15, 61*–66*.
191. *HALOT*, 1:251; *DCH*, 2:571.
192. Cf. also Josh. 10:10; 1 Sam. 7:10. The present statement casts Yahweh in the role of divine warrior, fulfilling his promise in Exod. 23:27: "I will send my terror ahead of you and throw into confusion every nation you encounter. I will make all your enemies turn their backs and run."
193. As translated by Grayson, *Assyrian Rulers of the Early First Millennium* B.C., 18 (iii 66–72).
194. Ibid., 197 (i 56b–58a).
195. Presumably it is Yahweh's sword (so also in v. 16b).
196. Compare 3:28–29, where the narration credits the success entirely to human activity, even though Ehud announces Yahweh's victory.
197. See B. Beitzel, "Roads and Highways (Pre-Roman)," *ABD*, 5:778–79; idem, *Moody Atlas*, 67–68.
198. Grayson, *Assyrian Rulers of the Early First Millennium* B.C., 203–4 (ii 30).
199. For a discussion and references, see S. C. Layton, "Yaʿel in Judges 4: An Onomastic Rejoinder," *ZAW* 109 (1997): 93–94.
200. On the structure of Israelite families and the role of the head of the household, see Block, "Marriage and Family in Ancient Israel," 40–61; King and Stager, *Life in Biblical Israel*, 21–39.
201. For full discussion, see V. A. Matthews, "Hospitality and Hostility in Judges 4," *BTB* 21 (1991): 13–21.
202. King and Stager, *Life in Biblical Israel*, 103.
203. For the Hebrew, see 1 Kings 6:7; Isa. 44:12; Jer. 10:4; for the Ugaritic, Gordon, *UT* §19:1533; for the Akkadian, *AHw* 607b.
204. See further D. F. Chalcraft, "Deviance and Legitimate Action in the Book of Judges," in *The Bible in Three Dimensions: Essays in Celebration of Forty Years of Biblical Studies in the Univ. of Sheffield*, ed. D. J. A. Clines et al. (JSOTSup 87; Sheffield: Sheffield Academic Press, 1990), 182–83.
205. J. G. Taylor, "The Song of Deborah and Two Canaanite Goddesses," *JSOT* 23 (1982): 99–108.
206. So also S. Niditch, "Eroticism and Death in the Tale of Jael," in *Gender and Difference in Ancient Israel*, ed. P. L. Day (Minneapolis: Fortress, 1989), 45.
207. See W. W. Hallo, "The Cultic Setting of Sumerian Poetry," in *Rencontre assyriologique internationale*, ed. Andre Fine (Brussels: Ham-sur-Heure, 1970), 132.
208. Thus N. K. Gottwald, *The Tribes of the Lord: A Sociology of the Religion of Liberated Israel, 1250–1050* B.C.E. (Maryknoll, N.Y.: Orbis, 1979), 539. For a detailed study of the root, see J. G. Janzen, "The Root *prʿ* in Judges V 2 and Deuteronomy XXXII 42," *VT* 39 (1989): 393–406. See also P. C. Craigie, "A Note on Judges V 2," *VT* 18 (1968): 397–99.
209. Moran, *Amarna Letters*, 331.
210. For the text see Kitchen, *Ramesside Inscriptions*.
211. *ANET*, 262.
212. Ibid., 298.
213. In Deut. 33:2, Yahweh comes from Sinai/Seir/Mount Paran; in Hab. 3:3, God comes from Teman/Mount Paran; in Ps. 7–8, God comes from the wasteland.
214. For a classical discussion of the hypothesis, see de Vaux, *The Early History of Israel*, 333–38; for recent surveys of the issue see K. van der Toorn, "Yahweh," *DDD*, 910–19; B. Halpern, "Kenites," *ABD*, 5:20–21.
215. Hebrew *zeh* with genitive, meaning "the one of," is cognate to Amorite *zu*, Ugaritic *d*, Old Sinaitic *d*, *dt*, and Arabic *dū*. For bibliography see *HALOT*, 264. For a contrary opinion, see Lindars, *Judges 1–5*, 233–34.
216. So also A. Globe, "The Text and Literary Structure of Judges 5,4–5," *Bib* 55 (1974): 178.
217. Thus N. Naʿaman, "Amarna *ālani pu-ru-zi* (EA 137) and Biblical *ʿry hprzyhprzwt* (Rural Settlements)," *Zeitschrift für Althebräistik* 4 (1991): 72–75. For discussion of the Hebrew expression, see L. E. Stager, "Archaeology, Ecology, and Social History: Background Themes to the Song of Deborah," *Congress Volume: Jerusalem, 1986*, ed. J. A. Emerton (VTSup 40; Leiden: Brill, 1988), 224–25; idem, "The Song of Deborah: Why Some Tribes Answered the Call and Others Did Not," *BAR* 15/1 (1989): 55.

218. Thus L. E. Stager, "Merenptah, Israel and Sea Peoples," *ErIsr* 18 (1985): 61*, and Freedman, *Pottery, Poetry and Prophecy* (Winona Lake, Ind.: Eisenbrauns, 1980), 176.
219. For discussions of military organization and warfare in the ancient Near East, see A. Schulman, "Military Organization in Pharaonic Egypt," *CANE*, 289–302; Dalley, "Ancient Mesopotamian Military Organization," *CANE*, 413–22; R. H. Beal, "Hittite Military Organization," *CANE*, 545–54. Conscription is discussed more specifically by J. N. Postgate, *Taxation and Conscription in the Assyrian Empire* (Studia Pohl: Series Maior 3, Rome: Biblical Institute, 1974).
220. Cf. O. Borowski, *Every Living Thing: Daily Use of Animals in Ancient Israel* (Walnut Creek, Calif.: AltaMira, 1998), 96–97.
221. Note how the Israelites speak of Moabites as "the people of Chemosh" (Num. 21:9; Jer. 48:46). Note too the obverse of this expression, "Chemosh, the god of Moab," and the Ammonite equivalent, "Milkom, the god of Bene-Ammon," in 1 Kings 11:33 (NIV, "Molech, the god of the Ammonites"). On the significance of these expressions, see Block, *Gods of the Nations*, 36–39.
222. For discussion and illustration, see Braun, *Music in Ancient Israel/Palestine*, 110–12.
223. Stager, "Song of Deborah," 229–32.
224. So also Rainey, "Who is a Canaanite?" 11.
225. For a popular illustrated study, see G. F. Bass, "Oldest Known Shipwreck Reveals Splendors of the Bronze Age," *National Geographic* 172/6 (1987): 692–733.
226. On Megiddo and Taanach see comment on 1:27–28.
227. M. Weinfeld suggests "a comet fell out of its fixed place" in "Divine Intervention in War in Ancient Israel and in the Ancient Near East," in *History, Historiography and Interpretation: Studies in Biblical and Cuneiform Literatures*, ed. H. Tadmor and M. Weinfeld (Jerusalem: Magnes, 1986), 127. J. F. A. Sawyer sees here a reference to the total eclipse of the sun in the vicinity of Megiddo and Taanach in 1131 B.C., in which case at least the nucleus of the song is to be dated early, its composer being an eyewitness of the eclipse, "From Heaven Fought the Stars," *VT* 31 (1981): 87–89.
228. As translated by J. K. Hoffmeier in COS, 2, 17. For full discussion of the motif, see Weinfeld, "Divine Intervention," 124–31.
229. Weinfeld, "Divine Intervention," 124, notes that all three of these elements also appear in the prose account of Yahweh's victory at the Reed Sea (Ex. 14:19–28). For a comparison of Judg. 5 and Ex. 15, see Hauser, "Two Songs of Victory," 265–84.
230. *UT ʿnt* II 41 (=*KTU* 1.3 II 41); see the translation by Pardee in *UNP*, 109.
231. Josh. 10:10, 12. Cf. Naʾaman, "The Battle of Kishon," 426; M. Hunt, "Meroz," *ABD*, 4:705–6; H.-D. Neef, "Meroz: Jdc 5,23a," *ZAW* 107 (1995): 118–22.
232. For discussion, see Bass, "Splendors of the Bronze Age," 714.
233. Third tablet of Aqhat, *CTA* 19:I:8–11 (*UNP*, 69). See also the first tablet of Aqhat, *CTA* 17:VI:26–28 (*UNP*, 61), and the second tablet of the Baal Cycle, *CTA* 2:II:36–37, as translated by M. S. Smith in *UNP*, 101.
234. *AHw*, 1107.
235. *CAD* 16.205.
236. Grayson, *Assyrian Rulers of the Early First Millennium* B.C., 217.
237. Gen. 25:2–4 presents them as descended from Abraham.
238. See further P. J. Parr, "Qurayya," *ABD*, 5:594–96; Kitchen, *Reliability of the Old Testament*, 214.
239. Gen. 29:1; Job 1:3. The *bᵉnê qedem* are often mentioned in the prophets: Isa. 11:14; Jer. 49:28; Ezek. 25:1–10.
240. COS, 1.38 (p. 78).
241. T. Hiebert, "Joel," *ABD*, 3:876; see also Borowski, *Every Living Thing*, 159–60.
242. See M. Ingraham et al., "Preliminary Report on a Reconnaissance Survey of the Northwestern Province (with a Brief Survey of the Northern Province)," *Atlas* 5 (1981): pl. 79/14.
243. On the use of these camels, see B. Rothenburg, "Egyptian Chariots, Midianites from Hijaz/Midian (Northwest Arabia) and Amalekites from the Negev in the Timna Mines: Rock Drawings in the Ancient Copper Mines of the Arabah—New Aspects of the Region's History II," *Institute for Archaeo-metallurgical Studies* 23 (February 2003): 14.
244. On the domestication and use of camels in the ancient Near East, see Borowski, *Every Living Thing*, 112–21; E. Firmage, "Zoology (Animal Profiles)," *ABD*, 6:1138–40.
245. For discussion and texts, see J. K. Hoffmeier, "The Arm of God Versus the Arm of Pharaoh in the Exodus Narratives," *Bib* 67 (1986): 378–87.
246. As translated by Nissinen, *Prophets and Prophecy*, 102.
247. Cf. J. M. Hamilton, "Ophrah," *ABD*, 5:28. On ʿAfula see M. Dothan, "ʿAfula," *NEAEHL*, 1:37–39.
248. Cf. J. M. Sasson, "King Hammurabi of Babylon," *CANE*, 902.
249. P. Bienkowski and A. Millard, *Dictionary of the Ancient Near East* (Philadelphia: Univ. of Pennsylvania Press, 2000), 39.
250. Sometimes ancient Near Easterners would also use threshing sledges, which consisted of boards with embedded flint or basalt studs and were drawn over the stalks of grain by donkeys or oxen. See King and Stager, *Life in Biblical Israel*, 89–90.
251. See ibid., 100–101.
252. For discussion, see J. H. Walton, *Ancient Near Eastern Thought and the Old Testament: Introducing the Conceptual World of the Hebrew Bible* (Grand Rapids: Baker, 2006), 87–112, 135–61.
253. *AHw*, 881.
254. Qere; cf. Kethib *prq*.
255. See also the large altar on Mount Ebal, on which see A. Mazar, "The 'Bull Site': An Iron Age I Open Cult Place," *BASOR* 247 (1982): 27–42.
256. For the procedure followed in Assyria, see C. Walker and M. Dick, "The Induction of the Cult Image in Ancient Mesopotamia: The Mesopotamian *mīs pî* Ritual," in *Born in Heaven, Made on*

Earth: The Making of the Cult Image in the Ancient Near East, ed. M. B. Dick (Winona Lake, Ind.: Eisenbrauns, 1999), 55–121. For a popular presentation, see M. B. Dick, "Worshiping Idols: What Isaiah Didn't Know," *BRev* 18/2 (April 2002): 30–37.

257. The issue is different in 1 Kings 18:21, where the purpose of the test proposed to Ahab is to determine whether Yahweh or Baal is God.
258. The jussive form used here translates lit., "Let the Baal contend against him." Note the change of preposition from "Will you plead for (*l*ᵉ) Baal" in v. 31 to *b*ᵉ ("against") in v. 32.
259. See M. Hunt, "Harod," *ABD*, 3:62.
260. Cf. Boling's, "Teacher's Hill," *Judges*, 144.
261. Thus A. Malamat, "The War of Gideon and Midian—A Military Approach," *PEQ* 84 (1952): 61–65; idem, "Period of the Judges," 143–47.
262. For further discussion, see Block, *Judges, Ruth*, 276–77.
263. For other examples of God's speaking to non-Israelites this way, see the dreams of Abimelech (Gen. 20:3, 6), Laban (31:24), Pharaoh and his servants (chs. 40–41), and Nebuchadnezzar (Dan. 2:1–3).
264. See J. Black and A. Green, *Gods, Demons and Symbols of Ancient Mesopotamia: An Illustrated Dictionary* (London: British Museum Press, 1992), 130–31.
265. GKC §147*c*.
266. C. R. Krahmalkov interprets this form as the soldier's oath of allegiance to God and ruler. See "The Foundation of Carthage, 814 B.C.: The Douïmès Pendant Inscription," *JSS* 26 (1981): 85–86.
267. For discussion of the inscription, see S. Gitin and M. Cogan, "A New Type of Dedicatory Inscription from Ekron," *IEJ* 49/34 (1999): 193–202.
268. Similarly K. L. Younger Jr., *Judges and Ruth* (NIVAC; Grand Rapids: Zondervan, 2002), 190–91.
269. H. O. Thompson discusses three of these in "Beth-Shittah," *ABD*, 1:698; "Zererah," *ABD*, 6:1082–83; "Tabbath," *ABD*, 6:291–92. On Abel Meholah see D. V. Edelman, "Abel-Meholah," *ABD*, 1:11–12.
270. So also Garsiel, "Name-Derivations," 308.
271. See further J. A. H. Seely, "Succoth," *ABD*, 6:217–18; G. van der Kooij, "Deir ʿAlla, Tell," *NEAEHL*, 1:338–42.
272. See Mazar, *Archaeology of the Land of the Bible*, 358.
273. For the first interpretation, see Soggin, *Judges*, 149; for the second, see G. E. Mendenhall, "Zebah and Zalmunna," *ABD*, 6:1055. Garsiel, "Homiletic Name-Derivations," 308, prefers an association with *ṣelem* ("image, shape").
274. See further C. L. Meyers, "Kinship and Kingship: The Early Monarchy," in *The Oxford History of the Biblical World*, ed. M. D. Coogan (Oxford: Oxford Univ. Press, 1998), 177–78.
275. So also Younger, *Judges and Ruth*, 197.
276. *AHw*, 292a; *CAD*, G, 99.
277. See Zohary, *Plants of the Bible*, 158–59; I. Jacob and W. Jacob, "Flora," *ABD*, 2:186. Also K. L. Younger Jr., "בַּרְקֹן," *NIDOTTE*, 1:770–71; idem, "קוֹץ," *NIDOTTE*, 3:907.
278. See *HALOT*, 218.
279. For discussions of Shishak's campaign, see B. Mazar, "Pharoah Shishak's Campaign to the Land of Israel," in *The Early Biblical Period*, ed. Shmuel Aḥituv and Baruch A. Levine (Jerusalem: Israel Exploration Society, 1986), 139–50; K. A. Kitchen, *The Third Intermediate Period in Egypt (1100–650 B.C.)* (Warminster, Eng.: Aris & Phillips, 1986), 298–99.
280. Cf. J. C. Slayton, "Penuel," *ABD*, 5:223.
281. Cf. *HALOT*, 1148.
282. Cf. H. O. Thompson, "Karkor," *ABD*, 4:6.
283. P. N. Franklyn, "Jogbehah," *ABD*, 3:880.
284. For analysis of the inscription and a discussion of its significance for the origin of the alphabet, see J. C. Darnell et al., "Two Early Alphabetic Inscriptions from the Wadi el-Ḥôl: New Evidence for the Development of the Alphabet from the Western Desert of Egypt," *BASOR* 59 (2005): 63–124.
285. See Gogel, *Grammar of Epigraphic Hebrew*, #6.1.5 (p. 404). For discussion of this text, see J. C. Vanderkam, "Calendars, Ancient Israelite and Early Jewish," *ABD*, 1:814–17.
286. The report of the discovery is available at www.zeitah.net/UpdateTelZayit.html.
287. See M. Kochavi, "An Ostracon of the Period of the Judges from ʿIzbet Ṣarṭa," *TA* 4 (1977): 1–13; Cross, "Newly Found Inscriptions in Old Canaanite and Early Phoenician Scripts," 8–15.
288. On literacy in ancient Egypt, see J. Baines and C. J. Eyre, "Four Notes on Literacy," *GM* 61 (1983): 65–96; B. M. Bryan, "Evidence for Female Literacy from Theban Tombs of the New Kingdom," *Bulletin of the Egyptological Seminar* 6 (1985): 17–32; L. H. Lesko, "Some Comments on Ancient Egyptian Literacy and Literati," in *Studies in Egyptology: Presented to Miriam Lichtheim*, ed. S. Israelit-Groll (Jerusalem: Magnes, 1990), 2:656–67. For Mesopotamia, see C. Wilcke, *Wer las und schrieb in Babylonien und Assyrien: Überlegungen zur Literalität im Alten Zweistromland* (SBAW Philosophisch-historische Klasse, Jahrgang 2000, Heft 6; Munich: Bayerische Akademie der Wissenschaften, 2000).
289. For the role and status of the *naʿar* in Israel, see J. MacDonald, "The Status and Role of the *NAʿAR* in Israelite Society," *JNES* 35 (1976): 147–70. MacDonald renders the term "squire."
290. Analysis of the diffusion of writing in ancient Israel has been a special project of A. R. Millard. See Millard, "Knowledge of Writing in Iron Age Palestine," *TynBul* 46 (1995): 207–17; idem, "The Question of Israelite Literacy," *BRev* 3 (1987), 22–31; idem, "Books in the Late Bronze Age in the Levant," in S. Izreʾel, I. Singer, and R. Zadok, eds., *Past Links: Studies in the Languages and Cultures of the Ancient Near East* (Israel Oriental Studies 18; Winona Lake, Ind.: Eisenbrauns, 1998), 171–81. See also A. Lemaire, "Writing and Writing Materials," *ABD*, 6:999–1008; R. S. Hess, "Literacy in Iron Age Israel," in *Windows into Old Testament History: Evidence, Argument, and the Crisis of "Biblical Israel"*

(Grand Rapids: Eerdmans, 2002), 82–102; I. M. Young, "Israelite Literacy and Inscriptions: A Response to Richard Hess," *VT* 55 (2005): 565–68; W. M. Schniedewind, *How the Bible Became a Book: The Textualization of Ancient Israel* (Cambridge: Cambridge Univ. Press, 2004).

291. For discussion of the role of elders in Israel, see Willis, *The Elders of the City*.
292. For references to Old South Arabic, see *HALOT*, 1311.
293. For further discussion, see Block, *Judges, Ruth*, 296–304.
294. Nili Fox, "Holy Piercing? The Connection between Earrings and Cult Images," a paper presented at the annual meeting of the American Schools of Oriental Research, November 18, 2004 (San Antonio, Tex.).
295. On the weight of a shekel, see Y. Ronen, "The Enigma of the Shekel Weights of the Judean Kingdom," *BA* 59/2 (1996): 122–26.
296. *CAD*, E.183. Cf. C. L. Meyers, "Ephod," *ABD*, 2:550.
297. H. A. Hoffner, "Hittite Equivalents of Old Assyrian *kumrum* and *epattum*," *WZKM* 86 (1996): 154–56.
298. In Judges we also read of the seventy kings subject to Adoni-Bezeq (1:7) and Abdon's seventy sons (12:14). Note also the seventy sons of Jacob (Gen. 46:27), seventy elders in Israel (Ex. 24:1), and the seventy sons of Ahab (2 Kings 10:1–7). The "Table of Nations" in Genesis 10 lists seventy descendants of Noah's three sons (not counting the names in the parenthetical comments).
299. See COS, 2.37 (p. 158); Gibson, *Aramaic Inscriptions*, 14:3.
300. *ANET*, 134; *UNP*, 134, on which see M. S. Smith, in ibid., 171, n. 135. See also F. C. Fensham, "The Numeral Seventy in the Old Testament and the Family of Jerubbaal, Ahab, Panammuwa and Athirat," *PEQ* 109 (1977): 113–15; J. C. de Moor, "Seventy," in *"Und Mose schrieb dieses Lied auf": Studien zum Alten Testament und zum Alten Orient: Festschrift für Oswald Loretz zur Vollendung seines 70. Lebensjahres mit Beiträgen von Freunden, Schülern und Kollegen*, ed. M. Dietrich und I. Kottsieper (AOAT 250; Münster: Ugarit Verlag, 1998), 199–203.
301. All were Philistines: Gen. 20; 26:1–33; Ps. 34, superscription. In the last case, the name replaces Achish (cf. 1 Sam. 21:10–15), the name of the king of Gath, lending support to the view that Abimelech functioned as a dynastic title for Philistine kings. Cf. V. H. Matthews, "Abimelech," *ABD*, 1:21.
302. Ten of the preserved letters (*EA* 146–55) were written by Abi-Milku. See Moran, *Amarna Letters*, 232–42.
303. The chief deity of Tyre was Melqart, a conflated form of *mlk* + *qrt*, "*MLK*/King of the City."
304. The national deity of the Ammonites was Milkom (cf. 1 Kings 11:5, 33; 2 Kings 23:13). For discussion of the deity Malik, see H.-P. Müller, "Malik," *DDD*, 538–42. On Milkom see E. Puech, "Milkom," *DDD*, 575–76.
305. Cf. Fowler, *Theophoric Personal Names*, 50–52; Layton, *Archaic Features of Canaanite Personal Names*, 116–17, 145–50; B. Halpern, "Abimelech," *ABD*, 1:21.
306. According to L. E. Stager, "Perhaps Abimelech's mother came from the most powerful founding family and leading clan of Shechem, the Hamorites (literally, the 'Donkey' clan), whose eponymous ancestor, Hamor, father of Shechem (Judg. 9:28), is also 'chief' of the land of Shechem in the patriarchal tale of Dinah (Genesis 34:2)." See "The Shechem Temple: Where Abimelech Massacred a Thousand," *BAR* 29/4 (July/August 2003): 66.
307. The ruins give evidence of a massive fire. Archaeologists have tended to associate this destruction with the end of the city of Labaʾyu and his sons (see L. E. Toombs, "Shechem," *ABD*, 5:1183), but Stager, "The Shechem Temple," has recently argued that the fire should be associated with events described at the end of Judges 9. See comment on 9:46.
308. For evidence of the pressure put on Jerusalem by the rulers of Shechem, see EA §§244–55, 280, 287, 289 (Moran, *Amarna Letters*, 298–308, 321, 328, 332–33).
309. Portrayed in iconographic images as a striding male figure brandishing a club and/or holding the lightning bolt in his hand (see *IBD*, 1:153). Cf. Ora Negbi's Type III warrior deities in *Canaanite Gods in Metal* (Tel Aviv: Univ. Institute of Archaeology, 1976), 29–41.
310. *ANET*, 134. The name El is prominent in the patriarchal narratives, often appearing in conjunction with other names: El Elyon, El Shaddai, El Roi, etc.
311. See the review of this position by T. J. Lewis, "The Identity and Function of El/Baal Berith," *JBL* 115 (1996): 403–4.
312. So ibid., 415. Cf. pp. 404–14 for a discussion of possible analogues to Yahweh's covenant with Israel, though none of these is unequivocal. For variations of Lewis's theory see R. E. Clements, "Baal-Berith of Shechem," *JSS* 13 (1968): 21–32, who interprets the "men/sons of Hamor" as "men/sons of the ass," the donkey being commonly slaughtered ritually in covenant ceremonies, and Y. Kaufmann, *Religion of Israel: From its Beginning to the Babylonian Exile*, trans. M. Greenberg (New York: Schocken, 1960), 138–39, who suggests that Israel drew its own understanding of Yahweh's covenant with them from Baal's relationship with Shechem.
313. On this temple, see further below.
314. For a study of the political situation in Canaan during the period of Israel's conquest and settlement, see J. P. van der Westhuizen, "The Situation in Syro-Palestine Prior to the Exodus/Conquest/Settlement as Reflected in the Amarna Letters," *JSem* 7 (1995): 196–231.
315. For a discussion of these elements, see A. F. Rainey, "Unruly Elements in Late Bronze Canaanite Society," in *Pomegranates and Golden Bells: Studies in Biblical, Jewish, and Near Eastern Ritual, Law, and Literature in Honor of Jacob Milgrom*, ed. D. P.

Wright et al. (Winona Lake, Ind.: Eisenbrauns, 1995), 481–96.

316. As translated by K. L. Younger Jr., in *COS*, 2.37. For a discussion of this text and its relation to Judges 9, see Fensham, "The Numeral Seventy in the Old Testament," 113–15.

317. Boling, *Judges*, 171; Gray, *Joshua, Judges and Ruth*, 318.

318. Thus M. Görg ("Beth-Millo," *ABD*, 1:690), who suggests a derivation from Egyptian m^3rw, which refers to a part of the king's court.

319. On the government of Shechem by an assembly of notables, see J. A. Soggin, "Il regno di'Abimelek in Sichem (Giudici 9) e leistituzioni della cittag-stato siro-palestinese nei secoli XV-XI avanit Cristo," *Studi in onore di Eduoardo Volterra* 6 (1973): 161–89; H. Reviv, "Early Elements and Late Terminology in the Descriptions of Non-Israelite Cities in the Bible," *IEJ* 27 (1977): 192–93; idem, "The Government of Shechem in the El-Amarna Period and in the Days of Abimelech," *IEJ* 16 (1966): 252–57.

320. For further discussion, see D. E. Fleming, *The Installation of Baal's High Priestess at Emar: A Window on Ancient Syrian Religion* (HSM 42; Atlanta: Scholars Press, 1992), 76–79; idem, *Time at Emar: The Cultic Calendar and the Rituals from the Diviner's Archive* (Mesopotamian Civilizations 11; Winona Lake, Ind.: Eisenbrauns, 2000), 82–85.

321. Thus L. Wachter, "Zur Lokalisierung des sichemitischen Baumheiligtums," *ZDPV* 103 (1987): 1–12.

322. Since it is associated with a tree rather than a temple, it is doubtful it should be associated with the large pillar (5 1/2 feet x 4 3/4 feet x 1 4/5 feet) standing stone before the entrance of the temple at Shechem. See G. E. Wright, *Shechem: The Biography of a Biblical City* (New York: McGraw Hill, 1965), fig. 28; Stager, "The Shechem Temple," 31–33. For further discussion, see E. Bloch-Smith, "Will the Real *Masseboth* Please Stand Up: Cases of Real and Mistakenly Identified Standing Stones in Ancient Israel," in *Text, Artifact, and Image*, ed. G. Beckman and T. Lewis (Brown Judaic Studies 346; Providence, R.I.: Brown Univ. Press, 2006), 38–63.

323. According to Deut. 11:29 and 27:12–13, Moses instructed the Israelites to recite antiphonally the blessings and curses of the covenant on Mounts Gerizim and Ebal, once the Israelites crossed into the Promised Land. For a study of the acoustical qualities of this site, see B. C. Crisler, "The Acoustics and Crowd Capacity of Natural Theaters in Palestine," *BA* 39/4 (1976): 138–39.

324. On the nature and significance of anointing in the ancient Near East, see T. N. D. Mettinger, *King and Messiah: The Civil and Sacral Legitimation of the Israelite Kings* (ConBOT 8; Lund: Gleerup, 1976), 185–232.

325. On the Hittite use of oil in anointing see H. A. Hoffner, "Oil in Hittite Texts," *BA* 58 (1995): 111–12.

326. For further information on Tirash, see J. F. Healey, "Tirash," *DDD*, 871–72. For a study of viticulture and the production of wine in ancient Israel, see V. H. Matthews, "Treading the Winepress: Actual and Metaphorical Viticulture in the Ancient Near East," in *Food and Drink in the Biblical Worlds*, ed. A. Brenner and A. W. van Henten (Semeia 86; Atlanta: SBL, 1999), 19–32.

327. *HALOT*, 37; *DCH*, 1:202. The word occurs elsewhere only in Gen. 50:10–11 and Ps. 58:10.

328. Thus M. Zohary, *Plants of the Bible*, 155.

329. For full discussion, see Tatu, "Jotham's Fable," 110–24.

330. Cf. 2 Sam. 17:18–21, which describes David's advisors Jonathan and Ahimaaz hiding in a well.

331. 1 Sam. 16:14–23; 18:10; 19:9. For discussion of these texts, see Block, "Empowered by the Spirit of God," 50–52.

332. For summaries of ancient Near Eastern conceptions, see Black and Green, *Gods, Demons and Symbols*, 63–65; G. J. Riley, "Demon," *DDD*, 235–40; J. K. Kuemmerlin-McLean, "Demons," *ABD*, 2:138–40.

333. The expression *rûaḥ rāʿâ* ("bad spirit") represents an exact equivalent to *rwḥh bšth* ("the evil spirit") mentioned in numerous Aramaic amulets from the early Christian period. For a study of these and other magical texts, see J. Naveh and S. Shaked, *Amulets and Magic Bowls: Aramaic Incantations of Late Antiquity* (Jerusalem: Magnes, 1985). See esp. text 7:6, but also 3:4 and 7:12. These demons could be either male or female.

334. Cf. Garsiel, *Biblical Names*, 55–57.

335. Cf. Obadiah, Obedʾel, Obedbaal, etc., in the Old Testament.

336. Cf. W. Herrmann, "Baal Zebub," *DDD*, 154–55.

337. The English rendering derives from the LXX's *omphalon*, via Vulgate's *umbilici terrae*. Based on Ezek. 38:12, the pseudepigraphic book of *Jubilees* (8:19), Josephus (*Wars* 3.3.5), and rabbinic writings (*b. Yoma* 54b, *Midrash Tanḥuma Qedoshim* 10, *b. Sanh.* 37a) treat Zion as the navel of the earth. The navel of the earth was supposedly the mythographical center, functioning as a link between heaven and earth (see Boling, *Judges*, 179). G. R. H. Wright, "The Mythology of Pre-Israelite Shechem," *VT* 20 (1970): 79, suggests the *ṭabbûr* identified some physical (stone?) object, which, as at Delphi, symbolized the cosmic *omphalos*.

338. B. W. Anderson, "The Place of Shechem in the Bible," *BA* 20 (1957): 10–11. H. Eshel and Z. Erlich, "Abimelech's First Battle with the Lords of Shechem and the Question of the Navel of the Land," *Tarbiz* 58 (1988–89): 111–16, identify the center with Ras el-Tagur, on the southwestern corridor of Jebel el-Kabir, northeast of Shechem; similarly Z. Ilan, "The Location of the Navel of the Land," *Beth Mikra* 27 (1981/82): 122–26 (Hebrew). For discussion and bibliography, see S. Terrien, "The Omphalos Myth and Hebrew Religion," *VT* 20 (1970): 315–38.

339. So also D. Winton Thomas, "Mount Tabor: The Meaning of the Name," *VT* 1 (1951): 230.

340. Cf. H. O. Thompson, "Arumah," *ABD*, 1:467–68; Boling, *Judges*, 121.

341. For discussion of these kinds of defensive temple-towers, see Mazar, *Archaeology of the Land of the Bible*, 248–57.
342. For earlier discussions of the temple, see G. E. Wright, *Shechem: The Biography of a Biblical City* (New York: McGraw-Hill, 1965), 95–100; M. Fowler, "A Closer Look at the Temple of El-Berith at Shechem," *PEQ* 115 (1983): 49–53; E. F. Campbell Jr., *Shechem II: Portrait of a Hill Country Vale* (ASOR Archaeology Reports 2; Atlanta: Scholars Press, 1991), 107–9; idem, "Judges 9 and Archaeology," in *The Word of the Lord Shall Go Forth: Essays in Honor of David Noel Freedman in Celebration of his Sixtieth Birthday*, ed. C. L. Meyers and M. O'Connor (Winona Lake, Ind.: Eisenbrauns, 1983), 263–67. For a survey of the archaeological exploration of Shechem (modern Tell Balatah), see E. F. Campbell Jr., "Shechem," *NEAEHL*, 4:1345–54.
343. See L. E. Stager, "The Fortress-Temple at Shechem and the 'House of El, Lord of the Covenant,'" in *Realia Dei: Essays in Archaeology and Biblical Interpretation in Honor of Edward F. Campbell, Jr., at His Retirement*, ed. P. H. Williams Jr. and T. Hiebert (Atlanta: Scholars Press, 1999), 228–49; idem, "The Shechem Temple," 26–35, 66–69.
344. Campbell, *Shechem II*, 107, suggests the name originally identified a tell two miles north of Tubas, but the name was transferred to the present sight in the Roman era.
345. So E. H. Dyck, "Thebes," *ABD*, 6:443. A. Malamat (*WHJP*, 3:320, n. 61) follows Y. Aharoni in treating *tēbeṣ* as a corruption of *tirṣâ*, "Tirzah" (Tell el-Farʾah), six miles northeast of Shechem.
346. See further King and Stager, *Life in Biblical Israel*, 94–95.
347. Cf. W. R. Kotter, "Shamir," *ABD*, 5:1157.
348. The boundary between *nāśîʾ* ("chieftain") and *melek* ("king") is unclear. See Meyers, "Kinship and Kingship," 221–72.
349. ARM 6.76:20–25, according to A. Malamat, "Mari," *BA* 34 (1971): 18; idem, *Mari and the Early Israelite Experience* (Oxford: Oxford Univ. Press, 1989), 2–4, 80.
350. B. Beem, "The Minor Judges: A Literary Reading of Some Very Short Stories," in *The Biblical Canon in Comparative Perspective*, ed. K. L. Younger et al. (Scripture in Context 4; Lewiston, N.Y.: Mellen, 1991), 152. For a detailed study of the significance of donkeys in the ancient world, see K. C. Way, *The Ceremonial and Symbolic Significance of Donkeys in the Biblical World*, Ph.D. dissertation, Hebrew Union College, Cincinnati, 2006.
351. Cf. H. O. Thompson, "Kamon," *ABD*, 4:5.
352. See I. Singer, *Hittite Prayers* (SBLWAW 11; Atlanta: Scholars Press, 2002), 58.
353. For translation of the prayers, see ibid., 47–69; cf. *ANET*, 394–96.
354. On prostitution in the ancient Near East and in Israel, see E. A. Goodfriend, "Prostitution," *ABD*, 5:505–10.
355. On the possibility/problem of cult prostitution, see ibid., 5:507–9; for a different interpretation see K. van der Toorn, "Cultic Prostitution," *ABD*, 5:510–13; ibid, "Female Prostitution in Payment of Vows in Ancient Israel," *JBL* 108 (1989): 193–205.
356. Cf. Rainey, "Unruly Elements in Late Bronze Canaanite Society," 481–97.
357. C. Redmount, "Bitter Lives: Israel in and out of Egypt," in *The Oxford History of the Biblical World*, ed. M. D. Coogan (Oxford: Oxford Univ. Press, 1998), 98.
358. O'Connell, *Rhetoric of the Book of Judges*, 195.
359. See J.-M. de Tarragon, "Ammon," *ABD*, 1:195.
360. See further R. W. Yonker, "Ammonites," in *Peoples of the Old Testament World*, ed. A. J. Hoerth et al. (Grand Rapids: Eerdmans, 1994), 296–97.
361. On the style and function of this formula (often referred to as "the messenger formula," see S. A. Meier, *Speaking of Speaking: Marking Direct Discourse in the Hebrew Bible* (VTSup 46; Leiden: Brill, 1992), 179–90.
362. See B. Routledge, *Moab in the Iron Age: Hegemony, Polity, Archaeology* (Philadelphia: Univ. of Pennsylvania Press, 2004), 41–48.
363. On this site, see L. T. Geraty, "Heshbon," *ABD*, 3:181–84; idem, "Heshbon," *NEAEHL*, 2:626–30.
364. Josh. 21:36 also identifies Jahaz as one of the eastern Levitical cities.
365. Routledge, *Moab in the Iron Age*, 143–45; J. A. Dearman, "Jahaz," *ABD*, 3:612.
366. As translated by K. A. D. Smelik, COS, 2.23 (p. 138).
367. For a listing of personal names deriving from Neo-Assyrian cuneiform texts as well as native Moabite inscriptions and seals, see H.-P. Müller, "Chemosh," *DDD*, 188.
368. See L. Herr, "The Servant of Baalis," *BA* 48 (1985): 169–72; L. T. Geraty, "Baalis," *ABD*, 1:556–57, who provides discussion and bibliography. The theophore also appears on the names *bdmlkm*, *mlkmgd*, and *mlkmʿz*. See E. Puech, "Milkom," *DDD*, 575–76, for discussion of this deity.
369. See D. M. Howard Jr., *An Introduction to the Old Testament Historical Books* (Chicago: Moody Press, 1993), 63–65; W. H. Shea, "Exodus, Date of the," *ISBE*, 2:233; J. J. Bimson and D. Livingston, "Redating the Exodus," *BAR* 13/5 (1987): 42; Washburn, "The Chronology of Judges," 414–25.
370. COS, 2.23.
371. Jacob's vow in Gen. 28:20–22; Israel's vow in Num. 21:2; Hannah's vow in 1 Sam. 1:11; Absalom's vow in 2 Sam. 15:7–8. For discussion of the forms of biblical vows, see D. Marcus, *Jephthah and His Vow* (Lubbock, Tex.: Texas Tech Press, 1986), 18–19.
372. For a helpful study of vows in the ancient world, see T. W. Cartledge, *Vows in the Hebrew Bible and the Ancient Near East* (JSOTSup 147; Sheffield: Sheffield Academic Press, 1992).
373. So also Malamat, "Period of the Judges," 157; G. L. Mattingly, "Aroer," *ABD*, 1:399.
374. Cf. R. W. Younker, "Minnith," *ABD*, 4:842.
375. Some identify the site with Naur, eight miles southwest of Amman. Cf. Malamat, "Period of the Judges," 157; Rasmussen, *NIV Atlas of the Bible*, 224. For a discussion of these names, see S. Mittmann, "Aroer, Minnith und Abel Keramim," *ZDPV* 85 (1969): 63–75; E. A. Knauf, "Abel

Keramim," *ZDPV* 100 (1984): 119–21; idem, "Abel-Keramim," *ABD*, 1:10–11.

376. Cf. Ex. 15:20; 1 Sam. 18:6; Ps. 68:25; Jer. 31:4.
377. For full discussion of the instrument itself and its usage, see Braun, *Music and Ancient Israel/Palestine*, 29–31, 117–33; also C. L. Meyers, "Of Drums and Damsels: Women's Performance in Ancient Israel," *BA* 54 (1991): 16–27.
378. See Saul's plea with David not to do this to him in 1 Sam. 24:21 and the widow's complaint in 2 Sam. 14:7 that by executing her only son for murdering his brother, her townspeople "would put out the only burning coal I have left, leaving my husband neither name nor descendant on the face of the earth." According to 2 Sam. 18:18 Absalom set up a memorial for himself because he had no children to proclaim his name after his death (see also Ps. 37:28; Isa. 14:20–21). For extrabiblical references to the same notion, see in particular the Vassal Treaty of Esarhaddon, where the curse of "blotting out the name/memory" of the enemy occurs repeatedly: §§140, 161, 255, 315, 435, 524, 537, 663.
379. See lines 140, 161, 255, 315.
380. As translated by Parpola, *Neo-Assyrian Treaties and Loyalty Oaths*, s.v. As in Hebrew, "name" is closely linked with "seed."
381. Scholars are not united in their interpretation of the idiom or the history of child sacrifice in Israel. For full discussion, see G. C. Heider, *The Cult of Molech: A Reassessment* (JSOTSup 43; Sheffield: Sheffield Academic Press, 1985); P. G. Mosca, "Child Sacrifice in Canaanite and Israelite Religion: A Study in *Mulk* and *mlk*," Ph.D. dissertation, Harvard Univ., 1975; J. Day, *Molech: A God of Human Sacrifice in the Old Testament* (Cambridge: Cambridge Univ. Press, 1989).
382. See the popular presentation of the archaeological evidence from Carthage by L. E. Stager and S. R. Wolff, "Child Sacrifice at Carthage—Religious Rite of Population Control," *BAR* 10/1 (1984): 30–51. This quotation is cited from p. 45.
383. *Aeneid* 11.264. Cf. 3:121.
384. As translated by Witter Bynner, "Iphegenia in Taurus," in *Euripides II*, ed. David Greene and Richmond Lattimore (Chicago: Univ. of Chicago Press, 1956), 117–87. Another Euripidean version ("Iphegenia in Aulis") has Iphegenia rescued in the end, but this ending is suspect. See Charles R. Walker, trans. "Iphegenia in Aulis," in *Euripides IV*, ed. David Greene and Richmond Lattimore (Chicago: Univ. of Chicago Press, 1958), 214. For a discussion of such stories, see Marcus, *Jephthah and His Vow*, 40–43; Burney, *Judges*, 332–33; Moore, *Judges*, 304–5.
385. Arthur S. Way, *Euripides*, vol. 2 (London: William Heinemann, 1919), 287. This ending is also found in Apollodorus (James G. Frazer, *Apollodorus: The Library*, vol. 2 [LCL; New York: Putnam, 1921], 191–93) and in Hesiod's "Cypria" (Hugh G. Evelyn-White, *Hesiod: The Homeric Hymns and Homerica* (Cambridge, Mass.: Harvard Univ. Press, 1943).
386. Cf. P. N. Franklin, "Zaphon," *ABD* 6:1040.
387. For explanations of the phonological merger see G. A. Rendsburg, "The Ammonite Phoneme /*T̲*/," *BASOR* 269 (1988): 73–79; idem, "More on Hebrew *šibbolet*," *JSS* 33 (1988): 255–58; P. Swiggers, "The Word *Šibbolet* in Jud. XII.6," *JSS* 26 (1981): 205–7; A. Lemaire, "L'Incident du sibbolet [Jg 12,6]: Perspective historique," in *Mélanges bibliques et orientaux en l'honneur de M. Mathias Delcor*, ed. A. Caquot et al. (AOAT 215; Neukirchen: Neukirchener Verlag, 1985), 275–81; A. F. L. Beeston, "Hebrew *Šibbolet* and *Šobel*," *JSS* 24 (1979): 175–77; J. Blau, "'Weak' Phonetic Change and the Hebrew *Œîn*," *HAR* 1 (1977): 67–119; and A. Faber, "Second Harvest: *šibboleth* Revisited [Yet Again]," *JSS* 37 (1992): 1–10.
388. So also J. A. Emerton, "Some Comments on the Shibboleth Incident (Judges XII 6)," in *Mélanges bibliques et orientaux en l'honneur de M. Mathias Delcor*, 150–57, and more recently R. S. Hendel, "Sibilants and *šibbōlet* (Judges 12:6)," *BASOR* 301 (1996): 69–75.
389. For the text, see H. A. Hoffner, "A Tale of Two Cities: Kanesh and Zalpa," in *Hittite Myths* (SBLWAW 2; Atlanta: Scholars Press, 1990), 62–63; idem, *COS*, 1.71. For discussion of the relationship between these texts, see M. Tsevat, "Two Old Testament Stories and Their Hittite Analogues," in *Studies in Literature from the Ancient Near East: By Members of the American Oriental Society Dedicated to Samuel Noah Kramer*, ed. J. M. Sasson (New Haven, Conn.: American Oriental Society, 1984), 321–26 (= *JAOS* 103 [1983]: 35–42).
390. See G. Galil, "Pirathon, Parathon and Timnatha," *ZDPV* 109 (1993): 49–53; E. A. Knauf, "*Pirathon—Farʿaṭ*," *BN* 51 (1990): 19–24; contra N. Naʾaman, who identifies Pirathon with Farkha in "Pirathon and Ophrah," *BN* 50 (1989): 11–16.
391. Cf. B. Halpern, *The Emergence of Israel in Canaan* (SBLMS 29; Chico, Calif.: Scholars Press, 1983), 74.
392. Cf. v. 25, which describes the Spirit of Yahweh stirring up Samson in Mahaneh Dan, between Zorah and Eshtaol, and 16:31, which has Samson buried in the tomb of his father between Zorah and Eshtaol.
393. Genesis 18:9–15 (Sarah); 25:19–26 (Rebekah); 30:1–24 (Rachel); 1 Sam. 1:1–20 (Hannah); Luke 1:5–25, 57–80 (Elizabeth).
394. For the text and translation by E. L. Greenstein, see *UNP*, 9–48.
395. See further V. H. Matthews, "Marriage and Family in the Ancient Near East," in *Marriage and Family in the Ancient World*, 17.
396. As cited by R. D. Biggs, "Medicine, Surgery, and Public Health in Ancient Mesopotamia," *CANE* 3:1917.
397. See H. A. Hoffner Jr., "Paskuwatti's Ritual against Sexual Impotence (CTH 406)," *AuOr* 5 (1987): 271–87; see also the discussion by G. Frantz-Szabó, "Hittite Witchcraft, Magic, and Divination," *CANE*, 3:2014.
398. *UNP*, 23.
399. *ANET*, 391.
400. See further J. Milgrom, *Leviticus 1–16: A New Translation with Introduction and Commentary* (AB 3; New York: Doubleday, 1991), 611–12. For a contrary position, see King and Stager, *Life in Biblical Israel*, 101–3,

who argue that *šēkār* can only be a grape product. On ancient viticulture Israel see C. E. Walsh, *The Fruit of the Vine: Viticulture in Ancient Israel* (HSM 60; Winona Lake, Ind.: Eisenbrauns, 2000).

401. Cognate to *nādar*, "to vow." Cf. 11:39. See *HALOT*, 674, 684.
402. See E. Stone, "The Social Role of the *Nadītu* Women in Old Babylonian Nippur," *JESHO* 25 (1982): 50–70; R. Harris, "Biographical Notes on the *Nadītu* Women of Sippar," *JCS* 16 (1962): 1–12.
403. Cf. 5:4 above. Compare *mišpaṭ hammalek* ("the pronouncement concerning the king") in 1 Sam. 8:10–11, which identifies Samuel's response to a formal inquiry by the people before the prophet.
404. Ug. V 6.3 and 12, as translated by F. C. Fensham, "The Ugaritic Root *ṯpṭ*," *JNSL* 12 (1984): 68. For another study of this text, see H. Cazelles, "*Mṯpṭ* à Ugarit," *Or* 53 (1984): 177–82.
405. Cazelles, "*Mṯpṭ* à Ugarit," 77.
406. On the significance of eating and drinking together and hosting a meal, see A. W. Jenks, "Eating and Drinking in the Old Testament," *ABD*, 2:250–54.
407. See Black and Green, *Gods, Demons and Symbols*, 130–31.
408. Of the 46 recorded instances of naming children in the Old Testament, in 28 the name is given by the mother. It is generally accepted that name-giving in the ancient world represented an expression of authority (cf. Gen. 2:19–20). On naming in the Old Testament, see D. Stuart, "Names, Proper," *ISBE*, 3:483–88.
409. J. A. Motyer, "Name," *IBD*, 2:1051–52.
410. Cf. 5:31; Ps. 19:5–6. Thus D. R. Hildebrand, "Samson," *ISBE*, 4:309.
411. See, e.g., O. Margalith, "The Legends of Samson/Heracles," *VT* 37 (1987): 63–70. Margalith proposes that the Israelites became familiar with the Greek legends through their contacts with the Philistines, whose roots are traced to the Aegean. For a summary of the supposed Heracles-Samson connection, see D. E. Aune, "Heracles," *DDD*, 404. But this interpretation was convincingly repudiated twenty-five years ago by G. G. Cohen, "Samson and Hercules: A Comparison between the Feats of Samson and the Labours of Hercules," *EvQ* 42 (1970): 131–41.
412. J. Gray, *Joshua, Judges and Ruth*, 220, concludes that "the role of the hero with the sun-name as the upholder of God's order against the enemies of his people is reminiscent of the Sun as the protagonist of Cosmos against Chaos, in the Egyptian myth of the sun-god nightly menaced by Apophis, the serpent of darkness.
413. This interpretation is rejected by Fowler, *Theophoric Names*, 167. On the divinity Shemesh (Shamash in Akkadian) see E. Lipinski, "Shemesh," *DDD*, 764–68; K. van der Toorn, "Sun," *ABD*, 6:237–39.
414. Cf. *HALOT*, 160. According to T. G. Crawford, a blessing involves a wish for someone to receive the things considered desirable in life: land, numerous progeny, sufficient food, clothing, etc. See *Blessing and Curse in Syro-Palestinian Inscriptions of the Iron Age* (American Univ. Studies 7/120; New York: Peter Lang, 1992), 16.
415. As translated by K. L. Younger Jr., *COS*, 2.31.
416. Cf. O'Connell, *The Rhetoric of the Book of Judges*, 215, n. 307.
417. On ancient Canaanite names of this type, see A. F. Rainey, "The Toponymics of Eretz-Israel," *BASOR* 231 (1978): 4–5 [1–17]; Layton, *Archaic Features*, 12.
418. See R. Greenberg, "Eshtaol," *ABD*, 2:617.
419. See W. R. Kotter, "Timnah," *ABD*, 6:557; A. Mazar and G. L. Kelm, "Batash, Tel (Timnah)," *NEAEHL*, 1:152–57.
420. J. M. Sasson, "Circumcision in the Ancient Near East," *JBL* 85 (1966): 473–76; R. G. Hall, "Circumcision," *ABD*, 1:1025–27; King and Stager, *Life in Biblical Israel*, 43–45. For ancient texts dealing with the rite, see *ANET*, 326; Herodotus, *Histories* 2.104; Josephus, *Antiquities* 8.10.3.
421. See W. Lemke, "Circumcision of the Heart: The Journey of a Biblical Metaphor," in *A God So Near: Essays in Biblical Theology in Honor of Patrick D. Miller*, ed. B. A. Strawn and N. R. Bowen (Winona Lake, Ind.: Eisenbrauns, 2003), 299–319; J. Goldingay, "The Significance of Circumcision," *JSOT* 88 (2000): 3–18; J. DeRouchie, "Circumcision in the Hebrew Bible and the Targumim: Theology, Rhetoric, and the Handling of Metaphor," *BBR* (2004): 175–204.
422. In the Old Testament the expression "uncircumcised NN" is used only of the Philistines (cf. 15:18; 1 Sam. 14:6; 17:26, 36; 31:4 [1 Chr 10:4]; 2 Sam. 1:20). See D. I. Block, "Beyond the Grave: Ezekiel's Vision of Life after Death," *BBR* 2 (1992): 122–29; idem, *The Book of Ezekiel Chapters 25–40* (NICOT; Grand Rapids: Eerdmans, 1998), 216–31.
423. Cf. Gen. 21:21 (Hagar arranges Ishmael's marriage); Gen. 24 (Abraham arranges Isaac's marriage); Judg. 1:12 (Caleb arranges Achsah's marriage). See further Block, "Marriage and Family in Ancient Israel," 56–57.
424. See H. Marsman, *Women in Ugarit and Israel: Their Social and Religious Position in the Context of the Ancient Near East* (OTS 49; Leiden: Brill, 2003), 49–53.
425. LE §27, as translated by M. T. Roth, *Law Collections from Ancient Mesopotamia and Asia Minor* (Atlanta: Scholar's Press, 1995), 63.
426. See M. Dick, "The Neo-Assyrian Royal Lion Hunt and Yahweh's Answer to Job," *JBL* 125 (2006): 245.
427. M. Streck, *Assurbanipal und die letzten assyrischen Könige bis zum Untergange Niniveh's* (VAB 7; Leipzig: J. C. Hinrichs, 1916), 309 line 1.
428. See the full discussion by Dick, "Neo-Assyrian Royal Lion Hunt," 243–70.
429. See William F. Albright, *The Archaeology of Palestine* (Harmondsworth: Penguin, 1961), 115; more recently Dothan and Dothan, *People of the Sea*, 90, 134.
430. See L. E. Stager, "The Fury of Babylon: Ashkelon and the Archaeology of Destruction," *BAR* 22/1 (January-February 1996): 54–77.

431. Cf. Soggin, *Judges*, 241.
432. So also Boling, *Judges*, 231; cf. S. Talmon, "The New Hebrew Letter from the Seventh Century B.C. in Historical Perspective," *BASOR* 176 (1964): 33.
433. As cited by W. W. Hallo, "Sumerian Literature: Background to the Bible," *BRev* 4/3 (June 1988): 31. For fuller discussion see M. Civil, "Sumerian Riddles: A Corpus," *AuOr* 5 (1987): 17–37.
434. Cf. the discussion by L. E. Stager, "When Canaanites and Philistines Ruled Ashkelon," *BAR* 17/2 (March-April 1991): 41. For a discussion of riddles in the Bible and the ancient Near East, see J. L. Crenshaw, "Riddles," *ABD*, 5:721–23.
435. The word appears elsewhere the Old Testament only in Isa. 3:23, where it refers to an element of female festal attire, and Prov. 31:24, where it identifies a garment made by a noble woman. In the Talmud and the New Testament, *sindōn* denotes a sleeping wrap or shroud (cf. Matt. 27:59; Mark 14:51–52; 15:46; Luke 23:53).
436. Cf. Burney, *Judges*, 362.
437. Cf. *HALOT*, 87.
438. Since the Philistines were Indo-Europeans living in a Semitic world, it is perhaps not surprising that apart from a couple of authentic Philistine names (Achish, Goliath), scholars have identified few words in biblical and modern Hebrew that may derive from the non-Semitic language the Philistines spoke when they arrived in Canaan.
439. This word for "heifer" recalls the name Eglon in ch. 3.
440. See *HALOT*, 319.
441. On which see Zohary, *Plants of the Bible*, 74; Borowski, *Agriculture in Iron Age Israel*, 88–91.
442. See *UT*, 397 (#881), for Ugaritic references; *DNWSI*, 363, for Imperial Aramaic, Yaudic, and Palmyrene references; for the Akkadian equivalent, *kibtu*, see *AHw*, 472; *CAD*, 8.340–41.
443. Thus Boling, *Judges*, 234.
444. For an analysis of the evidence for Old Babylonian marriage customs, see R. Westbrook, *Old Babylonian Marriage Law* (AfO Beiheft 23; Horn, Austria: Berger & Söhne, 1988).
445. Though the Ugaritic evidence from the thirteenth century B.C. does provide a bridge between these cultures. See the helpful study by Marsman, *Women in Ugarit and Israel*. For an analysis of the evidence for Neo-Babylonian marriage customs, see M. Roth, *Babylonian Marriage Agreements 7th–3rd Centuries B.C.* (AOAT; Neukirchen-Vluyn: Neukirchener Verlag, 1989).
446. The verb *śnʾ* ("to hate") functions as the antonym of *ʾāhab* ("to love, to be covenantally committed to"). See already Cf. M. San Nicolo, "Vorderasiatisches Rechtsgut in der Ägyptischen Eheverträgen der Perserzeit," *OLZ* 30 (1927): 218.
447. Contra Borowski, *Every Living Thing*, 203–4.
448. Cf. Judg. 16:23–24; 1 Sam. 5:1–7. For a discussion of the etymology of Dagon, see L. Feliu, *The God Dagan in Bronze Age Syria*, trans. W. G. E. Watson (Culture and History of the Ancient Near East 19; Leiden: Brill, 2003), 278–88.
449. See Felieu, *Dagan*, 295–306.
450. Cf. M. Lubetski, "Lehi," *ABD*, 4:275.
451. On the production of flax and derived products, see King and Stager, *Life in Biblical Israel*, 148–52; O. Borowski, *Agriculture in Iron Age Israel*, 98–99.
452. See M. Dothan, "Ashdod," *NEAEHL*, 1:98–99. For a mock-up of a city gate structure, see comment on 9:44. For discussion and illustrations of gate structures, see Z. Herzog, "Fortifications (Levant)," *ABD*, 2:844–52.
453. Ovadiah, "Gaza," 465.
454. So also Younger, *Judges*, 315. See further *CAD* D, 46–47; S. Parpola et al., eds., *The Prosopography of the Neo-Assyrian Empire* (Helsinki: The Neo-Assyrian Text Corpus Project, 1998-), 1/2:384. Some link the name to Arabic *dalla* ("to flirt"), in which case the name means "flirtatious" (Boling, *Judges*, 248).
455. Assuming an average modern wage is $30,000, this is equivalent to $16,500,000.
456. For Ugaritic evidence, see the Tale of Aqhat, *UNP* 4.vi:23 (p. 61); for Mesopotamia, see the later version of the Myth of Anzu II: 63–101. See also E. Reiner, *Your Thwarts in Pieces, Your Mooring Rope Cut: Poetry from Babylonia and Assyria* (Ann Arbor, Mich.: Univ. of Michigan, 1985), 64.
457. King and Stager, *Life in Biblical Israel*, 283.
458. See *DNWSI*, 2:612.
459. See R. Mayer-Opificius, "Simson, der sechslockige Held?" *UF* 14 (1982): 149–51: R. Wenning, "Der siebenlockige Held Simson: literarische und ikonographische Beobachtungen zu Ri 13–16," *BN* 17 (1982): 43–55.
460. The discovery of large numbers of loom weights at Iron Age Timnah (Tel Batash), Ashkelon, Ekron, and Ashdod confirms that weaving was an important industry in this region. See Stager, "Forging an Identity," 154.
461. Thus Walton, Matthews, and Chavalas, *IVP Bible Background Commentary*, 269.
462. Thus King and Stager, *Life in Biblical Israel*, 157.
463. Ibid., 154.
464. For discussion, see K. van der Toorn, "Judges XVI 21 in the Light of the Akkadian Sources," *VT* 36 (1986): 248–53.
465. *HKM*, 58:1–14, as cited by H. A. Hoffner Jr., "The Treatment and Long-term Use of Persons Captured in Battle according to the Maṣat Texts, in *Recent Developments in Hittite Archaeology and History*, ed. K. A. Yener and H. A. Hoffner Jr. (Winona Lake, Ind.: Eisenbrauns, 2002), 68–69.
466. Cf. K. van der Toorn, "Mill, Millstone," *ABD*, 4:831–32.
467. On this deity, see further Felieu, *Dagan*; J. F. Healey, "Dagon," *DDD*, 216–19; L. K. Handy, "Dagon," *ABD*, 2:1–3.
468. It is appropriate that Samson be humiliated at the festival of the grain god, since he had earlier burned the crops of the Philistines (cf. 15:4–5).
469. See A. Mazar, "A Philistine Temple at Tell Qasile," *BA* 36 (1973): 43–48; idem, *Archaeology of the Land of the Bible*, 319–23; idem, "Qasile, Tell," *NEAEHL*, 1207–11.

470. See further, King and Stager, *Life in Biblical Israel*, 364–65.
471. The name is borne by the later Israelite prophets Micaiah ben Imlah (1 Kings 22:8–28) and Micah of Moresheth (Mic. 1:1). On the name, see Fowler, *Theophoric Names*, 128–29, 152.
472. The Qal form appears elsewhere only in Hos. 4:2; 10:4; the Hiphil only in 1 Sam. 14:24; 1 Kings 8:31; 2 Chron. 6:22.
473. J. Scharbert, "אָלָה," *TDOT*, 1:262.
474. On these inscriptions, see J. Day, "Asherah," *ABD*, 1:484–85. Further bibliography is provided.
475. Pers. trans. See *COS*, 2.42.
476. For discussion of the calf, see L. E. Stager, "Canaanite Calf of Ashkelon," *Le Monde de la Bible*, (May/June, 1991): 50–52; idem, *NEAEHL*, 1:106.
477. Compare also the bronze bull, measuring seven inches long and five inches high, discovered at what is thought to have been a cult site in northern Samaria, four and one half miles east of Dothan. The bull is dated to the twelfth century B.C. See A. Mazar, "Bronze Bull Found in Israelite 'High Place' from the Time of the Judges," *BAR* 9/5 (Sept/Oct 1983): 34–40; idem, "'Bull' Site," *NEAEHL*, 1:266–67.
478. Exod. 28:41; 29:9, 29, 35; 32:29; Lev. 8:33; 16:32; 21:10; Num. 3:3; 1 Kings 13:33; 1 Chron. 29:5; 2 Chron. 13:9; 29:31. In Ezek. 43:26 the idiom applies exceptionally to the dedication of the altar.
479. See further Block, *Judges, Ruth*, 483–84.
480. See further Walton, *Ancient Near Eastern Thought*, 142–43.
481. Cf. Block, *Gods of the Nations*, 75–79.
482. See A. Malamat, "The Danite Migration and the Pan-Israelite Exodus-Conquest: A Biblical Narrative Pattern," *Bib* 51 (1970): 1–16.
483. ARM 26.420, translation by W. Heimpel, *Letters to the King of Mari*, 359.
484. Kitchen, *Reliability of the Old Testament*, 167; idem, *Pharaoh Triumphant: The Life and Times of Ramesses II, King of Egypt* (Warminster, Eng.: Aris & Phillips, 1983), 54–56.
485. ARM 26.209. Text and translation as given by Nissinen, *Prophets and Prophecy*, 44; cf. Heimpel, *Letters to the King of Mari*, 259.
486. Compare another oracle from Mari which opens with "The city of Mari, the pala[ce] and the district are well (*šalîm*)." ARM 26.201, as rendered by Nissinen, *Prophets and Prophecy*, 34; cf. Heimpel, *Letters to the King of Mari*, 255.
487. Cf. Amos 9:4. "To be before Yahweh" could be the obverse of "Yahweh has set his face against," as in Lev. 17:10; 20:3, 5; Jer. 21:10; 44:11.
488. For further discussion, see Block, "What Has Delphi to do with Samaria?" 189–216.
489. *ANET*, 329.
490. On the last name, see A. Malamat, "Northern Canaan and the Mari Texts," in *Near Eastern Archaeology in the Twentieth Century: N. Glueck Festschrift* ed. J. A. Sanders (Garden City, N.Y.: Doubleday, 1970), 164–77. On the excavation and pre-Danite history of the site, see A. Biran, *Biblical Dan* (Jerusalem: Israel Exploration Society, 1994), 27–58; idem, "Dan," *ABD*, 2:12–14; "Dan," *NEAEHL*, 1:323–26.
491. *ANET*, 242.
492. Thus A. Malamat, "After the Manner of the Sidonians and How They Were Far from the Sidonians," *EI* 23 (A. Biran volume; 1992): 194–94 [Heb; English summary p. 153*].
493. The Table of Nations, which omits Tyre, lists Sidon as the firstborn of Canaan (Gen. 10:15).
494. Deut. 3:9; Josh. 13:4,6; Judg. 3:3; 10:12; 18:7; 1 Kings 5:20; 11:5; 16:31; 2 Kings 23:13; 1 Chron. 22:4; Ezra 3:7; Ezek. 32:30. Homer interchanges "Sidonian" and "Phoenician," suggesting that the Greeks considered this city to be representative of the entire region. Cf. *Iliad* 6.290, 291; 23.743–44; *Odyssey* 4.83–85, 618; 13.270ff.; 14.288–91; 15:118, 415–17, 473. See further J. D. Muhly, "Homer and the Phoenicians," *Berytus* 19 (1970): 27; H. J. Katzenstein, *The History of Tyre* (Jerusalem: Magnes, 1973), 62–63; E. Gubel, "Aperçu historique de la civilization phénicienne," in *Les Phéniciens et le monde Méditerranéen* (Brussels: Catalogue de l'exposition, 1986), 20.
495. For further discussion, see A. Biran, "Tell Dan, Five Years Later," *BA* 43 (1980): 169–72; idem, *Biblical Dan*, 59–75.
496. Thus A. K. Grayson, *Assyrian Rulers of the Third and Second Millennia* B.C. *(to 1115* B.C.*)* (RIMA 1; Toronto: Univ. of Toronto Press, 1987), 236.
497. Biran, "Dan," *NEAEHL*, 1:327.
498. Most accept "Rehob" in 2 Sam. 8:3, 12 as an abbreviation of Beth Rehob.
499. Biran, "Dan," *NEAEHL*, 1:327.
500. For discussions of this inscription, see A. Biran, "To the God Who Is in Dan," in *Temples and High Places in Biblical Times* (Jerusalem: Magnes, 1981), 142–51; idem, *Biblical Dan*, 221–24. On the archaeological evidence for the Danite takeover of Laish see Biran, *Biblical Dan*, 125–46; "Dan," *NEAEHL*, 1:323–31.
501. For a contrary opinion, see D. G. Schley, *Shiloh: A Biblical City in Tradition and History* (JSOTSup 63; Sheffield: Sheffield Academic Press, 1989), 129–31. Schley argues that the chronological notes at the ends of vv. 30 and 31 ("the exile of the land" and "as long as the house of God was at Shiloh") refer to the same time period. Accordingly, either the structures defined by archaeologists as the cult site at Shiloh have been misidentified, or the site was rebuilt and continued to function as a northern place of worship after the division of the kingdom.
502. See I. Finkelstein, "Excavations at Shiloh," *TA* 12 (1985): 123–80. For the archaeological history of Shiloh, see A. Kempinski, "Shiloh," *NEAEHL*, 4:1364–66.
503. Judg. 19:10–11; 1 Chron. 11:4–5; Josh. 15:8 uses the gentilic form *yĕbûsû* ("Jebusite") as a toponym. Some have argued that the place name is primary and that "Jebusite" derives from this toponym. J. M. Miller ("Jebus and Jerusalem: A Case of Mistaken Identity," *ZDPV* 90 [1974]: 115–27) argues that Jebus identified the northern suburb of Jerusalem, modern *Šaʿfat*.

504. Cf. Hoffner, "The Hittites and Hurrians," 225.
505. N. L. Lapp, "Fûl, Tell El-," *NEAEHL*, 2:445–48.
506. P. M. Arnold, "Gibeah," *ABD*, 2:1007–9. For a detailed study of Gibeah in history and tradition see idem, "Gibeah in Israelite History and Tradition," Ph.D. dissertation, Emory University, Atlanta, 1987. Gibeah (not to be confused with Gibeon, modern el-Jib, six miles west) will play an important role in the Saul narratives of 1 Samuel 9–14.
507. Cf. P. M. Arnold, "Ramah," *ABD*, 5:613–14.
508. Cf. King and Stager, *Life in Biblical Israel*, 61–63.
509. See further, King and Stager, *Life in Biblical Israel*," 28–35.
510. ARM 2:48. For the Akkadian text, German translation, and commentary, see G. Wallis, "Eine Parallele zu Richter 19 29ff. und 1 Sam. 11 5ff. aus dem Briefarchiv von Mari," *ZAW* 64 (1952): 57–61.
511. On the archaeological and historical significance of Dan, see comment on 18:29.
512. Appropriately the phrase never appears in the historiographic writings in contexts dealing with realities after the division of the kingdom (cf. 1 Sam. 3:20; 2 Sam. 3:10; 17:11; 24:2, 15; 1 Kings 4:25; 1 Chron. 21:2), except in 2 Chron. 30:5, which describes Hezekiah's attempt to recapture pan-Israelite jurisdiction in his religious reforms (cf. Amos 8:14, which names Dan and Beersheba as a parallel pair). M. Sæbo observes that the expression concerns above all else the people and land of Israel as a whole and as a unity; see his "Grenzbeschreibung und Landideal im Alten Testament mit besonderer Beruucksichtigung der *min-ad* Formel," *ZDPV* 90 (1974): 21–22.
513. Cf. Josh. 18:13–20. See further P. M. Arnold, "Mizpah," *ABD*, 4:879–81; J. R. Zorn, "*Naṣbeh*, Tell en-," *NEAEHL*, 3:1098–102.
514. Although the account lacks an actual declaration of the verdict, the response of the men, and especially their declared goal to give the people of Gibeah what they deserved for their outrage in v. 10, assume the verdict, "Guilty as charged."
515. For a discussion of the issues involved see comment on 1:4.
516. ARM 6, 27:16, also cited by Boling, *Judges*, 284.
517. Cf. King and Stager, *Life in Biblical Israel*, 228–29.
518. For possible references see *CAD* L, 126, 1a.
519. *ABL*, 78, as translated by S. Parpola, *Letters from Assyrian and Babylonian Scholars* (SAA 10; Helsinki: Helsinki Univ. Press, 1993), 33.
520. This word derives from the image of the goddess Pallas, located in the citadel of Troy, on which the security of the city was thought to depend. On the use of the ark as a palladium and ancient Near Eastern analogues, see Milgrom, *Numbers*, 373–75.
521. Cf. the attack on Ai by the Israelites in Josh. 8:2–21; on Shechem by Abimelech's enemies in Judg. 9:30–45; by Jeroboam II on Abijah of Jerusalem in 2 Chron. 13:13–18.
522. For a description of the events, see Kitchen, *Pharaoh Triumphant*, 53–60.
523. See further S. E. McGarry, "Baal-Tamar," *ABD*, 1:553–54.
524. See further P. M. Arnold, "Rimmon," *ABD*, 5:773–74.

Sidebar and Chart Notes

A-1. Old Greek reads 50 years, yielding a total of 420 years.
A-2. The total does not include Shamgar (3:31), the duration of whose tenure is not specified.
A-3. In highlighting his age and vigor at 85 years of age, Caleb uses a round figure of 40 years from the time he was sent as a spy from Kadesh Barnea to the Israelites' arrival at the Jordan. Deut. 2:14 gives a more precise figure of 38 years, which means that the actual duration of the wars under Joshua was seven, rather than the five suggested by Caleb's comment.
A-4. Assuming the tenures of Shamgar, Samson, Samuel, and Eli are all included in the forty years of Philistine oppression (13:1). See further below.
A-5. The biblical text creates the impression of a long judgeship.
A-6. The number is taken from Acts 13:21, where Paul offers the only specific biblical statement on the duration of Saul's reign.
A-7. See below.
A-8. Josephus contradicts himself on the totals. Compare *Ant.* 8.3.1, 592 years; *Ant.* 20.10.1, 612 years.
A-9. B. Lindars speaks of "genuinely ancient, if legendary, scraps of tradition." See *Judges 1–5: A New Translation and Commentary*, ed. A. D. H. Mayes (Edinburgh: T. & T. Clark, 1995), 4–5.
A-10. See S. R. Driver, *Introduction to the Literature of the Old Testament* (ICC; 7th ed.; Edinburgh: T. & T. Clark, 1898), 162.
A-11. For further discussion, see D. I. Block, *Judges, Ruth* (Nashville: Broadman & Holman, 1999), 79–80.
A-12. For full discussion, see K. L. Younger Jr., "Judges 1 in Its Near Eastern Literary Context," in *Faith, Tradition and History: Essays on Old Testament Historiography in Its Near Eastern Context*, ed. J. K. Hoffmeier et al. (Winona Lake, Ind.: Eisenbrauns, 1994), 207–27.
A-13. As translated by A. K. Grayson, *Assyrian Rulers of the Early First Millennium* B.C., *vol. I (1114–859* B.C.*)* (RIMA 2; Toronto: Univ. of Toronto Press, 1991), 23–24.
A-14. Cf. Younger, "Judges 1," 208–12.
A-15. As translated by A. K. Grayson, *Assyrian Rulers of the Early First Millennium* B.C., *vol.* II (RIMA 3; Toronto: Univ. of Toronto Press, 1996), 201.
A-16. For additional references in an older source, see G. F. Moore, *A Critical and Exegetical Commentary on Judges*, 2nd ed. (ICC; Edinburgh: T. & T. Clark, 1908), 17–18.
A-17. For an illustrated study of the nature of ancient Assyrian mutilation in warfare, see E. Belibtreu, "Grisly Assyrian Record of Torture and

Death," *BAR* 17/1 (January/February 1991): 52–61, 75. For discussion of the shaming intent of this torture see T. M. Lemos, "Shame and Mutilation of Enemies in the Hebrew Bible," *JBL* 125 (2006): 225–41.

A-18. For discussion of the history of the use of chariotry in warfare in Mesopotamia see W. J. Hamblin, *Warfare in the Ancient Near East to 1600* B.C.: *Holy Warriors at the Dawn of History* (New York: Routledge, 2006), 129–53. Hamblin (p. 284) suggests that chariots were introduced to Canaan in Middle Bronze IIB (1750–1550). For discussion of the use of chariots in warfare at the end of the Bronze Age see R. Drews, *The End of the Bronze Age: Changes in Warfare and the Catastrophe ca. 1200* B.C. (Princeton: Princeton Univ. Press, 1993), 104–34.

A-19. For studies of the subject, see P. M. McNutt, *The Forging of Israel: Iron Technology, Symbolism, and Tradition in Ancient Society* (JSOTSup 108; Sheffield: Almond, 1990); P. Moorey, *Ancient Mesopotamian Materials and Industries* (Winona Lake, Ind.: Eisenbrauns, 1999), 278–92. For a popular presentation of the effect the introduction of iron had on military weaponry and the conduct of war, see J. D. Muhly, "How Iron Technology Changed the Ancient World and Gave the Philistines a Military Edge," *BAR* 8/6 (1982): 40–54. See also idem, "Metals," *OEANE*, 4:13–24.

A-20. Thus R. Drews, "The 'Chariots of Iron' of Joshua and Judges," *JSOT* 45 (1989): 15–23; McNutt, *The Forging of Israel*, 224–25; Lindars, *Judges 1–5*, 45–46.

A-21. Cf. A. R. Millard, "Back to the Iron Bed: Og's or Procrustes'?" in *Congress Volume, Paris 1992* (VTSup 61; Leiden: Brill, 1995), 194–95.

A-22. On Astarte, see J. Day, "Ashtoreth," *ABD*, 1:491–94; N. Wyatt, "Astarte," *DDD*, 109–14.

A-23. Heimpel, *Letters to the King*, 26:347 (p. 303).

A-24. ABL 136, 143, *et passim*.

A-25. EA 155.40–47, as translated by Moran, *Amarna Letters*, 241.

A-26. Lachish 4:2–4, as translated by S. L. Gogel, *A Grammar of Epigraphic Hebrew* (SBLRBS 23; Atlanta: Scholars Press, 1998), 417. For a discussion of these and other texts, see P. Kalluveettil, *Declaration and Covenant: A Comprehensive Review of Covenant Formulae from the Old Testament and the Ancient Near East* (AnBib 88; Rome: Biblical Institute Press, 1982), 153–59.

A-27. Gray (*Joshua, Judges, Ruth*, 261) sees the name as a scribal corruption of an original Cushan *rōʾš hattêmānî* ("the chief of the Temanites").

A-28. Papyrus Harris 1/75 (*ANET*, 260). Thus A. Malamat, "Cushan Rishathaim and the Decline of the Near East Around 1200 B.C.," *JNES* 13 (1954): 231–42.

A-29. On these and other suggestions, see B. Webb, *Book of Judges* (Sheffield: Sheffield Academic Press, 1987), 243, n. 5; Lindars, *Judges 1–5*, 131–34.

A-30. A. Malamat links Othniel's deliverance of Israel with the general defeat of this foreign invader of Egypt by Setnakht, the founder of the Twentieth Dynasty, at the end of the 13th century B.C. See A. Malamat, "The Egyptian Decline in Canaan and the Sea Peoples," in *Judges*, ed. B. Mazar (WHJP First Series: Ancient Times; Tel-Aviv: Massada, 1971), 26–27.

A-31. King and Stager, *Life in Biblical Israel*, 31–32.

A-32. The word for "key" is *maptēaḥ* ("opener"), from *pātaḥ* ("to open").

A-33. My interpretation of this event has changed significantly from that represented in my earlier commentary—which was heavily influenced by Halpern. See Block, *Judges, Ruth*, 166–69.

A-34. According to the archaeological record, the city's destruction is dated in the thirteenth century B.C. See further Y. Yadin, "Hazor," *NEAEHL*, 2:594–603.

A-35. See Manfred Weippert, "'Heiliger Krieg' in Israel und Assyrien: Kritische Anmerkungen zu Gerhard von Rads Konzept des 'Heiligen Krieges im alten Israel,'" *ZAW* 84 (1972): 472–76; R. J. van der Spek, "Assyriology and History: A Comparative Study of War and Empire in Assyria, Athens, and Rome," in *The Tablet and the Scroll: Near Eastern Studies in Honor of William W. Hallo*, ed. M. E. Cohen and D. B. Weisberg (Bethesda, Md.: CDL Press, 1993), 265–67; Nissinen, *References to Prophecy*, 164–65.

A-36. For discussion of these texts, see Block, "What Has Delphi to Do with Samaria?" 189–216. For a form critical study of charges to attack, see R. Back, *Die Aufforderung zur Flucht und zum Kampf in Alttestamentlichen Prophetenspruch* (Neukirchen-Vluyn: Neukirchener Verlag, 1962).

A-37. Herodotus, *Histories* 1.53.

A-38. Ibid., 1.55, as translated by Aubrey de Sélincourt, *Herodotus: The Histories* (Baltimore: Penguin , 1954), 33.

A-39. Ibid., 1.91 (p. 51).

A-40. *ANET*, 228. For a more recent translation and analysis, see K. A. Kitchen, *Poetry of Ancient Egypt* (Jonsered: P. Aströms Förlag, 1999), 71–74.

A-41. These are helpfully published and discussed by Kitchen, *Poetry of Ancient Egypt*, 165–96. See also M. Lichtheim, *Ancient Egyptian Literature*, vol. I, *The Old and Middle Kingdoms* (Berkeley: Univ. of California Press, 1975): Sesostris III, p. 119; vol. II, *The New Kingdom* (1976), Thutmosis III (pp. 36–37), Rameses II (pp. 62–70), Merneptah (pp. 74–77).

A-42. As translated by Lichtheim, *AEL*, 2:36–37. In the intervening strophes Amun-Re claims he hit a series of enemies; see Thutmose as a variety of animals: a youthful bull, crocodile, lion, falcon, jackal.

A-43. For introductory bibliography on the text, see K. L. Sparks, *Ancient Texts for the Study of the*

Hebrew Bible: A Guide to the Background Literature (Peabody, MA: Hendrickson, 2005), 389–90.

A-44. For the text in translation, see B. R. Foster, *Before the Muses: An Anthology of Akkadian Literature* (Bethesda, Md.: CDL Press, 1993), 1:209–29; idem, *From Distant Days: Myths, Tales, and Poetry of Ancient Mesopotamia* (Baltimore, Md.: CDL Press, 1995), 178–96.

A-45. P. C. Craigie, "The Song of Deborah and the Epic of Tikulti-Ninurta," *JBL* 88 (1969): 253–65. For additional helpful studies of the relationship between the present song and ancient victory odes, see K. L. Younger, "Heads! Tails! Or the Whole Coin! Contextual Method & Intertextual Analysis: Judges 4 & 5," *The Biblical Canon in Comparative Perspective: Scripture in Context IV*, ed. K. L. Younger et al (ANETS 11; Lewiston, NY: Mellen, 1993), 109–35; A. Globe, "The Literary Structure and Unity of the Song of Deborah," *JBL* 93 (1974): 495–99.

A-46. The shared features include (1) an introductory statement identifying the action of those who recited the poem with *syr* ("to sing"); (2) style: poetry following a prose account; (3) the involvement of female singers; (4) motif: the role of waters in the victory; (5) archaic language; (6) similar opening lines; (7) colorful and mythological imagery. For a closer comparison of these poems, see A. Hauser, "Two Songs of Victory: A Comparison of Exodus 15 and Judges 5," *Directions in Biblical Poetry*, ed. E. R. Follis (JSOTSup 40; Sheffield: Sheffield Academic Press, 1987), 265–84; also O'Connell, *The Rhetoric of the Book of Judges*, 133–37.

A-47. Thus M. D. Coogan, "A Structural and Literary Analysis of the Song of Deborah," *CBQ* 40 (1978): 165. Coogan's unitary interpretation is preferable to that of J. Blenkinsopp in "Ballad Style and Psalm Style in the Song of Deborah," *Bib* 42 (1961): 61–76, and followed by B. Lindars, "Deborah's Song: Women in the Old Testament," *BJRL* 65 (1983): 165–72, who propose that an originally secular ballad has been touched up with liturgical features to create a psalm celebrating the mighty acts of God.

A-48. A topographical list of Thutmose III (see *ANET*, 242–43) and a report Amen-hotep II's campaign in Asia (ibid., 245).

A-49. Cf. ibid., 259. On the Egyptian evidence for Edom, see K. A. Kitchen, "The Egyptian Evidence of Ancient Jordan," in *Early Edom and Moab—The Beginning of the Iron Age in Southern Jordan* ed. P. Bienkowski (Sheffield: Collis, 1992), 26.

A-50. The most important texts derive from reports of campaigns by Tiglath-pileser III (732 B.C.; *ANET*, 282), Sargon II (721–705 B.C., *ANET*, 287), Esarhaddon (680–669 B.C.), *ANET*, 291), and Ashurbanipal (668–633 B.C., *ANET*, 298, 301).

A-51. See T. Levy and M. Najjar, "Edom and Copper: The Emergence of Ancient Israel's Rival," *BAR* 32/4 (July/August, 2006): 24–35, 70.

A-52. Thus W. G. Lambert, *Babylonian Wisdom Literature* (Oxford: Clarendon, 1960), 42–43:71–72. *CAD*, A/1, 376a renders the statement, "The *alû*-demon has put on my body as if it were a garment."

A-53. N. M. Waldman, "The Imagery of Clothing, Covering, and Overpowering," *JANES* 19 (1989): 165.

A-54. For discussion, see D. I. Block, "Empowered by the Spirit of God: The Holy Spirit in the Historiographic Writings of the Old Testament," *The Southern Baptist Theological Journal* 1 (1997): 42–61.

A-55. *CT* 17, 6, iii, 31–32.

A-56. Block, "Empowered by the Spirit," 42–61; idem, "The Prophet of the Spirit: The Use of *rwḥ* in the Book of Ezekiel." *JETS* 32 (1988): 27–50.

A-57. E.g., Luke 24:49, "I am going to send you what my Father has promised [the Holy Spirit]; but stay in the city until you have been clothed [*endyēsthe*] with power from on high." Cf. Rom. 13:12; 1 Cor. 15:53; Gal. 3:27; Eph. 4:24; Col. 3:12.

A-58. Inasmuch as any given liver could simultaneously yield more than one binary response (it could have different markings relating to different issues), extispicy involved a complex binary mechanism.

A-59. See J. H. Walton, V. Matthews, and M. Chavalas, *The IVP Bible Background Commentary: Old Testament* (Downers Grove, Ill.: InterVarsity Press, 2000), 255.

A-60. Cf. Ezekiel's report of Nebuchadnezzar's triadic divinatory efforts in Ezek. 21:21–22.

A-61. For an excellent discussion of the nature, methods, and philosophical underpinnings of ancient Near Eastern divination, see Walton, *Ancient Near Eastern Thought and the Old Testament*, 239–74.

A-62. As translated by A. George, *The Epic of Gilgamesh: A New Translation* (Penquin Classics; London: Penguin, 2000), 10. For studies of ancient Near Eastern dream accounts, see A. L. Oppenheim, *The Interpretation of Dreams in the Ancient Near East* (Transactions of the American Philosophical Society; Philadelphia: American Philosophical Society, 1956); J. M. Lowery, "The Form and Function of Symbolic Vision Reports in the Hebrew Bible" (Ph.D. diss., The Southern Baptist Theological Seminary, 1999), 9–35, 183–200; S. A. L. Butler, *Mesopotamian Conceptions of Dreams and Dream Rituals* (AOAT 258, Neukirchener: Ugarit-Verlag, 1998). For studies of dream revelations in the Old Testament, see A. Jeffers, "Divination by Dreams in Ugaritic Literature and in the Old Testament," *IBS* 12 (1990): 167–83; R. Gnuse, "Dreams in the Night—Scholarly Mirage or Theophanic Formula?: The Dream Report as a Motif of the So-called Elohist Tradition," *BZ* n.s. 39 (1995): 28–53; and Jean-Marie Husser, *Dreams and Dream Narratives in the Biblical World* (Sheffield: Sheffield Academic Press, 1999).

A-63. Cf. Westbrook, *Babylonian Marriage Laws*, 111.
A-64. *UT* 1077:6–11.
A-65. Cf. 1 Kings 9:15–16 (Solomon and Pharaoh's daughter); 1 Kings 16:31 (Ahab's marriage to Jezebel, a princess of Tyre, though she appears to have been his primary wife).
A-66. Note the emphasis in Dan. 1:3–4 on the qualifications of candidates for the court of Nebuchadnezzar: youths without defect, handsome, intelligent in every branch of learning, discreet, wise, knowledgeable in the protocol of the court.
A-67. See J. A. Cuddon, *A Dictionary of Literary Terms and Literary Theory*, 3rd ed. (Oxford: Basil Blackwell, 1991), 322. On Old Testament fables, see K. J. Cathcart, "The Trees, the Beasts and the Birds: Fables, Parables and Allegories in the Old Testament," *Wisdom in Ancient Israel: Essays in Honour of J. A. Emerton*, ed. J. Day, R. P. Gordon, H. G. M. Williamson (Cambridge: Cambridge Univ. Press, 1995), 212–21.
A-68. For discussion of this and additional examples of Mesopotamian dispute literature, see S. Tatu, "Jotham's Fable and the *Crux Interpretum* in Judges IX," *VT* 56 (2006): 108–10; H. L. J. Vanstiphout, "The Mesopotamian Debate Poems: A General Presentation," *ActSum* 12 (1990): 271–318; idem, "The Mesopotamian Debate Poems: A General Presentation. Part II. The Subject", *ActSum* 14 (1992): 339–67.
A-69. Cf. S. Gevirtz, "Jericho and Shechem: A Religio-Literary Aspect of City Destruction," *VT* 13 (1963): 52–62.
A-70. As translated by Grayson, *Assyrian Rulers of the Early First Millennium* B.C., 24. Von Soden tentatively renders the hapax *ṣipu* as "salt?" *AHw*, 1104; cf. *CAD* 16 (1962), 205, which interprets the gesture as a "symbolic act signifying the annihilation of the destroyed settlement."
A-71. See Gevirtz, "Jericho and Shechem," 57–58.
A-72. As translated by J. A. Fitzmyer in COS, 2.82 (p. 214).
A-73. As translated by Gevirtz, "Jericho and Shechem," 53.
A-74. #16B §11, as translated by Beckman, *Hittite Diplomatic Texts*, 53.
A-75. 1 Kings 16:34; cf. Josh. 6:26. On salt as a symbol of barrenness and desolation, see Deut. 29:23; Ps. 107:34; Jer. 17:6; Zeph. 2:9.
A-76. As translated by S. B. Parker, *UNP*, 20.
A-77. Adapted from *ANET*, 394. For a study of these vows and a comparison with their biblical counterparts, see S. B. Parker, "The Vow in Ugaritic and Israelite Narrative Literature," *UF* 11 (1979): 693–700.
A-78. All birth narratives in the Bible involve boys (Moses, Samuel, Samson, John the Baptist, Jesus). Gen. 30:21 is the exception that proves the rule. Whereas many of the births of Jacob's sons are recounted as stories, Dinah's birth is simply announced, "Some time later she gave birth to a daughter and named her Dinah."
A-79. As translated by S. B. Parker, in *UNP*, 52–53.
A-80. Soggin, *Judges*, 240–41; de Vaux, *Ancient Israel*, 29.
A-81. Westbrook, *Old Babylonian Marriage Law*, 29.
A-82. O.R. Gurney and P. Hulin, *The Sultantepe Tablets* (London: British Institute of Archaeology at Ankara, 1964), II, no. 257 r. 2–9.
A-83. Apollodorus, *The Library* 3.15.8 (LCL 121; Cambridge, Mass.: Harvard Univ. Press, 1989), 2:117.
A-84. Ibid., 2.4.7 (1:173).
A-85. Robert Alter, *The Art of Biblical Narrative* (New York: Basic Books, 1981), 47–62.
A-86. The word occurs also in 1 Sam. 19:13; 2 Kings 23:24; Ezek. 21:21; Hos. 3:4–5; Zech. 10:2.
A-87. See further H. A. Hoffner, "The Linguistic Origins of Teraphim," *BSac* 124 (1967): 230–38; idem, "Hittite Tarpiš and Hebrew Terāphîm," *JNES* 27 (1968): 61–68. For a discussion of the options and an examination of the significance of the word in the Old Testament, see T. J. Lewis, "Teraphim," *DDD*, 844–50.
A-88. On their relation to the Israelite Urim and Thummim see W. Horowitz and V. Hurowitz, "Urim and Thummim in Light of a Psephomancy Ritual from Assur (LKA 137)," *JANES* 21 (1992): 110–11.
A-89. The verb *šāʾal* ("to ask, inquire") is associated with *t*ᵉ*rāpîm* in Ezek. 21:21.
A-90. See further K. van der Toorn, "The Nature of the Biblical Teraphim in the Light of the Cuneiform Evidence," *CBQ* 52 (1990): 203–22; idem, *Family Religion in Babylonia, Syria and Israel: Continuity and Change in the Forms of Religious Life* (Leiden: Brill, 1996), 218–25.
A-91. M. Stol, "Private Life in Ancient Mesopotamia," *CANE*, 1:494.
A-92. As translated in Roth, *Law Collections*, 159–60.
A-93. Thus Stol, "Private Life," 494.
A-94. See further H. A. Hoffner, "Incest, Sodomy and Bestiality in the Ancient Near East," in *Orient and Occident*, ed. H. A. Hoffner (AOAT 22; Neukirchen-Vluyn: Neukirchener Verlag, 1973), 83.

RUTH

by Dale W. Manor

Tomb painting of peasant couple gleaning in the fields
Erich Lessing/Art Resource, NY

Introduction

The opening statement of Ruth (1:1) embeds the events of the book in the chaotic era reflected in the book of Judges, when there was no central authority and "everyone did as he saw fit" (Judg. 21:25). Depending on when the Exodus occurred, the span can be either about 1400–1050 B.C. or about 1220–1050 B.C. Not only was Israel embroiled in chaos, most of the ancient world was as well. The Egyptians, Hittites, and Mesopotamians were in general decline; the Greeks were undergoing political upheaval; and the Sea Peoples (which included the Philistines) were wreaking havoc in the Mediterranean basin.

Israel and Moab

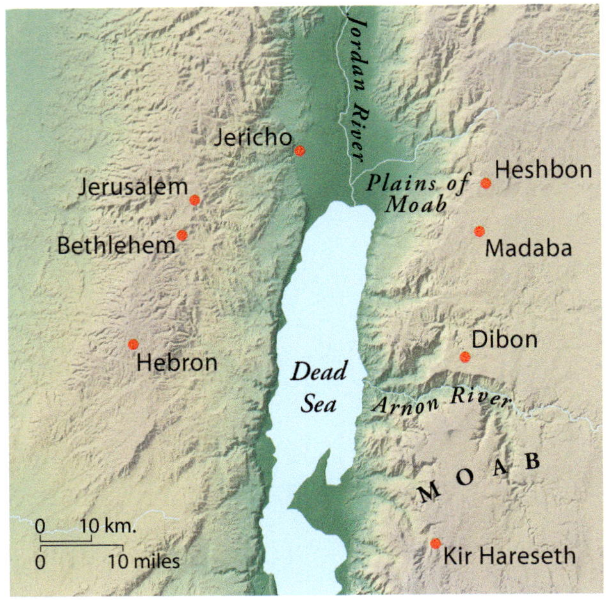

The reasons for these disruptions are difficult to determine, but environmental stresses of some kind, in conjunction with a flurry of earthquakes, may have contributed to the demise.[1] This deterioration of the major superpowers allowed a number of smaller peoples and states to germinate in the Levant. Among them are the Moabites, Phoenicians, Syrians, Ammonites, Philistines, and, of course, the Israelites.

Ruth Enters Judah (1:1–22)

A famine in the land (1:1). Famines were not uncommon in the Levant. Sometimes they could be local as prophesied by Amos (Amos 4:7–8), but the phrase normally implies a widespread famine. Several factors could precipitate a famine in addition to lack of rainfall. An adequate amount of rain, but at the wrong time, could destroy the crops.[2] Additionally, plant disease (Deut. 28:21; 1 Kings 8:37; Amos 4:9; Hag. 2:17), insect infestation (Joel 1; Amos 4:9–10), and warfare (2 Kings 6:24–25; Isa. 1:7) could effectively serve as famines. The Bible notes a number of famines, some of which precipitated departures from Canaan—Abraham went to Egypt (Gen. 12:10); Isaac sojourned in Gerar (26:1); and

Plains of Moab with Mount Nebo in background
Todd Bolen/www.BiblePlaces.com

Bethlehem region
Todd Bolen/www.BiblePlaces.com

Jacob and his family migrated to Egypt (chs. 43–50). Overall, the pattern of famine and plenty in the Levant is unpredictable.

A theological outgrowth of this unpredictability fueled devotion to various fertility deities (i.e., Baal, Asherah, Anat, etc.). The objective was to ensure the rains and productivity of the fields, flocks, and families. Another element likely contributed to their polytheism: Yahweh had promised to provide the full range of their sustenance if they served him faithfully (cf. Deut. 28:1–14). Thus, Israel may have perceived a famine as Yahweh's failure to provide, especially if they failed to recognize their own apostasy. This attitude seems reflected by Gideon: "If the LORD is with us, why has all this happened to us?" (Judg. 6:13). Similarly, the women informed Jeremiah that when they quit worshiping the Queen of Heaven, famine and disaster had come upon them (Jer. 44:18). From a practical standpoint, the people would attempt to reduce their risk by diversifying their crops and flocks.

Bethlehem (1:1). Bethlehem means "house of bread." Ironically, the house of plenty has failed Elimelech, forcing his exodus to Moab.

Bethlehem is about five miles south of Jerusalem on the main north-south road that passes along the ridge of the central mountains. The area is generally productive with wheat, barley, almonds, and grapes, which may have factored into the significance of the town's name.[3] This diversification of crops would normally be a valuable survival defense in the otherwise precarious agricultural setting.

Excavations in Bethlehem have been few and no ruins have been found for the period of Ruth, nor has a well been located to which David referred when he yearned for water from the well at the gate of the city (2 Sam. 23:15). Surveys, however, have revealed sherds from the period of the united monarchy.[4]

Went to live (1:1). The Hebrew word for "live" (*gûr*) is often rendered "sojourn" and is a technical term applied to a class of people who are neither native nor simply foreigners living in the land. They had no blood ties to the residents and only had legal rights as the dominant peoples permitted,[5] which were often whimsically granted and withdrawn. The people of Sodom refer to Lot as an alien (*gûr*) and use it as a slur (Gen. 19:9).

Moab (1:1). Moab, situated east of the Jordan River and Dead Sea, received an annual rainfall of about sixteen inches a year, which provided a number of perennial springs and rivers. The sudden rise of the winds from the depths of the Jordan Valley could wrest more moisture out of the clouds.[6] Hence, Moab often sustained or escaped a famine.

Moab, as a geographical or political entity, receives confirmation as early as Rameses II, who refers to Moab on a pylon at Luxor.[7] Moab consisted of three main regions. The northernmost section was the plains of Moab to the northeast of the Dead Sea. The middle extended from the plains of Moab southward to the Arnon and was generally a fairly level tableland at 2,000 to 2,400 feet elevation. The third and southernmost section was higher with elevations over 4,000 feet and extending from the Arnon to the Zered at the southern end of the Dead Sea.[8]

The relationship between Moab and early Israel is difficult to clarify. The Bible notes that Reuben and Gad lived in some of the area later attributed to Moab (Num. 32; Josh. 13:15–28). Mesha, king of Moab (late ninth century), states that the people of Gad had lived in the area "forever."[9] Excavations at Tall al-ʿUmayri in modern Jordan have revealed a town that seems to reflect an early Israelite occupation that was likely Reubenite.[10] Since the core of Moab seems to have been to the south, the northern regions may have been much more fluid and multicultural in nature.

The text gives no indication of where Elimelech settled in Moab. To reach the borders, however, would have taken several days since the maximum rate of travel on foot was about twenty miles a day.[11] The distance involved in the move made the decision a serious one, inhibiting easy access to the homeland. If he took the family to northern Moab, he would have traveled northward to Jerusalem and descended to Jericho, where he crossed the Jordan into Moab. Alternatively, he may have traveled southward to Hebron, descended eastward to the Dead Sea, crossed the sea to the Lisan (i.e., the peninsula that extends into the Dead Sea) and climbed into the interior of Moab. This would have been the shortest route to Moab.[12]

The remnants of a wide thoroughfare (ca. 4–5 meters wide) with stone demarcations have been identified in Moab; it appears to date at least to the time of Mesha and almost certainly was built over an earlier road.[13] The width of this road is characteristic of the roads throughout the Mediterranean and Mesopotamian regions and is corroborated from the evidence of wagons, chariots, and carts from the ancient world.[14]

Names (1:2). With the exception of the wordplay that Naomi injects regarding her own name, the names of the major personalities—Elimelech, Naomi, Mahlon, Kilion, Ruth, and Orpah—have neither meanings nor etymologies that play literary roles in the narrative. The equivalents of Elimelech, Naomi, and Kilion are preserved in Ugaritic, Amorite, and/or Akkadian, while Mahlon, Ruth, and Orpah have not been identified elsewhere.[15]

Ephrathites (1:2). The matriarch Rachel had died on the way to Ephrath (Gen. 35:16–19), which was an earlier name of Bethlehem. The use of Ephrathite may reflect an old aristocratic family of Ephrath/Bethlehem from which Elimelech descended.[16]

Elimelech ... died (1:3). After Elimelech died, Naomi was left a widow, and after the deaths of her two sons, we may infer that she is stripped of all male protection except reliance on Yahweh (see sidebar on "The Widow in Ancient Society"). Her plight, then, was similar to that of the orphan and sojourner (e.g., Mal. 3:5) and the poor (e.g., Isa. 10:2). The lapse of ten years (Ruth 1:4) implies that Naomi is past childbearing, or at least near the end of such, and hence her prospect of finding a husband is significantly reduced. Her decision to return to Bethlehem was the most reasonable option, where she might at least find sustenance by gleaning if no extended family members were to care for her.

Sons ... become your husbands (1:11). The Bible provides specific legislation for

The Widow in Ancient Society

The hazards of widowhood in antiquity were great. In most rural areas, women had little opportunity to pursue independent careers, but overwhelmingly depended on their husbands for sustenance. Women certainly had significant roles in their household, but these usually did not extend to commercial enterprises, contrary to the idealized description of the noble woman of Proverbs 31. After her husband's death, normally a widow had to rely on her sons for support; if she had none, she might have to sell herself into slavery, resort to prostitution, or die.

From Alalakh comes a receipt for the purchase of a female debt slave with the provision that there be no emancipation.[A-1] Amos declares to Amaziah that after his exile and death, his wife will be forced into prostitution, especially since their children will be killed (Amos 7:17). It is in part against this kind of harshness that the redeemer-kinsman legislation exists (Lev. 25:39–55). Van der Toorn has suggested that if a widow made a vow she could not pay (cf. Num. 30; Prov. 7:14–20), she might resort to prostitution to fulfill her vow.[A-2] It is probably against these desperate prospects that an ostracon from the period of the monarchy preserves the plea of a childless widow who writes to her lord to honor his promise of an inheritance.[A-3]

Yahweh, however, was concerned for the widows and the poor (Deut. 10:17–18; Ps. 68:5; 146:9; Jer. 49:11) and issued instructions for their preservation (Ex. 22:22–24; Deut. 14:28–29; 24:17–20; 26:12–13; 27:19). Many of these concerns with widows, the poor, and orphans are mirrored in surrounding cultures from whom laws and customs have been preserved. Among them are laws from the Code of Hammurabi,[A-4] instructions relative to widows and orphans in Egypt,[A-5] and judgment for the widow and orphan in the gate at Ugarit.[A-6] The prophets, however, had to remind Israel of her responsibilities (Isa. 1:23; 10:1–2).

If the marriages in the narrative of Ruth 1 followed typical ancient Near Eastern tradition,[A-7]Naomi probably had married in her mid-teens and had likely borne her two sons by age twenty. The sons would have married little earlier than age twenty to young women similarly in their mid-teens. By the time she decides to return to Judah, Naomi is likely in her mid-forties and Ruth and Orpah in their mid-to-upper twenties.

Kings would regularly gather an audience to hear the complaints and cases brought by the people at places like this ruler's podium in the gate at Dan.
Todd Bolen/www.BiblePlaces.com

family preservation, often called levirate marriage (Deut. 25:5–10): If a man married a woman and he died before there were offspring, his brother would marry the widow and raise up children in the name of the deceased (see sidebar on "Levirate Marriage"). Since Naomi does not mention the prospect of marrying her husband's brother, technically, her proposed scenario would not be levirate marriage since the husband she might hypothetically secure would not, in a patrilineal society, produce levirate brothers to her deceased sons. However, in Naomi's distraught state, she is likely unconcerned with the nuances of law; instead, she emphasizes how futile is any prospect of securing any husband for her widowed daughters-in-law.

A relief on the false door of Nikaure shows Nikaure's mother-in-law Hetepheres and his wife Ihat embracing.
Werner Forman Archive/The Egyptian Museum, Cairo

Her people and her gods (1:15). While "people" and "gods" may refer to Orpah's personal allegiances, they also may extend to her tribe's social and religious associations.[17] Ancient societies often had a hierarchical slate of deities who resided in their area—sometimes connected with geography or geographic features. This is indicated when the Aramaean king's servants described Israel's gods as "gods of the hills" and not of the valleys (cf. 1 Kings 20:23–25). A god's domain, however, might expand geographically through conquest as indicated in Assur-nasirpal's bombastic self-description and the sponsorship of a host of Assyrian deities.[18] These national gods apparently were often considered beyond the reach of the common person, who alternatively appealed to an array of lesser deities and spirits more easily accessible and task specific[19]—hence, the proliferation of personal family worship that may have been at odds with the national religious expression.

The national god of Moab was Chemosh. Mesha, a later Moabite king, commented that Chemosh had been angry with the land and permitted Omri to subdue the country.[20] Chemosh was an ancient god in the Levant for whom we have evidence as early as the late third millennium B.C. at Ebla. We have no evidence of what he looked like at the period, although he may have been a god of war similar to the Mesopotamian god Nergal.[21]

But Ruth replied (1:16–17). Ruth's commitment to leave her family for a land where she apparently has never been, potentially totally isolating herself from her own kin, commands admiration and respect. While she has probably become familiar with some Hebrew customs and beliefs, to saturate herself in the different culture has dimensions that one can only appreciate by experience. Some suggest that her loyalty surpasses that of Abraham, who was called by divine direction (Gen. 12:1–5); Ruth was not.[22]

To most Westerners, there is usually little emotional trauma in being buried away from the family plot. Such a casual approach to death was unknown to the people of ancient Canaan. Ruth's declaration is emphatic—"*there* I will be buried"—that is, with you, Naomi.

The whole town was stirred (1:19). The Hebrew word rendered "stirred" elsewhere denotes considerable excitement and commotion (cf. 1 Sam. 4:5; 1 Kings 1:45). The women's reaction (which the text indicates) implies that Naomi has made few, if any, visits to her hometown in the intervening ten years. News of Naomi's arrival probably buzzed through the town. Ancient towns were little more than small villages. Demographic studies indicate that the typical village had a population of only a few hundred.[23] Moreover, the population of the town may have diminished because of the famine—either by death or by emigration (as Elimelech and his family had done).

Levirate Marriage

Levir is a Latin word meaning "brother-in-law" (Heb. *yābam*). Middle Assyrian laws (ca. 1100 B.C.) provided for custody of a childless widow to pass through the family, but the concerns focus on the dowry protection more than producing offspring.[A-8] Hittite law (ca. 1650–1500 B.C.) had a similar provision to marry the widow to either a brother-in-law or, under some circumstances, a father-in-law.[A-9] While these laws do not explicitly indicate that the purpose is to produce an heir, an heir would essentially be the woman's source of welfare.

Similar customs appear among the Nuzi (ca. 1400 B.C.).[A-10] An episode involving levirate marriage appears in the narrative of Judah and Tamar (Gen. 38). The Sadducees later used the levirate legislation to try to make the resurrection look incredulous (cf. Matt. 22:23–28).[A-11] A full resolution of all the nuances of application of levirate and levirate-type marriages is difficult. One author contends that the concern in the biblical examples is primarily to perpetuate the property title in the family of the deceased[A-12] by providing an heir for the deceased.[A-13]

Middle Assyrian laws (A)
Emily Katrencik, courtesy of the Vorderasiatisches Museum, Berlin

Barley harvest (1:22). Barley and wheat were usually sown at the same time, but barley matured a month before wheat and was harvested in mid-to-late April. Barley was not the preferred grain of consumption—it yielded a course, hearty bread. Since barley matures first, though, it was suitable as the firstfruit offering (Lev. 23:10). The arrival of the barley was a time of rejoicing and heralded the prospect of security as the remaining crops came in.[24]

Ruth Meets Boaz (2:1–23)

Clan of Elimelech (2:1). The "clan" (Heb. *mišpāḥâ*) was a social grouping in size between that of the tribe (Heb. *šēbet* or *matteh*), such as Judah, and the extended family (Heb. *bêt ʾāb*; lit., "house of the father"). The clan definition was based on descent from a common ancestor, and from within this context the function of the kinsman-redeemer (Heb. *gōʾēl*; Lev. 25) in the narrative will unfold. The clan was normally responsible for maintaining the social and economic survival of the relatives and in time of crisis even contributed personnel to the defense of the emerging tribal-based nation.[25]

A man of standing (2:1). The Hebrew phrase (*gibbôr ḥayil*) is often rendered "mighty man of valor" (cf. Josh. 6:2; 2 Kings 5:1), but sometimes it simply refers to a person of ability (1 Kings 11:28) or of wealth (2 Kings 15:20).[26] The connection with

Ancient Burial Practices

The Bible often refers to death as being gathered to one's people (cf. e.g., Gen. 25:8, 17; 35:29; 49:33; Num. 20:24, 26; Deut. 32:50), and Jacob and Joseph gave specific instructions that their remains be conveyed to the family homeland (Gen. 49:29–32; 50:24–26). These requests are apparently not unique to the Israelites. Archaeology has uncovered a number of cemeteries, many of which yield evidence that the deceased passed away elsewhere and their bones were interred in the cemetery some time after death and decarnation had occurred. Ruth 1 gives no indication that Naomi brought her husband's and sons' remains back to the family plot in Bethlehem, but if she had not, she likely was returning with them on this journey.[A-14]

A proper burial was a matter of great concern for people in the ancient world. The maintenance of the dead was a common practice, as implied in the often elaborate tombs designed to accommodate the extended family. Many tombs have been excavated in the regions of ancient Canaan and Israel; these usually contain various grave offerings such as lamps, bowls, jars, and personal items, implying some concept of an afterlife.[A-15]

It was commonly considered necessary for the descendants to care for the deceased with proper burial and occasional ritual to ensure their transition from the world of the living into that of the deceased.[A-16] Among these practices were sacrifices to the dead that often included meals in their honor (cf. Deut. 26:14). Additionally, some survivors thought the deceased might provide some revelation (cf. Isa. 8:19–20; 65:4; Jer. 16:6–9). While these passages indicate that some Israelites observed rituals for the dead, Moab also had such a tradition that had been part of the Peor apostasy (cf. Ps. 106:28–31).

Iron Age tomb at Ketef Hinnom
Christie J. Goulart

The Gezer Calendar

Excavations at Gezer in 1908 yielded a small stone inscription dating from ca. 925 B.C. with a sort of calendar poem geared to harvest expectations. Albright suggests that it may have been a school writing exercise. The tablet reads:

> His two months are (olive) harvest,
> His two months are planting (grain),
> His two months are late planting;
> His month is hoeing up of flax,
> His month is harvest of barley,
> His month is harvest and feasting;
> His two months are vine-tending,
> His month is summer fruit.[A-17]

The tablet does not refer to the months by calendar names but by the work expectations associated with them, probably because the lives of the people so heavily depended on the yield from the soil. In similar fashion, the reference to barley harvest in 2 Samuel 21:9–10 and the wheat harvest in 1 Samuel 12:17, along with Amos's reference to the harvest "just as the second crop was coming up" (7:1), refers to seasons and not specifically to months. The weather cycles likely differed slightly in Gezer as compared to Bethlehem, but the sequence of the work would have been similar.

Gezer Calendar
Todd Bolen/www.BiblePlaces.com

wealth suggests that the "man of valor" was wealthy enough to leave his place of livelihood, having his own weapons of war to serve as necessary when there was not a standing army. Even though there is no evidence of military conflict or turmoil in the book of Ruth, Boaz's description as a *gibbôr ḥayil* may be significant since the events are placed within the context of the chaos and anarchy of Judges (Ruth 1:1), when there was occasional need to call people for military duty (cf. Judg. 3:37; 4:10; 7:1, 23).

Pick up the leftover grain (2:2). This is commonly called gleaning. Mosaic law had decreed that landowners were not to harvest the full extent of their fields, but they were to leave produce in the hard-to-reach areas. The remaining harvest was for the poor and foreigners who might be in the land (Lev. 19:9–10; Deut. 24:19–22). Ruth expects to gather the cut remnants that the reapers have accidentally dropped. Obadiah (Obad. 6) and Jeremiah (Jer. 49:9) allude to the expectations of gleaning in their indictments of Edom.

In whose eyes I find favor (2:2). Even though Mosaic law prescribed the landowner to permit gleaning, part of the challenge of the period of the judges was that the people did not generally follow God's law. Ruth's statement implies not only an awareness of etiquette to request permission, but

Flint sickle blades from the Iron Age
Kim Walton, courtesy of the Oriental Institute Museum

also the danger to herself, particularly as a foreigner. Later prophets reveal that the Israelites did not always follow God's direction relative to the poor and oppressed (cf. Isa. 1:17; Amos 5:10–15; 8:4–6; Mic. 3:1–3), and almost certainly this abuse would often manifest itself in the refusal to allow them to glean.

Corroboration of this is the Egyptian instruction from the Ramesside period: "[Do not] pounce on a widow when you find her in the fields. And then fail to be patient with her reply."[27] It is not clear if this instruction reflects a widespread custom or law in Egypt or if it simply represents Amenemope's perception of civility and humanitarianism.

Behind the harvesters (2:3). Whether the harvesters were from Boaz's household cannot be ascertained. The Bible notes that natives and foreigners might hire themselves out for work (Deut. 24:14), either on a daily basis (Lev. 19:13; Deut. 24:15; cf. also Matt. 20:1–16) or annually (Lev. 25:53). The Laws of Eshnunna specified a shekel of silver for a month's wages, plus a grain provision.[28] The Code of Hammurabi decrees a per diem wage[29]—for the first half of the year, it was to be six barleycorn of silver per day and for the second half, five barleycorn per day.[30]

We do not know the pay scale for the time of Ruth in Judah. Harvesting crops apparently was not a favored occupation (cf. Job 7:1–2; 14:6), and the harvester's welfare would inevitably be at the mercy of the overseer (Jer. 22:13; Mal. 3:5). An inscription from the time of Josiah preserves the petition to the regional magistrate of a reaper whose cloak had been appropriated by the overseer.[31]

The harvesters probably used flint sickles to cut the grain. Numerous flint sickle blades have been discovered at sites all over Israel from the Iron Age I period (i.e., 1200–1000 B.C.),[32] the probable period of the events of Ruth. Even though the period is often referred to as the Iron Age, use of iron was initially rare. Weapons and tools were usually of bronze or, in the case of harvest work, flint. During Saul's reign, the Philistines dominated ironworking (1 Sam. 13:19). Recent excavations at Tel Beth-Shemesh have uncovered the earliest ironsmith workshop (tenth to ninth century B.C.) found in the Near East.[33]

Tel Beth-Shemesh: earliest iron smith workshop
Kim Walton

A field belonging to Boaz (2:3). People typically lived in a small town or village, which provided safety as well as a sense of community, especially since the people were usually tribally related. The population of the town seldom exceeded a few hundred. The fields were away from the town, and it was necessary for the people to leave the security of town to work in the fields.

The fields were marked off in family plots, often with small piles of stones serving as the boundary markers. It would be somewhat easy for an unscrupulous person to move these stones over a little at a time to increase his land holdings at the expense of a neighbor. Reflecting this reality, the Bible has injunctions against illicitly moving the boundary markers (Deut. 19:14; 27:17; Prov. 22:28; 23:10; cf. Job 24:2; Hos. 5:10). A similar prohibition against land theft with instructions for compensation appears in Hittite laws.[34] The small piles of stones and sometimes low walls were convenient means by which to remove the stones from the cultivable fields.

"The LORD be with you!" "The LORD bless you!" (2:4). This exchange of greetings imploring the Lord is not unusual. It may denote an element of devotion, but it may also simply have been a customary greeting; however, the tone of the book implies more than a cultural accommodation. The psalmist in Psalm 129 uses agricultural imagery to describe the interaction with his enemies; the final verse (129:8) implies that a blessing including the divine name was common. One greeting in the Hebrew Bible was simply "shalom" (*šālôm*), meaning "peace" (cf. Judg. 6:23; 1 Sam. 25:6; 2 Sam. 18:28).[35] Some inscriptions have been preserved that implore blessing from both Yahweh of Samaria and his Asherah.[36]

The foreman (2:5). The Hebrew word *naʿar* is sometimes translated "young man," but the term encompasses much more. Ugaritic and Egyptian sources use a cognate word to refer to people of military rank.[37] Similarly, people in the Bible who are so designated are often servants or retainers of some kind (cf. Num. 22:22; Judg. 7:10–11; 19:3; 2 Kings 4:12) or military personnel (Gen. 14:24; 1 Sam. 25:5; 2 Sam. 2:14; 1 Kings 20:14). The term can apply to someone who manages an estate, as was the case with Ziba, who had custody of Saul's estate (2 Sam. 9:9; 19:17 [19:18]).

As far as age is concerned, the age of demarcation varies depending on the function of the person involved—for military service, it was age twenty (cf. Ex. 30:14; Num. 1:3, 18); for Levitical service outside the Tent of Meeting it was twenty-five (Num. 8:24); and for service in the Tent of Meeting it was thirty (see Num. 4). Several signet impressions with the term *naʿar* have been found from the biblical world. Four read "Belonging to Elyaqim steward [*naʿar*] of Yokin"—two are from Tell Beit Mirsim, one from Tel Beth-Shemesh, and one from Ramat Rahel.[38] The term also appears on an Ammonite seal.[39]

From morning till now (2:7). The Hebrew text is difficult to decipher. The NIV opts for a rendering that describes the agricultural custom of rising early to work in the fields. Farmers typically rise at or before dawn to take advantage of the cooler morning temperatures. In preindustrial societies and especially in a hot climate like Israel's, it would be normal to take an afternoon break or siesta during the heat of the day and resume the field work in the later afternoon. This is part of the tradition behind

One of the boundary stones of Gezer from around the first century B.C.
Todd Bolen/www.BiblePlaces.com

David's late afternoon walk on his roof after his rest (cf. 2 Sam. 11:2).

Short rest in the shelter (2:7). Again the Hebrew is difficult. The NIV renders this verse to reflect Ruth's industriousness: She has not stopped working "except for a short rest in the shelter." Work in the hot sun can quickly drain one's energy. The shelter was a kind of brush arbor set up as a break shade for the workers. Because of Israel's low humidity, retreat into the shade yields a dramatic differential in temperature since the dry air rapidly evaporates the perspiration and accentuates the cooling effects.

Follow ... after the girls (2:9). In the division of labor, the men did the cutting (2:15) and the women (*n^{e}ʿārôt*, feminine plural form *of naʿar*) did the binding (2:8–9), although this separation is not necessarily absolute.[40]

I have told the men not to touch you (2:9). Ruth's presence on the scene as a stranger and especially as an alien would naturally draw attention and almost invite abuse by some in society. The word "touch" (*nāgaʿ*) carries several nuances, including to strike (Gen. 32:26, 33 [32:25, 32]; Josh. 8:15; Job 1:19), to inflict injury (Gen. 26:11, 29), and to have sexual relations (Gen. 20:6; Prov. 6:29). Unless Boaz suspected his employees to be of the basest sort, it is unlikely that sexual relations (i.e., rape) would be the point of prohibition; more likely it is not to strike or abuse her and may prohibit verbal abuse (cf. comments on 2:2).

Water jars (2:9). Instead of touching her, the young men were to permit her to drink from the jars that the young men had filled. Without a readily available water supply in the field, it was necessary to prepare for the day's activities. The water source was likely the well at the gate of Bethlehem that David longed for later during his flight from Saul (2 Sam. 23:15–16 = 1 Chron. 11:17–18). The location of the well has not been identified.

While not necessarily exclusively so, drawing water was commonly a woman's job (Gen. 24:11, 13; 1 Sam. 9:11); note Ugaritic materials here.[41] The Israelites sometimes coerced foreigners into the job (Deut. 29:10; Josh. 9:21–27). The jars were likely somewhat porous and allowed the water to seep through the pores. The low humidity accelerated the evaporation from the surface of the jar and cooled the contents of the jar significantly.

Her face to the ground (2:10). While we cannot be sure of the posture involved, the Black Obelisk depicts Jehu of Israel bowing before Shalmaneser III with his face on the ground.[42] Yamauchi suggests that the posture is similar to the modern Moslem who places his forehead to the ground in his daily prayers.[43]

Under whose wings (2:12). The Hebrew word for "wing" is *kānāp*, which is rendered "corner of your garment" in 3:9, when Ruth broaches the subject of marriage. In the present case, Boaz likely simply alludes to the protective covering of the Lord's care. The Lord elsewhere is portrayed as providing

Egyptian painting from the tomb of Menna shows a supervisor standing in a shelter while harvesting work is being done.
Manfred Näder
Gabana Studios, Germany

Goddess spreading her wings over two children who nurse at her breasts
Scala/Art Resource, NY, courtesy of the National Museum, Damascus, Syria

such protection (see Ps. 36:7; 57:1; 61:4; 91:4). Occasional artistic depictions of deities spreading their wings over their subjects can be seen in a Syrian goddess spreading her wings over two children who nurse at her breasts.[44] An Egyptian statue depicts Horus as a falcon hovering behind the king, Khafre,[45] and another shows Isis's wings surrounding Osiris protectively.[46] Boaz's imagery might draw from the wing-protected ark of the covenant with its cherubim (Ex. 25:17–22).[47]

At mealtime (2:14). The day's meals normally began with a light breakfast and a light noon meal, such as reflected in this narrative. The evening meal was the main meal of the day and usually consisted of basically a one-pot stew of mainly vegetables; the stew was sopped with bread.[48] The wine vinegar (*ḥōmeṣ*) was a soured wine that was among the prohibitions for Nazirites (Num. 6:3). In this passage it may have been a vinegar-based sauce.[49]

An inscription preserved from Arad lists *ḥōmeṣ* as a requisitioned commodity along with wine;[50] however, earlier Ugaritic materials seem to list it as a synonym of wine.[51] Linguistically, the item could render a commonly used chick pea sauce (hummous), prevalent throughout the Mediterranean world, into which bread is dipped.[52] The roasted grain was a common addition to the meal (1 Sam. 17:17; 25:18; 2 Sam. 17:28). Robinson had noted in his travels in 1838 that "the grains of wheat not yet fully dry and hard are roasted in a pan or on an iron plate,"[53] although Borowski suggests that the parching was done because the grain was too hard to be eaten raw without breaking the kernel.[54]

Threshed the barley (2:17). To thresh this personal harvest for her and Naomi, Ruth beat the grain with a stick to separate the grains from the chaff (cf. Gideon in Judg. 6:11). It would be necessary then to winnow it as well. Her take for the day was impressive—an ephah (ca. twenty-two liters = two-thirds of a bushel) is an exceptional quantity and implies that the workers complied with Boaz's request. This was the same amount that Jesse instructed David to deliver to his three brothers serving in Saul's army (cf. 1 Sam. 17:13–17).

The living and the dead (2:20). Some cultures worked to maintain the dead by giving food offerings and sacrifices on their behalf.[55] There is no indication that Naomi has this in mind; she more likely alludes to God's preservation of the memory of the dead (i.e., Elimelech, Mahlon, and Kilion) by taking care of their widows (i.e., Naomi and Ruth). She recognizes that Boaz is a potential source of hope as their kinsman-redeemer (*gōʾēl*). The role of the kinsman-redeemer was multifaceted and served to stabilize a disrupted family circumstance.

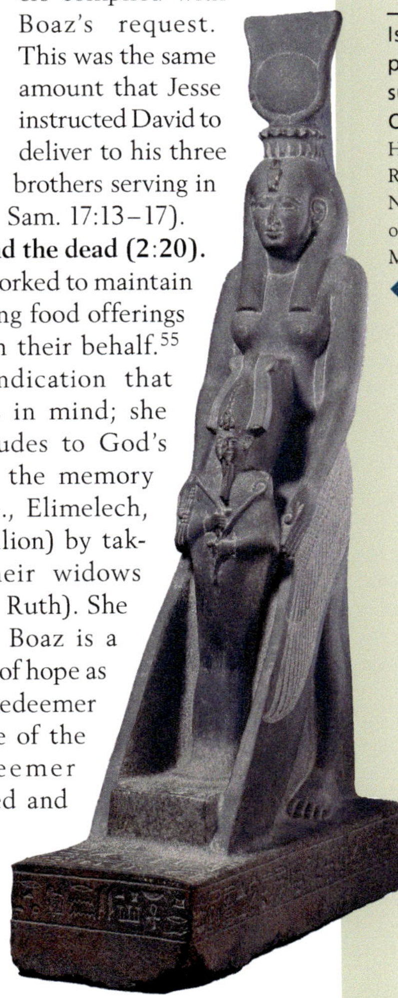

Isis's wings protectively surrounding Osiris
HIP/Art Resource, NY, courtesy of the British Museum

Xēstes	Greco-Roman	1/2 cab	1 1/6 pints
Cab	Hebrew	1/18 ephah	1 quart
Choinix	Greco-Roman	1/18 ephah	1 quart
Omer	Hebrew	1/10 ephah	2 quarts
Seah/Saton	Hebrew/Greek	1/3 ephah	7 quarts
Modios	Greco-Roman	4 omers	1 peck or 1/4 bushel
Ephah [Bath]	Hebrew	10 omers	3/5 bushel
Lethek	Hebrew	5 ephahs	3 bushels
Cor [Homer]/Koros	Hebrew/Greek	10 ephahs	6 bushels or 200 quarts/14.9 bushels or 500 quarts

Barley and wheat harvests (2:23). The time involved would normally be two to two and a half months, taking the wheat harvest into June. If the narrative is chronological, the barley winnowing (see ch. 3) was apparently put on hold until the wheat harvest had come in. If this is the case, it implies a significant harvest in view of the recently terminated famine.

Ruth Proposes Marriage to Boaz (3:1–18)

Winnowing barley (3:2). Winnowing was often done as a community activity. Winnowing takes place after the threshing (see below), and it is a labor-intensive process to separate the grains from the plant stalks. The process was conducted typically outside of the town where the person, using a pitchfork, threw the mixture into the air. The breezes blew away the unwanted, lighter components (cf. Hos. 13:3), allowing the heavier grains to fall to the ground. The process would be repeated until the grains were relatively free from the plant stalks.[56] The breezes usually came up in the mid-afternoon and died out about sunset; it is possible that Naomi's reference to Boaz winnowing at night (3:2) accommodates the festivities that normally followed a successful harvest and winnowing.

Transport of the grain to the threshing and winnowing floor was either on animal-drawn carts (cf. Amos 2:13) or in baskets.[57] The threshing floor was a large flat area, usually bared bedrock and slick from the polishing effect of the intensive activity with the straw acting as a polishing agent.[58] They were situated to take advantage of the prevailing winds, which were critical. Sometimes these were near the city gates (cf. 1 Kings 22:10; Jer. 15:7).[59]

Egyptian painting from the tomb of Nakht with farmers carrying baskets full of wheat
Erich Lessing/Art Resource, NY

Threshing could be done several ways. Ruth had beaten out

The Role of Kinsman-Redeemer

Mosaic law prescribed that the kinsman-redeemer (*gōʾēl*) reacquire property lost by family members who had fallen on hard times (Lev. 25:25–30; Jer. 32:6–15). He also was to redeem relatives who, because of poverty, had sold themselves into slavery (Lev. 25:47–55). In addition, he was to avenge relatives who had died at the hands of others (Num. 35:12, 19–27; Deut. 19:6, 12; Josh. 20:2–3, 5, 9), to be the recipient of payments owed to deceased relatives (Num. 5:8), and generally to alleviate wrongs that relatives might not be able to accomplish for themselves (Job 19:25; Ps. 119:154; Prov. 23:11; Jer. 50:34; Lam. 3:58).[A-18]

The legislation says nothing explicitly regarding taking the wife of the deceased as part of the redemption procedure, although it appears that the Israelites sometimes understood a connection between the two. Elements of redemption appear in laws from Eshnunna[A-19] and Hammurabi,[A-20] but they do not focus on a specific family member serving as the redeemer.

her fairly small volume with a stick (2:17). A larger volume, however, required more intensive and efficient threshing. Sometimes animals would walk over the grain and their hooves beat the grain to separate the grain from the stalk (cf. a metaphorical allusion in Mic. 4:13). Mosaic legislation demanded that the animals be allowed to eat of the harvest (Deut. 25:4). A more efficient tool was a threshing sledge, which was pulled by an animal or two (cf. metaphor in Isa. 41:15). This consisted of two to three wide boards with upturned ends to slide easily over the grain; the underside of the boards would have holes drilled or slots cut into them into which teeth of flint or iron were driven. The teeth separated the components of the grain. Isaiah also alludes to the wheels of carts along with the animals' hooves being used to thresh (Isa. 28:28).

Uncover his feet (3:4). The instruction can be seen as a double entendre. Sometimes "feet" (*rᵉgālîm*) is a euphemism for the genital region (cf. Isa. 7:20; Ezek. 16:25;[60] some extend it to Ex. 4:25; Judg. 3:24; 1 Sam. 24:3), but most of the time *rᵉgālîm* means feet. Complicating the interpretation, however, is the use of "uncover" (*gālâ*), which sometimes referred to sexual relations (Lev. 18 and 20 numerous times; Deut. 23:1 [22:30]; 27:20; Ezek. 16:35–39). More specifically, though, Naomi instructs Ruth to uncover "the place of his feet" (*margᵉlôt*),[61] and given the character reflected of both Boaz and Ruth, there is no reason to infer that anything more than uncovering the feet occurs.[62]

Far end of the grain pile (3:7). Probably Boaz remained at the threshing floor to protect against thieves.

Spread the corner of your garment … kinsman-redeemer (3:9). As to what startled Boaz awake is not revealed, but it likely

Egyptian painting from the tomb of Menna showing workers winnowing grain
Manfred Näder, Gabana Studios, Germany

Threshing floor with sledge
Todd Bolen/www.BiblePlaces.com

was the subconscious realization that someone was nearby. Ruth's request is an idiom for marriage. The phrase "corner of your garment" is (*kānāp*), which applies to either a wing or the edge of a garment. The phrase is the same as applies to marriage when God later described his marriage to Israel (Ezek. 16:8).[63] The imagery brings to mind Boaz's own blessing of coming under the Lord's wing for protection (2:12). Ruth explains that the invitation is important because he is her kinsman-redeemer. Boaz appears to understand the request as no more than a marriage proposal.

All my fellow townsmen (3:11). The Hebrew phrase literally translates "all the gate of my people." It is a metonymy to the organization of ancient towns—all the people passed through the gate to work out in the fields, and at least in the case of Bethlehem, the well was near the gate (2 Sam. 23:15–16); hence, the phrase alludes to all the people. See sidebar on "Ancient City Gates" at 4:1–2.

Six measures (3:17). The measure is not identified, but it would not have been six ephahs, which would equal approximately two hundred pounds. The seah is more likely, six of which would equal sixty to ninety pounds. An alternative would be an omer, which was approximately one-tenth of an ephah, in which case the amount would be a little over half the quantity she had gleaned in her first outing (cf. 2:17).

Boaz Marries Ruth (4:1–22)

The town gate (4:1). Most Canaanite and Israelite towns were on hills and were walled in some way; hence, they required a gate for access and egress. Since the fields and usually the water supply were outside the town (the water supply was usually outside the city near the foot of the hill; cf. 1 Sam. 9:11), most people passed through the gate sometime during the day. The gate of the town, therefore, became a scene of social significance.

Kinsman-redeemer (4:1). See sidebar on "The Role of the Kinsman-Redeemer" at 2:20.

Ten of the elders (4:2). References to elders who oversee the people of antiquity appear in the Epic of Gilgamesh[64] and in Hittite law.[65] The Bible indicates that Moab and Midian had elders (Num. 22:4, 7), as did the Gibeonites (Josh. 9:11). The term "elder" (*zāqēn*) derives from a word mean-

Egyptian painting from the tomb of Menna with grain heaped up on the threshing floor
The Yorck Project/Wikimedia Commons

ing "beard" and alludes to one who is of advanced age.[66] Over time, however, the term came to apply as well to administrators of the affairs of the community. They are assumed to be people who have experienced sufficient vicissitudes of life to be able to tap into those experiences to guide the community (cf. 1 Kings 12:6–11; Job 12:20; Jer. 26:17–19). Elders also sometimes represented the people before God (Lev. 4:13–15) and oversaw murder trials and questions of asylum (Deut. 19:11–12; 21:1–9; Josh. 20:1–6) and disputes regarding virginity (Deut. 22:15–19). They also served as social witnesses to issues of the kinsman-redeemer and levirate marriages (Deut. 25:5–10; Ruth 4:9–11).

The Bible notes that there were elders over tribal and clan affairs (e.g., Judg. 11:5) as well as nationally (cf. Deut. 31:28). In addition, cities had their own appointments (cf. Deut. 19:11–12). How many elders a town should have is not indicated in the Bible. Gideon was informed that Succoth had seventy-seven elders and officials (Judg. 8:14). Ruth 4:2 indicates that there were more than ten for Bethlehem (i.e., "ten of the elders").

The dead man's widow (4:5). See sidebar on "Levirate Marriage" at 1:11.

Name of the dead (4:10). A similar explanation appears in the levirate marriage legislation (Deut. 25:6). "Name" (*šēm*), however, does not serve just as nomenclature; it also refers to being remembered and honored, a kind of eternal life in having offspring to connect with the deceased.[67] Its broader use has to do with inheritance and "the reality and significance of a man's deeds and life."[68] If a man had no sons, the name might be preserved through daughters, as implied in the request of Zelophehad's daughters and their petition to Moses (Num. 27:1–11); however, they were required to marry only within their own tribe (Num. 36).

Might endanger my own estate (4:6). This closer relative fails to elaborate how serving as the *gōʾēl* with Ruth as part of the deal would endanger his estate. Since the purpose of the levirate marriage concern was to perpetuate the name of the deceased, the inheritance would be through another's line rather than the redeemer himself. An investment to redeem the land for Naomi, who was apparently past child-bearing (cf. 1:11–13), would likely keep the property in his own line, but the prospect of marrying Ruth, who came with the property and the implied responsibilities, would indicate that not only would the investment to redeem the property be forfeited to any offspring that might be born, but there would be the added burden of supporting Ruth and Naomi, as well as any additional offspring that might come from the union.

Removed his sandal (4:7–8). The introductory phrase of verse 7 indicates that some time has passed from the events of the narrative and its retelling, although the term "earlier times" (*lᵉpānîm*) can refer to a single generation's separation (cf. Job 42:11). The text implies that the kinsman-redeemer relinquished his sandal to Boaz. The image derives from property rights and the right of the person who owns a piece of land to be the one who walks on it. God had revealed to Abraham that wherever he might walk in Canaan, the land would belong to him (Gen. 13:17). This foot placement motif is reflected in the Nuzi materials in which "to make a transfer of real estate more valid, a man would 'lift up his foot from his property,' and 'placed the foot of the other man on it.'"[69]

With similar imagery, God declares possession of Edom with the metaphor of casting his sandal over the land (Ps. 60:8; 108:9).[70] The difference between the widow's snatching the sandal off the foot of the reluctant brother-in-law (Deut. 25:9) and the demeanor exhibited in Ruth is likely that the legal focus of the transaction is property redemption and not levirate marriage. Furthermore, Ruth has someone who has agreed to be the redeemer; therefore there is no need to humiliate the next of kin.

Ancient Egyptian sandal
Kim Walton, courtesy of the Oriental Institute Museum

Ancient City Gates

The Bible notes a number of activities associated with the gate. Among them are occasions of pomp and ceremony (1 Kings 22:10), speeches (Neh. 8:1–2; Jer. 17:19–20; 36:10), economic transactions as people were able to increase the visibility of their wares (Gen. 23:10, 18; 2 Kings 7:1), and judicial proceedings (Deut. 21:19; Josh. 20:4; 2 Sam. 15:2; Prov. 22:22; Amos 5:10), which might include executions (Deut. 17:5; 22:24) and legal/social negotiations (Deut. 25:7). They were also the scenes of worship activities (2 Kings 23:8).

The Israelite town of Dan has preserved several shrine areas in the gate.[A-21] Ugaritic literature similarly notes judicial activity in association with the gate.[A-22] Hittite literature mentions the "king's gate," which, given the context, probably refers to the judicial body of elders who are mentioned in the same paragraph.[A-23] The gate of the Iron Age in which Ruth lived was likely different than the gates of other periods. The Middle Bronze Age gates (ca. 2000–1650 B.C.) were massive structures with passages through them in which there were piers creating rooms where people might gather for meetings. The Late Bronze Age (ca. 1650–1200 B.C.) did not commonly see creation of new fortifications, but typically reused the fortifications from the Middle Bronze Age.[A-24]

During the period of the judges, the Israelites reused fortifications from earlier periods. The numerous new establishments in the central hill country[A-25] were towns that typically consisted of a ring of houses adjoining each other with their shared side walls. The back wall extended from house to house with no windows, by default creating a sort of defensive wall. Examples of these can be seen at Khirbet Radanna, Tel Masos, and ʿIzbet Ṣarṭah.[A-26] Since excavations at Bethlehem have not uncovered the walls or gates, it is not possible to know exactly how the events transpired; however, since even these Iron Age I ad hoc defensive walls required an opening for access, it was the convenient location to flag down the next of kin for negotiations. If Bethlehem reused a Middle Bronze Age gate, the meeting may have been inside one of the rooms of the gate complex.

Gate chamber at Arad showing bench where people would sit to conduct business
Kim Walton

Affectionate couple
Caryn Reeder, courtesy of the British Museum

May the LORD make ... like that of Perez (4:11–12). Boaz's declaration elicits recognition from the witnesses (i.e., the elders), who pronounce a tripartite blessing on the pair. The first blessing seeks fruitfulness: May the Lord make the bride fruitful, as Rachel and Leah were, from whom the tribes of Israel came. The second blessing seeks recognition and respect in their community, Bethlehem (Ephrathah parallels Bethlehem; cf. Gen. 35:16; see comment on Ruth 1:2). The third blessing repeats the second seeking recognition and respect—it appeals to Perez, who was the Judahite son through whom the Bethlehemites had come and through whom they perceived their own greatness (and through whose line King David would come; cf. Ruth 4:18–22).

This tripartite type of blessing mirrors a similarly structured blessing in Ugaritic literature, when Kirta marries Hurraya and El pronounces a blessing first of fertility on Hurraya and then twice for greatness for Kirta.[71]

Your home like Rachel and Leah ... have standing in Ephrathah (4:11). The appeal is to Rachel and Leah, who were the wives of Jacob/Israel, their progenitor (Gen. 29–30). Four of the tribes claimed their heritage specifically through the handmaids, Zilpah and Bilhah (Gen. 30:1–13), but these women would not be mentioned since the children born to them were considered the offspring of the respective wives, similar to Hagar's relationship to Sarah (Gen. 16). Some ancient cultures (e.g., Alalakh and Nuzi) permitted the arrangement of a surrogate mother through whom an heir could be produced.[72]

The desire for a large family was not simply the prestige implied in the numbers, but the practical element of survival. The available archaeological evidence reflects an approximately 35 percent mortality rate by age five; thus, the production of numerous children tended somewhat to compensate for the deaths. Added wealth could be realized by the fact that from an early age, almost all people had roles in the family economy.[73] The blessing also imports Perez, the son of Judah and Tamar, from whom the tribe of Judah was descended (Gen. 38). Perez had been born out of trying circumstances demanding the less-than-ideal levirate relationship; hence the people seem to perceive a similarity between Boaz and Ruth with Judah and Tamar.

Better to you than seven sons (4:15). The imagery of seven emphasizes the greatness of Ruth's contribution to Naomi's survival and especially as compared to sons. Patrilineal and patrilocal societies place more emphasis on having sons because the women are married off into other families, removing their economic contribution from the father's family. With patrilineal descent, property tends generally to remain in the male line.[74] The compliment of Ruth is therefore especially significant. She has brought Naomi's life to completion in providing the male heir who would keep the property in the family; they also recognize her underlying devotion to Naomi, which was demonstrated in forsaking her homeland to come to the foreign land of Judah to adopt a new family and a new God.

BIBLIOGRAPHY

Block, Daniel I. *Judges, Ruth*. NAC. Nashville: Broadman & Holman, 1999. A thorough discussion from an evangelical perspective, responding responsibly to a wide range of alternative interpretations.

Bush, Frederic. *Ruth/Esther*. WBC. Dallas: Word, 1996. Excellent commentary from an evangelical perspective, providing background, textual, and grammatical analysis along with some explanation of structure. Its discussion lends itself well to exegetical application.

Campbell, Edward F., Jr. *Ruth*. AB. Garden City, N.Y.: Doubleday, 1975. From a typically liberal perspective, but very good commentary dealing heavily with the grammatical and background discussion.

Cundall, Arthur E., and Leon Morris. *Judges & Ruth*. TOTC. Downers Grove, Ill.: InterVarsity Press, 1968. Ruth is written by Morris, who does an outstanding job compressing a wealth of information in a small and inexpensive volume.

Hubbard, Robert L., Jr. *The Book of Ruth*. NICOT. Grand Rapids: Eerdmans, 1988. A responsibly done commentary with good historical, literary, and linguistic discussion, with more theological discussion and application than most.

Sasson, Jack M. *Ruth: A New Translation with a Philological Commentary and a Formalist-Folklorist Interpretation*. 2nd ed. Sheffield: Sheffield Academic Press, 1995. Sasson brings a broad literary and cultural background to his remarks, dealing with the text more from literary perspectives than theological ones. It is probably somewhat difficult for the non-Hebrew reader since much of it is based directly on the Hebrew text.

Younger, K. Lawson, Jr. *Judges and Ruth*. NIVAC. Grand Rapids: Zondervan, 2002. An excellent commentary explaining the structure and background of Ruth. It is particularly helpful in bridging the transition from its original setting to modern application.

Main Text Notes

1. A good overall discussion of the period from a geographical and political perspective appears in R. Drews, *The End of the Bronze Age: Changes in Warfare and the Catastrophe ca. 1200* B.C. (Princeton: Princeton Univ. Press, 1993).
2. For a discussion of the weather patterns and particularly rainfall effects, see E. Orni and E. Efrat, *Geography of Israel*, 3rd ed. (Philadelphia: Jewish Publication Society of America, 1973), 146–49.
3. J. Sasson, *Ruth: A New Translation with a Philological Commentary and a Formalist-Folklorist Interpretation*, 2nd ed. (Sheffield: Sheffield Academic Press, 1995), 15.
4. S. Gutman and A. Berman, "Bethléem," *RB* 77 (1970): 583–85.
5. See D. Kellerman, "גּוּר *gûr*," *TDOT*, 2:439–49.
6. See Orni and Efrat, *Geography*, 110–11; J. Rogerson, *Atlas of the Bible* (New York: Facts on File, 1985), 204; Y. Aharoni, *The Land of the Bible: A Historical Geography*, rev. and enlarged, trans. and ed. A. F. Rainey (Philadelphia: Westminster, 1979), 36–37; E. F. Campbell Jr., *Ruth* (AB; Garden City, N.Y.: Doubleday, 1975), 51.
7. K. A. Kitchen, "The Egyptian Evidence on Ancient Jordan," in *Early Edom and Moab: The Beginning of the Iron Age in Southern Jordan*, ed. P. Bienkowski (Sheffield Archaeological Monographs 7; Sheffield: J. R. Collis Publications, 1992), 21–34.
8. F. Bush, *Ruth, Esther* (WBC; Dallas: Word, 1996), 61–62.
9. A. J. Dearman, "Historical Reconstruction and the Mesha Inscription," in *Studies in the Mesha Inscription and Moab*, ed. A. J. Dearman (Atlanta: Scholars Press, 1989), 155–210.
10. L. G. Herr and D. R. Clark, "Excavating the Tribe of Reuben," *BAR* 27/2 (2001): 36–47, 64–66.
11. D. A. Dorsey, *The Roads and Highways of Ancient Israel* (Baltimore: Johns Hopkins Univ. Press, 1991), 12–13.
12. Aharoni, *Land of the Bible*, 60.
13. A. Kloner and C. Ben-David, "*Mesillot* on the Arnon: An Iron Age (Pre-Roman) Road in Moab," *BASOR* 330 (2003): 65–81.
14. See Dorsey, *Roads and Highways*, 17–24.
15. Good discussions of the names and etymologies may be found in Bush, *Ruth/Esther*, 64–65; Sasson, *Ruth*, 17–19; and Campbell, *Ruth*, 53.
16. A. E. Cundall and L. Morris, *Judges and Ruth* (TOTC; Downers Grove, Ill.: InterVarsity Press, 1968), 249.
17. A good, brief discussion of the term for "people" is in R. H. O'Connell, "עַם *ʿam*," *NIDOTTE*, 3:429–32.
18. D. D. Luckenbill, ed., *Ancient Records of Assyria and Babylonia*, vol. 1: *Historical Records of Assyria* (reprint; London: Histories and Mysteries of Man Ltd., 1989), 138–41.
19. G. del Olmo Lete, *Canaanite Religion according to the Liturgical Texts of Ugarit*, trans. W. G. E. Watson (Bethesda, Md.: CDL, 1999), 44–45.
20. *COS*, 2:23.
21. See G. Pettinato, *The Archives of Ebla: An Empire Inscribed in Clay* (Garden City, N.Y.: Doubleday, 1981), 291–92; G. Mattingly, "Chemosh," *ABD*, 1:895–97.
22. K. D. Sakenfeld, *Ruth* (Interpretation; Louisville: John Knox, 1999), 33.
23. L. E. Stager, "The Archaeology of the Family in Early Israel," *BASOR* 260 (1985): 1–35; W. G. Dever, "Israel, History of (Archaeology and the 'Conquest')," *ABD*, 3:545–58.
24. A good discussion of the agricultural calendar and cycles may be found in O. Borowski, *Agriculture in Iron Age Israel* (Winona Lake, Ind.: Eisenbrauns, 1987), 31–44.
25. For a brief orientation of the clan, see R. de Vaux, *Ancient Israel*, vol. 1: *Social Institutions* (New York: McGraw-Hill, 1965), 21, 28, 216.
26. H. Eising, "חַיִל *ḥayil*," *TDOT*, 4:350–55.
27. *COS*, 1:47 (ch. 28).
28. *COS*, 2:130 (§11).
29. *COS*, 2:131 (§273).
30. The weight of a shekel consisted of 180 barleycorn (Akk: *še*), hence the salary was roughly 1/30 of a shekel. A shekel on average was about 10 grams or about 1/3 of an ounce.
31. *COS*, 3:41.
32. Borowski, *Agriculture*, 61.
33. S. Bunimovitz and Z. Lederman, "Tel Beth Shemesh, 2001–2003," *IEJ* 53 (2003): 233–37.
34. *COS*, 2:19 (§§168–169). Cf. also Sumerian references in *COS*, 1:162 (line 139, n.28).
35. The NIV renders the Samuel passages "Good health" and "All is well" respectively.
36. See conveniently the inscription and translation in Z. Meshel, "Teman, Horvat," *NEAEHL*, 4:1462. Scholars debate exactly what is meant by "Asherah" in this inscription (see John Day, "Asherah," *ABD*, 1:483–87).
37. H. F. Fuhs, "נַעַר *naʿar*," *TDOT*, 9:474–85. For further discussion, see N. Avigad, "New Light on the *Naʿar* Seals," in *Magnalia Dei: The Mighty Acts of God: Essays on the Bible and Archaeology in Memory of G. Ernest Wright*, ed. F. M. Cross, W. E. Lemke, and P. D. Miller Jr. (Garden City, N.Y.: Doubleday, 1976), 294–300.
38. Conveniently see N. Avigad, *Corpus of West Semitic Stamp Seals*, rev. B. Sass (Jerusalem: Israel Academy of Sciences and Humanities, The Israel Exploration Society, 1997), 243–44. He also lists unprovenanced seals in which the same term appears (25–26).
39. Ibid., 324.
40. An excellent discussion of the role of women in Israelite society can be found in Carol Meyers, *Discovering Eve: Ancient Israelite Women in Context* (New York: Oxford Univ. Press, 1988), esp. 139–64.

41. COS, 1.102 (p. 335, ll.103–23; cf. p. 336, ll.154 to end): "The women drawing water will flee from the spring, from the fountain the women filling (jugs)."
42. See *ANEP*, figs. 351, 355.
43. *TWOT*, 1:268.
44. See *ANEP*, fig. 829.
45. See *ANEP*, fig. 377.
46. See *ANEP*, fig. 544.
47. For discussion of the wing imagery, see O. Keel, *The Symbolism of the Biblical World: Ancient Near Eastern Iconography and the Book of Psalms*, trans. T. J. Hallett (Winona Lake, Ind.: Eisenbrauns, 1997), 190–92.
48. For more discussion of the meals of ancient Israel, see P. J. King and L. E. Stager, *Life in Biblical Israel* (Louisville: Westminster John Knox, 2001), 64–68.
49. R. L. Hubbard Jr., *The Book of Ruth* (NICOT; Grand Rapids: Eerdmans, 1988), 173.
50. Y. Aharoni, *Arad Inscriptions*, trans. J. Ben-Or (Jerusalem: Israel Exploration Society, 1981), 15–16, inscription #2.
51. D. Kellerman, "חמץ *ḥmṣ*," *TDOT*, 4:487–93.
52. Ibid., 490–92.
53. Quoted in C. F. Keil and F. Delitzsch, *Commentary on the Old Testament in Ten Volumes*, vol. 2: *Joshua, Judges, Ruth, I & II Samuel*, trans. J. Martin (Grand Rapids: Eerdmans, n.d.), 479, n.1.
54. Borowski, *Agriculture*, 88.
55. See conveniently T. J. Lewis, "Ancestor Worship," *ABD*, 1:240–42; C. A. Kennedy, "Dead, Cult of the," *ABD*, 2:105–8.
56. Borowski (*Agriculture*, 65–69) describes several steps to the process, including the initial winnowing, which was followed by the more refined grain cleaning procedures.
57. Cf. in Egypt, *ANEP*, fig. 91.
58. The oxen carrying the ark of the covenant at the threshing floor of Nacon (2 Sam. 6:6) probably had slipped on this slick surface to cause the ark to shake.
59. Ugaritic literature cites the placement of a threshing floor near the gate (COS, 1:103 [*CTA*, 17, v 3–33]).
60. Literally, the passage reads: "You opened wide your feet to all the passers-by."
61. BDB, 920; this seems to imply the extremity rather than the genital area. See also V. P. Hamilton, "רֶגֶל," *NIDOTTE*, 3:1048–49. However, see F. J. Stendebach, "רֶגֶל *regel*," *TDOT*, 13:309–24.
62. Bush (*Ruth/Esther*, 152–56) offers a good discussion of the terms and their nuances, indicating a more literal meaning of the phrase. See also D. I. Block, *Judges, Ruth* (NAC; Nashville: Broadman & Holman, 1999), 683–88.
63. The same Heb. word appears in Deut. 23:1 [22:30] and 27:20 to refer to the husband's relationship to his wife.
64. COS, 1:132.
65. COS, 2:19 (§71).
66. See discussion in K. T. Aitken, "זָקֵן," *NIDOTTE*, 1:1137–39.
67. A. P. Ross, "שֵׁם," *NIDOTTE*, 4:147–51.
68. T. Thompson and D. Thompson, "Some Legal Problems in the Book of Ruth," *VT* 18 (1968): 86.
69. E. R. Lacheman, "Note on Ruth 4:7–8," *JBL* 56 (1937): 53–56.
70. See further E. A. Speiser, "Of Shoes and Shekels," *BASOR* 77 (1940): 15–20.
71. See S. B. Parker, "The Marriage Blessing in Israelite and Ugaritic Literature," *JBL* 95 (1976): 23–30; for Ugaritic translation, see COS, 1:102 (*CTA*, 15, ii 12–iii 19).
72. See introduction to letter in COS, 3:101B.
73. Meyers, *Discovering Eve*, 112–13; King and Stager, *Life in Biblical Israel*, 15. Cf. also M. Harris and E. B. Ross, *Death, Sex, and Fertility: Population Regulation in Preindustrial and Developing Societies* (New York: Columbia Univ. Press, 1987), 10–13, 39–40, 172.
74. The concern about Zelophehad's daughters losing the family inheritance because of no males addresses this issue (cf. Num. 27:1–11). The legislation indicates that male inheritance rights have priority.

Sidebar and Chart Notes

A-1. COS, 3:100.
A-2. Karel van der Toorn, "Female Prostitution in Payment of Vows in Ancient Israel," *JBL* 108 (1989): 193–205.
A-3. The authenticity of the ostracon is debated; for discussion and translation, see COS, 3:44.
A-4. COS, 2:131 (§§117–18, 171–74).
A-5. COS, 1:35 (spec. 62); COS, 1:36.
A-6. COS, 1:103 (*CTA*, 17, v 3–33). See also further discussion in F. C. Fensham, "Widow, Orphan, and the Poor in Ancient Near Eastern Legal and Wisdom Literature," *JNES* 21 (1962): 129–39.
A-7. For a discussion of the ages of marriage in various ancient cultures see V. Hamilton, "Marriage (OT and ANE)," *ABD*, 4:559–69.
A-8. COS, 2:132 (§§30, 33, 43).
A-9. COS, 2:19 (§193).
A-10. M. Burrows, "The Ancient Oriental Background of Hebrew Levirate Marriage," *BASOR* 77 (1940): 2–15.
A-11. For a survey of the law and its application, see D. W. Manor, "A Brief History of Levirate Marriage as It Relates to the Bible," *RQ* 27 (1984): 129–42.
A-12. R. Westbrook, *Property and the Family in Biblical Law* (JSOTSup 113; Sheffield: Sheffield Academic Press, 1991), 69–89.
A-13. H. J. Marsman, *Women in Ugarit and Israel: Their Social and Religious Position in the Context of the Ancient Near East* (Leiden: Brill, 2003), 299–317.
A-14. For further discussion, see E. M. Meyers, "Secondary Burials in Palestine," *BA* 33/1 (1970): 2–29.
A-15. For a catalogue of graves and grave goods from the Iron Age in Judah, see conveniently E. Bloch-Smith, *Judahite Burial Practices and*

Beliefs about the Dead (JSOTSup 123; Sheffield: Sheffield Academic Press, 1992), 152–245.

A-16. For a background discussion of these beliefs, see T. Abusch, "Ghost and God: Some Observations on a Babylonian Understanding of Human Nature," in *Self, Soul and Body in Religious Experience*, ed. A. I. Baumgarten, J. Assmann, and G. G. Stroumsa (Leiden: Brill, 1998), 363–83. Their application in the Old Testament world is discussed in T. J. Lewis, "Dead," in *Dictionary of Deities and Demons in the Bible*, ed. K. van der Toorn, B. Becking, and P. W. van der Horst (Leiden: Brill, 1995), 421–38.

A-17. *ANET*, 320. Additionally, see Borowski, *Agriculture*, 31–44.

A-18. H. Ringgren, "גָּאַל *gāʾal*," *TDOT*, 2:350–55. For further discussion, see M. S. Moore, "*Haggoʾel*: The Cultural Gyroscope of Ancient Hebrew Society," *RQ* 23/1 (1980): 27–35, and R. L. Hubbard, "The *gōʾēl* in Ancient Israel: The Theology of an Israelite Institution," *BBR* 1 (1991): 3–19.

A-19. *COS*, 2:130 (§39).

A-20. *COS*, 2:131 (§117).

A-21. See A. Biran, *Biblical Dan* (Jerusalem: Israel Exploration Society, 1994), 235–54.

A-22. Danʾel judges the case of a widow in the gate with the elders of his town; *COS*, 1:103 (*CTA*, 17, v 3–33).

A-23. *COS*, 2:19 (§71).

A-24. Z. Herzog, "Fortifications (Levant)," *ABD*, 2:844–52.

A-25. A brief discussion of the settlement explosion for the period can be found in W. G. Dever, *Who Were the Early Israelites and Where Did They Come From?* (Grand Rapids: Eerdmans, 2003), 96–100.

A-26. See conveniently discussion and drawings of plans in ibid., 75–88.

1 SAMUEL

by V. Philips Long

Captive Sea Peoples in Egyptian relief at Medinet Habu

Z. Radovan/www.BibleLand Pictures.com

Introduction[1]

Few Old Testament books have attracted more attention than 1 and 2 Samuel, and for good reason! The stories of Hannah, Eli, Samuel, Saul, David, Absalom, and many others are riveting, often praised as among the finest narratives to be found anywhere in world literature.[2] In addition, the events that these books trace—namely, those involved in Israel's transition from tribal league to monarchy—are among the most momentous in the history of ancient Israel. Given the societal and theological ramifications of these changes—and especially in the light of the prominent place that the famous king David occupies in them—it is hard to overstate the significance of the books of Samuel.

But 1 and 2 Samuel were written long ago and in a culture different in many respects from the world in which we live. In order to understand them, therefore, and to discern their historical and theological import, we must discover what we can of the cultural context in which these books took shape. Our focus in what follows will be on how knowledge of the ancient Near Eastern cultures and literatures of Israel's near and far neighbors can elucidate our understanding of the text and how the growing body of archaeological knowledge can help us understand the places and "life-ways" that figure in the biblical narratives. Before launching into our specific explorations of the texts, a few general comments about the historical and literary settings of these two books are in order.

Historical Setting

The events described in 1 and 2 Samuel took place in the eleventh and early tenth centuries B.C. This time period (which archaeologists call Iron Age I, ca. 1200–1000 B.C.) was one in which the superpowers of the preceding Bronze Ages had little impact in Syria-Palestine. The Anatolian kingdom of the Hittites had been essentially destroyed by "the 'Sea Peoples' and other land-based movements."[3] The Egyptians exercised limited control along the coast of Canaan until the mid-twelfth century and then withdrew.[4] The Assyrians were occupied with troubles closer to home, especially their rivalry with Babylonia to their south. The Assyrian king Tiglath-pileser I did push as far westward as the northern Mediterranean coast near the end of the twelfth century, defeating some Aramean territories along the way, but he did not move southward into Palestine itself.

Babylonia, too, was incapable at this time of giving much attention to Syria-Palestine, finding plenty to keep it busy protecting its interests against neighboring Assyria and Elam.[5] Thus, as 1 Samuel opens, the land in which the Israelites are set was experiencing an eclipse of the Great Powers. Conditions were ripe for the emergence of smaller territorial powers—mini-empires, as Kitchen calls them[6]—such as the kingdom ascribed to David in the text of Samuel (see sidebar on "The 'Empire' of David" at 2 Sam. 8).

The transition to monarchy was a new departure in the political and religious life of tribal Israel. But it was not a surprising or unanticipated development. The concept of kingship was well known in the ancient Near East from at least early in the third millennium and was widely practiced not only by the major powers in Egypt, Anatolia, and Mesopotamia, but also by Israel's immediate neighbors, whose kings are regularly mentioned (e.g., Judg. 3:8, 12; 4:2; 8:5).[7] The Israelite tribes themselves had experienced at least one abortive attempt to introduce monarchy (i.e., Abimelech in Judg. 9).

Fertile Crescent

King (here Sargon) with all the symbols of power
Marie-Lan Nguyen/ Wikimedia Commons, courtesy of the Louvre

The opening books of the Bible, moreover, clearly hint of a coming time in which Israel will have a human king (e.g., Gen. 49:10; Num. 24:7, 17–19). In Deuteronomy, Moses even prescribes how the eventual Israelite kings are to be chosen and how they are to behave (Deut. 17:14–20). More surprising, then, than Israel's eventual installation of a king is its reluctance for so long to do so. The words of the judge-deliverer Gideon, when offered an opportunity to establish dynastic rule, are suggestive of what may have underlain Israel's hesitancy: "I will not rule over you, nor will my son rule over you. The LORD will rule over you" (Judg. 8:23).

How human kingship could exist within an authority structure that allowed Yahweh to remain the "Great King" is one of the key questions addressed by the books of Samuel. Understanding ancient Near Eastern patterns of royal accession and vassal kingship, the interplay of religion and politics, the interaction of prophets with kings, and so forth will aid us in grasping the social and religious dynamics reflected in these two books.

Literary Setting

In order to read any text with understanding, one must have some sense of the genre or genres represented in the text. Otherwise, misunderstandings and misinterpretations will result. Determining precisely what genre(s) one is reading is not always an easy task, especially when one is reading texts from a distant time and place. A good way to begin is to become familiar with the various literary genres available at the time and in the place that the text was written. Here again knowledge of the ancient Near Eastern background of the Old Testament can help us.

In seeking to discover what 1 and 2 Samuel should be "read as," we must bear in mind the broader ancient Near Eastern literary culture in which the texts were first written. Difficulty in putting a date on texts that refuse to date themselves is self-evident, and 1 and 2 Samuel have been assigned dates across a wide spectrum—from early, close to the tenth-century events they describe, to late, in the exilic period. It is not our purpose to resolve the questions of time or place of writing, nor is it likely that these questions can be resolved. A possible scenario sees them as containing early sources edited to one degree or another in order to incorporate them into a larger corpus, such as the conventionally designated Deuteronomistic History (Deuteronomy to 2 Kings) or the Primary History (Genesis to 2 Kings). For current purposes, the best we can do is to view 1 and 2 Samuel against the broad background of ancient Near Eastern literatures.

Underneath the broad genre categories of story (narrative) and poem, these books seem to incorporate a number of more specific literary forms or subgenres, such as birth narratives, call narratives, dream theophanies, prophetic judgement speeches, battle reports, accession accounts, court intrigues, and regnal formulae/summaries. Many of these subgenres are attested not only in the Bible but also in the ancient Near East more generally. Where consideration of these subgenres illuminates the biblical text, I will note them in the entries below.

Taking a slightly wider view, scholars in search of the building blocks of 1 and 2 Samuel have variously isolated larger, hypothetical entities, such as an Ark Narrative, a Samuel Cycle, a Saul Cycle, a History of David's Rise, a Court History (or Succession Narrative), and so forth. Some scholars contend that these entities enjoyed an independent existence before being incorporated into the larger narrative as we have it. Difficulty in actually delimiting these hypothetical entities, however, and their current high degree of integration into the larger text in which they now stand suggest that our time is better spent exploring the text we have rather than texts that are assumed to have once existed.

While familiarity with extrabiblical ancient Near Eastern literature can enlighten our reading of the books of Samuel in many ways, taken as a whole these books are *sui generis*. They are without parallel, at least in terms of literary and theological breadth and depth. Should we be forced to offer one genre description, apart from such general descriptions as "narrative" or "Scripture," then "royal apology" is a candidate worth considering.

David is without doubt the central human character in 1 and 2 Samuel. Although the biblical writers show no reticence in exposing his serious failings, David is defended from start to finish as rightly occupying the throne of Israel. Royal apologies are well known from the ancient Near East,[8] and though no example of the genre comes close to the books of Samuel in terms of length, depth, complexity, or tone, there are some shared traits. Ancient Near Eastern royal apologies offer a defense of the right of a certain individual to occupy the throne. This individual is typically not the hereditary heir and often comes to the throne by a path that some, then as now, regard as suspicious. That charge of usurpation is often a catalyst for writing a royal apology. Some ancient Near Eastern royal apologies are, to be sure, little more than deceptive political propaganda. But the mere fact that circumstances may be such that an individual, such as David, requires defense in no way proves that the individual is unworthy of defense.[9]

Samuel's Birth and Dedication (1:1–28)

There was a certain man from Ramathaim, a Zuphite from the hill country of Ephraim (1:1). The manner of Elkanah's introduction, including his rather full genealogy, suggests he was an important individual.[10] That Elkanah is called a Zuphite may reflect his descent from Zuph (1 Chron. 6:35; cf. 6:26), or it may reflect the district in Ephraim from which Elkanah's people came (see 1 Sam. 9:5)—or possibly both.[11] According to the genealogies of 1 Chronicles 6:16–30, 33–37, Elkanah was a Levite, not an Ephraimite. But as we learn from Joshua

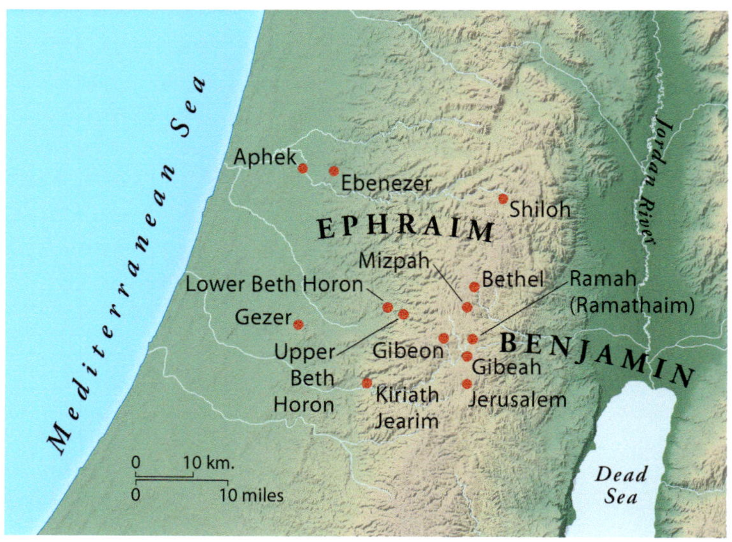

Ephraim and Benjamin

Ramah
Todd Bolen/www.
BiblePlaces.com

Family group statue, thirteenth century
Manfred Näder, Gabana Studios, Germany

21:1–26, the Levites received no tribal territory of their own but were allotted "Levitical cities" within each of the other tribal territories. Thus Elkanah's Levitical forebears may well have lived in the district of Zuph in Ephraim.

More puzzling in Elkanah's introduction is the name Ramathaim ("twin heights"). This name occurs nowhere else in the Old Testament, whereas the hometown of Elkanah (and later his son Samuel) is elsewhere consistently called Ramah (probably the Ramah alloted to the tribe of Benjamin in Josh. 18:25). To Ramah Elkanah returns in 1:19 and 2:11.[12] This suggests that Ramathaim and Ramah refer to the same place and should probably be associated with modern er-Ram, some five miles north of Jerusalem.[13]

He had two wives (1:2). The biblical creation account envisages monogamy as God's design for marriage, in which one man and one woman forsake all others to become "one flesh" (Gen. 2:24). Nevertheless, polygamy, or more accurately polygyny (having more than one wife), is attested already as early as Genesis 4:19, in the story of Lamech. Polygyny was less prevalent among commoners than among the well-to-do; in fact, Elkanah is the only commoner described in the books of Samuel or Kings as having more than one wife.[14] This social situation is implicit in Nathan's parable—told in the aftermath of David's adultery with Bathsheba and murder of Uriah—in which the poor man has but one lamb (signifying one wife), while the rich man has many (2 Sam. 12:1–3).

Polyandry (a woman having more than one husband at

Gold leaf fertility figurines used to enable child-bearing
Z. Radovan/www.BibleLandPictures.com

the same time) is not attested in the Bible. From the biblical and extrabiblical examples we have, it appears that taking more than one wife was prompted less by romantic desire than by concerns about having offspring to continue the family line and having a large enough family (wives and children) to do the work involved in seminomadic and agricultural living.[15] Having multiple wives or concubines (and thus many children) was also sometimes intertwined with status issues. For a woman to remain childless, therefore, was a cause of grief and shame (see the next comment).

Polygamy is recognized in the Old Testament as a common practice and is regulated (Deut. 25:15–17), but it is not endorsed or encouraged. Similarly, ancient Near Eastern law codes do not necessarily promote polygamy; rather, the detailed regulations are intended to lessen its abuses.[16] Compared to the systematic treatment of marriage in some extrabiblical texts, the Old Testament's treatment is more occasional and ad hoc. For this reason, one should not seek to infer God's standards of marital conduct from the (mis)adventures of biblical characters any more than one should infer traffic laws from the behaviors of individual drivers.[17]

Peninah had children, but Hannah had none (1:2). Hannah finds herself not only in the difficult position of having a rival wife, but in the pitiable position of having no children. Given the order in which she and Peninnah are named, Hannah is probably Elkanah's first wife, and it may have been her barrenness that prompted Elkanah to take a second wife. In the ancient Near East generally, as indeed in many agrarian societies today, fertility was a major concern for women[18] and even for men,[19] the more so as fertility was regarded as under the control of God (see 1:5) or the gods, and lack of fertility could be understood as a curse. A curse is not necessarily implied, however, in the Bible. It refers to numerous women whose initial barrenness becomes the backdrop for God's demonstration of his grace and power.

Year after year this man went up from his town to worship and sacrifice (1:3). Religious life in the ancient Near East was marked by feasts or festivals. For example, a year in the life of the Egyptian city of Thebes might include as many as fifty or sixty religious festivals.[20] The number of festivals mentioned in the Bible is modest. The Pentateuch refers to three annual pilgrim festivals: the Feast of Unleavened Bread, the Feast of Weeks, and the Feast of Tabernacles (Deut. 16:16; cf. Ex. 23:14–17; 34:18–23; Deut. 16:1–15). An "annual festival of the LORD in Shiloh" (Judg. 21:19) may be the festival to which Elkanah and his family go here, or they may have gone to Shiloh simply to observe a family ceremony (the existence of family ceremonies is suggested by David's excuse in 1 Sam. 20:6).

LORD Almighty (1:3). This divine appellation occurs here for the first time in the Old Testament. Generally in the Hebrew Bible, the word "LORD" (i.e., *yhwh*, perhaps pronounced Yahweh) represents the God of Israel in his personal, covenantal character (and is thus more specific and intimate than the general designation "God"). The second word (*ṣ*^{e}*bāʾôt*) is the subject of ongoing debate, but has traditionally been understood as a military term meaning "hosts" or "armies." This term seems to encompass, depending on the context, the hosts of Israel (cf. 17:45), the cosmic hosts (i.e., the celestial bodies; Deut. 4:19), or the angelic hosts (Josh. 5:14). The title is then expressive of Yahweh's sovereignty over all earthly and heavenly powers.[21] Alternatively, or perhaps additionally, *ṣ*^{e}*bāʾôt* may be taken as an abstract noun, yielding "LORD of Might" or "LORD, the Almighty."[22] In any case, a reminder of the Lord's might, military and otherwise, is not inappropriate at the beginning of 1 Samuel.

Shiloh (1:3). Shiloh is to be identified with modern Khirbet Seilun, which lies midway between Shechem to the north and Bethel or Jerusalem to the south. First mentioned in Joshua 18:1, Shiloh was the place where Joshua designated the tribal allotments after the initial conquest (19:51) and the place where the "cities of refuge" and the "Levitical cities" were named (chs. 20–21). Shiloh became the site of an annual festival during the time of the Judges (Judg. 21:19), and by the end of that period it was the home of the priestly family of Eli and of the ark of the covenant (1 Sam. 4:3; 14:3). Psalm 78:60 and especially Jeremiah 7:12 suggest that Shiloh may have served as Israel's first "central sanctuary," and Jeremiah 7:14 and 26:6, 9 imply the city was destroyed or at least abandoned after Israel's defeat by the Philistines in 1 Samuel 4.

With this scenario the archaeological evidence converges nicely. The most recent excavations (between 1981 and 1984) have led to the tentative conclusion that Shiloh may have been "primarily a sacred *temenos* [sacred enclosure] rather than an ordinary village." The eventual destruction of the city in a "fierce conflagration" was probably, according to the site's excavator, "the work of the Philistines in the aftermath of the battle of Ebenezer in the mid-11th century B.C.E." (i.e., the battle described in 1 Sam. 4).[23]

Hophni and Phinehas, the two sons of Eli, were priests of the LORD (1:3). That Eli is simply mentioned without further introduction suggests that he must have been well known to the original audience(s) of this story. He appears to have been both judge (cf. 4:18) and high priest as the period of the judges was drawing to a close—though he is never explicitly called high priest. Combining the evidence of several biblical passages (1 Sam. 22:9, 11, 20; 14:3; 1 Chron. 24:3), we may conclude that Eli descended from Aaron's fourth son, Ithamar, rather than from his third son, Eleazar, whose line occupied the high priestly office at the beginning of the period of the judges (see, e.g., Josh. 22:31–32; Judg. 20:28).

How the transfer of responsibility from the house of Eleazar to the house of Ithamar took place remains obscure. In any case, the sons of Eli, with their Egyptian names, Hophni ("Tadpole") and Phinehas ("The Nubian"),[24] prove as unworthy and disappointing as Aaron's sons Nadab and Abihu (Lev. 10:1–7; Num. 26:61).

Whenever the day came for Elkanah to sacrifice, he would give portions of the meat (1:4). While some sacrifices were completely consumed by fire (e.g., whole burnt offerings; see Lev. 1), others (e.g., fellowship offerings, Lev. 3; 7:11–34) stipulated portions to be eaten by those participating in the sacrifice. That similar practices existed among Israel's neighbors is clear from the Ugaritic ʾAqhatu Legend, which includes among the duties of a son the following lines: "To eat his grain (-offering) in the temple of Baʿlu, his portion in the temple of ʾIlu."[25]

But to Hannah he gave a double portion (1:5). Deuteronomy 21:19 speaks of a "double share" being given to the firstborn son, even if he is the son of an unloved wife. Many commentators assume a similar meaning here of a "double portion" given to the beloved but barren wife. The Hebrew expression here is, however, different from the one in Deuteronomy 21:19, and its sense is much debated. Some argue that Hannah must have received a particularly special or

Shiloh

honorable portion.[26] The LXX reads simply, "to Hannah he would give a single portion, still it was Hannah he loved," and this rendering is probably closest to the original sense.

In any case, Elkanah's attempts to lessen Hannah's sorrow by expressions of his own love (see v. 8) are ineffectual, inasmuch as his love alone cannot compensate for other factors, such as the social stigma associated with barrenness, the need for offspring to assure the social security of aging parents, and so on.[27]

Eli the priest was sitting on a chair by the doorpost of the LORD's temple (1:9). Mention of "the LORD's temple" at this stage in Israel's history may seem anachronistic, inasmuch as Solomon's temple in Jerusalem will not be built until more than seventy years later; moreover, 2 Samuel 7:6 indicates that the Lord's house prior to King David's time is a tent. This is confirmed by Psalm 78:60, which speaks unmistakably of the Lord's "tent" at Shiloh. The best approach is to understand the "temple" here (cf. also 1 Sam. 3:3) as referring to the "tabernacle" (see NIV text note).

Given the fact that the tabernacle is designated in several different ways in Samuel—e.g., "the house of the LORD" in 1:7; 3:15; "the tent of meeting" in 2:22—and the fact that other portions of Scripture exhibit a similar variety of expression (e.g., Ps. 27:4–5 uses "house of the LORD," "temple," "dwelling," and "tabernacle" as virtual synonyms), one should not make too much of the fact that the tabernacle is called the Lord's temple. The mention of "doorposts" in 1:9 and "doors" in 3:15 does seem to suggest a more permanent structure than has typically been associated with the tabernacle; indeed, there may have a been a more substantial "house" at Shiloh that held the tabernacle inside it,[28] though no archaeological evidence of such a structure has been uncovered at Shiloh.[29]

Golden portable shrine from the tomb of Tutankhamun
Scala/Art Resource, NY, courtesy of the Egyptian Museum, Cairo

The biblical tabernacle was once regarded by some scholars as a fictional retrojection from a later time period, created perhaps on the model of the temple itself. But archaeological evidence of portable shrines similar in construction to the biblical description of the tabernacle has generally silenced such speculations.[30] While portable shrines are known from various parts of the ancient Near East, particularly striking are several examples from Egypt, ranging from the time of Moses to about a thousand years earlier.[31] Though the Egyptian examples do not match the construction of the tabernacle precisely, they do demonstrate that the idea of tent shrines and the methods of constructing them—wooden framework wrapped in gold and covered with embroidered fabric or animal skins—were well known long before Israel's day.[32]

She made a vow (1:11). The making of vows was common in the Old Testament and in the ancient Near East (they are widely attested among Mesopotamians, Hittites, Phoenicians, Egyptians, etc.).[33] Often the vow was made to God (or a god) and involved an agreement by the one making the vow to do a particular thing (offer

> ## ▸ The Melqart Stele
>
> A succinct translation of this stele is as follows:
>
> The stela which Bir-Hadad the son of
> Attarhamek,
> [ ] king of Aram, set up for his lord
> Melqart,
> to whom he made a vow and who
> heard his voice.[A-1]

a sacrifice, erect a stele, etc.) on the condition that the deity fulfill a request. The Old Aramaic Melqart Stele of Bar-hadad, which dates from the last decades of the ninth century B.C., attests to this kind of vow-making among one of Israel's closest neighbors (see sidebar on "The Melqart Stele").

The Bible itself attests many instances of vow-making. It is worth noting that apart from vows described in biblical narratives (e.g., Hannah's vow here), vow-making is strikingly attested also in the "lament psalms" of the Psalter. In these laments (the most common of the Psalter's genres), the psalmist typically cries out to God in time of need, expresses confidence that God can meet the need, and vows to praise God in the assembly (or to fulfill some other vow) once God has answered. "Songs of thanksgiving" often make reference to the fulfillment of these vows (see sidebar on "A Vow in the Psalms"). Thus, Hannah is not so much bargaining with God as pouring out her soul in her distress, asking for a son, and vowing to give him over to the Lord, probably as a Nazirite (see next comment), for his entire life.

> ## ▸ A Vow in the Psalms
>
> Psalm 66:13–14 makes clear reference to a vow with the promise of fulfillment:
>
> I will come to your temple with burnt
> offerings
> and fulfill my vows to you—
> vows my lips promised and my mouth
> spoke
> when I was in trouble.

Figurines of pregnant women used to bring fertility
Z. Radovan/www.BibleLand Pictures.com

No razor will ever be used on his head (1:11). Hannah's vow that no razor will ever be used on her son's head recalls the second prohibition of the so-called "Nazirite" vow (described most fully in Num. 6:1–21). The term "Nazirite" apparently derives from the Hebrew verb *nzr,* meaning "to separate, consecrate, abstain"; thus, the nature of the vow has to do with being set apart, or consecrated, to God.

The evidence of this consecration is the avoidance of certain things. According to Numbers 6:1–8, the man or woman who takes the vow carefully avoids any consumption of the fruit of the vine (vv. 3–4), any cutting or shaving of the hair of the head (v. 5), and any contact with corpses (vv. 6–7). While the origin of Israel's Nazirite vow is obscure, votive individuals—individuals voluntarily set apart to the deity—are common in ancient Near Eastern religions. Distinctive in Israel's practice is not the Nazirite vow itself so much as the God to whom the individual is set apart. That the practice continued in some form into the New Testament period is evidenced by passages such as Acts 18:18 and 21:23–24.[34]

While Nazirite vows were commonly made for a limited period of time (the end of which was marked by shaving the head and returning to "normal" status),[35] Hannah consecrated her son for "all the days of his life." In this respect, Hannah's vow is reminiscent of the Nazirite charge included in the annunciation of Samson's birth (Judg. 13:3–7).

Hannah was praying in her heart (1:13). While spontaneous prayer is common in the Bible, silent prayer is mentioned explicitly only here. An interesting parallel is found in the Egyptian Instruction of Any, a portion of which reads as follows:

> Do not raise your voice in the house of a god,
> He abhors shouting;
> Pray by yourself with a loving heart,
> Whose every word is hidden.
> He will grant your needs,
> He will hear your words,
> He will accept your offering.[36]

Hannah apparently has nothing to offer, which must have made Eli's favorable response to her—once he realizes that she has been praying, not drinking (1:13–17)—all the more comforting and reassuring (v. 18).

She named him Samuel (1:20). Names in the Bible and in ancient Near Eastern texts are usually more than simple labels; rather, they denote the "essence of a thing."[37] Theophoric names (names bearing the name of a deity) are common. In the Bible, characters sometimes state the significance of a name, as in the present instance where Hannah explains why she gives her child the name "Samuel": "Because I asked the LORD for him." Sometimes names are changed (Abram ["exalted father"] was changed to Abraham ["father of multitudes"]; Hoshea ["salvation"] to Joshua ["the LORD saves"]; Naomi ["pleasant"] to Mara ["bitter"], etc.). And sometimes the biblical narrators themselves creatively exploit the semantic potential of homophony (what a name sounds like) in the telling of their tales: "punning upon names ... functions [in the Bible] as a significant literary device to enrich and intensify the plot through a correspondence between names and themes."[38] Naming in the Old Testament seldom operates on the basis of etymology; rather, it is on the basis of the potential of a name to be invested with meaning in keeping with the historical or literary context of the episode.

After the boy is weaned (1:22). In antiquity, a child might be nursed for three years or more. In the Egyptian Instruction of Any, a father instructs his son to care for his mother:

> She had a heavy load in you,
> But she did not abandon you.
> When you were born after your months,
> She was yet yoked <to you>,
> Her breast was in your mouth for three years.[39]

Similarly, 2 Maccabees 7:27 states, "I carried you nine months in the womb, suckled you three years." Because the return of ovulation after giving birth can be delayed by breast-feeding, an extended period of nursing may have served as a kind of natural contraceptive.[40] In any case, weaning may have been celebrated by a feast (Gen. 21:8).

A three-year-old bull, an ephah of flour and a skin of wine (1:24). The Hebrew text reads "three bulls," but a majority of modern translations and commentators follow 4QSam[a], the LXX, and the Peshitta in reading a "three-year-old bull," assuming that the Hebrew text has wrongly divided two words.[41] The Masoretic text as it stands is not without defenders, however. Wenham, for example, in commenting on Hannah's offering, suggests that "one bull was for the burnt offering, one for the purification offering that was expected after childbirth (Lev. 12), and the third for the peace offering, in payment of her vow."[42]

According to the stipulations of Numbers 15:8–10, a young bull for sacrifice was to be accompanied by "a grain offering of three-tenths of an ephah of fine flour" mixed with oil, as well as a drink offering of wine. That Hannah's offering included "an ephah of flour"—more than three times the amount stipulated—may support the notion that she brought three bulls. On present evidence, it is best to leave the question open.

Tomb painting of bull being brought for offering
The Yorck Project/ Wikimedia Commons

Hannah's Prayer (2:1–11)

Horn (2:1). On a literal level the word "horn" refers to the antlers or horns that serve as weapons for various animals; the Old Testament uses *qeren* to describe the natural headgear of rams and wild oxen, and even for the tusks of elephants. In addition, horns tend to give their possessors a majestic, even regal, appearance. The raised horn sometimes suggests prosperity or progeny, or both. Throughout the ancient Near East, "the wild ox himself was symbol of strength and virility."[43]

It is not surprising, therefore, that horns regularly appear in depictions of Mesopotamian deities and kings. As a general metaphor, one's horn represents one's strength, pride, and security. Hannah clearly understands Psalm 75:10, that the Lord is the One who exalts the horn of the righteous but cuts off the horn of the wicked. Thus, she rejoices in the Lord that her "horn is lifted high"—an expression that may sometimes refer to having posterity.[44]

At the end of her song (1:10) Hannah speaks of the Lord as exalting the horn of his anointed, his king. Later on, David, the king of God's own choosing, extols the Lord as "my shield and the horn of my salvation" (2 Sam. 22:3). Grasping the metaphorical use of "horn" in the Old Testament and in ancient Near Eastern literature and iconography is vital for understanding the horn imagery in Daniel 7–8, Revelation 12–13, and elsewhere.[45]

There is no Rock like our God (2:2). The term "rock" (or "mountain"; *ṣûr*) occurs in theophoric personal names in both the ancient Near East and the Old Testament.[46] As a title (and not a mere metaphor) for the God of the Bible, *ṣûr* is concentrated in poetic passages (e.g., the song of Moses, Deut. 32; the song of David, 2 Sam. 22; Psalms; Isaiah). Modern readers, familiar with the use of explosives and heavy machinery to move or even pulverize rocks, must use their imaginations to grasp the sense of "impervious solidity" that a large rock evoked in the minds of ancient people.[47]

In the Bible, "rock" is suggestive of God's strength and sovereignty and of the security, stability, and salvation of those who trust in him. Hannah's focus here is on the uniqueness of the one true Rock as opposed, presumably, to all false sources of security (cf. Isa. 44:8 and the contrast with false gods, also called "rock," in Deut. 32:31, 37). That the same God who affords sanctuary to some is to others a stone of stumbling and a rock that makes them fall is clear in Isaiah 8:14 (cf. Rom. 9:33; 1 Pet. 2:8).

The Lord brings death and makes alive; he brings down to the grave and raises up (2:6). The conviction that the fate of human

Winged genie from dur-Sharrukin wears a horned helmet. In Assyrian art, gods and genies are the ones who wear horned helmets rather than the kings.
Marie-Lan Nguyen/ Wikimedia Commons, courtesy of the Louvre

beings is in the hands of God (or the gods) runs deep in ancient Near Eastern cultures. In the Akkadian creation epic known as *Enuma Elish*, we read the following lines: "Thou, Marduk, art the most honored of the great gods, thy decree is unrivaled, thy word is Anu [i.e., it has the authority of the sky-god Anu]. From this day unchangeable shall be thy pronouncement. To raise or bring low—these shall be (in) thy hand."[48] From the Egyptian Instruction of Amenemope comes the following: "He [the deity] tears down and builds up every day, he makes a thousand poor as he wishes, and makes a thousand people overseers, when he is in his hour of life."[49]

To this general notion of the sovereignty of the deity, Hannah adds the nuance that the true and living God acts compassionately toward the humble, arming with strength those who stumble (2:4), filling those who are hungry (2:5a), blessing the one who is barren with a full complement of children (seven being the number of perfection; 2:5b), and, conversely, abasing the proud. In short, Hannah knows and trusts the God who can reverse human fortune and bring blessing out of hardship.

Storm god
Kim Walton, courtesy of the Oriental Institute Museum

He will thunder against them from heaven (2:10). Few displays of nature evoked such a sense of power and danger among ancient people as a severe thunderstorm. Not surprisingly, the ancients perceived booming thunder as evidence of the powerful presence and judgment of the deity. In the Akkadian flood stories, it is the weather god Adad who rumbles and thunders in the clouds.[50] In Hittite mythology, Telipinu, also a weather god, comes raging with lightning and thunder.[51] In Ugaritic texts, the Canaanite god Baal makes "his voice ring out in the clouds, by flashing his lightning to the earth"; he opens "a rift" in the clouds and makes "his holy voice" resound.[52]

The poets and psalmists of Israel use similar imagery in describing their God, both because they share the same cultural milieu as their neighbors and perhaps to express Yahweh's superiority over the false gods of their neighbors. A prime example is Psalm 29, in which the bulk of the psalm (vv. 3–9) is a celebration of the powerful "voice" (thundering) of Yahweh[53] (see comment on 2 Sam. 22:14).

He will give strength to his king (2:10). That Hannah should refer to the Lord's "king" may seem surprising, inasmuch as kingship has not yet been introduced in Israel. Kingship was certainly well known among Israel's neighbors, and it was widely practiced in Egypt and Mesopotamia from at least the third millennium B.C.[54]

Israel itself had flirted with the idea of kingship in the days of Abimelech (Judg. 9). Jotham's fabled response to Abimelech's bid for power explicitly mentions anointing a king (9:8). Prior to Judges, numerous references in the Pentateuch make clear that God intended for Israel one day to have a king (e.g., Gen. 17:6; 49:10; Num. 24:7, 17–19; Deut. 17:6, 16; 35:11). Hannah's anticipation that the time for a king draws nigh is, therefore, not so surprising. Her invocation of blessing on the Lord's king makes clear that kingship per se need not be a problem in Israel—only kings who refuse to rule as vassals of the Great King (see next comment).

Exalt the horn of his anointed (2:10). Anointing with oil was practiced in ancient Israel and the ancient Near East. Egyptian officials were anointed to high office, though it is unclear whether the Egyptian pharaoh himself was anointed. From the Amarna letters, it appears that local kings in Palestine were anointed as an expression of vassalage to their Egyptian suzerain. Among the Hittites, the suzerain commonly bound his vassals to him by formal rites undergirded by religious

This anointing scene from Kom Ombo dates to the first couple of centuries B.C. The motif of the gods anointing the king with life (ankh signs) was a long-standing motif in ancient Egypt.
Steve Nicholls

sanctions. Among these rites was the anointing of the vassal ruler. Hittite kings themselves were anointed with the "holy oil of kingship," and their titles sometimes referred to their anointed status (e.g., "Tabarna, the Anointed, the Great King").[55]

Similar practices are represented in the Old Testament. While both religious objects and religious personnel were anointed (Ex. 30:22–33), it was the king who ultimately held the title "the LORD's anointed" or, in shortened form, "the anointed [one]." This title expressed the king's vassal status as the Lord's earthly representative and his consecration to and authorization for divine service (on vassal kingship, see also comments on 1 Sam. 8:7; 16:13; 24:6). The king's status as "the anointed" implied his divine enabling and his inviolability.

Eli's Sons (2:12–26)

The servant of the priest would come with a three-pronged fork in his hand (2:13). Implements such as tongs and, as here, three-pronged forks were used in cultic practice for various purposes, such as adjusting sacrifical animals on the altar. Here Eli's wicked sons are simply plunging the forks into the pot of sacrificial meat, contrary to procedures prescribed in the Pentateuch, in which only certain portions of the sacrificial animal were to be eaten by the priests (Lev. 10:14–15). Three-pronged forks, shovels, and other cultic instruments have been discovered in archaeological excavations from a wide range of time periods.[56]

Even before the fat was burned (2:15). Throughout the ancient Near East, the

Three-pronged fork from Gezer
Todd Bolen/www.BiblePlaces.com

Linen clothing worn in ritual contexts
Fredduf/Wikimedia Commons, courtesy of the Louvre

Egyptian model of man cooking the meat from a sacrifice in a stew pot
Kim Walton, courtesy of the Oriental Institute Museum

offering of sacrifices was a common feature in religious observance, though conceptions of their meaning and purpose varied considerably. In Mesopotamia, for example, sacrifices were thought to feed the gods. Although one occasionally hears an echo of this notion in the Bible (e.g., Lev. 21:6, "offerings made to the LORD by fire, the food of their God"), this is probably little more than a figure of speech; in fact, the idea that God eats "the flesh of bulls" or drinks "the blood of goats" is explicitly denied (Ps. 50:13). In ancient Israel, sacrifices were offered to express contrition or thanksgiving, to honor God, and for other purposes.[57] Certain portions of the sacrificial animal carried special significance, and the portions reserved for God were to be burned.

Israel was not unique in this regard; a Hittite temple dedication text, for instance, after describing how the image of a new deity is to be smeared with the blood of a sacrifical sheep, concludes by stating that "the fat is burned up. No one eats it."[58] In the biblical tradition, beginning with Abel's pleasing offering of "fat portions from some of the firstborn of his flock" (Gen. 4:4), the fat portion came to represent the best portion (cf. Num. 18:29–32, where "best" renders the Hebrew word "fat"; cf. also the expression "fat of the land" in Gen. 45:18). As the best portion, the fat (along with the blood) belonged to the Lord.

Why the fat portions take on this metaphorical significance remains a mystery, especially in light of the fact that the "fat" may refer to inedible "suet" derived from the "the layers of fat beneath the surface of the animal's skin and around its organs ... in contrast to the fat that is inextricably entwined in the musculature." There is evidence along the Mediterranean littoral of sacrificial flesh being burned in kidney fat, but in Mesopotamia proper the use of suet in sacrifices is not attested, "probably for the reason that in Mesopotamia the food offerings to the gods were not burned but were subsequently eaten by the priests."[59]

Perhaps the offering of inedible suet to Yahweh was deemed appropriate precisely because it was understood that Yahweh did not need to be fed (though this remains no more than a speculation). In any case, the priest's duty was to burn the fat on the altar as a pleasing aroma to the Lord (Lev. 3:16; 7:31). Both fat and blood were barred from human consumption (3:17; cf. 7:33; Ezek. 39:19; 44:7, 15), and anyone who offended in this matter was to be "cut off from his people" (Lev. 7:25). Against this background, the abuses of the sons of Eli, described as "wicked men" here (1 Sam. 2:12), were grave indeed (2:17).

A boy wearing a linen ephod (2:18). "Ephod" refers to three distinct but related items in the Bible: (1) the "simple linen garment worn by priests" (as here); (2) the "very elaborate high-priestly ephod" described especially in Exodus 28 and 39, on which was attached a breastplate containing the Urim and Thummim (see comments on 14:3, 18–19); and (3) some other object, perhaps an idol or, more likely, a sacred garment that clothed an idol.[60] What all three types of ephod have in common is their character as a sacred vestment of some sort. Old Assyr-

▸ Robes in 1–2 Samuel

In 1–2 Samuel, robes play a significant role in numerous places. Note, among others:

1 Sam. 15:27 (Samuel's torn robe marking Saul's loss of the kingdom)
1 Sam. 18:3–4 (Jonathan transferring his princely robe to David)
1 Sam. 19:24 (Saul's divestment of his royal robe)
1 Sam. 24:4–5 (David's carving a corner off of Saul's robe)
1 Sam. 28:14 (Samuel recognized by his robe)
2 Sam. 1:11 (David and his nobles tearing their robes in mourning for Saul and Jonathan)
2 Sam. 13:18–19 (Tamar's torn robe marking her violation and loss of virginity).

ian texts from Cappadocia attest the possibly cognate term *epattu*, which designates a "rich and costly garment."[61] Samuel's wearing a linen ephod indicates he has entered the priestly service as an apprentice.

His mother made him a little robe (2:19). The "little robe" provided by Hannah is probably an outer garment of some sort to be worn over the linen priestly ephod. In both the Bible and the ancient Near East generally, special garments often carried symbolic significance or marked the wearer as holding a particular office or status (see comment on 18:3–4).

Women who served at the entrance to the Tent of Meeting (2:22). The "Tent of Meeting" (cf. Ex. 27:21) frequently refers to the pre-Solomonic portable sanctuary where the Lord appeared to his people and their leaders, initially and especially to Moses. Here the designation may be virtually synonymous with the tabernacle. Portable shrines have been discovered by archaeologists excavating in the ancient Near East.[62]

The comment that Eli's sons slept with the women who served at the entrance of the Tent of Meeting, while aptly contributing to the depiction of Eli's sons as wicked men (see 2:12), is uncertain in several respects. First, the comment may not belong to the original text.[63]

Second, even should the reference be genuine, its meaning is not clear. Some commentators have assumed that the women were engaged in cultic prostitution and have compared their activities to those of fertility cults believed to have existed in Canaan. Recent studies have questioned the link between prostitution and fertility, however, and have expressed doubt about the prevalence of cultic prostitution in the ancient Near East—cultic prostitution being defined as "religiously legitimated intercourse with strangers in or in the vicinity of the sanctuary ... [that] had a ritual character and was organized or at least condoned by the priesthood, as a means to increase fecundity and fertility."[64]

To be sure, a kind of "sacred" prostitution of women and sometimes men was practiced in the ancient Near East, sometimes as a means of bringing funds into the temple coffers and sometimes as a way for an individual to earn money to fulfill a religious vow; but such activities are condemned in the Old Testament. For example, Deuteronomy 23:17–18 reads:

> No Israelite man or woman is to become a shrine prostitute. You must not bring the earnings of a female prostitute or of a male prostitute into the house of the LORD your God to pay any vow, because the LORD your God detests them both.

Finally, unlike many of its neighbors, ancient Israel seems not to have included women in the priesthood. In fact, Hebrew does not have a word for "priestess," in contradistinction to references to priestesses among the Assyrians, Phoenicians, and others.[65]

In sum, while much uncertainty surrounds the notice that Eli's sons "slept with the women who served at the entrance to the Tent of Meeting," there is no uncertainty about the fact that "Eli's sons were wicked men" (2:12).

Eli's Rejection (2:27–36)

A man of God came to Eli (2:27). The descriptor "man of God" is often used in the Old Testament as a synomym for "prophet" (cf. 9:8–11). The phenomenon of prophecy is widely attested in the ancient Near East, from Mesopotamia (Uruk, Mari, Assyria, etc.) to Anatolia (where the Hittites also referred to prophets as "men of God")[66] to Syria-Palestine (Ebla, Emar, Ugarit, Phoenicia, Aram, Ammon) to Egypt (though in Egypt, distinguishing prophets from priests and sages is of uncertain validity: "In actuality there is very little known from Egypt that illustrates the prophet as an inspired speaker of divine oracles").[67] Although definitions of "prophecy" range from "foretelling the future" to "decrying injustice," the key element in biblical (and some ancient Near Eastern) prophecy is that it constitutes "inspired speech at the initiative of a divine power."[68] The key distinction between biblical and ancient Near Eastern prophecy is the identity of the divine power at whose behest the prophet speaks—the true God Yahweh or one of the gods of the nations around Israel (see also comments on 3:1).

Zakkur Stele
Rama/Wikimedia Commons, courtesy of the Louvre

To wear an ephod in my presence (2:28). On the three senses in which "ephod" is used in the Bible, see comment on 2:18. The present context, which speaks of Eli's house approaching the altar and burning incense, suggests that the high priestly ephod is in view.

He will minister before my anointed one always (2:35). On the Lord's anointed, see comment on 2:10.

Samuel's Vision and Initiation as a Prophet (3:1–21)

Not many visions (3:1). Judging from the extant evidence, ancient Near Eastern cultures were deeply theological, whether their allegiance was to the myriad of local deities or, as in the case of ancient Israel, to the one true God. It is not surprising, therefore, that "visionaries," or prophets, who (ostensibly) brought messages from the gods to the people, were a regular feature in most such societies (see comment on 2:27).

The biblical terms for prophetic individuals find parallels in other ancient Near Eastern literatures, as in the Old Aramaic inscription of Zakkur, king of Hamath (c. 800 B.C.): "Now I raised my hands to Baʿlshamayn and Ba'lshamayn answered me. Baʿlshamayn [spoke] to me through seers and diviners."[69] The Aramaic word for "seer" is cognate with the Hebrew word for "seer" (*ḥōzeh*), which is related to the noun "vision" (*ḥāzôn*) in 3:1. In 3:20, Samuel is called a "prophet" (*nābîʾ*). While the Bible also applies this term to prophets of Baal, this sharing of terminology must not obscure the distinction between true and false prophecy, any more than the worship of false gods should be confused with worship of the true God. For a dramatic illustration of the difference, see the contest between the prophet Elijah and the prophets of Baal in 1 Kings 18.

Samuel was lying down in the temple of the LORD (3:3). On "the temple," see comment on 1:9. That Samuel is described as "lying down in the temple of the LORD, where the ark of God was" (3:3), has led some to speculate that he may have been engaging in a well-attested ancient Near Eastern practice called "incubation."[70] Incubation involves spending a night in the temple precinct in the hope of receiving a divine vision or oracular dream. The practice is attested among the Egyptians, with manuals of dream interpretation being used as early as the New Kingdom period,[71] among the Hittites of Anatolia,[72] and in Canaan during the biblical period.[73]

An early example of oracular dreams prior to temple building is that of Gudea of Lagash (near the end of the third millennium). As Averbeck notes, "Dreams, dream incubations, and dream interpretation are a major concern in the Gudea Cylinders."[74] Significantly, Averbeck observes that while the second and third dreams of Gudea involved ritual procedures, "it is not certain that Gudea's first dream was incubated."[75] In this respect, we are reminded of Samuel's experience, as there is no hint here that Samuel intends to incubate a revelatory dream; quite the contrary, for he repeatedly assumes that the voice he hears is Eli's. Samuel's experience is best called an (unanticipated) auditory dream theophany.

Extrabiblical examples of such theophanies, or auditory message dreams as they are sometimes called, come from Egypt (Thutmose IV, fifteenth century),[76] Ugarit (in both the Kirta Epic and the ʿAqhatu Legend),[77] Hatti (Ḫattušiliš, thirteenth century),[78] and Babylonia (Nabonidus, sixth century).[79]

Ark of God (3:3). Built during the time of Moses (see Ex. 25:10–22), the ark of God (also called the ark of the testimony and the ark of the covenant) was a relatively small box (about 45 inches long, 27 inches wide, and 27 inches high) made of acacia wood, overlaid with gold, and fitted with rings so it could be carried with poles. Items of similar size and construction have been discovered in the tomb of the Egyptian pharaoh Tutankhamun (ca. 1336–1327). The biblical ark was a visible symbol of God's presence with his people; when not mobile (e.g., accompanying Israel into battle or leading them through the Jordan), it was kept in the Most Holy Place of the tabernacle, later the temple.[80] The ark was not a magical object and was not to be trifled with, as is made apparent especially in 1 Samuel 4–6 and 2 Samuel 6.

Samuel was attested as a prophet of the Lord (3:20). On prophecy in the ancient Near East and the Bible, see comments on 2:27 and 3:1.

The Ark of God Lost to the Philistines (4:1–11)

The Israelites camped at Ebenezer (4:1). No site called Ebenezer is mentioned in the extant ancient Near Eastern corpus, and archaeologists have been unsuccessful in positively identifying Ebenezer's location. The biblical text in view here indicates that Ebenezer must have been in the vicinity of Aphek (see next comment), because it describes the Israelites at Ebenezer spoiling for a fight with Philistines nearby at Aphek.

The discovery in 1973 of a small Iron Age I settlement some two miles east of Aphek, across the Aphek Pass, has led some scholars to suggest that this settlement (called ʿIzbet Ṣarṭâ) or perhaps one of several similar sites nearby may well be biblical Ebenezer. Excavated in four seasons, from 1976 to 1978, ʿIzbet Ṣarṭâ revealed three strata, which show potential convergences with early Israelite history as known from the books of Samuel. The oldest settlement was founded at the end of the thirteenth or beginning of the twelfth century B.C. and abandoned in the early eleventh—perhaps in the aftermath of the battle of Ebenezer recounted in 1 Samuel 4.

The site was reoccupied in the late eleventh century but was abandoned again after one or two decades—perhaps as a result of "the Philistines' consolidation of power in their war with Saul" (1 Sam. 13–14). The site was occupied yet again at the beginning of the

▸ Philistines

"Don't be such a Philistine!" For centuries in the English language, and still today, the word "Philistine" has been used as a term of opprobrium. To be called a Philistine is to be branded as uncultured or concerned only for the material and the commonplace. Given the biblical depiction of the Philistines as Israel's archenemies during the periods of the judges and the early monarchy, it is not surprising that they have been viewed negatively.

Archaeological excavations, however, and indeed the Bible itself, hardly justify calling the Philistines uncultured. A careful reading of the biblical texts suggests not so much that the Philistines lack culture—in many respects their material culture surpasses Israel's—as that they are staunch enemies of Israel and, by extension, of Israel's God.[A-2] They are, to use the biblical censure, the "uncircumcised" (e.g., 1 Sam. 14:6; 17:26, 36; 31:4; 2 Sam. 1:20).[A-3] They are the quintessential foreign adversary, a fact that may be reflected in LXX's rendering of the word "Philistine" most often simply as *allophylos* ("foreigner, Gentile, heathen, pagan").[A-4]

The Philistines are reasonably well attested in extrabiblical ancient Near Eastern literature, the earliest known references coming from the time of the Egyptian pharaoh Ramesses III (ca. 1184–1153 B.C.). Inscribed on the walls of his temple at Medinet Habu in Thebes is an account of a war he fought against various Sea Peoples, among whom the Philistines are included: "Their confederation was the Philistines, Tjeker, Shekelesh, Denye(n), and Weshesh, lands united."[A-5] According to Ramesses III's inscription, "The foreign countries made a *conspiracy* in their islands," and they proved almost an irresistible force as they migrated into the eastern Mediterranean: "No land could stand before their arms, from Hatti, Kode, Carchemish," and so on.[A-6]

It was a different story, however, when they approached Egypt: "Those who reached my frontier, their seed is not, their heart and their soul are finished forever and ever."[A-7] The walls of the temple at Medinet Habu celebrate Ramesses III's victory over the Sea Peoples not only verbally but visually, as in the wall relief shown in the accompanying picture (the Philistine warriors can be identified by their characteristic headdress).

The Philistines are also frequently mentioned in eighth- and seventh-century Assyrian records, the earliest reference coming from an account of a north-to-south expedition down along the eastern Mediterranean by Adad-Nirari III (810–783 B.C.): "I subdued from the bank of the Euphrates, the land of Ḫatti, the land of Amurru in its entirety, the land of Tyre, the land of Sidon, the land of Israel (Ḫumri), the land of Edom, the land of Philistia, as far as the great sea in the west."[A-8] Under Tiglath-pileser III (744–727 B.C.), Assyria reduced Philistia to tributary status, along with Judah and other neighboring states.[A-9]

While the Philistines loom large in both the biblical record—particularly

tenth century—perhaps reflecting "a resumption of Israelite expansion to the west under David."[81] The final abandonment of the site may have been due simply to the increasing freedom of the Israelites under David to move into the more fertile Yarkon Basin.[82]

One of the more interesting finds at ʿIzbet Ṣarṭâ is an ostracon inscribed with eighty-three alphabetic signs in proto-Canaanite/Hebrew script.[83] The final line is most deeply inscribed and contains a twenty-two-letter alphabet, suggesting that the Samson narratives (Judg. 13–16) and 1–2 Samuel—and ancient Near Eastern texts, the question of their origin remains something of a mystery.[A-10] The general view is that the Philistines, along with other Sea Peoples, migrated in large numbers from "the islands and coastlands of the Aegean Sea, including the island of Crete,"[A-11] as part of a general social upheaval that characterized the latter part of the second millennium B.C.

The Bible confirms the Philistines' association with the Aegean and with Crete (biblical Caphtor; Jer. 47:4; Amos 9:7), but this may not be the end—or, more precisely, the beginning—of their story. The Table of Nations in Genesis 10 ties the Philistines to the little-known Casluhites (10:14), who "may have been the Philistines' progenitors before the Philistines went to Caphtor."[A-12] Furthermore, the Table of Nations traces the Philistines back to Noah's son Ham (forbear of, among others, the Canaanites) and not to his son Japheth (forbear of the Indo-Europeans associated with the Aegean). Perhaps, then, "the Philistines actually were an amalgamation of several different peoples and ... the Philistines descended from the Casluhites were different from those who came from Caphtor."[A-13]

Pertinent to this issue may be the controversial theory of C. H. Gordon, based on his putative decipherment of Linear A as a (West) Semitic language, that Minoan civilization of the island of Crete must have had Semitic as well as Greek (Linear B) roots.[A-14] Though Gordon's theory has not gained general acceptance, if it should prove true it would help to explain, for example, how Samson, an Israelite, could have communicated with Delilah, a Philistine, as both would have been of Semitic stock.[A-15]

What we do know is that at least by the beginning of the Iron Age (ca. 1200 B.C.) the Philistines were settling along the southwest coast of Canaan from somewhere south of modern Jaffa to the border of Egypt. Their five most important cities, the so-called Philistine pentapolis, were Ashdod, Gaza, Ashkelon, Gath, and Ekron (Josh. 13:3; 1 Sam. 6:17). Beyond their so-called pentapolis, the Philistines exhibited expansionist tendencies—already in the time of Samson and increasingly in the period of Samuel and the early monarchy—which brought them into direct conflict with their Israelite neighbors to the north and east.[A-16]

Sea Peoples captives in Egyptian relief from Medinet Habu
Z. Radovan/www.BibleLandPictures.com

the ostracon is a practice abecedary (alphabet list). The letters in the preceding lines appear to be random and rather repetitive, again suggesting a practice text. The significance of this find is that it attests alphabetic writing—and someone attempting to learn it—in a small Iron I (probably Israelite) village. Given the simplicity of alphabetic writing (as opposed to pictographic or syllabic writing), and given this evidence of literacy in a small village, it is not unreasonable to assume that literacy may well have been more widespread in early Israel than is often assumed.[84]

Philistines at Aphek (4:1). Of several biblical Apheks, the city in view here is to be identified with modern Ras el-ʿAin (now sometimes referred to as Aphek-Antipatris).[85] The site lies some seven and a half miles east of Tel Aviv in the plain of Sharon near the source of the Yarkon River and is strategically located on an important trade route.[86] Aphek is mentioned in various extrabiblical sources, beginning with the nineteenth-century B.C. Execration texts from Egypt[87] and including the fifteenth-century topographical lists of the pharaohs Thutmose III[88] and Amenhotep II,[89] and various later documents.[90] Lying less than twenty-five miles north of the Philistine city of Ekron, the city of Aphek naturally was of interest to the Philistines and provided a strategic launching pad for further military excursions to the north and east.

Archaeological investigations of the site, especially in the 1970s and 1980s, discovered large quantities of Philistine pottery from the Iron Age (1200 B.C. and following), as well as "the heads of Ashdoda-type statuettes and a fragment of a clay tablet containing an inscription in an unknown and as yet undeciphered script."[91] The discovery at Aphek of eight Akkadian cuneiform texts or fragments from the end of the Late Bronze Age (1200 B.C.) further underscores the importance of the site, as the number of such texts so far discovered in Israel/Palestine is limited.[92]

Let us bring the ark of the LORD's covenant from Shiloh (4:3). On the ark, see comment on 3:3; on Shiloh, see comment on 1:3.

Enthroned between the cherubim (4:4). Not to be confused with the portly baby-like "cherubs" of Western art, the "cherubim" (plural of Heb. *kᵉrûb*) of the ancient Near East and the Bible were fanciful, celestial, composite creatures, often with the head of a lion or a human (sometimes both), with two or four legs, and always with wings. Cherubim were, by virtue of their unnatural number and nature of features, symbols well suited to their associations with divinity. While the constellation of features varied from one depiction or description to another, the one constant feature was wings, suggestive of the unusual mobility of cherubim. This and other characteristics of cherubim made them, as C. Meyers observes, "apt symbols for divine presence, since deities moved where humans could not and were something other than either animals or humans."[93]

Aphek
Todd Bolen/www.BiblePlaces.com

The Hebrew text does not explicitly indicate whether Yahweh is enthroned "between" or "upon" the cherubim, but the latter seems more likely, as the ark with its cherubim served in biblical symbolism as the footstool of the invisible deity.[94] Visual representations of winged creatures fitting the description and symbolic function of cherubim have been brought to light by archaeological investigation throughout the ancient Near East.[95]

You will be subject to the Hebrews, as they have been to you (4:9). As evidenced by biblical references to Philistine outposts in Isra-

Cherub-flanked throne on Ahiram sarcophagus
Werner Forman Archive/The National Museum, Beirut

elite territory (e.g., 10:5; 13:3), the Philistines were for a time successful in expanding beyond the Philistine heartland in which the Philistine Pentapolis was located. Particularly "with the breakdown of Egyptian hegemony in Canaan after the death of Ramesses III (1153 B.C.), the Philistines [began] to expand in all directions beyond their original territory, north to the Tel Aviv area, east into the foothills (Shephelah), and southeast into the Wadi Gaza and Beersheba basin."[96] By the middle of the eleventh century, the Philistines were putting enough pressure on the highlands of Israel to trigger a major shift in Israelite polity, namely, the demand for and granting of a king.

Israel lost thirty thousand foot soldiers (4:10). The question of how to interpret the large numbers of the Old Testament has elicited extensive debate among biblical scholars. No approach has been generally agreed upon, although several plausible theories have been suggested. This question is bound up with estimates of the general population that the land of Israel could have supported in antiquity.[97]

One approach is to take all the numbers literally, but this sometimes runs into seemingly insuperable problems. For example, the census numbers of Numbers 1 and 26, if read literally, imply a total Israelite population of some two to three million people. But passages such as Deuteronomy 7:7 insist that in comparison to the Canaanites, the Israelites were "the fewest of all peoples."[98]

Attempts to resolve the difficulties of the large numbers in the Old Testament have observed that the Hebrew word rendered "thousand" can also mean "chieftain, family leader, clan, military unit" (assuming appropriate revocalizations of the consonantal Hebrew text). Further, some numerals seem to function as round numbers or to carry symbolic value.[99] In military reportage, there is even some evidence that numbers may have been multiplied by a factor of ten to underscore the magnitude of victories or losses.[100] Inconsistencies between numbers in parallel passages can sometimes be explained on the basis of textual corruptions.

Philistine Territory

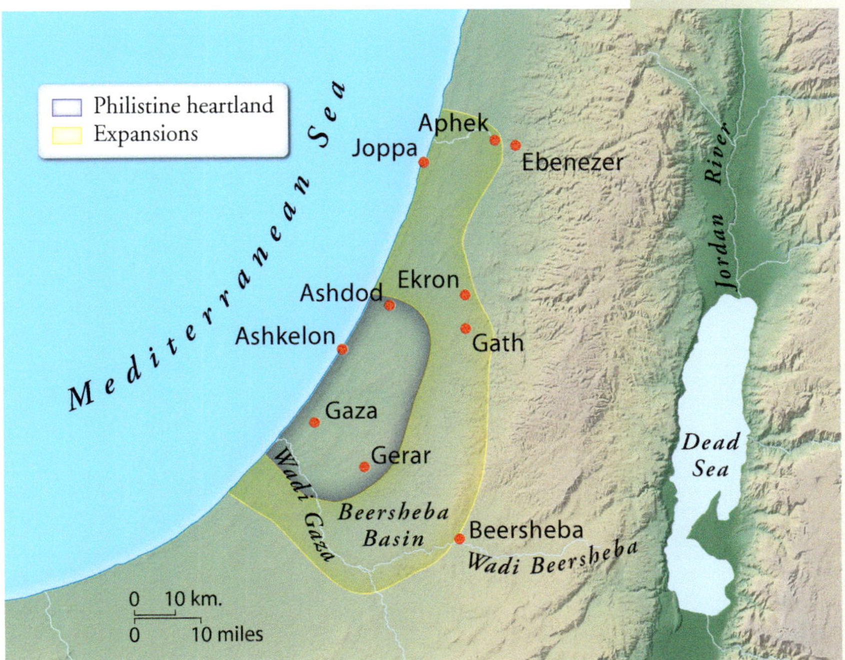

▸ Hebrew/Habiru

The Philistines' query regarding the "shouting in the Hebrew camp" (4:6) marks the first occurrence of the designation "Hebrew" in the books of Samuel, and it is perhaps not surprising that this label is found on the lips of a non-Israelite people. Throughout 1–2 Samuel, as well as elsewhere in the Hebrew Bible, the designation "Hebrew(s)" is often used by foreigners or in the presence of foreigners. A possible explanation for this phenomenon has to do with the much-debated link between the "Hebrews" and the so-called Habiru (variously spelled *ʿapirû, Ḫabirû, Ḫapiru*, or using the Sumerian logogram SA.GAZ) known from many documents throughout the ancient Near East, particularly in the second millennium B.C.[A-17]

It was the discovery in 1888–89 of the now famous Amarna letters that first sparked debate over possible links between the Habiru and the "Hebrews" of the Canaanite conquest. More than 380 tablets were discovered in the royal archives at el-Amarna, the site of ancient Akhetaten, in Egypt.[A-18] Covering less than a thirty-year period, mostly during the reign of the "monotheist" Amenophis IV (called Akhenaten, ca. 1352–1336 B.C.), the bulk of the letters (over 300) "were exchanged between Egypt and vassal kingdoms in Canaan and northern Syria."[A-19] Some 16 letters from city-states within Canaan mention the troublesome Habiru (spelled *ʿapiru*) and appeal to Egypt for assistance.[A-20] These Habiru "appear as marauding mercenaries who at times pose a threat to all the Canaanite states and at other times are to be found on opposing sides of intercity warfare."[A-21]

Not surprisingly, as N. Naʾaman wrote in a 1986 study,[A-22] "the resemblance between the names Ḫabiru and Hebrew, the proximity of their location, as well as the close chronological relationship between the Amarna *Ḫabiru* and the Israelites aroused the imagination of scholars, bringing about the immediate equation of the two groups."[A-23] The excitement was to be short-lived, however, for it soon became apparent that the Habiru, as noted already above, were virtually ubiquitous in the Fertile Crescent throughout much of the second millennium.[A-24]

It became equally clear that the Habiru did not represent an ethnic group per se, but landless and often troublesome people who had been "uprooted from their original political and social framework and forced to adapt to a new environment."[A-25] Arguing from evidence at Mari, Naʾaman suggested that the Habiru should be understood as "migrants."[A-26] More recently, D. Fleming has argued that a better etymology for biblical "Hebrews" is provided by Mari's *ʿibrum*, a designation for backcountry herders that was particularly popular among the Binu Yamina tribespeople of southwest Syria.[A-27] Fleming maintains that his *ʿibrum* hypothesis offers a better etymology for biblical "Hebrew" (*ʿibrî*; "the *qitl* noun form offers an exact match"), and a better social fit for biblical "Hebrews" than either the Eberite derivation of Genesis 10:21 or the Habiru linkage.[A-28]

So what, in the end, have the biblical "Hebrews" to do with the Habiru? And why would the Philistines use the label "Hebrews" for the Israelites? It is now clear that a straight equation of Hebrews and Habiru is impossible—not all Habiru could possibly have been Israelites; the geographical and temporal distribution is simply too great.[A-29] But this does not mean that there can be no relationship whatsoever. Perhaps the

Israelites, as they are described in the books of Joshua, Judges, and Samuel, were *viewed as* Habiru by some of their Canaanite opponents. As Naʾaman notes, "With their status as uprooted people living on the margins of society, the bands described in the books of Judges and Samuel are identical to the *Ḫabiru* of the ancient Near Eastern texts."[A-30]

Quite conceivably, therefore, threatened Canaanites (in this instance, Philistines) may have viewed menacing Israelites as Habiru, and this perception may have been reinforced by the *coincidental* similarity of the term Habiru to the gentilic *ʿibrî* ("Hebrew").[A-31] Worth noting is the fact that the designation "Hebrew" is often applied to Israelites by those wishing to cast aspersions on them (e.g., Potiphar's spurned wife in reference to Joseph in Gen 39:14, 17; Pharaoh's daughter in reference to Moses in Ex. 2:6; the Philistines in reference to Israelites in general in 1 Sam. 4:6, 9). Even the biblical narrators seem at times to distinguish between Hebrews and Israelites, as in 14:21: "The Hebrews who previously had been with the Philistines and had gone up with them into the camp turned and joined the Israelites who were with Saul and Jonathan." It is perhaps, then, as a term of opprobrium that the Philistines refer in 4:6 to the Israelite camp as the camp of the "Hebrews."

Amarna Letter number 299 is one of many that refers to the Apiru.
Todd Bolen/www.BiblePlaces.com

In the end, each case must be decided on its own merits, and some problems remain to challenge future researchers. In the present context, an approach other than the strictly literal seems justified—for example, that Israel suffered the loss of thirty "units" of foot soldiers, which would yield a number of anywhere between three hundred and three thousand soldiers, is still a significant loss. The narrator's point in reporting the military damage seems to be to stress how disastrous was Israel's attempt to manipulate Yahweh to their own advantage.

Slaughter on the battlefield in relief depicting the Assyrian victory at Til-Tuba
Alan Saunders, courtesy of the British Museum

Eli's Death and Ichabod's Birth (4:12–22)

His clothes torn and dust on his head (4:12). The Benjamite messenger's appearance leaves no doubt that he brings bad news. Grief and distress are often indicated in the Bible by actions such as fasting, wailing, breast-beating, tearing of one's garments, putting on sackcloth, or throwing dust (dirt or ashes) on one's head.[101] While such practices were common among Israel's neighbors, their origin remains a matter of debate. For instance, E. F. de Ward comments regarding the practice of throwing dust on the head:

> The use of earth or ash in all types of mourning rites is widespread, its original motives obscure. In moments of disaster, it may have been a dramatic reaction to shock; in funeral customs the dust may have been taken from the grave, the ash from the pyre, in some kind of covenant with the dead; or the motive may have been to seek anonymity at times of numinous portent.[102]

The origin of tearing one's garment is equally obscure. Perhaps it is simply as a sign of self-abasement, as an attempt to disguise oneself from impending doom, or even as an alternative to the harsher practice of self-mutilation.[103] Whatever the logic of each of these actions, they were certainly widespread in the ancient Near East. An interesting example is offered in the Ugaritic Myth of Baal. Upon hearing that Baal is dead,

> Beneficent El the Benign
> Descends from his seat, sits on the footstool,
> [And] from the footstool, sits on the earth.
> He pours dirt on his head for mourning,
> Dust on his crown for lamenting;
> For clothing he puts on sackcloth.[104]

The Ark's Wanderings in Philistia (5:1–12)

Ashdod (5:1). Later called Azotus (cf. Acts 8:40), Ashdod in the Old Testament was one of the cities of the Philistine Pentapolis (see sidebar on "Philistines" at 4:1). The city, along with "its surrounding settlements and villages," was assigned to the tribe of Judah in Joshua 15:47, but from the arrival of the Sea Peoples at the end of the Late Bronze Age (late thirteenth/early twelfth century B.C.) until the time of King David (tenth century), the city seems to have been in Philistine hands. Tel Ashdod, which today lies some two miles inland from the Mediterranean coast (north of Ashkelon and on about the same latitude as Jerusalem), was "a major seaport in the Late Bronze and Iron Ages."[105]

The first mentions of Ashdod outside the Bible come from Ugarit in Late Bronze II. A commercial text, writ-

Ashdod
Todd Bolen/www.BiblePlaces.com

ten in Akkadian, suggests that Ashdod was "a textile center from which purple dyed garments were traded," while an alphabetic Ugaritic text includes an Ashdodite among a group of "tin merchants."[106] Nine seasons of excavation at Tel Ashdod between 1962 and 1972, under the direction of M. Dothan, uncovered twenty-three strata, giving evidence of occupation from the Middle Bronze Age to the Byzantine period.

At its height, the city included an acropolis of some twenty acres and a lower city of seventy acres.[107] The city "was violently destroyed by fire toward the end of the thirteenth century B.C. and covered by a thick ash layer, apparently by the 'Sea Peoples.'"[108] Thereafter, throughout Iron Age I, the site exhibits typically Philistine material culture, including two seals that constitute some of the "earliest written evidence found in a Philistine context."[109]

In the half-century preceding the rise of the Israelite monarchy, Ashdod expanded beyond the acropolis and eventually developed a fortified area within the lower city. A rather substantial gate (13.7m long and 16.2m wide), attached to a five-meter wide wall, "was destroyed in the first half of the tenth century, perhaps at the end of the reign of King David or during the expedition of Pharaoh Siamon, in about 960 B.C.E."[110] No temple from the Philistine period has yet been discovered at Ashdod, though some Philistine "cult installations" have been found.[111]

Perhaps the most significant cultic artifact uncovered at Ashod is the so-called "Ashdoda," a female figure merged into the form of a chair or throne and painted in typically Aegean style.[112] The "Ashdoda" "probably represents a Philistine goddess whose prototype seems to be the figurines of the Mycenean Great Mother."[113]

They carried the ark into Dagon's temple and set it beside Dagon (5:2). Whether worshipers of the one true God, Yahweh, or of the false gods of the nations, ancient Near Eastern people were convinced that their fates were ultimately in the hands of the gods. In keeping with this (poly)theistic mindset, battles were viewed as contests not just between the human opponents but especially between the deities of the respective sides. A defeat, therefore, was a humiliation not only for the human participants but also for the gods of the losing side. As part of the victor's despoiling the vanquished, the gods of the losing side were typically carried off and deposited in the temple of the winning god(s) as adjunct deities and/or as a sign of the inferiority and subordination of the captured gods. References to this practice are ubiquitous in ancient Near Eastern battle reports (see sidebar "The Treatment of Defeated Deities").[114] Although not an idol, the ark of God was treated as such by the Philistines — and with disastrous results for their own chief deity Dagon (see comment on 5:3–4).

There was Dagon, fallen on his face.... His head and hands had been broken off (5:3–4). Decapitation of defeated foes was a common practice in the ancient Near East and, indeed, in the books

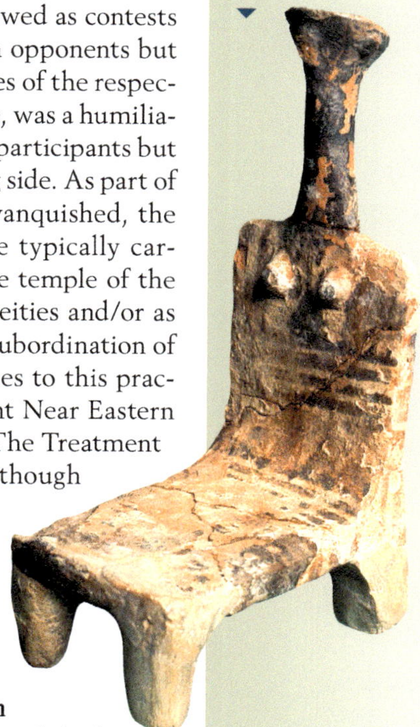

Ashdoda
Z. Radovan/www.BibleLandPictures.com

Hands broken off from a statue at the Ramesseum in Luxor
Manfred Näder, Gabana Studios, Germany

The Ubiquitous God Dagon/Dagan

The worship of Dagon—or Dagan, as he is typically called in ancient Near Eastern literature outside the Bible—is widely attested in Mesopotamia from as early as the third millennium B.C. In the West Semitic city of ancient Ebla, for example, "temples, festivals and even a section of the city were dedicated to Dagan."[A-32] In Palestine, the existence of a Dagon cult already in the second half of the second millennium is evidenced by a proper name in the Amarna Letters, which includes the theophoric element Dagon.

In Philistia—judging from biblical evidence—Dagon was the head of the pantheon of gods. Judges 16:23 speaks of the rulers of the Philistines assembling to offer a "great sacrifice to Dagon their god" after their capture and humiliation of Samson. After King Saul's death, the Philistines place his armor in the temple of their gods and hang his head "in the temple of Dagon" (1 Chron. 10:10). (On archaeological evidence of this temple, see comment on 31:10.)

Extrabiblical confirmation of the importance of Dagon for the Philistines is sometimes sought in the sarcophagus inscription of ʾEshmunʿazor, a fifth-century B.C. king of Sidon, which "refers to Dor and Joppa (modern Jaffa) in the Plain of Sharon as 'the mighty lands of Dagan.' "[A-33] Uncertainty in translation, however, renders this confirmation dubious; a more recent critical edition reads "Dor and Joppa, the majestic corn lands that are in the Plain of Sharon."[A-34] The translational uncertainties arise from the fact that the name of the deity Dagon and the West Semitic word for "grain" involve the same three consonants, *dgn*.

The vexed question of what kind of deity Dagon must have been has elicited several etymological theories. The first, favored by Jerome and some Jewish traditions and promoted by Wellhausen in the nineteenth century, is that Dagon was a fish god, the chief evidence being the similarity of the deity's name to the Hebrew word for fish, *dāg*. As further support, some postulated a relationship between the god Dagon and one "Odakon, a fish-man character in Berossus' *Babyloniaca*."[A-35] While intriguing, not least because this theory enabled Wellhausen (after a slight textual emendation) to propose a solution to the difficult phrase in 1 Samuel 5:4, "only Dagon was left upon him" (Wellhausen read "only his fish-part ..."), this etymology of Dagon has not gained general acceptance.

Sarcophagus of Eshmunazor II, king of Sidon
Brian J. McMorrow

A second theory links the name to the word *dāgān* ("grain"), but again there are problems. Healey points out, for instance, that "the grain-related meaning of the root *dgn* is distinctively West Semitic ... and would not have been known to a Mesopotamian worshipper of the deity."[A-36] There is some evidence, however, that Dagon/Dagan may have been regarded in Mesopotamian religion as inventor of the plow and that his consort may have been the goddess Shala, "an agricultural deity ... represented symbolically by a barley stalk."[A-37] This would lend some support to the "grain" etymology.

A third theory, which goes back to W. F. Albright, links the name Dagon to an Arabic root *dajana* ("to be gloomy, cloudy") and makes Dagon a storm god, a notion that finds some support in the positioning of Dagon as the father of Baʿal, also a god of storm.[A-38]

None of these three major theories has gained a consensus, and while Dagon/Dagan is frequently attested in Mesopotamian literature, these attestations do little to clarify his specific character and role. In a zukru festival tablet from Emar, for instance, Dagan is variously referred to as "Lord of the Brickwork," "Lord of the Firstborn," "Lord of Creation," "Lord of the Camp," "Lord of Habitations," "Lord of the Valley," "Lord of Shade and Protection," "Lord of the Fortress," "Lord of the Quiver," and "Lord of" several villages.[A-39]

Given this evidence, many specific questions regarding Dagon remain open. What can be said is that Dagon was widely worshiped in Mesopotamia over a vast stretch of time (Dagon worship being attested as late as the second-century B.C. Maccabean period; see 1 Macc. 10:83–85), and that his ascendancy to the head of the Philistine pantheon possibly took place after the Sea People's arrival in Canaan.[A-40]

of Samuel (cf. 17:51; 31:4; cf. 18:24). The Assyrian king Tiglath-pileser I (1114–1076 B.C.), for instance, boasts of his defeat of twenty thousand men-at-arms and five kings of the land of Kadmuhu: "Like a storm demon I piled up the corpses of their warriors on the battlefield (and) made their blood flow into the hollows and plains of the mountains. I cut off their heads (and) stacked them like grain piles around their cities."[115] Severing hands (and sometimes other body parts; see comment on 18:24) was a convenient way of tabulating and demonstrating enemy casualties. Dagon's loss of head and hands, therefore, was a sign of unmistakable defeat by the supposedly captive Israelite God, Yahweh, as symbolized by the ark.

Statues and idols of this period were often constructed in several parts, with head, hands, and feet attached to the trunk, so that loss of head and hands would have followed natural breaking points.

Altar and threshhold of Philistine temple at Tell Qasile

Kim Walton, courtesy of the Eretz Israel Museum

Dagon fallen before the ark
Jonathan Walton

Occurrences involving statues, whether of gods or kings, were often interpreted as omens in the ancient Near East, as the following text from Seleucid-period Uruk suggests:

> (An omen reads:) If the image of the king of a country in question or the image of his father or the image of his grandfather falls over and breaks, or its *shape warps*, (this means that) the days of the king of that country will be few in number.[116]

Step on the threshhold (5:5). Peoples of the ancient Near East had a sense of sacred

▸ The Treatment of Defeated Deities

The practice of capturing the gods (i.e., their images or symbols) of vanquished enemies and depositing them in the temples of the victorious deities was widespread in the ancient Near East. In a study of Neo-Assyrian instances of "godnapping," for instance, Holloway remarks that "contrary to the niggardly reports of burnt temples, Assyrian royal inscriptions and palace reliefs are almost voluble with their tales of plundered idols."[A-41] The following texts offer a brief sampling from various quarters. From a royal inscription of the Assyrian king Tiglath-pileser I (1115–1076) comes this inscription:

> With the mighty power of the god Ashur, my lord, I marched to the land of Sugu of the land of habhu, (people) insubmissive to the god Ashur my lord.... I conquered the entire land of Sugu. I brought 25 of their gods, their booty, their possessions, (and) their property.... At that time I donated the 25 gods of those lands, my own booty which I had taken, to adorn the temple of the goddess Ninlil, beloved chief spouse of the god Ashur, my lord, (the temple of) the gods An (and) Adad, (the temple of) the Assyrian Ishtar, the temples of my city, Ashur, and the goddesses of my land.[A-42]

Here is a statement from the chronicle of the fall of Nineveh by the Neo-Babylonian king Nabopolassar (626–605):

> In the month of Ab the king of Akkad (and) his army went upstream to Mane, Sahiri, and Balihu. He plundered them, sacked them extensively, (and) abducted their gods. In the month of Elul the king of Akkad and his army returned and on his way he took (the people of) Hindanu and its gods to Babylon.[A-43]

As a diplomatic or magnanimous gesture, captured deities that fell into the hands of a third party were sometimes returned to their original cities, as in the following notice from the accession year of Nabopolassar (626–605): "The accession year of Nabopolassar: In the month Adar Nabopolassar returned to Susa the gods of Susa whom the Assyrians had carried off and settled in Uruk."[A-44]

Images of deities being carried off as booty
Mark Borisuk/www.BiblePlaces.com

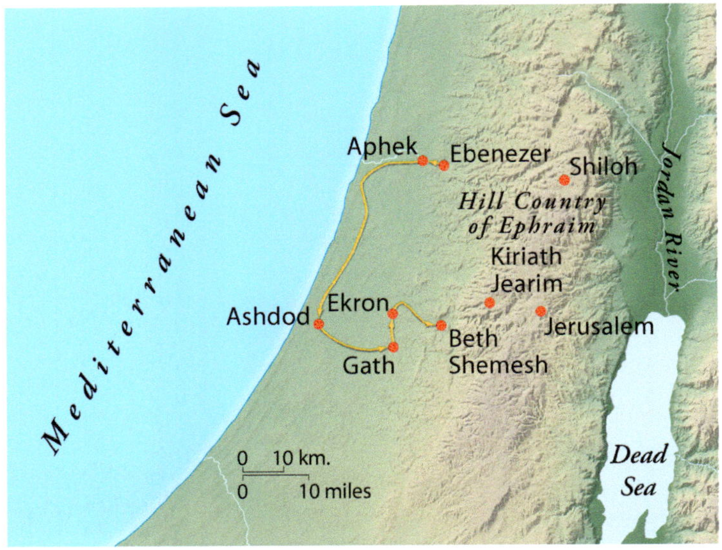

Travels of the Ark

precincts and especially of sacred spaces within the sacred precincts. In Israel, for instance, one may think of the Most Holy Place within the temple. In the book of Ezekiel, thresholds appear to be of special significance (cf. Ezek. 9:3; 10:4, 18; 46:2; 47:1). The avoidance of stepping on the threshold of a sacred precinct was known, if not approved, in Israel (see Zeph. 1:9). Philistine avoidance of thresholds may have begun with the humiliation of Dagon described in the present episode, or it may have been a preexisting practice that the biblical narrator, for purposes of irony and ridicule, links to the fall and destruction of Dagon at the threshold.

Afflicted them with tumors (5:6). Debate over the nature of the Philistine affliction has revolved around two main possibilities: bacillary dysentery and bubonic plague (characterized by tumors, or swellings of the lymph nodes).[117] Both afflictions could be caused by pathogen-bearing rodents,[118] a particular bane for coastal cities such as Ashdod, where infected rodents could arrive by ship. The LXX's longer reading for this verse (cf. NIV text note) mentions rats appearing in the land and bringing "death and destruction." That the Philistines suspected their woes to be the result of infestation may be inferred also from the Hebrew text of the next chapter, which mentions rodents several times (6:4, 11, 18).[119]

Fresco from third century A.D. synagogue of Dura Europos shows the ark of the covenant and the temple of Dagan. Z. Radovan/www.BibleLandPictures.com

Have the ark of the god of Israel moved to Gath (5:8). While the identification of Philistine Gath with the site of Tel Zafit (Tell es-Safi) is not absolutely certain, the balance of evidence seems to support it.[120] The earliest excavation of the site dates back to 1899 and was limited in scope because of human occupation of significant portions of the site and cemeteries in other portions. A surface survey in 1955 yielded pottery evidence sufficient to confirm the occupation of the site in the Bronze and Iron Ages. Ample quantities of Philistine pottery along with the discovery of Hebrew materials (stamps bearing personal names or the phrase l^{e}*melek*, "for/belonging to the king," etc.) attest to the shifting fortunes of this border town, indicated also in the biblical texts (e.g., 7:14). Excavation of the site resumed in the mid-1990s, and the current

Gath (Tell es-Safi)
Joshua Walton, courtesy of Tell es-Safi excavations

excavators are convinced that Tel Zafit is Gath, though the case is not yet proven.[121]

Tel Zafit/Gath lies some twelve miles east-southeast of Ashdod, the city to which the Philistines first brought the ark in the aftermath of the battle of Ebenezer (4:1–5:1). While the biblical text explains why the citizens of Ashdod want to rid themselves of the ark—the "LORD's hand was heavy" upon them, bringing devastation and disease (5:6)—it does not explain why sending the ark to another Philistine city is deemed sensible. According to the LXX (and the Vulgate), the citizens of Gath themselves suggest that the ark be sent to them. Perhaps the answer has to do with the fact that Ashdod was a port city, while Gath lay inland. It is well known that shipping can contribute to the spread of disease by transporting infected carriers such as rodents.

The LXX of 5:6 even mentions rodents bursting forth from ships at Ashdod and precipitating a "deathly panic" in the city. Later references to rats and tumors (6:4–5) confirm the nature of the problem. Perhaps some Philistines were skeptical of any link between the distress in Ashdod and the ark's presence there and preferred a natural explanation of the outbreak of plague. After all, such outbreaks were common enough in port cities. By taking the ark inland to Gath they perhaps hoped to confirm this natural explanation. Immediately and dramatically, however, their experiment failed (5:9).[122]

So they sent the ark of God to Ekron (5:10). The Gittites lose no time in sending the ark on its way, this time to Ekron, another member of the Philistine Pentapolis. Ekron has now been decisively identified with Tel Miqne, a site lying some five miles north of Gath and about eight miles west of Beth Shemesh. As evidence of the frequent difficulty in identifying sites, in the early twentieth century Albright thought Tel Miqne to be the biblical Eltekeh (Josh. 19:44; 21:23). After a survey in 1957, however, Naveh challenged this identification on the grounds that the modest importance of Eltekeh in the Bible seemed inconsistent with the archaeological evidence at Tel Miqne—a fifty-acre site and one of Israel's largest in the Iron Age. At around the same time, an alternate site for Eltekeh was proposed by B. Mazar.[123]

It was not until 1996, however, that an inscription discovered at Tel Miqne effectively put the site's identification as Ekron beyond dispute. In their thirteenth season, directors T. Dothan and S. Gitin discovered the now-famous Ekron Inscription in the destruction debris of a seventh-century temple complex. The inscription reads as follows:

> The temple (house) that Akhayus, son of Padi, son of Ysd, son of Ada, son of Yaʿir, ruler of Ekron, built for PTGYH, his lady. May she bless him, and prote[ct] him, and prolong his days, and may she bless his [l]and.[124]

Ekron (Tel Miqne)
David Hully, Tel Miqne-Ekron Excavation and Publications Project

I. Sztulman, the Tel Miqne-Ekron Excavation and Publications Project

The inscription is complete and appears to be a royal dedicatory inscription.[125]

Two of the individuals named in the inscription appear in other ancient Near Eastern texts. Padi appears as the erstwhile king of Ekron in the Neo-Assyrian annals of Sennacherib:

> The officials, the nobles, and the people of Ekron who had thrown Padi, their king, (who was) under oath and obligation to Assyria, into iron fetters and handed him over in a hostile manner to Hezekiah, the Judean, took fright because of the offense they had committed.[126]

Further on in the inscription, Sennacherib takes credit for restoring Padi to his throne in Ekron:

> I advanced to Ekron and slew its officials and nobles who had stirred up rebellion and hung their bodies on watchtowers all about the city.... I freed Padi, their king, from Jerusalem and set him on the throne as king over them and imposed tribute for my lordship over him.[127]

Akhayus (Achish, though not the Achish of 1 Sam. 21ff.) is listed as "Ikausu, king of Ekron" in Esarhaddon's (680–669 B.C.) account of his Syro-Palestinian campaign.[128] On the basis of this and other evidence, "there is no doubt in the mind of all qualified scholars," as Rainey puts it, that the Ekron Inscription is authentic and "a discovery of the first magnitude."[129]

Tel Miqne, therefore, establishes the location of biblical Ekron in relation to the other cities of the Philistine pentapolis. Only five miles north of Gath, the Ekronites must surely have been aware of the devastation wrought by the ark in both Ashdod and Gath, and they were dismayed that the ark was coming in their direction (5:10b).

Ekron Inscription
Z. Radovan/www.BibleLandPictures.com

The Ark's Return to Israel (6:1–7:1)

Philistines called for the priests and diviners (6:2). In the ancient world, an outbreak of plague was often considered the work of an angry deity, perhaps the god of an enemy people. From ancient Ḫatti, for instance, we have rituals designed to appease an angry god and remove a plague. One begins this way:

> Thus says Uḫḫamūwa, man of Arzawa. If in the land there is continual dying and if some god of the enemy has caused it, then I do as follows: They bring in one wether [i.e., a castrated ram] and they combine blue wool, red wool, yellow-green wool, black wool and white wool and they make it into a wreath and they wreathe the one wether and they drive the wether forth on the road to the enemy and they say to him (the god) as follows: "What god of the enemy has made this plague, now this wreathed wether we have brought for your pacification, O god! Just as a fortress is strong and (yet) is at peace with this wether, may you, the god who has made this plague, be at peace in the same way with the land of Ḫatti. Turn again in friendship to the land of Ḫatti." Then they drive the wreath-sheep into the enemy territory.[130]

In this text, an enemy god is assumed responsible for an outbreak of plague, and in response a chosen animal is decorated and driven back into enemy territory in the hope of pacifying the angry god and ending the plague. This procedure loosely parallels the Philistines' actions in 1 Samuel 6.

A second Hittite ritual text offers further parallels, except that it involves human beings (enemy captives) as scapegoats. The text begins by describing a situation in which a king, having won a victory, leaves the conquered territory only to discover that a plague has broken out among his people, the action perhaps of an angered male or female deity of the enemy land. This is what he is to do:

> As he [is marching a]way from the border of the land of the enemy, they take one prisoner and one woman of the (enemy's) land. [On which(ever) road] the ki[ng] came from the land of the enemy, the king tr[avels] on that road. All of the lords travel with him.

The text then describes how the male prisoner is to be clothed in the king's own garments and addressed as follows:

> If some male god of the enemy land has caused this plague, for him I have just given an adorned man as a substitute. This o[ne is gr]eat with respect to his head, this one is great with respect to his heart, and this [one is gr]eat with respect to his limb. You male god, be pacified with t[his ad]orned man. Turn [agai]n in friendship to the king, the [lords], the ar[my, and] to the land of Ḫatti. […] but [let] this prisoner be[ar] the plague and transport (it) ba[ck into the land of the enemy.][131]

The last lines above describe a kind of apotropaic (turning away) ritual that vaguely resembles the scapegoat ritual in Leviticus 16:7–10, 21–22 and is even closer (though certainly not identical) to the procedure enacted by the Philistines in 1 Samuel 6: Both the Philistines and the Hittites express some uncertainty regarding whether their plague has been caused by an offended deity (cf. 6:9); both return something or someone representative of the plague or its agents back to enemy territory, accompanied by "all the lords" (cf. "the rulers of the Philistines" in 6:12); both are concerned that the apotropaic objects or persons be of value sufficient to pacify the offended deity. The Philistine account is distinctive in its references to sending a "guilt offering" (6:3) and paying "honor to Israel's god" (6:5). See also next comment.

Five gold tumors and five gold rats (6:4). While commentators have traditionally assumed, as do the NIV translators, that a total of ten golden objects are returned with

Egyptians use a calf to get the cows across the Nile River. In the Philistines' test they expected the cows to go to their calves.
Werner Forman Archive

the ark, Tsumura has recently argued on the basis of the structure of ancient Near Eastern lists (specifically in Ugaritic economic texts) that the actual number of objects is probably five. Such lists typically involve several parts: title, item list, and narrative summary. Inspecting 6:17–18 in the light of this structure, Tsumura concludes that verse 18a should be translated not "and the golden mice" but "namely, the golden mice," making this phrase a parallel explication of the golden tumors of verse 17. In other words, the five golden objects are referred to "both as 'golden tumors' and 'golden mice.'"[132] The bubos (tumors) caused by plague sometimes approach the size of a chicken's egg and thus about the size of a mouse. Thus, the golden objects may have in some general sense resembled both mouse and tumor.

More important than the number of golden objects is the Philistine understanding of their function. It seems likely, especially given their stated intent to "pay honor to Israel's god" (v. 5), that the use of gold is a sign of honor and submission. Further, the golden objects (tumors/mice) probably serve an apotropaic function.[133] As Tsumura explains, "making and sending off the golden mice was 'sympathetic magic' whose purpose was to get rid of the disease itself, as represented by the tumor-shaped mice, not to get rid of mice as the cause of the disease."[134] Like the Israelite scapegoat of Leviticus 16 that was to "carry on itself all their sins to a solitary place" (v. 22), the golden tumors/mice are meant to bear away the plague afflicting the Philistines.

A similar procedure involving a mouse is attested in the Hittite Ambazzi ritual, described by Wright[135] and reported by Tsumura. In this Hittite ritual, "the practitioner, after attaching to a mouse a bowstring 'symbolic of the patients' pollution,' declares: 'I have taken away from you evil and I have put it on the mouse. Let this mouse take it to the high mountains, the deep valleys and the distant ways!' (Ambazzi ii 37–40)."[136]

Get a new cart ready (6:7). In keeping with the ritual character of the proceedings, the Philistines prepare a new cart (thus ritually clean), to which they attach cows that have recently calved. The point of the exercise is to determine whether their distress is wrought by Israel's God or has come upon them simply by chance (v. 9). If, contrary to nature, they forsake their calves and, accepting the yoke, pull the cart toward Israelite territory, this will be a sure sign that Yahweh is

Bronze votive statue of a rodent from Twenty-Sixth Dynasty Egypt
Erich Lessing/Art Resource, NY, courtesy of the Kunsthistorisches Museum, Vienna, Austria

Philistine cart from the relief at Medinet Habu of the Sea Peoples' battle with the Egyptians
Todd Bolen/www.BiblePlaces.com

the cause of their recent distress (cf. comment on 6:2). The aims of the Philistine procedure are to ascertain the cause of their affliction, to pacify the offended deity if necessary, and by sympathetic magic to bear the plague away.

Beth Shemesh (6:9). Of several towns bearing the name Beth Shemesh ("house/temple of the sun"), the one in view here was strategically located in the Valley of Sorek, in the northeastern Shephelah (foothills), overlooking a major ancient route linking the coastal plain and the central hill country near Jerusalem. As a border town between Philistine and Israelite territory (see 6:12), Beth Shemesh is a logical destination for the pestilent ark, once the Philistines have tired of feeling the heavy hand of Yahweh and wish to return the ark (5:10–12).

While Beth Shemesh is not mentioned in any known extrabiblical texts, the name seems to have survived in the name of the modern Arabic village, ʿAin Shems ("spring of the sun"). Just to the west of this village lies Tell er-Rumeilah, identified already in 1838 by Edward Robinson as ancient Beth Shemesh. This identification, which locates Beth Shemesh a few miles south of Zorah and Eshtaol and some eight miles east of Ekron, comports nicely with the biblical association of Beth Shemesh with these other sites (Josh. 19:41–42).

Two series of excavations (1911–1912; 1928–1933) unearthed evidence of more or less continuous occupation of the site from the Middle Bronze period to the Byzantine period. The Late Bronze city appears to

Beth Shemesh
Todd Bolen/www.BiblePlaces.com

have been prosperous, yielding archaeological evidence of "fine domestic structures, many cisterns, a smelting furnace, a Proto-Canaanite ostracon, a jewelry hoard, and several tombs."[137] In addition to the Proto-Canaanite ostracon, this level also yielded a cuneiform tablet in Ugaritic.[138] It has been suggested that both texts may be abecedaries, but this remains uncertain.

The Iron Age I period evidences "a large but relatively unplanned village, still somewhat in the Late Bronze tradition, but with Philistine bichrome ware."[139] This Iron Age village, with its apparent Philistine presence, experienced a massive destruction near the beginning of the eleventh century, and it may have been at that time that it returned to the more complete Israelite control indicated by the text before us. That Beth Shemesh was frequently disputed by the Philistines and the Israelites seems clear from 2 Chronicles 28:18.[140]

Kiriath Jearim (6:21). The location of Kiriath Jearim ("city of the forests)" has not been positively identified, though some authorities believe it to be "Tell el-Azhar, near modern Qaryet el-ʿEnab."[141] This would place Kiriath Jearim almost nine miles east-northeast of Beth Shemesh in the general direction of Jerusalem, seven or eight miles farther east. First mentioned as one of the Gibeonite cities in Joshua 9, Kiriath Jearim housed the ark for twenty years (7:2) following its return to Beth Shemesh by the Philistines, until King David brought it to Jerusalem (2 Sam. 6). That the site is sometimes called Kiriath Baal (Josh. 15:60; 18:14), Baalah (15:9), and Baalah Judah (2 Sam. 6:2) may reflect a Canaanite cultic background—Baal was one of Canaan's chief deities, and Baalah is a feminine counterpart. The name change to Kiriath Jearim may be intended to mute this association.[142]

Possible site of Kiriath Jearim
Bible Scene Multimedia/Maurice Thompson

Samuel's Defeat of the Philistines at Mizpah (7:2–17)

Put away their Baals and Ashtoreths (7:4). Samuel's exhortation in 7:3 and the people's response here is indicative of just how syncretistic Israelite worship had become on the eve of the monarchy. But this was not a recent development. Already in the period of the judges, forsaking Yahweh and serving the Baals and the Ashtoreths was a recurrent problem (Judg. 2:11–13 and passim). Baal, whose name means "lord, owner, husband," was the Canaanite god of fertility and storm and as such corresponded to the Mesopotamian god Hadad, whose name means "thunderer."[143] The father of Baal/Hadad according to Mesopotamian and Syrian sources was Dagan/Dagon (see comment on 5:2).

Ashtoreth, or Astarte as she was generally known, was a goddess of fertility and war. Along with Anat, she was a consort of Baal, as is widely attested in biblical and extrabiblical (especially Ugaritic) literature.[144] The vocalization of Ashtoreth is peculiarly biblical and likely represents the replacement of the name's original vowels with the vowels from the Hebrew word *bōšet* ("shame"). The same intentional distortion may lie behind Molech, the biblical name of another Canaanite deity known in Ugaritic as Milku and in Ammonite as Milcom.[145] Perhaps the clearest instances of intentional distortions involve such personal names as Esh-Baal and Merib-Baal (1 Chron. 8:33–34), which appear elsewhere in the Old Testament as Ish-Bosheth and Mephibosheth (2 Sam. 2:8; 9:6).

Baal and, less frequently, Ashtoreth were sometimes associated with specific locations (e.g., Baal Hazor, Baal Hermon, Baal Gad, Baal Meon, Baal Peor), but this should not be construed as suggesting a multiplicity of Baals or Ashtoreths. Ugaritic texts now confirm that the compound names refer simply to "local manifestations" of the two deities.[146] Frequent biblical reference to the Baals and Ashtoreths (as here) may reflect these local manifestations but more likely "is simply a way of speaking about Canaanite gods and goddesses generally."[147] Samuel's exhortation, then, is aimed at the Israelites' ridding themselves of *all* "foreign gods" (cf. 7:3).[148]

Mizpah (7:5). Because Mizpah means something like "place of watching," implying a lookout or high vantage point, it is not surprising that several biblical sites bear the name (e.g., 22:3 mentions a Mizpah in Moab).[149] The site in view here is probably Tell en-Naṣbeh, located some eight miles north of Jerusalem and nine miles northeast of Kiriath Jearim (see comment on 6:21).[150] Support for this identification consists not only of topographical fit but also of the fact that the Arabic name Naṣbeh seems to reflect the original Hebrew name Mizpah.[151]

Five seasons of excavation between 1926 and 1935 uncovered about two-thirds of the 7.7 acre site, revealing occupation as early as the Chalcolithic and Early Bronze I periods, but there is a gap in occupation from the end of this period to the beginning of the Iron Age. Despite extensive erosion of the central part of the site, "the remains uncovered at Tell en-Naṣbeh correlate with what is known of Mizpah" from the biblical text.[152] Mizpah played a prominent role in premonarchic Israel (Judg. 20:1; 21:1–24; 1 Sam. 10:17) and became one of the regular stops in Samuel's circuit (7:16).

They drew water and poured it out before the LORD (7:6). Although this apparently ritual act of pouring out water before the Lord (called a "libation") is without parallel elsewhere in the Old Testament, its association with fasting and confession in the present context (see next comment) suggests that in this instance at least it is meant to imply repentance and a desire to do serious business with God. One is reminded of Hannah's metaphorical reference to "*pouring out* my soul to the LORD" in 1:15. In 2 Samuel 23:15–16, David receives "water from the well near the gate of Bethlehem" but refuses to drink it, choosing rather to pour it out "before the LORD." Given the distinctive circumstances of David's action, this does not offer a valid parallel to the water libation in the present episode.

Water (as well as beer and wine) libations are attested in the ancient Near East. An Old Babylonian libation prayer, for instance, includes the following: "Sin [a god], you are god of heaven and earth. In the morning I am

Baal above the waters with lightning bolt
Marie-Lan Nguyen/Wikimedia Commons, courtesy of the Louvre

▸ A Hymn to Baal

Baal sits enthroned like the sitting of
a mountain
Haddu li[es in wait] like the subterranean waters,
In the midst of his mountain, the
divine Zaphon,
On his [pleasant] mountain of victory.
Seven lightnings [are in his hand],
Eight storehouses of thunder—
The shaft of lightning he [brandishes.][A-45]

Mizpah (Tell en-Naṣbeh)
Todd Bolen/www.BiblePlaces.com

pouring water to you for the family of Sin-nasir son of Ipqu-Annunitum. Release the family of Sin-nasir son of Ipqu-Annunitum, that they may eat his bread and drink his water."[153] This was apparently a water libation over the grave of an ancestor, probably repeated at regular intervals. Because of its distinctive context, it does little to elucidate the significance of the Israelites' water libation in the present episode, other than to attest to the general practice of pouring out water libations.

More generally, water libations in Mesopotamia and in Syria-Canaan seem to be offered as drink for the gods,[154] just as animal sacrifices represented food for the gods. For ancient Israel, however, such practices appear to have been emptied of their literal significance even while being retained as ritual features.

Luxor relief of priest pouring out libation
Frederick J. Mabie

They fasted (7:6). On fasting in the ancient Near East, see comment on 2 Samuel 1:12.

Samuel was leader of Israel (7:6). The word rendered "leader" (*šōpēṭ*) is elsewhere rendered "judge," and indeed the Semitic word in view has been shown in various contexts to denote a leader in the sense of ruler or deliverer, as well as judge in the more administrative sense.[155] At Mari, for instance, the *šāpiṭum* is described as a provincial or district ruler or administrator. Thus, Samuel is depicted as combining several roles, namely, prophet, priest, and judge. The transitional period in which Samuel serves, along with his own personality and divine calling, may well account for his combining of roles that later in Israel's development are kept separate.[156]

When the Philistines heard that Israel had assembled (7:7). That word of an Israelite assembly in progress raises concern among the Philistines is understandable, given the fact that in the ancient Near East impending battles were typically preceded by cultic assemblies designed to entreat the deity for a favorable oracle. Babylonian and Assyrian historical texts ranging in time from Hammurabi (eighteenth century) to the siege of Jerusalem by Sennacherib a thousand years later make frequent reference to (trust-inspiring) oracles of the deity/deities prior to battle.[157] Mediation of the oracle through prophets or priests is not explicitly mentioned in these passages, though the king sometimes assumes the title of high priest.[158]

An inscription from the reign of Ashurnasir-apli II (884–858 B.C.), however, distinguishes "king" and "diviner" among the conquered forces of Karduniash, and it is particularly noteworthy that the diviner is also described as a "commanding officer," suggesting a combined religious and military role.[159] Mesha, king of Moab, is commanded by Chemosh to attack Nebo in Israel,[160] but again the means by which this message was delivered is not described.

Of special interest is the eighth-century Zakkur Inscription written in Old Aramaic, in which King Zakkur of Hamath and Luᶜath, under threat from Barhadad of Aram and an alliance of seventeen kings, receives an "oracle of salvation" through the mediation of "seers" and "messengers."[161] It is in the Mari letters, however, that prophetic involvement in military affairs is most apparent.[162] The Ugaritic Prayer-Song of El[163] provides a parallel example of the offering of prayer and sacrifices in a situation of (apparently military) crisis (see next comment).

In the Old Testament it was customary to "consecrate" war and to speak of warriors as "consecrated." An attempt to consult Yahweh, through priest or prophet or otherwise, generally preceded a battle and was sometimes accompanied by sacrifice and/or prayer.[164] In the light of this, it is understandable that the Philistines are concerned that the assembly of Israelites to Mizpah at a time unconnected to a regular festival may signal an imminent war.

Samuel took a suckling lamb and offered it up as a whole burnt offering (7:9). Samuel's sacrifice accompanies his crying out to Yahweh in a time of military distress. This combination of prayer and sacrifice in a context of military crisis is found also in a Ugaritic prayer-song to the god El, excerpts from which read as follows:

> Be gracious, O El!
> Be a support, O El!
> Be salvation, O El!
> O El, hasten, come swiftly!
> To the help of Zaphon,
> to the help of Ugarit.
> With the lance, O El,
> with the upraised (?), O El,
> With the battle-axe, O El,
> with the shattering, O El.
> Because of the burnt offering, O El,
> because of the appointed sacrifice (?), O El,
> because of the morning sacrifice, O El.[165]

Assyrian camp with sacrifice being offered at top left
Todd Bolen/www.BiblePlaces.com

The LORD thundered ... against the Philistines (7:10). See comment on 2:10.

Beth Car (7:11). The location of Beth Car, not mentioned elsewhere in the Old Testament, is unknown, unless we are to assume a corruption of another name, such as Beth Horon, which lay some six miles west of Mizpah.

Samuel took a stone and set it ... named it Ebenezer (7:12). The use of (often inscribed) boundary stones was widespread throughout the ancient Near East.[166] The stones were sometimes named and believed to be under divine protection. Curses against those who moved them were sometimes included in the inscription. This stone erected by Samuel is named Ebenezer, which is not to be confused with the site called Ebenezer in 4:1 and 5:1 (see comment on 4:1). The present Ebenezer does, however, recall that earlier episode in which the Israelites, having tried to force Yahweh's hand by bringing his ark into battle, suffered defeat at the hands of the Philistines. Having now (for the time being at least) learned their lesson (cf. 7:4, 6, 8), the Israelites realize a great victory over the Philistines.

Samuel's setting up of a memorial stone with the name Ebenezer—which sounds like "Stone of Help"—and with the explanation "thus far the LORD has helped us" both acknowledges Yahweh's decisive role in the victory and serves as an oblique reminder of the strikingly different results brought about by presumption, on the one hand, and by penitence, on the other. Samuel's explanation may carry both a spatial and a temporal meaning. Spatially, Samuel is proclaiming that Yahweh has given Israel victory up to the place marked by the boundary stone. Temporally, the sense may be that to this point in time Yahweh has helped Israel against its foes. The temporal sense takes on ironic significance in the light of the succeeding chapter, in which the Israelites insist that they be given a human king, such as other nations have, "to lead us and to go out before us and fight our battles" (8:20).

The towns from Ekron to Gath that the Philistines had captured from Israel (7:14). As border towns between Philistine territory to the west and Israelite territory to the east, the towns in the vicinity of Ekron and Gath doubtless changed hands from time to time, depending on which power was in the ascendancy. On Ekron and Gath, see comments on 5:10 and 5:8 respectively.

There was peace between Israel and the Amorites (7:14). In 1–2 Samuel, the Amorites are mentioned only here and at 2 Samuel 21:2 (the Gibeonites being survivors from a former Amorite population). Along with the Canaanites, the Amorites are frequently mentioned as among the early inhabitants of the land of promise prior to the arrival of Israel. The full geographic range of the Amorites is much wider, including northern Syria and Mesopotamia from as early as 3000 B.C. Mendenhall argues, in fact, that "from the Middle Bronze Age on there was no region of the Levant that had not been influenced by the Amorite language and culture in various ways and to various degrees."[167] Their name is attested in Sumerian and Akkadian, and sounding like "west(erner)" seems at times to have geographic as well as ethnic significance.

Amorite power and geographic distribution peaked in the middle of the second millennium and declined thereafter, so that by this episode they are counted among the several minor powers in Canaan.[168] When the term is nevertheless used in a general sense in the biblical narratives, it may refer to inhabitants of the more mountainous regions of the land, while the "Canaanites" inhabit the coast and valleys.[169] Thus, this notice seems to suggest that in Samuel's day Israel experiences a degree of peace with those populations remaining in its heartland.

Samuel continued as judge ... went on a circuit (7:15–16). Assuming that "Bethel" is to be located at or near Beitin (but see comment on 10:3) and that "Gilgal" is located in the vicinity of Jericho (see comment on 10:7–8), Samuel's circuit takes him on a

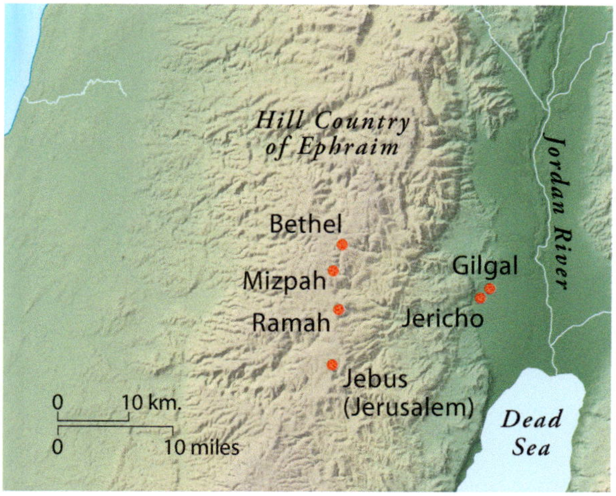

journey of more than thirty miles. As a possible analog to this circuit, Malamat has drawn attention to a letter from Asqudum, "the chief diviner at the Mari palace in the Old Babylonian period," to Yasmah-Addu, "the viceroy of Mari," that appears to describe a four-town circuit in which Asqudum performs extispicies (inspections of the entrails of sacrificial animals for purposes of divination).[170] The towns he visited were Saggaratum (near the confluence of the Habur and Euphrates), Terqa (Tell Ashara), Ṣuprum or Šuprum (Tell Abu Hassan? on the east bank of the Euphrates near Mari), and his home-base at Mari (Tell Hariri on the west bank of the Euphrates). A circuit among these four cities covered over a hundred miles.[171] The relevant portion of the Mari text in question is translated by W. Heimpel as follows:

> [To] *my* lord] Yasmah-Addu *speak*! Your servant Ašqudum (says), "As of my arrival in Terqa, Tarim-Šakim arrived, and I asked him the following: I (said), 'Did Zunan perform extispicies for the well-being of the land and the strong cities?' He answered me as follows: 'He did not make (them).' I returned with him to Saggaratum at the clearing of this month, and I made extipicies for the well-being of the city of Saggaratum for 6 months, and the extispicies were sound. And prior to my (departure) I will make (extispicies) for the fortress of my lord, Terqa, Ṣuprum, and Mari, and I will promptly *write* a full report to my lord.

The text continues for a few lines describing the favorable extispicy.[172] Heimpel's rendering implies that Asqudum intended to complete extispicies for the other three cities while still in Saggaratum, but it rests on a textual emendation. The text as it stands may suggest that Asqudum desired to perform extispicies in each of the towns, beginning with the northernmost (see map). At the end of the day, it remains uncertain whether Malamat's suggested analogy to Samuel's circuit is apt, especially when one considers the general mobility of administrative officials from Mari: "Many officials spent their careers moving back and forth between Mari and the provincial centers."[173] Samuel's circuit, in any case, was a regular, annual affair.

He built an altar there to the LORD (7:17). With Shiloh being destroyed at the hands of the Philistines in the aftermath of Israel's loss in 1 Samuel 4, sacrifices can no longer be offered there (on Shiloh, see comment on 1:3). Whether Samuel's altar at Ramah is intended for sacrifice or merely as a memorial is not specified by the text, but the former seems more likely. While the proliferation of local altars is discouraged after the establishment of Jerusalem as Israel's central sanctuary, there was no absolute prohibition at earlier periods, only a command not to sacrifice in the Canaanite way (cf. Deut. 12).

Israel Demands a King (8:1–22)

Samuel ... appointed his sons as judges ... they served at Beersheba (8:1–2). While Samuel's sons bear pious Israelite names (v. 2), their behavior proves anything but pious (v. 3). Unless Samuel has grown as dull as Eli, his appointment of men of such poor character to judge Israel raises questions.

Perhaps an answer is suggested by the rather remote location of Beersheba and its

Relief of ruler (Hammurabi) making report of his justice to the god Shamash
Soumit Nandi, courtesy of the Louvre

insignificance in Samuel's day. In the biblical tradition, Beersheba, in the Negev, was early considered the southern extremity of the territory of Israel, in the same way that Dan was considered the northernmost city (note the expression "from Dan to Beersheba" in, e.g., Judg. 20:1; 2 Sam. 3:10). The modern identification of Beersheba's precise location, however, is debated. The ancient name seems to be preserved in the modern name Bir es-Seba^c, which designates a section of the industrial heart of the modern city of Beersheba, but the most likely location of biblical Beersheba now appears—in the light of current knowledge—to be Tell es-Seba^c located some three miles to the east.[174]

It may be, as Manor observes, that Beersheba was "a dual site consisting of the royal city (i.e., the tell) along with a civilian settlement further W on the banks of the wadi (where the modern city now stands)."[175] Rainey argues the two sites (Bir es-Seba^c and Tell es–Seba^c) may both have had the same name in antiquity, thus placing Beersheba among other ancient examples of two cities with the same name.[176] Tell es-Seba^c is a small mound of only 2.5 acres, and excavation at the site suggests that the population in Samuel's day (eleventh century B.C.) was small, perhaps fewer than two hundred people.[177] Excavator Herzog estimates that a community of perhaps twenty families could have lived in the settlement in the first half of the eleventh century and notes that the first houses at the site appear to have been built in the third quarter of the eleventh century,[178] the approximate time of Samuel's judgeship. Given this situation, Samuel's appointment of his two sons as judges in Beersheba is a minor appointment indeed.[179]

Beersheba
Todd Bolen/www.BiblePlaces.com

Accepted bribes and perverted justice (8:3). It is not just in the Bible that accepting bribes and perverting justice are considered serious offenses. In a well-attested Hittite text containing instructions from "His Majesty Arnuwanda the great king" to his officials in border towns, the king insists that "border governors" (or "margraves") are to judge each "case properly and make things right" or else refer it to the king himself. The margrave is specifically warned against perverting justice: "Let no one take a bribe. He is not to make the stronger case the weaker, or the weaker the stronger one. Do what (is) just."[180]

They have rejected me as their king (8:7). Not just in Israel, but in the ancient Near East generally, kingship was intertwined with religion. While in Egypt the king himself was worshiped as divine, in Mesopotamia kingship was regarded as "one of the basic institutions of human life devised by the gods for mankind." The opening words of the famous Sumerian King List (ca. 2100), for example, read, "When the kingship was lowered from heaven, the kingship was in Eridu."[181] The concept of divine sponsorship of kingship was foundational in the cognitive environment of the ancient Near East. Commenting on the Neo-Assyrian period, Holloway writes:

> The Neo-Assyrian royal titularies, narrative inscriptions, astrological prognostications and unctuously flattering correspondence hammer away at the theme of the unique proximity of the king to the divine realm and extol his god-like powers. The kings were summoned prenatally to kingship, suckled by goddesses, warned by eclipses and other portents of imminent personal hazards, and succored by upbeat, motherly prophecies uttered by goddesses. Kings, like the gods, strode into battle surrounded by the *melammu*, a radiant, terrifying nimbus devastating to foes ... and kings embodied godlike wisdom and could be characterized as the very image of the gods. The kings were not members of the state pantheon, but they dwelt in closer physical and ontological proximity to the gods than any other mortals.[182]

In Israel, the emphasis falls on God himself as the Great King, with the human king to serve not as a demigod, but as vice-regent (vassal) to the Great King (cf. comments on 2:10). The "law of the king" (Deut. 17:14–20) makes it clear that the king in Israel is to be subservient to the divine law and must not "consider himself better than his brothers" (v. 20). Though 1 Samuel 8:7 does not elaborate, something in the elders' demand for a king "such as all the other nations have" represents a rejection of the supreme kingship of Yahweh, and this is a serious sin indeed (cf. 10:19; 12:17, 19, 25).

This is what the king ... will do (8:11–17). Whatever advantages the elders imagine a king like those of the nations will bring, Samuel—speaking for Yahweh—is intent on making plain the disadvantages that a human king, particularly if self-serving, will bring.

Samuel begins his warning with a word about sons. Sons were particularly important in the ancient Near East—for reasons relating

Runners by ruler's chariot
Todd Bolen/www.BiblePlaces.com

to the security and continuity of the family line—but, as Samuel warns, the king "will take your sons and make them serve with his chariots and horses, and they will run in front of his chariots" (8:11). The practice Samuel describes finds a loose analogy in a Hittite text prescribing the protocol to be followed by the royal guard when the king travels. One section reads: "The guard sets up the stool. The king comes forth. The chief of the palace staff is holding him by the hand. The king sits in the carriage. The officers of the spear-men bow. Then they run (up) and walk in front. They march with the man of the [golden] spear."[183]

Apart from the fact that the sons will be taken from the family to serve the king, Samuel's warning that they will be required to run in front of the king's chariot may not have sounded particularly negative to Israel's elders. Indeed, a couple of eighth-century Aramaic inscriptions seem to suggest that "running at the wheel" of one's lord was an honor,[184] though the fact remains that the absence of sons will prove a hardship, for example, at harvest time. Perhaps Samuel's warning progresses from the less obviously to the more obviously abusive royal practices (cf. 8:18).

In any case, a centralized monarchical government will require courtiers and servants of the court, agricultural workers for the king's fields, artisans to craft the king's weapons (v. 12), domestic workers to prepare meals for the court and to keep the palace (v. 13), and a standing army to protect it all (vv. 11–12). To make all this happen, there will be royal taxation and expropriation of "the best" of the fields, flocks, and servants of the people (vv. 14–17). The end result, Samuel warns, is that "you yourselves will become his slaves" (v. 17).

While some older biblical commentators supposed that the abuses Samuel describes in this passage reflect the bitter experiences of a later writer familiar with Israel's own kings, Mendelsohn insists that Samuel's "summary of 'the manner of the king' does not constitute 'a rewriting of history' by a late opponent of kingship but represents an eloquent appeal to the people by a contemporary of Saul not to impose upon themselves a Canaanite institution alien to their way of life."[185] Specifically, he shows on the basis of texts from Alalakh and Ugarit that Samuel's warnings about the costs of a standing army with chariot forces, royal expropriation of land, taxation including the royal tithe, and corvée labor all reflect an accurate understanding of "the semi-feudal Canaanite society as it existed prior to and during the time of Samuel."

Tribe of Benjamin

As regards Samuel's warnings about a chariot force, we know that Israel's neighbors were already making use of chariots when the Israelites arrived in Canaan (cf. the coalition of northern kings in Joshua 11 and the Canaanites of Josh. 17 who lived in the plain), but we are not told whether King Saul ever acquired them. David captured many and destroyed most (2 Sam. 8:4; 10:18), but the actions of his sons Absalom and Adonijah, both of whom made a bid for the throne, strongly recall Samuel's warning (see 2 Sam. 15:1 and 1 Kings 1:5, respectively).

Samuel Anoints Saul (9:1–10:8)

A Benjamite, a man of standing ... Kish (9:1). As a small tribe wedged between the two more powerful tribes—Judah to the south and Epharaim to the north—and as the home of the yet to be conquered city of Jerusalem, Benjamin was an ideal choice as home of Israel's first centralized regime, since it would be less likely to provoke jealousy among the other tribes.

Saul, an impressive young man without equal (9:2). While commentators usually assume that Saul at this point in his life was a diffident youth, the emphasis in his introduction is on physical stature and good looks, not youth.[186] In the ancient Near East, a high priority was placed on the commanding appearance and heroic qualities of leaders. For example:

- Sargon of Akkad receives the appellation "King of Battle."[187]
- King Tukulti-Ninura of Assyria is described as "glorious in his heroism ... reckoned as flesh godly in his limbs ... cast sublimely from the womb of the gods."[188]
- Nebuchadnezzar I of Babylon is described as a "valiant male whose strength is directed towards doing battle."[189]
- Of the legendary Gilgamesh it is said, "Two-thirds of him is god, [one-third of him is human]. The form of his body [...] He is made fearful like a wild ox, lofty."[190]

By ancient Near Eastern standards, therefore, Saul shows great potential. By biblical standards, however, the focus of his introduction exclusively on external qualities, with no reference to Yahweh being with him (contrast the introduction of David in 16:18), is unsettling.

Go and look for the donkeys (9:3). While donkeys may not enjoy a high reputation among nonagrarian people (who associate them more with stubbornness than utility), they were valued in the ancient Near East. The early second-millennium Egyptian Protests of the Eloquent Peasant revolves around the peasant's loss of donkeys (through his opponent's trickery) and their eventual recovery.[191] Also worth mentioning is a letter from Alalakh seeking the return of stolen donkeys.[192] Most noteworthy is a letter from the diviner Asqudum to King

King Ashurnasirpal II holding the symbols of sovereignty
Werner Forman Archive/The British Museum

Donkey relief from tomb of Urirenptah
Lenka Peacock, courtesy of the British Museum

Zimri-Lim of Mari, in which Asqudum reports on the king's acquisition of a donkey and then describes the loss of some other donkeys in a provincial town in the far north of the kingdom of Mari.[193]

What these parallels demonstrate is that while Saul's search for lost donkeys over a large area may strike the modern reader as odd, it is fully in keeping with life in the ancient Near East, where animals "at times went astray and search parties were sent out in order to return the missing animals."[194] But as important as recovering his father's lost livestock is, it pales in comparison to the truly momentous events of the day, when Saul encounters Samuel.

Ephraim ... Shalisha ... Shaalim (9:4). Ephraim refers to the tribal territory of that name. Shalisha and Shaalim have generally eluded identification.[195] Among the most popular speculations are Baal Shalisha and Shaalbim, respectively, lying at the northwest and southwest extremities of Ephraimite territory. If these identifications are correct, then Saul's search covers some sixty miles over its three-day duration.[196]

What can we give the man? (9:7). In the ancient Near East, prophets, prophetesses, diviners, and the like were sought out for consultation on all manner of issues ranging from health and fertility to cultic observance, political fortune, military enterprises, and lost items. Recipients of services naturally expected to pay and generally did so without need of reminder.[197] Remuneration for solicited prophetic services is well attested in the Mari corpus,[198] where payment is occasionally even demanded. In one text, a "shock-head of Dagan" ("shock-head" refers to a female given to trances and with unkempt hair), after delivering a prophetic message concerning the king, requests "a straight ewe-wool garment and a nose-rope."[199]

Unsolicited prophetic revelations, which describe most biblical prophecies, were often delivered without expectation of payment. In fact, the biblical writing prophets express disapproval of those who prophesy for money; Amos denies being such a prophet (Amos 7:12), and Micah explicitly condemns prophets who divine for money (Mic. 3:5, 11; cf. Jer. 6:13). The attitude of preliterary Yahwistic prophecy is less clear, however, making it difficult to decide whether Saul's concern to pay the "man of God" is normal or is, as Josephus suggests (*Ant.* 6.48), yet another hint of religious ignorance.[200]

Stone weights inscribed with their values
Michael French, courtesy of the British Museum

Quarter of a shekel of silver (9:8). Silver was a common form of currency in Canaan as well as in Assyria and Babylonia. In Hebrew, the word for "silver" eventually came to mean "money." Coinage was not invented until the seventh century B.C., but as Youngblood observes, "it is likely that much earlier there were pieces of silver of fixed weight ... for use in trade and commerce."[201] A quarter shekel weighed less than a half-ounce and likely represented several days' wages for any ordinary worker. (David later pays fifty shekels for the oxen and threshing floor of Araunah [2 Sam. 24:24].) It seems likely, then, that the quarter shekel available to Saul would be an appropriate payment for a solicited inquiry.[202]

They met some girls coming out to draw water (9:11). At least until underground water systems were developed (see comment on 2 Sam. 2:13; 5:8), village dwellers had to make periodic trips to draw water from the nearest source, often near the base of the hills on which most towns were situated. Wells or springs, located on the outskirts of towns, were often the places where newcomers to town first met townspeople; they were usually women, who typically bore the responsibility of porting water.

The people have a sacrifice at the high place (9:12). "High places" (Heb. *bāmôt*; sg. *bāmâ*) are mentioned over a hundred times in the Old Testament, but their precise "nature, appearance, and architecture are disputed."[203] The word is used in the Old Testament in its mundane senses to mean "hill, height, ridge," and in a cultic sense to mean a sacred "high place," either a cultic site on a natural elevation or a raised platform.[204] Whether high places were open-air or enclosed structures is debated.[205] Often sites of Canaanite worship, "high places" were viewed in the Old Testament as endangering the purity of Israelite worship (see, e.g., Num. 33:52; Deut. 12:2–3; Jer. 2:20).

Nevertheless, in the period between the destruction of the sanctuary at Shiloh and the building of the temple in Jerusalem, worship of Yahweh at "high places" was sometimes conducted without explicit censure, as here. After the division of the kingdom, worship at "high places" constituted a severe problem both in the north (cf. 1 Kings 12:31–32; 13:32–34) and the south (cf. 14:22–24). Removal of "high places" became a major goal of reform movements under southern kings such as Hezekiah (e.g., 2 Kings 18:4) and Josiah (e.g., 23:5).

The LORD had revealed this to Samuel (9:15). On the various modes of divine revelation, see comment on 28:6.

Eat, because it was set aside for you for this occasion (9:24). Having instructed the cook to set aside a special cut of meat (v. 23), namely, the "shank" (v. 24; NIV reads "leg"), Samuel has it placed before Saul. Special portions of meat were often reserved for important personages, such as an officiating priest, who was to receive the right shank of the sacrificial animal (Lev. 7:32–34). That a special portion has been set aside for Saul in advance of his arrival suggests both the momentousness of the occasion and its providential direction.

Samuel talked with Saul on the roof of his house (9:25). While archaeologists are generally only able to excavate the foundations of houses,[206] Israelite houses at the time of David typically included a second story and a flat roof. The main living space may have been on the second floor, with the ground floor serving for storage, stabling of animals, and the like. In warm weather, the upper story and even the flat roof of the house offered cooler living and sleeping conditions because of better ventilation.[207]

Samuel took a flask of oil and poured it on Saul's head (10:1). The word rendered "flask" connotes a small jug or vial. Special oils and cosmetics, because of their preciousness, were often held in tiny containers in antiquity, as today.[208] An archaeological find made in the 1980s in

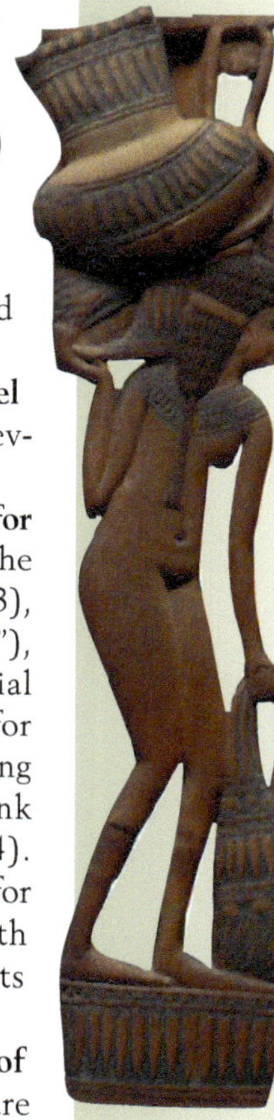

Egyptian carving of woman carrying water
Rama/Wikimedia Commons, courtesy of the Louvre

Philistine-era anointing vessel
Z. Radovan/www.BibleLandPictures.com

the Judean desert, though dated to a thousand years after Saul, may offer an example of a small jug containing ceremonial oil. Archaeologists working in the vicinity of Qumran discovered a small pottery flask (five inches in diameter) carefully hidden three feet underground in a cave some two miles north of Qumran. Astonishingly, the juglet still contained oil after two thousand years! Tests indicated the oil to be of vegetable origin, possibly balsam, because rare balsam trees grew in the area in antiquity. The jug was wrapped in palm fibers, some of which still survive. The care with which the flask was wrapped and hidden underground suggests that the oil it contained was special, perhaps oil for some kind of anointing.[209]

Has not the LORD anointed you leader over his inheritance? (10:1). See comments on anointing at 2:10 and 16:1. The term rendered "leader" in this context means something like "king-elect"[210] or "one who is designated as ruler of the people."[211] Yahweh's "inheritance" comprised both the land and the people of Israel (see Deut. 32:9). In acceding to the people's demand for a king, Yahweh does not relinquish his rights as the Great King over his inheritance to the human monarch. Rather, the human king is to be Yahweh's vice-regent and is to subordinate himself within an authority structure that Yahweh himself will stipulate (10:25).

Prior to the monarchy, judge-deliverers were raised up by Yahweh on an ad hoc basis and both received and carried out Yahweh's instructions. With the inauguration of kingship, however, the tasks of receiving and carrying out Yahweh's instructions were usually divided between prophet and king. The former were Yahweh's mouthpiece to the king, and the king was to carry out Yahweh's instructions as received through the prophet. This authority structure is evidenced in the first charge Saul receives in 10:7–8, and grasping its significance is essential to understanding the nature of the eventual breach between Saul and Samuel (and Yahweh!).

Rachel's tomb (10:2). The location of Rachel's tomb has, understandably, not been positively identified. One theory places it near Kiriath Jearim (see comment on 6:21), some eight miles west of Samuel's home in Ramah.[212] Well-known places, tombs, trees, and even geographical features often served in antiquity to give orientation.

Portion of an Egyptian relief shows a king being anointed as life is pouring forth from the jars.
Manfred Näder, Gabana Studios, Germany

Gibeah of God, where there is a Philistine outpost (10:5). The association of "Gibeah of God" with a Philistine outpost suggests that it should probably be equated with "Geba" of 13:3, also associated with a Philistine outpost (see sidebar on "Outposts in Subject Territories"). Geba, in turn, is probably to be equated with Gibeah of Benjamin/Gibeah of Saul (see comment on 10:26). Thus, Saul must be well aware that his hometown hosts an occupying Philistine force. The significance of Samuel's explicit reference to the Philistines may be understood in relation to 9:16 and to Saul's first charge as "king-elect" (see comment on 10:7–8).

▸ Outposts in Subject Territories

The stationing of outposts, or garrisons, in subject territories was a common means in the ancient Near East of maintaining some measure of control over subject territories (cf. David's own stationing of garrisons in "the Aramean kingdom of Damascus" [2 Sam. 8:6] and "throughout Edom" [2 Sam. 8:14]). The precise meaning of the Hebrew word *n^eṣîb* ("garrison, outpost") is debated, as it can also mean something like "governor" or even "stele" (something set in place).[A-46] In any case, the presence of the one may have entailed the presence of the other. King Shamshi-Adad I of the Old Assyrian period (early second millennium) mentions all three at some point in his inscriptions:

> I established my great name and my steles in the land of Lebanon on the shore of the Great Sea.[A-47] I kissed the feet of the god Adad, my lord, and reorganized that land. I installed my governors everywhere.... I captured all the fortified cities of the land of Arbela. I established my garrisons everywhere.[A-48]

Relatively few such garrisons, or small fortresses, have been excavated in the ancient Near East, as archaeologists have tended to focus on larger sites. But a few locations may be mentioned. For Mesopotamia, Roaf describes a "small hilltop settlement at Yemniyeh on the Euphrates [which] has been interpreted as a ninth-century military guardpost," as well as a "square, compact mud-brick fortress on the top of Tell Gubba," which "may have marked the border between Media and Babylonia in the early sixth century."[A-49] In Israel, the Iron Age II fortress at Arad in the Negev is worthy of mention.[A-50]

Iron Age outpost fort at Arad
Todd Bolen/www.BiblePlaces.com

Prophetic Bands and Music

On the eve of the monarchy in Israel, prophetic bands described as "sons of the prophets" began to appear, often under the leadership of a prominent individual. Samuel himself presided over such a group of prophets (19:20), in a role similar to that of Elisha in 2 Kings 2; 6:1; 9:1. Particularly in times of spiritual decline and apostasy, this company of prophets constituted zealous defenders of true religion. As the monarchy developed, these prophetic bands "served as a refreshing counterpoise to the potential despotism of the monarchy and the tendency toward formalism in the priesthood."[A-51] It is one such band that Saul will encounter at Gibeah of God, and they will be playing musical instruments and prophesying.

That "music was often associated with prophecy in antiquity," as King and Stager note,[A-52] seems a reasonable assumption, though extrabiblical evidence of this association is difficult to come by. Some have suggested that music may have induced a kind of prophetic ecstasy, such as is attested among Mari prophets.[A-53] The Bible does attest to a role for music in inducing prophetic receptivity (2 Kings 3:15–16), but in contexts where prophecy devolves into erratic behavior the focus tends not to be on true worshipers of Yahweh but on those at odds with him (e.g., Saul in 1 Sam. 18:10; the prophets of Baal in 1 Kings 18:29). Biblical prophets are occasionally referred to as "madmen" (2 Kings 9:11; Jer. 29:26; Hos. 9:7), though never by the authoritative narrator with respect to true prophets of Yahweh.

Whatever may have been the effect, the procession of prophets that Saul was to encounter at Gibeah of God, according to Samuel, would be bearing musical instruments—lyres, tambourines, flutes, and harps—and be making music as they went. Much mystery surrounds the specific connotations of the rather extensive vocabulary of music in the Bible, but Israel's stock of musical instruments included stringed, percussion, and wind instruments, such as were known among Israel's ancient Near Eastern neighbors generally. A particularly interesting archaeological find from the Philistine city of Ashdod is a terra cotta cult stand with five figures, four of which appear to be playing musical instruments: "cymbals, double pipe, lyre, and tambourine."[A-54]

Philistine cult stand from eleventh-tenth-century Ashdod is decorated with musicians
Z. Radovan/www.BibleLandPictures.com

The "flute" was likely a "double pipe," such as is illustrated by a terra cotta figurine discovered at Tel Malḫata. The "tambourine" was a "small, shallow, handheld frame drum," stretched with animal skin and played with the hand.[A-55] The metal disks of modern tambourines were almost certainly absent. Archaeologists in Mesopotamia and the Levant have discovered numerous female figurines holding disk-like objects that, according to the detailed studies of Carol Meyers, represent tambourines.[A-56] On the harp and the lyre, see comment on 16:16.[A-57]

A procession of prophets ... with lyres, tambourines, flutes and harps being played before them ... prophesying (10:5). Though prophets and prophecy were certainly not unknown in Israel's premonarchical period—e.g., Abraham, Moses, and Miriam are described as prophets—it was with the inception of the monarchy that the prophetic office and the prophetic guild came into their own. This statement reflects the fact that prophets such as Samuel, Elijah, and Elisha served in the election, rejection, and instruction of the king. F. M. Cross observes that "the institution of prophecy appeared simultaneously with kingship in Israel and fell with kingship," though of course prophets such as Haggai and Zechariah continued to function in the postexilic period.[213] See sidebar on "Prophetic Bands and Music."

The Spirit of the LORD will come upon you in power ... prophesy ... be changed into a different person (10:6). The range of activities of the "Spirit of God" or "Spirit of Yahweh" in the Old Testament can be understood by consulting such passages as Genesis 1:2; 41:38; Exodus 31:3; Numbers 24:2; Judges 3:10. Bestowal of the divine Spirit often connoted God's empowering of an individual to accomplish a particular task. Conversely, the Spirit of God might thwart someone intent on a particular action (e.g., 1 Sam. 19:23).

Verse 10 describes the "Spirit of God" coming upon Saul "in power," a verbatim repetition of what is often said of Samson (Judg. 14:6, 19; 15:14). Such visitations of the Spirit appear to have been temporary and designed to empower (or prevent) a particular action. Dignity and the power to command authority were in the ancient Near East often linked to divine prerogative and were endowments for which one might pray.[214] In Akkadian, oath formulae often invoked or implied the *adû* (majesty?) of the king. This *adû* was not the oath itself but was "regarded as a special supernatural manifestation of royal power comparable but not identical to 'life' in the Hebrew oath."[215]

In the present epsiode, the divine Spirit fundamentally—if temporarily—alters Saul ("different person" [v. 6]; "changed Saul's heart" [v. 9]) in order that "all these signs" might be "fulfilled that day" (v. 9). Only of David is it later said that his enduement with the Spirit was permanent (16:13). In her discussion of prophecy in the Bible and the ancient Near East, Kitz observes that the results of "anthropomancy [divine manipulation of human beings] could be permanent or transitory."[216]

Cylinder seal impression of Mushezib-Ninurta, ninth century B.C. The king, shown in mirror image, is protected by guardian genii sprinkling holy water from a bucket using what may be a fir cone or sponge. Above a stylized tree is a god in the winged disc probably representing the sun god Shamash or the supreme god of Assyria, Ashur. In this way the god is depicted giving power and authority to the king.
HIP/Art Resource, NY, courtesy of the British Museum

Once these signs are fulfilled, do whatever your hand finds to do. ... Go down ahead of me to Gilgal (10:7–8). While ancient Gilgal has not been identified, it must have been near Jericho in the Jordan Valley and would have had special significance for Israel ever since Joshua built there a memorial of twelve stones from the middle of the Jordan (Josh. 4:19–20). Commentators have generally found Samuel's instructions to Saul to be confusing, even contradictory. Is Saul to "do what lies at hand," or is he to "go down to Gilgal" and wait?

A coherent understanding of Samuel's instructions is possible, however, if one recognizes that Saul's charge entails two tasks, the second to be undertaken only after the first.[217] Taking his cue from Samuel's otherwise unnecessary mention of a Philistine outpost at Gibeah of God where the final sign will be completed, Saul is to understand that his first task ("what lies at hand") is to strike the Philistine outpost. Such an action will provoke—not defeat—the Philistines. Saul's second task, therefore, is to repair to Gilgal and await Samuel, who will come, offer prebattle sacrifices (see comment on 7:7), and give Saul further instructions from Yahweh. This procedure constitutes an important test for Saul, as the successful accomplishment of both parts of his first charge will demonstrate not only Saul's courage but, more importantly, his willingness and ability to subordinate himself to an authority structure whereby Yahweh can continue to reign. In the event, Saul doesn't attack the Philistine garrison and thus derails the process by which he is to come to public attention. This in turn necessitates the lot-casting described in 10:17–27 (see below).

Saul's Response (10:9–16)

God changed Saul's heart, and all these signs were fulfilled (10:9). See comment on 10:6.

The Spirit of God came upon him in power (10:10). See comment on 10:6.

Saul Selected by Lot (10:17–27)

At Mizpah (10:17). On the probable location of the Mizpah in view here, see comment on 7:5. There is perhaps a touch of irony in the fact that the assembly to select Israel's first king—the demand for which was interpreted as a rejection of Yahweh's kingship (ch. 8)—is called at the very place where Yahweh earlier wrought a great deliverance, leading Samuel to proclaim, "Thus far has the LORD helped us" (7:12).

Samuel explained to the people the regulations of the kingship ... wrote them down on a scroll and deposited it before the LORD (10:25). This verse raises three interesting questions: What were these "regulations of the kingship"? What was the state of writing and literacy in Samuel's day? What did it mean to deposit something "before the LORD"? None of these questions can be answered with certainty, but studied conjectures can be offered.

(1) The "regulations of the kingship" likely stipulated the responsibilities of the people to the king, the king to the people, and, most significantly, the king to Yahweh (perhaps similar to the "law of the king" in Deut. 17:14–20). Assyrian kings sometimes made formal agreements (*adû*-agreements) with their servants "in front of the great gods."[218] Something similar may be implied here, but the text offers little detail.

(2) The question of popular literacy in ancient Israel is widely debated,[219] but there are grounds for optimism that, after the invention of the easily mastered phonetic alphabet in the second millennium, literacy could have spread rapidly (see comment on 4:1).[220] In any case, Samuel's upbringing as a priest in the house of Eli likely afforded educational opportunities beyond the ordinary.

(3) The statement that the document was deposited "before the LORD" suggests that it was deposited in the sanctuary. In the ancient Near East (e.g., among the Hittites),[221] covenant documents were frequently deposited

Geba
Todd Bolen/www.BiblePlaces.com

in sanctuaries. In fact, as Ben-Barak points out, the events recounted in 10:25 share features with Hittite vassal treaties: "a ritual ceremony, a legal document read in public and deposited in the sanctuary."[222] Similarly, the Mizpah covenant of 20:25 appears to be "a suzerainty covenant between two unequal parties, the king and the people, in which the latter undertake an obligation to the former. The covenant has the character of a politico-social pact bearing the seal of religious sanction."[223] Other biblical references to documents deposited before the Lord include Deuteronomy 31:26 and Joshua 24:26.

Saul also went to his home in Gibeah (10:26). While several sites with the name Gibeah ("height, hill") are mentioned in the Old Testament, by far the most prominent is Gibeah of Benjamin, home of Saul. The location of this Gibeah has been a matter of lengthy debate, not least in respect to its relationship to "Geba" (mentioned, e.g., in 13:3, and called "Geba of Benjamin" in 13:16; "Geba" and "Gibeah" are variant spellings of the same word).

This debate has been well summarized by Arnold,[224] but a few highlights are worth noting here. In 1841 E. Robinson launched the search for Gibeah of Benjamin by suggesting that Gibeah and Geba should be regarded as variant toponyms for the same site, or at least as closely proximate sites, to be associated with modern Jebaᶜ, which lies about six miles north of Jerusalem, south of the Wadi Swenit and across from modern Mukhmas (biblical Micmash). Robinson subsequently altered his view in the light of Judges 19:10–14 and linked Gibeah with Tell el-Fûl (3.5 miles north of Jerusalem), continuing to identify biblical Geba with Jebaᶜ.

W. F. Albright's excavations at Tell Tell el-Fûl in the 1920s and 1930s reinforced an emerging scholarly consensus that King Saul's capital at Gibeah of Benjamin was indeed to be associated with Tell el-Fûl, not least because excavators found a large architectural structure that was plausibly associated with a fortress Saul may have built (it is worth noting, however, that the biblical text makes no mention of such a fortress).[225]

Publication by L. Sinclair (1960) of detailed results of Albright's 1933 expedition, however, along with subsequent archaeological study of the site by P. Lapp (1965), caused scholars to question the identification. Today many are returning to the earlier view that Gibeah and Geba are both to be associated with Jebaᶜ.[226]

But some troublemakers said, "How can this fellow save us?" (10:27). While culpable for refusing to accept the one whom Yahweh chose, the "troublemakers" ("insurrectionists") nevertheless ask a valid question, especially when viewed against the typical process by which leaders in the ancient Near East often came to power. As several studies have shown, the accession process in the ancient Near East typically comprised three stages: (1) divine designation of the new leader; (2) some kind of demonstration by the new leader that gains public attention and rallies support; (3) public confirmation of the new leader.

The essential case for such a pattern was first made by B. Halpern, basing his analysis on the book of Judges (e.g., Jephthah) and on ancient Near Eastern texts such as the Babylonian epic *Enuma Elish*, in which Marduk is first chosen in the divine assembly to confront Tiamat, does so, and, after his victorious return, is enthroned.[227] If all had gone according to plan, Saul's anointing and first charge (10:1–8) would have served as his designation (stage 1); an attack on the Philistine outpost in Gibeah of God would have served as the demonstration (stage 2); and a public confirmation of Saul as Israel's first king would have followed (stage 3).

Saul's failure to execute stage 2 means that he did not come to public attention. To rectify this situation, Samuel convenes the assembly at Mizpah, where Saul is selected by lot. This means, however, that Saul has still done nothing to distinguish himself or gain public confidence; in fact, he has been dragged from behind the baggage, where he was hiding. Eventually (ch. 11) Saul's victory over the Ammonites will silence the dissenters, but it will leave his first charge—intended to test his fitness as a vassal-king to Yahweh—yet unfulfilled. Only in chapter 13 does the first charge come back into play, and there Saul fails.

Tell el-Fûl (believed by some to be the ancient site of Gibeah) and the ruins of what some have associated with Saul's kingship
David Bivin/www.Lifeinthe Holyland.com

Saul Rescues the City of Jabesh Gilead (11:1–15)

Nahash the Ammonite (11:1). The first extra-biblical references to the Ammonites are found in Neo-Assyrian documents beginning with the reign of Tiglath-pileser III in the late eighth century[228] and include the reigns of Sargon II,[229] Sennacherib,[230] and Assurbanipal.[231] The latter mentions an Ammonite king whose name, Amminadab, appears also on the Tell Sīrān bottle inscription from ca. 600 B.C.[232]

Tell Sīrān Inscription: "May the produce of 'Amminadab king of the Ammonites, the son of Hissal'il king of the Ammonites, the son of 'Amminadab king of the Ammonites—the vineyard and the garden(s) and the hollow and cistern—") *COS*, 2.25
Todd Bolen/www.BiblePlaces.com

The territory of the Ammonites lay in Transjordan, south of the Jabbok River, with a capital at Rabbath Ammon (modern Amman in Jordan). Archaeological excavations at Rabbath Ammon have unearthed ample evidence—in the form of tombs, pottery, a temple, and fortifications—of the Ammonites' presence and prominence from the eighteenth century B.C. onward.[233] One interesting find is the Amman Citadel Inscription,[234] discovered on the acropolis of the city. This inscription, though partially damaged, is sufficiently preserved to show the close similarity between Ammonite and Hebrew. To learn more of the earlier history of the Ammonites, we must turn to the Bible.

From the latter part of the period of the judges into the early monarchy, the Israelites were harassed from the west by the territorially ambitious Philistines and from the east by the Ammonites. Not until David's reign were both the Philistines and the Ammonites decisively defeated (2 Sam. 8:11–12). Rather than seeing the Ammonite and Philistine oppressions as occurring sequentially, we should probably understand them as occurring concurrently.[235]

Amman citadel inscription
Todd Bolen/www.BiblePlaces.com

The Ammonites, according to biblical tradition, were descendants of Abraham's nephew Lot (Gen. 19:36–38) and enjoyed protected status during Israel's initial approach to the Promised Land (Deut. 2:19). Even during the early monarchy period, there were periods of friendly relations with Israel (e.g., 2 Sam. 10:2), but for the most part the Ammonites' stance was hostile. Here the Ammonite king Nahash is besieging Jabesh Gilead (see next comment), in the heart of the territory of the Israelite tribe of Gad.

According to a longer reading of 1 Samuel 10:27 attested at Qumran (4QSam[a]), and reflected in Josephus (*Ant.* 6.5.1), the siege of Jabesh Gilead was part of a larger offensive by Nahash against the tribes of Gad and Reuben. The longer reading is adopted by several modern translations, including NAB, NEB, and NRSV, which renders the text as follows:

> Now Nahash, king of the Ammonites, had been grievously oppressing the Gadites and the Reubenites. He would

> gouge out the right eye of each of them and would not grant Israel a deliverer. No one was left of the Israelites across the Jordan whose right eye Nahash, king of the Ammonites, had not gouged out. But there were seven thousand men who had escaped from the Ammonites and had entered Jabesh-gilead.[236]

Jabesh Gilead (11:1). Jabesh Gilead was a city in Transjordan with an eventful relationship with the Cisjordanian tribes, particularly Benjamin. In the period of the judges, the city was virtually annihilated because its inhabitants failed to join in the general retaliation against the Benjamites in the aftermath of the outrage at Gibeah (see Judg. 19–21). Only four hundred women of Jabesh Gilead were spared to provide wives for the decimated tribe of Benjamin (21:12–14). Perhaps in part because of this Benjamite connection, and especially because of the city's rescue by Saul in the present chapter, the citizens of Jabesh Gilead later retrieved the bodies of Saul and his sons from Beth Shan, after journeying through the night (1 Sam. 31:11–13).

The precise location of Jabesh Gilead is still under debate, but the likeliest suggestion is Tell Maqlub. This is the only known site that (1) "lies within the range of travel time described in 1 Sam 31:11–13," (2) "has yielded evidence of Iron I occupation in surface survey," (3) lies along the Wadi el-Yabis in northern Gilead ("Yabis" seems to preserve the name Jabesh), and (4) comports reasonably well with Eusebius, *Onomasticon*.[237]

Jabesh Gilead (Tell Maqlub)
Todd Bolen/www.BiblePlaces.com

Gouge out the right eye (11:2). In the ancient Near East, losing a battle sometimes resulted in physical mutilation of one sort or another, and punitive action by regimes against those considered rebels often included mutilation such as the removal of eyes, ears, or hands.[238] In the present context, submission to mutilation is presented as a precondition for avoiding battle.

Threats of physical mutilation appear frequently in ancient Near Eastern treaty documents, specifically in the curse sections that describe what will befall treaty violators. These threats were not only pronounced but sometimes, at least, symbolically enacted, as in the following excerpt from a mid-eighth-century, Old Aramaic treaty from Sefire: "Just as (this) bow and these arrows are broken, so may Inurta and Hadad break [the bow of Matiᶜel], and the bow of his nobles! And just as the man of wax is blinded, so may Mati[ᶜel] be blinded!"[239]

The purposes of blinding the vanquished varied, as the Bible itself indicates. Samson was blinded by the Philistines to humiliate and incapacitate him (Judg. 16:21); King Zedekiah of Judah was blinded by the king of Babylon in order that his last visual memory might be the slaughter of his own sons (2 Kings 25:7; cf. Jer. 39:6–7). In the case before us, the Ammonite king's intention was certainly to humiliate the Jabesh Gileadites, but also, it seems likely, to render the fighting men ineffectual in battle. As Josephus (*Ant.* 6.68–72) explains, "since the left eye was covered by the buckler" (i.e., the shield), blinding the right would render the warriors "utterly unserviceable." Right-handed warriors (the majority) would be able to see little in battle, unless they were willing to lower their shields or literally stick their necks out. In any case, with only one eye, they would lack depth perception and thus be at a severe disadvantage in hand-to-hand combat. Sparing the left eye would leave them capable of agricultural work and menial tasks, but little else.[240]

When the messengers came to Gibeah of Saul (11:4). The Hebrew text of this verse can also be rendered, "So the messengers came to Gibeah of Saul." It seems likely that the messengers are in fact sent directly to Gibeah and not "throughout Israel" (the elders' request in v. 3 involving an element of deception). Not only would this have been a logical action after the assembly in Mizpah in which Saul was selected as Israel's king-elect, but pragmatic considerations make a more general dispersal of messengers unlikely. The rate of marching for armies in the ancient Near East was about fifteen to twenty miles a day.[241] Messengers on an urgent mission could probably double that rate.

The distance from Jabesh Gilead to Gibeah was between fifty and sixty miles, depending on the route taken. This places the messengers in Gibeah late on the second day. Their subsequent dispersal "throughout the territory of Israel" (v. 7) would have taken another two or three days, leaving two or three days of the permitted seven days for the general muster at Bezek (vv. 7–8).[242]

The Spirit of God came upon him in power (11:6). On empowering by the Spirit of God, see comment on 10:6. In the present context, the Spirit propels Saul into action, who, though king-elect, has apparently gone back to farming.

He took a pair of oxen, cut them into pieces, and sent the pieces by messengers throughout Israel (11:7). The intent is to evoke a strong reaction, reinforced by the threat that those who do not respond may suffer similar treatment. As Gordon observes, the dismemberment of the oxen "evokes the world of execration and treaty curse where the threat was directed not so much at the individual's property as at the individual himself."[243] The ancient Near East was accustomed to gruesome actions intended to prompt a certain response. A text from Mari, for example, records a request for permission to sever the head of a prisoner and parade it throughout the territory so as to shock reticent warriors into assembling for battle.[244]

Saul mustered them at Bezek (11:8). While it is tempting to identify Bezek with Khirbet Ibziq, which lies nine miles west of the Jordan on approximately the same latitude as Jabesh Gilead, Zertal maintains that the name has shifted and that the original site of Bezek was at Khirbet Salhab, about two miles southeast.[245] In either case the distance between Gibeah and Bezek is about seventeen miles. Judges 1:4–5 mentions a different Bezek, near Jerusalem.

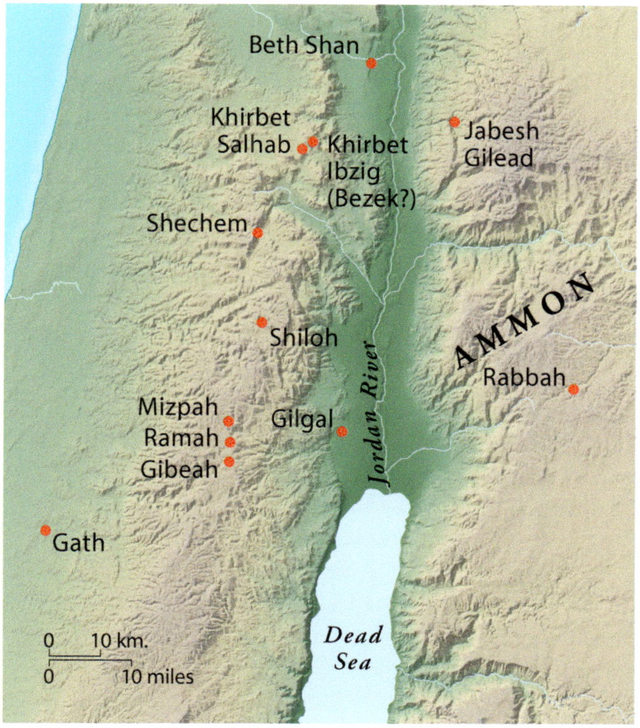

Area of Saul's activities

Region of Bezek
Todd Bolen/www.BiblePlaces.com

Samuel's Instructions and Warnings concerning Kingship (12:1–25)

Testify against me in the presence of the LORD and his anointed (12:3). It was widely understood in the ancient Near East that those in positions of power were responsible to execute justice and to protect the vulnerable in society (see comment on 2 Sam. 8:15; 15:4; cf. 5:12; 12:1–4). When rulers were deposed, it was not uncommon for those who replaced them to trump up charges of injustice against them and seek to eliminate them. Thus, Samuel is intent on clearing his name before redefining his leadership role.

While the context is markedly different, the so-called "negative penance" section of the Egyptian Book of the Dead employs phrases in some respects similar to Samuel's protestations: for example, "I have committed no injustice against men. I have not mistreated the cattle (of God).... I have not done violence to a poor man.... I have neither increased nor diminished the bushel."[246] Similar protests are attested in the archival records of Hittite court cases,[247] as well as in Hittite canonical compositions: "What have I done? What? I haven't taken anything from anyone. I haven't taken an ox from anyone."[248]

Is it not the wheat harvest now? (12:17). Wheat harvest took place early in Israel's dry season (in May-June). In this period of almost complete drought, Yahweh's sending of "thunder and rain" at Samuel's request serves both as a sign of divine approval for Samuel and as a mild punishment for Israel's sin, as rain is never welcome at harvest time. Rain at harvest time can cause what is called preharvest sprouting—water is absorbed into the head of the grain, stimulating hormone production leading to germination and thus a lower-quality yield.

Saul's Disobedience at Gilgal (13:1–15)

Saul was thirty years old when he became king, and he reigned over Israel forty-two years (13:1). As the half-brackets in the NIV indicate, "thirty" and "forty" do not actually appear in the Hebrew text, which reads literally, "Saul was a year old when he became king, and he reigned over Israel two years." This appears to be a (defective?) regnal formula. In the historiography of the Old Testament, regnal formulae stating the age of the king at accession and the length of his reign typically mark the official beginning of a king's reign (cf., e.g., 2 Sam. 2:10; 5:4; 1 Kings 14:21). Clearly, Saul could not have been literally a year old when he began to reign. Perhaps the number is to be understood differently—for instance, it may have been a year since Saul's anointing, when he was "changed into a different person" (see comment on 10:6); perhaps the two-year reign refers to the time elapsed between Saul's inauguration and his definitive rejection by God in 1 Samuel 15:23, 28.[249]

If the regnal formula is to be read literally, however, we must assume that one or two numerals are missing from the text. Examples of omitted numerals do occur in the ancient Near East—for example, in two economic texts from Ur, in a list of personal names from the Old Babylonian period, in the Sumerian King List, and in the Babylonian Chronicles.[250] At present the question of Saul's age at accession must remain open, but a rough estimate would make

Fertile wheat fields are seen in the foreground with Mount Zaphon, the Canaanite mount of assembly for the divine council, towering in the back as clouds form behind it. Baal was considered the "Rider on the Clouds" who came from Mount Zaphon and brought fertility to the ground so crops would grow. But for Israel, Yahweh was the one who brought rain and who caused the fields to yield their harvest, or sent destructive storms.
John Monson

him at least forty, assuming that the events of chapter 13, in which his son Jonathan is already in charge of troops, take place early in his reign.

As for the length of Saul's reign, twenty(-two) years is a good estimate. In one place, Josephus accords Saul a reign of twenty years (*Ant.* 10.143). In another place, the text of Josephus states that Saul reigned eighteen years during Samuel's lifetime and "two and twenty" thereafter. But the "twenty" is text-critically and logically dubious; if Saul reigned twenty-two years after Samuel's death, and David became king at age thirty (2 Sam. 5:4), then at the time of Samuel's death David was only eight years old—having already killed Goliath, served as a commander in Saul's army, incurred Saul's jealousy, escaped to the Philistines, gathered a troop of six hundred men while on the run in the wilderness, and so on. Full discussion is not possible here, but a reign of about twenty or twenty-two years for Saul seems to work best.[251]

Micmash (13:2). This is a hilltop village to be identified with the present-day city of Mukhmas, some seven miles northeast of Jerusalem and just a couple of miles from Geba/Gibeah to the southwest, across the Wadi Swenit. Micmash has not been excavated.

Jonathan attacked the Philistine outpost at Geba (13:3). On the link between this action and Saul's first charge at the time of his anointing, see comment on 10:7–8. For the location of Geba, see comment on 10:26.

Saul had the trumpet blown (13:3). The word rendered "trumpet" is *šôpār*, which designates a "sounding horn" crafted (usually) from the horn of a ram. Such horns were frequently used in battle contexts for summoning troops or for signalling advances or retreats.[252] Use of trumpets for battle signals is attested in the battle scenes in ancient Egypt. Two trumpets were found in the tomb of Tutankhamun, which are likely war trumpets for they bear the names of some of the army divisions known to have been used in Egypt.[253] Other instances of trumpet blasts as signaling devices in military situations include Judges 3:27 (Ehud vs. Moab); 6:34 (Gideon vs. Midian); and 2 Samuel 20:1 (Sheba vs. Judah).

Michmash
Todd Bolen/www.BiblePlaces.com

The *šôpār* must be distinguished from metal trumpets, also used in the monarchical period, but which, unlike the modern instrument of the same name, had no valves. The latter would have been more like a straight bugle. Both the ram's horn and the trumpet "were signal and alarm instruments, much like today's military bugles, automobile horns, emergency vehicle sirens, or fire and civil defense alarms." They "could not play a wide variety of notes and, hence, could not easily contribute melodically to music," but "they could produce a loud and piercing sound, which, when of a higher pitch or played in a higher register, could be heard over other noises. This contributed to their use in cultic contexts as noisemakers."[254]

The Philistines assembled to fight Israel, with three thousand chariots (13:5). Whether Jonathan's attack on the Philistine outpost was a solo performance or part of a larger strategy, it succeeded in provoking a massive Philistine reaction. The phraseology of verse 5—namely, the notice that the Philistines first assemble for battle, presumably in "safe" (Philistine?) territory,[255] and then advance to take up battle positions in Micmash, east of Beth Aven[256]—suggests a procedure similar to what Saul followed in mustering troops in Gilgal (v. 4), away from the scene of the impending conflict. The Philistine muster, however, is reported as markedly more successful than Saul's (v. 5). On the chariots, see sidebar on "Chariots."

You acted foolishly (13:13). The precise nature of Saul's folly has elicited considerable debate among commentators, most assuming that his offense must have been in arrogating to himself the priestly privilege of offering sacrifices. It should be noted, however, that both biblical and ancient Near Eastern kings often served some priestly functions (see comment on 2 Sam. 8:18). Furthermore, the text does not accuse Saul of cultic infraction but rather of failing to keep the "command/charge" of Yahweh.

The "charge" that Saul failed to keep is the two-part first charge that he received at the time of his anointing by Samuel (see comment on 10:7–8). Jonathan did the first part ("what lay at hand") by attacking the

It was common in the ancient world for kings to serve in the role of priest and to make offerings to deity. Here in the Hall of Offerings at Luxor a multitude of bulls are being offered by the king, including the offering in front of him that is comprised of a trussed-up bull at the bottom, a thigh, and some fowl.
Mike Murrill

Chariots

The Hebrew text of 13:5 refers to 30,000 chariots, while LXX and Syriac attest the number 3,000. Even the lower figure seems high by ancient Near Eastern standards, though not impossible: for example, Sisera had 900 (Judg. 4:3); David killed 700 Aramean charioteers (2 Sam. 10:18); Solomon had 1,400 chariots (1 Kings 10:26); Tukulti-Ninurta II had "2,702 horses in teams [and chariots], more than ever before."[A-58] If the NIV is correct in reading "six thousand charioteers," this would further confirm that the Philistines had 3,000 (not 30,000) chariots. The word translated "charioteer" can also be rendered "horseman/cavalryman" and "(chariot) horse."

In view of the fairly late introduction of cavalry in Canaan[A-59] and the pictorial evidence of travelling bands of Philistines comprising "three main elements: chariots, infantry, and noncombatants,"[A-60] but no cavalry, the decision of many modern translations to read "cavalry" or "horsemen" seems misguided. Moreover, if the Philistines, like the Hittites, employed three-man chariot crews,[A-61] then the number 6,000 best refers to the chariot *horses*, not charioteers (which would number about 9,000).[A-62] But some variation of the chariot team is certainly possible. Assyrian chariot crews could consist of two, three, or even four men.[A-63] And there is possible evidence of two-man chariots among the Mycenaeans, to whom the Philistines are thought to be related.[A-64]

Assuming that chariots would have been of little use in hilly terrain, some (especially older) commentators have doubted the accuracy of the present verse.[A-65] Such judgments, however, overlook the fact that one of the chief functions of chariots in antiquity was to terrorize the enemy.[A-66] Moreover, we have the explicit witness of numerous Assyrian royal inscriptions that chariots were indeed sometimes transported into "unsuitable/impassable" terrain. In an inscription of Tiglath-pileser I, for example, we read: "Taking my chariots and warriors I hacked through the rough mountain range and difficult paths with copper picks and made a good way for the passage of my chariots and troops."[A-67]

This is not to imply that geographic features never necessitated the abandoning of chariotry,[A-68] but even in "impassable" regions, a way was sometimes found. Note this statement again from Tiglath-pileser's inscription: "In the high mountains, which cut like the blade of a dagger and which were impassable for my chariots, I put the chariots on (the soldiers') necks (and thereby) passed through the difficult mountain range."[A-69] While allowing for the hyperbolic nature of such reports, we are still left with the impression that the Assyrians could be persistent in overcoming obstacles in order to get their chariotry to the scene of battle. We probably underestimate the Philistines if we imagine that they were less so. In any case, the present verse dramatizes the odds facing the Israelites.

Chariots portrayed on the Balawat Gate
Z. Radovan/www.BibleLandPictures.com

Philistine outpost at Geba (cf. 10:7; 13:3), Saul initiated the second, going "down to Gilgal" to await Samuel's arrival (cf. 10:8; 13:4, 8). But he fails to wait *until Samuel arrives*, which is not a minor infraction. Yahweh's "charge" to Saul at the time of his anointing was intended as a test of Saul's willingness and ability to understand and abide by the all-important authority structure whereby Yahweh could continue to rule, with the human king remaining obedient to the divine will (as mediated, often, by the prophet).

Saul's sweeping aside of this arrangement when under pressure is a culpable act of folly, the consequences of which are that his kingdom will not be established (v. 14). This understanding of Saul's failure finds further confirmation in 1 Chronicles 10:13–14.[257]

A man after his own heart (13:14). McCarter has argued that the phrase "after his own heart" says nothing of "any great fondness of Yahweh's for David or any special quality of David"; rather, it should be rendered "of his own choosing."[258] Reserving judgment on McCarter's first assertion for the moment, we may add in support of the suggested rendering "of his own choosing" the following excerpt from the Babylonian Chronicle concerning the early years of Nebuchadnezzar II:

> The seventh year: In the month Kislev the king of Akkad mustered his army and marched to Hattu. He encamped against the city of Judah and on the second day of the month Adar he captured the city (and) seized (its) king. A king of his own choice [*šarra šá libbi-šu* = lit., "a king according to his heart"] he appointed in the city (and) taking the vast tribute he brought it into Babylon.[259]

Compare also the following: "Enlil will install a king of his own choosing (*šà sa*ᶜ-*šua*).[260]

The evidence validates putting the accent on Yahweh's sovereign election of David, but in the light of such passages as 2:35 and 16:7, the idea that Yahweh's king, David, has a heart attuned to Yahweh's will and purposes should not be diminished (cf. the similar usage in 14:7).

Israel's Predicament (13:16–23)

Raiding parties went out from the Philistine camp in three detachments (13:17). Having established their base of operations at Micmash, the Philistines send out raiding parties to the north, west, and east. The first party moves north toward Ophrah (identified with modern et-Taiyiba, some six miles north of Micmash), where according to a theory proposed by Garsiel[261] they turn east-southeast along a route leading down into the Jordan Valley near Jericho.[262] Another party moves west toward Beth Horon, probably in order to secure access to Philistine territory. A third travels east along the "border road."[263] Garsiel, assuming that the Philistines must have learned that Saul is centralizing his forces in Gilgal, argues that the strategic aim of the two eastbound parties may be to create a "pincer movement" to put pressure on Saul's camp. Alternatively, these two eastbound units may have been to control two major passes into the hill country from the Jericho region and thus to eliminate the

Philistine raiding parties

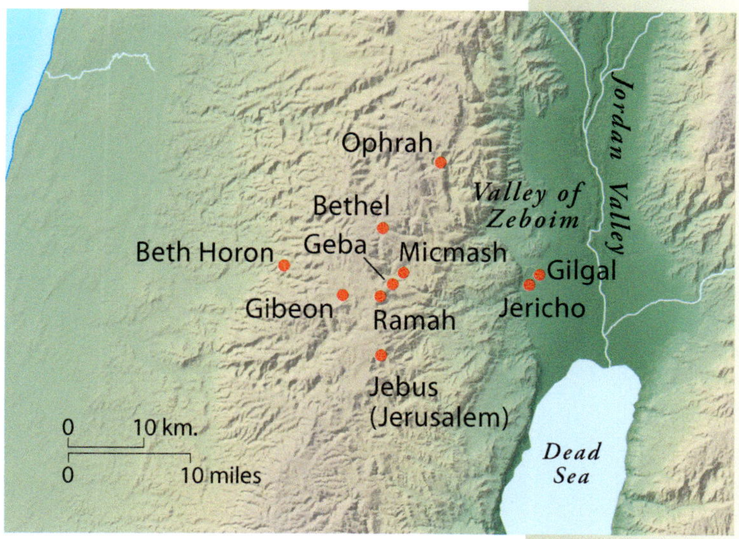

▸ Iron Technology

Iron objects are not unknown prior to the so-called Iron Age,[A-70] but at earlier periods iron was generally not preferred to bronze (an alloy of copper and tin), because bronze was stronger than simple wrought iron. Only when iron was "carburized" (had carbon added to it) and "quenched" (doused in cold water) did it become steel. Because of its higher melting temperature (1528° C, as opposed to 1200° C for copper), iron could not be melted and cast; ancient furnaces could achieve at best 1300–1400° C. The only solution was "forging"—repeatedly heating and then hammering the spongey hot iron to remove slag and compact the metallic iron.[A-71]

In most parts of the ancient Near East, iron ore was in fact more common and available than copper or tin, but the technological challenges of smelting iron meant that its use for weapons and tools did not become widespread until shortages of (often imported) copper and tin created a necessity that could not be ignored.[A-72]

Iron technology may have developed first in Hittite Anatolia, as evidenced by increasing textual references to iron towards the end of the so-called Late Bronze Age. An interesting example from the first half of the thirteenth century is the following excerpt from an Akkadian letter sent to an Assyrian king by a Hittite king:

> In the matter of the good iron about which you wrote, good iron is not (currently) available in my storehouse in Kizzuwatna. I have already told you that this is a bad time for producing iron. They will be producing good iron, but they won't have finished yet. I shall send it to you when they have finished. At present I am sending you an iron dagger-blade.[A-73]

Weight inscribed with the word *pym*
Z. Radovan/www.BibleLand Pictures.com

possibility of a flanking action by Israelite forces coming up from the Jordan Valley.

In any case, the obvious freedom of movement enjoyed by the Philistines in 13:16–18 signals their military superiority in the area and contributes to the impression that the diminutive Israelite forces at Geba are in an almost hopeless situation. Division of troops into three detachments is a frequently attested practice in the premonarchical and monarchical period (cf. Judg. 7:16; 9:43; 1 Sam. 11:11; 2 Sam. 18:2).

Not a blacksmith could be found in the whole land of Israel (13:19). Whether the Philistines led their neighbors in iron-working technology or simply were militarily powerful enough in this period to deny Israel access to blacksmiths remains an open question. The point, in any case, is that the Philistines prevent the Israelites from arming themselves properly. See sidebar on "Iron Technology."

The price was two thirds of a shekel ... a third of a shekel (13:21). The Hebrew word *pym*, rendered "two thirds of a shekel," occurs only here in the Old Testament, and it baffled interpreters until archaeologists uncovered stone weights with the word inscribed. These stones weighed .268 oz., or "two thirds of a shekel," the shekel being the standard monetary weight at that time. If the average monthly wage was one shekel,[264] then this charge was exorbitant.

There are even earlier references to metallic iron, which treat it as a luxury item, obtained most often from meteors (the Egyptian word for iron is "metal of heaven"[A-74]). The following excerpt is from a letter dating to the Old Assyrian period (early second millennium):

> Please do not smuggle anything. If you pass through Timilkia leave your iron which you are bringing through in a friendly house in Timilkia, and leave one of your lads whom you trust, and come through yourself and we can discuss it here.[A-75]

One of the earliest allusions to the quenching of carburized iron is found in Homer's description of the blinding of Cyclops by Odysseus and his men, using a massive olive stake made red-hot in the flames:

> So we seized our stake with its fiery tip and bored it round and round in the giant's eye till blood came boiling up around that smoking shaft and the hot blast singed his brow and eyelids round the core and the broiling eyeball burst—its crackling roots blazed and hissed—as a blacksmith plunges a glowing ax or adze in an ice-cold bath and the metal screeches steam and its temper hardens. (*Odyssey* 9.433–52).[A-76]

Iron ingots were considered precious metal in this period.
Kim Walton, courtesy of the Oriental Institute Museum

Jonathan's Valor (14:1–14)

Saul was staying on the outskirts of Gibeah under a pomegranate tree in Migron (14:2). Migron is to be associated with the Wadi Swenit, which ran between Micmash to the north and Geba to the south. The word "tree" is not present in the Hebrew text, and Arnold has proposed the attractive theory that the "pomegranate" refers to a large cave in the south wall of the wadi (the Migron). The cave's pitted interior gives it the resemblance of an open pomegranate and may have earned it the name Rimmon (Heb. for "pomegranate"). Judges 20:45 speaks of a Rock of Rimmon to which six hundred Benjamites fled, and so it is conceivable that the six hundred men with Saul could have been stationed "under the Pomegranate." Saul's location in a cave also explains his need for lookouts to inform him of activities in the Philistine camp (14:16).

Ahijah, who was wearing an ephod ... son of Ichabod's brother Ahitub (14:3). On the three senses in which "ephod" is used in the Bible, see comment on 2:18. In the present context, the ephod that Ahijah is "wearing" (or "carrying"—the Heb. verb can mean either) is probably the high priestly ephod containing the Urim and Thummim, devices used in divine inquiry (see Ex. 28:15, 30 and comment on 1 Sam. 14:18–19). The presence of these oracular instruments among Saul's entourage might encourage hope that Saul will seek and receive divine guidance, as David later did on several occasions, using the ephod (23:9–12; 30:7–8). Ahijah, the bearer of the ephod, is provided with a genealogy that not only identifies him as a member of the rejected priestly house of Eli, but makes a rather unusual step sideways to mention an uncle, Ichabod, whose name means something like "No glory, no weight" (4:21). Commentators have struggled to explain this genealogy, but its purpose is probably to recall, if only indirectly, that Saul's glory, too, is much diminished after the events of 1 Samuel 13.[265]

On either side of the pass ... was a cliff ... Bozez ... Seneh (14:4). The topography of the area around Geba and Micmash, especially where the Wadi Swenit begins to develop the steep sides of a gorge, is well suited to the bold exploit of Jonathan and his armor-bearer. The meanings of Bozez and Seneh are debated, but if the suggestions of "slippery" for the former and "thorny" for the latter are correct, these names may have been mentioned to dramatize the challenge facing Jonathan.[266]

Let's go over to the outpost of those uncircumcised fellows (14:6). To be called "uncircumcised" was a strong censure in the thought world of ancient Israel (see comment on 4:1). Here Jonathan uses "uncircumcised" as a derogatory synonym for the Philistines (cf. the parallel injunction of 14:1). Circumcision was instituted in Genesis 17:10–14 as a sign of the covenant between Yahweh and Israel, but Israel was not the only ancient Near Eastern people to engage in the practice. As Jeremiah 9:25–26 (which mentions Egypt, Edom, Ammon, and Moab, as well as Judah) indicates, many of Israel's neighbors circumcised their males.[267] There is no evidence,

Micmash
Todd Bolen/www.BiblePlaces.com

Pass of the Wadi Swenit near Micmash
Todd Bolen/www.BiblePlaces.com

however, that the practice served as a covenant sign outside Israel.[268]

While in Israel the rite was administered to male babies at eight days old, in Egypt circumcision appears to have been more a rite of passage, administered either prior to marriage or at puberty. An Egyptian inscription from the twenty-third century B.C. provides a first-person description of the circumcision of a young man along with 120 others:

Flint knife
Kim Walton, courtesy of the Oriental Institute Museum

> I was one beloved of his father, favored of his mother, whom his brothers and sisters loved. When I was circumcised, together with one hundred and twenty men, there was none thereof who hit out, there was none thereof who was hit, there was none thereof who scratched, there was none thereof who was scratched.[269]

The large number of men circumcised at one time suggests a kind of "circumcision festival," such as is depicted on a relief from the Sixth Dynasty (2350–2000 B.C.) tomb of Ankhmahor at Saqqara.[270] The legend to the relief mentions not only the Egyptian word for circumcision, but gives evidence also that a flint knife was used[271] (a practice attested also in Josh. 5:2–3). The left side of the relief appears to show an attendant supporting and perhaps restraining the arms of a young man as he is being circumcised. Perhaps the statements in the inscription that no one "hit out" or "was hit," "scratched" or "was scratched" should be understood in the light of the fear that such a painful operation would engender and the discipline required not to react.[272] That all Egyptian males were to be circumcised—as were their Israelite counterparts—seems unlikely,[273] but priests were required to be; traces of the circumcision of priests can still be detected on Egyptian mummies.[274]

Circumcision does not appear to have been practiced among the east Semitic peoples of Mesopotamia. Judging from the gruesome tale of the circumcision and subsequent slaughter of the Shechemites by Simeon and Levi in Genesis 34, circumcision was apparently not a universal practice in Canaan.[275] That the Philistines did not practice circumcision is often attributed to their apparent Aegean origin. Perhaps some such explanation may apply also to the Shechemites.

Egyptian relief of an army in panic being decimated
Aaron and Estelle Morton

Nothing can hinder the LORD from saving, whether by many or by few (14:6). Though distinctive in its monotheism, Israel's belief that the Divine Warrior ultimately decided the outcome of battles was not without analogy among neighboring peoples. The ancient Near Eastern pantheons included gods or goddesses of war—Baal and Anat in Canaan, Nergal and Ishtar in Assyria, Marduk in Babylon, and so forth.[276] Battles were regarded as ultimately decided by the gods, the stronger god defeating the weaker.

Thus, an inferior human force led by a superior deity could defeat a superior human force led by a weaker deity. In this instance, Jonathan's faith in the power of Yahweh emboldens him to go over, accompanied only by his armor-bearer, to confront an entire Philistine troop. This action causes the reader to revisit Saul's earlier excuse for his not waiting for Samuel at Gilgal—"the men were scattering" (13:11)—and to view it in a more negative light.

Saul's Folly (14:15–48)

The ground shook. It was a panic sent by God (14:15). In keeping with the belief that in warfare the gods actually did battle (see comment on 14:6), people of the ancient Near East associated this divine activity with dramatic manifestations in nature—the shaking of the earth, the splitting of the heavens, thunder and storm, and so forth (cf. 2 Sam. 22:8–10). From Ugaritic writings, for instance, we read:

> Ba[al gives] forth his holy voice,
> Baal discharges the ut[terance of his li]ps.
> His h[oly] voice [convulses] the earth ...
> the mountains quake,
> A-tremble are ...
> East and west, the earth's high places
> reel.[277]

Such descriptions are widespread in the ancient Near East.[278] Weinfeld cites the following examples:

- in Akkadian: "which at the sound of his voice the heavens shake, the earth quakes, the mountains tremble"; "who set his voice in the heavens like Adad, and all the earth trembles at his voice."
- in Egyptian: "the earth trembles when (Amon) sends forth his voice."
- In Greek: "Zeus, whose voice is borne afar, himself sat upon his throne of gold, and beneath his feet great Olympus quaked" (*Iliad* 8.442–43); "the high mountains trembled and the woodland beneath the immortal feet of Poseidon as he went" (*Iliad* 8.18–19).[279]

In the present passage, Yahweh manifests himself by causing the ground to shake and throwing the Philistines into confusion so that their swords turn on each other (14:20). It was indeed a "panic sent by God"! The Hebrew expression can also be read as a superlative, in the same way that English speakers use expressions of divinity as superlatives: e.g., "the food was divine." Thus, some translations read, "an exceedingly great panic."

Bring the ark ... withdraw your hand (14:18–19). Having learned that Jonathan and his armor-bearer have left the camp, Saul orders Ahijah to "bring the ark of God." Mention of the "ark" is surprising at this point in the narrative: (1) in 14:3 Ahijah is in possession of an "ephod," not the ark; (2) judging from 7:1 and 2 Samuel 6, the ark appears to have remained at the town of Kiriath Jearim throughout the reign of Saul (1 Chron. 13:3 confirms that the ark was not sought during Saul's reign); (3) Saul's order that Ahijah "bring near" the object seems appropriate in reference to an ephod (cf. 23:9; 30:7) but not in reference to the ark; (4) Saul's command in 14:19 to "withdraw your hand" makes little sense if the ark is in view but excellent sense if Ahijah is in the process of grasping the Urim and Thummin, or the container holding them,[280] in the breastplate of the priestly ephod.[281]

Based on Akkadian evidence, it is possible that oracular inquiry using Urim and Thummim was a form of psephomancy ("divination by means of white and black stones").[282] Considerations such as these have led a majority of commentators to follow the LXX (cf. also Josephus, *Ant.* 6.115) in reading "ephod" instead of "ark" in the present context—the two words are orthographically fairly similar in Hebrew.[283] It seems likely, then, that Saul initiates an oracular inquiry involving the ephod but almost immediately aborts the process when it becomes apparent that the battle is heating up. Having failed to wait for Samuel in 1 Samuel 13, Saul now finds it difficult even to wait the few minutes necessary to inquire of Yahweh regarding the battle in progress, and this trend of increasing indifference to gaining divine direction adds to the unfavorable portrayal of Saul.[284] On the customary practice in the Bible and the ancient Near East of seeking divine guidance before entering battle, see comment on 7:7.

Hebrews who had previously been with the Philistines ... went over to the Israelites (14:21). This statement seems to distinguish "Hebrews" from "Israelites." The "Hebrews" here may refer to the "Habiru," landless, troublesome mercenaries who may have shifted allegiances opportunistically (see sidebar on "Hebrews/Habiru" at 4:6).

Beth Aven (14:23). See comment on 13:5.

Cursed be any man who eats food (14:24). In the ancient Near East, fasting is often associated with mourning, but it is unattested in battle contexts such as this. See comments on 7:16; 2 Samuel 1:12; 12:16.

From Micmash to Aijalon (14:31). Reference to Aijalon is lacking in the LXX, and the shorter text is preferred by some commentators.[285] The precise location of Aijalon has not been determined, but it lies somewhere in the valley of the same name. Two possible sites have been suggested: Yalo (which seems to reflect the ancient name) and Tell

Qoqa. Surface surveys reveal that both sites were occupied in Iron Age I (time of Saul and Jonathan).[286] Whichever site is correct, the Israelite pursuit of the Philistines after the initial victory at Micmash covers sixteen miles. Outside the Bible, Aijalon is mentioned in the fourteenth-century Amarna letters as Ayyaluna and in a list of conquered territories by Pharaoh Shoshenq I (945–924 B.C.).[287]

Sinning against the LORD by eating meat that has blood in it (14:33). Not just in the Old Testament but throughout Egypt, Mesopotamia, and the Levant, blood was regarded with awe as the "true life substance," the "bearer of life." As such, it gave rise to seemingly conflicting attitudes: "On the one hand, [people treated] blood with reverential awe and surround[ed] it with a series of taboos; on the other hand, [they hoped] to make use of these powers in appropriate rites."[288]

In the Old Testament, control over the lifeblood belongs to God, the giver of life, and prohibitions against eating blood are pervasive (Gen. 9:4; Lev. 3:17; 7:26–27; 17:10, 12; 19:26; Deut. 15:23; Ezek. 33:25). The juxtaposition in Leviticus 19:26 of prohibitions against eating meat with the blood still in and the practice of divination or sorcery suggests that the two were linked, and it was probably this link rather than any dietary restriction that stood behind the breech of protocol by Saul's troops. (For more on occultic practices involving blood, see comment on 28:8.)

Aijalon Valley
Todd Bolen/www.BiblePlaces.com

Saul's Disobedience in Battle with the Amalekites (15:1–11)

I will punish the Amalekites (15:2). To date, no explicit reference to the Amalekites has been discovered in the ancient Near Eastern corpus. Archaeologically, some scholars have suggested links between the Amalekites and certain "small fortified settlements in the Negeb highlands," while others have debated whether "the city of Amalek" in 15:5 is to be identified with Tel Masos, a site some seven miles east-southeast of Beersheba.[289] For explicit information about the Amalekites, however, the Bible is our only source.

According to Genesis 36:12, the eponymous ancestor of the Amalekites was Amalek, a grandson of Esau, a "chief" (*ʾallûp*) in the land of Edom (36:15), while Numbers 13:29 locates the Amalekites in the Negev, south of Judah and in the proxim-

Tel Masos, possible site of the city of Amalek
David Bivin/www.LifeintheHolyland.com

ity of Edom. As a nomadic or seminomadic people, the Amalekites seem to have ranged widely, from the hill country of Ephraim in the north (Judg. 12:15) to the Philistine territory around Ziklag in the west (1 Sam. 30:1–2). The description of Saul's victory over the Amalekites "from Havilah to Shur, to the east of Egypt" (15:7) places them in a broad territory stretching from the western Sinai eastward, possibly to the Arabah of Arabia (the location of Havilah is uncertain).[290]

It was in the wilderness of Sinai at Rephidim that the Israelites, after escaping from Egypt, first encountered the Amalekites, and this encounter, like virtually every subsequent one between Israel and Amalek, was hostile (Ex. 17:8–13). What was so abhorrent in Amalek's first attack on Israel was, according to Stern, its timing. Yahweh had just "exercised his cosmogonic powers, allowing Israel to safely pass through the *Un-Welt* in two manifestations, Egypt and the Sea." The Amalekite aggression threatened to return Israel to "the *Un-Welt*," to chaos, to nonexistence. Because of this heinous act, Amalek "became officially set apart as the 'enemies of YHWH' and deserving of being fought against from generation to generation."[291]

A battle ensued in which Joshua led the Israelites to victory, while Moses sat atop a nearby hill with his hands raised. After the victory, "the LORD said to Moses, 'Write this on a scroll as something to be remembered and make sure that Joshua hears it, because I will completely blot out the memory of Amalek from under heaven' " (Ex. 17:14). The severity of the treatment of the Amalekites commanded by Yahweh here must be seen in the light of their initial and ongoing opposition to Israel (see, e.g., Judg. 3:13; 6:3–5, 33; 7:12; 10:12).

Attack the Amalekites and totally destroy everything that belongs to them (15:3). The curse pronounced against the Amalekites in Exodus 17 is now to be worked out. The order of "total destruction" (*ḥērem*), sometimes referred to in English as placing someone or something under the "ban" or as "devoting to destruction," is clearly attested outside the Old Testament only in the ninth-century Mesha Inscription (line 17). The Moabite king Mesha recounts how he was sent by the god Chemosh to attack "Nebo from Israel," and having done so how he "slew all in it, seven thousand men and women, both natives and aliens, and female slaves; for I had devoted it to Ashtar-Chemosh."[292] In both Hebrew and Moabite the root *ḥrm* describes the act of "totally destroying" or "devoting" to the deity that which is under the ban.

Elsewhere in the ancient Near East, it was believed that the gods controlled the outcome of battles and that they therefore also controlled the spoils of battle. In Israel, failure to treat banned persons or objects properly drew the offenders under the ban as well and left them liable to destruction (cf. Achan in Josh. 7). Simply put, contact with "devoted/banned" objects was "contagious, the transgressor becoming devoted in turn—and as such, foredoomed to death."[293]

Telaim (15:4). This is probably to be equated with Telem, listed in Joshua 15:24 as one of the cities of Judah. The LXX mentions Gilgal here instead, which some have suggested may have been the site of Samuel's instructions to Saul.

Two hundred thousand foot soldiers (15:4). See comment on 4:10.

Kenites (15:6). On linguistic grounds the Kenites have been associated with metalworking, their name perhaps meaning something like "(metal)smith."[294] In Genesis 4:22, Tubal-Cain ("Cain" and "Kenite" are variant English spellings of the same Hebrew root) is described as a forger of metal tools. If Tubal is to be identified with the nation of Tabal mentioned in Assyrian texts, then the link with metalworking and the copper trade is strengthened.[295]

Mesha Stele
Jill Walton, courtesy of the Louvre

According to Judges 1:16, Moses' father-in-law was a Kenite; his descendants went up from the "City of Palms [Jericho] with the men of Judah to live among the people of the Desert of Judah in the Negev near Arad."[296] A late seventh/early sixth-century Hebrew ostracon from Arad[297] mentions a site called Qinah/Kinah (cf. Kenite) along with Arad, possibly confirming the association of Kenites with Arad. The first half of the ostracon is mostly unreadable, though the addressee's name, Elyashib, is preserved. The line mentioning Qinah reads: "from Arad fifty (or five) and from Qina[h]." The succeeding lines state that this quantity of something (?) from Arad and Qinah is to be sent to Ramat-Negeb, by order of the king.[298]

The Kenites are attested mostly in the southern parts of Palestine—such as Midian, Edom, Amalek, and Sinai. They were likely seminomadic; for instance, Judges 4:11 recounts how "Heber the Kenite had left the other Kenites ... and pitched his tent by the great tree in Zaanannim near Kedesh." Not only in the present context of Saul's battle against the Amalekites but elsewhere in the Bible (e.g., Num. 24:20–21) Kenites and Amalekites are mentioned together. But whereas the Amalekites were consistently hostile toward Israel, the Kenites were consistently friendly, and so Saul is careful to send the Kenites away from danger before attacking the Amalekites.

Havilah to Shur (15:7). See comment on 15:2.

Saul's Trial and Rejection (15:12–35)

Saul has gone to Carmel. There he has set up a monument in his own honor (15:12). On Carmel, see comment on 25:2 (cf. 23:24). It was common practice in the ancient Near East for victorious kings to set up monuments, or victory stelae, with inscriptions celebrating their glorious achievements and crediting their success to their god(s). The ninth-century Assyrian king Ashur-nasir-apli II, for instance, makes repeated reference to erecting stelae or statues in praise of his mighty power. After describing his massacre and decapitation of enemy troops, as well as the execution of the son of the ruler of the city Nishtun by flaying and draping his skin over the city wall, he writes: "At that time I made an image of myself (and) wrote thereon the praises of my power."[299]

Relief of a hilltop with a stele at the top, a monument to the king
Zen Liu/www.flickr.com/photos/zenra

In the aftermath of another victory, apparently not content with a single monument to himself, Ashur-Nasir-Apli II erected a "colossal royal statue of myself" in the palace of his vanquished foe and also deposited "steles" in praise of his own might in the enemy's gate.[300] Saul's monument may have been such a victory stele, but that it was erected "in his own honor" is disconcerting. Absalom will later honor himself similarly with a monument (2 Sam. 18:18).

Arrogance like the evil of idolatry (15:23). The word rendered "idolatry" is *t^erāpîm*; see comment on 1 Samuel 19:13.

Saul caught hold of the edge of his robe, and it tore (15:27). Although the Hebrew text does not state explicitly *who* caught hold of *whose* robe, the context suggests it was Saul who took hold of Samuel's robe (so NIV).[301] More uncertain is the precise significance, or intent, of Saul's seizing the hem of Samuel's robe. Several Akkadian texts from Mari[302] attest the practice of cutting a lock of hair and a piece of hem from the garment of one who has prophesied and sending these items to the king of Mari.

Some have argued that taking and sending hair and hem expressed distrust of the one who prophesied and that Saul, by grasping and tearing Samuel's robe, is challenging Samuel.[303] This argument overlooks both the fact that the tearing of the robe seems to have been accidental (as indicated by the Hebrew grammar) and the fact that in one text a prophetess *voluntarily* sends hair and hem: "Here then I have given you my hair and hem, that one may [ritually] cleanse them."[304] That the prophetess would be expressing self-distrust is hardly likely.

In the present episode, moreover, no lock of hair is mentioned but only the grasping of the hem of a robe. Closer parallels may be offered, therefore, by texts that mention only the grasping of the hem. In addition to several texts in Akkadian,[305] at least one can be found in Old Aramaic[306] and one other in Zechariah 8:23: "This is what the LORD Almighty says: 'In those days ten men from all languages and nations will take firm hold of one Jew by the hem of his robe and say, "Let us go with you, because we have heard that God is with you."'" In the light of these texts, Saul's grasping of Samuel's hem may be read positively, indicating supplication or submission.[307] But this positive construal of Saul's action assumes more regarding Saul's motives than the context will support.

A further instance of grasping the hem is found in the Ugaritic Myth of Baal and Mot, in which Anat seizes the hem of Mot's garment in order to constrain him.[308] Anat's action, in context, is suggestive of supplication but hardly of penitence or submission; when she next "seizes" Mot,[309] Anat "hacks him up, pulverizes him, and scatters his remains for the birds to eat."[310] Taking this evidence together, we may conclude that grasping the hem can mean various things in various contexts.[311]

In the present context, Saul's grasping and (inadvertently?) tearing the hem of Samuel's robe is best understood as a last desperate attempt to rescue a situation that has gone badly awry and to wrest from the prophet a word of comfort or concession.[312] As it happens, however, the torn robe becomes a symbol of the kingdom now "torn" from Saul (15:28).[313]

King's elaborate hem can be seen in contrast to the hem of his attendant
Caryn Reeder, courtesy of the British Museum

Glory of Israel does not lie or change his mind (15:29). The ninth-century Assyrian king Ashur-nasir-apli II begins one of the longest extant Assyrian royal inscriptions with line after line of praise to the god Ninurta, whom he describes as, among other things, "the splendid god who never changes (his mind)."[314] In a subsequent edition of the same text, Grayson alters his earlier translation slightly, reading "the splendid god who never once changes."[315]

The question that arises is whether Ninurta is being described as immutable generally (in his character and general decrees) or specifically (in his judicial judgments). The Akkadian verb *enû* III, with the general meaning of "turn (around), change," has a broad range that includes both these senses.[316] Therefore, the specific sense in which Ninurta "never once changes" must be determined from the immediate context, where he is called "the god without whom no decisions are taken in heaven and underworld ... the one whose command is unalterable ... the one whose command none of the gods in the divine assembly can alter."[317] Particularly the latter statement suggests the supremacy of Ninurta's commands over against any attempts by others to alter them.

Also worthy of consideration are a few lines from a Sumerian Hymn to Enlil:

> You are lord An and king Enlil (in one),
> judge and decision maker
> for (both) heaven and earth,
> you know no rescinder of your great
> decrees.[318]

In the context of Saul's trial, the sense seems to be similar—no amount of cajoling or manipulation will succeed in mitigating the sentence pronounced against him, for it has been issued by Yahweh, whose judgment is supreme. As Eichrodt noted long ago, "the purpose of Num 23.19 and 1 Sam 15.29 ... is to combat the erroneous idea that it is easy to talk God round, and that his threats and promises need not be taken seriously."[319]

Samuel Anoints David (16:1–13)

Fill your horn with oil (16:1). Whereas Samuel anointed Saul in 10:1 from a "flask" or small jug (see comment on 10:1), here he is instructed to take his "horn" of oil and go to Jesse to anoint one of his sons as Saul's replacement. The horn in view is probably an animal horn fitted out to contain oil. The word for oil is a general one, but here it probably refers to a vegetable oil of an aromatic variety.[320] While anointing per se was fairly widespread in the ancient Near East and served various functions (see comment on 2:10),[321] Keel suggests that "anointing from an *oil-horn* seems to have been distinctive to Syria-Palestine,"[322] and current evidence does not suggest otherwise.

Ivory anointing horn
Erich Lessing/Art Resource, NY, courtesy of the Israel Museum (IDAM)

A depiction from the tomb of the Egyptian Sebekhotep in Thebes (ca. 1420 B.C.) shows a Semitic/Syrian envoy (recognizable by his clothing and beard) carrying an ornate anointing horn.[323] Also mentioning an oil-horn is a letter from a king of Ugarit (in Syria) to his Queen Mother. The central issue has to do with the king's designs on an Amurrite princess, although lacunae in the text obscure the king's precise intentions. The lines pertinent here state that one Yabninu, who has been dispatched to the court of Amurru bearing gifts, "has also taken oil in a horn and poured it on the head of the daughter of the king of Amurru."[324] The significance of this anointing is not stated, but perhaps it was meant, among other things, to establish a kind of "first contact, however remote," between groom and bride.[325]

Bethlehem (16:1). Because of its rich associations—e.g., vicinity of Rachel's tomb (Gen. 35:19), setting of the book of Ruth, hometown of David, birthplace of Jesus (Matt. 2:5–6; John 7:42; cf. Mic. 5:2)—Bethlehem figures more prominently in biblical history than its size merits. Located less than six miles south-southwest of Jerusalem, the ancient site is today occupied by a modern town, limiting the possibility of excavation. Only in the vicinity of the Church of the Nativity, or where fresh construction is undertaken, has excavation been attempted. Enough has been

In top register, one envoy carries ivory horn perhaps for anointing oil.
Z. Radovan/www.BibleLand Pictures.com

Bethlehem

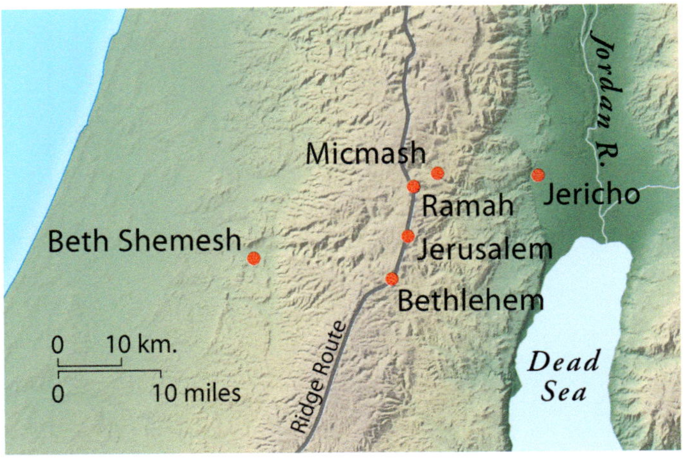

lehem, "house of bread." This theory, while interesting, remains unproven.[327]

The LORD looks at the heart (16:7). In the ancient Near East, the heart was viewed as far more than the seat of the blind passions. In Mesopotamia, it was "the locus of the emotions that are more subject to the will (desire, love, friendship, mercy, faithfulness, etc.), of consciousness, wisdom, and understanding." In Egypt, the heart was "the focus of the individual—body, spirit, soul, and will—the center of the entire personality and its relationship to God." As the "locus of an individual's ethical competence," the heart "was weighed in the judgment of the dead."[328] Some texts speak of the deity seeing into or searching the heart.[329]

found to confirm the presence of an Iron Age town in the time of David.

A fourteenth-century B.C. Amarna letter mentions "a town belonging to Jerusalem, Bit-^{d}NIN.URTA by name, a city of the king."[326] Reading the city name as "Bit-Laḫmu" or the like, which is possible in the syllabic Akkadian language, some have suggested that this may be an early reference to Bethlehem. The name may originally have meant "house of Lahmu," a Mesopotamian god, and only later been transposed to Beth-

The Hebrew concept of the heart as the center of intellectual, ethical, moral, and religious consciousness is similar. Unlike human appraisal that judges by external appearances, Yahweh passes over the tall, impressive older brothers (indeed, he "rejects" them, subtly recalling the rejection of Saul, who exceeded his fellows by a head) and chooses the youngest (in Heb., the smallest), David.

Jesse had seven of his sons pass before Samuel. . . . "There is still the youngest" (16:10–11). While this passage and 17:12–13 make David the youngest of Jesse's eight sons, 1 Chronicles 2:13–15 lists David as the young-

Bethlehem with flocks still wandering the hills
Bible Scene Multimedia/Maurice Thompson

est of seven sons. It seems likely that David is in fact the eighth son and that the Chronicler lists only seven in order for David to occupy the favored seventh position. Alternatively, the "seven" in the present passage may be intended simply to connote the full complement (see comment on 2:6; 13:8). Ascendancy of a younger brother is a common motif in the Bible and in the ancient Near East. One interesting parallel is offered by a mid-third millennium Sumerian epic in which the eighth son, Lugulbanda, joins seven older brothers and performs heroically in an attempt to conquer a city.[330]

Rise and anoint him; he is the one (16:12). On the anointing of kings in ancient Israel and in the ancient Near East, see comment on 2:10.

From that day on the Spirit of the LORD came upon David in power (16:13). The statement that David is endowed with the Spirit of Yahweh "from that day on" is meant either to suggest a contrast with the more occasional coming of the Spirit of God on Saul (e.g., 10:10; 11:6; 19:23) or simply to underscore that David is henceforth the king through whom Yahweh will work, since Saul's royal status has been revoked. Prior to the monarchy, the Spirit of Yahweh came on certain individuals to empower them to perform certain tasks, military or otherwise. These Spirit-endowments were occasional, aimed at specific competencies, and impermanent—one need only think of the way in which the Spirit came on Samson "in power" to enable a specific feat of strength or deliverance and then departed (Judg. 14:6, 9; 15:14).

Against this backdrop, David's apparently more permanent endowment with the Spirit, commensurate with the more permanent nature of his role as Yahweh's anointed and future king, is striking. By the same token, the departure of the Spirit from Saul (see comment on 16:14) is commensurate with his rejected status.

Kingship was a sacral office, sanctioned and empowered by the deity, which was a widespread notion in the ancient Near East, though with considerable variation in specifics.[331] The Egyptian pharaohs were regarded as divine and to be worshiped. Mesopotamian kings were sometimes regarded as divine by adoption, or at least as bearers of the *melammu* of the gods, that is, the "radiance, supernatural awe-inspiring sheen (inherent in things divine and royal)."[332]

Israel's notion was different, for the Israelite king was regarded simply as Yahweh's Spirit-endowed *human* representative on earth, who, as God's vassal ruler, was like any ordinary Israelite citizen in having a duty to "fear the LORD and serve and obey him and ... [not] rebel against his commands" (12:14–15). Failure in this duty could lead to rejection from office and withdrawal of the empowering Spirit, as in the case of Saul.

David Enters Saul's Service (16:14–23)

The Spirit of the LORD had departed from Saul, and an evil spirit from the LORD tormented him (16:14). The Hebrew adjective *ra*ᶜ ("evil") has a broad range of possible meanings, including the following: "of bad quality, inferior, disagreeable, displeasing, vicious, harmful, bad, evil."[333] The noun *rûaḥ* ("spirit") also has a broad range, including: "wind, breath, transitoriness, volition, disposition, temper, spirit, Spirit."[334] Of particular note for the present context is the use of *rûaḥ* to mean "the natural spirit of humanity, as **sense, mind, intellectual frame of mind**."[335] Thus, the "evil spirit" visited on Saul may connote not a malevolent spiritual being per se, but an ill temper or even psychological affliction.[336]

That music provides some relief for Saul (see 16:15–17) seems to support this more mundane interpretation of the "evil spirit" that comes on Saul after the departure of the "Spirit of the LORD." In the ancient Near East, unworthy kings could provoke similar displeasure and disciplinary actions from

Philistine jug with shepherd playing lyre as he watches his animals
Z. Radovan/www.BibleLandPictures.com

their deities. For instance, near the end of his law code, Hammurabi invokes a curse on anyone who disobeys his law. Should the offender be a king, then "may mighty Anum, the father of the gods, who proclaimed my reign, deprive him of the glory of sovereignty, may he break his scepter, may he curse his fate!"[337] The Akkadian notion of "a spirit or demon representing the individual's vital force," which could become alienated from the individual or driven away by evil, may offer some degree of conceptual parallel, as also to a lesser degree the Akkadian phrase *mukīl rēš damiqti/lemutti* (good spirit/evil spirit).[338]

Harp (16:16). Music played a major royal in ancient societies, both in private and in public spheres, in the royal court as well as the cult.[339] In the Bible, music and musical instruments are mentioned as early as Genesis 4:21 and 31:27. From the inception of monarchy in Israel, music would have been a part of court life. The present reference offers evidence of this fact, as David's skill as a harpist is the chief reason for his induction into Saul's court.

The precise significance of some Hebrew musical terms is uncertain (see sidebar on "Prophetic Bands and Music" at 10:5). The word rendered "harp" in the NIV (*kinnôr*) probably refers to a "lyre," of which there were several types in antiquity (see illustrations).[340] (Conversely, the term that the NIV renders "lyre" [*nēbel*] probably refers to a "harp.")[341] The type of lyre David played was presumably the "Eastern," or "thin," lyre, which was strung with four to eight strings and was played with a plectrum. The "thick" lyre had ten to thirteen strings and was played with the fingers. No evidence of thick lyres has been discovered in Palestine.[342]

Lyres were constructed using "a rectangular soundbox, two asymmetrical arms, and an oblique yoke,"[343] with strings stretched between the soundbox and the yoke. Archaeological discovery has yielded many representations of lyres, such as the

Valley of Elah
Todd Bolen/www.BiblePlaces.com

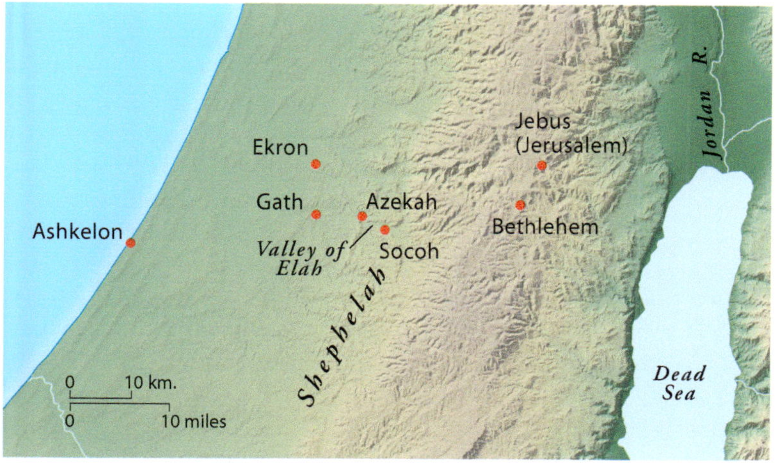

determined, the locations of the other sites mentioned are reasonably certain. The Valley of Elah (Wadi es-Sant) was part of a major east-west corridor from the Judean hill country through the Shephelah westward down into Philistine territory. There is evidence that in biblical times a road running westward from Jerusalem picked up the Elah Valley as it ran past Socoh and Azekah, then continued on to the Philistine cities of Gath and Ashkelon.[345]

remains of nine lyres from the Sumerian royal cemetery at Ur (ca. 2500 B.C.), a depiction of "an Amorite/Canaanite lyre player entering Egypt with his clan" (ca. 1900 B.C. wall painting at Beni Hasan in Egypt), a depiction of a female lyre player on an ivory plaque from Megiddo (twelfth century B.C.), and a male lyre player on a Philistine bichrome jug (Megiddo, eleventh century B.C.).[344]

David Kills Goliath (17:1–58)

Philistines (17:1). See comments on 4:1.

Pitched camp at Ephes Dammim, between Socoh and Azekah. Saul and the Israelites ... in the Valley of Elah (17:1–2). While the precise location of Ephes Dammim has not been

Socoh, identified with modern Khirbet ʿAbbad, lay almost fifteen miles due west from Bethlehem, Azekah (modern Tell Zakariya) is three miles northwest of Socoh, and Gath (Tel Zafit; Tell es-Safi; see comment on 5:8) another five miles west of Azekah. Socoh has not been excavated, but pottery collected on the surface confirms its occupation in the requisite period.[346] Just to the east of Khirbet ʿAbbad is Khirbet Shuweikeh, which seems to preserve the ancient name Socoh, and the two sites together may have formed twin villages, as Eusebius supposed, called Socoth (plural of Socoh).[347]

Azekah was excavated in 1898–1899, revealing continuous occupation from 1500 B.C. to the Byzantine period. A sense of its strategic location overlooking the Elah Valley is conveyed in an Assyrian source from the time of Sargon II: a "stronghold, which is situated in the mid[st of the mountains …] located on a mountain ridge like a pointed dagger."[348] Ephes Dammim, located somewhere between Azekah and Socoh and within a few miles of Philistine territory presented a logical and dramatic location of the confrontation between the Israelite David and the Gittite Goliath.

Apology of Ḫattushili
Istanbul Archaeological Museum; © Dr. James C. Martin

Champion named Goliath (17:4). The contest joined between the "champion" Goliath and the temerous young David is perhaps the best-known example from antiquity of a military conflict decided by "single combat," namely, a fight between representatives of the warring factions intended to avoid a more general engagement. The logic behind such contests was grounded in the belief that battles were ultimately decided by God or the gods; thus, the champion representing the more powerful deity would triumph.

In his 1959 seminal essay, R. de Vaux drew attention to numerous examples of single combat in the Bible and to several from other ancient sources. Among the latter, de Vaux cited Homer's *Iliad* (Paris versus Menelaus, Hector versus Ajax) and the Egyptian Tale of Sinuhe, in which Sinuhe triumphs over a Syrian challenger, felling him with an arrow and dispatching him with his own sword.[349]

While certain similarities with the story of David's triumph over Goliath are striking, H. A. Hoffner in a 1968 essay correctly observed that some of the presumed ancient Near Eastern parallels are better described as *duels*, not representative combat, inasmuch as the grievances to be settled were personal and the fates of larger contingents were not at stake. A better parallel, Hoffner argued, is to be found in the Hittite Apology of Ḫattušiliš III. Massively outnumbered in one particular engagement—the enemy boasting 800 chariot teams and countless infantry versus Ḫattušiliš's 120 chariot teams and no infantry—Ḫattušiliš nevertheless "personally" defeated the enemy: "For when I slew the man who was the *piran ḫuyanza*, the (rest of the) enemy fled."[350]

The literal meaning of the Hittite *piran ḫuyanza* is "one who runs/marches in front," which offers a remarkable parallel to both the Greek and Hebrew words for champion, both of which "are descriptive of persons who have *gone out in front* of their own host in order to engage an opponent." The technical term in Homer's *Iliad* is the Greek word *promachizein*, "of which the preverb *pro* signifies that he fights in a cleared area in front of the host." The Hebrew term, used of Goliath in the present context is *ʾîš habbēnayim*, the "man between two (armies)."[351] Thus, David's confrontation with Goliath, and the resulting flight of the Philistines, fits nicely within the frame of "single combat" as attested particularly "in Western Asia Minor and along the Levantine coast."[352] For a biblical example of representative combat between two select teams of champions, see 2 Samuel 2:12–16.

Gath (17:4). See comment on 5:8.

Goliath ... was over nine feet tall (17:4). The Hebrew text records Goliath's height as six cubits (a cubit being the distance from the elbow to the tip of the middle finger) and a span (the distance from the tip of the thumb to the tip of the smallest finger of a hand fully spread). There was considerable variation in the precise lengths of cubits and spans in antiquity, but by any standard Goliath would have been "over nine feet tall," as the NIV has it.

Codex Vaticanus of the LXX, as well as numerous manuscripts of the Lucianic recension, reduces Goliath's height by a third to "four" cubits and a span, making him about six feet six inches—still tall by ancient standards, to be sure, but not a giant (a claim that the biblical text never makes). If this lesser height should be correct, then the Hebrew text (or its copyists) are perhaps engaging in narrative hyperbole commensurate with the larger than life character of the story. It should be noted, however, that examples of giantism on the order of what the Hebrew text claims for Goliath are attested in numerous sources both ancient and modern.[353]

Within the Bible itself, both giant individuals (e.g., King Og of Bashan; Deut 3:11) and entire races of giants are described (e.g., the Nephilim, Anakim, and Rephaim [the latter being the race of which Og was a remnant]). A noteworthy extrabiblical reference is found in the thirteenth-century Egyptian Papyrus Anastasi I, which "describes bedouin in Canaan, 'some of whom are of four cubits or five cubits (from) their nose to foot and have fierce faces.' "[354] The spies sent by Moses to reconnoitre the land of Canaan also encountered fearsome giants: "We saw the Nephilim there (the descendants of Anak come from the Nephilim). We seemed like grasshoppers in our own eyes, and we looked the same to them" (Num. 13:33). Joshua was largely successful in wiping out the Anakim, but with some survivors in the Philistine cities of Gaza, Gath, and Ashdod (Josh. 11:21–22). As Mattingly has observed, "It is most probable that Goliath of Gath and the other giants of 2 Sam. 21:16–22 (cf. 1 Chr. 20:4–8) were regarded as descendants of the Anakim remnant in Philisitia."[355]

Bronze helmet ... scale armor ... bronze greaves ... spear shaft (17:5–7). The character and significance of Goliath's armor has elicited considerable discussion. See sidebar on "Goliath's Armor."

Ephrathite (17:12). While Ephrathite may be used as a synonym for Ephraimite,[356] in the present case it designates a kinship group within the larger tribe of Judah and is associated with the town of Bethlehem.[357] In fact, Ephrath(ah) was sometimes used as an alternate name for Bethlehem in Judah, as distinct from Bethlehem in Zebulun (Josh. 19:10, 15).[358]

Scale armor
Todd Bolen/www.BiblePlaces.com

▸ Goliath's Armor

By biblical standards, Goliath's defensive and offensive equipment is described in far greater detail than is typically dedicated to physical objects. Such elaborate description of a hero's panoply is far more typical of the writings of Homer (eighth century B.C.). Some have cited this as evidence that the Goliath episode is a later addition to the text of Samuel, or at least an editorial recasting of the episode, under the influence of Greek culture.[A-77] It is further argued that Goliath's armor and weaponry were not common among the Philistines at the time of David; for instance, Philistines in the reliefs from Medinet Habu sport feathered headdresses, not bronze helmets, and Goliath's shield, apparently large enough to require a shield-bearer, is unlike the small shields born by Philistines in Egyptian reliefs.[A-78]

On the basis of these and related arguments, recent studies have taken exception to Yigael Yadin's earlier opinion that "the detailed Biblical description of the weapons of Goliath is one of the most important documents for an understanding of Philistine armaments, their features and attributes, at the beginning of the Davidic period."[A-79] It may well be the case that Goliath's armaments reveal little or nothing about *normal* Philistine military equipment, but this does not necessarily mean that Goliath's description is anachronistic. Even Finkelstein, who strongly disagrees with Yadin, allows that "every single item in the description of Goliath's armament can be compared to Aegean weapons and armour from the Mycenaean period to Classical times.... In all periods within this time-frame one can find metal helmets, metal armour and metal greaves."[A-80]

Finkelstein's point is not that such gear is absent but that it is not prevalent in the time of David: "At any given period until the seventh century BCE, each of these items was not the most common of its kind."[A-81] Azzan Yadin,

Bethlehem (17:12). On the history and importance of Bethlehem, see comment on 16:1. David's trek from Bethlehem to the battle scene in the Valley of Elah covers over fifteen miles (see comment on 17:1–2).

Take an ephah of roasted grain ... ten loaves of bread ... ten cheeses (17:17–18). Throughout history, resupplying troops in the field has always presented logistical challenges. In the ancient Near East it often fell to local populations to resupply troops campaigning in their regions. Among the Hittites, for instance, troops on the march, along with their horses, were typically provided with food from strategically placed supply depots, but once outside Hittite-controlled territory, the soldiers either foraged and lived off captured booty or were resupplied by the host country, if it was a treaty partner.[359] In the present instance, Jesse's provisions may have gone to a supply officer rather than to his sons directly (see next two comments).

Bring back some assurance from them (17:18). The English translation of this instruction from Jesse to David suggests that he is to bring back assurance that his brothers are faring well. This is one possible understanding of *ʿărubbātām* ("their pledge, token").[360] There may also be a sense that David is to bring back some indication that he has fulfilled his mission and delivered the goods.[361] In view of the responsibility of local populations to supply troops in their area (see preceding comment), a further possibility is that David is to bring back a token as "proof that Jesse had met his obligations to supply the army," which would in turn be "the brothers' way of collecting their rations."[362]

Mycenaean warrior vase
N. Croll, courtesy of the Athens National Archaeological Museum

Saul offers David the use of his own "bronze helmet" in v. 38, though such helmets were not likely to be standard issue for Israelite soldiers.)

G. Philip notes that "both the javelin and the greaves are unusual for Syro-Palestinian warriors" of the Iron Age, but this may simply "hint at [Goliath's] foreign connections."[A-83] The fact is that his equipment is *not* out of keeping with the Aegean background of the Philistines.[A-84] The well-known twelfth-century Mycenaean Warrior Vase depicts Mycenaean warriors whose armor resembles Goliath's in at least some significant respects: for example, they apparently wear (bronze) greaves, which were probably lined with leather and protected the entire calf.[A-85]

who also disagrees with the earlier Yadin, similarly argues that Goliath's gear "is not common in the Bible."[A-82] But is this not precisely the point the biblical narrator is trying to make, with his unusual amount of descriptive detail? Goliath is not a typical Syro-Palestinian warrior; indeed, he is not even a typical Philistine warrior, either in stature or in military hardware. (We may note in passing that

David left his things with the keeper of supplies (17:22). If the grain and loaves brought by David are for the resupply of the troops, his depositing them with the "keeper of supplies"[363] marks the fulfillment of that part of the errand. But if his task is to deliver the grain and loaves directly to his brothers (and the cheeses to the commanding officer), then he is simply placing them in safe-keeping as long as attention is directed toward the battle lines. In either case, the context favors the view that David acts responsibly both in the case of the supplies and in the case of the sheep he earlier entrusted to a shepherd (lit., "keeper"; v. 20),

Mealtime in an army camp
Z. Radovan/www.BibleLandPictures.com

contrary to the charge of irresponsibility laid against him by his older brother Eliab (v. 28).

Exempt his father's family from taxes in Israel (17:25). Taxes are not explicitly mentioned in the Hebrew text; rather, "exempt ... from taxes" is simply "free" (*ḥopšî*), most often used to distinguish those who are not slaves. Attempts have been made on the basis of similar sounding terms in Akkadian and Ugaritic to liken these "free" people to social classes in ancient Near Eastern societies (craftsmen, farmers, serfs, etc., who fell midway between slaves and landowners),[364] but as McCarter observes, "this is contrary to Israelite usage, where there is no evidence of a distinct *ḥopšî* class."[365] McCarter finds Rainey's paralleling the current context with the situation attested in Ugaritic of a soldier who by his exploits is "granted freedom by the king from service to the palace" (RS 16.269:14–16) to be more persuasive.[366]

In the end, certainty of what precisely the promised freedom would be is elusive, but it may well have involved exemption from further obligations to the king (including the obligation to pay taxes). Perhaps it even involved the right of the hero's family to live "as pensioners of the royal house."[367]

Uncircumcised Philistine (17:26). See comments on 14:6 and 31:4. David's words reflect a theologically based confidence similar to that of Jonathan when he, too, went up against the Philistines despite apparently unfavorable odds (see 14:1–14).

Heroes and kings are often portrayed as fighting lions
Caryn Reeder, courtesy of the British Museum

Your servant has killed both the lion and the bear (17:36). The land of the Bible today is remarkably diverse in its ecological zones with their respective flora and fauna, and perhaps was even more so in antiquity. This diversity is especially noteworthy in a land so modest in size. Just as ancient Palestine was the bridge of the Fertile Crescent, connecting Mesopotamia on the north and east with Egypt on the south and west, it was also the meeting place of very different ecological zones: "the Palearctic, the Irano-Turanian, the Tropical, and the Saharo-Arabian, each with its own characteristic climate, flora, and fauna."[368]

Within these zones, the diverse climates in Israel/Palestine have apparently remained fairly constant from biblical times to the present. That progressive deforestation and the resultant erosion of hilltops have changed the landscape and certain ecosystems since biblical times seems likely.[369] Such changes inevitably affected animal habitat and range. Thus, although references to lions and bears may seem implausible to those familiar with the land today, in biblical times these creatures were well known and rightly feared.[370]

The lion that David encountered was probably of the Asiatic variety (*Panthera leo persica*), which closely resembles the African lion but is now virtually extinct—there are less than three hundred still in the wild in the Gir Forest of northwestern India and two hundred or so in zoos worldwide. The last sure evidence of a lion in Palestine was one killed in the thirteenth century A.D.[371]

The bear David defeated was likely a brown bear of the subspecies *Ursus arctos syriacus*, a somewhat smaller and paler relative of the well-known grizzly bear (*Ursus arctos horribilis*). These bears can still be found in parts of the Middle East, but they disappeared from Palestine in the first half of the twentieth century. Preferring fruits and wild forage, bears would likely have menaced livestock mostly in winter months when such vegetarian fare was scarce. Despite their seemingly gentler eating habits, bears may have been even more feared than lions because of their greater strength and more erratic behavior.[372]

Tangible evidence of lions and bears—in the form of their remains—has been unearthed by archaeologists excavating Iron Age levels in Palestine (the period of the settlement and monarchy).[373] The obvious point of David's words to Saul is not to boast in his own prowess but to stress that the God who delivered him from the most terrifying of beasts can surely deliver him from the terrifying Philistine giant.

Saul dressed David in his own tunic (17:38). On the use of armor in antiquity, see sidebar on "Goliath's Armor" at 17:5–7. Whether Saul's motive was to help David or vicariously to share in any possible victory (or something else), dressing David in the royal armor presents an ironic, if unintentional, foreshadowing of things to come (cf. Jonathan's willing transfer of royal regalia to David in 18:3–4).

With his sling in his hand, [he] approached the Philistine (17:40). One is not to think of a forked stick with an elastic catapult stretched between it, which is a modern invention, but of a leather or cloth pouch to which two cords were attached. A slingstone, either crafted by hand or, as in the present instance, rounded by water action, was placed in the pouch and then, after swinging the sling overhead or to the side to gain momentum, was released at great speed by letting go of one of the cords. Slings were affordable but effective weapons used, for instance, by shepherds to drive off predators. David's background as a shepherd would have afforded him opportunity to develop considerable skill in the use of a sling. In time, slings became (along with bows and arrows) a regular part of the long-range arsenal of ancient Near Eastern armies.

Am I a dog, that you come at me with sticks? (17:43). Dogs were not highly esteemed in the ancient Near East (see comment on 24:14). Goliath's taunting words were typical in prebattle situations, especially when a contest of champions was involved (see comments on 17:4; 2 Sam. 2:14). In such situations, an exchange of insults, termed "flyting," was intended to ridicule and shame the opponent. Flyting has been variously defined as "a verbal contest in which opponents try to outdo one another, often by hurling 'cutting words' at one another or words that will shame the opponent";[374] "antiphonal insults from opposing forces"; or "an exchange of verbal provocations between hostile speakers in a predictable setting."[375] Often, "the boasts and insults are traditional, and their arrangement and rhetorical form is highly stylized."[376]

Not surprisingly, flyting takes place in numerous contexts both ancient and modern (today, the term "trash-talking" captures the idea). One kind of flyting ("ludic") consists of words only, while a second kind ("heroic") leads to physical combat.[377] The

Slinger on Orthostat from Tell Halaf

Bible contains numerous examples of flyting, mainly of the "heroic" variety (e.g., the altercation between Abijah and Jeroboam [2 Chron. 13:2–17], between Amaziah and Jehoash [2 Kings 14:8–14], and in a modified sense between Elijah and prophets of Baal [1 Kings 18:21–40, esp. v. 27]).[378]

Captured Philistine on relief of Ramesses III at Medinet Habu
Erich Lessing/Art Resource, NY

Goliath's specific taunt to David, "Am I a dog that you come at me with sticks?" may suggest that he does not see David's sling, which he would certainly know to be a dangerous weapon in skilled hands (see comment on v. 40). Among the ailments that often attend giantism is poor eyesight, often a kind of tunnel vision.[379] The shepherd's simple sling hanging limp in his hand may have appeared to Goliath as no more than a stick, though we know from verse 40 that David has both a staff and a sling in his hands.

Warrior holding head of enemy
Kim Walton, courtesy of the Oriental Institute Museum

The battle is the LORD's (17:47). See comment on 14:6.

Struck the Philistine on the forehead (17:49). Questions have been raised concerning whether a stone from David's sling could have struck Goliath's forehead, given the kinds of helmets that Philistines are depicted as wearing (see illustration).[380] But the biblical text does not suggest that Goliath's armor was *typical* Philistine hardware but exceptional (see sidebar on "Goliath's Armor" at 17:5–7). That said, it is interesting to note that the Hebrew word rendered "greave" in verse 6 (*miṣḥâ*), which occurs only here in the Hebrew Bible, is very close, if not identical, to the Hebrew word for "forehead" (*mēṣah*).[381] Noting this curiosity, A. Deem has suggested that David's stone finds its mark not in Goliath's forehead but at the "greave" in the gap required for walking.[382] It is difficult to decide between these two interpretations; in either case Goliath is toppled and quickly dispatched by David, using Goliath's own sword (v. 51).

He cut off his head (17:51). Decapitation of enemy dead was a common practice in the ancient Near East and a recurrent motif in Samuel (see comments on 5:3–4; 31:4; cf. 18:2). Sometimes, as here, the enemy's own weapon is used. Having bested his opponent with an arrow in his neck, the Egyptian hero Sinuhe boasts: "He cried out and fell on his nose. I felled him with his (own) battle-axe and raised my cry of victory over his back, while every Asiatic roared"[383] (cf. also Benaiah's killing of a "huge Egyptian" with his own spear in 2 Sam. 23:21).

Their dead were strewn along the Shaaraim road to Gath and Ekron (17:52). On Gath, see comment on 5:8; on Ekron, see comment on 5:10. Shaaraim has been identified with modern Khirbit esh-Sharia, which lies some six miles east of Gath, seven miles east-southeast of Ekron, and a couple of miles northeast of Azekah.

Saul Fears David (18:1–30)

Jonathan made a covenant with David ... took off the robe he was wearing and gave it to David (18:3–4). The covenant described here is probably made "on an equal basis between Jonathan and David, with a certain stress on the initiative of Jonathan."[384] Jonathan's transfer of his robe, tunic, sword, bow, and belt to David is a subsequent, symbolic act. In the light of Jonathan's later references to David's ascendancy (20:14–15; 23:17), the act here seems to symbolize "a deliberate and free transference of the right to the throne by Jonathan to David."[385]

Jonathan's action may be likened to symbolic acts performed by the prophets, but it almost certainly also has legal significance. Texts from Ugarit and Emar, for instance, illustrate the symbolic significance of mantles (robes) in matters relating to inheritance or even royal succession. Two texts describe how "a son who refuses to obey his father is forced to leave the house and deposit his mantle on the stool or the door-bolt."[386] The implication is that the son no longer holds legal status as a member of the family. Another addresses a situation in which a prince must choose whether to stay with his father, Ammistamru, king of Ugarit, or follow his divorced mother. Should he choose to follow his mother, he must leave his mantle on the throne and depart,[387] the implication being that he has relinquished his legal status as prince.

These and other extrabiblical examples do not fully match Jonathan's action, as they mention only the relinquishment of the mantle, not its transference to another, but the general point seems clear. A special robe or mantle could serve as a symbol of a person's identity and status; thus, to transfer it to another signified a transfer of status. In this instance and the later ones, Jonathan acknowledges David's right to the throne.

Women came out ... to meet King Saul with singing and dancing (18:6). Judging from both the (biblical) textual evidence and artifactual evidence unearthed by archaeologists, we may conclude that dancing, often accompanied by music, was a common feature in religious and secular celebrations in tenth-century Israel, as well as in other periods. Indeed, dancing seems to have been

Musicians greet the king on his return from battle as the dead float down the river.
Todd Bolen/www.BiblePlaces.com

an integral part of ritual ceremonies among Israel's neighbors as well, such as Philistia and Phoenicia.

Representations of dancers and musicians are found throughout the ancient Near East. Mazar has drawn attention to the complementary nature of the so-called "Dancer's Stand" from Tel Qasile and the "Musician's Stand" from Ashdod.[388] The biblical writers employ a dozen different verbal roots to designate dancing but do not describe the dances in any detail.[389] For more on dancing in ancient Israel, see comment on 2 Samuel 6:14.

All Israel and Judah loved David (18:16). On the character of "love" as political loyalty and service, see comment on 2 Samuel 19:6.

Price for the bride (18:25). Twice Saul offers to make David his son-in-law. This second time he seems less mindful of the promise made earlier (17:25), which he may have regarded as no longer valid, and he is more intent on David's proving his martial skill (or dying in the attempt!). Payment of a bride price was common in the Old Testament world, as it is still in some cultures today. It was the prerogative of the bride's father to set the price, and Saul sets it dangerously high at a hundred Philistine foreskins. Body parts (heads, hands, etc.) often served as trophies of war, and Saul's unusual choice is designed to assure that David actually kills *Philistines*—other of Israel's neighbors were likely circumcised (see comment on 14:6).

Merenptah's Great Libyan War Inscription from Karnak repeatedly mentions that the "phalli with foreskins" were being collected from slain enemies. This shows that the request made of David is not that odd.[390] David meets Saul's challenge twice over, presenting two hundred foreskins (v. 27). Saul views this success as evidence that Yahweh is with David (v. 28), and his fear of him grows into full-blown enmity (v. 29).

Armies would remove body parts from the slain enemy to number the casualties. Though often heads or hands, in this relief it is a pile of phalli reminiscent of David's collection of Philistine foreskins.
V. Philips Long

Saul Seeks David's Life (19:1–24)

Michal took an idol and laid it on the bed (19:13). The nature of Michal's "idol" (*t^erāpîm*) is somewhat mysterious. Attempts to clarify the character of "teraphim" etymologically have not proved successful. More fruitful has been a phenomenological approach, focusing on the apparent function of teraphim in their fifteen biblical occurrences. The general consensus that teraphim must have been "household gods"[391] has been challenged recently by van der Toorn, who prefers the notion that teraphim were "ancestor statues."[392]

The latter theory may help to explain the Bible's somewhat ambivalent attitude toward teraphim, but a definitive answer to the question of what the teraphim were remains elusive.[393] Even their size seemed to vary considerably. While Rachel was able to conceal Laban's teraphim in the camel's saddle on which she was sitting (Gen. 31:34–35), Michal's teraphim are apparently large enough to simulate a reclining David. About all that can be said with relative certainty is that teraphim figured more prominently in "folk religion" than in the official cult.

Naioth (19:18). This word, which occurs only in 1 Samuel 19–20, is associated with the place name Ramah and is probably a noun signifying "camps," where the prophets at Ramah were active (the prophets' lodge in 2 Kings 6:1–2 may provide an analog).

A group of prophets prophesying (19:20). For discussions of prophecy in the Old Testament and the ancient Near East, see comments on 3:1 and 10:5.

The great cistern at Secu (19:22). Secu is probably not a proper noun but a common noun meaning a "bare height," perhaps here associated with a threshing floor near Ramah.[394]

He stripped off his robes (19:24). As discussed at 18:3–4, both in the Bible and the ancient Near East more broadly, special garments often marked a person's identity, status, or rank. Saul's (involuntary) divestment of his royal robes here serves as yet another reminder that, in Yahweh's eyes, he is no longer the rightful king (cf. 15:28).

Jonathan Aids and Encourages David (20:1–42)

Tomorrow is the New Moon festival (20:5). The Mesopotamian calendar included various festivals, or special days. Many were celebrated on certain days of the month—the seventh day, the fifteenth, or the beginning of the month (the new moon).[395] In Israel, too, the New Moon festival was a time of rejoicing. Marked by special sacrifices (Num. 28:11–15) and the sounding of trumpets (10:10; cf. Ps. 81:3), the festival is often mentioned in conjunction with the most regular of special days, the Sabbath (2 Kings 4:23), and it may have been subject to similar regulations (Amos 8:5). Judging from the prominence of the king in ancient Near Eastern festival celebrations[396] and from passages such as Ezekiel 45:17, David's absence from Saul's table may have had political repercussions. Observance of the New Moon festival continued into the postexilic period (Neh. 10:33; cf. also Col. 2:16).[397]

Ceremonially unclean (20:26). The issue is not so much one of physical as of ritual purity, though the boundary between these two was vague in the ancient Near East.[398] Thus, any uncleanness, whether incurred by contact with bodily fluids, unclean objects, or dead bodies, typically required more than a bath, often some kind of sacrifice, or a waiting period. Cleanliness legislation is presented most fully in Leviticus 11–15. On the present circumstance of uncleanness barring one from a festal meal, cf. 7:19–21.

They kissed each other (20:41). On possible connotations of a kiss in the ancient Near East, see comment on 2 Samuel 20:9. Here Jonathan and David, in the face of the dire situation they face, kiss each other as an expression of their friendship and the covenant existing between them. The Gilgamesh Epic speaks of a similar exchange between the hero Gilgamesh, apparently about to embark on a dangerous venture, and Enkidu, who has failed to dissuade him: "They kissed each other and formed a friendship."[399]

David Deceives Abimelech at Nob and Escapes to Gath (21:1–15)

Nob (21:1). The exact location of Nob is uncertain, but several sites within a couple of miles of Jerusalem are plausible candidates. Isaiah 10:32 speaks of an invader standing at Nob and shaking his fist at Jerusalem, which confirms the proximity of the two sites. After the destruction of Shiloh as a cultic center (see comment on 1:3), Nob became the "town of the priests" (22:19).

Consecrated bread ... provided the men have kept themselves from women (21:4). Consecration, or purification, of soldiers prior to battle was a common practice in the ancient Near East,[400] as in the Old Testament. Ritual purity would be all the more required before handling "consecrated bread," usually reserved for the priests. Uncleanness could be brought about in various ways (see comment on 20:26). Sexual intercourse could lead to a state of ritual uncleanness (Lev. 15:18), and abstention was often ordered for a period prior to an auspicious occasion (Ex. 19:15). Fear of

Bread was often part of offerings and would have been consecrated to be used ritually.
Guillaume Blanchard/Wikimedia Commons, courtesy of the Louvre

contaminating the camp may have played some part in Uriah's refusal to visit his wife, Bathsheba, in 2 Samuel 11:11–12.

Goliath's sword ... behind the ephod (21:9). On the three senses of "ephod" in the Bible, see comment on 2:18. All three designate sacred garments of some sort, from simple linen ephods worn by regular priests to the highly elaborate ephod worn by the high priest to costly garments not associated with a human wearer. In the ancient Near East, ornate vestments not only were worn by high officials but also sometimes adorned the statues of deities.[401] It has been suggested that the ephod here in Nob is not a garment at all but "some kind of object of veneration, perhaps even a divine image."[402]

This suggestion may be unnecessary, however, as the more ornate garments, often containing gold threads, would likely have been draped over something—either a statue or a stand—when not being worn. In the present context, with the ark unavailable (see comment on 6:21), the ephod at Nob may have been "the holiest relic of the sanctuary," lending plausibility to the notion that "captured articles of power such as Goliath's sword" would have been placed near it, as the ark had earlier been placed in the temple of Dagon (cf. 5:2).[403]

Achish king of Gath (21:10). On Gath, see comment on 5:8. "Achish" may be a title rather than a proper name; in either case it appears to be, like "Goliath," of Philistine origin.[404] A later "Achish" (Akhayus) is attested on the recently discovered Ekron Inscription (see comment on 5:10).

David Gathers a Company (22:1–5)

Escaped to the cave of Adullam (22:1). In biblical times, caves often provided refuge for those in distress (cf., e.g., 13:6). Adullam has

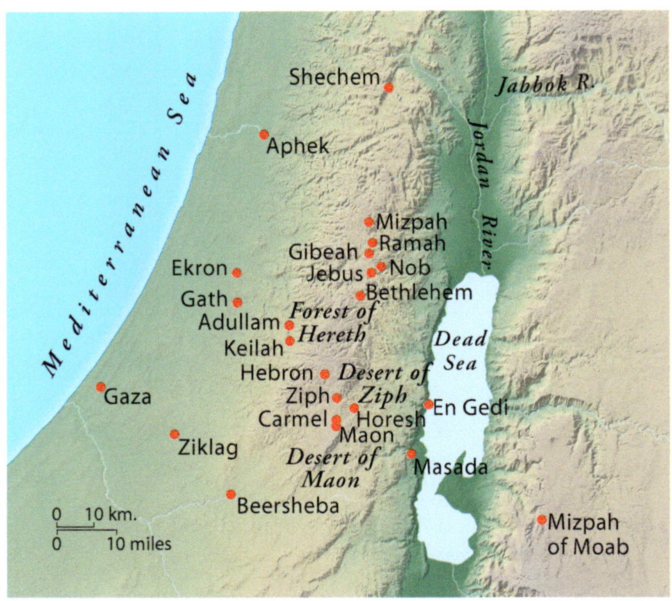

Region of David's movements

▸ Future King on the Run

The following is excerpted from The Story of Idrimi, King of Alalakh: "I am Idrimi.... An evil deed happened in Halab, the seat of my family, and we fled to the people of Emar, brothers of my mother, and we lived (then) in Emar."[A-86] Aspiring to better his standing, Idrimi leaves Emar and begins to attract followers.

In Canaan, a band including some of his own countrymen gathers around him. "They discovered that I was the son of their overlord and gathered around me. There I grew up and stayed a long time. For seven years I lived among the Hapiru-people." When oracular signs (i.e., the entrails of sheep and the flight direction of released birds) prove favorable, Idrimi returns to his native territory and begins to establish his rule.

long been identified with Khirbet esh-Sheikh Madhkur,[405] which lies near Socoh and Keilah in the Shephelah, roughly nine miles southeast of Gath, seven miles south of Beth Shemesh, and sixteen miles southwest of Jerusalem.[406] The king of Adullam was among the thirty-one Canaanite kings defeated by Joshua (see Josh. 12:15), and the town is listed among Judah's holdings in the western foothills (15:35).[407] As a border town, Adullam was doubtless contested from time to time by the Philistines. Adullam may have been the "stronghold" mentioned in 22:4 (see comment), but this is not the only possibility.

Those who were in distress or in debt or discontented gathered around him (22:2). Shifting alliances were characteristic of the ancient Near East, as is illustrated by the behaviors of the marginalized Habiru in the second millennium (see sidebar on "Hebrew/Habiru" at 4:6). The judge Jephthah, during his own period of marginalization, was joined by a band of "adventurers" (Judg. 11:3 NIV; NRSV has "outlaws"; JPS has "men of low character"). To David comes a "motley band of marginal people," who are suffering in various ways; perhaps some are "smarting under the oppression of tyranny," some are "victims of the neglect of laws forbidding usury," and some are "in despair at the way the country was being run."[408] The "discontented" are (lit.) those "bitter in spirit" (i.e., have suffered some great loss, are economically deprived, are homeless, etc.) and as a result are eager for change.[409] David's attraction to these disenfranchised people is far more than a partisan attraction to southerners against northerners.

David went to Mizpah in Moab (22:3). Several sites named Mizpah, which means something like "lookout point" or "watchtower," are mentioned in the Bible (see comment on 7:5). Moabite Mizpah is mentioned only here and its specific location is unknown, though

▲ This statue of King Idrimi of Alalakh was inscribed with 104 lines in the mid-fifteenth century. It apparently stood in the sactuary at Alalakh, but was discovered carefully buried nearby, probably in an effort to prevent its destruction by invaders.
Todd Bolen/www.BiblePlaces.com

the Jordanian sites of Kerak and Rujm el-Meshrefeh lying southwest of Madaba in Jordan have been suggested.[410] David's reception by the Moabite king may be related generally to the "practice of providing sanctuary for adversaries of enemies"[411] and, more specifically, to David's Moabite ancestry through Ruth (Ruth 4:13–17).

The Bible offers several examples of individuals seeking refuge in foreign territories (e.g., Jacob, Joseph, Moses, Absalom). An interesting ancient Near Eastern example is the story of Idrimi, King of Aleppo, who was forced to flee his native land, found refuge among his mother's kin, and eventually took up with the Habiru in northern Canaan for seven years, before returning to become king of Alalakh in northwestern Syria[412] (see sidebar on "Future King on the Run").

David was in the stronghold (22:4). While David's "stronghold" may have been at Adullam (see comment on 22:1),[413] other possibilities include an unspecified site somewhere in Moabite territory—note Gad's injunction to David "not [to] stay in the stronghold" but to "go into the land of Judah" (22:5)—or perhaps the natural fortress of Masada. On the latter possibility, Aharoni has observed that the best route between Judah and Moab involved crossing the Jordan at a ford opposite Masada, thus making Masada a candidate for the "fortress used by David as his base in the wilderness."[414] The discovery of Iron Age potsherds at Masada confirms that the site was used during the

Masada
Todd Bolen/www.BiblePlaces.com

Israelite period,[415] but the route itself has "not [yet] been confirmed archaeologically either side of the Dead Sea."[416]

David left and went to the forest of Hereth (22:5). Mentioned only here in the Bible, this forest's specific location is unknown, the problem of identification being exacerbated by uncertainties regarding the location of the "stronghold" David is to leave. At a minimum, the forest must have been west of the Dead Sea in the tribal territory of Judah. McCarter notes that a modern village called "Kharas" (cf. Hereth?) lies near "Khirbet Qîlā, which preserves the name of ancient Keilah";[417] this places the forest in the vicinity of Adullam (see comment on 22:1).

Saul Massacres the Priests at Nob (22:6–23)

Saul, spear in hand, was seated under the tamarisk tree ... at Gibeah (22:6). On the location of Gibeah, see comment on 10:26. Saul's position seated under a (tamarisk) tree recalls many such scenes involving ancient Near Eastern rulers. Often cited is the Ugaritic ʾAqhatu Legend, in which the hero Danʾel is found

> Sitting before the gate,
> Beneath a mighty tree on the threshing floor,
> Judging the cause of the widow,
> Adjudicating the case of the fatherless.[418]

The rendering "mighty tree" is uncertain, however, and a more recent translation by Pardee reads "among the leaders."[419] One is reminded also of Deborah holding court beneath the "Palm of Deborah between Ramah and Bethel" (Judg. 4:5).

In the present context, Saul sits beneath a tamarisk (*Tamarix*), a smallish tree which had several varieties in Palestine and which was typically found in drier regions. In Mesopotamian incantations, the tamarisk was a holy tree with purifying qualities. Images were made from its wood, and it was at times connected with cosmic stability. With its roots toward the underworld and its branches toward the sky, the tamarisk symbolized mediation "between the temporal world and the divine domains."[420] Whether this tree held such significance in Saul's day is uncertain, but Saul's overriding concern seems to be to scold his troops for their supposed disloyalty.

Will the son of Jesse give all of you fields and vineyards? (22:7). The practice of both rewarding and encouraging loyalty to the king by royal grants of land, houses, vineyards, wells, and the like was widespread in the ancient Near East. Royal rewards and incentives are evidenced in Babylonian, Assyrian, Hittite, and Ugaritic documents.[421] As Saggs

Tamarisk tree
Z. Radovan/www.BibleLand Pictures.com

explains in a discussion of the Early Dynastic period (ca. 2900–2400 B.C.), "Once kingship had developed, there also came to be royal estates.... The king would normally reward those who served him with a grant of land; legally the ownership of such land remained with the king, but it could become de facto an hereditary holding if the grantee had a son able to succeed to his duties."[422]

Tablet granting restoration of land by King Nabu-apla-iddina, ninth century B.C.
Michael Greenhalgh/ArtServe, courtesy of the British Museum

Even a foreigner such as the Edomite Doeg could become the beneficiary of royal largesse. The following thirteenth-century Ugaritic text provides an example of an Egyptian receiving a royal grant:

> From this day Ammistamri, son of Niqmepa, king of Ugarit, has given to Pa'ahi the Egyptian the house of Abdi-ba'al [*sic*?] son-in-law of Kunabilu, and the field of Sahteya and three iku [just over 2 1/2 acres] of field from the field of Ilimmasiru. And no one shall take it from the hand of Pa'ahi or from the hand of his son or the son of his sons. This gift is given for ever.[423]

Although the primary motives for awarding land grants are not often spelled out in the extant documents, they "were presumably reward for service, encouragement of the careful fulfillment of duties, and the desire to tie the recipients closely to the monarchy."[424]

Ahimelech inquired of the LORD for him (22:10). In the ancient Near East, one of the duties of (at least certain classes of) priests was to inquire of the deity on behalf of the king and others. In Mesopotamia, for instance, priests were trained in the omen texts and in the art of reading omens from animal entrails (e.g., sheep livers), from oils, from birds, and so on.[425] In Israel, too, priests were often involved in divine inquiry, although using the Urim and Thummim rather than the means just listed (see comments on 14:3; 14:18–19).

Whether Ahimelech had in fact inquired of the Lord for David is unclear. The statement in this verse to the effect that Ahimelech had done so comes from Doeg the Edomite, and so it is not necessarily to be trusted. The NIV's rendering of 22:15 ("Was that day the first time I inquired of God for him? Of course not!") seems to suggest that Ahimelech himself admits to making inquiry for David. But the verse may also be rendered, "Did I begin now to inquire of God for him? Far be it from me!"[426]

Put to the sword Nob, the town of the priests (22:19). The massacre of the inhabitants of the priestly town of Nob—"men

Enemy being slaughtered at the battle of Til-Tuba
Werner Forman Archive/The British Museum

and women, its children and infants, and its cattle, donkeys and sheep"—strikes the modern reader as an illegal outrage. A recent study considering the present episode in the light of Hittite literature, however, maintains that priests in Israel were "obliged by oaths of loyalty to the royal authority," just as were Hittite priests.[427] A text from Mari entitled The Protocol of the Diviner illustrates what such an oath of loyalty might look like. A relevant excerpt in which the diviner swears loyalty to Zimri-Lim, the king, reads as follows:

> And the one who makes an evil rebellion
> [against the life]
> of Zimri-Lim, [my] lord,
> who speaks to me about taking oracles,
> or who speaks to a diviner, my colleague,
> [and I he]a[r] or I see in the oracles
> [performed by the h]and of a diviner, my colleague,
> [I swear I will not] conceal it. In that very day
> I will surely tell [Zim]ri-Lim, my lord.[428]

The penalty for disloyalty could be extreme. In the Hittite Instructions to Priests and Temple Officials, for example, offenses against human superiors or a god are punished severely, potentially including the "total annihilation of the 'sinner' and his house."[429] A section using the slave/master relationship to illustrate the kinds of punishments an offender could expect concludes with the threat that "if he ever dies, he does not die alone, but his family (is) included with him." The next section spells out the fate of one who offends a god:

> If then, on the other hand, anyone vexes the feelings of a god, does the god punish him alone for it? Does he not punish his wife, his children, his descendants, his family, his slaves male (and) female, his cattle, his sheep, (and) his harvest for it, and remove him utterly?[430]

On the basis of such comparisons, one might argue that Saul's annihilation of the inhabitants of Nob is neither illegal nor outrageous. For Taggar-Cohen, "the act was expected of Saul: this is the way to punish treacherous and disloyal servants." Yet features of the biblical text, especially the unwillingness of Saul's courtiers to stretch out their hands against the priests, suggest a "tension between the religious feelings of the courtiers and the king's law."[431]

What must not be forgotten in this discussion is that Saul is no longer rightful king from the perspective of the author, having been rejected by Yahweh in 15:28; thus, he has no right either to expect loyalty or to punish those who lack it. In the end, Saul's actions remain an outrageous sacrilege on a number of counts, and their heinousness is only underscored by the fact that the list of those whom he destroys at Nob matches almost verbatim the list of those he failed to destroy, by his own disobedience, in his battle against the Amalekites (see 15:3). The irony of this comparison highlights the extent of Saul's depravity and his lack of seriousness in dealing with Yahweh (see also ch. 28).

David Saves the Citizens of Keilah (23:1–6)

Philistines are fighting against Keilah (23:1). On the Philistines as Israel's adversary to the southwest, see comment on 4:1. Keilah has been identified with Khirbet Qila, some eight miles northwest of Hebron and at the eastern extremity of the foothills (Shephelah) separating the coastal plain to the west from the central hills to the east (see comment on 22:5). One of a string of border towns often contested by the Philistines, the site of Keilah has not yet been excavated. While the comment of David's men in verse 3, distinguishing Keilah from Judahite territory, expresses the tenuous status of Keilah as a border town between vying forces, David's saving of the people of Keilah out of the hand of the Philistines (v. 5) attests their Judahite connection (as does their allocation to Judah in Josh. 15:44).

▸ The Changing Fate of Border Town Keilah

As a border town, Keilah appears to have been fortified (see Saul's reference to "gates and bars" in 23:7). Several of the fourteenth-century Amarna letters mention Qiltu (or Qiʿiltu), which is probably to be identified with the later biblical site of Keilah:

- EA 279: Śuwardata, the ruler of the city, speaks of having to "go fo[rt]h to Qiltu [again]st the *t[raitors]*."
- EA 280: Śuwardata reports having successfully waged war against Qiltu, with the result that "my city is restored to me."
- EA 289: the city of Qiltu is accused by ʿAbdi-Ḥeba, governor of Jerusalem, of having engaged in a conspiracy to isolate Jerusalem.
- EA 290: ʿAbdi-Ḥeba names Qiltu, Gazru (biblical Gezer), and Gimtu (biblical Gath) as towns making trouble in the area. He urges the Pharaoh to send archers, lest the "land of the king ... desert to the Ḫapiru."

Such references attest to the frequently changing status of Keilah and other border towns.

Looting the threshing floors (23:1). In the agricultural societies of the ancient Near East, grain was a highly valued commodity. Grain that reached the threshing floor was at the end of a lengthy process of labor-intensive cultivation and harvesting; thus, the looting of the threshing floors was a particularly effective means of weakening an adversary. The story of Gideon offers a parallel example of agricultural looting and destruction (Judg. 6:3–6, 11).

Keilah
Todd Bolen/www.BiblePlaces.com
▸

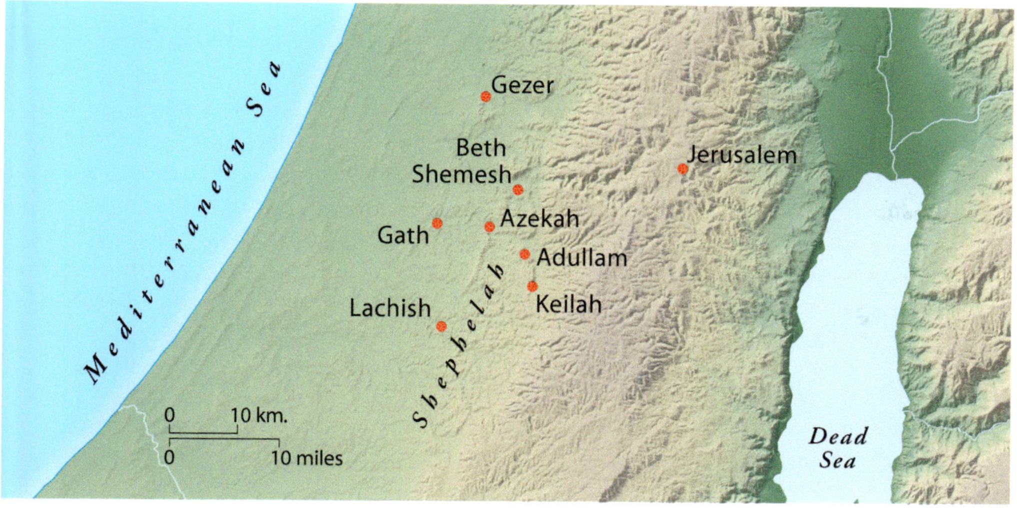

Keilah and its region

He inquired of the LORD (23:2). As in Israel it was understood that human destinies were in God's hands, so also throughout the ancient Near East the gods were regarded as controlling human affairs. Thus before any major undertaking, it was customary to consult the deity or deities. Before launching a military campaign, the king of the Hittites, for instance, consulted "his superiors, the gods," asking questions such as the following:

> "Do you, O god, approve a campaign this year for His Majesty on the Durmatta front?" or "Do you, O god, approve a campaign this year by His Majesty on the Nerik front?" The king might inquire about his control of land while on campaign: "If while My Majesty is returning from a campaign (in the east) against Assyria, will these (northern) borderlands not defect and no harm come to the holy city of Nerik?" Or the king might ask the very outcome of a campaign: "Will you give me the gods of the king of Assyria and will I defeat him in battle?"[432]

Formally, David's inquiry of Yahweh is along the same lines, though from the biblical perspective, David's God is the one true God, as distinct from the pagan gods regarded in the Bible as "nothings." David was diligent in consulting Yahweh before making any important moves (e.g., 30:7; 2 Sam. 2:1; 5:19), although not without some failures (see comment on 1 Sam. 27:2). By contrast, Saul's commitment to gaining direction from Yahweh was marginal from the beginning and declined over time (see 14:18–19, 36–42; 28:3–25). On some of the accepted modes of divine inquiry in Israel, see comment on 28:6.

Egyptian tomb of Menna showing oxen threshing grain
Manfred Näder, Gabana Studios, Germany

LMLK seals from Lachish with "Ziph" inscribed
Todd Bolen/www.BiblePlaces.com

Saul Pursues David but Is Thwarted by the Philistines (23:7–29)

Bring the ephod (23:9). On the use of the ephod as an oracular device, see comment on 2:18.

David stayed in the desert strongholds and in the hills of the Desert of Ziph (23:14). The town of Ziph (associated with Tell Zif, some five miles southeast of Hebron and thirteen miles southeast of Keilah) occupied a high vantage point overlooking the wilderness of Judah. Archaeologically, Ziph is attested several times on stamped jar handles from the late eighth century (the time of King Hezekiah).[433] These are of the *lmlk*—"belonging to the king"—variety, over eight hundred of which have been recovered from some twenty Judean sites.

In addition to those with Ziph, others attest the names Sucoh, Hebron, and *mmst*.[434] It has been postulated that these four sites were "the chief towns of four administrative districts where Hezekiah of Judah built stores which could be drawn upon in the event of an Assyrian invasion."[435] Ziph may also be mentioned in Arad ostracon 17, though the reading is uncertain.[436]

Horesh in the Desert of Ziph (23:15). While *ḥōreš* can mean a "forest" or "wooded area," such a meaning seems unlikely in a desert region; thus, Horesh is probably a place name, perhaps to be associated with modern Khirbet Khoreisa, some two miles south of Ziph.[437]

Hill of Hakilah, south of Jeshimon (23:19). Mentioned only here and in 26:1, 3, the Hill of Hakilah has not been identified. Jeshimon is used in two senses: as a general designation for a desert or wasteland, and as specific name for certain such places. Here Jeshimon may designate a particularly "desolate and dangerous region" of the Judean wilderness,[438] whose foreboding features tended to draw desperate people on the run—note Saul's concern to gather intelligence about "all the hiding places [David] uses" (v. 23).

The Ziphites' betrayal of David's whereabouts to Saul does not appear to have been driven by an "instinct for self-preservation,"

Desert of Ziph
Todd Bolen/www.BiblePlaces.com

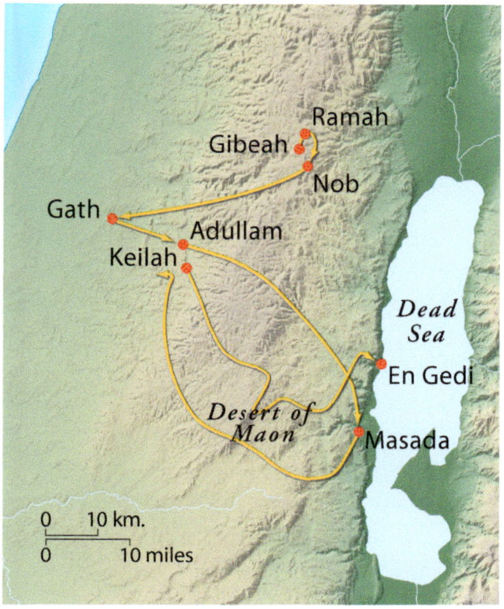

David's flight from Saul

as was the case with the citizens of Keilah, but by "outright antipathy."[439] The Amarna letters give ample evidence of how troublesome to settled populations roving bands such as the Habiru could be, and the Ziphites may well "not have welcomed the idea of such a large contingent of freebooters in their neighbourhood."[440]

Desert of Maon, in the Arabah south of Jeshimon (23:24). Continuing his flight southward, David reached Maon, a site some five miles south of Ziph that has been identified with modern Khirbet el-Maᶜin. A mile or so north of Maon lay Carmel (not to be confused with Mount Carmel on the north coast), and it was in this region that David came into conflict with the wealthy livestock owner Nabal (25:2–3). Baly describes the countryside around Maon and Carmel as consisting largely of "broad open hills with wide, open valleys" and grading off into desert on the south and east.[441]

Maon, which means something like "den, haunt, refuge, dwelling,"[442] may reflect either the ruggedness and remoteness of the area bordering it to the south and east or, more likely, the characteristic dwellings of the herdsmen who occupied the site.[443] As Aharoni has noted, many biblical sites "are named after particular buildings characterizing the settlement in its earlier stages or after the general form of its dwellings."[444] Archaeologically, Maon is attested on at least one ostracon.[445]

Saul and his forces were closing in on David (23:26). The Hebrew word rendered "closing in" means to "surround, encircle," suggesting that Saul may have been seeking to catch David in a pincer movement by sending troops around the "crag" in two directions.[446]

Strongholds of En Gedi (23:29). The name En Gedi means "spring of the young goat" and aptly designates an oasis on the western side of the Dead Sea some thirty-five miles south of Jerusalem and fifteen miles

En Gedi
Kim Walton

or more east of Ziph and Maon. The main spring of En Gedi (there are others in the area) issues from a height along the shore of the Dead Sea, emerging more than six hundred feet above the level of the sea. Both the presence of water in this arid region and the rugged terrain made En Gedi an ideal haunt for wild goats (see comment on 24:1–2) and for David on the run, offering him and his men both provision and protection.

Not surprisingly, the oasis of En Gedi has a long settlement history, beginning as early as the fourth millennium B.C.—a temple from that period has been discovered[447]—and continuing throughout the biblical period.[448] Excavations have yielded ample evidence of the cultic, military, and commercial significance of the En Gedi region.[449] According to excavator B. Mazar, the "strongholds of En Gedi" may refer to "walled camps at the top of the mountains,"[450] but the cavernous terrain itself may have provided refuge; in the next chapter, David will be found hiding in a cave at En Gedi.

David Spares Saul's Life in the Cave (24:1–22)

Desert of En Gedi ... Crags of the Wild Goats (24:1–2). En Gedi means "spring of the young goat" (see comment on 23:29). That a region within the Desert of En Gedi bore the name "Crags of the Wild Goats" is further indication of the kind of wildlife that inhabited the area in biblical times, and even today. The Hebrew word rendered "wild goat" (*yāʿēl*) actually identifies an ibex (*capra ibex nubiana*), which typically inhabits craggy terrain in desert regions and is noted for its agility and cliff-climbing ability (the Heb. name may be related to the verb *ʿlh*, "to go up").[451] It is reported that locals can even today identify the ibex cliffs at En Gedi and that herds of ibexes still thrive in the region.

Ibex from En Gedi area
Copyright 1995–2009 Phoenix Data Systems

A cave was there, and Saul went in to relieve himself (24:3). While caves certainly are in the area, attempts to identify the specific cave in question have not succeeded.[452] The literal meaning of the Hebrew expression translated "relieve oneself" is to "cover one's feet." Its occurrence in Judges 3:24 (in the story of Ehud and Eglon) confirms its use as a euphemism. The logic of the expression is not certain, but it may relate to "the Israelite practice of disposing of human excrement in a sanitary manner through covering it over with dirt (cf. Deut. 23:13)."[453] That Saul enters alone into the very cave where David and his men are hiding is an unmistakably providential irony.

David ... cut off a corner of Saul's robe ... was conscience-striken (24:4–5). For the significance of robes and hems and their removal see comment on 15:27, which notes that grasping or removing the hem of a garment can mean different things in different contexts. Moreover, in the discussion of Jonathan's transfer of his robe to David in 18:3–4, we noted that in the ancient Near East a "special robe or mantel could serve as a symbol of a person's identity and status, so that to transfer it to another signified a transfer of status." In the present episode, David displays the severed hem of Saul's robe as evidence that he had been close enough to Saul to kill him but had refrained to do so, despite the encouragement of his men (24:10–11).

But the fact that no sooner had David "cut off the corner of Saul's robe" than his conscience began to strike him (24:5) suggests that his motive may not have been first

Pharaoh in the presence of four deities conveying the gods' sponsorship of the king
Brian J. McMorrow

or foremost to demonstrate his innocence to Saul but, rather, to divest Saul symbolically of his rule.

The LORD forbid that I should do such a thing to my master, the LORD's anointed (24:6). On the significance of Saul as "the LORD's anointed," see comments on 2:10. In brief, the king's anointing expressed his vassal relationship to the Great King, from whom his authority was derived, under whose protection he stood, and to whom he was beholden. Not only in the Bible but generally in the ancient Near East, "royal authority was seen to have a heavenly origin and destiny; where authority was at issue, the gods were believed to be nearby."[454]

To cite but a few examples, Eannatum, ruler of Lagash in its Early Dynastic period (early third millennium), speaks of himself as one "whose name was called by Enlil; endowed with strength by Ningirsu; envisaged by Nanshe in (her) heart; truly and rightly suckled by Ninhursaga; named by Inanna." Gudea (near the end of the third millennium), also of Lagash, betrays a similarly polytheistic orientation in describing himself as the "Shepherd envisaged by Ningirsu in (his) heart ... endowed with dignity and sublime scepter by Ig-alima ... he whom Ningiszida his god has made to appear in the assembly with (proudly) raised head." The famous Hammurabi (early second millennium) alludes to his divine election when he speaks of a time when "Shamash ... with radiant face had joyfully looked upon me—me, his favourite shepherd, Hammurabi."[455]

Nearer the time of David, an inscription of the Assyrian king Tiglath-pileser I (1114–1076 B.C.) credits the king's rule to divine appointment:

> Great gods, managers of heaven (and) underworld, whose attack means conflict and strife, who make great the sovereignty of Tiglath-pileser, beloved prince, your select one, attentive shepherd, whom you chose in the steadfastness of your hearts; upon him you set the exalted crown, you grandly established him for sovereignty over the land of the god Enlil, to him you granted leadership, supremacy, (and) valour, you pronounced forever his destiny

> of dominion as powerful and (the destiny) of his priestly progeny for service to Ehursagkurkurra.[456]

Such was the consistent tenor of royal inscriptions in the ancient Near East; all these (and many more) give the flavor of ancient Near Eastern thinking with respect to the link between royal authority and divine authorization. As a worshiper of the one true God, David is rightly respectful of the status of Yahweh's anointed (cf. 26:9) and, despite the fact that Saul is clearly out to kill him, regrets having lifted his hand, even symbolically, against Saul.

David bowed down and prostrated himself with his face to the ground (24:8). Bowing facedown on the ground was a common way in the ancient Near East of showing submission, reverence, and sometimes fear. A notable instance in the archaeological record is found on the so-called Black Obelisk, which shows King Jehu of Israel doing obeisance before the Assyrian king Shalmaneser III (see photo).

In the El Amarna correspondence, local rulers in Canaan often begin their letters to their Egyptian superior with a standard greeting including the phrase, "I fall at the feet of the king." A typical example, which mentions the troublesome *ʿapiru*, reads: "Say to the king, my lord, my god, my Sun: Message of Milkilu, your servant, the dirt at your feet. I fall at the feet of the king, my lord, 7 times and 7 times. May the king, my lord, know that the war against me and against Śuwardata is severe. So may the king, my lord, save his land from the power of the ʿApiru."[457] Many of the letters clarify what "7 times and 7 times" may signify, saying something like the following: "I fall at the feet of the king, my lord, 7 times and 7 times, both on the stomach and on the back."[458] Ugaritic letters to the king or queen employ similar greetings. One letter varies the standard phrase to read "two times seven times," suggesting that the essential element is repetition, not necessarily front and back.[459]

Obeisance before the king

A dead dog? A flea? (24:14). Since the dog was not considered "man's best friend" in the ancient Near East but was regarded with some disdain, "dog" was a favorite term both in insults and in expressions of self-abasement. To be a "*dead* dog" was worse still (see also 2 Sam. 9:8; 16:9, the only other occurrences in the Bible). David's self-deprecation before Saul is meant to assure Saul that his pursuit of him is neither necessary nor worthy.

Reference to oneself as a "dog" was a stereotypical way of showing deference to one in a superior position, as is evidenced in the Lachish and Amarna letters.[460] If to be a (dead) dog was to be insignificant, then to be a "single flea" (so the Hebrew reads) was to be almost nothing at all. This usage of "single" to connote something like "mere" is paralleled in several Amarna letters that refer to a "single dog" (e.g., "Who am I, a *mere* dog, that I should not go?").[461]

Abigail Saves David from Blood-Guilt (25:1–44)

David moved down into the Desert of Maon (25:1). See comment on 23:24.

Carmel (25:2). Not to be confused with Mount Carmel, a mountain range along the coast to the northwest of Samaria, the town of Carmel with which Nabal is identified lay about a mile north of Maon and eight miles southeast of Hebron. Although this site (probably to be identified with modern Khirbet el-Kirmil) is today rather unimpressive from an agricultural perspective, it was well suited for grazing livestock in David's day.[462]

Moreover, Carmel was both politically and economically important in the biblical period. Its political importance derived from its strategic position as "part of the defense system of the Judean desert," and its economic importance was based on its suitability to animal breeding.[463] In the aftermath of his battle against the Amalekites, Saul had raised a monument to himself at Carmel (see comment on 15:12). In so doing, he laid claim to sovereignty over the area. This fact, perhaps with some sense of indebtedness to Saul for expelling the Amalekites, may have contributed to Nabal's utter disregard for David.[464]

His name was Nabal and his wife's name was Abigail (25:3). On naming and the various significances of names among the ancient Hebrews, see comment on 1:20. The name Abigail sounds something like "(my) father rejoices," and the description of Abigail in the present verse as "an intelligent and beautiful woman" is certainly commensurate with such a meaning. The name of her husband, Nabal, sounds like a Hebrew adjective meaning "churlish, foolish," and again his portrayal throughout the chapter confirms the appropriateness of the name (explicitly confirmed by Abigail in v. 25: "his name is Fool, and folly goes with him).

It seems hardly likely, however, that Nabal's parents would have saddled him with a name of such negative connotation, nor is it likely that the name arose as a nickname by those who knew Nabal—nicknames do not typically focus on character deficiencies. Rather, the meaning(s) associated with "Nabal" in the minds of his parents were probably favorable. On various linguistic grounds, J. Barr offers four suggestions: (1) fire/flame/arrow; (2) one sent; (3) noble/noble-minded/generous; (4) skilled/clever.[465] Barr prefers the second option, but whatever one's preference Barr is almost certainly correct that there was some positive connotation in the mind of Nabal's parents when they named their son.

Abigail herself probably heard the name as expressing something positive or at least neutral at the time of her marriage. But, as Barr remarks, "years of marriage to this miserly and cantankerous man made her think about his name in another way, and made her realize how close he came to expressing the quality which the Israelites normally designated as *nabal*."[466]

Calebite (25:3). Since the time of Israel's conquest and settlement of the Negev, Hebron was associated with the hero Caleb (Josh. 14:13–15; Judg. 1:20), who like Joshua had brought back a faithful report to Moses after the initial sending of twelve spies into the land of Canaan (Num. 13–14). Possibly (cf. the genealogical information in 1 Chron. 2:18–55, which links the settlement of Bethlehem with the descendants of Caleb; see esp. vv. 19, 50–51, 54) Nabal the Calebite was a distant kinsman of David,[467] making David's request of him all the more reasonable. The name Caleb resonates with the Hebrew word for "dog," leading some ancient versions as well as modern commentators to detect a disparaging pun in Nabal's epithet, yielding something like "Nabal, that dog!"[468] (cf. comment on 24:14).

He heard that Nabal was shearing sheep (25:4). King and Stager boldly state, "The

Flocks captured by invaders demonstrate the need for protection.
Todd Bolen/www.BiblePlaces.com

▸ Shepherding in the Ancient World

Subcontracting the tasks of shepherding is well illustrated in an Old Babylonian text first published by Finkelstein.[A-87] After a brief listing of the numbers of sheep and goats of various types, genders, or stages of development, the text (as adapted by Postgate) reads as follows:

> Total 158 sheep, 64 goats, which Sin-šamuh has entrusted to Dada the shepherd. He takes liability for them, and will replace any lost animal. If Nidnatum his shepherd-boy makes off, he shall be responsible for the loss. Dada will pay (the boy) 5 gur [1,500 l] of grain. (3 witnesses. 18th day of 4th month, Samsu-iluna Year 1).

As Postgate observes, "the terms of the contract reflect the inescapable fact that the shepherd is beyond the control of the owner."[A-88] At certain times of the year, it may have been possible for the flocks to graze near the home of their owner, returning each evening, but in the dry summer months shepherds often had to travel considerable distances to find suitable pasturage for the flocks and be gone for long stretches of time. As a reward for fulfilling their duties, the shepherds could expect a certain amount of wool per adult sheep, as well as milk while in the field, meat at slaughter time, and so forth.

For their part, shepherds assumed liability for the welfare of the sheep and were responsible to return the correct total at shearing time (calculated on the basis of normal rates of birth and natural attrition, and with agreed-upon means of proving loss by disease or animal attack). This proof typically involved some animal part (skin, ears, tendons, or the like) that demonstrated that the animal had in fact perished and had not simply been sold or negligently lost.[A-89] Should the shepherds come up short, they would have to make up the lack.[A-90]

economies of the biblical world were, to a large extent, based on wool."[469] Shearing time (in the spring)[470] was a time of abundance and gladness and, one would hope, of generosity. If, as early second-millennium texts from the Babylonian city of Larsa indicate, one sheep produced over two pounds of wool at shearing time,[471] Nabal's three thousand sheep (25:2) would have produced over three tons of wool. Further evidence of Nabal's wealth is the quantity of the goods that Abigail brings to David in 25:18.

Night and day they were a wall around us (25:16). With these words, one of Nabal's servants explicitly confirms to Abigail that David's claim in verses 7 and 15 to have safeguarded Nabal's flocks is true. For this service, Nabal's servants have as much reason to be grateful to David as Nabal himself. In the ancient Near East, sheep owners often contracted with shepherds to tend their flocks (who in turn might contract out the actual care of the sheep to shepherd boys; see sidebar on "Shepherding in the Ancient World").

Abigail lost no time. She took two hundred loaves of bread (25:18). These gifts are in keeping with a time of festival and are suggestive of hospitality, not simply of repayment. In ancient societies, gift-giving, as distinct from the simple exchange of goods (which constituted commerce), played an important and complex role. Among the dynamics of gift-giving summarized by Stansell in a recent study, the following seem pertinent to the present situation: "Gifts are bound up in the honor/shame system and establish or deny rank; gifts establish inti-

Supplies brought for a banquet
Kim Walton, courtesy of the Oriental Institute Museum

mate ties between persons or groups ... gifts amend or appease."[472]

Abigail's immediate concern, of course, is to make amends for her foolish husband's actions and to appease the affronted David. David is affronted not simply by Nabal's unwillingness to compensate for services rendered (even if they were technically unsolicited), but also by the dishonor/shame that Nabal's refusal to recognize him as more than a runaway slave heaped on David. Though not its original intent, Abigail's gift, which both honors David and repays him for his services, also smooths the way for David, after Nabal's death, to woo and to wed Abigail. On his part, David would have given gifts as part of the courtship process and, in due course, also gave Abigail children (2 Sam. 3:3).[473]

Bound securely as in the bundle of the living... hurl away as from the pocket of a sling (25:29). Abigail engages in two brilliant metaphorical wordplays. The first, "bound ... bundle" (root *ṣrr*), is evident in English translation, while the second in Hebrew is something like "sling ... [from a] sling" (root *qlᶜ*).

Two main theories have been proposed to elucidate the "bundle of the living." One is that it is a document that has been bound or tied up—thus, "Document of the Living." McCarter understands this to be equivalent to the "Book of the Living," that is, "the heavenly book in which all living people are recorded; exclusion from which means death."[474] The concept of a heavenly ledger is present in the ancient Near East from earliest times. As S. M. Paul remarks, "Divine bookkeeping also began in Sumer."[475] In Mesopotamia, destinies were determined by the gods, and their decisions were inscribed on "tablets of destiny."[476] Thus, prayers included petitions such as the following by Nebuchadrezzar: "On your [Nabu's] unchangeable tablet, which establishes the boundaries of heaven and earth, proclaim length of days for me, inscribe long life."[477]

A second theory is that shepherds kept a tally of their sheep by carrying a bag of small stones, each of which represented one of the sheep. When a sheep was bought or sold, a stone was added or removed.[478]

David sent word to Abigail, asking her to become his wife (25:39). While modern, Western readers might read these lines as a tale of romance, in the ancient Near East marriage and politics were often intertwined. In the colorful words of S. N. Kramer, marriage in the ancient Near East was typically "a practical arrangement in which the carefully weighed shekel counted more than love's hot desire."[479]

Amarna letter from Tushratta, king of Mitanni, lists gifts associated with the diplomatic marriage of his daughter to the Egyptian pharaoh.
bpk/Vorderasiatisches Museum, SMB/Olaf M.Teßmer

In third millennium Ebla, for instance, political alliances were often solidified by establishing blood ties through giving princesses in marriage to foreign rulers.[480] Similarly, the Neo-Sumerian King of Ur, Shulgi (2046–1998 B.C.), sought to expand his influence and control through diplomatic marriages; some one hundred princes or princesses of the Third Dynasty of Ur are on record, many filling official state positions.[481] Hittite texts also attest political marriages, as evidenced by the web of relations established by the thirteenth-century king Ḫattušiliš III, who having reinstalled a certain Benteshima on the throne of Amurru gave him one of his daughters, Gasshulawiya, in marriage. A son born of this union later married another of Ḫattušiliš's daughters, with the result that the son's wife was also his aunt.[482]

Among the Assyrians, rulers such as Assur-uballit I (ca. 1364–1329 B.C.) and Shalmaneser III (858–824 B.C.) married daughters to Babylonian puppet kings in an attempt to manipulate the Babylonians.[483] Predictably, arranged diplomatic marriages were not always the happiest. The Mari letters include several from Kirum, a daughter of King Zimri-Lim of Mari, who along with her older sister had been given in marriage to a vassal ruler named Haya-Sumu. So unhappy was Kirum in her marriage with Haya-Sumu, who according to one of Zimri-Lim's servants "could not care less about her," that she wrote, "If my lord [her father] does not conduct me to Mari, I will not hesitate to throw myself from the roof."[484]

Whatever may have been David's personal feelings for Abigail—"an intelligent and beautiful woman" (v. 3)—he undoubtedly benefited politically from this, as well as other, marriages.[485] David's earlier marriage to Saul's daughter Michal (18:27) brought him into the royal family; his marriages to Ahinoam of Jezreel (25:43, see next comment) and to Abigail would have strengthened his ties to the southern region around Hebron. On polygamy in antiquity, see comment on 1:2.

David had also married Ahinoam of Jezreel (25:43). While first mentioned here, David's marriage to Ahinoam of Jezreel apparently preceded his marriage to Abigail, bringing the sum of David's wives, including Saul's daughter Michal, to three so far. Ahinoam has piqued the curiosity of scholars. Combining the fact that the Old Testament mentions only one other Ahinoam (the wife of Saul listed in 14:50) with Nathan's statement to David in 2 Samuel 12:8 that the Lord had given "your master's wives into your arms," one scholar has suggested that David's Ahinoam may have once been Saul's wife.[486] As D. Edelman has remarked, however, "such a presumption would require David to

Carmel
Z. Radovan/www.BibleLandPictures.com

have run off with the queen mother while Saul was still on the throne, which seems unlikely."[487]

More likely, Nathan's comment refers in a formulaic fashion to David's inheritance of all that belonged to Saul, once David became king over both Judah and Israel (see 2 Sam. 5:1–5). The Jezreel from which David's Ahinoam came was almost certainly not the Jezreel Valley but a town in the hill country of Judah somewhere in the vicinity of Maon, Carmel, and Ziph (see Josh. 15:55–56). The precise location of this town is uncertain.

Saul had given his daughter Michal, David's wife, to Paltiel son of Laish, who was from Gallim (25:44). The location of Gallim is unknown, but based on Isaiah 10:30, which mentions Gallim in parallel to Anathoth (a town three miles northeast of Jerusalem), the town of Gallim probably lay in that general region. Isaiah 10:30 also mentions a town called Laishah in the area, which recalls Paltiel's father Laish. Saul's giving of Michal to Paltiel must have been, in part at least, politically motivated, effectively distancing David from the royal family—a situation that David will be quick to rectify at the earliest opportunity (2 Sam. 3:14).

David Spares Saul's Life in the Camp (26:1–25)

Ziphites ... Hakilah ... Jeshimon (26:1). On the Ziphites and on David's location in the Judean wilderness, see comments on 23:14, 19. It is understandable that the citizens of Ziph, which lay only a few miles north of Carmel (the setting of the preceding chapter), would keep tabs on David's whereabouts and report these to Saul (cf. their similar action in 23:19).

Ahimelech the Hittite and Abishai son of Zeruiah (26:6). That Ahimelech is described as a "Hittite" raises the question whether he is to be associated with the Hittites who founded an empire in the eighteenth century B.C. and dominated Anatolia in the fourteenth and thirteenth centuries, or was simply a member of a Canaanite people group who happened also to be called Hittites. The latter Hittites were counted among the Canaanite peoples whom Israel was to displace (e.g., Gen. 10:20; 15:18–21). Ahimelech's name is Semitic, which suggests Canaanite origin, although other explanations are possible.[488]

The vexed question of the relationship between Anatolian Hittites and the Canaanite enclave of the same name has not been resolved.[489] At the very least, most references in the Old Testament to Hittites appear to refer to "a local people of Palestine, settled in the area around Hebron before Abraham's arrival."[490] Ahimelech, then, is a Canaanite recruit. Abishai, however, was a kinsman—specifically, a nephew through David's sister Zeruiah (see family tree at 2 Sam. 16:10–11).

Who can lay a hand on the LORD's anointed (26:9). As in his earlier close encounter with an unsuspecting Saul (ch. 24), David is again urged to kill his pursuer. David's reaction is the same as before—the anointed of Yahweh is sacrosanct (see comment on 24:6). Furthermore, having seen Yahweh deal with Nabal (25:38), David is more confident than ever that Saul's "time [lit., 'day'] will come and he will die" (26:10). The expression "his day will come," followed by its rather grave interpretation, is neatly paralleled in a prophetic text from Mari.[491] This expression seems to relate to death not caused by obvious injury, as David distinguishes it from death by the sword in battle; in either case, Yahweh is seen as doing the striking. The same distinction is made in the Apology of Ḫattušiliš III.[492]

Get the spear and water jug that are near his head, and let's go (26:11). Again

Royal spear head
Marie-Lan Nguyen/Wikimedia Commons, courtesy of the Louvre

Pilgrim flask
Joshua Walton, courtesy of the Joseph P. Free Collection and Wheaton College

Saul is found with his spear at his side or, in this instance, "stuck in the ground near his head" (v. 7) while he sleeps. The regular association of Saul with his spear (see 22:6; 2 Sam. 1:6) suggests that it may have served as a kind of royal emblem, but it also recalls his earlier acts of violence against others and adumbrates his final act of violence against himself (1 Sam. 31:4). The loss of spear and water jug in the Judean desert could be life-threatening, and David uses the items effectively to demonstrate that even though Saul has again fallen into his hands, David has refused to lay a hand on him. That David does not intend to harm Saul, even indirectly, is evidenced by his return of the spear in 26:22.[493]

Go, serve other gods (26:19). While peoples of the ancient Near East often associated their deities with particular territories and even particular holy places, Yahweh, according to mainstream Old Testament thinking, is not so limited.[494] In their recent history, Israel had seen Yahweh lay his heavy hand on the Philistines and the Ammonites (chs. 6; 11), to say nothing of David's encounter with the Philistine Goliath (ch. 17). The sense of David's complaint that he is being forced to serve other gods and is being driven from the presence of Yahweh should not be understood in any absolute sense but in the purely practical sense that, as a fugitive, he is being driven from the familiar places where Yahweh is worshiped.[495]

A flea ... a partridge in the mountains (26:20). On "flea," see comment on 24:14. Here David's self-description may suggest not only humility but also the difficulty of Saul's accomplishing his goal, "looking for a flea."

Barren region in the Judean wilderness where David hid away from Saul
Kim Walton

Then, having begun his exchange with Saul by "calling out" to Abner from atop a distant hill (v. 13), David now likens himself to "a partridge in the mountains." This second metaphor is apt on several grounds. (1) The word for "partridge" in Hebrew is (lit.) "caller"; just as a hunter might pursue a single partridge ("caller") in the mountains with little hope of success, so Saul is in futile pursuit of David, himself a caller in the mountains (cf. v. 14). (2) The type of partridge found in this part of the Judean desert is probably the sand partridge (*Ammoperdix heyi*), which is "a great runner and speeds along the ground when it is chased, until it becomes exhausted and can be knocked down by the hunter's stick."[496] As adroit as David's movements are, Saul's relentless chasing after him must have been exhausting.

David Flees to the Philistines (27:1–12)

David ... went over to Achish son of Maoch king of Gath (27:2). As a fugitive seeking refuge in foreign territory and perhaps employment as a mercenary, David is following a widely attested practice in the ancient Near East. The landless or disenfranchised, such as the Habiru (with whom David and his men have been compared),[497] sometimes hired themselves out as fighters in order to obtain favors such as land (see also sidebar on "Hebrews/Habiru" at 4:6). In response to David's request for "one of the country towns," Achish gives him Ziklag (27:5–6), but his motivation is hardly generosity. As Postgate remarks, "it has always proved political for a state to secure the continued attachment of its fighting men by finding plots of land for them."[498]

In addition to the desire to better their own circumstances, mercenaries were also sometimes motivated by their grievances toward a former ruler. At the famous battle of Marathon, for instance, the Persian army benefited from the defection of Greek tyrants who, having been expelled from their positions, joined the ultimately unsuccessful Persians in fighting against the Greeks.[499] David's departure to the Philistines (though not a full defection, as subsequent events demonstrate) is largely prompted by his grievous treatment at the hands of Saul. Later, after David becomes king, he too uses mercenaries, the Kerethites and Pelethites (i.e., Cretans and Philistines), who serve as his personal bodyguard (2 Sam. 8:18; cf. 23:22–23).

Although David's sojourn among the Philistines has rightly been characterized as "one of the most disreputable in David's career,"[500] from a pragmatic standpoint it accomplishes several things: It places him out of Saul's reach; it allows him to learn Philistine ways, including their technologies and military practices; it puts him in a position surreptitiously to destroy some of Israel's longtime foes, while benefiting from their wealth and using some of it to curry favor with leaders in Judah, who will one day be his subjects.[501] (For more on Achish, see comments on 5:10; 21:10. On Gath, see comment on 5:8.)

Ahinoam of Jezreel and Abigail of Carmel (27:3). See comments on 25:39, 43.

Achish gave him Ziklag (27:6). To say that the precise location of biblical Ziklag is uncertain is an understatement. See sidebar on "The Identity of Ziklag."

David lived in Philistine territory a year and four months (27:7). During this period Saul dies, and following it David becomes king in Hebron at the age of thirty (2 Sam. 5:4). Thus, David is about twenty-eight years old when he flees to Philistine territory.

Geshurites (27:8). Not to be confused with Geshur in Transjordan (see, e.g., Josh. 12:5), the Geshurites here are neighbors of the Philistines (note their association in Josh. 13:2). Absalom, David's third son, is born to Maacah, daughter of Talmai king of Geshur in Transjordan, and it is to that Geshur, not this region in southwest Canaan, that he flees after killing Amnon (2 Sam. 13:37–38; 15:8 ["Geshur in Aram"]).

Girzites (27:8). The identification of the Girzites, mentioned only here in biblical or

The Identity of Ziklag

J. D. Currid chooses the quest for the geographic location of Ziklag as his prime example of the difficulties of site identification.[A-91] J. D. Seger began an earlier quest for the site with the observation that "after almost a full century of intensive archaeological exploration and study, no firm consensus has yet emerged."[A-92] He argued in favor of Tell Halif (Tell Khuweilifeh), but his case was weakened by the "minimal amount of Iron I remains at the mound."[A-93]

Subsequently, Oren sought to identify Tel Seraᶜ (Tell esh-Shariᶜa) as Ziklag and has been followed in this judgment by many scholars.[A-94] This site lies almost twenty-five miles south-southwest of Gath, in the transition zone between the southern foothills (Shephelah) and the northern Negev. Such a location is appropriate to the biblical evidence, which suggests that Ziklag is in a border zone between Philistine and Israelite territory—assigned to the tribe of Simeon in Joshua 19:5, later counted as part of Judah (Judg. 15:31), and perhaps still later brought under the control of Gath as a result of Philistine expansion in the period just prior to David's time. The biblical evidence also suggests that Ziklag must have been sufficiently far from Gath for David's military exploits (about which he lied to Achish) to have escaped scrutiny. Tell esh-Shariᶜa meets these criteria.

The problem, however, is that no evidence of a tenth-century destruction of the site has been uncovered, contrary to what one expects from 30:3, 14.[A-95] Conclusions based on what has *not* been found archaeologically are to be drawn with caution, however, and the conquests of cities, even where burn-

Ziklag (Tell Sera)
Todd Bolen/www.BiblePlaces.com

ing is involved, do not always leave recoverable evidence.[A-96] The general area offers other potential sites, such as "Tell Haror, Khirbet Zuheiliqah, and even Tell Beith Mirsim," mentioned by Currid.[A-97]

Fritz has argued that Tell es-Seba^c, normally identified as Beersheba, is possibly Ziklag and that biblical Beersheba lies buried beneath the modern city of Beersheba, some four miles west of Tell es-Seba^c.[A-98] Fritz makes an interesting case, noting in particular that the Iron Age village on the site "was replaced in the early 10th century by a fortified town—just at the beginning of the monarchy," a change that would be in keeping with David's interest in the site. But for now, we remain as we began, uncertain as to the precise location of Ziklag.[A-99]

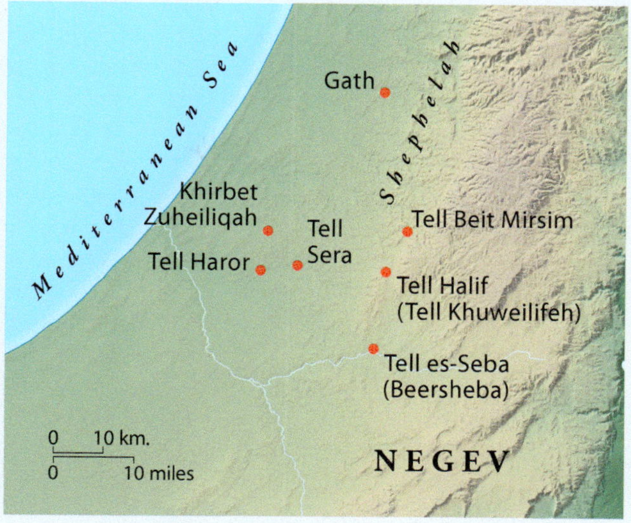

Possible sites of Ziklag

extrabiblical sources, has baffled scholars. Some have suggested reversing two letters to read "Gizrites" (inhabitants of Gezer), but the town of Gezer lay some twelve miles north of Gath and thus over thirty-five miles north of Ziklag (if it is Tell esh-Shari^ca, more if Tell es-Seba^c; see comment on 27:6), well north of the likely area of David's raiding activities (and perhaps too close to Gath to escape Achish's notice). One of the chief witnesses of the LXX (i.e., LXX[B]) includes only two, not three, peoples against whom David conducts his raids: the Amalekites and (probably) the Geshurites. The reading "Girzites" in the Hebrew text may thus be a corruption, having arisen by a conflation of variants.[502]

Amalekites (27:8). See comment on 15:2.

The land extending to Shur and Egypt (27:8). See comment on 15:2.

Negev of Jerahmeel (27:10). Jerahmeel is named in 1 Chronicles 2:9–15 as a descendant of Judah and a brother of David's ancestor Ram. The Negev of Jerahmeel may have been south of Beersheba, but this is not known with certainty. McCarter notes that the "arid

Region of David's raids

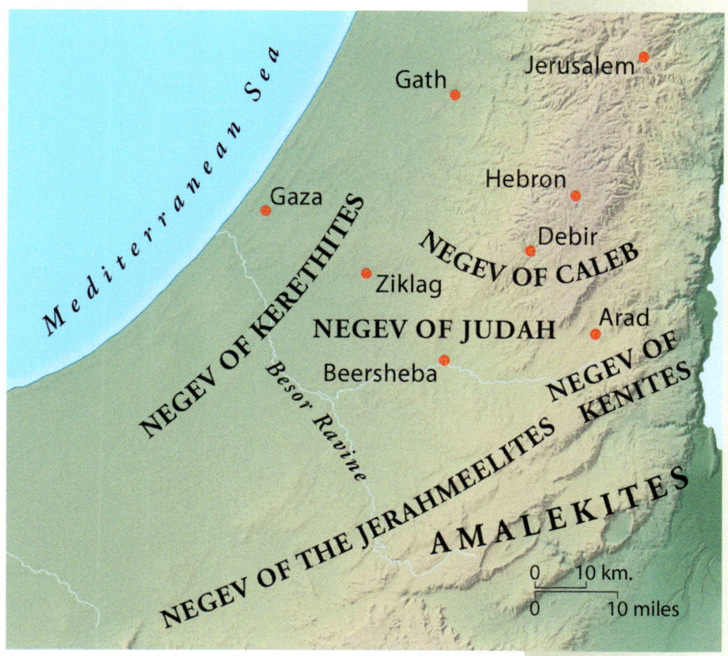

negeb or 'Southland' of Palestine was traditionally divided into districts by population," with the Negev of Judah likely centered around Beersheba, and the Negev of the Jerahmeelites further south,[503] or possibly east.[504] David's response to Achish's query regarding what he has been up to is entirely false, claiming to have been attacking Judahites and their friends, while in fact he is annihilating foes of Israel and leaving neither man nor woman alive to report him to Achish.

Negev of the Kenites (27:10). On the Kenites, see comment on 15:6.[505] That David mentions the Negev of the Kenites in a list including the Negev of Judah, along with the later notice that David sends gifts to the Kenites (30:29), confirms that they remain on friendly terms with Israel, as they were since the time of Israel's wandering in the wilderness.

Saul Inquires of the Medium of Endor (28:1–25)

I will make you my bodyguard for life (28:2). David's deception of Achish is supremely successful, so much so that Achish instates David as his bodyguard for life. The word Achish uses for "bodyguard" is not the word used elsewhere in Samuel (22:14; 2 Sam. 23:23). The phrase literally reads "keeper/guard of my head" and perhaps carries a sense similar to the colloquial expression in English, "You've got my back." The irony of this choice of words—given the fact that David has already collected the head of Goliath, another citizen of Gath—is heightened by the complaint of the Philistine commanders in 29:4 that David may turn in battle and "regain his master's favor … by taking the heads of our own men"!

Saul had expelled the mediums and spiritists (28:3). Cultures throughout the ancient Near East desired to make contact with the spirit world, and a complex array of rites and practitioners arose in an effort to satisfy this desire. For Israel, however, participation in these kinds of rites was condemned in the strongest possible terms, both in Deuteronomy (see Deut. 18:9–13) and the priestly legislation of Leviticus (Lev. 19:31; 20:27). The basis of proscribing occult practices may in part have had to do with the distinction between magic and religion—that is, between the occult magical arts, which seek to harness knowledge and power for selfish ends, and religious observance, which seeks to bring the worshiper into communion with God.

But the distinction between magic and religion is not always easy to maintain,[506] and the Old Testament itself reports without censure certain acts that may be considered magic (a staff becoming a snake, the casting of lots, causing an axehead to float, etc.).[507] The more fundamental reason for banning occult practices in Israel is that they involved engaging false gods or demonic powers rather than the one true God, Yahweh.

In any case, Saul's explusion of mediums and spiritists is fully in accord with Mosaic law and, as Gordon observes, "could have been inspired by zeal for the Yahwistic religion." But, as Gordon also allows, other motivations may have been behind Saul's action.[508] Commentators often cite Gudea, king of the Sumerian city of Lagash, as an example of a (non-Yahwistic) king who, for his own reasons, expelled "sorcerers and witches" from his domain. The relevant lines in the Gudea Cylinder (cyl. A, col. xiii, lines 14–15) are notoriously difficult to translate, however, and today few Sumerologists believe that they refer to occult practitioners.[509] So this example offers no help in assessing Saul's action.

About all that can be said at present is that purging the land of occult specialists may have been motivated by a variety of reasons, but whatever Saul's initial motivation, he loses no time in seeking out a medium when the accepted methods of divine inquiry fail him, nor does he show any doubt that a medium can easily be found despite his purge.[510]

Shunem … Gilboa (28:4). Having first assembled their troops at Aphek (see also comments on 29:1), the Philistines move north and set up camp at Shunem. Meanwhile Saul brings his troops to (Mount) Gilboa. Shunem has been identified with modern Solem, a site lying on the southwestern slope of the Hill of Moreh toward the eastern end of the rich Valley of Jezreel. The valley is bordered on the north by Mount Tabor and some twelve miles to the south by Mount Gilboa, with the Hill of Moreh midway between, dividing the valley into two passes running east toward the Jordan.

Shunem
Todd Bolen/www.BiblePlaces.com

The village of Shunem figures in several well-known biblical accounts[511] and is attested also in ancient Near Eastern texts from as early as the Late Bronze period.[512] From Mount Gilboa Saul's troops move to encamp at the spring of Jezreel (see comment on 29:1), less than five miles south of their Philistine foes at Shunem. Throughout history the Jezreel Valley has been a strategic crossroads for travelers seeking passage from the coastal plain through the Carmel range and on to the east and north. A question that the current episode raises is how the Philistines manage to travel unmolested by Israelite troops through the passes in the Carmel range and into the Jezreel Valley. Herzog and Gichon, both with extensive military experience in the British and Israeli armies, reason as follows:

> After their many unsuccessful attempts to penetrate the central mountain massif from the west, the Philistines planned a major enveloping movement by marching northwards along the Plain of Sharon (the coastal plain) and then through one of the passes of the Carmel range into the Jezreel Valley, so as to enter the central mountain massif at Ir-ganim (present-day Jenin) and move southwards along the plateau.

Saul's last stand

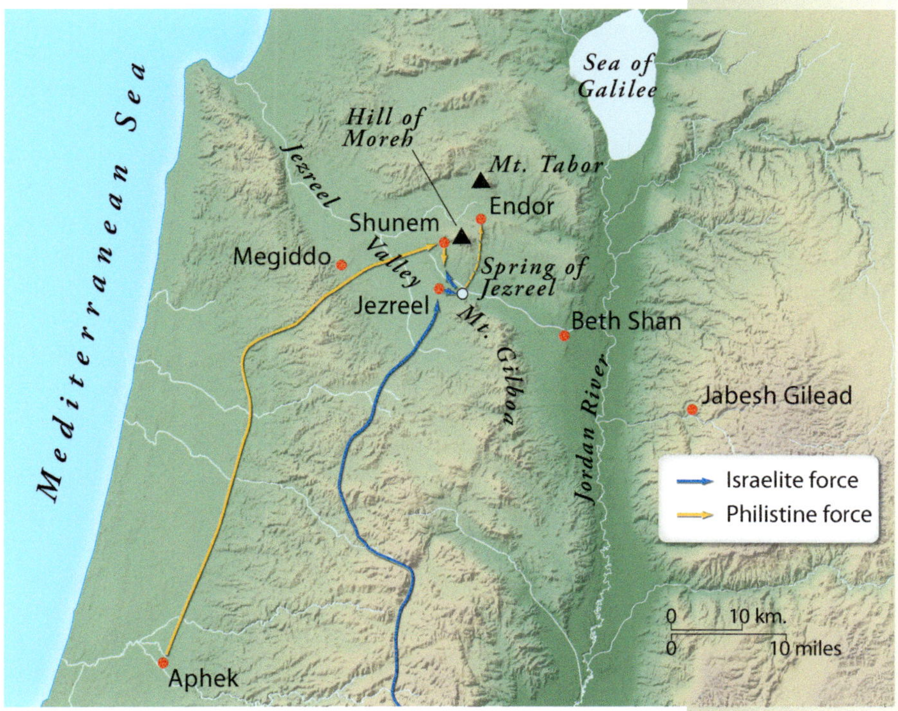

Herzog and Gichon speculate that the Philistines may have hoped for some support from Canaanite cities in the Jezreel Valley that the Israelites had failed to conquer. They continue:

> Saul had the advantage of the interior lines. Accordingly, he waited to see in what direction the Philistines would move. After he was sure of their intentions, he moved his forces parallel to theirs on the plateau and then took up a blocking position that flanked the ascent to Ir-ganim in the lower foothills of the Gilboa range.
>
> Why was no attempt made to block the Philistine passage through the difficult Carmel defiles? The answer can be inferred from the choice of Aphek as the assembly point for the Philistine host. By convening on Aphek, the Philistines posed a direct threat to the Judean mountains, which must have caused Saul to detach at least some of his observation forces to guard the western approaches.

Herzog and Gichon, as military strategists, suggest that this would have been an ideal situation for the Philistines to use some kind of diversionary tactic, but no such plan is mentioned. But the forced return of David and his troops from Aphek to Ziklag (1 Sam. 29) may well have (unintentionally) served as such a diversionary movement, as David would pass by several "obvious invasion routes into Judah" (e.g., the Elah Valley and the Sorek Valley), "which must have kept Saul's men on their guard." Only when they were sure that "no stab in his back was intended could Saul rush to meet the northern threat, which gave the Philistine host the time necessary to effect an unmolested passage through the Carmel range."[513]

The LORD did not answer him by dreams or Urim or prophets (28:6). These three means of inquiry were all acceptable options in ancient Israel, as well as elsewhere in the ancient Near East. A remarkable parallel is found in the Second Plague Prayer of Muršili II, a fourteenth-century Hittite king, son of Šuppiluliuma I. Both Muršili's father and his brother had died from a devastating and ongoing plague that ravaged the Hittite population for years. In his prayers to the gods of Hatti, Muršili confesses both corporate and personal sins and pleads that the plague be lifted. And should it be that the "people are dying for some other reason" than those confessed, Muršili begs, "either let me see it in a dream, or let it be found out by an oracle, or let a prophet declare it, or let the priests find out by incubation whatever I suggest to them."[514]

Saul's attempt to gain a word from the Lord is prompted more by anxiety (v. 5) than by piety (especially judging from his behavior before and after this event). His failure to receive any answer must be read in the light of the warnings uttered by Samuel in 8:18 ("the LORD will not answer you in that day") and 12:15, 25 and against the backdrop of his rejection in 15:28 (cf. 16:1). On dreams as a means of divine guidance see comment on 3:3; on Urim (and Thummim) see comment on 2:18; 14:3, 18–19; on prophets see comment on 3:1; 10:5.

Find me a woman who is a medium (28:7). The term "medium" is most often paired with "spiritist" in biblical references (e.g., vv. 3, 9); the chief function of such practitioners was evidently to communicate with the spirit world, particularly with the dead. In the present instance, the Hebrew for "medium" reads literally "ghostwife" or perhaps "ghostmistress."[515] The "ghost" (Heb. *ʾôb*; on which see comment on 28:8) was understood as the spirit of the dead, and the function of the medium was to call up the spirit through necromancy, in order that it might speak.

Necromancy was practiced throughout the ancient Near East.[516] In Mesopotamia, the necromancer rubbed salve on his or her face in an effort to contact or perhaps embody the spirit of the dead, or used "skulls or figurines as temporary houses for the spirit which was being summoned."[517] Although evidence of specifics is sparse, similar practices took place in Hittite Anatolia, where a distinguishing feature was the prominent role played by "old women."[518]

In Egypt the cult of the dead included offerings to the dead. Offering tables such as this one were often placed by a false door in the tomb that allowed the spirit to come out and receive sustenance.
Guillaume Blanchard/Wikimedia Commons, courtesy of the Louvre

In Egypt necromancy is first attested in the first half of the first millennium B.C., but there is evidence, such as in the Letters to the Dead, that necromancy may have been practiced much earlier. Egyptian necromancy sometimes used cadavers or scrying (gazing) cups.[519] From Ugarit, the so-called Protocol of a Necromancy offers direct evidence of the practice, and there is indirect evidence as well.[520] The only direct evidence of necromancy being practiced in Israel is the present encounter between Saul and the medium at Endor, and in this context the practice is evaluated negatively.

Endor (28:7). The precise location of Endor remains a matter of some dispute. Its former identification with present-day Indur (which clearly reflects the name) has been rejected since archaeological survey work at the site has failed to turn up ancient artifacts. Currently favored, rather, is Khirbet Ṣafṣâfeh, a site near Indur and northeast of the Hill of Moreh. If this identification is correct, Saul's nocturnal visit to the medium would have taken him behind enemy lines and landed him only about four miles from the Philistine camp at Shunem.

Such a scenario is not impossible, as Saul is traveling in disguise, and he could have passed along the eastern side of the Hill of Moreh, while the Philistines were encamped on its western slopes.[521] There may be other grounds for seeking Endor on the south side, rather than the north side, of the Jezreel Valley, and several alternative identifications have been suggested.[522]

Consult a spirit for me (28:8). The word for "spirit" is *ʾôb* (see first comment on v. 7). The etymological origin of this term is much debated,[523] but one attractive proposal in the light of the present context (note, e.g., the spirit coming up "out of the ground," v. 13) is that the word derives from a non-Semitic loanword

Area of Moreh and Endor
Todd Bolen/www.BiblePlaces.com

meaning "sacrificial pit." Proposed by Hoffner first on the basis of the occurrence of a cognate word meaning "pit" in Hittite religious texts,[524] he finds additional cognates in Sumerian, Akkadian, Hurrian, and Ugaritic.[525] He argues that the Hebrew term, like its Hittite cognate, is to be understood as designating

> a pit dug in the ground, which served as a means of access between infernal spirits of gods or deceased persons and the upper world. Among the Hittites, rituals were carried out which involved the opening up of such pits in places selected by oracle, the lowering of offerings into the pits, and the luring up of spirits out of the pit to eat the sacrifices and drink the blood libations and show their favour and superior knowledge to the sacrificers.[526]

Among the offerings lowered in the pit were foodstuffs, often including a black sacrificial animal (a hog or a dog), silver objects such as a model of a human ear (symbolizing the practitioner's desire to hear from the underworld), and a ladder or staircase (to encourage the spirit to ascend).[527] Sumerian and Akkadian versions of the Gilgamesh Epic also attest the use of pits or holes in the ground as portals through which the dead could ascend from the underworld; Gilgamesh used such a pit to summon his departed companion Enkidu.[528] In the Old Testament, the Hebrew term *ʾôb* is extended to connote not only the "ghost" that comes out of the pit but also the necromancer who calls forth the spirit.

As regards Saul's night visit to the necromancer at Endor, opinion is divided over whether the real Samuel appeared or a mere apparition. The startled reaction of the woman in verse 12, her immediate realization that she has been deceived (she is not dealing with her "familiar" spirits), and the narrator's unqualified statement that the woman "saw Samuel" all suggest that Samuel really appears. That in this instance Yahweh should deign to return Samuel from the grave—to the surprise of the woman and the dismay of Saul—in no way represents a validation either of the efficacy or the acceptability of necromancy.

A spirit coming up out of the ground (28:13). See comment on 28:8.

An old man wearing a robe (28:14). We have frequently encountered the use of robes or special garments to signify particular roles or offices in 1 Samuel (e.g., 2:19; 15:27; 18:3–4; 19:24; 24:4–5). For discussion of ancient Near Eastern instances of this general custom, see comment on 18:3–4. Saul's recognition that the "spirit coming up out of the ground" (v. 13) is Samuel seems to be triggered by his robe (with which Saul has had prior, bitter experience, 15:27–28). The medium's description of the spirit as an "old man" may also suggest the prophet Samuel, if Malamat is correct in his assertion that in Akkadian texts from Mari, the epithet "old man" was occasionally used to designate a "diviner-prophet."[529]

David's Help Is Refused by the Philistines (29:1–11)

Aphek ... spring in Jezreel (29:1). Of the several towns named Aphek mentioned in the Bible,[530] the one in view here, identified with Ras el-ʿAin, is located in the plain of Sharon in the vicinity of Philistine territory (see also comments on 4:1). After their general muster at Aphek, the Philistines would have traveled some thirty miles (as the crow flies) north-northeast to encamp at Shunem (28:4). Meanwhile, Saul's troops encamp "by the spring in Jezreel," probably En-Harod, about two miles east of Jezreel and less than five miles south of Shunem. See sidebar on "Jezreel."

What about these Hebrews? (29:3). As we have already observed (see sidebar on "Hebrews/Habiru" at 4:4), the Israelites are often referred to by the Philistines (probably pejoratively) as "Hebrews." This may be because in their eyes, the Hebrews were indistinguishable from the trouble-

▸ Jezreel

Jezreel is not mentioned outside the Bible, but it has been identified archaeologically with Tel Jezreel, excavated in six seasons (1990 to 1996) by D. Ussihkin and J. Woodhead. Iron I pottery at the site gives evidence of its occupation during the united monarchy period. The most impressive architectual feature of the site is a grand-scale royal enclosure probably dating to the period of the ninth-century Omride Dynasty. The maximal outer dimensions of the enclosure are approximately 350 by 200 yards, and the area enclosed is about eleven acres, with a rock-cut moat surrounding three sides.[A-100]

The site occupies a commanding position some hundred yards above the valley floor and undoubtedly controlled the important "ancient Megiddo and Beth Shean road that linked Egypt to Syria and Mesopotamia and runs east-west along the valley floor to the north of the site."[A-101] It also controlled the road running north-south from Shunem to the Dothan Valley.[A-102]

Thus, Saul's troops may have intended to block any Philistine attempt to move southward into the Israelite hill country. Similarly, the position of the Philistines at Shunem would have "threatened to cut Saul off from the Israelite tribes further north," and this, as Gordon opines, "perhaps explains why he was induced to join battle in an area where the Philistines' chariots and cavalry (cf. 2 Sam. 1:6) gave them a decisive advantage."[A-103]

Harod Valley from Jezreel
Todd Bolen/www.BiblePlaces.com

some Habiru, landless free-booters known throughout the ancient Near East, especially in the second millennium.

Taking the heads of our own men (29:4). See comment on 28:2.

David Pursues the Amalekites and Rescues His People (30:1–31)

The Amalekites had raided the Negev and Ziklag (30:1). On the Amalekites, see comment on 15:2; on Ziglag and the Negev, see comments on 27:6, 10.

Reached Ziklag on the third day (30:1). The distance from Aphek to Ziklag was around fifty or sixty miles (depending on which of the likeliest locations for Ziklag is assumed: Tell esh-Shariʿa or Tell es-Sebaʿ). The average marching rate for armies in the ancient Near East has been estimated at about fifteen to twenty miles per day.[531] The arrival in Ziklag of David and his troops "on the third day" comports well with these figures and suggests, further, that David must have wasted no time along the way. Perhaps it was with some uneasiness that he had left his town of Ziklag unprotected in order to follow Achish. After all, Ziklag had been David's "base of operations against the Amalekites (27:8), the archetypal bandits of biblical tradition,"[532] and David may have feared that his aggressions would not go unrequited.

David said to Abiathar the priest ... "Bring me the ephod" (30:7). On Abiathar, see comment on 22:20; on the ephod as an oracular instrument, see comment on 2:18. Compare also Saul's instructions to Ahijah in 14:18.

Besor Ravine (30:9). The Besor Ravine is generally identified as the Wadi Ghazzeh that runs northwestward some twelve to fifteen miles south of Ziklag (if Tell esh-Shariʿa) to empty into the Mediterranean Sea south of Gaza. Several wadis (seasonal rivers) flow from the vicinity of Tell esh-Shariʿa to join the Wadi Ghazzeh (Nahal Besor on some maps). From Tell es-Sebaʿ (another candidate for Ziklag) flows the Wadi Bir es-Sebaʿ (Nahal Beer Sheva), eventually becoming the Wadi Ghazzeh.

If we assume the Amalekites traveled an established route after ravaging Ziklag, several possibilities present themselves. An apparently major route ran south-southwest by Tell esh-Shariʿa to cross the Besor Ravine in the vicinity of Tell el Farʿa.[533] Along this route the distance from Ziklag to the Besor Ravine is about fourteen miles. A second route followed the Wadi esh-Shariʿa (Nahal Gerar) due west out of Ziklag to reach the ravine near Tell Jemma, again about fourteen miles away.[534] The fact that the other main candidate as Ziklag, Tell es-Sebaʿ, is essentially at the ravine and would have required little further travel may be a strike against this identification, though it remains a possibility.

Of David's six hundred men, two hundred are too exhausted to continue by the time they reach the Besor Ravine, so they stay behind. Having covered some fifty to sixty miles in three days from Aphek to Ziklag, David and his men

Nahal Besor
Todd Bolen/www.BiblePlaces.com

probably remain in Ziklag only long enough to inquire of Yahweh whether they should pursue the Amalekites (vv. 7–8). Without rest, then, it is not surprising that some of the men are too exhausted to continue the pursuit.

Negev of the Kerethites ... Negev of Caleb (30:14). The Negev, or arid southland, designated an expansive region beginning on about the latitude of Beersheba in Judah and stretching southward, bounded on the west by the Mediterranean and on the east by Edom. In biblical times the Negev was inhabited by various people groups, many of whom, like the Amalekites, ranged widely, but were nevertheless associated with particular regions within the Negev (see comment on 27:10).

The Kerethites (or Cherethites) were an ethnic people, probably from Crete, often mentioned alongside the Philistines (e.g., in Ezek. 25:16; Zeph. 2:6; and in many other places if "Pelethites" is a linguistic variation of "Philistines"; see 2 Sam. 8:18). The "Kerethites and Pelethites" served under the command of Benaiah son of Jehoiada as professional troops loyal to David (2 Sam. 8:18; 15:18; 20:7, 23) and, for a short time at least, to Solomon (1 Kings 1:44). Their particular function seems to have been as the king's bodyguard (see 2 Sam. 23:20, 23).

The Calebites were descended from Caleb, son of Jephunneh, first mentioned in Numbers 13:6 as one of the spies chosen to scout out the land of Canaan. He is commended in Numbers 14:24 as one who followed the Lord "wholeheartedly" and who, therefore, was to have an inheritance in the Promised Land. His inheritance included Hebron and its environs (Josh. 14:13–14; Judg. 1:20). Nabal's designation as a Calebite (25:3) and his association with Carmel and Maon (25:2), seven and eight miles south of Hebron, respectively, suggest that these, and possibly other, cities in the vicinity of Hebron were included in Calebite territory (see comment on 30:27).

Rode off on camels (30:17). On the possession of camels by the Amalekites see 15:3. Of the six living species of camels, only two appear to have inhabited the world of the ancient Near East—the one-humped dromedary (*Camelus dromedarius*) and the two-humped bactrian (*Camelus bactrianus*). The term for camel used in the Bible is generic, like its English equivalent, and does not clearly identify the species of camel in view (though the one-humped, or Arabian, camel is most likely in this range).[535] Biblical references to domesticated camels in the patriarchal period continue to be challenged as anachronistic by some scholars, but other scholars point out that pentateuchal references to *riding* camels are quite limited, and there is some evidence for the domestication of camels as early as 3000 B.C.[536]

More pertinent to the time period of the text before us, both extrabiblical textual evidence and material archaeological evidence (e.g., camel bones) leave little doubt

Stone relief from the palace of Ashurbanipal showing raiders riding camels
Werner Forman Archive/The British Museum

The Spoils of War

In the thought world of the ancient Near East, both victory in battle and the spoils of battle were regarded as gifts of the gods. Furthermore, soldiers who were not mercenaries were often not paid directly for their services but, rather, "lost property during the war, abandoned their work, and endangered their lives." Logically, therefore, the taking of plunder could be viewed as "fair compensation for the damages they suffered."[A-104]

In the Old Testament, Yahweh was regarded as the Divine Warrior (see comment on 14:6), who led his people into battle, gave them victory, and along with victory, the spoils. According to the biblical ethic, however, the taking of spoils was not to be the primary motivation for going to war (but see comment on 2 Sam. 3:22).

A similar attitude prevailed among Israel's neighbors, though with marked exceptions. The Assyrian king Adad-nirari II (912–889), for example, boasts: "At the time by the edict of the great gods, my sovereignty (and) dominion were decreed (and) they named me *to plunder the possessions of the lands*."[A-105] Apparently the Assyrian king saw the plundering of other nations as central to his job description. For the most part, however, plundering the vanquished foe was regarded as a legitimate *aspect* of warfare, not in itself a legitimate *ground* for initiating a conflict. The quantity of spoils captured, whether measured in human captives, livestock, or material goods, served as a measure of the magnitude of the victory and bolstered the prestige of the triumphant army, especially its leader, and was often celebrated in inscriptions and reliefs.

Usually the spoils of war were collected and carefully distributed in the aftermath of a battle, according to guidelines established either before or after the battle.[A-106] As a general rule, significant quantities of spoils went to the temple and the temple service. Any allies involved in the conflict or in certain covenantal relationships also received a

that "domesticated camels were in use in the northwestern portion of the Arabian peninsula sometime in the mid-second millennium B.C. among pastoral people with whom the Israelites had some acquaintance."[537] This evidence converges nicely with the biblical texts, in which cameleering is associated mainly with peoples such as the Amalekites and Midianites (Judg. 6:5; 7:12; 8:21, 26), who lived in the arid regions to the south and east of Judah. Because of their ability to go several days without drinking and their speed, camels made effective mounts for travel and for battle. In the present episode, they also prove invaluable for the escape of four hundred Amalekites.

All will share alike (30:24). While the taking of plunder in battle is subjected to ethical questioning nowadays, in antiquity it was regarded as a legitimate aspect of warfare.[538] See sidebar on "The Spoils of War."

David ... sent some of the plunder to the elders of Judah (30:26). The message that David sends with the plunder—"Here is a present for you from the plunder of the LORD's enemies"—underscores the theological significance of David's conflict with the Amalekites. The Amalekites are viewed not simply as a marauding people group in the Negev but, more fundamentally, as the enemies of Yahweh (see comment on 15:2). David confronts them and defeats them not simply as a Judahite chieftain, but as Yahweh's anointed/messiah.[539]

Though described as a "present" (lit., "blessing"), David's presentation of plunder to the share—one may think in this regard of David's "sending some of the plunder to the elders of Judah" (v. 26), among whom he found refuge for a time during his fugitive period. The king or leader, of course, received a significant share, and the soldiers along with auxiliary personnel also received distributions.[A-107]

Among such auxiliary personnel in the present episode might be counted the two hundred soldiers who remained behind at the Wadi Besor (vv. 9–10; cf. the two hundred who "stayed with the supplies" as David and four hundred others went up against Nabal in 25:13). Thus, David's insistence that those who stayed behind were not to be denied a share was in keeping with wider practices in the ancient Near East and in the Bible (e.g., Num. 31; Josh. 22). The specific rationale David gave, however, was deeply theological: Yahweh "has protected us and handed over to us the forces that came against us" (v. 23). Both victory in battle and the spoils of battle ultimately belonged to Yahweh, and so, irrespective of the specific role one had played in the battle, "all will share alike" (v. 24).

Booty and tribute being presented to Ashurbanipal after the capture of Babylon
Todd Bolen/www.BiblePlaces.com

elders of Judah may have followed the ancient Near Eastern custom, practiced for instance by the Hittites, of restoring to its original owner booty taken in a conflict with a third party.[540] According to the logic whereby spoils were seen as a legitimate by-product of warfare that therefore became the rightful possession of the conquerors, David had a right to keep what he had taken from the Amalekites. But knowing that the Amalekites had plundered not only Ziklag but also "the Negev of the Kerethites and the territory belonging to Judah and the Negev of Caleb" (as reported by the Egyptian slave in v. 14), David chooses to return some of the plunder to its original owners.

Interestingly, no mention is made of any "present" being sent to the Kerethites, though David recovered much plunder that had been taken not only from Judah but from "the land of the Philistines" (v. 16; on the Philistine associations of the Kerethites, see comment on v. 14). This may reflect the distinction in David's mind between "members of God's covenant community"[541] and peoples opposed to that community (cf. David's actions and words in 27:8–11). The specific recipients of David's largesse are named in 30:27–31.

He sent ... to those in all the other places where David and his men had roamed (30:27–31). While the geographic locations of a few of the specific sites mentioned have not been positively identified, verse 31 makes clear that they lay in the general areas frequented by David while on the run from Saul (see comments on 27:2, 7), namely, the southern hill country of Judah and the northern Negev.[542]

"Bethel" (the first site mentioned) is not the well-known Ephraimite Bethel, north of Jerusalem, but is perhaps a different Bethel—possibly the "Bethuel" of 1 Chronicles 4:30 (cf. "Bethul" in Josh. 19:4).[543] Its precise location has not been determined, but Joshua 19:4 appropriately lists it with Ziklag and Hormah.[544] Alternatively, perhaps we should read (with LXX^{B}) "Beth-zur," which as McCarter notes would be "quite at home in this list."[545] Beth-zur is identified as Khirbet et-Tubeiqah, three or four miles north of Hebron, near the ancient road between Hebron and Jerusalem. Judging from biblical and archaeological evidence, Beth-zur would have been occupied by Calebites (see comments on 25:3 and 30:14) in David's day.[546]

For the location of other sites in the list, so far as these are known, see the accompanying map.[547] David's ability to distribute "presents" to different geographic regions would have increased his prestige and popularity in the area around Hebron, where he is first made king (see comment on 2 Sam. 2:4). Distribution of spoils to various geographic regions is attested also, for example, among the Assyrians.[548]

Revenge on the Amalekites

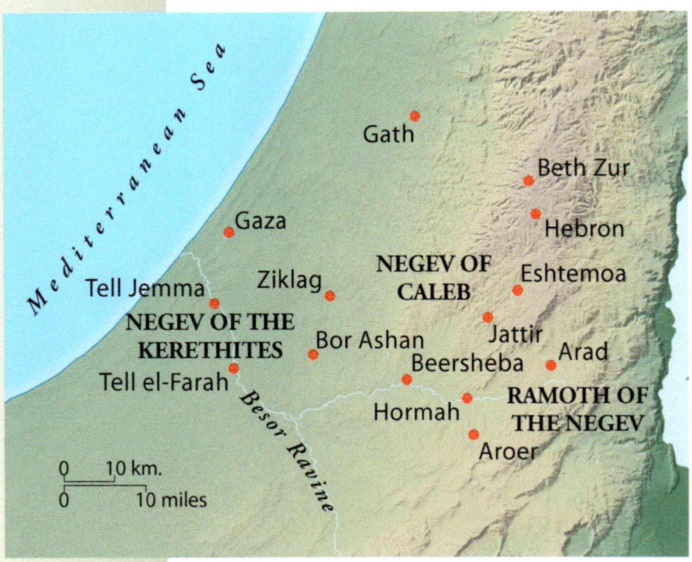

Saul Is Wounded on Mount Gilboa and Takes His Own Life (31:1–13)

Mount Gilboa (31:1). The Gilboa range runs north to border the Jezreel Valley on the southeast side. For information on the deployment of Philistine troops at Shunem and Israelite troops near Gilboa at the spring of Jezreel, see comment on 28:4. The military superiority that chariots afforded the Philistines in the relatively flat battleground of the Jezreel Valley led to a rapid Philistine victory. Many Israelites were slain on Mount Gilboa, perhaps as they sought to gain the advantage of high ground or rougher terrain where chariots would be less effective, or simply because they were overmatched and had been routed. In antiquity, chariots often served as mobile firing platforms.

Saul said to his armor-bearer, "Draw your sword and run me through" (31:4). In view of the kind of treatment ancient Near Eastern prisoners of war in general, and defeated kings in particular, could expect, Saul's fear of being abused by the Philistines was well founded. From Assyrian inscriptions around the time of David and later, we gain "an impression of unremitting cruelty" to prisoners of war: "Most were slaughtered or blinded, some hung on stakes or fortifications around city walls, as a warning to others. Heads, hands, or lower lips were cut off to facilitate counting."[549] One particularly gruesome relief from the reign of Sargon II shows the vanquished king of Hamath literally being flayed alive in public.[550]

Although Saul managed to end his life before falling into the hands of the Philistines, their treatment of his corpse confirms the cruelty that Saul feared (see vv. 8–10). Some commentators praise Saul's suicide as a courageous act, worthy of a tragic hero seeking to gain mastery of his own fate, even in death. But the tenor of 1–2 Samuel, and indeed the Bible as a whole, points in another direction.[551] The truly courageous are, rather, those who like David in times of distress find strength in God (23:16; 30:6) and who, like Jonathan, yield fully to his

Mount Gilboa and environs
Copyright 1995–2009 Phoenix Data Systems

will (18:4; 23:17). Saul's attempt to have his armor-bearer run him through finds its closest analogy in the death scene of the less-than-admirable Abimelech of Judges 9 (see v. 54). Outside the Bible, Assyrian texts also attest a king asking his armor-bearer to finish him off.[552] For more on attitudes towards suicide in ancient Egypt and Mesopotamia, see comment on 2 Samuel 17:23.

Uncircumcised fellows (31:4). See comments on 14:6 and 17:26. Saul's fear of the Philistines stands in marked contrast to the bold confidence of Jonathan (14:6) and David (17:26), anchored by their faith in Yahweh.

They cut off his head (31:9). In the ancient Near East, "a king's head was a prized trophy."[553] See comment on 5:3–4.

They put his armor in the temple of the Ashtoreths (31:10). On depositing armor and weapons in temples, note the placement of Goliath's sword behind the ephod in the sanctuary at Nob (21:9). Note also the general practice of deporting enemy gods/idols and depositing them in one's own sanctuary (see sidebar on "Treatment of Defeated Deities" at 5:2). On the "temple of the Ashtoreths," see comments on 7:4 and next note.

Fastened his body to the wall of Beth Shan (31:10). Beth Shan is one of the oldest continuously occupied sites in Canaan. Identified with Tell el-Ḥuṣn, Beth Shan guarded the eastern end of the Valley of Jezreel, at the intersection of two main trade routes. Dominated by Egypt from as early as the fifteenth century, Beth Shan later came under Philistine and ultimately Israelite control. Archaeological excavation of the site has been extensive. The eleventh century, the period of Saul, is well attested, and particularly noteworthy is the discovery of a pair

Heads hung on the city wall from the Balawat Gate
Werner Forman Archive/The British Museum

Cutting the head off the enemy
Edward Silver, University of Chicago, courtesy of the British Museum

of public buildings that the excavators have identified as "twin temples," tentatively identified as "the House of Ashtoreth" (1 Sam. 31:10) and "the House of Dagon" (1 Chron. 10:10).[554]

Positive identifications are, of course, difficult, so it is best to remain cautious. What one can say is that there appear to have been temples at Beth Shan at the time of Saul's death into which his armor, and presumably his head, could have been deposited. The bodies of Saul (sans head) and his sons were reserved for public display on the wall of the city. On the exposure of enemy dead, see comments on 21:6, 10.

Jabesh Gilead ... journeyed through the night (31:11–12). On the likely location of Jabesh Gilead, see comment on 11:1. The distance between Jabesh Gilead and Beth Shan was about thirteen miles.

They took down the bodies ... burned them (31:12). Cremation was not a common burial practice in most parts of the ancient Near East, though it is attested especially among the Hurrian-influenced Hittites of Anatolia.[555] There is some evidence of cremation burials in Judah from as early as the second half of the eleventh century, though this meager evidence may be a result of accidental causes, such as tomb fires.[556] In the Old Testament, "burning in/with

Beth Shan
Todd Bolen/www.BiblePlaces.com

Remains of one of the temples on the tell of Beth Shan
Kim Walton

the fire" is associated mostly with purification (Lev. 13:57), with the punishment of capital offenders (Lev. 20:14; 21:9), or both (Josh. 7:25).

Cremation as a burial custom per se is unknown in the Old Testament, unless the present episode in which the mutilated bodies of Saul and his sons are burned provides an exception. As Matthews notes, however, the burning may have been made necessary simply because of the "dismemberment and advanced state of decay of the bodies."[557] On burial customs in general, see comment on 2 Samuel 2:32.

BIBLIOGRAPHY

Commentaries

Gordon, Robert P. *I & II Samuel: A Commentary*. Library of Biblical Interpretation. Grand Rapids: Zondervan, 1986. An insightful and accessible commentary of 1 and 2 Samuel in one volume. The best in its class.

McCarter, P. Kyle. *I Samuel: A New Translation with Introduction and Commentary*. AB. Garden City, N.Y.: Doubleday, 1980. McCarter's commentary is expansive in scope, particularly strong in text-critical matters, but attentive also to ancient Near Eastern background issues.

Special Studies

De Vaux, Roland. *The Bible and the Ancient Near East*. Translated by Damian McHugh. London: Darton, Longman & Todd, 1972 (French orig. 1959). Especially useful are the sections on single combat and on the king of Israel as a vassal of Yahweh.

Dever, William G., and Seymour Gitin, eds. *Symbiosis, Symbolism, and the Power of the Past: Canaan, Ancient Israel, and Their Neighbors from the Late Bronze Age through Roman Palaestina*. Proceedings of the Centennial Symposium, W. F. Albright Institute of Archaeological Research and American Schools of Oriental Research, Jerusalem, May 29–31, 2000. Winona Lake, Ind.: Eisenbrauns, 2003. A wide-ranging collection of essays by prominent biblical and ancient Near Eastern scholars. Several articles treat topics pertinent to 1 and 2 Samuel, such as the Philistines, state formation, and Israelite religion.

Halpern, Baruch. *The Constitution of the Monarchy in Israel*. HSM 25. Chico, Calif.: Scholars Press, 1981. Seeks to elucidate the ideological and sociopolitical environment in which the first monarchy in Israel was instituted. Halpern is attentive to the role that ancient Near Eastern myth and ritual may have played in this historical development.

_____. *David's Secret Demons: Messiah, Murderer, Traitor, King*. Grand Rapids: Eerdmans, 2001. While attempting to write a historical biography of King David, Halpern offers a wealth of background information on matters ranging from the ideology of kingship in the ancient Near East to the geography of the Davidic state, to the archaeology of the reign of David.

Herzog, C., and M. Gichon. *Battles of the Bible*. 2nd ed. New York: Random House, 1997. Both with extensive military experience, Herzog and Gichon offer detailed, readable accounts of the technology, topography, and strategy of the battles recounted in Samuel and throughout the rest of the Bible. Alongside Yadin's classic *Art of Warfare in Biblical Lands*, this work provides vivid understanding to the character of ancient warfare.

Isserlin, B. S. J. *The Israelites*. New York: Thames & Hudson, 1998. A sparsely documented but masterful treatment of the material culture and intellectual and spiritual climate in which ancient Israel emerged and existed. Well illustrated, well organized, and well written.

Knoppers, Gary N. "The Historical Study of the Monarchy: Developments and Detours." Pages 207–35 in *The Face of Old Testament Studies: A Survey of Contemporary Approaches*, ed. D. W. Baker and B. T. Arnold. Grand Rapids: Baker, 1999. Particularly strong in respect to the role of archaeology in reconstructing the history of the Israelite monarchy.

Malamat, Abraham. *Mari and the Bible*. Ed. B. Halpern and M. H. E. Weippert. SHCANE 12. Leiden: Brill, 1998. A leading authority on the Mari corpus (some of the most significant ancient Near Eastern texts in relation to biblical studies), Malamat collects in this volume some twenty-two previously published essays, many of which relate to the books of Samuel.

Richard, Suzanne, ed. *Near Eastern Archaeology: A Reader*. Winona Lake, Ind.: Eisenbrauns, 2003. A collection of brief essays covering a plethora of subjects ranging from Levantine geography to Canaanite gods and goddesses, from weapons and warfare in ancient Syria-Palestine to women in the ancient Near East. Many entries, contributed by authorities in their respective fields, provide useful background to the study of 1 and 2 Samuel.

Roberts, J. J. M. *The Bible and the Ancient Near East: Collected Essays*. Winona Lake,

Ind.: Eisenbrauns, 2002. Part 4 of this collection of essays is especially helpful in relation to biblical concepts of kingship, messianism, and Zion theology within the thought world of the ancient Near East.

Saggs, H. W. F. *Civilization before Greece and Rome*. New Haven, Conn.: Yale Univ. Press, 1990. Organized topically, this volume provides handy reference for a variety of subjects, including ancient Near Eastern medicine, law, trade, urban life, and kingship.

Vaughn, Andrew G., and Ann E. Killebrew, eds. *Jerusalem in Bible and Archaeology: The First Temple Period*. Atlanta: Society of Biblical Literature, 2003. An important collection of essays, many of which exhibit the potential and limitations of archaeology for shedding light on the city of Jerusalem in the united monarchy period.

CHAPTER NOTES

Main Text Notes

1. At the outset of this study, I would like to express my sincere gratitude to my two exceptionally gifted research assistants, Andrew Krause and Matt Lynch, who by their endeavors have not only speeded my progress but also enriched the work in many ways. I would also like to thank general editor John Walton for his helpful suggestions at many points.
2. Strictly speaking, 1 and 2 Samuel are not "literary" in a merely (or even primarily) aesthetic sense but, rather, in a "rhetorical" sense—designed to be persuasive; cf. M. Z. Brettler, "Biblical Literature as Politics: The Case of Samuel," in *Religion and Politics in the Ancient Near East*, ed. A. Berlin (Bethesda, Md.: Univ. Press of Maryland, 1996), 71–92.
3. K. A. Kitchen, "The Controlling Role of External Evidence in Assessing the Historical Status of the Israelite United Monarchy," in *Windows into Old Testament History: Evidence, Argument, and the Crisis of "Biblical Israel,"* ed. V. P. Long, G. J. Wenham, and D. W. Baker (Grand Rapids: Eerdmans, 2002), 120. This essay covers a concise, yet detailed survey of the political state of affairs in Canaan at the time of David and Solomon. Cf. also E. H. Merrill, *Kingdom of Priests: A History of Old Testament Israel* (Grand Rapids: Baker, 1987), 154.
4. Kitchen, "Controlling Role," 112, observes that from the time of Ramesses III (whom Kitchen dates to ca. 1184–1153 B.C.) until the invasions of Siamun (ca. 970) and Shoshenq I (biblical "Shishak," ca. 925 B.C.), no pharaoh of Egypt was engaged militarily in Canaan. Cf. Merrill, *Kingdom of Priests*, 156.
5. K. A. Kitchen, *On the Reliability of the Old Testament* (Grand Rapids: Eerdmans, 2003), 89.
6. Kitchen, "Controlling Role," esp. 113–25; cf. also idem, *Reliability*, 98–104.
7. For a brief treatment of the rise of kingship, see H. W. F. Saggs, *Civilization before Greece and Rome* (New Haven, Conn.: Yale Univ. Press, 1991), 35–38.
8. The following is but a sampling of pertinent treatments of the topic: M. B. Dick, "The 'History of David's Rise to Power' and the Neo-Babylonian Succession Apologies," in *David and Zion: Biblical Studies in Honor of J. J. M. Roberts*, ed. B. F. Batto and K. L. Roberts (Winona Lake, Ind.: Eisenbrauns, 2004), 3–19; H. A. Hoffner Jr., "Propoganda and Political Justification in Hittite Historiography," in *Unity and Diversity: Essays in the History, Literature, and Religion of the Ancient Near East*, ed. H. Goedicke and J. J. M. Roberts (Baltimore: Johns Hopkins Univ. Press, 1975), 49–62; T. Ishida, "The Succession Narrative and Esarhaddon's Apology: A Comparison," in *Ah, Assyria: Studies in Assyrian History and Ancient Near Eastern Historiography Presented to Hayim Tadmor*, ed. M. Cogan and I. Ephʾal (ScrHier 33; Jerusalem: Magnes, 1991), 166–73; P. K. McCarter Jr., "The Apology of David," *JBL* 99 (1980): 489–504; S. L. McKenzie, *King David: A Biography* (Oxford: Oxford Univ. Press, 2000), 25–46; H. Tadmor, "Autobiographical Apology in the Royal Assyrian Literature," in *History, Historiography and Interpretation*, ed. H. Tadmor and M. Weinfeld (Jerusalem: Magnes, 1984), 36–57.
9. On the issue, for instance, of how accurately David is portrayed in the books of Samuel, see I. Provan, V. P. Long, and T. Longman III, *A Biblical History of Israel* (Louisville: Westminster/John Knox, 2003), 217–21.
10. Cf. the similar introductions in Josh. 1:1; Judg. 1:1; 13:2; 1 Sam. 9:1.
11. Cf. R. Youngblood, "Elkanah," *ABD*, 2:475–76.
12. For Samuel's association with Ramah, see, e.g., 1 Sam. 7:17; 8:4; 15:34; 16:13; 19:18; 25:1.
13. So, e.g., P. M. Arnold, "Ramah," *ABD*, 5:613–14. An alternative theory associates Ramathaim with Arimathea of New Testament times (see Matt. 27:57; John 19:38), noting that a "Ramathaim" in the territory of Samaria (thus Ephraim) is mentioned in 1 Macc. 11:34 and identified as Arimathea by Eusebius's *Onomasticon*. On this and other attempts to solve the Ramathaim puzzle, see Arnold, "Ramah," 613.
14. So Youngblood, "Elkanah," 2:475.
15. For further factors encouraging the practice of polygamy, see *IVPBBC-OT*, at 1 Sam. 1:2.
16. See, e.g., Hammurabi's Code, sections 128–84 (*ANET*, 171–74) and the Middle Assyrian Laws, sections 25–39 (*ANET*, 182–83). For a concise summary of polygynous practices in ancient Mesopotamia, see S. Greengus, "Legal and Social Institutions of Ancient Mesopotamia," *CANE*, 478–79. For a similar treatment of Egyptian practices, see G. Pinch, "Private Life in Ancient Egypt," *CANE*, 373–75. A list of polygamy contracts is presented in R. Westbrook, *Old Babylonian Marriage Law* (AfOB 23; Horn: Berger, 1988), 103–8. For an excursus on the whole issue, see H. J. Marsman, *Women in Ugarit and Israel: Their Social and Religious Position in the Context of the Ancient Near East* (OtSt 69; Leiden: Brill, 2003), 122–40.
17. Further, see V. P. Hamilton, "Marriage," *ABD*, 4:559–69 (esp. 565).
18. As evidenced by the prevalence of female fertility figurines discovered by archaeologists throughout the Levant. In the Phoenician Karatepe inscriptions, Azitawada, vizier of Baal, invokes the blessing of Baal on him and his people, requesting that the latter may "give birth to many (children) and by virtue of the many ... be powerful" (W. Beyerlin, ed., *Near Eastern Religious Texts Relating to the Old Testament* [OTL; London: SCM, 1978], 242).
19. See, e.g., the Hittite Ritual against Impotence, *ANET*, 349–50.
20. See K. A. Kitchen, *The Bible in Its World: The Bible and Archaeology Today* (Exeter: Paternoster, 1977), 86.

21. Cross has argued that the title makes grammatical sense in Hebrew only if the first element "carries verbal force and takes an object," thus yielding the sense "He who creates the (heavenly) armies." This he compares to epithets for the Canaanite god El such as "Father of the gods," "creator of creatures"; F. M. Cross, *Canaanite Myth and Hebrew Epic* (Cambridge, Mass.: Harvard University Press, 1973), 69–70.
22. See T. Fretheim, "Yahweh," *NIDOTTE*, 4:1295–300 (esp. 1297–98).
23. I. Finkelstein, "Seilun, Khirbet," *ABD*, 5:1069–72, on 1072. See also idem, *Shiloh: The Archaeology of a Biblical Site* (Tel Aviv: Institute of Archaeology, 1993); reviewed by W. G. Dever in *BAR* 21/6 (1995): 6–10.
24. So R. Youngblood, "Eli," *ABD*, 2:456.
25. "The ʾAqhatu Legend," trans. D. Pardee (*COS*, 1:103:344 [section i 27–34]).
26. See, e.g., F. Deist, "ʾ*APPAYIM* [1 Sam I 5] אפים," *VT* 27 (1977): 205–9.
27. Cf. *IVPBBC-OT*, at 1 Sam. 1:8.
28. On this point, see R. E. Friedman, "Tabernacle," *ABD*, 6:292–300 (esp. 298–99).
29. For an interesting, if speculative discussion, see A. S. Kaufman, "Fixing the Site of the Tabernacle at Shiloh," *BAR* 14/6 (1988): 46–52.
30. Friedman, "Tabernacle," 294–95; cf. C. H. Gordon and G. A. Rendsburg, *The Bible and the Ancient Near East* (New York: Norton, 1997), 166.
31. See K. A. Kitchen, "The Tabernacle: A Bronze Age Artifact," *ErIsr* 24 (1993): 119–29.
32. See A. Millard, *Treasures from Bible Times* (Tring, Belleville, Sydney: Lion, 1985), 73; Kitchen, *Bible in Its World*, 85–86.
33. See T. W. Cartledge, "Vow," *ISBE*², 4: 998–99; cf. also idem, *Vows in the Hebrew Bible and the Ancient Near East* (JSOTSup 147; Sheffield: Sheffield Academic Press, 1992).
34. On this point and on Nazirites in general, see R. de Vaux, *Ancient Israel*, 2 vols. (New York: McGraw-Hill, 1961), 2:466–67.
35. For the view that "the shaving rite occurs as one component of the series of aggregation rites which move the votary out of a state of separation back into the common life of Israel," see S. M. Olyan, "What Do Shaving Rites Accomplish and What Do They Signal In Biblical Ritual Contexts?" *JBL* 117 (1998): 611–22.
36. Trans. M. Lichtheim (*COS*, 1.46:111 [section 4.1ff.]).
37. De Vaux, *Ancient Israel*, 1:43. For a thorough rebuttal of the notion that for the ancient Hebrews a name possessed power and virtually determined the character of the one given the name, see J. Barr, "The Symbolism of Names in the Old Testament," *BJRL* 52 (1969–70): 11–29.
38. M. Garsiel, "Puns upon Names as a Literary Device in 1 Kings 1–2," *Bib* 72 (1991): 379–86 (on 386); cf. idem, *Biblical Names: A Literary Study of Midrashic Derivations and Puns*, trans. Phyllis Hackett (Ramat Gan, Israel: Bar-Ilan University, 1991). See also D. Stuart, "Names, Proper," *ISBE*², 3:483–88.
39. *COS*, 1.46:113 (section 7.15ff.); cf. *ANET*, 420d.
40. P. J. King and L. E. Stager, *Life in Biblical Israel*, ed. D. A. Knight (Library of Ancient Israel; Louisville: Westminster John Knox, 2001), 41.
41. See P. K. McCarter, *I Samuel* (AB; Garden City, N.Y.: Doubleday, 1980), 56–57; cf. also R. P. Gordon, *1 & 2 Samuel* (Grand Rapids: Zondervan, 1988), 78.
42. G. J. Wenham, *The Book of Leviticus* (NICOT; Grand Rapids: Eerdmans, 1979), 79 n.12. Other defenders of the Masoretic text's reading include R. Ratner, "Three Bulls or One? A Reappraisal of 1 Samuel 1,24," *Bib* 68 (1987): 98–102; followed by R. Bergen, *1, 2 Samuel* (NAC; Nashville: Broadman & Holman, 1996), 73. Among modern translations, JPS also follows "three bulls."
43. McCarter, *I Samuel*, 71–72.
44. Cf. 1 Chron. 25:5 (where "exalt" renders "lift the horn"); Ps. 132:17; see also McCarter, *I Samuel*, 72; M. L. Brown, "קֶרֶן" *NIDOTTE*, 3:991.
45. On the topic generally, see M. L. Süring, *The Horn-Motif in the Hebrew Bible and Related Ancient Near Eastern Literature and Iconography* (Berrien Springs, Mich.: Andrews Univ. Press, 1982). More briefly, see *DBI*, 400.
46. On the presence of the words meaning "mountain" and "rock" in Aramaic and Hebrew names, see J. D. Fowler, *Theophoric Personal Names in Ancient Hebrew: A Comparative Study* (JSOTSup 49; Sheffield: Sheffield Academic Press, 1987), 221; cf. also H. B. Huffmon, *Amorite Personal Names in the Mari Texts: A Structural and Lexical Study* (Baltimore: Johns Hopkins Univ. Press, 1965), 258.
47. For discussion, see "Rock," *DBI*, 732–33.
48. *ANET*, 66a.
49. W. Beyerlin, *Near Eastern Religious Texts Relating to the Old Testament* (OTL; London: SCM, 1978), 61.
50. Ibid., 93, 95.
51. Ibid., 163.
52. Ibid., 209, 211.
53. For the view that in Ps. 29 "elements of the ancient Near Eastern veneration of the god of thunderstorms ... [are] taken up and transferred to Yahweh," see H.-J. Kraus, *Psalms 1–59*, trans. Hilton C. Oswald (Minneapolis: Augsburg, 1988), 347. Cf. also Y. Avishur, *Studies in Hebrew and Ugaritic Psalms* (Jerusalem: Magnes, 1994), 88; A. R. W. Green, *The Storm-God in the Ancient Near East* (Winona Lake, Ind.: Eisenbrauns, 2003).
54. See Saggs, *Civilization*, 25–26, 35–38.
55. See de Vaux, *Ancient Israel*, 1:104 and Saggs, *Civilization*, 179; for more thorough treatments, see R. de Vaux, "The King of Israel, Vassal of Yahweh," in *The Bible and the Ancient Near East* (London: Darton, Longman & Todd, 1972), 152–66; T. N. D. Mettinger, *King and Messiah: The Civil and Sacral Legitimation of Israelite Kings* (ConBot 8; Lund: Gleerup, 1976).
56. See, e.g., G. E. Wright, *Biblical Archaeology*, rev. ed. (Trowbridge and Esher, UK: Duckworth, 1962), 143.
57. For a concise discussion of sacrifice in Israel and among its neighbors, see King and Stager, *Life in Biblical Israel*, 357–63. For more detail, see B. A.

Levine, "Ritual as Symbol: Modes of Sacrifice in Israelite Religion," in *Sacred Time, Sacred Place: Archaeology and the Religion of Israel*, ed. B. M. Gittlen (Winona Lake, Ind.: Eisenbrauns, 2002), 125–35.

58. B. J. Collins, "Establishing a New Temple for the Goddess of the Night," *COS*, 1.70:176 §32.
59. On all this, see J. Milgrom, *Leviticus 1–16* (AB 3a; New York: Doubleday, 1991), 205–6.
60. For a brief discussion and a listing of further literature, see P. Jenson, "אֵפוֹד," *NIDOTTE*, 1:476–77.
61. C. Meyers, "Ephod," *ABD*, 2:550, citing *CAD*, 4:183; cf. *AHw*, 1:222a; cited in Jenson, "אֵפוֹד," 1:476.
62. See A. Tomasino, "אֹהֶל," *NIDOTTE*, 1:301; R. E. Friedman, "Tabernacle," *ABD*, 6:294; Cross, *Canaanite Myth*, 72.
63. It is missing in the Qumran text 4QSam[a] and in some recensions of the LXX (specifically LXX[B]). For further discussion of the textual difficulties, see McCarter, *I Samuel*, 81.
64. K. van der Toorn, "Cultic Prostitution," *ABD*, 5:510; see ibid., 510–13 for full discussion.
65. De Vaux, *Ancient Israel*, 2:383–84.
66. See, e.g., I. Singer, *Hittite Prayers* (SBLWAW 11; Atlanta: Society of Biblical Literature, 2002), 58 (§2; though the phrase "man of god" is restored).
67. So H. B. Huffmon, "Prophecy (ANE)," *ABD*, 5:477–82, on 481. See ibid. for a concise description of titles and functions, with appropriate primary source references. For a fuller summary treatment, see the section on "Divination and Prophecy," in *Religions in the Ancient World*, ed. S. I. Johnston (Cambridge, Mass.: Belknap Press of the Harvard Univ. Press, 2004), 370–82. Cf. also the important study by R. R. Wilson, *Prophecy and Society in Ancient Israel* (Philadelphia: Fortress, 1980), esp. the section on "Prophecy in the Ancient Near East," 89–134.
68. Huffmon, "Prophecy (ANE)," 5:477.
69. "The Inscription of Zakkur, King of Hamath," trans. A. Millard (*COS*, 2.35:155).
70. On Samuel's experience as a "dream theophany," see R. K. Gnuse, "A Reconsideration of the Form-Critical Structure in 1 Samuel 3: An Ancient Near Eastern Dream Theophany," *ZAW* 94 (1982): 379–90; idem, *The Dream Theophany of Samuel: Its Structure in Relation to Ancient Near Eastern Dreams and Its Theological Significance* (Lanham, Md.: Univ. Press of America, 1984). For an evaluative review of the latter, see V. P. Long, "Review of R. K. Gnuse, *The Dream Theophany of Samuel: Its Structure in Relation to Ancient Near Eastern Dreams and Its Theological Significance*," *JETS* 28 (1985): 230–31. For more recent treatments, see S. A. L. Butler, *Mesopotamian Conceptions of Dreams and Dream Rituals* (AOAT 258; Munster: Ugarit Verlag, 1998); J.-M. Husser, *Dreams and Dream Narratives in the Biblical World* (Sheffield: Sheffield Academic Press, 1999).
71. J. F. Borghouts, "Witchcraft, Magic, and Divination in Ancient Egypt," *CANE*, 1783. For the oldest surviving example of such a manual, see the Chester Beatty "Dream Book," trans. R. K. Ritner (*COS*, 1.33:52–54); this Egyptian text is attested in a thirteenth-century B.C. copy, but it may stem from a much earlier original from as early as the first half of the second millennium B.C.
72. G. McMahon, "Theology, Priests, and Worship in Hittite Anatolia," *CANE*, 1991, 1994.
73. K. van der Toorn, "Theology, Priests, and Worship in Canaan and Ancient Israel," *CANE*, 2055.
74. R. E. Averbeck, "The Cylinders of Gudea," *COS*, 2.155:419 n.7.
75. Ibid.
76. *ANET*, 449b.
77. See D. Pardee, *COS*, 1.102 and 103, respectively.
78. Cf. Husser, *Dreams*, 56–58.
79. *ANET*, 562c.
80. On the tabernacle of Moses and the ark's place within it, see *OEANE*, 1:324–30.
81. On these convergences between text and archaeology, see I. Finkelstein, *NEAEHL*, 652–53.
82. So ibid.
83. For photo, drawing, and brief description of the ostracon, see M. Kochavi, *NEAEHL*, 654.
84. For discussion of this point, see R. S. Hess, "Literacy in Iron Age Israel," in *Windows into Old Testament History: Evidence, Argument, and the Crisis of "Biblical Israel,"* ed. V. P. Long, G. J. Wenham, and D. W. Baker (Grand Rapids: Eerdmans, 2002), 86. See also A. Demsky, "A Proto-Canaanite Abecedary Dating from the Period of the Judges and Its Implications for the History of the Alphabet," *Tel Aviv* 4 (1977): 14–27. For further description of the ostracon itself, see McCarter, *Ancient Inscriptions*, 77–78; note his interesting, if highly speculative suggestion regarding line 4: "It is possible that the first eight signs in line 4 of the ʿIzbet Ṣarṭah ostracon preserve the name of the scribe, *ʾrp bn nḥm*, 'Oreph son of Nahuym.' If this is correct, it is interesting to note that the name of this 12th-century scribe is the masculine equivalent of biblical Orpah, the name of Ruth's sister-in-law, who, according to biblical tradition, lived 'in the days when the judges judged' (Ruth 1:1)—that is, in the 11th or 12th century B.C.E., the time period from which the ostracon also derives" (ibid., 78).
85. For a summary essay by excavation director M. Kochavi, see *OEANE*, 1:147–51.
86. More or less midway between Gaza in the south and Megiddo in the north on the Great Trunk Road; see Beitzel, *Atlas*, 68.
87. See *ANET*, 329 n.8: "the Ruler of Aphek, Yankiilu"; cf. also D. B. Redford, "Execration and Execration Texts," *ABD*, 2:682; for other execration texts, see "Execration Texts," trans. R. K. Ritner (*COS*, 1.32:50–52); and on the nature of execration texts generally, see McCarter, *Ancient Inscriptions*, 42–43.
88. Cf. *ANET*, 242–43.
89. "The Memphis and Karnak Stelae of Amenhotep II," trans. J. K. Hoffmeier (*COS*, 2.3:21; cf. *ANET*, 246).
90. E.g., a report of the Assyrian king Esarhaddon's seventh-century march towards Egypt mentions

"the town of Apku which is in the region of Samaria" (*ANET*, 292c). Other later references to Aphek outside the Bible are noted in R. Frankel, "Aphek," *ABD*, 1:276.

91. *NEAEHL*, 68–69.
92. See W. W. Hallo's introduction to "The Letter of Takuhlina" (COS, 3.94:243).
93. C. Meyers, "Cherubim," *ABD*, 1:900.
94. Some have suggested that the phrase should be read together as a title, "LORD of Hosts Enthroned on the Cherubim" (so JPS).
95. See, e.g., T. N. D. Mettinger, *The Dethronement of Sabaoth: Studies in the Shem and Kabod Theologies* (ConBOT 18; Lund: Gleerup, 1982), 19–37; idem, "YHWH SABAOTH—The Heavenly King on the Cherubim Throne," in *Studies in the Period of David and Solomon and Other Essays: Papers Read at the International Symposium for Biblical Studies, Tokyo, 5–7 December, 1979*, ed. T. Ishida (Winona Lake, Ind.: Eisenbrauns, 1982), 109–38.
96. L. E. Stager, "Forging an Identity: The Emergence of Ancient Israel," in *The Oxford History of the Biblical World*, ed. Michael D. Coogan (Oxford: Oxford Univ. Press, 1998), 123–75 (on 153–54). See also idem, "The Impact of the Sea Peoples in Canaan (1185–1050 B.C.E.)," in *The Archaeology of Society in the Holy Land*, ed. T. E. Levy (London: Leicester Univ. Press, 1997), 332–48, 583–85.
97. On which, see W. G. Dever, *What Did Biblical Writers Know, and When Did They Know It? What Archaeology Can Tell Us about the Reality of Ancient Israel* (Grand Rapids: Eerdmans, 2001), 126–27.
98. Such *biblical* evidence contrary to the assumption of an Israel numbering in the millions can easily be multiplied. For a succinct summary of evidence, see C. J. Humphreys, *The Miracles of Exodus: A Scientist's Discovery of Extraordinary Natural Causes of the Biblical Stories* (San Francisco: HarperSanFrancisco, 2003), 104–5.
99. A selection of important studies includes the following: D. M. Fouts, "A Defense of the Hyperbolic Interpretation of Large Numbers in the Old Testament," *JETS* 40 (1997): 377–87; C. J. Humphreys, "The Number of People in the Exodus from Egypt: Decoding Mathematically the Very Large Numbers in Numbers I and XXVI," *VT* 48 (1998): 196–213; idem, *Miracles of Exodus*, 103–10; A. R. Millard, "Large Numbers in the Assyrian Royal Inscriptions," in *Ah, Assyria: Studies in Assyrian History and Ancient Near Eastern Historiography Presented to Hayim Tadmor*, ed. M. Cogan and I. Ephʿal (ScrHier 33; Jerusalem: Magnes, 1991), 213–22; J. W. Wenham, "The Large Numbers in the Old Testament," *TynBul* 18 (1967): 19–53. For brief discussion and further bibliography, see D. Howard, *Joshua* (NAC; Nashville: Broadman & Holman, 1998), 189 n. 76; Provan, Long, and Longman, *A Biblical History of Israel*, 130–31, n. 95.
100. So R. B. Allen, "Numbers," *EBC*, 686–91 ("The Large Numbers—Toward a Solution").
101. *DBI*, 574; King and Stager, *Life in Biblical Israel*, 372–73.
102. E. F. de Ward, "Mourning Customs in 1, 2 Samuel," *JJS* 23 (1972): 1–27 (on p. 8). For more recent, thorough treatments of the subject, see S. M. Olyan, *Biblical Mourning: Ritual and Social Dimensions* (New York: Oxford Univ. Press, 2004); X. H. T. Pham, *Mourning in the Ancient Near East and the Hebrew Bible* (JSOTSup 302; Sheffield: Sheffield Academic Press, 1999).
103. See de Ward, "Mourning Customs," 8–10.
104. S. B. Parker, ed., *Ugaritic Narrative Poetry* (SBLWAW 9; Atlanta: Scholars, 1997), 149. For another translation, see "The Baʿlu Myth," trans. D. Pardee (COS, 1.86:267–68). Earlier translations of these lines by S. R. Driver and J. C. L. Gibson differ slightly, reading, e.g., "straw" instead of "dirt" in the phrase describing what the mourner pours on his head; see *CML*[1], Baal I*.vi.12–24 and *CML*[2], "Baal and Mot," 5. vi.12–24, respectively.
105. W. G. Dever, *OEANE*, 1:219.
106. M. Dothan, *NEAEHL*, 93d.
107. Ibid., 93b.
108. *OEANE*, 1:219.
109. *NEAEHL*, 98b; cf. *OEANE*, 1:219.
110. *NEAEHL*, 98d.
111. *NEAEHL*, 97a; cf. esp. *CANE*, 1276–77.
112. For fuller description, see *CANE*, 1277.
113. *NEAEHL*, 98b.
114. For other examples and discussion, see A. F. Campbell, *The Ark Narrative (1 Sam. 4–6; 2 Sam. 6): A Form-Critical and Traditio-Historical Study* (SBLDS 16; Missoula, Mont.: Scholars, 1975), 179–91; P. D. Miller and J. J. M. Roberts Jr., *The Hand of the Lord: A Reassessment of the 'Ark Narrative' of 1 Samuel* (Baltimore: Johns Hopkins Univ. Press, 1977), 9–17; P. K. McCarter, *II Samuel: A New Translation with Introduction and Commentary* (AB; Garden City, N.Y.: Doubleday, 1984), 178–82.
115. *ARI*, 2.12:7.
116. *ANET*, 340b.
117. On both, see J. Scurlock and B. R. Anderson, *Diagnoses in Assyrian and Babylonian Medicine: Ancient Sources, Translations, and Modern Medicine* (Urbana, Ill.: Univ. of Illinois Press, 2005), 51–52, 73–74.
118. In the case of plague, the bacterium *Yersinia pestis* is introduced by the bites of infected rat fleas (see ibid., 73).
119. For a convenient review of the plague debate, see McCarter, *I Samuel*, 123.
120. For the state of the question, see E. Stern, *NEAEHL*, 1522. Cf. also J. D. Seger, "Gath," *ABD*, 2:908–9.
121. A. M. Maeir and C. S. Ehrlich, "Excavating Philistine Gath: Have We Found Goliath's Hometown?" *BAR* 27/6 (2001): 22–31.
122. For additional evidence of the Philistines' empirical spirit, see 6:9.
123. Namely, Tell esh-Shalaf. On all this, see T. Dothan and S. Gitin, *NEAEHL*, 1051–52.
124. "The Ekron Inscription of Akhayus," trans. K. L. Younger Jr. (COS, 2.42:164). On internal grounds, the inscription should be dated ca. 680–665 B.C. (so ibid.).

125. For the initial publication of the Ekron Inscription, describing the circumstances of its discovery and aspects of its translation and significance, see S. Gitin, T. Dothan, and J. Naveh, "A Royal Dedicatory Inscription from Ekron," *IEJ* 47 (1997): 1–16. For a discussion of how the name (actually an appellation) of the Ekronite king "may be of great importance to the discussion of the origin of the Philistines," see J. Naveh, "Achish-Ikausu in the Light of the Ekron Dedication," *BASOR* 310 (1998): 35–37. Naveh links "Akhayus" to "Achaean," meaning "Greek" (ibid., 35). Further support for the Greek connection may exist if A. Demsky is correct in reading the name of the goddess in the inscription not as PTGYH but as PTNYH, vocalized "Potnia," "meaning 'mistress' or 'lady,' the formal title used for various goddesses in archaic Greek and Minoan and Mycenaean writings dating back to the Late Bronze Age. The root *pot* means 'lord' or 'master,' as in des*pot*. Potnia is simply the feminine form, which sometimes accompanies the name of a particular goddess" ("Discovering a Goddess: A New Look at the Ekron Inscription Identifies a Mysterious Deity," *BAR* 24/5 [1998]: 53–58 [on 57]).
126. "Sennacherib's Siege of Jerusalem," trans. M. Cogan (*COS*, 2.119B:303).
127. Ibid. Padi is mentioned also in another Ekronite inscription, which reads, "for Baʿal and for Padi" (see V. Sasson, "The Inscription of Achish, Governor of Ekron, and Philistine Dialect, Cult and Culture," *UF* 29 [1997]: 627–39 [on 632]) and in a docket from 699 B.C. recording the contribution of one "Pidi of Anqaruna" = Padi of Ekron (see Gitin, Dothan, Naveh, "A Royal Dedicatory Inscription from Ekron," 9).
128. Ibid. For text, see *ANET*, 291b.
129. A. F. Rainey, "Syntax, Hermeneutics and History," *IEJ* 48 (1998): 239–51 (on 242).
130. "Uḫḫamūwa's Ritual against Plague," trans. B. J. Collins (*COS*, 1.63:162).
131. "Pulisa's Ritual against Plague," trans. B. J. Collins (*COS*, 1.62:161).
132. D. T. Tsumura, "List and Narrative in 1 Samuel 6, 17–18a in the Light of Ugaritic Economic Texts," *ZAW* 113 (2001): 353–69 (on 365).
133. On the nature of apotropaic rituals, see O. R. Gurney, "Babylonian Prophylactic Figures and Their Rituals," *AAA* (1935), 21–96; A. R. Green, "Neo-Assyrian Apotropaic Figures," *Iraq* 45 (1983): 87–96; and the brief comments by A. R. Millard, "Keeping Evil at Bay [Queries and Comments]," *BAR* 27/1 (2001): 10.
134. Tsumura, "List and Narrative in 1 Samuel 6, 17–18a," 366–67.
135. D. P. Wright, "The Gesture of Hand Placement in the Hebrew Bible and in Hittite Literature," *JAOS* 106 (1986): 446.
136. Tsumura, "List and Narrative in 1 Samuel 6,17–18a," 367.
137. *OEANE*, 1:311.
138. For photographs, see *NEAEHL*, 250.
139. *OEANE*, 1:311.
140. For fuller discussion of the site and its excavation, see F. Brandfon, "Beth Shemesh," *ABD*, 1:696–98; S. Bunimovitz and Z. Lederman, *NEAEHL*, 249–53; W. G. Dever, *OEANE*, 1:311–12.
141. McCarter, *I Samuel*, 137; cf. Y. Aharoni, *Land of the Bible* (Philadelphia: Westminster, 1979), 255 ("Tell Deir el-ʾAzar in Abu Gosh").
142. See J. M. Hamilton, "Kiriath Jearim," *ABD*, 4:85; Boling, *Joshua*, 267, 369.
143. J. Day, "Baal," *ABD*, 1:545–49. On divine thunder and lightning, see comment on 2:10.
144. For discussion of extrabiblical allusions to Astarte, see J. Day, "Ashtoreth," *ABD*, 1:492–94, who notes, among other things, that "precursors of the Canaanite goddess Astarte are to be found in the Mesopotamian Ishtar and the Eblaite Ashtar" (492); cf. idem, *Yahweh and the Gods and Goddesses of Canaan* (Sheffield: Sheffield Academic Press, 2000), 128ff. See also N. Wyatt, "Astarte," *DDD*², 110–12.
145. Day, "Ashtoreth," *ABD*, 1:492; G. C. Heider, "Molech," *DDD*², 581; but note also the latter's discussion of alternative construals of Molech (582–83). For a brief summary of debates regarding biblical references to Molech, see *CANE*, 2054, under "Human Sacrifice."
146. Day, "Baal," *ABD*, 1:547.
147. So Day, "Ashtoreth," *ABD*, 1:492, who compares the Akkadian use of *ilāni u ištarāti* to signify simply "gods and goddesses."
148. For a succinct and admittedly "oversimplified" discussion of the nature of Canaanite idolatry, see Merrill, *Kingdom*, 159–61. For a more thorough treatment of Canaanite religion, see M. S. Smith, "Myth and Mythmaking in Canaan and Ancient Israel," *CANE*, 2031–41, and van der Toorn, "Theology, Priests, and Worship," 2043–58.
149. On the various Mizpahs or Mizpehs, see P. M. Arnold, "Mizpah," *ABD*, 4:879–81.
150. Some earlier scholars assumed Nebi Samwil to be the Mizpah in view here, but scholarly opinion now favors Tell en-Naṣbeh; see ibid., 4:880. On the excavation history of Tell en-Naṣbeh, see J. R. Zorn, *NEAEHL*, 1098–102; idem, *OEANE*, 4:101–3.
151. Arnold, "Mizpah," *ABD*, 4:880.
152. Zorn, *OEANE*, 4:102; cf. idem, "Mizpah: Newly Discovered Stratum Reveals Judah's Other Capital," *BAR* 23/5 (1997): 28–38, 66.
153. J. N. Postgate, *Early Mesopotamia: Society and Economy at the Dawn of History* (London: Routledge, 1992), 100.
154. See, e.g., Johnston, ed., *Religions*, 331–32.
155. Cf. T. Ishida, "The Leaders of the Tribal Leagues: 'Israel' in the Pre-Monarchical Period," *RB* 80/1 (1973): 514–30 (repub. in idem, *History and Historical Writing in Ancient Israel: Studies in Biblical Historiography* [Leiden: Brill, 1999], 37–56).
156. For further discussion, see Provan, Long, and Longman, *A Biblical History of Israel*, 205–7.
157. E.g., *ANET*, 270, l. 31; 275 §a; 277 §§a,b; 281 §5; 287 §8; cf. 279, 285.
158. E.g., *ANET*, 277, 281, 289.
159. *ARI*, 2.577:138.
160. *SSI*, 1:76 l. 14.
161. *NERT*, 231; *ANET*, 655.
162. *NERT*, 122–28; *ANET*, 623–32. On ancient Near Eastern prophecy outside Israel, see M.

Nissinen, *Prophets and Prophecy in the Ancient Near East* (SBLWAW 12; Atlanta: Scholars, 2003). More briefly, cf. J. Blenkinsopp, *History of Prophecy in Israel* (Louisville: Westminster John Knox, 1996), 54–58.
163. *NERT*, 222.
164. Cf. Judg. 20:26–28; 1 Sam. 13:8–12; 1 Kings 8:44–45. For further discussion and literature, see V. P. Long, *The Reign and Rejection of King Saul: A Case for Literary and Theological Coherence* (SBLDS 118; Atlanta: Scholars, 1989), 62–63.
165. *NERT*, 222.
166. See, e.g., the discussion of Babylonian *kudurrus* ("boundary stones") from the Kassite period (late second millennium) in W. Sommerfeld, "The Kassites of Ancient Mesopotamia: Origins, Politics, and Culture," *CANE*, 920–22. For fuller discussion, see K. E. Slanski, *The Babylonian Entitlement Narûs (kudurrus): A Study of their Form and Function* (ASOR Books 9; Boston: American Schools of Oriental Research, 2003).
167. G. E. Mendenhall, "Amorites," *ABD*, 1:199–202.
168. See A. Negev and S. Gibson, eds., *Archaeological Encyclopedia of the Holy Land*, rev. ed. (New York/London: Continuum, 2003), 31–32; more fully, M. Liverani, "The Amorites," *POTW*, 100–133.
169. As suggested by Liverani, "Amorites," 125–26.
170. See A. Malamat, *Mari and the Bible*, ed. B. Halpern and M. H. E. Weippert (SHCANE 12; Leiden: Brill, 1998), 102. The letter cited is *ARM* 26/1.88.
171. See the descriptions of and the map locating these sites in W. Heimpel, *Letters to the King of Mari: A New Translation with Historical Introduction, Notes, and Commentary* (Winona Lake, Ind.: Eisenbrauns, 2003), xxii–xxiii.
172. Ibid., 210–11.
173. P. Villard, "Shamshi-Adad and Sons: The Rise and Fall of an Upper Mesopotamian Empire," *CANE*, 877.
174. On the question of identification, see Z. Herzog, *NEAEHL*, 168a; idem, *OEANE*, 1:288; D. W. Manor, "Beersheba," *ABD*, 1:641–42.
175. Manor, "Beersheba," *ABD*, 1:642.
176. A. F. Rainey, "Early Historical Geography of the Negeb," in *Beer-Sheba II: The Early Iron Age Settlements*, ed. Zeʾev Herzog (Tel Aviv: Tel Aviv Univ. Institute of Archaeology, 1984), 88–104. The fact that several different sites may have borne the name Beersheba relieves the tension created by the fact that, while Beersheba figures in the lives of the patriarchs (e.g., Gen. 21:33; 46:1), Tell es-Sebaʿ evidences little occupation before the twelfth century B.C.; see H. W. Vos, "Beersheba," *NIDOTTE*, 4:439.
177. See *IVPBBC-OT*, 291c.
178. *OEANE*, 1:288c.
179. *IVPBBC-OT*, 291c.
180. "Instructions to Commanders of Border Garrisons," trans. G. McMahon (*COS*, 1.84:221–25 [§§1, 36–37]).
181. Saggs, *Civilization*, 36.
182. Holloway, *Aššur is King!* 181–82.
183. "Instructions to the Royal Guard," trans. G. McMahon (*COS*, 1.85:225–30 [§18]).
184. "The Panamuwa Inscription," trans. K. L. Younger Jr. (*COS*, 2.37:159 [section 11b–19a]; "The Bar-Rakib Inscription," trans. idem (*COS*, 2.38:161 [section 7b–15]).
185. I. Mendelsohn, "Samuel's Denunciation of the Kingship in the Light of Akkadian Documents from Ugarit," *BASOR* 143 (1956): 17–32. Cf. also S. Talmon, "'The Rule of the King'—1 Samuel 8:4–22," in *King, Cult and Calendar in Ancient Israel*, ed. S. Talmon (Jerusalem: Magnes, 1986), 53–67.
186. For a full discussion of this issue, see Long, *Reign and Rejection*, 204–5.
187. J. G. Westenholz, *Legends of the Kings of Akkade* (Mesopotamian Civilizations; Winona Lake, Ind.: Eisenbrauns, 1997), 119; cf. also the text "Sargon, the Conquering Hero" (ibid., 59–77).
188. B. R. Foster, *Before the Muses: An Anthology of Akkadian Literature*, 3rd ed. (Bethesda, Md.: CDL, 2005), 301.
189. G. Frame, *Rulers of Babylonia: From the Second Dynasty of Isin to the End of Assyrian Domination (1157–612 B.C.)* (RIMB 2; Toronto: Univ. of Toronto Press, 1995), 34.
190. *ANET*, 73.
191. See N. Shupak, "The Eloquent Peasant," *COS*, 1.43:98–104; *ANET*, 407–10.
192. R. S. Hess, "Letter Asking for the Return of Stolen Donkeys," *COS*, 3.91:236.
193. *ARM*, 26/1, 63. For discussion, see Malamat, *Mari and the Bible*, 103.
194. Ibid.
195. But for a studied attempt, see McCarter, *I Samuel*, 174–75.
196. Cf. *IVPBBC-OT*, 293.
197. See S. M. Paul, "1 Samuel 9:7: An Interview Fee," in *Divrei Shalom: Collected Studies of Shalom M. Paul on the Bible and the Ancient Near East 1967–2005*, ed. S. M. Paul (CHANE 23; Leiden: Brill, 2005), 95–98.
198. For summary and discussion, see Malamat, *Mari and the Bible*, 124–27.
199. For the text in translation, with explanations of items requested, see Heimpel, *Letters*, 252–54 (26.199).
200. See Long, *Reign and Rejection*, 201, n. 26.
201. Youngblood, "1 and 2 Samuel," *EBC*, 620, citing B. Kanael, "Ancient Jewish Coins and Their Historical Importance," *BA* 26 (1963): 39.
202. Cf. King and Stager, *Life in Biblical Israel*, 194–95.
203. Ibid., 320; see 320–30 for a good discussion of "high places."
204. For an extrabiblical example of the cultic sense, see Mesha's statement in the Mesha Inscription that he "built this high place for Chemosh" (*SSI*, 1:16.3).
205. E.g., King and Stager (*Life in Biblical Israel*, 320) assume the former, while Zevit at least allows for the latter (*The Religions of Ancient Israel*, 263).
206. Rarely, as in the case of Akrotiri of the island of Thera, volcanic ash may preserve more, even

second stories, but such preservation is the exception. For a brief online introduction to Akrotiri, visit www.culture.gr/2/21/211/21121a/e211ua08.html [accessed 17 August 2005].

207. See A. Faust and S. Bunimovitz, "The Four Room House: Embodying Iron Age Israelite Society," *NEA* 66 (2003): 22–31.
208. For discussion, see King and Stager, *Life in Biblical Israel*, 280–82. D. V. Edelman (*King Saul in the Historiography of Judah* [Sheffield: Sheffield Academic Press, 1991], 52) suggests that Samuel's use of a "vial" rather than a "horn," as was customary in royal anointings (cf. 16:1, 13), is vaguely unsettling.
209. On this discovery, see J. Patrich, "Hideouts in the Judean Wilderness," *BAR* 15/5 (1989): 32–42 (esp. 35).
210. So Edelman, *King Saul*, 44.
211. T. Ishida, *History and Historical Writing in Ancient Israel* (SHCANE 19; Leiden: Brill, 1999), 67.
212. For further discussion and literature, see McCarter, *I Samuel*, 181.
213. Cross, *Canaanite Myth*, 223.
214. Cf. *CAD*, 2:142.
215. *CAD*, 1/1:134–35.
216. A. M. Kitz, "Prophecy as Divination," *CBQ* 65 (2003): 22–42 (on 31).
217. See Long, *Reign and Rejection*; more briefly, idem, "How Did Saul Become King? Literary Reading and Historical Reconstruction," in *Faith, Tradition and History*, ed. A. R. Millard, J. K. Hoffmeier, and D. W. Baker (Winona Lake, Ind.: Eisenbrauns, 1994), 271–84. Cf. also Edelman, *King Saul*, whose reading differs from that presented here in some important respects.
218. See *CAD*, 1/1:131–34.
219. See Provan, Long, and Longman, *A Biblical History of Israel*, 58–60.
220. A. R. Millard has made a strong case for literacy in early Israel; see, e.g., "The Question of Israelite Literacy," *BRev* 3 (1987): 22–31; "Books in the Late Bronze Age in the Levant," in *Past Links: Studies in the Languages and Cultures of the Ancient Near East*, ed. S. Izreʾel, I. Singer, and R. Zadok (Israel Oriental Studies 18; Winona Lake, Ind.: Eisenbrauns, 1998), 171–181. Others arguing for early literacy include Hess, Isserlin, Dever, Hoffmeier, etc. (for bibliography, see Provan, Long, and Longman, *A Biblical History of Israel*, 314, n. 20).
221. See Z. Ben-Barak, "The Mizpah Covenant (I Samuel 10 25)—The Source of the Israelite Monarchic Covenant," *ZAW* 91 (1979): 30–43, esp. 35–37.
222. Ibid., 36.
223. Ibid., 37.
224. P. M. Arnold, *Gibeah: The Search for a Biblical City* (Sheffield: Sheffield Academic Press, 1990), 39–54.
225. See, e.g., N. L. Lapp, "Ful, Tell el-," *OEANE*, 2:346–47. Cf. also idem, "Fûl, Tell el-," *NEAEHL*, 446–47.
226. E.g., Arnold, *Gibeah*; H. S. Wentz, "The Monarchy of Saul: Antecendents, 'Deuteronomic' Interpretations and Ideology" (PhD diss., Univ. of Exeter, 1970/71); J. M. Miller, "Geba/Gibeah of Benjamin," *VT* 25 (1975): 145–66; V. P. Long, "Gibeah," *NIDOTTE*, 4:678–81 (from which the above discussion is adapted); Walton, *IVPBBC-OT*, 296.
227. The basic pattern has been further developed in works by D. Edelman and V. P. Long. For discussion and bibliography, see Long, *Reign and Rejection*, 185–90.
228. *ANET*, 282b.
229. "A Letter Reporting Matters in Kalaḫ," trans. K. L. Younger Jr. (*COS*, 3.96:245).
230. "Sennacherib's Siege of Jerusalem," trans. K. L. Younger Jr. (*COS*, 2.119B; cf. *ANET*, 287c).
231. *ANET*, 294b.
232. See *NEAEHL*, 1247; "The Tell Sīrān Inscription," trans. W. E. Aufrecht (*COS*, 2.25:139–40); for other brief Ammonite inscriptions, see *COS*, 2.24 and 2.26.
233. See J.-M. de Tarragon, "Ammon," *ABD*, 1:194, and esp. M. Burdajewicz, *NEAEHL*, 1243–49.
234. *COS*, 2.24:139.
235. See, e.g., Judg. 10:6–8, and discussion of this issue in Provan, Long, and Longman, *A Biblical History of Israel*, 164–65.
236. For more on the Ammonites, see R. W. Younker, "Ammonites," in *POTW*, 293–316.
237. As argued by D. Edelman, "Jabesh-Gilead," *ABD*, 3:594–95.
238. K. A. Kitchen, *Ramesside Inscriptions, vol. IV: Merenptah and the Late Nineteenth Dynasty* (Oxford: Blackwell, 2003), text on 1–2, the Nubian War Stele.
239. "The Inscriptions of Bar-gaʾyah and Matiʿel from Sefire," trans. Joseph A. Fitzmyer (*COS*, 2.82:214). Further on the Aramaic inscriptions discovered at Sefire (a village in Syria some 16 miles southeast of Aleppo), see Fitzmyer, *OEANE*, 4:512–13.
240. See Bergen, *1, 2 Samuel*, 135. Further on the large-scale blinding of prisoners-of-war, see Postgate, *Early Mesopotamia*, 255.
241. See I. Ephʾal, "On Warfare and Military Control in the Ancient Near Eastern Empires: A Research Outline," in *History, Historiography and Interpretation: Studies in Biblical and Cuneiform Literature*, ed. H. Tadmor and M. Weinfeld (Jerusalem: Magnes, 1983), 88–106 (on 99).
242. For full argumentation, see Long, *Reign and Rejection*, 219–24.
243. Gordon, *1 & 2 Samuel*, 124.
244. *ARM*, 2.48. The parallel to 1 Sam. 11:7 was first proposed by G. Wallis, "Eine Parallele zu Richter 19.29ff. und 1 Sam. 11.5ff aus den Briefarchiv von Mari," *ZAW* 64 (1952): 57–61.
245. Zertal bases this judgment on the presence of Iron Age pottery at the latter; see A. Zertal, "The Trek of the Tribes as They Settled in Canaan," *BAR* 17/5 (1991): 48–49, 75.
246. *NERT*, 65–66.
247. See *COS*, 3.33:59 §22.
248. H. A. Hoffner Jr., "Crossing the Taurus," *COS*, 1.73:184 §§1–2. Cf. also *COS*, 2.15:80 §14.

249. An interpretation like this was suggested by the medieval Jewish commentator Isaac Abrabanel (see Long, *Reign and Rejection*, 75, n. 30).
250. For these and other examples, see G. Buccelati, "1 Sam 13:1," *BeO* 5 (1963): 29; A. K. Grayson, "1 Sam 13:1," *BeO* 5 (1963): 86, 110. For a recent alternative approach, see S. Kreuzer, "'Saul war noch zwei Jahre König ...' Textgeschichtliche, literarische und historische Beobachtungen zu 1 Sam 13,1," *BZ* 40 (1996): 263–70.
251. For more, including comments on Acts 13:21, see Long, *Reign and Rejection*, 71–75; Provan, Long, and Longman, *A Biblical History of Israel*, 199–201.
252. The *šôpār* was also used in cultic contexts to "summon people together ... signal an announcement ... mark the beginning of cultic events and times ... acclaim a king ... introduce a theophany," etc. (D. P. Wright, "Music and Dance in 2 Samuel 6," *JBL* 121 [2002]: 201–25 [on 210]).
253. K. S. Gilbert et al., ed., *Treasures of Tutankhamun* (New York: Ballantine, 1976), 103 and color plate 8.
254. So Wright, "Music and Dance," 210–11, which see for full discussion.
255. Cf. 29:1–2, 11, where the Philistines gather their forces in Aphek before advancing to do battle with Israel in Jezreel.
256. In the present context, Beth Aven probably does not represent a disparaging transformation of the name Bethel (as in Hos. 10:5; cf. 1 Kings 12:28–29) but a different site, possibly Burqa, south of Beitîn (Bethel?). The site is mentioned in order to clarify the location not of Micmash, but of the Philistine encampment.
257. For discussion, see Provan, Long, and Longman, *A Biblical History of Israel*, 212–14; more fully, Long, *Reign and Rejection*, 85–96.
258. McCarter, *I Samuel*, 229. Describing a king this way is attested as early as the mid-third millennium in the royal inscriptions of Eanatum, which repeatedly identify him as "chosen in the heart by the goddess Nanshe" (D. Frayne, *Presargonic Inscriptions* [RIME 1; Toronto: Univ. of Toronto Press, 2008], 146, 150, 155, 157).
259. *ABC*, 102.
260. *CAD*, 9:171 (libbu 3b §2′), which see for many other examples of this usage. Similar in concept, though employing different terminology, cf. "the political situation will change, Šamaš will install a king of his own choice for his land" (*CAD*, 15:405 [B §3′b].
261. M. Garsiel, "The Battle of Michmash: An Historical-Literary Study (1 Sam 13–14)," in *Studies in Bible and Exegesis: Arie Toeg in Memoriam*, ed. M. Goshen-Gottstein and U. Simon (Ramat-Gan: Bar-Ilan Univ. Press, 1980), 15–50 [Hebrew].
262. On the route in question, see D. A. Dorsey, *The Roads and Highways of Ancient Israel* (ASOR Library of Biblical and Near Eastern Archaeology; Baltimore: Johns Hopkins Univ. Press, 1991), 202.
263. On archaeological evidence for this road marking the northern border of Benjamin, see ibid., 204.
264. So *IVPBBC-OT*, 300.
265. Cf. D. Jobling, "Saul's Fall and Jonathan's Rise: Tradition and Redaction in 1 Sam 14:1–46," *JBL* 95 (1976): 368.
266. Long, *Reign and Rejection*, 107 and n. 28.
267. On the origins and history of the practice of circumcision in the ancient Near East, see J. M. Sasson, "Circumcision in the Ancient Near East," *JBL* 85 (1966): 473–76. Sasson argues that circumcision did not arise first in Egypt but was already "known to the inhabitants of North Syria during the early third millennium B.C." (476).
268. Gordon, *1 & 2 Samuel*, 137.
269. *ANET*, 326.
270. On the notion of an Egyptian "circumcision festival," see G. Pinch, "Private Life in Ancient Egypt," *CANE*, 363–81 (on 378).
271. *ANET*, 326, n.2.
272. A second possibility is that these statements refer simply to the general good conduct of those undergoing the rite, but this interpretation seems less likely (see *ANET*, 326, n.2).
273. In some periods at least, such as the New Kingdom period, some adult males remained uncircumcised (see Pinch, "Private Life in Egypt," *CANE*, 378). There is little to suggest that female circumcision was practiced in Egypt (ibid., 378–79).
274. So J. F. Quack, "Religious Personnel (Egypt)," in *Religions of the Ancient World: A Guide*, ed. S. I. Johnston (Cambridge, Mass.: Belknap Press of the Harvard Univ. Press, 2004), 289–92. Quack notes further that when at a much later period, "the emperor Hadrian prohibited circumcision in the Roman Empire, Egyptian priests were among the few groups who could, by application and proof of priestly descent, obtain permission to continue the practice" (291).
275. For a discussion of this and other biblical evidence, see King and Stager, *Life in Biblical Israel*, 43–45. Cf. also P. J. King, "Circumcision—Who Did It, Who Didn't and Why," *BAR* 32/4 (2006): 48–55.
276. On the topic generally, see P. D. Miller Jr., *The Divine Warrior in Early Israel* (Cambridge, Mass.: Harvard Univ. Press, 1973); T. Longman III and D. G. Reid, *God Is a Warrior* (Grand Rapids: Zondervan, 1995).
277. *ANET*, 135a.
278. M. Weinfeld, "Divine Intervention in War in Ancient Israel and in the Ancient Near East," in *History, Historiography and Interpretation: Studies in Biblical and Cuneiform Literature*, ed. H. Tadmor and M. Weinfeld (Jerusalem: Magnes, 1983), 121–47.
279. See ibid., 121–22, for further citations and bibliography.
280. A. M. Kitz argues on the basis of lexical and comparative evidence that "lots" (Urim and Thummim?) were likely held in a container that was shaken until one lot was cast out and fell to the ground. The meaning assigned to that lot was understood to be the decision of the deity ("The Hebrew Terminology of Lot Casting and Its Ancient Near Eastern Context," *CBQ* 62 [2000]: 207–14).
281. See de Vaux, *Ancient Israel*, 2:351.

282. W. Horowitz and V. Hurowitz, "Urim and Thummim in Light of a Psephomancy Ritual from Assur (*LKA* 137)," *JANESCU* 21 (1992): 95–115. Horowitz and Hurowitz suggest that any religious aspects of psephomancy were minimal and secondary, in contrast to other forms of ancient Near Eastern divination, making this form of divination acceptable to ancient Yahwists, while other, more religiously laden forms were abhorrent (114–15).
283. For an instance of confusion of ארון and אפוד outside the Old Testament, see 2 Bar. 6:7 (cf. the note on this verse in *APOT)*. For further discussion, see Long, *Reign and Rejection*, 112.
284. Cf. A. F. Kirkpatrick, *The First Book of Samuel* (CB; Cambridge: Cambridge Univ. Press, 1981), 133; K. A. D. Smelik, *Saul, de voorstelling van Israels eerste Konig in de Masoretische tekst van het Oude Testament* (Amsterdam: Drukkerij en Uitgeverij P. E. T., 1977), 125; Stoebe, *Das erste Buch Samuels*, 264; McCarter, *I Samuel*, 240.
285. E.g., McCarter, *I Samuel*, 246.
286. J. L. Peterson, "Aijalon," *ABD*, 1:131.
287. See EA 273, 287; *ANET*, 242.
288. B. Keder-Kopfstein, "דָּם," *TDOT*, 3:237–38. For speculation regarding a possible distinction in the perception of blood's significance between Israel and Mesopotamia more generally, see T. Abusch, "Blood in Israel and Mesopotamia," in *Emanuel: Studies in Hebrew Bible, Septuagint and Dead Sea Scrolls in Honor of Emanuel Tov*, ed. S. M. Paul (VTSup 94; Leiden: Brill, 2003), 675–84.
289. See G. L. Mattingly, "Amalek," *ABD*, 1:171.
290. Ibid., 1:170.
291. P. D. Stern, *The Biblical ḤEREM: A Window on Israel's Religious Experience* (BJS 211; Atlanta: Scholars, 1991), 173–74.
292. *SSI*, 1:16.14–17.
293. A. Malamat, *Mari and the Early Israelite Experience* (Oxford: Oxford Univ. Press, 1989), 70; see also 70–75 for Malamat's discussion of how the term *asakkum* was used at Mari "to designate consecrated property belonging exclusively to a divinity or to royalty" (72).
294. See *HALOT*, sub קַיִן II.
295. So Negev and Gibson, *Archaeological Encyclopedia*, 281.
296. On Kenites in the vicinity of Arad, see Y. Aharoni, "The Negeb," in *Archaeology and Old Testament Study*, ed. D. W. Thomas (Oxford: Clarendon, 1967), 390, 401 and map on 384; idem, *Land of the Bible*, 201.
297. I.e., Tell Arad Ostracon 24; see Y. Aharoni, *Arad Inscriptions* (JDS; Jerusalem: Israel Exploration Society, 1981), 46–47.
298. For full text in transliteration, see G. I. Davies, *Ancient Hebrew Inscriptions* [Volume 1]: *Corpus and Concordance* (Cambridge: Cambridge Univ. Press, 1991), 19–20 (2.024); for translation as well, see S. L. Gogel, *A Grammar of Epigraphic Hebrew* (SBLRBS 23; Atlanta: Scholars, 1989), 392–93.
299. *ARI*, 2.546:123.
300. *ARI*, 2.547:125. Further references could easily be cited; see, e.g., *ARI*, 2.222–23:49; 2.550:126–27.
301. See Long, *Reign and Rejection*, 157–58.
302. E.g., *ARM*, 6.45; 10.7.23ff.; 10.8.20ff.; 10.50.29ff.; 10.81.16ff.; 13.112. English translations of several of these texts are conveniently available in *NERT*, 122–28. See also Nissinen, *Prophets and Prophecy in the Ancient Near East.*
303. So D. Conrad, "Samuel und die Mari-'Propheten': Bemerkungen zu I Sam. 15:27," *ZDMG* Sup. 1 (1969): 273–80.
304. *ARM*, 10.81.
305. See *ARM*, 6.26.3'f., 8'f.; 8.148.8; and perhaps the following from Ashurnasirpal's hymn to Ishtar: "I, Ashurnasirpal, the frightened, who fear you, who seize the fringe of your divinity, who pray to you as mistress" (*NERT*, 115).
306. *SSI*, 2:14.11 (= *KAI*, 215.11): "Then did he grasp the skirt of his lord, the [great] king of Assyria."
307. So R. A. Brauner, " 'To Grasp the Hem' and 1 Samuel 15:27," *JANES* 6 (1974): 35–38.
308. *CML*[2], 6.ii.9b–11a. On these lines, see E. L. Greenstein, " 'To Grasp the Hem' in Ugaritic Literature," *VT* 32 (1982): 217–18.
309. *CML*[2], 6.ii.30b–31a.
310. Greenstein, " 'To Grasp the Hem,' " 218.
311. See also the discussion of David's action in 24:4.
312. For a similarly "neutral" (that is, not "religious or magical") use of the phrase in a different context, see Greenfield's discussion of a proverb of Aḥiqar that begins, "if the wicked man takes hold of the corners of your garment, leave it in his hand . . ."; J. C. Greenfield, "Two Proverbs of Aḥiqar," in *Lingering Over Words: Studies in Ancient Near Eastern Literature in Honor of William L. Moran*, ed. T. Abusch, J. Heuhnergard, and P. Steinkeller (Atlanta: Scholars, 1990), 195–201.
313. For a more thorough discussion, see Long, *Reign and Rejection*, 157–64.
314. *ARI*, 2.536:119.
315. RIMA, 2/1:194 (A.0.101.1 line 7).
316. *AHw*, 221a (sub *enû* III, "umwenden, ändern"). On the sense of changing a judicial verdict, see sec. G, 2.b. of the entry cited.
317. RIMA, 2/1:193–94 (A.0.101.1 lines 3–4, 8).
318. Lines 139–42 in T. Jacobsen, *The Harps That Once . . . : Sumerian Poetry in Translation* (New Haven, Conn.: Yale Univ. Press, 1987), 109.
319. W. Eichrodt, *Theology of the Old Testament*, trans. J. A. Baker, 2 vols. (OTL; Philadelphia: Westminster, 1975), 1:216. For further discussion, see Long, *Reign and Rejection*, 163–64.
320. See King and Stager, *Life in Biblical Israel*, 280–82. Ex. 30:22–25 prescribes the makeup of the aromatic oil that was to be used to anoint, and thus consecrate, the tabernacle, its furnishings, and the ark.
321. See also the brief descriptions in *IVPBBC-OT*, 304–5; *DBI*, 33; and the more thorough treatment in Mettinger, *King and Messiah*, 185–232.
322. O. Keel, *Symbolism of the Biblical World* (New York: Seabury, 1978), 258.
323. Cf. J. A. Motyer, "Anointing, Anointed," *IBD*, 1:68–69.
324. "The King and the Queen-Mother in the Matter of the Amurrite Princess," trans. D. Pardee (*COS*, 3.45D:91).

325. So T. P. J. van den Hout, commenting on the Hittite king Ḫattušiliš III's request, in anticipation of his daughter's marriage to the Egyptian Pharaoh Ramesses, that (in van den Hout's words) "sweet-scented oil be brought from the groom's country to anoint the bride-to-be" ("Khattushili III, King of the Hittites," *CANE*, 1116).
326. Moran, *Amarna Letters*, 333–34 (EA 290).
327. See D. W. Manor, "Bethlehem," *OEANE*, 1:302; M. Avi-Yonah, "Bethlehem," *NEAEHL*, 204; the cautionary remarks of G. C. Heider, "Lahmu," *DDD*^{2}, 502; and the alternative suggestion by H. Cazelles, "Bethlehem," *ABD*, 1:712.
328. H.-J. Fabry, "לֵב," *TDOT*, 7:401–3.
329. See, e.g., *CAD*, 9:170b (where Shamash is said to see "into the heart of man"); Jacobsen, *Harps That Once . . .* , 474, lines 430–34.
330. H. Vanstiphout, *Epics of Sumerian Kings* (SBLWAW 20; Atlanta: SBL, 2003), 107–9.
331. In addition to the notes on 2:10 and 8:7, see, e.g., D. Launderville, *Piety and Politics: The Dynamics of Royal Authority in Homeric Greece, Biblical Israel, and Old Babylonian Mesopotamia* (Grand Rapids: Eerdmans, 2003).
332. So *CAD*, 10:9–10 (sub *melammu*, §1). A. Green ("Ancient Mesopotamian Religious Iconography," *CANE*, 1842) notes that "living gods and other supernatural beings are said, in literary accounts, to 'wear,' and sometimes to 'take off,' a radiant light called ME.LÁM or *melammu*." Cf. also M. Weinfeld, "כָּבוֹד," *TDOT*, 7:29–30.
333. D. W. Baker, "רעע," *NIDOTTE*, 3:1154.
334. M. V. Van Pelt, W. C. Kaiser Jr., D. I. Block, "רוּחַ," *NIDOTTE*, 3:1073.
335. *HALOT*, sub רוּחַ, §7.
336. Cf. other uses of "spirit" that may be suggestive of a state of mind or even a physical condition: Judg. 9:23; 1 Kings 22:22; Isa. 19:14; 29:10.
337. *ANET*, 179a; cf. *COS*, 2.131:352.
338. See *CAD*, 15:257 (sub *šēdu* A, §1); 10/2:185 (sub *mukīl rēši*, §3).
339. See, e.g., the following summary essays and their bibliographies: R. Anderson, "Music and Dance in Pharaonic Egypt," *CANE*, 2555–68; A. D. Kilmer, "Music and Dance in Ancient Western Asia," *CANE*, 2601–13; S. de Martino, "Music, Dance, and Processions in Hittite Anatolia," *CANE*, 2661–69.
340. For a thorough and enlightening study, see B. Lawergren, "Distinctions among Canaanite, Philistine, and Israelite Lyres, and Their Global Lyrical Contexts," *BASOR* 309 (1998): 41–68. For a well-illustrated brief treatment, see K. A. Kitchen, "Music and Musical Instruments," *IBD*, 2:1031–40.
341. See Youngblood, "1 and 2 Samuel," 625.
342. For discussion, see King and Stager, *Life in Biblical Israel*, 291–94.
343. Ibid., 291.
344. For a convenient summary of all these, see King and Stager, *Life in Biblical Israel*, 292–94.
345. See Dorsey, *Roads and Highways*, 189–91 and map on 182.
346. H. D. Lance, "Socoh," *ABD*, 6:99.
347. Ibid.
348. Cited in J. D. Seger, "Azekah," *OEANE*, 1:243.
349. R. de Vaux, "Single Combat in the Old Testament," in *The Bible and the Ancient Near East* (London: Darton, Longman & Todd, 1972), 122–35.
350. H. A. Hoffner Jr., "A Hittite Analogue to the David and Goliath Contest of Champions," *CBQ* 30 (1968): 220–25 (on 222).
351. Ibid., 224.
352. Ibid., 225.
353. For a fascinating survey, see D. Kellermann, "Die Geschichte von David und Goliath im Lichte der Endokrinologie," *ZAW* 102 (1990): 344–57.
354. So R. S. Hess, *Joshua: An Introduction and Commentary* (TOTC; Downers Grove, Ill.: InterVarsity Press, 1996), 218, n. 3 (citing E. Wente, *Letters from Ancient Egypt* [SBLWAW; Atlanta: Scholars, 1990], 108).
355. G. L. Mattingly, "Anak," *ABD*, 1:222. For concise discussions of the giant peoples in the Bible, see R. S. Hess, "Nephilim," *ABD*, 4:1072–73; M. S. Smith, "Rephaim," *ABD*, 5:674–76.
356. *HALOT* (sub verb.) cites Judg. 12:5; 1 Sam. 1:1; 1 Kings 11:26 as examples.
357. Other key instances of this usage include Gen. 35:19; 48:7; Ruth 1:2; 4:11; 1 Chron. 4:4; Mic. 5:2.
358. Youngblood, "1 and 2 Samuel," 696.
359. See R. H. Beal, "Hittite Military Organization," *CANE*, 545–54, esp. 550–52. On the topic generally, and for more examples, see *IVPBBC-OT*, 307.
360. See R. Wakely, "ערב," *NIDOTTE*, 3:517.
361. Cf. de Vaux, *Ancient Israel*, 1:171.
362. *IVPBBC-OT*, 307d. Bergen (*1, 2 Samuel*, 191–92) speculates that the token may have constituted "a sort of promissory note redeemable for a certain portion of plunder that might be taken from the Philistines in the event of an Israelite victory."
363. Bergen (*1, 2 Samuel*, 192) calls him the "supply officer."
364. So de Vaux, *Ancient Israel*, 1:88, who disagrees with these attempts.
365. McCarter, *I Samuel*, 304.
366. Ibid., which see for fuller discussion and bibliography.
367. Gordon, *1 & 2 Samuel*, 156, referring to N. P. Lemche, "חפשׁי in 1 Sam. XVII 25," *VT* 24 (1974): 373–74.
368. E. Firmage, "Zoology (Fauna)," *ABD*, 6:1109–67 (on 1109).
369. It is debated whether this deforestation may have preceded the emergence of Iarael in Canaan, but the biblical texts themselves attest to plant and animal life different in significant regard from what one encounters in Palestine today. For discussion by one who holds that deforestation took place during the Old Testament period, see J. Rogerson, *Atlas of the Bible* (New York: Facts on File, 1985), esp. 58–62. Throughout his atlas, Rogerson attempts to infer from topographical and climatological factors where forests may have existed in the biblical period.
370. For a broad survey of the plants and animals of the ancient Near East in antiquity, see A. S. Gilbert,

"The Flora and Fauna of the Ancient Near East," *CANE*, 153–74. On animals specifically mentioned in the Bible, see G. S. Cansdale, "Animals of the Bible," *IBD*, 1:52–68; Firmage, "Zoology."

371. Cansdale, "Animals of the Bible," 58.
372. On all this, see ibid., 59–60.
373. L. Martin, "The Faunal Remains from Tell es-Saʾidiyeh," *Levant* 20 (1988): 83–84 (Martin's brief report is Appendix D of J. N. Tubb, "Tell es-Saʾidiyeh: Preliminary Report of Renewed Excavations," *Levant* 20 [1988]: 23–88); cited by Firmage ("Zoology," 1143), who also mentions the discovery in the southeastern Negev of several ingenious leopard traps. The recovery of lion and bear bones in an archaeological dig is rare, as Martin notes. Only three such bones were reported by Martin: "a proximal radial and a tarso-scaphoid of bear (*Ursus* sp.), and the medial phalanx of a lion (*Panthera leo*)." Martin remarks that the "presence of these two wild animals on the site suggests that hunting was still practised, even though it may not have played an important part in the economy" (Martin, "Faunal Remains," 83). The animals may also have been killed in defense of the village, in which case their remains would likely have been retained as trophies or for ritual purposes.
374. Launderville, *Piety and Politics*, 61; citing the fuller treatment of "flyting" in R. P. Martin, *The Language of Heroes: Speech and Performance in the Iliad* (Ithaca, N.Y.: Cornell Univ. Press, 1989), 68, 80.
375. So M. R. Eaton, "Some Instances of Flyting in the Hebrew Bible," *JSOT* 61 (1994): 3–14 (on 3, quoting P. Bawcutt and W. Parks respectively).
376. Ibid.
377. Ibid., 7.
378. On the latter, see G. A. Rendsburg, "The Mock of Baal in 1 Kgs 18.27," *CBQ* 50 (1988): 414–17.
379. So Kellermann, "Die Geschichte von David und Goliath im Lichte der Endokrinologie," 354–55.
380. For depictions of typical Philistine (feathered?) headgear, see *ANEP*², figs. 7, 57, 341, 813; Dothan, *The Philistines*, figs. 4–7.
381. According to *HALOT*, *mēṣaḥ* means "brow," and its grammatically feminine counterpart *miṣḥâ* means "front-side>shin," and so perhaps, by extension, greave (that which covers the shin).
382. A. Deem, "'... And the Stone Sank into His Forehead.' A Note on 1 Samuel XVII 49," *VT* 28 (1978): 349–51.
383. *ANET*, 20c; cf. *COS*, 1.38:79.
384. See Å. Viberg, *Symbols of Law: A Contextual Analysis of Legal Symbolic Acts in the Old Testament* (ConBOT 34; Stockholm: Almqvist & Wiksell, 1992), 129–30.
385. Ibid., 131.
386. RS, 8.145 and *Ugaritica V*, 83; both cited in ibid., 132.
387. *PRU IV*, 17.159; cited in ibid., 132. For a convenient, brief summary, see S. Rummel, "Clothes Make the Man—An Insight from Ancient Ugarit," *BAR* 2/2 (1976): 6–8.
388. A. Mazar, "Ritual Dancing in the Iron Age," *NEA* 66 (2003): 126–32.
389. For discussion, see ibid., 126; King and Stager, *Life in Biblical Israel*, 298–300.
390. The inscription is translated in K. A. Kitchen, *Ramesside Inscriptions, vol. IV: Merenptah and the Late Nineteenth Dynasty* (Oxford: Blackwell, 2003), quotes from pages 6–7.
391. So, e.g., M. Heltzer, "New Light from Emar on Genesis 31: The Theft of the Teraphim," in *Und Mose schrieb dieses Lied auf*, ed. M. Dietrich and O. Loretz (Münster: Ugarit-Verlag, 1998), 357–67.
392. K. van der Toorn, "The Nature of the Biblical Teraphim in the Light of the Cuneiform Evidence," *CBQ* 52 (1990): 203–22. See also idem, *Family Religion in Babylonia, Syria, and Israel: Continuity and Change in the Forms of Religious Life*, ed. B. Halpern and M. H. E. Weippert (SHANE; Leiden: Brill, 1996), 218–25; G. A. Bruce and K. van der Toorn, "From Holy Mountains to the New Earth: The Nature of the Biblical Teraphim in the Light of the Cuneiform Evidence," *Theologia Evangelica* 23 (1990): 27–34.
393. For a nuanced, recent discussion of teraphim as figurines possibly representing gods or people, see Zevit, *Religions of Ancient Israel*, 267–76.
394. See McCarter, *II Samuel*, 328–29.
395. Postgate, *Early Mesopotamia*, 123. Van der Toorn (*Family Religion*, 211–18) argues that the Israelite New Moon (*ḥōdeš*) festival may be best understood as corresponding to the Babylonian *bubbulum*, celebrated not at the new moon but in the "interlunium," the period at the end of the month just before the new moon. He further theorizes that the biblical reference may contain a hint of an erstwhile ancestor cult.
396. Postgate, *Early Mesopotamia*, 265.
397. For a book-length treatment of ancient calendrical systems, see M. E. Cohen, *The Cultic Calendars of the Ancient Near East* (Bethesda, Md.: CDL, 1993).
398. On notions of sin, pollution, and purity across the ancient world, see Johnston, ed., *Religions*, 496–513.
399. *ANET*, 79a.
400. Postgate, *Early Mesopotamia*, 265.
401. See, e.g., A. L. Oppenheim, "The Golden Garments of the Gods," *JNES* 8 (1949): 172–93; cited by C. Meyers, "Ephod," *ABD*, 2:550.
402. McCarter, *I Samuel*, 350; citing also Gideon's ephod in Judg. 8.
403. *IVPBBC-OT*, 312b.
404. McCarter, *I Samuel*, 356.
405. W. F. Albright, "Researches of the School in Western Judaea," *BASOR* 15 (1924): 2–11.
406. On these sites, see comments at the following references: Socoh (17:1–2); Keilah and the Shephelah (23:1); Gath (5:8); Beth Shemesh (6:9); Jerusalem (2 Sam. 5:6).
407. See further Negev and Gibson, *Archaeological Encyclopedia*, 17.
408. So R. Wakely, "נשׂא," *NIDOTTE*, 3:177.
409. Ibid.; cf. also R. Klein, *1 Samuel* (WBC; Waco, Tex.: Word, 1983), 223.

410. P. M. Arnold, "Mizpah," *ABD*, 4:880.
411. So Bergen, *1, 2 Samuel*, 225, citing as further examples 1 Sam. 27:4–5; 1 Kings 11:17–18; 12:2; 2 Kings 25:26.
412. On this site, see D. L. Stein, "Alalakh," *OEANE*, 1:55–59; and on the texts discovered there, see E. L. Greenstein, "Alalakh Texts," *OEANE*, 1:59–61.
413. Wellhausen (cited approvingly by McCarter, *I Samuel*, 355) even suggested emending "cave [Heb. *mʿrt*] of Adullam" in 22:1 to "stronghold [Heb. *mṣdt*] of Adullam," thus identifying Adullam with the "stronghold" mentioned in 22:4–5. The relevant letters might be easily confused in the Hebrew square script (only two of them so easily in Paleo-Hebrew). Given the use of caves as natural strongholds (see comment on 22:1), however, and the fact that David enters the "stronghold" *after* his journey to Moab, there is no necessity of linking the stronghold of 22:4–5 to Adullam.
414. Aharoni, *Land of the Bible*, 290.
415. Ibid., 318, n.9.
416. Dorsey, *Roads and Highways*, 148.
417. McCarter, *I Samuel*, 357. Kharas lies to the northwest of Hebron. A second site, Khirbet Khoreisa, which lies southeast of Hebron, has also been suggested (*IVPBBC-OT*, 313).
418. *ANET*, 151a.
419. *COS*, 1.103:346.
420. See G. Cunningham, *"Deliver Me From Evil": Mesopotamian Incantations 2500–1500 B.C.* (Studia Pohl: Series Maior 17; Rome: Pontificio Insituto Biblico, 1997), 27–28.
421. So A. Taggar-Cohen, "Political Loyalty in the Biblical Account of 1 Samuel XX–XXII in the Light of Hittite Texts," *VT* 55 (2005): 251–68.
422. Saggs, *Civilization*, 39.
423. Ibid., 192 (citing *Le palais royal d'Ugarit* III, 142, no. 16.136).
424. So W. Sommerfeld, "The Kassites of Ancient Mesopotamia: Origins, Politics, and Culture," *CANE*, 922. On the topic of "land grants and 'feudalism'" in ancient Mesopotamia, see ibid., 920–25.
425. See Johnston, ed., *Religions*, 295.
426. So Taggar-Cohen, "Political Loyalty," 262, which see for further discussion.
427. Ibid., 267.
428. For full text, translation, and discussion of the relevance of this text to the account of Saul's slaughter of the priests at Nob, see J. Roberts, "The Legal Basis for Saul's Slaughter of the Priests of Nob (1 Samuel 21–22)," *JNSL* 25 (1999): 21–29. A different translation of the text is available in Heimpel, *Letters*, 174 (26.1).
429. Ibid., 264.
430. E. H. Sturtevant and G. Bechtel, *A Hittite Chrestomathy* (Philadelphia: Univ. of Pennsylvania Press, 1935), 149. See also G. McMahon, *COS*, 1.83:217–18, for a similar, more recent translation.
431. Taggar-Cohen, "Political Loyalty," 264–65.
432. Beal, "Hittite Military Organization," *CANE*, 545–54 (on 550).
433. See Davies, *Ancient Hebrew Inscriptions*, 246–48 (105.006–105.010); for discussion, see A. Lemaire, "Classification des Estampilles Royales Judéennes," *ErIsr* 15 (1981): 54–60; see also the article on this by Y. Garfinkel in *BASOR* 271 (1988): 70.
434. See Negev and Gibson, *Archaeological Encyclopedia*, 453.
435. Ibid.
436. See Aharoni, *Arad Inscriptions*, 32; cf. Davies, *Ancient Hebrew Inscriptions*, 17; Gogel, *Grammar*, 390.
437. Gordon, *1 & 2 Samuel*, 177.
438. So D. Baly, *The Geography of the Bible: A Study in Historical Geography* (New York: Harper & Brothers, 1957); cited by L. F. DeVries, "Jeshimon," *ABD*, 3:769.
439. Gordon, *1 & 2 Samuel*, 177.
440. Ibid.
441. Baly, *Geography*, 164. Baly notes an obvious division in the area between the eastern and the western slopes: "To the east ... lies the barren wilderness, and to the west are the cultivated lands."
442. So K. N. Schoville, "מָעוֹן," *NIDOTTE*, 2:1013.
443. On the latter, cf. L. B. DeVries, "Maon," *ABD*, 4:512–13.
444. Aharoni, *Land of the Bible*, 109.
445. Arad 25; for this brief text listing quantities of barley, see Gogel, *Grammar*, 393.
446. On this tactic, see McCarter, *I Samuel*, 378–79.
447. D. Ussishkin, "The Ghassulian Shrine at En-Gedi," *Tel Aviv* 7 (1980): 1–44.
448. For a brief summary of occupations, see E. Stern, "'Ein-Gedi," *OEANE*, 2:222–23.
449. For more detail, see J. M. Hamilton, "En-Gedi," *ABD*, 2:502–3; and esp. B. Mazar, "En-Gedi," *NEAEHL*, 399–409.
450. Mazar, "En-Gedi," 399.
451. See A. Danin, "'Do You Know When the Ibexes Give Birth?'" *BAR* 5/6 (1979): 50–51. On the derivation, see M. S. Moore and M. L. Brown, "יָעֵל / יַעֲלָה," *NIDOTTE*, 2:488.
452. See "The Ark That Wasn't There," *BAR* 9/4 (1983): 58–61.
453. Bergen, *1, 2 Samuel*, 238.
454. Launderville, *Piety and Politics*, 47.
455. For these and many more examples, see H. Frankfort, *Kingship and the Gods: A Study of Ancient Near Eastern Religion as the Integration of Society and Nature* (Chicago: Univ. of Chicago Press, 1978), 238–40. For information on the rulers and gods mentioned, see, e.g., W. von Soden, *The Ancient Orient: An Introduction to the Study of the Ancient Near East*, trans. Donald G. Schley (Grand Rapids: Eerdmans, 1994 [German orig. 1985]).
456. *ARI*, 2:5–6.
457. EA 271; Moran, *Amarna Letters*, 317. For further examples, see ibid., *passim*; *COS*, 3:237–42.
458. EA 282; ibid., 323; also 322 (EA 281), 324 (EA 284), 340 (EA 298, 299), 343 (EA 305), 344 (EA 306), etc.
459. *COS*, 3.45V:105; cf. also *COS*, 3.45T–U:104; 3.45Y:106.

460. For examples from Lachish, see COS, 1.3.42A:79; COS, 1.3.42E:80; *ANET*, 322 (3x); and from Amarna see, among many others, EA 129, 134, 201, 319, 320, 322. For further discussion, see G. W. Coats, "Self-Abasement and Insult Formulas," *JBL* 89 (1970): 14–26 (esp. 16–17); McCarter, *I Samuel*, 384–85.
461. See Moran, *Amarna Letters*, 277–78 (*EA* 201 [and n.2], 202).
462. King and Stager, *Life in Biblical Israel*, 148.
463. L. F. DeVries, "Carmel (Place)," *ABD*, 1:873.
464. Cf. *IVPBBC-OT*, 315d.
465. J. Barr, "The Symbolism of Names in the Old Testament," *BJRL* 52 (1969–70): 11–29 (on 25–27).
466. Ibid., 27. For further discussion, see Garsiel, *Biblical Names*, 246–48.
467. Cf. Bergen, *1, 2 Samuel*, 245–46.
468. The LXX translates the Heb. as "dog-like"; on modern commentators, see Gordon, *1 & 2 Samuel*, 182.
469. King and Stager, *Life in Biblical Israel*, 147. See Postgate, *Early Mesopotamia*, 158–63, for a fuller discussion.
470. King and Stager, *Life in Biblical Israel*, 113.
471. Ibid., 147. Cf. Postgate, *Early Mesopotamia*, 161.
472. G. Stansell, "The Gift in Ancient Israel," *Semeia* 87 (1999): 65–90 (see 86 for the complete summary). Stansell begins the essay with a succinct summary of anthropological research on gift-giving.
473. Ibid., 82.
474. McCarter, *I Samuel*, 399, citing esp. Ps. 69:28 (Heb. 69:29) and Ex. 32:32–33. This theory draws on the work of N. H. Tur-Sinai (*The Book of Job: A New Commentary* [rev. ed.; Jerusalem: Kiryath Sepher, 1967], 240–41), who argues that Job 14:17's "bag" in most English translations actually refers to a "tied document."
475. S. M. Paul, "Heavenly Tablets and the Book of Life," in *Divrei Shalom: Collected Studies of Shalom M. Paul on the Bible and the Ancient Near East 1967–2005*, ed. S. M. Paul (Leiden: Brill, 2005), 59–70 (on 59).
476. Ibid., 60.
477. Ibid. Paul cites further examples, as does W. W. Hallo in an appendix to Paul's essay.
478. See A. L. Oppenheim, "On an Operational Device in Mesopotamian Bureaucracy," *JNES* 18 (1959): 121–28. Beginning with a description of an egg-shaped, inscribed clay container discovered at Nuzi, Oppenheim presents a detailed discussion of the use of stones as counters and of how counter-stones would have been deposited in specific containers in a central accounting office. On both theories, see Gordon, *1 & 2 Samuel*, 185–86. V. Hurowitz ("Queries and Comments," *BAR* 23/5 [1997]: 12) cites the traditional "wish for the dead ... often engraved on Jewish tombstones" as harking back to this biblical reference and speculates that the custom of visitors to a gravesite leaving a stone may originally have symbolized the soul of the departed who is bound up in God's pouch/bundle.
479. S. N. Kramer, *The Sumerians: Their History, Culture, and Character* (Chicago: Univ. of Chicago Press, 1963), 250. Kramer does go on to admit that there is evidence also that "there was no little wooing and cooing before marriage." In other words, it should not be denied that "ancient Mesopotamians fell deeply in love" (so K. R. Nemet-Nejat, *Daily Life in Ancient Mesopotamia* [Peabody, Mass.: Hendrickson, 2002], 132).
480. L. Milano, "Ebal: A Third-Millennium City-State in Ancient Syria," *CANE*, 1219–30 (on 1224).
481. J. Klein, "Shulgi of Ur: King of a Neo-Sumerian Empire," *CANE*, 843–57 (on 844).
482. T. P. J. Van den Hout, "Khattushili III, King of the Hittites," *CANE*, 1107–20 (on 1117, which see for further examples of political marriage alliances).
483. A. K. Grayson, "Assyrian Rule of Conquered Territory in Ancient Western Asia," *CANE*, 959–68 (on 965).
484. *ARM*, 26.304; 10.33. For a succinct discussion of Kirum's unhappy marriage, see Heimpel, *Letters*, 80–81. For fuller discussions of the marriages of Kirum and her sister, see J.-M. Durand, "Trois études sur Mari," *MARI* 3 (1984): 127–80; N. Ziegler, *Le Harem de Zimrî-Lîm* (Mémoires de N.A.B.U. 5: FM 4; Paris: SEPOA, 1999), 64.
485. See, e.g., J. D. Levenson and B. Halpern, "The Political Import of David's Marriages," *JBL* 99 (1980): 507–18; J. Kessler, "Sexuality and Politics: The Motif of the Displaced Husband in the Books of Samuel," *CBQ* 62 (2000): 409–23.
486. J. Levenson, "1 Samuel 25 as Literature and History," *CBQ* 40 (1978): 11–28; cf. also J. D. Levenson and B. Halpern, "The Political Import of David's Marriages," *JBL* 99 (1980): 507–18.
487. D. Edelman, "Ahinoam," *ABD*, 1:118.
488. E.g., Bergen (*1, 2 Samuel*, 256) infers from Ahimelech's Semitic name that "his family had adopted Israelite cultural and religious practices, including the worship of Yahweh." This may well have been the case, though it would still not necessitate the assumption that Ahimelech was a Hittite of the Anatolian variety.
489. See H. A. Hoffner, "The Hittites and Hurrians," in *POTT* 197–228; more recently, idem, "Hittites," in *POTW*, 127–55 (esp. the nuanced discussion on 152–54); cf. also G. McMahon, "Hittites in the Old Testament," *ABD*, 3:231–33.
490. McMahon, "Hittites in the Old Testament," *ABD*, 3:233.
491. See J.-G. Heintz, "Aux origines d'une expression biblique: *ūmūšū qerbū*, in A.R.M., X/6, 8?," *VT* 21 (1971): 528–40.
492. COS, 1.77:203 [§12a].
493. The lack of mention of Saul's water jug is curious, though it may simply have been assumed to accompany the spear, or it may not have been returned, or it may have been recognized as unusable by Saul once it had been in David's hands; cf. Gordon, *1 & 2 Samuel*, 190.
494. See ibid., 189.

495. On the "local nature of the cult of the personal god" in the ancient Near East, see van der Toorn, *Family Religion*, 83–85.
496. *Fauna and Flora of the Bible* (London: United Bible Societies, 1972), 64; cited by Youngblood, "1 and 2 Samuel," 771. Cf. McCarter, *I Samuel*, 408.
497. E.g., N. P. Lemche, "David's Rise," *JSOT* 10 (1978): 2–25 (on 12–14).
498. Postgate, *Early Mesopotamia*, 87. As regards David's motivation, Wiseman ("Alalakh," in *AOTS*, 125) suggests, on the basis of a practice in ancient Syria whereby an individual would "dwell in the house of the king" as a slave in exchange for a loan or other favor, that David may have been anxious *not* to "dwell with Achish" lest it be assumed that he stood in a similar slave-relationship to Achish.
499. *IVPBBC-OT*, 317.
500. Gordon, *1 & 2 Samuel*, 191.
501. Cf. *IVPBBC-OT*, 317.
502. See McCarter, *1 Samuel*, 413.
503. Ibid., 415.
504. See Y. Aharoni, "The Negeb," in *AOTS*, 401 and map on 384.
505. Textual evidence for reading "Kennizites" instead of "Kenites" here and in 30:29 is considerable (LXX^{B} and 4QSam^{a}; see McCarter, *1 Samuel*, 434), but whatever the reading, the same general area is involved and the gist of the passage remains the same: David is duping Achish regarding the true objects of his aggression.
506. See S. I. Johnston, "Magic," in Johnston, ed., *Religions*, 141.
507. Cf. J. K. Kuemmerlin-McClean, "Magic (OT)," *ABD*, 4:469.
508. Gordon, *1 & 2 Samuel*, 193.
509. As Sumerologist R. Averbeck explains in a personal correspondence received July 9, 2005, only partial renderings are attempted by most recent authorities, but there is a general agreement that the issue is ritual uncleanness in the city, not occultism. Taking a cue from a parallel in Gudea Statue B (iii 15–iv 2), Averbeck in his dissertation proposes a reading such as the following: "The impure man, the one terrifying to look at, (and) the man inflamed (with venereal disease) he drove out from the city." (I wish thank Dr. Averbeck for providing counsel on this issue.)
510. For description of the full range of forbidden practices, see J. K. Kuemmerlin-McLean, "Magic (OT)," *ABD*, 4:468–69; J. G. McConville, *Deuteronomy* (Apollos Old Testament Commentary 5; Downers Grove, Ill.: InterVarsity Press, 2002), 299–302; E. H. Merrill, *Deuteronomy* (NAC; Nashville: Broadman & Holman, 1994), 270–72.
511. E.g., David's attendant Abishag of 1 Kings 1:3 was from Shunem, and the prophet Elisha often visited a well-to-do couple there, both predicting the birth of and raising back to life their only son (2 Kings 4:8–37).
512. In the itineraries of the fifteenth-century Egyptian Thutmose III and the tenth-century Shoshenq I (see *ANET*, 243) and in the fourteenth-century Amarna letters (*ANET*, 485).
513. C. Herzog and M. Gichon, *Battles of the Bible*, 2nd ed. (New York: Random, 1997), 93–94.
514. *ANET*, 396; cf. *NERT*, 174; *COS*, 1.60:159 (note that the translation by G. Beckman in COS begins a new sentence with the final clause, which he renders as an indicative—"Or the priests will sleep ..."—not an injunctive; the result is that the triad attested in 1 Sam. 28:6 is preserved, but the parallel would hold in any case).
515. McCarter (*1 Samuel*, 418, 420) assumes a conflation of both readings in the Hebrew of 28:7.
516. As well as in the Greco-Roman world: "Greek and Latin literature contains a whole series of necromancies, starting from the Homeric *Nekyia* ... and Aeschylus's rite of *The Persians* down to the fictions in the late novels and the parodies of Lucian" (F. Graf, *Magic in the Ancient World*, trans. Franklin Philip [Cambridge, Mass.: Harvard Univ. Press, 1997], 194).
517. J. A. Scurlock, "Magic (ANE)," *ABD*, 4:465, which see for literature, esp. I. Finkel, "Necromancy in Ancient Mesopotamia," *AfO* 29/30 (1983–84): 1–17.
518. Scurlock, "Magic (ANE)," *ABD*, 4:465–66. See, e.g., the "Old Woman" practitioner of Hittite rituals presented in *ANET*, 347, 350–51.
519. Ibid., 466; cf. C. L. Nihan, "1 Samuel 28 and the Condemnation of Necromancy in Persian Yehud," in *Magic in the Biblical World: From the Rod of Aaron to the Ring of Solomon*, ed. T. E. Klutz (London: T. & T. Clark, 2003), 23–54 (see 28, n. 13). Nihan offers a succinct and well-documented discussion of necromancy in the ancient Near East and the Hebrew Bible (esp. 24–32).
520. *KTU*, 1:124, mentioned by Nihan, "1 Samuel 28," 28, n. 13, referring to the critical edition of the text by M. Dietrich and O. Loretz, *Mantik in Ugarit: Keilalphabetische Texte der Opferschau, Ommensammlungen, Nekromantie* (Abhandlungen zur Literatur Alt-Syrien-Palästinas 3; Munich: Ugarit-Verlag, 1990).
521. See *IVPBBC-OT*, 318.
522. On the whole question, see D. V. Edelman, "En-Dor," *ABD*, 2:499–501.
523. The chief theories variously connect the word to an Arabic verb meaning "to return" (thus, the spirit is "one who returns"); to a Hittite term meaning "pit"; to the Heb. word "father, ancestor" (thus relating the practice to ancestor worship). For discussion by one who prefers the latter, see Nihan, "1 Samuel 28," 30–32.
524. Hoffner, "Hittites and Hurrians," *POTW*, 216; cf. idem, "Second Millennium Antecedents to the Hebrew *ʾôb*," *JBL* 86 (1967): 386–401.
525. H. A. Hoffner, "אוֹב," *TDOT*, 1:131.
526. Hoffner, "Hittites and Hurrians," 216.
527. So Hoffner, "אוֹב," 1:132.
528. Ibid., 1:131.
529. Malamat, *Mari and the Bible*, 103–4.
530. R. Frankel ("Aphek," *ABD*, 1:275–77) names five sites: Aphek in Asher, in Aram, in Lebanon, in Sharon, and Aphekah in Judah.
531. Ephʿal, "On Warfare and Military Control in the Ancient Near Eastern Empires," 99.

532. McCarter, *I Samuel*, 434.
533. See Dorsey, *Roads and Highways*, 68–69 and map on 58.
534. Ibid., 199 and map on 194. See also maps in G. A. Smith, *The Historical Geography of the Holy Land*, 25th ed. (London: Hodder & Stoughton, 1931), 195; J. Monson, ed., *Student Map Manual: Historical Geography of the Bible Lands* (Grand Rapids: Zondervan, n.d.), regional map 1–3.
535. On a possible linguistic distinction in Assyrian between the one-humped camel (*gammalu*) and the two-humped bactrian camel (*udru*), see T. C. Mitchell, *The Bible in the British Museum: Interpreting the Evidence*, new ed. (Matwah, N.J.: Paulist, 2004), 54.
536. See K. A. Kitchen, "Camel," *IBD*, 1:228–30. Further on the early domestication of the camel—e.g., by 2300 B.C. in the Indus Valley—see J. Zarins, "Camel," *ABD*, 1:824–26.
537. So Zarins, "Camel," *ABD*, 1:825, which see for specific descriptions of the evidence.
538. For a nuanced and thorough study of the subject, see D. Elgavish, "The Division of the Spoils of War in the Bible and in the Ancient Near East," *ZABR* 8 (2002): 242–73.
539. For further reflections, see Bergen, *1, 2 Samuel*, 280–81.
540. On the Hittite practice, see V. Korošec, "The Warfare of the Hittites from the Legal Point of View," *Iraq* 25 (1963): 159–66 (on 162); and the succinct discussion, comparing Abraham's restoration of property to the king of Sodom, in Elgavish, "Division of the Spoils," 271–73.
541. So Bergen, *1, 2 Samuel*, 280.
542. The NIV's "other places" might seem to distinguish these places from the sites just listed, but it is probably better to read the final clause as a generalizing summary of the sites listed (so, e.g., NRSV, JPS).
543. H. Brodsky, "Bethel (Place)," *ABD*, 1:711.
544. For more on Bethuel, see G. Herion, "Bethuel (Place)," *ABD*, 1:715.
545. McCarter, *I Samuel*, 434.
546. See W. I. Toews, "Beth-zur (Place)," *ABD*, 1:701–2.
547. For brief discussion, see also Gordon, *1 & 2 Samuel*, 201.
548. See Elgavish, "Division of Spoils," 261.
549. S. Dalley, "Ancient Mesopotamian Military Organization," *CANE*, 419.
550. Ibid., 420.
551. Bergen (*1, 2 Samuel*, 282, n.163), after listing the six suicides or assisted suicides mentioned in the Bible, comments that the Bible views these as desperate acts by deeply troubled individuals: "None of the individuals who resorted to this action is portrayed as a role model for the pious."
552. *ARAB*, II:312 §815.
553. Dalley, "Ancient Mesopotamian Military Organization," 420.
554. Negev and Gibson, *Archaeological Encyclopedia*, 84.
555. See V. Haas, "Death and the Afterlife in Hittite Thought," *CANE*, 2021–30, esp. 2023.
556. For a cataloguing and evaluation of extant evidence, see E. Bloch-Smith, *Judahite Burial Practices and Beliefs about the Dead* (JSOTSup 123; Sheffield: Sheffield Academic Press, 1992), 52–55.
557. V. H. Matthews, *Manners and Customs of the Bible* (Peabody, Mass.: Hendrickson, 1988), 128.

Sidebar and Chart Notes

A-1. *COS*, 152–53.
A-2. On Iron-Age Philistine religious practice, as evidenced in the archaeological record at Tel Miqne–Ekron, see S. Gitin, "Israelite and Philistine cult and the Archaeological Record in Iron Age II: The 'Smoking Gun' Phenomenon," in *Symbiosis, Symbolism, and the Power of the Past: Canaan, Ancient Israel, and Their Neighbors from the Late Bronze Age through Roman Palaestina*, ed. W. G. Dever and S. Gitin (Centennial Symposium, W. F. Albright Institute of Archaeological Research and American Schools of Oriental Research, Jerusalem, May 29–31, 2000; Winona Lake, Ind.: Eisenbrauns, 2003), 279–95.
A-3. On circumcision in the ancient Near East, see comment on 1 Sam. 14:6.
A-4. J. P. Louw and E.A. Nida, *Greek-English Lexicon of the New Testament* (New York: UBS, 1988), 11.43. Prior to the book of Judges (i.e., in Genesis, Exodus, and Joshua), the LXX simply transliterates the Heb. term *p^elištîm* ("Philistines") as *phylistiim*. Another term used by some Greek sources is *pelasgoi* ("sea peoples"; see J. Olivier, "פְּלִשְׁתִּי," *NIDOTTE*, 3:631).
A-5. *ANET*, 262c; see also ibid., 263a.
A-6. Ibid., 262c.
A-7. Ibid., 262c.
A-8. "Calah Orthostat Slab," trans. K. Lawson Younger Jr. (*COS*, 2.114G:276; cf. *ANET*, 281; see also *ANET*, 282).
A-9. See *ANET*, 282–84. On the further reduction of Philistine sovereignty under subsequent Assyrian and Egyptian monarchs, see H. J. Katzenstein, "Philistines (History)," *ABD*, 5:326–38. For convenient summaries of ancient Near Eastern texts mentioning the Philistines, see T. Dothan, "Philistines (Archaeology)," *ABD*, 5:328–29; Olivier, "פְּלִשְׁתִּי," 3:633.
A-10. See, e.g., T. Dothan, *The Philistines and Their Material Culture* (Jerusalem: Israel Exploration Society, 1982), 21–23. For a popular summary, see idem, "What We Know about the Philistines," *BAR* 8/4 (1982): 20–44.
A-11. D. M. Howard Jr., "Philistines," *POTW*, 232.
A-12. Ibid., 232; see his discussion of the identification of biblical Caphtor with Crete and of the biblical Cherethites (Cretans) with the Philistines.
A-13. Ibid. Such complex origins might shed light on the appearance of "Philistines" in Canaan during the ancestral period (e.g., Gen. 21:32, 34; 26:1; Ex. 13:17), unless references to Philistines are simply instances of updating names.

A-14. See C. H. Gordon, *Evidence for the Minoan Language* (Ventnor, N.J.: Ventnor, 1966); for brief treatments, see C. H. Gordon and G. A. Rendsburg, *The Bible and the Ancient Near East* (New York: Norton, 1997), 22–23; G. A. Rendsburg, "'Someone Will Succeed in Deciphering Minoan': Cyrus H. Gordon and Minoan Linear A," *BA* 59 (1996): 36–43; idem, "Is Linear A Semitic?" *BAR* 26/6 (2000): 60–61; H. Shanks, "Against the Tide: An Interview with Maverick Scholar Cyrus Gordon," *BAR* 26/6 (2000): 52–63, 71.

A-15. Gordon's thesis would also help explain the apparent cross-influence of the Semitic and Greek worlds from early on.

A-16. For recent book-length treatments, see N. Bierling, *Giving Goliath His Due: New Archaeological Light on the Philistines* (Grand Rapids: Baker, 1992); C. S. Ehrlich, *The Philistines In Transition: A History from ca. 1000–730 B.C.E* (Leiden: Brill, 1996).

A-17. The earliest known references to the SA.GAZ (Habiru) are found in Sumerian texts from the middle of the third millennium B.C. and the latest in Mesopotamian texts from near the end of the second millennium; so E. Yamauchi, "Habiru," *NIDBA*, 223–24, which contains a convenient summary and assessment of the evidence. For fuller discussion, see also Provan, Long, and Longman, *A Biblical History of Israel*, 170–72, from which the following is adapted.

A-18. For the history of the discovery, see N. Naʾaman, "Amarna Letters," *ABD*, 1:174–81. The best English edition of the letters is W. L. Moran, *The Amarna Letters* (Baltimore: Johns Hopkins Univ. Press, 1992). A selection of letters is also available in *ANET*, 483–90.

A-19. Naʾaman, "Amarna Letters," 1:174.

A-20. See EA (=El-Amarna) 243, 246, 254, 271, 273–74, 286–290, 298–99, 305, 318, and AO 7096 (for a convenient listing and summary of contents, see Merrill, *Kingdom of Priests*, 105).

A-21. Ibid., 100.

A-22. N. Naʾaman, "*Ḫabiru* and Hebrews: The Transfer of a Social Term to the Literary Sphere," *JNES* 45 (1986): 271–88.

A-23. Ibid., 271. For the history of this attempted equation, see M. Greenberg, *The Ḫab/piru* (New Haven, Conn.: American Oriental Society, 1955), 3–12.

A-24. N. P. Lemche, "Ḫabiru, Ḫapiru," *ABD*, 3:7. For a convenient listing of attestations, see John Bright, *A History of Israel*, 4th ed. (Louisville: Westminster John Knox, 2000), 94–95. Bright concludes that the Habiru were "a people found all over western Asia from the end of the third millennium to about the eleventh century" (95).

A-25. Naʾaman, "*Ḫabiru* and Hebrews," 272. So also A. Kuhrt, *The Ancient Near East, c. 3000–330 BC* (London: Routledge, 1995), 1:320: "It is unlikely that they were a culturally and linguistically coherent group. Intensive studies of contexts in which the term appears suggest that it was applied to a range of people: runaway slaves, political exiles, brigands and landless peasants, i.e. people on the margins of society."

A-26. Naʾaman, "*Ḫabiru* and Hebrews," 275.

A-27. D. Fleming, "Refining the etymology for 'Hebrew': Mari's *ʿIBRUM*," paper delivered at the SBL Annual Meeting in Denver, November 2001, and currently being prepared for publication. We here express appreciation to Fleming for making his paper available to us.

A-28. Ibid., 8–9. Fleming's theory would support the notion that Israel's background was indeed tribal and pastoralist, as the Bible suggests.

A-29. For the view that neither etymology nor social status and activities offer any grounds for linking the *ʿapîru* and the *ʿibrî* , see A. F. Rainey, "Unruly Elements in Late Bronze Canaanite Society," in *Pomegranates and Golden Bells: Studies in Biblical, Jewish, and Near Eastern Ritual, Law, and Literature in Honor of Jacob Milgrom*, ed. D. P. Wright, D. N. Freedman, and A. Hurvitz (Winona Lake, Ind.: Eisenbrauns, 1995), 481–96.

A-30. Naʾaman, "*Ḫabiru* and Hebrews," 285.

A-31. For discussion, see Merrill, *Kingdom of Priests*, 101.

A-32. J. F. Healey, "Dagon," *DDD*², 216.

A-33. So *CANE*, 2047, apparently reflecting the translation of the text in *ANET*, 662d.

A-34. "The Sarcophagus Inscription of ʾEshnmunʿazor, King of Sidon," trans. P. K. McCarter (*COS*, 2.57:183 [sec. 13–20]).

A-35. L. K. Handy, "Dagon," *ABD*, 2:2.

A-36. Healy, "Dagon," 217.

A-37. *CANE*, 1846.

A-38. On these three prominent theories, see Handy, "Dagon," *ABD*, 2:2; Healy, "Dagon," 216–18.

A-39. "The *Zukru* Festival," trans. D. Fleming (*COS*, 1.123:431–36).

A-40. For a recent book-length treatment, see L. Feliu, *The God Dagan in Bronze Age Syria* (CHANE 19; Leiden: Brill, 2003).

A-41. S. W. Holloway, *Aššur is King! Aššur is King! Religion in the Exercise of Power in the Neo-Assyrian Empire* (CHANE 10; Leiden: Brill, 2002), 144–51. See also M. Cogan, *Imperialism and Religion: Assyria, Judah, and Israel in the Eighth and Seventh Centuries B.C.E.* (SBLMS 19; Missoula, Mont.: Scholars, 1974), 22–41; Z. Bahrani, "Assault and Abduction: The Fate of the Royal Image in the Ancient Near East," *ArtH* 18 (1995): 363–82.

A-42. *ARI*, 2.28:11–12.

A-43. *ABC*, 91.

A-44. Ibid., 88.

A-45. *CANE*, 2053–54, citing *Die keilalphabetischen Texte aus Ugarit*, 1.101:1–4.

A-46. For discussion, see Long, *Reign and Rejection*, 44, n. 9.

A-47. *ARI*, 1.128:21.

A-48. *ARI*, 1.158:26. For other references to the stationing of garrisons and/or governors, see *ARI*, 2.641:162; 2.651:166; 2.729:187; 2.766:195; 2.867:209.

A-49. M. Roaf, "Palaces and Temples in Ancient Mesopotamia," *CANE*, 438.

A-50. See G. W. Ahlström, "Administration of the State in Canaan and Ancient Israel," *CANE*, 602.

A-51. Youngblood, "1 and 2 Samuel," 624.

A-52. King and Stager, *Life in Biblical Israel*, 287.

A-53. See the cautious treatment of the subject by Abraham Malamat in "Prophetic Revelations in Mari and the Bible: Complementary Considerations" (in *Mari and the Bible*, 83–101). After noting sporadic evidence of "ecstatic prophecy" in "the western cultural sphere extending across Palestine, Syria and as far as Asia Minor," Malamat remarks: "Yet without attempting to divest Mari or Israelite prophecy of any ecstatic features, primacy must be given here to the sense of mission" (85). Of the two Akkadian terms used to designate diviners at Mari, *muḫḫûm* and *āpilum*, the former seems to be "derived from a root meaning 'to rave, to become frenzied' " (86) and appears to refer to diviners who worked alone. By contrast, the latter term, which may possibly be related to the Akkadian word meaning "he who responds, respondent" (88), occurs in at least one text in the plural, indicating, according to Malamat, "that these diviners acted in groups as well, similar to the prophetic band or coterie known from the Bible" (87). Further on the issue of terminology, see M. Nissinen, "The Socioreligious Role of the Neo-Assyrian Prophets," in *Prophecy in Its Ancient Near Eastern Context: Mesopotamian, Biblical and Arabian Perspectives*, ed. M. Nissinen (SBLSymS 13; Atlanta: SBL, 2000), 89–114; idem, *Prophets and Prophecy in the Ancient Near East*, 5–8.

A-54. So King and Stager, *Life in Biblical Israel*, 287. For further descriptions, drawings, and photos, see Dothan, *Philistines*, 249–51; Keel and Uehlinger, *Gods, Goddesses, and Images*, 123–24.

A-55. So King and Stager (*Life in Biblical Israel*, 297–98), who mention also an Arabic instrument of similar name that "consists of goatskin stretched over a frame of wood, about twenty-five centimeters in diameter and five centimeters deep" (about ten inches by two inches).

A-56. C. L. Meyers, "A Terracotta at the Harvard Semitic Museum and Disc-holding Female Figures Reconsidered," *IEJ* 37 (1987): 116–22; idem, "Of Drums and Damsels: Women's Performance in Ancient Israel," *BA* 54 (1991): 21–22.

A-57. For a full treatment of music and musical instruments in ancient Israel, see J. Braun, *Music in Ancient Israel/Palestine: Archaeological, Written, and Comparative Sources*, trans. D. W. Stott (Grand Rapids: Eerdmans, 2002).

A-58. *ARI*, 2.477:104–5.

A-59. Cf. J. Wiesner, *Fahren und Reiten in Alteuropa und im alten Orient* (Leipzig: Hinrichs, 1939), 44–90; W. F. Albright, *Archaeology and the Religion of Israel* (Baltimore: Johns Hopkins Univ. Press, 1946), 135–36, n. 25; Y. Yadin, *The Art of Warfare in Biblical Lands in Light of Archaeological Study* (New York: McGraw-Hill, 1963), 5, and the reliefs on 403.

A-60. Yadin, *Art of Warfare*, 249–50.

A-61. Cf. ibid., 250; N. K. Sandars, *The Sea Peoples: Warriors of the Ancient Mediterranean, 1250–1150 B.C.* (London: Thames & Hudson, 1978), 120 and illustrations on 28–29, 30–31.

A-62. For the view that the Hebrew word in question consistently in the Old Testament refers to chariot horses, not horsemen, see W. R. Arnold, "The Word פרש in the Old Testament," *JBL* 24 (1905): 43–53; J. A. Montgomery and H. S. Gehman, *The Book of Kings* (ICC; Edinburgh: T. & T. Clark, 1951), 82–83; and the comprehensive treatment by S. Mowinckel, "Drive and/or Ride in O.T.," *VT* 12 (1962): 289–95.

A-63. K. Galling, *Biblisches Reallexikon* (HAT 1; Tübingen: Mohr, 1937), 1:424.

A-64. Sandars, *Sea Peoples*, 188–89.

A-65. H. P. Smith, *A Critical and Exegetical Commentary on the Books of Samuel* (ICC; Edinburgh: T. & T. Clark, 1899), 95; K. D. Budde, *Die Bücher Samuel* (KHC 8; Tübingen: Mohr, 1902), 85; H. J. Stoebe, *Das erste Buch Samuels* (KAT 8.1; Gütersloh: Gerd Mohn, 1973), 244.

A-66. Cf. Wiesner, *Fahren und Reiten*, 71; H. W. Hertzberg, *I & II Samuel* (OTL; Philadelphia: Westminster, 1964), 105; C. E. Hauer, "The Shape of Saulide Strategy," *CBQ* 31 (1969): 153–67 (on 155, n. 8). Cf. also Sandars' comments (*Sea Peoples*, 72) regarding the importance of Mycenaean chariotry as "symbol." For discussion of various other deployments of chariotry, e.g. in protecting advancing infantry, in pursuing an enemy in flight, or in providing a mobile firing platform, see A. Malamat, "How Inferior Israelite Forces Conquered Fortified Canaanite Cities," *BAR* 8/2 (1982): 24–35 (on 28); Yadin, *Art of Warfare*, 4–5. On the latter deployment, cf. perhaps the references to Philistine archers (31:3) and chariots (2 Sam 1:6) in the accounts of Saul's last battle.

A-67. *ARI*, 2.13:7; cf. also *ARI*, 2.216:48 (Ashur-bel-kala), 2.430:90 (Adad-nirari II), 2.544:122, 2.565:132, 2.635:160 (Ashur-nasir-apli II).

A-68. E.g., in the same inscription from Tiglath-pileser I we read: "Riding in my chariot when the way was smooth and going by foot when the way was rough, I passed through the rough terrain of mighty mountains. In Mount Aruma, a difficult area which was impassable for my chariots, I abandoned my chariotry" (*ARI*, 2.16:8). Cf. also *ARI*, 2.222:49 (Ashur-bel-kala), 2.468:100 (Tukulti-ninurta II).

A-69. *ARI*, 2.21:10.

A-70. For an informative survey, see Saggs, *Civilization*, 202–10.
A-71. Ibid., 203.
A-72. For an interesting discussion of the topic, see J. D. Muhly, "How Iron Technology Changed the World and Gave the Philistines an Edge," *BAR* 8/6 (1982): 40–54. On Philistine ironworking, see also Dothan, *The Philistines*, 91. For more thorough treatments, see P. M. McNutt, *The Forging of Israel: Iron Technology, Symbolism, and Tradition in Ancient Society* (SWBA 8; Sheffield: Almond, 1990); P. R. S. Moorey, *Ancient Mesopotamian Materials and Industries: The Archaeological Evidence* (Oxford: Clarendon, 1994), esp. 278–91.
A-73. Saggs, *Civilization*, 205.
A-74. So G. F. Hasel, "Iron," *ISBE*, 2:880–82; cf. McNutt, *Forging of Israel*, 108.
A-75. Postgate, *Early Mesopotamia*, 214.
A-76. As trans. by R. Fagles (New York: Penguin, 1996).
A-77. E.g., I. Finkelstein ("The Philistines in the Bible: A Late-Monarchic Perspective," *JSOT* 27 [2002]: 131–67) likens Goliath's armor to that of "the Greek hoplites [armored infantry soldiers] of the seventh to the fifth centuries B.C.E." (143). In a more detailed study, A. Yadin ("Goliath's Armor and Israelite Collective Memory," *VT* 54 [2004]: 373–95) argues that "the literary representation of Goliath and the contest of champions is thoroughly Homeric" (389).
A-78. So, e.g., K. Galling, "Goliath und seine Rüstung," *VT* 15 (1966): 150–69. Cf. A. Yadin, "Goliath's Armor," 375–76.
A-79. Yadin, *Art of Warfare*, 265.
A-80. Finkelstein cites A. M. Snodgrass, *Early Greek Armour and Weapons from the End of the Bronze Age to 600 B.C.* (Edinburgh: Edinburgh Univ. Press, 1964), and idem, *Arms and Armour of the Greeks* (London: Thames & Hudson, 1967).
A-81. Finkelstein, "Philistines in the Bible," 143.
A-82. Yadin, "Goliath's Armor," 380. Yadin also cites the "contest of champions" in which Goliath and David engage as "a form of battle known almost exclusively from the Greek epic tradition" (379), but Hoffner's Hittite analogue suggests otherwise (see comment on 17:4).
A-83. G. Philip, "Weapons and Warfare in Ancient Syria-Palestine," in *Near Eastern Archaeology: A Reader*, ed. S. Richard (Winona Lake, Ind.: Eisenbrauns, 2003), 184–92 (on 187–88).
A-84. On Philistine origins, see comment on 4:1; for an authoritative survey see T. Dothan, "The 'Sea Peoples' and the Philistines of Ancient Palestine," *CANE*, 1267–79.
A-85. For a convenient description of the technical aspects of some of Goliath's gear, see *IVPBBC-OT*, 307a.
A-86. *ANET*, 557.
A-87. J. J. Finkelstein, "An Old Babylonian Herding Contract and Genesis 31:38 f," *JAOS* 88 (1968): 30–36.
A-88. Postgate, *Early Mesopotamia*, 160.
A-89. For discussion, see Postgate, *Early Mesopotamia*, 160; *HANEL*, 1:409–10.
A-90. That a careful distinction was made between losses because of negligence and those because of events beyond the shepherd's control is well illustrated in the Code of Hammurabi (Laws 261–67); see *ANET*, 177.
A-91. J. D. Currid, *Doing Archaeology in the Land of the Bible: A Basic Guide* (Grand Rapids: Baker, 1999), 62–65.
A-92. So J. D. Seger, "The Location of Biblical Ziklag," *BA* 47/1 (1984): 47–53 (on 47); cited by Currid, *Doing Archaeology*, 63.
A-93. Currid, *Doing Archaeology*, 64.
A-94. E.g., Press, Mazar, Aharoni, Kallai, Rainey, Naʾaman, and perhaps Seger himself by 1988, identified Tell esh-Shariʿa as Ziklag; so E. D. Oren, "Ziklag," *ABD*, 6:1090. For a report on Oren's excavation of the site from 1972 to 1979, see E. D. Oren, "Seraʿ, Tel," *NEAEHL*, 1329–35. See also J. D. Seger, "Ḥalif, Tel," *NEAEHL*, 553–59; esp. 554, where Seger moves away from his earlier identification of Tel Halif as Ziklag.
A-95. See Currid, *Doing Archaeology*, 64.
A-96. On this general point, see B. S. Isserlin, "The Israelite Conquest of Canaan," *PEQ* 115 (1983): 85–94; cf. Provan, Long, and Longman, *A Biblical History of Israel*, 140–41 and n.15.
A-97. Currid, *Doing Archaeology*, 64.
A-98. V. Fritz, "Where Is David's Ziklag?" *BAR* 19/3 (1993): 58–61, 76.
A-99. See also comment on 8:2.
A-100. For a summary of excavation results at Tel Jezreel, see D. Ussishkin, "Jezreel, Tel," *OEANE*, 3:246–47.
A-101. Negev and Gibson, *Archaeological Encyclopedia*, 270. For specifics, see Dorsey, *Roads and Highways*, 110–12 and map on 104.
A-102. For specifics on the "Dothan Valley–Jezreel–Shunem Road," see Dorsey, *Roads and Highways*," 98–100 and map on 94.
A-103. Gordon, *1 & 2 Samuel*, 194.
A-104. Ibid., 266.
A-105. Ibid., 267 (italics added).
A-106. For details, see ibid., 246–49. See also Malamat's discussion of the distribution of the spoils of war at Mari (A. Malamat, *Mari and the Early Israelite Experience* [The Schweich Lectures of the British Academy 1984; Oxford: Oxford Univ. Press, 1989], 75–79).
A-107. On these distributions, see Elgavish, "Division of the Spoils," 255–57 (to allies), 257–60 (to temples), 260–61 (to king or leader), 261–62 (to soldiers), 257, 262–65 (to auxiliary personnel).

2 SAMUEL

by V. Philips Long

"House of David" inscription from Tel Dan

Z. Radovan/www.BibleLandPictures.com

Introduction

See the introduction of 1 Samuel.

David Learns of Saul's Death (1:1–16)

Amalekites (1:1). See comment on 1 Samuel 15:2.

Ziklag (1:1). See comment on 1 Samuel 27:6.

With his clothes torn and with dust on his head (1:2). On these and other signs of distress and mourning, see comment on 1 Samuel 4:12.

Bronze figurine with gold is a warrior leaning on a spear. The figurine is from the temple of Baalat-Gebal, Byblos, Lebanon, second millenium B.C.
Erich Lessing/Art Resource, NY, courtesy of the Louvre

He fell to the ground to pay him honor (1:2). As noted in 1 Samuel 24:8, bowing facedown on the ground was a common way in the ancient world of showing submission, reverence, and sometimes fear. In this situation, the messenger doubtless expresses all three.

Leaning on his spear (1:6). Bronze or iron spearheads (along with arrowheads, etc.) are regularly uncovered in archaeological excavations in Palestine. The spear was primarily a stabbing or thrusting weapon and was typically heavier than the javelin, which was hurled at the enemy.[1]

Chariots and riders almost upon him (1:6). On Philistine chariots, see comment on 1 Samuel 13:5. In the light of the late introduction of cavalry to Syria-Palestine, the "riders" (lit., "horse-masters" or "master horsemen"), a phrase that occurs only here in the Hebrew Bible, are probably "charioteers." While chariots are not mentioned in the account of Saul's death in 1 Samuel 31 (where Saul's injuries are inflicted by archers, 31:3), there is no necessary discrepancy here, as chariots often served as mobile firing platforms for archers.

Crown that was on his head and the band on his arm (1:10). From evidence of reliefs, it is apparent that crowns of many shapes and sizes were worn by gods, kings, and other important individuals throughout the ancient Near East from earliest times (see illustrations). The specific character of Saul's crown and armband is unknown, but given the fact that Saul was able to wear them into battle, it is fair to assume that they were of lightweight construction.

Further support for this assumption comes from the fact that the Hebrew word *nēzer* ("crown") more properly connotes something like a "diadem" (i.e., a circular, ornamental headdress sometimes bearing precious stones).[2] The related Hebrew word *nāzar* means "to dedicate," and so the diadem worn by Israel's kings and priests was a symbol not only of their exalted position but of their dedication to God.[3]

Diadems could be added to the turbans frequently worn by ancient Near Eastern kings, priests, and others. Israel's high priest wore not only a fine linen turban but a diadem as well, from the front of which hung a gold plate engraved with the words "holy to the LORD" (Ex. 28:36–38).[4] Saul's crown may have been a similar diadem with royal insignia attached. The nature of his armband is also uncertain; there is only one other mention of such an "armlet" in the Bible (Num. 31:50), but this band must have also served to symbolize Saul's royal status.

David and all the men with him took hold of their clothes and tore them (1:11). The origin of tearing one's clothes is uncertain (see comment on 1 Sam. 4:12). De Ward has speculated that it may signify self-abasement, an attempt to disguise oneself in the face of woe, or a milder form of self-mutilation.[5] Whatever its origin, it is clear in the present context that tearing one's clothes is a way of expressing grief and sorrow. The practice is widely attested in the ancient Near East. For instance, crown prince Esarhaddon (681–669), upon hearing of the "sorry happenings" related to his brothers' violent attempts to take over the kingship, reports: "I cried 'Woe!' rent my princely robe and began to lament loudly."[6]

Mourned and wept and fasted till evening (1:12). On this occasion of mourning and weeping, David also proclaimed a fast. Fasting, "the deliberate, temporary abstention from food,"[7] is not widely attested in the ancient Near East, and where fasting is attested, it is associated with mourning.[8] In the Bible, fasting was connected either with religious rites (being prescribed, e.g., on the Day of Atonement) or with "rites of mourning, personal penance, or the reinforcement of supplicatory prayer."[9]

Mourners
Michael Greenhalgh/ArtServe, courtesy of the British Museum

David's Elegy (1:17–27)

David took up this lament (1:17). Among the various lamentations and elegies known from the ancient Near East,[10] the best known is Gilgamesh's lament for his dead friend Enkidu. A portion of his elegy reads as follows:

> Hear me, O young men, hear [me!]
> Hear me, O elders [of teeming Uruk,] hear me!
> I shall weep for Enkidu, my friend,
> like a hired mourner-woman I shall bitterly wail.
> The axe at my side, in which my arm trusted,
> the dirk at my belt, the shield at my face,
> my festive garment, my girdle of delight:
> a wicked wind rose up and robbed me.
> O my friend, wild ass on the run, donkey of the uplands, panther of the wild,
> my friend Enkidu, wild ass on the run, donkey of the uplands, panther of the wild!
> Having joined forces we climbed the [mountains,]
> seized and [slew] the Bull of Heaven,
> destroyed Humbaba, who [dwelt in the] Forest [of Cedar.]
> Now what is this sleep that has seized [you?]
> You've become unconscious, you do not [hear me!]
> But he, he lifted not [his head.]
> He felt his heart, but it beat no longer.[11]

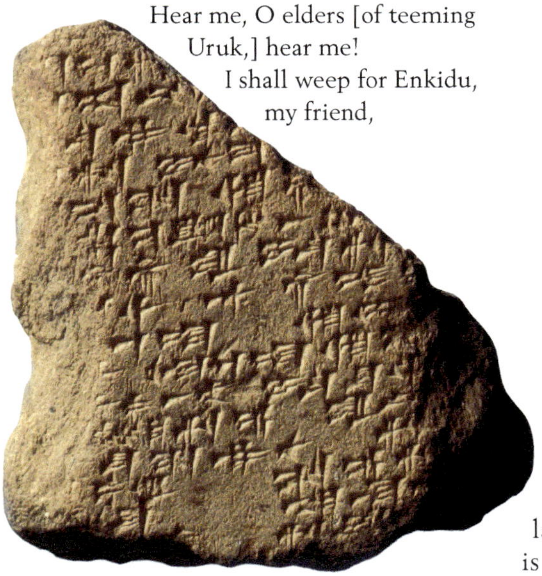

Fragment of the Gilgamesh Epic found at Megiddo
Z. Radovan/www.BibleLandPictures.com

David's lament over Saul and Jonathan exhibits a number of general similarities—for example, a broad public is addressed (v. 19); martial imagery is prevalent and deeds of valor are celebrated (vv. 21–22); physical prowess is highlighted (v. 23); deep affection and grief are expressed (v. 26); and there is a recurring refrain (vv. 19, 25, 27).

Lament of the bow (1:18). The sense of this title has puzzled commentators and sparked several explanations.[12] The word "lament" is not explicitly stated in the Hebrew text, and the LXX omits the word "bow" as well. The sense then is that David is ordering that the following lament should be taught to the children of Israel. If the word "bow" is retained, however, it may refer to Jonathan (whose bow is mentioned in v. 22) and serve as a title for the lament. Referring to Jonathan or Saul by the weapon(s) they wield seems apparent in the closing line (v. 27), where "weapons of war" probably stands for Saul and Jonathan. The later designation of Elijah and Elisha as "the chariots and horsemen of Israel" (2 Kings 13:14) offers an analogy.

Book of Jashar (1:18). This book appears to have been a book of early Israelite poetry, now lost (see also Josh. 10:12–13, Joshua's exceptional day in defense of the Gibeonites). The name is generally assumed to derive from the Hebrew word meaning "upright, just, righteous," suggesting that the Book of Jashar may have celebrated the exploits of heroic individuals in Israel or of the Israelites as a whole, as the Lord's "upright" people. Alternatively, the name may reflect the Hebrew word for "song," yielding simply the "Book of Song."[13]

Tell it not in Gath ... Ashkelon (1:20). Gath and Ashkelon were—along with Ashdod, Gaza, and Ekron—member cities of the Philistine Pentapolis. On Gath, see comment on 1 Samuel 5:8. Ashkelon occupied a favorable coastal site, amply supplied with fresh water from an aquifer that coursed some twenty meters below the surface of the ground. Located on the coast some thirty-nine miles south of Tel Aviv and ten miles north of Gaza, Ashkelon was settled as early as the Neolithic and Chalcolithic periods. The city was taken over by the Philistines sometime around 1175 B.C. and remained in their hands until its destruction by Nebuchadnezzar in 604 B.C.

Ashkelon was a thriving commercial seaport in the Philistine period, a role aptly reflected not only in its name, which appears to derive from a Canaanite word meaning "to weigh" (from which the word *shekel* also derives),[14] but also in David's reference to the "streets" of Ashkelon, which should probably be read as "bazaars" or "marketplace."[15]

Conquest of Ashkelon at Karnak
Todd Bolen/www.BiblePlaces.com

Like its sister cities Ashdod and Ekron (see comments at 1 Sam. 5:1, 10), Ashkelon was a major city with heavy fortifications. It is frequently mentioned in extrabiblical texts, beginning with the nineteenth- and eighteenth-century B.C. Execration Texts from Egypt.

In the fourteenth-century el-Amarna correspondence, at least nine letters involve Ashkelon (*ašqaluna*) or its ruler Yidya/Idiya: some assuring the pharaoh of Yidya's care in guarding "the place of the king, my lord, and the city of the king, my lord, [w]here I am"; others promising to supply "food, strong drink, oil, grain, oxen, sheep and goats" to the king's troops; one from ʿAbdi-Ḫeba of Jerusalem accusing the ruler of Ashkelon of supplying provisions for the feared ʿApiru; and one from the pharaoh to Yidya (spelled Idiya), directing him to "guard the place of the king where you are."[16]

Ashkelon finds further mention—along with Gezer, Yanoam, and the Israelites—in the famous Merneptah Stele (ca. 1207). An Egyptian siege of Ashkelon is depicted visually on a relief at Karnak. As David begins his elegy for Saul and Jonathan, he cannot bear the thought that their defeat should be celebrated among Israel's archenemies, the Philistines.

Uncircumcised (1:20). On "uncircumcised" as a derogatory term for the Philistines, see comments on 1 Samuel 4:1; 14:6.

Gilboa, may you have neither dew nor rain (1:21). David curses the mountains of Gilboa, the place where Saul and Jonathan's blood was spilled, almost as if "the mountain range itself had been responsible for the disaster."[17] Drought, crop failure, and other natural disasters were often connected with (illicit) spilling of blood upon the ground. After Cain's murder of Abel, for instance, the latter's blood cries out to Yahweh from the ground (Gen. 4:10), and Yahweh announces to Cain, "When you work the ground, it will no longer yield its crops for you" (4:12).

Outside the Bible, a similar pattern of nature responding to the (illicit) shedding of blood is attested. In the Legend of ʾAqhat, for example, the murder of the youth ʾAqhat causes the "*[fr]uits* of summer" to wither, "the ear [in] its husk." There is "No dew, No rain; No welling-up of the deep, No sweetness of Baal's voice."[18] In the Bible, natural events, whether favorable or unfavorable, are understood to be a part of Yahweh's ongoing conversation with his people.[19]

Shield of Saul—no longer rubbed with oil (1:21). Ancient Near Eastern shields came in a variety of shapes and sizes. One of the most prevalent constructions involved a wooden shield covered with leather.[20] Fifteenth-century wall paintings from the tomb of the Egyptian Rekhmire illustrate the various steps in the construction of such shields. To preserve and condition leather shields, oil was periodically rubbed into them (cf. Isa. 21:5). An Old Babylonian text from Tell Asmar records "one sila of oil to rub the shield(s)."[21]

I grieve for you, Jonathan my brother ... your love ... more wonderful than that of women (1:26). Some modern readers, unaware or neglectful of the biblical and ancient Near Eastern background to such expressions of love, have tried to read a homosexual nuance into David's words. But not only is such a reading unwarranted and inadmissible in terms of the broader biblical context (cf., e.g., Lev. 18:22; 20:13) and ancient Near Eastern attitudes toward homosexual practice generally, so far as the minimal evidence allows us to determine,[22] it also flies in the face of the fact that "love language" was often used to express loyalty in legal contexts. For example, the Hittite Bronze Tablet from the thirteenth century B.C., which records a treaty between the Hittite king Tudḫaliya IV and his cousin Kurunta, who ruled over a vassal kingdom, contains the following lines:

Funerary model from the Twelfth Dynasty tomb of Mesehti shows soldiers carrying shields covered with leather.
Giraudon/Art Resource, NY, courtesy of the Egyptian Museum, Cairo

I Tudḫaliya, the Great King, before I became king,
the god had already earlier brought me and Kurunta together in friendship
And already we were dear and beloved to each other.
And we had an oath between us (saying): "one shall be loyal to the other."[23]

The legal (and not sexual) connotations of words such as "dear" and "beloved" is evident. The same is true of the Hebrew word "love" (*ʾhb*) in many contexts.[24] Commentators have perhaps been led astray by David's extolling of Jonathan's love as "more wonderful than the love of women," but David's intent may simply have been to underscore the remarkably selfless character of Jonathan's loyalty to David and willingness to defer to him with regard to the kingship (see comment on 1 Sam. 18:3–4).

Areas of control of David, Ishbosheth, and the Philistines

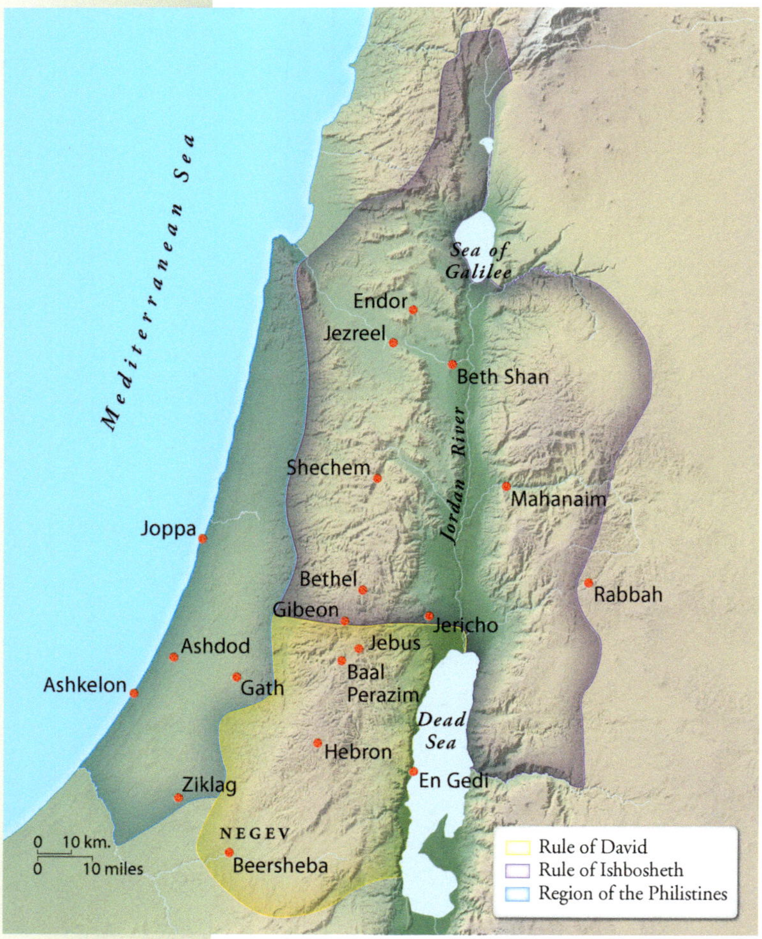

David Becomes King over Judah (2:1–7)

David inquired of the LORD (2:1). The likely method of David's inquiry is through the use of the Urim and Thummim kept in the ephod, first brought to David by the sole survivor of the priests of Nob, Abiathar (see comment on 1 Sam. 23:6). On the function of the ephod as an oracular device, see comments on 1 Samuel 2:18; 14:3, 18–19.

Hebron (2:1). The ancient name of Hebron, Kiriath Arba (Gen. 23:2), may originally have meant something like "tetrapolis,"[25] a name commensurate with the fact that "there are several archaeological sites in the vicinity of the ancient nucleus of Hebron."[26] We may note also that verse 3 reports that David and his men "settled in Hebron and its towns." See sidebar on "Hebron."

Ahinoam of Jezreel and Abigail ... of Carmel (2:2). On these two wives of David, see comments on 1 Samuel 25:39.

The men of Judah ... anointed David king (2:4). On anointing, see comment on 1 Samuel 2:10. Several factors converge to make the anointing of David as king by the major southern tribe of Judah understandable. (1) The recent successes of the Philistines in the battle of Gilboa may have limited the ability of more northerly tribes to participate, even had they wanted to. (2) The death of most of Saul's house created uncertainty regarding the succession, even for those unaware of or unwilling to accept the fact that Saul's house had been rejected. (3) Government by city-kings was well known in Canaan, and a previous attempt to establish a king had been initiated by a tribe (Judg. 9).[27]

Men of Jabesh Gilead who had buried Saul (2:4). See comments on 1 Samuel 11:1; 31:11, 12, 13.

Hebron

Situated along the major route running between Beersheba and Jerusalem (some twenty-four miles north of the former and nineteen miles south of the latter), Hebron occupied "the most important crossroads in southern Judea"[A-1] and enjoyed one of the highest elevations of any city in Israel. Prominently and strategically located, and well supplied with water by some twenty-five springs, Hebron was an important city throughout its history.

Hebron was a Canaanite royal city when Israel arrived in Canaan (cf. Josh. 10:3), and its links with God's people extended back to the patriarchs (e.g., Gen. 13:18; 23:2, 19; 35:27). The Arabic name for Hebron (El-Khalil) means "the friend" and may reflect the biblical commendation of Abraham (who sojourned in Hebron) as the "friend" of God.[A-2] Given its importance and its safe distance from Philistine-controlled territory, Hebron was an ideal location for David to launch his rule over Judah. (The importance of the site is further reflected in the fact that Absalom's later rebellion was also launched from Hebron; 2 Sam. 15:10.)

Major excavations of Tel Hebron were conducted first from 1964–1966 under the direction of P. C. Hammond and again in 1984 under the direction of A. Ofer.[A-3] There is archaeological evidence that the site was occupied continuously from the Early Bronze Age to the time of David and beyond, with the city reaching its "zenith ... between the eleventh century and the end of the tenth century." Ofer attributes this "golden age at Hebron" to "the city's position as a tribal and religious center for the people of the Judean Hills and the first royal capital of King David."[A-4] Significant individual finds include a seventeenth- to sixteenth-century Akkadian cuneiform tablet containing a list of animals and royal *lmlk* jar handles with the name Hebron.

Hebron area
Copyright 1995–2009 Phoenix Data Systems

Mahanaim
Todd Bolen/www.BiblePlaces.com

Hostilities between the Houses of David and Saul (2:8–3:5)

Abner ... had taken Ish-Bosheth son of Saul ... to Mahanaim (2:8). In the aftermath of Israel's defeat by the Philistines at the battle of Gilboa, Abner had little choice but to seek to establish a rump kingdom in Transjordan. The former heart of the kingdom of Saul west of the Jordan was too vulnerable to repeated Philistine attack.

Mahanaim is identified, with varying degrees of confidence, with Telul ed-Dhahab el-Garbi, on the northern bank of the Jabbok River, near a natural ford. "The site's strategic location as a gateway to the iron resources of the adjacent Ajlun probably led to its establishment as the administrative seat for Gilead in the early monarchy."[28] The site has not been excavated, but surface surveys have yielded ample quantities of Iron I and II pottery to square with the biblical testimony.

Located on the border between the tribes of Gad and Manasseh (Josh. 13:26, 30), Mahanaim's centrality and importance in the premonarchical period is reflected in the fact that it served as a Levitical city and a city of refuge (Josh. 21:38). This city is mentioned along with many others in the Karnak relief of Shoshenq I (945–924; biblical Shishak?).[29]

He made him king over ... all Israel (2:9). Both the specific sites over which Ish-Bosheth is to have been made king as well as the summary of his domain as "all Israel" probably represent merely "the territories to which Ish-Bosheth laid claim, irrespective of whether he actually exercised control over them."[30] The scenario of a "military strongman" (i.e., Abner) propping up a "weak heir to the throne" is not without precedent in the ancient Near East.[31]

Ish-Bosheth ... forty years old when he became king over Israel (2:10). See comment on 1 Samuel 13:1.

Meeting at Gibeon

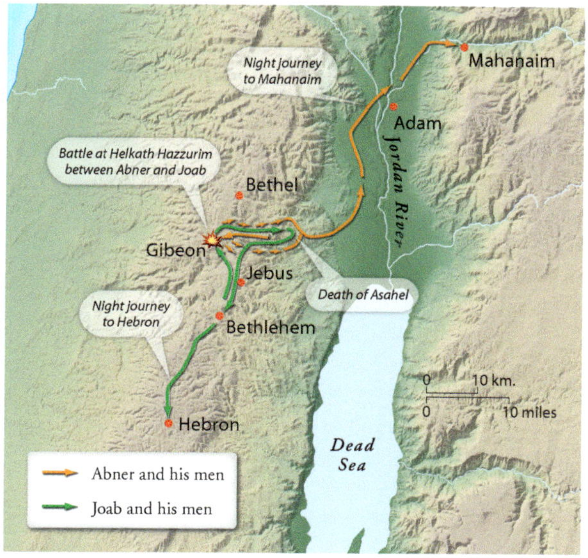

Left Mahanaim and went to Gibeon (2:12). The town of Gibeon played an important role in Israel's history, beginning with the covenant Joshua made with the Gibeonites in Joshua 9:15. Along with its associated Hivite cities, Gibeon is described in Joshua 11:19 as the only city that made peace with the Israelites at the time of the conquest of Canaan. In addition to being the site of the current episode—the remarkable contest between the house of Saul under Abner and the house of David under Joab—Gibeon was designated a Levitical city (Josh. 21:17), was the place where Joab murdered Amasa (2 Sam. 20:8–10), and was the place where God first appeared to Solomon and granted him wisdom (1 Kings 3:4–12).

Gibeon was first identified with present-day el-Jib (ca. six miles north of Jerusalem) by Edward Robinson in 1833, on the basis of the similarity of the names. Robinson's identification was confirmed by four seasons of excavation (1956–1962) under the direction of J. B. Pritchard, who unearthed thirty-one jar handles bearing the name Gibeon in Paleo-Hebrew script.[32] The importance of Gibeon in the premonarchical period is indicated in a campaign report of Amenhotep (Amenophis) II (1447–1400), which mentions the defeat of "36,300 Kharu, or Horites, the very term used in Joshua 9:7, according to the Greek version, for the Gibeonites,"[33] as well as in Thutmose III's (1479–1425) record of an encounter with Hurrians ("Hurru") in a coalition gathered by Megiddo.[34] Gibeon appears to have been an important producer of wine. On the pool at Gibeon, see comment on 2:13.

Joab son of Zeruiah (2:13). Joab, who serves as commander of David's forces (8:16), is mentioned here for the first time in the Bible. He is a nephew of David, being one of three sons of David's sister Zeruiah (2:18; 1 Chron. 2:13–16). Ardently supportive of David, Joab nevertheless at times proves uncontrollable (2 Sam. 3:39). He is not averse to acting independently and in his own self-interest (3:26–27), and he even defies David's direct orders in the matter of Absalom's life (18:5, 9–14). At times, though, he is a savvy advisor in matters political (12:26–29; 19:7) and even religious (24:1–3).

Pool of Gibeon (2:13). At the time of his identification of el-Jib as Gibeon (see comment on 2:12), Robinson drew attention to a rectangular pool he thought must have been the "pool of Gibeon." Pritchard subsequently determined that the pool was of far too late a date to qualify, but his own excavations discovered two further pools, one of which

Pool at Gibeon
Z. Radovan/www.BibleLandPictures.com

▸ Representative Combat

The concept of representative combat was encountered in the contest between David and Goliath, where David gained a decisive victory, killing Goliath and putting the Philistine army to flight (see comment on 1 Sam. 17:4). With respect to the term "play" or "sport," Hoffner suggests that Abner "employed a euphemistic *terminus technicus* for such a contest."[A-5] As de Vaux noted earlier, the term "young men refers here, as in other military contexts, to professional soldiers."[A-6]

The line between mock fighting or a contest of champions should perhaps not be too sharply drawn—one need only think of medieval jousting to understand that the line between sport and battle may be thin. In antiquity, battles were sometimes perceived as festivals of sorts. Early in the text Sargon, the Conquering Hero, for example, we encounter the following lines:

> Now (?), the champion speaks,
> "Restore to your body your jewelry, your festive garb!
> "Certainly, you are endowed with ṭēmu, your attacker is the enemy of . . .
> "Let your mouth command your mind,
> "and let your mind command your legs!"
> Tomorrow, Akkade will commence battle.
> A festival of men at arms will be celebrated.[A-7]

The purpose of "single combat" or "representative combat," whether by individuals or, as here, by a group of elite soldiers, was to decide victory without the necessity of wider bloodshed. The outcome in the present context was decidedly inconclusive, however—"each man grabbed his opponent by the head and thrust his dagger into his opponent's side, and they fell down together" (2:16)—with the result that "the battle that day was very fierce" (2:17). Second Samuel 3:1 records that "the war between the house of Saul and the house of David lasted a long time."

Hand-to-hand combat from Medinet Habu
Manfred Näder, Gabana Studios, Germany

probably was the pool mentioned here.[35] This pool was created by carving a cylinder some thirty-nine feet in diameter and thirty-five feet deep into limestone bedrock, removing some 3,000 tons of limestone in the process. A five-foot-wide staircase spirals down the side of the cylinder, providing access to the flat floor of the large cylinder. The stairs do not end here, however, but continue in a narrower shaft some forty-five feet further down, until they reach the water table.

The purpose of this two-part construction is somewhat mysterious, but Cole suggests that the large cylinder may have been a first phase, intended to serve as a cistern. (Given the dry summer season, larger settlements in Canaan found it necessary to find ways to capture and preserve water.) The narrower shaft may have been dug when it was determined that the spring feeding the other water system at Gibeon must lie somewhere below the large cylinder.[36]

Let's have some of the young men get up and fight hand to hand in front of us (2:14). The Hebrew terminology used here has led

Rock shelves for bodies in the Iron Age tomb at St. Etienne's, Jerusalem
Christie J. Goulart

some interpreters to assume that the event involved some kind of sport or exhibition that became overly serious and turned out badly. The word rendered "young men" can mean "youths," and the word rendered "fight" often means "play" or "sport"; thus, Abner's suggestion may be that youths from the opposing sides arise and make sport (perhaps engage in mock fighting) for the entertainment of the others. More likely, however, what we have in this passage is an example of representative combat by a team of select warriors to decide the fates of the opposing armies (see sidebar on "Representative Combat").[37]

Helkath Hazzurim (2:16). The spot in Gibeon where the twenty-four fell was called in Hebrew "Helkath Hazzurim" (the precise sense of which is debated, suggestions ranging from "field of flint [knives/daggers]" to "field of hostilities" to, with slight textual emendation, "field of sides").[38] A remarkably telling, if poorly carved, pre-ninth-century relief from the Aramaean site of Gozan (Tell Halaf) on the banks of the Khabur River in northeastern Syria depicts two men in precisely the position described here, "each man grabb[ing] his opponent by the head and thrust[ing] his dagger into his opponent's side."[39]

Abner thrust the butt of his spear into Asahel's stomach (2:23). Unless the text should read "with a backward thrust,"[40] Abner's ability to kill a man with the butt of his spear reflects both his own physical prowess and the fact that the butt end of spears would have typically been fitted out with a metal casing useful for prodding and for sticking the spear in the ground (without damaging the spearhead itself); recall the statement in 1 Samuel 26:7 that Saul's spear was "stuck in the ground near his head." Archaeological excavations have uncovered numerous such end casings, and they can be seen also in wall paintings.[41]

Spear butt
Kim Walton, courtesy of the Oriental Institute Museum

Hill of Ammah, near Giah (2:24). The specific locations have not yet been identified,[42] but the general direction of troop movements during and after the battle can be surmised (see map).

Joab blew the trumpet (2:28). For the trumpet (*šôpār*) as a signaling device, see comment on 1 Samuel 13:3.

Arabah ... Bithron ... Mahanaim (2:29). The Arabah is the rift valley running north-south from the Sea of Galilee, called the Jordan Valley north of the Dead Sea and the Wadi el ʿArabah between the Dead Sea and the Gulf of Aqabah. The word "Bithron," from a root meaning "to divide," may be a proper place name, or it may be a common noun meaning either a "ravine" (perhaps the ravine of the Jabbok River along which Mahanaim is situated) or "half a day" (i.e., "all morning"). If the latter meaning is correct, the sense is that Abner's troops traveled all night northward along the Jordan Valley and then, after crossing the Jordan, all morning before reaching Mahanaim (on which see comment on 2:8).

Buried him in his father's tomb at Bethlehem (2:32). In the ancient Near East generally, "tombs took on a number of different forms that reflected the nature of building materials, topography, social status, ethnic or tribal affiliations, and spiritual beliefs."[43] In Israel's monarchy period it was common for important families to bury succeeding generations of their dead in cave or rock-cut tombs or tomb complexes—thus, perhaps, the expression "to be gathered to one's fathers." The bones of earlier burials would be either collected in a "charnel pit" or simply pushed to the periphery of the tomb, while the most recently deceased would be placed on a bench shelf, often surrounded by personal items.[44]

Sons were born to David in Hebron (3:2). The numeric growth of David's family attests to the growing strength of his house, in contrast to the house of Saul (v. 1). David has six sons with four additional wives (or concubines),[45] and after David's arrival in Jerusalem (5:13–16), he obtains more wives/concubines and conceives eleven more children (cf. 1 Chron. 3:1–9). It was common practice among powerful kings in the ancient Near East to multiply wives and children; the biblical narrator withholds judgment for the time being on David's "royal" behavior. But in the light of the instruction in Deuteronomy 17 to future kings of Israel—that they "must not take many wives" (17:7)—David's family planning at least raises an eyebrow.[46]

Abner Defects to David and Is Murdered by Joab (3:6–21)

Why did you sleep with my father's concubine? (3:7). In the ancient Near East, a household often included a primary wife and one or more subordinate wives or concubines, the latter being defined as women by whom a man might father children but who brought no dowry into the relationship and thus did not enjoy the status of full wife.[47] While monogamy may have been the (flexible) norm among common folk in the ancient Near East,[48] polygamy was common among the powerful, especially kings (on polygamy in the ancient Near East generally, see comments on 1 Sam. 1:2; for the beginnings of David's harem, see comment on 25:39).

A king's wives and concubines reflected his power and position, often involving political alliances through marriage. Thus for an outsider to sleep with one of these women was, among other things, a direct assault on the king's status and position.[49] In the Bible, to sleep with a royal wife or concubine was tantamount to usurping the throne (2 Sam. 16:21–22), and merely to ask to marry a concubine of a deceased king was considered treason (see esp. 1 Kings 2:22). In the present episode, the narrator does not state explicitly whether Abner had slept with Saul's concubine Rizpah, but he does state that "Abner had been strengthening his own position in the house of Saul" (3:6), perhaps aggravating Ish-Bosheth's suspicions. Abner's incensed response in 3:8 to Ish-Bosheth's charge—unless he is simply feigning indignation—suggests that he is innocent of the specific charge.[50]

Dog's head (3:8). This expression is found nowhere else in biblical or ancient Near Eastern literature, and so its significance can only be surmised.[51] Dogs were not highly regarded in the ancient Near East (see comment on 1 Sam. 24:14). To be a "dog" was at best to be insignificant, a "dead dog" less significant still, and a "dog's head" perhaps worst of all (particularly if "head" is being used euphemistically for the opposing end of the dog!).[52] In the Old Testament specifically, dogs were considered unclean (Lev. 11:26–28), aggressive scavengers (2 Kings 9:35–36), and disgusting (Prov. 26:11 speaks of their returning to their own vomit);[53] thus, Abner's choice of image aptly captures his sense of outrage at Ish-Bosheth's accusation.

Bring Michal daughter of Saul when you come (3:13). Several ancient Near Eastern law codes stipulate what should be done when a husband was either voluntarily or involuntarily absent from his wife for a long period. The Mesopotamian Law Code of Eshnunna, for instance, states that if a man is taken prisoner by an invading force and carried away to a foreign country, he shall receive his wife back upon his return, even if she has been taken by another man; but if a man "repudiates his city and his master and then flees," he shall have no right to reclaim his wife upon his return.[54]

The Law Code of Hammurabi addresses the issue similarly, adding that a woman incurs no blame by entering the house of another man, but only if "there are not sufficient provisions in [her absent husband's] house."[55] If the husband has voluntarily deserted his city and his wife and she "enters another's house," then upon his return "because he repudiated his city and fled, the wife of the deserter will not return to her husband."[56]

Middle Assyrian laws run along similar lines, but qualify the code in further respects. To give one example, even if a woman was voluntarily deserted by her husband and was left without "oil or wool or clothing or provisions or anything else," she was still required to "remain (the exclusive object of rights) for her husband for five years" before considering other options.[57]

In the light of ancient Near Eastern legal tradition, David is within his rights to demand the return of his wife Michal—his absence from her has been involuntary, necessitated by Saul's attempts to kill him—and Saul should probably be faulted for giving her to another man (1 Sam. 25:44).[58]

Laws of Eshnunna
Scala/Art Resource, NY, courtesy of the Iraq Museum

Saul's treatment of Michal was almost certainly motivated more by political considerations than by concern for her best interests, and the same can probably be said of David's motivation in demanding her back.[59] Michal is David's tie to the former royal house of Benjamin, and her return to his own house will serve his own royal ambitions. Further, the text's poignant picture of Paltiel "weeping behind her all the way" (v. 16) seems intended to contrast Paltiel's affection with David's political maneuvering.[60]

Well of Sirah (3:26). Judging from the context, the well of Sirah must have lain somewhere in the vicinity of Hebron, probably to the north, as Abner reaches it while presumably traveling northward toward Mahanaim. Driver suggests identifying Sirah with "an *ʿAin Sārah*, about a mile north of Hebron, on the road to Jerusalem."[61] McCarter, citing Josephus (*Ant.* 7.34), posits an oasis about 2.5 miles north of Hebron, perhaps in the vicinity of modern Ṣîret el-Bellaʿ.[62] In either case, Abner has not traveled far before being brought back by Joab's messengers to meet his untimely end at the hands of Joab (v. 27).

Joab took him aside into the gateway (3:27). City gateways in ancient Israel were not simple entrances to a city but complex affairs often involving several chambers, where elders sat and business was transacted. Joab's action of taking Abner aside would probably not have aroused the latter's suspicion. Given the prominence of the city of Hebron in David's day (see comment on

Chambers in the city gate at Megiddo
Kim Walton

that would "inflict upon him in his body a grievous malady, an evil disease, a serious wound that never heals, whose nature no physician knows, which he cannot allay with bandages, which like a deadly bite cannot be rooted out."[64] David concludes his curse by invoking death ("falls by the sword") and poverty ("lacks food") on Joab's house.

2:1), it likely had a sizeable gate complex in which Joab could catch Abner unawares. (For more on Iron Age gate complexes, see comments on 18:24ff.)

May Joab's house never be without someone who ... (3:29). In distancing himself from Joab's egregious murder of Abner, David curses Joab using formulaic language familiar in the ancient Near East. First, he calls down on Joab's house the worst of chronic and socially ostracizing diseases. Leprosy (more accurately "scale disease") led to "the banishment of their carriers from the community."[63] This disease in particular was regarded as resulting from divine displeasure, and the threat of scale disease was often a prominent component of the curse formulae that accompanied treaty documents or law codes.

Assyrians at hard labor
Z. Radovan/www.BibleLand Pictures.com

Appended to the Code of Hammurabi, for instance, is a curse threatening any potential offender with divine action

Less certain in its interpretation is the middle element in which David expresses his desire that the house of Joab never be without someone "who leans on a crutch" (NIV). While this rendering is traditional, it seems less likely than two other possibilities. One is that David is condemning Joab's male descendants to "turn out effeminate, i.e., unfit for the manly business of warfare."[65] This reading is based on the fact that the Hebrew word rendered "crutch" is, in view of Semitic cognates and its rendering in Proverbs 3:29, more likely to mean "spindle" or "distaff," a weaving tool associated in the ancient Near East with female activities. The Hittite so-called Soldier's Oath offers an example of the curse of effeminacy on disloyal soldiers:

> Let them [the oaths] change his [disloyal] troops into women, let them dress them in the fashion of women and cover their heads with a length of cloth! Let them break their bows, arrows (and) clubs in their hands and [let them put] in their hands distaff and mirror.[66]

Holloway, though recognizing that the effeminacy interpretation is "both philologically and culturally possible"[67] and certainly more likely than the "crutch" interpretation, nevertheless offers a further possibility.

Funerary stele shows the priest Remi with his wife and child. Remi is depicted with a shorter and thinner right leg, apparently the result of poliomyelitis. Priests with physical defects could not serve in Israel.
Ole Haupt, courtesy Ny Carlsberg Glyptotek, Copenhagen

Taking the key word to mean "work-duty" or "tax in the form of conscripted labor," as suggested by A. Demsky for the same word in Nehemiah 3:9, 12, 14, 15, 16, 17 (2x), 18, Holloway proposes that David's curse may have been that Joab's house will never be without someone working on a "chain gang." Since corvée labor was usually performed by captive foes, it "represented not the bottom of idealized Israelite society, but something beneath it." Joab's military ambitions would have involved not just destruction of enemy forces but "the creation of captive populations from whom corvée battalions could be assembled with impunity." So David's malediction that the house of Joab "never be without corvée-worker" constitutes, as Holloway maintains, an "excellent irony."[68]

Ish-Bosheth Assassinated (4:1–12)

From the tribe of Benjamin (4:2). By stressing the Benjamite origin of the two men who will soon assassinate Ish-Bosheth, the narrator underscores the fact that even members of Saul's own tribe have become disillusioned with the house of Saul, confirming the judgment of 3:1 that "the house of Saul grew weaker and weaker."

The people of Beeroth fled to Gittaim (4:3). One of the four major cities of the Gibeonite enclave (Josh. 9:17), Beeroth (tentatively identified with el-Burj, two miles south of Gibeon) was undoubtedly included in the treaty that Israel made with the Gibeonites in Joshua 9. In Joshua 18:25, however, Beeroth is allotted to the tribe of Benjamin. King Saul apparently attempted to annihilate the Gibeonites during his reign (cf. 2 Sam. 21:1–2), and it may well have been in response to that aggression that the people of Beeroth fled to Gittaim.

Gittaim is a dual form of Gath, which means winepress—thus "Twin-Gath" or "Twin-Winepresses." Its location is uncertain, as numerous places bore the name Gath or equivalents. One suggestion is Tell Ras Abu-Hamid.[69] If correct, the original Beerothites' flight and relocation placed them some eighteen miles west of Beeroth. In any case, the city of Beeroth remained in the possession of the Benjamites. Whether Ish-Bosheth's assassins were from the original Beerothites or the Benjamite settlers remains unclear.

Son who was lame in both feet (4:4). That Jonathan's son Mephibosheth (called Merib-Baal in Chronicles; on intentional name distortions, see comment on 1 Sam. 7:4) is described as lame in both feet may suggest a spinal cord injury. It is also possible that he received (compound) fractures that either were not or could not be set properly.

Medicine designed to treat illness and injury was practiced in the ancient Near East from early times. An Egyptian medical papyrus copied by scribes from older texts (ca. 1700 B.C.), for example, provides systematic instructions for the diagnosis and treatment of a host of injuries, beginning with the head and moving downward (the text is discontinued and reaches no further than the upper arm and ribs). One section describes a serious spinal cord injury:

> If you examine a man having a dislocation in a vertebra of his neck, if you find him

Mutilated enemy shown on the Balawat Gate
Werner Forman Archive/The British Museum

paralysed in both arms and both legs because of it ... you shall say concerning him ... an ailment which I will not treat.

A later section describes "a man having a fracture in his collarbone ... an ailment which I will treat." There follows, then, a careful and rational description of how the patient is to be splinted. Broken limbs were also splinted and wrapped with linen. Archaeologists have even recovered from Egyptian graves examples of splints designed to deal with long-bone fractures.[70] Medicine was also practiced in Mesopotamia, though not without some admixture of irrational superstition. One could predict, for instance, whether a patient would recover by what he saw while hallucinating: "If, when he was suffering from a long illness, he saw a dog, his illness will return to him; he will die.... If he saw a gazelle, that patient will recover."[71]

They went into the inner part of the house as if to get some wheat (4:6). There is wide agreement among commentators that a textual variant represented by the LXX should be preferred here. Thus, while in-house storage facilities were common enough in the ancient Near East, the text should actually read along the lines of McCarter's suggestion: "The portress (female porter) of the house had been gathering wheat; she had nodded and fallen asleep."[72]

They cut off their hands and feet and hung the bodies by the pool (4:12). On the dismemberment of enemy dead or, as here, the executed, see comment 1 Samuel 31:4 (cf. 5:3–4). Though mutilation of this sort was not uncommon in the ancient Near East, there may be a special significance here, that is, the removal of the offending members—hands that committed the murder and feet that brought the news.

David's Kingdom Established (5:1–25)

When all the elders of Israel had come (5:3). "The elders constituted a leadership institution within societies in the ancient Near East, in all the countries and during all periods."[73] As a tribal and patriarchal society, ancient Israel looked to the collective leadership of "elders," drawn from "the fathers of the basic family units" called fathers', or ancestral, houses.[74] Mothers also participated in some judicial proceedings, as in those involving children (e.g., Deut. 21:18–20; 22:15),[75] and occasionally assumed leadership on an ad hoc basis in times of crisis (e.g., 2 Sam. 20:16), but in general the elders comprised the male heads of the household.[76]

In short, "the elders were the governing body of the clan by virtue of being its leading householders."[77] As military and judicial leaders in village society, the elders were viewed as the accepted representatives of their respective families, clans, and tribes; thus David's acceptance as king by the northern tribes of Israel is dependent on his endorsement by the "elders of Israel."

The king made a compact with them (5:3). Elsewhere this Hebrew terminology (cf. 3:21) is rendered "to make a covenant." The compact/covenant David makes with the elders of the northern tribes probably contains regulations for the kingship (see comment on 1 Sam. 10:25), including the duties and responsibilities of the respective parties to one another and to the Lord (cf. 2 Kings 11:17, where Jehoida makes a three-way covenant between Yahweh, the king, and the people). Even under the new arrangement, old divisions—particularly the one between the tribes in the north and those in the south—persist, as evidenced by the short-term success of Sheba's revolt (2 Sam. 20:1) and the eventual division of the kingdom during the reign of Solomon's son Rehoboam (1 Kings 12:16).

They anointed David king over Israel (5:3). See comments on 2:4; 1 Samuel 2:10.

David was thirty years old when he became king (5:4). Regnal formulae such as this one, which give a monarch's age at the time of his accession and the length of his reign, are common in the books of Samuel and Kings (e.g., 1 Sam. 13:1; 2 Sam. 2:10; 1 Kings 14:21; 22:42). The placement of David's regnal formula here, though it includes his seven-and-a-half-year reign, appropriately marks the inauguration of his reign over all Israel.

The king and his men marched to Jerusalem (5:6). David's interest in Jerusalem (where he eventually established his royal capital) likely stemmed from its strategic location and relatively independent status. Occupied already in the third millennium B.C. (and even earlier), Jerusalem in David's time lay within the territorial allotment of the small tribe of Benjamin, close to the northern border of Judah, but it never came under full Israelite control. The city had been conquered by Judah in the period of the judges (Judg. 1:8), but neither Judah nor Benjamin had been successful in occupying the city or in driving out its Jebusite inhabitants (Josh. 15:63; Judg. 1:21). Thus, David probably viewed Jerusalem as an ideal candidate for a national capital—centrally located between the northern and southern tribes within one of the smaller tribes that would be unlikely to evoke jealousy from the others, and not yet conquered.

To attack the Jebusites (5:6). Jebusites are first mentioned in Genesis 10:16, in the Table of Nations, where they are listed between Hittites and Amorites as descendants of Canaan. Beyond this general association with Canaan, little is known with certainty regarding their ethnic origins. B. Mazar has suggested that Ezekiel 16:3 may offer a hint: "This is what the sovereign LORD says to Jerusalem: Your ancestry and birth were in the land of the Canaanites; your father was an Amorite, and your mother a Hittite."

In support of the notion that the Jebusites may have had Hittite roots, Mazar draws attention to two prominent individuals who figure in the story of David: Uriah and Araunah. With respect to the latter, he observes that "Araunah (or *the* Araunah, as the Hebrew has it in 24:16) seems not to have been a personal name but rather the Hurrian word *ewrine* (lord), found in Hittite (and as a personal name in Ugaritic)."[78] Thus, the Jebusites should perhaps be associated with Hurrians or Hittites. Whatever the case, most authorities at least believe the Jebusites to have been of non-Semitic origin and to have retained control of Jerusalem (glossed as the city of Jebus) throughout the settlement period until the time of David—despite temporary setbacks (such as the Judahite raid and burning of the city recounted in Judg. 1:8).[79]

Even the blind and the lame can ward you off (5:6). An exchange of taunts or insults prior to a battle (referred to as "flyting") was common in the ancient Near East (see comment on 1 Sam. 17:43). The meaning of the Jebusites' taunt has elicited considerable discussion and numerous suggestions, but no interpretation has achieved a consensus. Perhaps it is suggestive of overconfidence ("even our handicapped can keep you at bay") or simply of a determination to fight to the last man ("even be he blind or lame"). Or perhaps this expression involves some kind of hex, or it harks back to a prior treaty between David and the Jebusites in which the blind or lame were invoked in the ratification ceremony.[80] It

Fragment of a cult object perhaps portraying a Jebusite
Z. Radovan/www.BibleLand Pictures.com

▸ Jerusalem in Literary Sources and Archaeology

Given its importance in biblical history, Jerusalem has enjoyed the attention of archaeologists from the middle of the nineteenth century down to the present.[A-8] Some have even described Jerusalem as the most excavated city in Israel. The archaeological results, however, particularly as they relate to the city at the time of David, have been mixed—or at least they have given rise to a heated debate over whether tenth-century B.C. Jerusalem was a city worthy of David's attention or a mere "cow-town."[A-9]

Whatever questions arise from the material remains, extrabiblical literary evidence leaves little room for doubting Jerusalem's prominence even in the controversial Late Bronze and Iron Age I periods, for which sparse material remains have been recovered. Jerusalem is mentioned already in the nineteenth- and eighteenth-century Egyptian Execration texts (where it is called "Urushalimum"),[A-10] in the fourteenth-century Amarna letters (similarly called "Urusalim"),[A-11] and in later Assyrian texts (where the name is "Urusalimmu").[A-12] In the fourteenth-century Amarna period, Jerusalem seems to have been particularly prominent, vying with Shechem for control of the central hill country. This literary evidence of an important Late Bronze Age city of Jerusalem prior to the Israelite settlement in Canaan is significant not only in its own right but also for its bearing on the question of whether there was (as the biblical text asserts) an Iron Age I city at Jerusalem for David to conquer. As noted, archaeological excavations in and around the modern city of Jerusalem have not yielded much that proves *either* the Late-Bronze *or* Iron-Age-I prominence of the settlement, but the literary evidence, whether from Amarna or the biblical text, is unequivocal.[A-13]

The basic contours of the archaeological debate are summarized in a number of places and need not be repeated here.[A-14] But a few cautionary remarks are in order.

1. One must be cautious in drawing conclusions from what archaeology has *not* found—"absence of evidence is not evidence of absence."
2. Because Jerusalem has been continuously occupied throughout the age of archaeological exploration of Palestine, many sections are unavailable for excavation or sounding.
3. The archaeologists who have conducted major excavations in accessible areas in and around the city (e.g., K. Kenyon and Y. Shiloh) seem never to have questioned the importance of the city in the time of David; this to some degree undercuts more recent arguments that archaeological results indicate the city to have been of little importance in David's day.
4. Because Jerusalem is situated in a defensible, well-watered location near arable land and along major ancient trade routes (east-west and north-south),[A-15] the notion that it would have lacked significant occupation in any ancient period seems unlikely.

In short, as B. Halpern has remarked, one must be cautious in drawing conclusions "from the vagaries of material survival and recovery alone," especially "in a site such as Jerusalem, where monumental construction especially in the Persian through Herodian periods was repeatedly carried down to bedrock, and where the overburden of modern settlement and political constraints prohibit extensive soundings."[A-16]

Aerial of the City of David extending south from the current city wall.
Z. Radovan/www.BibleLandPictures.com

▸ Jerusalem in Literary Sources and Archaeology (continued)

It is no surprise, therefore, that material and architectural evidence from some periods may be minimal. This is not to say that nothing remains from Davidic Jerusalem. For instance, the Jebusite city captured by David was surrounded by a ten-foot-thick wall that had been constructed in Middle Bronze II (eighteenth-century B.C.), and which continued in use throughout the united and divided monarchies, with some additions along the way.

Notable also is the much-discussed "stepped-stone structure" on the northeast side of the city, overlooking the Kidron Valley. This structure is believed to have been built in the Jebusite period prior to David and augmented by David himself. Comprising a terraced fill involving dressed and undressed stones, stamped soil, and rubble, and still preserved to a height of some fifty-five feet, the stepped-stone structure is the largest Iron I structure to have been excavated in Israel. It apparently supported an important civic structure, perhaps the "fortress of Zion" mentioned in 5:7.

Having captured the fortress of Zion and taken up residence in it, David "built up the area around it, from the supporting terraces inward" (5:9). Not until the time of David's son Solomon was the city's administrative center moved north to Temple Mount.[A-17] Ancient Jerusalem can be divided into three regions: (1) the formerly Jebusite City of David; 2) the so-called Ophel, a narrow ridge jutting north from the hill of David and joining (3) the Temple Mount area. The actual size of the original "City of David," as it was renamed (5:9), was modest, occupying only about ten acres along the ridge running southward from the present-day walled city, but it likely controlled other towns and outlying areas.

Close-up of the excavations on the eastern flank
Kim Walton
▸

No discussion of the archaeology of Jerusalem is complete without mention of Eilat Mazar's excavation of a "large-stone structure" located between the Temple Mount and the stepped-stone structure, in about the place that—according to Mazar's interpretation of verses such as 5:17 (see comment)—David's palace may have been located.[A-18] At the time of this writing, it is too early for definitive interpretations of these material remains, but initial indications are that the earliest level may stem from the tenth century, the early monarchy period.

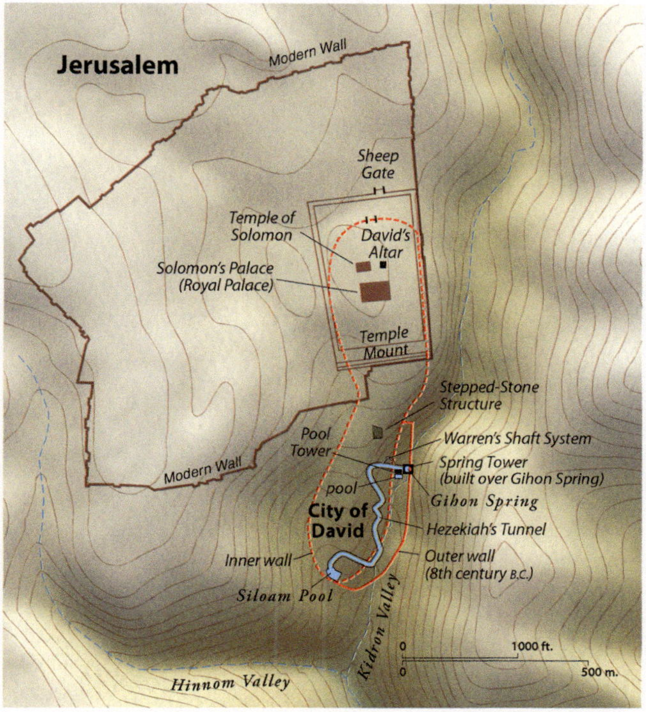

With the walls of the Old City visible at the top, the eastern flank of the City of David features the stepped-stone structure near the top right, the entrance to the Warren's Shaft (center, left of the steps), and the spring house at the entry to Hezekiah's Tunnel at the bottom in the center.

has even been suggested that the sense of the taunt is that "only someone capable of curing the blind and the lame could breach [the city's] defenses"[81] (though this seems difficult to square with the grammar of the Hebrew).

Perhaps the precise meaning of the taunt is beyond recovery (apart from the basic biblical explanation that by it the Jebusites mean "David cannot get in here" [v. 6]). In any case, the taunt fits a pattern of ongoing hostility between the Jebusites and their Bethlehemite neighbor David (cf. v. 8, where David's enmity with the Jebusites is mentioned; also 1 Sam. 17:54).

Fortress of Zion (5:7). The etymology of "Zion," which occurs here for the first time in the Bible, has not been firmly established; suggestions include "castle," "bare place," "bare hill," and so on.[82] The fortress of Zion probably referred originally to a stronghold atop the stepped-stone structure (see sidebar on "Jerusalem in Literary Sources and Archaeology" at 5:6). The name eventually was extended to designate Jerusalem itself (e.g., 2 Kings 19:21; Isa. 2:3) or even the entire nation of Israel (e.g., Ps. 149:2; Isa. 46:3). In Israel's poetical and prophetical literature, "Zion" is often presented as the locus of God's mighty acts of salvation and judgment (cf. Ps. 14:7; Isa. 4:4; Lam. 4:11).

Water shaft (5:8). Since Charles Warren's discovery in 1867 of an approximately fifty-foot vertical shaft not too far from the Gihon Spring but within the walls of the ancient City of David (see map), many scholars have assumed that David's instructions to "use the water shaft to reach those 'lame and blind' who are David's enemies" must relate to what came to be called "Warren's shaft." This view was never universally accepted, however, and has recently been rejected by many scholars.

One problem has to do with the rare Hebrew word translated "water shaft" (*ṣinnôr*). Elsewhere

Warren's Shaft
Kim Walton

Bel-harran-bel-usur stele commemorating a city and temple that he built, which was granted freedom from taxation (in grain, water, and straw)
Todd Bolen/www.BiblePlaces.com

in the Bible, *ṣinnôr* occurs only in Psalm 42:7: "Deep calls to deep in the roar of your *waterfalls* [plural of *ṣinnôr*; NRSV and JPS render *cataracts*]; all your waves and breakers have swept over me." A meaning along the lines of "water shaft" works here,[83] but lack of certainty has nevertheless spawned a number of alternative theories, based largely on cognate Arabic and Aramaic words and yielding meanings ranging from "grappling-hook" to "throat."[84]

Recent work by T. Kleven, however, has sought to strengthen the case for reading *ṣinnôr* as "water shaft" or something similar. He cites in particular a cognate word (*ṣnr*) found in a Ugaritic text (early second millennium B.C.) describing the guilds involved in building houses. Kleven follows C. Gordon in reading the Ugaritic word *ṣnr* as designating a guild of "pipe" makers, who were responsible for water systems related to the new construction.[85] Not only does this Ugaritic evidence lend support to the traditional reading of Hebrew *ṣinnôr* as perhaps "water shaft," but it also suggests that water works were utilized in Canaan already in the second millennium, well before the time of David.

This leads us to the second major objection to the traditional understanding. Y. Shiloh, convinced that water works such as Warren's shaft should be dated no earlier than Iron II (tenth–ninth century) and perhaps influenced by philological theories that rejected the meaning "water shaft" for *ṣinnôr*, doubted that Warren's shaft could have been known in David's day.[86] The most recent archaeological explorations of Jerusalem's water systems (by R. Reich and E. Shukron)[87] have come to a very different conclusion regarding the initial construction of Jerusalem's water system(s), which they believe to have taken place in the Middle Bronze II period (ca. 1700–1550), but they too doubt that "the natural vertical cavity" known as Warren's shaft could have been Joab's point of entry; in their view, the shaft "was not visible or accessible to the local people until the eighth century B.C.E."[88]

In the end, it is difficult to retrace with any confidence Joab's daring entry into the Jebusite city. Certainly, the general notion

Entry to Gihon Spring
Peter White

that he entered through some kind of water shaft or water tunnel system seems reasonable enough, especially given the new support for the traditional reading of *ṣinnôr.* If Reich and Shukron are correct that the shaft discovered by Warren would have been unknown to inhabitants of Jerusalem until the eighth century, then "the shaft proper could not have taken part in the biblical story." Their own suggestion, rather, is that "the rock-cut 'Pool' [near the spring house (see diagram)] and the tunnels connected to it (in its first phase of use) might well qualify" as the venue for Joab's exploit.[89]

Called it the City of David (5:9). The practice of renaming a captured (or purchased) city and making it one's capital and principal residence is attested elsewhere in the ancient Near East. McCarter mentions as examples the establishment by the Assyrian Sargon II (721–705) of a "new capital at modern Khorsabad, which he called *dūr šarru-kīn,* 'Sargonsburg,'" and the founding of "Tukulti-ninurta City" by the thirteenth-century Assyrian king Tukulti-ninurta I.[90]

Such cities, which were often considered part of the ruler's personal estate, not only enjoyed the most ambitious building projects but also, as far as the administrative personnel were concerned (typically relatives of the king), enjoyed such privileges as exemption from taxation, military duty, or corvée labor.[91] These latter privileges stemmed not least from the fact that from Mesopotamia to Egypt such cities were typically "temple cities," which were to be "free of oppression and of obligations toward the government, since it was to be governed by the god alone," places where justice and righteousness prevailed.[92]

Supporting terraces (5:9). See discussion of the "stepped-stone structure" in the sidebar on "Jerusalem in Literary Sources and Archaeology" at 5:6.

Hiram king of Tyre (5:11). Tyre was a major Phoenician seaport city situated on an island off the Mediterranean coast some thirty miles north of Mount Carmel and twenty-five miles south of Sidon. Only about a hundred miles north of Jerusalem, Tyre's commercial and cultural influence was felt throughout the ancient world and throughout the duration of Israel's history. Eventually rising to the position of "ruler of the sea," Tyre had commercial relations with most places in the known world.[93]

Not surprisingly, Tyre is often mentioned in texts from the ancient Near East, including the Ebla texts (third millennium), the Egyptian Execration texts (nineteenth–eighteenth centuries), and the Amarna letters (fourteenth century), down to classical sources.[94] In the time of David, Tyre under King Hiram I experienced its first golden age. Hiram's generosity to David is a testimony to the impressiveness of David's own accomplishments, but it was likely also motivated by self-interest; Hiram may well have been concerned that David not deny him access to inland trade routes and necessary agricultural produce (cf. the goods supplied to Sidon and Tyre in Ezra 3:7).

Cedars of Lebanon floating down river
Marie-Lan Nguyen/ Wikimedia Commons, courtesy of the Louvre

Hiram's friendship with Israel continued well into Solomon's reign (1 Kings 5:1–12; 9:11). Hiram I is not mentioned in ancient Near Eastern texts outside the Bible, but the much later Assyrian king Tiglath-pileser III (745–727) includes a different Hiram of Tyre in a list of those from whom he received tribute.[95] A third Hiram is attested in the early tenth-century sarcophagus inscription of ʾAhirom (Hiram), king of Byblos.[96]

Hiram ... sent cedar logs (5:11). The cedars of Lebanon (*Cedrus libani*), which could grow to heights of 130 feet and live as long as three thousand years, were much admired in the ancient Near East, and their timbers were much coveted for the construction of temples and palaces. The beauty, aroma, and durability of the wood were unsurpassed, and the kings of Mesopotamia and Egypt imported cedar timbers from the Lebanese region as early as the fourth millennium.[97] About a century before David's reign, the Assyrian king Tiglath-pileser I (1115–1076 B.C.) included the following in a report of an expedition to Lebanon and the Mediterranean: "I went to Lebanon (*Lab-na-a-ni*). I cut (there) timber cedars for the temple of Anu and Adad, the great gods, my lords, and carried (them to Ashur)."[98]

Exalted his kingdom for the sake of his people Israel (5:12). On the chief responsibility of the king in the ancient Near East to establish justice and equity for the people, see comments on 8:15; 15:4; cf. 12:1–4; also see 1 Samuel 12:3.

David took more concubines and wives (5:13). On the topic of diplomatic marriage, see comment on 1 Samuel 25:39. On the implications of David's growing harem, see comment on 2 Samuel 3:2.

The Philistines ... went up in full force ... David ... went down to the stronghold (5:17). David's rule over Judah from Hebron was not contested by the Philistines, but the extension of his domain to include the northern tribes pose a threat to their interests that they could not ignore. The identity of the "stronghold" to which David "went down" is debated. In the present context, one naturally thinks of the "fortress [same Heb. word] of Zion" captured by David in verse 7 and occupied by him in verse 9. But some regard the expression "to go down" as inappropriate in reference to Jerusalem and suggest that David returns to a stronghold of prior acquaintance, perhaps at Adullam[99] (see comment on 1 Sam. 22:4).

In view of the other geographical reference points in the context, the newly acquired fortress of Zion remains a favored option.[100] Recent excavation led by Eilat Mazar in the area just north of the stepped-stone structure has uncovered evidence of an impressive Iron-Age "large-stone structure" that some suggest may represent David's palace[101]—an association that must, of necessity, remain suppositional pending further discovery and dating. If correct, however, then from his palace David would indeed have gone "down" to the fortress of Zion.

Valley of Rephaim (5:18). Generally identified with the Wadi el-Ward, the Valley of Rephaim ran essentially east-west about a mile south of the present-day Old City of Jerusalem. The deployment of Philistines in this valley makes good strategic sense, as it would hinder Judahite reinforcements from joining David in Jerusalem.[102]

David inquired of the LORD (5:19). See comments on 1 Samuel 22:10; 23:2; 28:6.

Baal Perazim (5:20). The location of Baal Perazim is uncertain; suggestions include a site somewhere on the southern or western border of the Valley of Rephaim (if the stronghold to which David descends in v. 17 is the stronghold of Adullam) or a site nearer to Jerusalem (if the stronghold is the fortress of Zion).[103]

Philistines abandoned their idols (5:21). On ancient Near Eastern conceptions of the involvement of the god(s) in warfare and on the common practice of carrying off defeated deities, see comments on 1 Samuel 5:2 and the sidebar, "The Treatment of Defeated Deities." While the captured gods of defeated foes were often placed in the temples of the more powerful, victorious deities, the biblical text here gives no indication that David follows this practice. The parallel account in Chronicles completes the picture: "The Philistines had abandoned their gods there, and David gave orders to burn them in the fire" (1 Chron. 14:12; cf. the instructions of Deut. 7:5, 25).

While less common than subordinating (or simply adding) captured gods to the existing pantheon, the practice of denigrating the power of and even destroying captured gods is known in the ancient Near East. Assurbanipal, for instance, exemplifies the former practice with his remark regarding the gods of the Elamites: "I counted their gods and goddesses as powerless ghosts." In another place, he writes about the Elamite gods: "I smashed their gods and thereby soothed the heart of the lord of lords."[104]

Circle around behind them ... sound of marching in the balsam trees (5:23–24). Though there are uncertainties of interpretation in these verses—e.g., are we to read "balsam trees" or, perhaps, a place name?[105]—two typical aspects of Israelite warfare are evident: clever strategies capitalizing on deception and surprise,[106] and divine assistance through the orchestration of natural or supernatural events (cf. 2 Kings 7:6, where Yahweh caused "the Arameans to hear the sound of chariots and horses and a great army").

The LORD has gone out in front of you (5:24). The concept of the Divine Warrior was not unique to Israel (see comment on 1 Sam. 14:6). A major tenet of Divine Warrior theology was that God or the gods went before the troops to enable victory by demoralizing, confusing, or terrifying the enemy. At times the deity would "thunder" against the enemy (see 1 Sam. 2:10), cause the earth to shake (see 14:15), or in other ways befuddle, trick, and dispirit the enemy. David's "song of praise" combines many images associated with the awesome character of Yahweh as Divine Warrior and rescuer (2 Sam. 22:8–16). If Israel's belief in a Divine Warrior was not unique conceptually, it was ontologically, as Israel worshiped the only true God, Yahweh.

From Gibeon to Gezer (5:25). David's rout of the Philistines was more extensive and far more decisive than Jonathan's in 1 Samuel 14:31. Whereas Jonathan drove the Philistines as far as Aijalon, David drove them all the way to Gezer—seven miles further west and, significantly, right out of the hill country.[107] David's defeat of the

Battle and pursuit to Gezer ▶

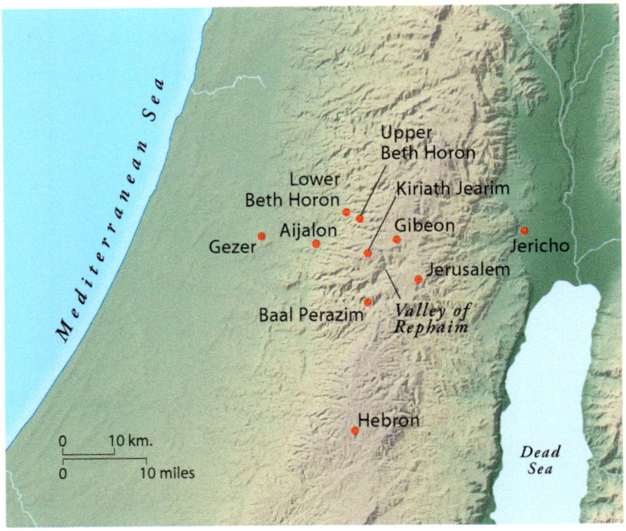

Philistines was of great moment, because these archenemies of Israel were central to the commissions of both Saul and David (cf. 1 Sam. 9:16; 2 Sam. 3:18). David succeeded (cf. 2 Sam. 8:1) where Saul failed, and the weight of David's achievement was not lost on the people or on the later Chronicler (1 Chron. 14:17).

The Ark Established in Jerusalem (6:1–23)

Baalah of Judah (6:2). This is another name for Kiriath Jearim (see comment on 1 Sam. 6:21). If the site has been correctly identified, the journey from Baalah to Jerusalem was seven or eight miles.

To bring up from there the ark of God (6:2). On the ark of God, see comment on 1 Samuel 3:3. Various studies have compared the present episode to ancient Near Eastern accounts of ceremonies accompanying the return of a deity to its temple.[108] While aspects of these studies are illuminating, McCarter is correct in pointing out that the more pertinent analogues to David's bringing the ark up to Jerusalem are "ancient Near Eastern accounts of the introduction of a national god to a new royal city." As examples, he cites inscriptions of the Assyrian kings Sargon II (721–705 B.C.), Sennacherib (704–681), and Esarhaddon (680–669), each of which recounts the arrival or restoration of a deity in a (new) royal city. The basic pattern of each account comprises the following elements: "ceremonial invitation of the national god into a royal city, the presentation of sacrifices, and the preparation of a feast for the people of the land."[109] Most lavish of all is the account of Assurbanipal II's inauguration of the palace in Calah. First, "he invited into it Ashur, the great lord and the gods of his entire country," to whom he next offered sacrifices of extraordinary quantity and variety; third, he "treated for ten days with food and drink 47,074 persons, men and women," along with other guests, bringing the total to 69,574.[110] David's actions in 2 Samuel 6 follow a similar pattern: Yahweh, as represented by the ark of God, is brought into the new royal city of David, sacrifices are offered, and the people are treated to a banquet.

Enthroned between the cherubim (6:2). See comment on 1 Samuel 4:4.

New cart (6:3). While the choice of a "new" cart is doubtless motivated by a desire for ritual purity, it was still an inappropriate choice. Recalling Philistine precedent set in 1 Samuel 6:7, this mode of transporting the ark entirely neglects the divine directive that the ark, equipped with rings and poles (e.g., Ex. 25:12–14; 37:5), is to be carried, not carted (see Num. 4:15, 19; 7:9; Deut. 10:8; Josh. 3:8; etc.).

House of Abinadab (6:3). See comment on 1 Samuel 7:1.

Harps, lyres, tambourines, sistrums and cymbals (6:5). The musical instruments mentioned are for the most part well known both in the Bible and in the ancient Near East generally (see comments on 1 Sam. 10:5; 16:16). The "sistrum" occurs only here in the Bible, and so is more difficult to describe with cer-

Procession of musicians
Michael Greenhalgh ArtServe, courtesy of The Istanbul Museum

tainty. A sistrum was a metallic instrument known particularly among the ancient Egyptians. The handle of what may have been an Egyptian sistrum from around the fifteenth century B.C. was discovered at Beitin. To the handle was attached an oval hoop made of metal. Several wires were attached to the hoop in such a way that shaking the instrument produced a jingling sound.

The etymology of the Hebrew word used here suggests that the key aspect of the instrument was that of a "shaker" of some sort.[111] This has led to the alternative suggestion that the instrument may have been a "(pottery) rattle."[112] Dozens of pottery rattles, averaging about four inches in height, have been discovered in ancient Palestine. Used from as early as the second millennium until they

Procession with musical instruments, including sistrum
Lisa Jean Winbolt

were generally replaced by metal bells in the ninth century, these rattles consisted of enclosed hollow pottery vessels containing one or more small pellets.[113]

Threshing floor of Nacon (6:6). On the nature of threshing floors, see comments on 24:18, 22. The precise location of this threshing floor is unknown, though it was probably near Jerusalem. The name "Nacon," which sounds like a Hebrew term denoting that which is stable, steadfast, or sure, may have been mentioned to underscore the dramatic irony of the oxen stumbling just at that spot.

Six steps (6:13). The nature of the ritual procedure described in this verse has been described in two distinct ways. The first, reflected in the NIV, is that after those carrying the ark took their first six steps without incident, a sacrifice was performed in thanksgiving for the apparent divine approval of David's second attempt to transport the ark to Jerusalem.

The second, likelier interpretation is that a sacrifice was offered each time the bearers of the ark had taken six steps. While the number of sacrificial animals would have been considerable and the ritual procession slow moving, Assyrian sources offer a possible analogue to such a procession. An inscription of King Esarhaddon (681–669) describes a procession by which divine images were brought to their restored sanctuaries in Babylon: "From Assur to the quay of Babylon, brushwood piles were lit every third of a mile, and every double mile they slaughtered fat bulls." Esarhaddon died, in fact, "before he could carry out the festive procession described in his inscriptions," so it fell to his son Assurbanipal (669–633) to do so.[114]

The following is exerpted from Assurbanipal's fuller inscription:

> In my first year of reign, when Marduk, king of the universe, *put into* my hands the rule *of Assyria* ... I besought my creator in the matter of his godhead's going (back to Babylon).

Having apparently received a favorable reply, Assurbanipal describes the procession:

> From the quay of Assur to the quay of Babylon, where they were taking him, lambs were slaughtered, bulls sacrificed (cut down), sweet-smelling (herbs) scattered about ... all that one could mention was brought [lit., they brought] to the morning and evening meal.... Brushwood was kindled, torches lighted. Every *bêru* ["double-hour's journey"], a beacon was set up. All of my troops kept going round it, like a rainbow, making music day and night.[115]

While the idea that David's procession halted every six paces to offer a sacrifice may stretch credulity, McCarter insists that "one can hardly object that the number of sacrificial animals seems excessive here in view of the statistics given for the ceremony accompanying Solomon's installation of the ark in the temple in 1 Kings 8:5, 63—twenty-two thousand victims from the herds and one hundred twenty thousand from the flocks!"[116]

David, wearing a linen ephod, danced (6:14). For the three senses of the word "ephod" in the Bible, see comment on

Hittite mythological scene from Megiddo with dancers celebrating before deities
Kim Walton, courtesy of the Oriental Institute Museum

1 Samuel 2:18; David apparently lays aside his royal insignia and clothes himself in a priestly garment (or perhaps the attire of a dancer) in order to participate in the cultic procession. Scrutiny of the words used to describe David's dancing suggests that it is an exuberant, energetic leaping and whirling about.[117]

While ancient Near Eastern literature provides no other examples of kings dancing in such processions, instances of the queen joining in a ritual dance, followed by other dignitaries, are known from Hittite sources.[118] Depictions of dancers in a broad range of ancient Near Eastern pictorial sources give some sense of what this dancing may have been like. Dancing was done either in groups or singly and was often quite acrobatic.[119] Dancing took place in a variety of settings and for a variety of reasons, as it has in most cultures up to the present time. It could be a spontaneous expression of joy and playfulness; on occasion it could verge into eroticism; and it was often a component of cultic ceremonies.

Dancing was not always evaluated positively. An Akkadian letter from the first half of the second millennium criticizes a woman who had "greatly aggravated the matter." The letter explains: "In addition to dancing about every day, she has slighted us by consistently behaving thoughtlessly."[120] Mostly, though, dancing was deemed a reflex of joy and well-being. A letter to the Assyrian king Assurbanipal lauds his reign as a golden age:

> A good reign, righteous days, years of justice, plentiful rains, enormous floods, a good market price! The gods are appeased, there is much reverence of god, the temples abound; the great gods of heaven and earth have been exalted in the time of the king, my lord! The old men dance, the young men sing, the women and the girls are merry and happy; women are married and provided with rings, boys and girls are brought forth, the births thrive![121]

David's whirling dance apparently combines personal exuberance with cultic performance. For more on dancing in ancient Israel, see comment on 1 Samuel 18:6.

Shouts and the sound of trumpets (6:15). As in 2:28 and 1 Samuel 13:3 (see comments), the kind of "trumpet" in this context is the *šôpār,* a horn made usually from a ram's horn. Because its piercing sound could be heard from a great distance or above the din of other noises, the *šôpār* was often used as a signaling device in military contexts. For the same reasons, the *šôpār* was also used, as here, in celebratory ritual contexts; its rather limited musical range meant that its contribution to the music was more dramatic than melodic.[122]

Bread ... dates and ... raisins to each person (6:19). On the provision of a royal feast for the people as part of the ceremony accompanying the "introduction of a national god to a new royal city," see comment on 6:2.[123]

How the king of Israel has distinguished himself today (6:20). Michal's criticism of David shows a fundamental misunderstanding of the requirements of Israelite kingship and effectively seals the fate of the house of Saul (6:23). David's humbling himself before Yahweh not only comports nicely with the consistent emphasis in 1–2 Samuel on the honor of Yahweh, but it also finds at least general analogy in Mesopotamian ritual texts. A ritual text from the reign of late thirteenth- to early twelfth-century Assyrian king Tukulti-Ninurta I, for instance, describes the king's divestment of royal insignia and humble appearance as supplicant before the god Assur. Following his humiliation, the king is "reinvested with the symbols of office, is crowned, and is extolled with praises and wishes for a long reign."[124]

David Promised an Enduring Kingdom (7:1–29)

The LORD had given him rest (7:1). The biblical emphasis on Yahweh's giving his people rest is unusual in the ancient Near Eastern context, where it was generally deemed the responsibility of the people to provide a place of rest for the deity—a temple, in other words. In ancient Mesopotamia, the chief purpose of the state was to provide shelter and food for the gods; to fail to do so was high treason. Such provision was made through the cult, and the center of the cult was the temple, the house of the gods (or the main god). The building and repair of the temple was the responsibility of the ruler.[125]

All these activities were aimed at appeasing the gods and keeping them at rest. The Assyrian king Sennacherib, for instance, in an account of his building a "Temple of the New Year's Feast," speaks of his desire to "quiet the heart of Assur, my lord."[126] Other aspects of his temple building parallel David's. He writes: "My heart moved me, the command of Shamash and Adad I sought by oracle, a favorable reply they gave me, and commanded (me) to build."[127]

Gudea Temple Cylinder B
Rama/Wikimedia Commons, courtesy of the Louvre

David too desires to build a house for Yahweh, and he too seeks and receives approval (later reversed) from the person responsible for oracular inquiry, the prophet Nathan. The striking distinctive of the biblical account is, as just noted, the fact that, rather than the king building a house and providing rest for the god(s), Yahweh provides rest and builds a house for Israel's king, David (see next comment).

He said to Nathan the prophet (7:2). Nathan is mentioned here for the first time. He will play a significant role also in 2 Samuel 12 and in 1 Kings 1. That David should approach a prophet to seek (oracular) approval for his intent to build a temple is in keeping with general ancient Near Eastern practice.[128] From the late third millennium, we have the example of Gudea of Lagash, who set out to build a temple for his god, but not without first receiving divine approval:

> ... in order to build the temple of Ningirsu—Gudea brought (these materials) together in his town Girsu.... After the god Ninzagga had given him a (pertinent) order, they brought copper for Gudea, the temple-builder ... after the god Ninsikila had given him a (pertinent) order, they brought great willow-logs ... to the ensi, the temple-builder.[129]

Examples of kings seeking divine sanction for temple building can be multiplied, and there are also instances of divine sanction being withheld.[130] The biblical accounts are unique in the ancient Near East, however, in offering an explanation as to "why the deity responded negatively to the request of a king who is otherwise viewed in a positive light."[131] Building a temple in a capital city and thus bringing together the religious and political would ostensibly strengthen David's hand. But Yahweh rejects David's plan to build a temple and chooses, rather, a more radical method of affirming his support of David. First comes the divine election of David as a man of Yahweh's own choosing, a man for whom Yahweh will build a house (dynasty). Only later are the political aspects—the merger of political and cultic centers in Jerusalem—brought into effect.

Living in a palace of cedar (7:2). The mention of cedar is suggestive of the refinement and luxury of David's palace (see comment on 5:11). David evidently views his palace as in some sense symbolic of his now-established rule (cf. 5:11–12) and thinks it only appropriate that God's rulership be similarly symbolized by a permanent dwelling for the ark. In wishing to build a temple for the God who has given him victory, David is not unlike other ancient Near Eastern monarchs, who liked to crown their achievements with temples to their patron deities.[132] David's focus on the ark links the present chapter with the immediately preceding one, which recounted David's bringing of the ark to Jerusalem.

I will make your name great (7:9). Attempts to liken the great name promised David to the Egyptian term "great name" (*ren wer*) are now regarded as misguided, inasmuch as David's great name seems to have to do with renown, while the Egyptian term functions as a titulary.[133] Similarly, attempts to liken the prophecy of 2 Samuel 7 to Egyptian *Königsnovellen* (royal tales) have also been refuted.[134]

Much more enlightening are proposed Mari parallels to the dynastic oracle. Malamat has drawn attention to a prophecy from Mari that exhibits a number of features of a "dynastic oracle."[135] These features include divine installation of the king, father-son imagery, reference to a tent-shrine (?), reference to a sanctuary as a house, house as a palace/dynasty, mention of throne, land/kingdom, and extent of rule. However, the Mari and the biblical dynastic oracles also differ markedly in some respects; chiefly, the Mari oracles are "obligatory" (i.e., conditional), placing the king under obligation, while the Davidic oracle is promissory and thus unconditional. Furthermore, while Yahweh rejects David's desire to build him a temple, the deity of the Mari oracles (Adad) is adamant that the king, Zimri-Lim, should build him a temple.

I will be his father, and he will be my son (7:14). The father/son terminology that Yahweh uses to describe his relationship to David's royal descendant is in keeping with the bond of intimacy that God feels toward David. Unlike in Egypt, where the pharaoh was considered divine, the king in ancient Israel was "not truly a god but one who metaphorically [partook] of a familial relationship" with God.[136] Sometimes termed "sacral kingship," this concept

Transport of cedar
Marie-Lan Nguyen/Wikimedia Commons, courtesy of the Louvre

Gods giving the pharaoh life
Frederick J. Mabie

was transformed into a far deeper reality with the incarnation of Jesus.

While the ancient Near East offers no true parallels to the profundity of the full biblical picture, familial father/son language was sometimes used to describe the relationship of a patron deity to an earthly monarch. In the Late Bronze Age Ugaritic epic of King Kirta, for example, Kirta is referred to as "the 'lad' and the 'son' of El, the high god of the Ugaritic pantheon," and in one passage is even called a "god."[137] A claim to divine sonship is apparent even in some of the throne names of Aramean kings (e.g., Barhadad [Ben-Hadad in the Bible] means "son of [the god] Hadad").[138] Instances of royal claims to divine heritage are evident in most places and periods of the ancient Near East.[139]

When a dynastic line fell out of power, the new regime made every attempt to expunge memory of those kings and even reliefs of them were often effaced.
Hansjoerg Klein

My love will never be taken away from him (7:15). "Love" language is often used in ancient Near Eastern contexts to express "covenant loyalty" (see the "love" of Israel and Judah for David in 1 Sam. 18:16 and of David's praise of Jonathan's love in 2 Sam. 1:26; cf. also 2 Sam. 19:6). Biblical expressions of God's love for his people or his king certainly do not exclude notions of emotional attachment and affection, but such

Treaty between King Ḫattušiliš III and Ulmi-Teshshup

I, My majesty, will [not depose] your son. [I will accept] neither your brother nor anyone else. Later your son and grandson will hold [the land] which I have given [to you]. It may not be taken away from him. If any son or grandson of yours commits an offense, then the King of Hatti shall question him. And if an offense is proven against him, then the King of Hatti shall treat him as he pleases. If he is deserving of death he shall perish, but his household and land shall not be taken from him and given to the progeny of another.[A-19]

expressions should be understood, first and foremost, in covenantal terms. Similar to the way that "love" in the Amarna letters connotes loyalty and service,[140] Deuteronomy, for instance, sees love "defined by and pledged in the covenant—a covenantal love."[141]

Covenantal use of love language is well illustrated in a later biblical passage describing the relationship of Hiram, king of Tyre, to David: "When Hiram king of Tyre heard that Solomon had been anointed king to succeed his father David, he sent his envoys to Solomon, because he had always been on friendly terms with [lit., had been one loving, or a lover of] David" (1 Kings 5:1 [Heb. 5:15]). The point in 2 Samuel 7 is that while Yahweh, as father, may find it necessary to discipline David's royal son when he does wrong (7:14), he will never remove his covenantal love from the Davidic line. Though the punishment be severe, extending even to the loss of land and temple (1 Kings 9:6–9), God's promise to establish forever the throne of David will not fail.

Over time this promise came to be understood in messianic terms (cf. Isa. 9:7; 11:1–5; Jer. 33:14–26; Mic. 5:1–5). A noteworthy conceptual parallel to this passage, though involving a covenant agreement between two human rulers, is found in the Hittite Bronze Tablet (see comment on 1:26).[142] The "Great King" Tudḫaliya IV promises the vassal Kurunta that the treaty between them will remain in force and will apply even to Kurunta's descendants. Even should a son or grandson of Kurunta commit treason, the covenant will remain inalienable: "I ... will not throw out your son." The offender, if proven guilty, will be punished, to be sure; "they shall do to him whatever the king of the land of Ḫatti decides. But they may not take from him his 'house' [i.e. dynasty] and land."[143] Similar with respect to succession is a section of a treaty between the Hittite king Ḫattušiliš III and Ulmi-Teshshup (see sidebar).[144]

There is no one like you (7:22). Awed by what Yahweh has said to him, David utters what many have rightly understood as an explicit monotheistic confession: "There is no God like you" (cf. Hannah's confession in 1 Sam. 2:2).[145] Other important reminders of Israel's monotheistic faith include the first commandment ("You shall have no other gods before me," Ex. 20:3; Deut. 5:7) and the Shema ("Hear [Heb. *šᵉmaᶜ*], O Israel: The LORD our God, the LORD is one," Deut. 6:4). The belief that there is but one true God is evidenced also in Israel's attitude toward idols, which are regarded as worthless nothings, burdensome blocks of wood, stone, or metal that have eyes but cannot see, ears but cannot hear, and so forth (cf. Ps. 115:1–8; Isa. 45:15–17; 46:1–7; Jer. 2:11; see sidebar on "Israel's Monotheism and Ancient Theisms").

David's Growing Empire (8:1–18)

David defeated the Philistines and subdued them (8:1). Given the prominence of the

Israel's Monotheism and Ancient Theisms

Akhenaten
Richard Beck, courtesy of the Alexandrian Museum

Israel's ancient Near Eastern neighbors were almost entirely polytheistic, occasionally perhaps bordering on henotheism (the worship of one god while granting the existence of others). For instance, the Neo-Babylonian king Nabonidus (555–539 B.C.) extolled the moon god Sin as "the king of the gods, the lord of lords who dwells in heaven, whose name surpasses that of (all) the (other) gods in heaven, (i.e.) of Shamash, who is *installed* by him, Nusku, Ishtar, Adad (and) Nergal who have (only) executed the command of the Divine Crescent, who surpasses them (all)."[A-20]

The best-known, if short-lived, exception to the polytheistic rule is the experiment with monotheism that took place during the reign of the Egyptian Pharaoh Akhenaten (Amenhotep IV, 1352–1336). Akhenaten's hymn to the sun god Aten refers to Aten as "sole God beside whom there is none."[A-21] An intriguing question is whether there may have been some connection between Akhenaten, the Egyptian monotheist, and the assumed monotheism of Israelites in Egypt. The question is often posed in terms of a possible connection between Akhenaten and Moses (whether the latter is believed to have lived in the fifteenth century or the thirteenth). On present evidence, however, influence cannot be established in either direction.

While monotheistic experiments such as Akhenaten's were extremely rare, more common was the tendency to collapse together deities from various locations who had similar functions but different names. As Saggs explains,

> within any region, the original local pantheons had arisen from very similar backgrounds, and therefore in many cases the supernatural powers worshipped (the numen behind the storm, the corn, the sun, etc.) differed in little more than name. It was thus easy in later periods to recognize the identity of such deities, and we find in Egypt and Mesopotamia, texts which explicitly state that deity A of one city is deity B of another.[A-22]

The effect of such equations was to reduce the actual number of deities assumed to exist. This reduction could be viewed as contributing a nascent monotheistic tendency, but in the end Israel's exclusive commitment to one God remains unique in the ancient Near East.

Philistines as Israel's archenemy from the time of the judges, David's success in subduing them is notable (contrast Saul's failure, 1 Sam. 14:52). F. M. Cross draws attention to a seventh-century ostracon excavated at Ashkelon, which may shed light on the little-known Philistine language and script. Surprisingly, the ostracon shows greater affinities

David's "Mini-Empire"

▸ The "Empire" of David

To call the kingdom ruled by David (and later Solomon) an "empire" can be misleading, if one's points of comparison are the massive empires of the ancient Egyptians, Assyrians, Persians, or Romans. The Bible does not describe such an empire for David but, rather, what has been termed a "mini-empire" of limited expanse and duration.[A-23] The summary of David's victories in 2 Samuel 8 speaks of David's "subduing" (lit., "humbling"; Hiphil of *knʿ*) the Philistines (v. 1), of his fighting and conquering the Moabites (v. 2), Zobahites (vv. 3–4), and Arameans (vv. 5–8), and of his receiving congratulatory greetings from Tou, the king of Hamath, who sends gifts by the agency of his son Joram (vv. 9–10). In 8:11–12 the Edomites, Ammonites, and Amalekites are added to the list of peoples "subdued" (Piel of *kbš*) by David.[A-24]

The summary in 2 Samuel 8 of David's kingdom suggests various distinctions. While the Philistines were "humbled," there is no mention of their becoming "servants" of David or of their sending tribute. By contrast Moab and Aram are explicitly reduced to tributary status, as are also, apparently, Edom and Ammon. Hamath welcomes David's defeat of Aram and allies itself to David without the necessity of conquest. Taken together, these data present a multitiered Davidic "empire" comprising *heartland* (Judah and Israel, but not Philistia), *conquered territories* (Edom, Moab, Ammon, and Aram), and *subject-allies* (Hamath).[A-25]

Over these constituent parts of his empire, David gains political control by various means and exercises dominion in different ways. The general concept of a multitiered empire is appropriate to David's time and place in the southern Levant. Three other "mini-empires" in the Late Bronze Age Levant have been inferred from biblical and extrabiblical evidence (especially Hittite hieroglyphic and Mesopotamian cuneiform texts): Aram (with Hadadezer as king), Carchemish, and Tabal.[A-26]

to Hebrew script and orthography than to Phoenician, as might have been expected. Cross remarks that this "points to a period of strong Israelite cultural influence on—and most likely political domination of—the Philistines." He cites the "era of the United Monarchy of David and Solomon" (i.e., "the period when, according to Biblical accounts,

Israel exercised hegemony over the Philistine city-states") as providing the likeliest context.[146]

He took Metheg Ammah from the control of the Philistines (8:1). Whether Metheg Ammah is to be understood as a place name or as two simple common nouns is unclear. If the former, the site is attested only here (but cf. "hill of Ammah" in 2:24) and its location remains unknown. If it is a combination of two common nouns, various readings are possible. One can read the words as "the reins of the forearm," an idiomatic usage suggesting control or supremacy, in this instance over the Philistines. Or, with slight emendation, one can read "the common lands," yielding the sense that David took control of the outlying (nonurban) lands from the Philistines. The parallel phrase in 1 Chronicles 18:1 reads "Gath and its villages [lit., daughters]." Gath was viewed by early rabbinical scholars as the foremost of Philistine cities, so that supremacy over Gath constituted effective supremacy over the Philistines.[147]

Every two lengths of them were put to death (8:2). Unparalleled in biblical and extrabiblical literature, David's method of casting lots[148] to reduce the soldiers of Moab by two-thirds strikes modern readers as cruel and arbitrary, especially in view of the fact that David had earlier trusted the Moabites (1 Sam. 22:3). A case can be made, however, that, in an ancient Near Eastern context in which combatants were often either all sold into slavery or all executed, the sparing of one third of the enemy soldiers to return to their homes is not without mercy.[149] Furthermore, even where defeated combatants were retained as slaves, they were often mutilated (e.g., blinded) to keep them under control (see comment on 1 Sam. 11:2); long-term imprisonment of large numbers of prisoners was not an option, though brief internment was sometimes practiced when repatriation or political negotiations were anticipated.[150]

The Moabites became subject to David and brought tribute (8:2). In the ancient Near East, subjugated territories were expected to send various kinds of tribute (e.g., precious metals and other goods, agricultural produce, livestock, even labor forces). In addition to the symbolic and, indeed, economic value of the conqueror's receiving tribute, this system had the effect of depressing the economy of the conquered land and helping to assure its continued submission, much in the same way that deportation (or, as in the present instance, execution) depleted the workforce and defense forces of the conquered land.

From as early as Sumerian times, references to tribute can be found in the extant literature. Among Egyptian records, the annals of Thutmose III (1479–1425 B.C.) recount not only that the conquered chieftains of Megiddo brought tribute but that they carried it along with the Egyptian army

Subdued enemies lined up on ground; Ramesses II, Karnak
Vanni/Art Resource, NY

Black Obelisk of Shalmaneser III, collecting tribute from Patina
Todd Bolen/www.BiblePlaces.com

as it continued southward: "Now [all] the chieftains, [ca]rried off by the awe of his majesty, bore their tribute of silver, gold, lapis lazuli and copper, bearing grain, wine, cattle and flocks for the army of his majesty; one company of them carried tribute on the journey south."[151]

Assyrian sources contain numerous references to Israel's paying tribute. The most famous instance—that of Jehu bringing tribute and bowing before Shalmaneser III (858–824)—is depicted on the well-known Black Obelisk. Other explicit references to Assyria's exacting tribute from Israel can be found in the records of Adad-nirari III (810–782 B.C.), Tiglath-pileser III (745–727), Sargon II (722–705), Sennacherib (705–681), Esarhaddon (681–669), and Ashurbanipal (668–627).[152]

Hadadezer, son of Rehob, king of Zobah (8:3). Hadadezer (sometimes written Hadarezer) was the name of at least two kings of the Arameans who occupied territory to the north of the Israelite heartland (on the Arameans, see comment on v. 5). The name Hadadezer sounds like "(the god) Hadad is (my) helper." Hadadezer II is mentioned in Assyrian sources as an ally of Ahab, the ninth-century king of Israel, at the battle of Qarqar,[153] while the present Hadadezer, son of Rehob, is mentioned only in the Bible.[154]

The name Rehob, in addition to designating the father (or ancestor) of Hadadezer I, sometimes appears to designate a city central to the Aramaean kingdom of Zobah (cf. 10:6). Its precise location has not been determined, though some assume on the basis of Judges 18:28 (which mentions Dan/Laish in

David's success and influence was such that he was recognized as the founder of the long-lasting dynastic line both in the Bible and in ancient Near Eastern records such as this Aramaic inscription from a century and a half after his time. This inscription contains the clearest reference to David yet found in extra-biblical documents from the Iron Age.
Z. Radovan/www.BibleLand Pictures.com

the vicinity of Beth Rehob) that it must have been situated near the source of the Jordan River. The kingdom of Zobah occupied the northern Beqaᶜ Valley between the Lebanon Mountains on the west and the Anti-Lebanon Mountains on the east.[155]

He went to restore his control along the Euphrates River (8:3). Ambiguity regarding the antecedent of "he" has caused scholars to debate whether David or Hadadezer went to "restore control" (or possibly "set up a monument").[156] On the one hand, it can be argued that, because David would have passed through the territory of Hadadezer en route to the Euphrates River (probably in the vicinity of Emar) and would otherwise not likely have encountered Hadadezer so far north, David went to "restore his control." On the other hand, however, if it was Hadadezer who had to restore order in his northern territories, David may have seized the opportunity of Hadadezer's preoccupation with the north to attack him from the south.[157]

He hamstrung all but a hundred of the chariot horses (8:4). For the general character and uses of chariots in the time of David, see comment on 1 Samuel 13:5. Hamstringing a horse involved cutting the tendon equivalent to the Achilles tendon in humans. By this means David disabled the horses so that they could no longer pull chariots, though they may still have been capable of minor tasks.

The motivation behind David's action is debated. Some have argued that David's military apparatus already had a chariot force and that it was either so well-supplied with horses or so small that he could use only a hundred of the captured horses; the rest, then, were incapacitated, lest they fall again into enemy hands.[158] Alternatively, David's hamstringing of the majority of the horses may have followed historical and theological precedent. According to the so-called "law of the king" in Deuteronomy 17:16, Israel's kings were not to "acquire great numbers of horses." Yahweh had instructed Joshua to hamstring the horses and burn the chariots of the northern coalition of kings, which he did (Josh. 11:6, 9). David's action is thus largely in keeping with these precedents, though retaining a hundred of the chariot horses is perhaps disconcerting, as it may suggest an early stage in a growing reliance on military might (see comment on 24:1).

Two sons of David, Absalom and Adonijah, later dramatize their bids for the throne by preparing chariots and horses and having fifty men run before them (15:1; 1 Kings 1:5; cf. Samuel's warning in 1 Sam 8:11). A third son, Solomon, will become particularly well known for his chariot forces (1 Kings 4:26–28; 9:22; 10:26–29) as well as for the accumulation of wives and wealth, also forbidden by Deuteronomy 17's "law of the king."

He put garrisons in the Aramean kingdom of Damascus (8:6). On the placing of garrisons in conquered territories, see comment on verse 14. The Arameans occupied a broad swath of Mesopotamian territory from the second millennium on. They are frequently mentioned in ancient Near Eastern sources, including texts from Mari and Ugarit, and a city named Aram located in the region of the upper Tigris River is attested already at the beginning of the second millennium. The Bible names Aram among the descendants of Shem (Gen. 10:22–23).[159]

At the beginning of David's reign, various Aramean tribes occupied areas to the north and east of the Israelite heartland. These tribes were distinguished and designated according to the territory they occupied—thus, Aram-Zobah, Aram-Damascus, and so forth.[160] As was the case with many important cities in the ancient Near East, Damascus was located in a favorable spot—an oasis at the crossroads of the two main international highways.[161] At least in part owing to its favored location, Damascus has been continuously occupied up to the present, making serious excavation impracticable and archaeological finds rare and generally late.

Gold shields ... to Jerusalem (8:7). "Gold shields" should probably read "bow (and arrow) cases," a judgment based on Aramaic technical terminology and supportive Semitic cognates.[162]

Tebah and Berothai, towns that belonged to Hadadezer (8:8). As towns of Hadadezer, Tebah and Berothai lay within the territory of Zobah (v. 3).[163]

Tou king of Hamath (8:9). Hamath was a city situated 130 miles north of Damascus along the Orontes River that served as the capital of a Neo-Hittite state stretching from Zobah on the south to the Euphrates River on the northeast. King Tou appears to be of Hurrian (as opposed to Aramean) origin. News of David's defeat of Hadadezer prompts Tou to seek a more amicable, if nevertheless subordinate, relationship with David. On the multitiered character of David's empire, see comment on verse 11.

Sent his son Joram (8:10). That the king of Hamath's son should bear the name Joram ("Yahweh is exalted") seems surprising, and indeed his original name may have been Hadoram ("[the god] Haddu/Hadad is exalted," as in 1 Chron. 18:10).[164] Perhaps the name Joram was adopted or imposed in keeping with Israel's growing dominance under David. The adoption of a second name is a practice "well attested in royal circles throughout the Near East."[165]

King David dedicated these articles to the LORD (8:11). Not only in Israel but in the ancient Near East generally, the "dominant worldview" was that "the gods [or in Israel's case the true God, Yahweh] went before the army, fought the enemy, and awarded the victor his success and the spoils that fell into his hands."[166] Such thinking is clearly implied here by the refrain, Yahweh "gave David victory wherever he went" (vv. 6, 14). In keeping with the belief that God or the gods gave victory, it was appropriate and expected that a valuable portion of the spoils of victory would be dedicated to the deity.

While no battle was fought against Hamath to gain the gifts brought by Joram—"articles of silver and gold and bronze" (v. 10)—it was David's victory over Hadadezer that prompted the king of

Bow (and arrow) case depicted in a Persian relief
Brian J. McMorrow

Hamath to subordinate himself voluntarily to David (see comment on v. 9). While in some instances that which was dedicated to God was killed or destroyed, precious metals were typically placed in the sacred precinct, under the administration of the priests and for the maintenance of the sanctuary (cf. 1 Chron. 26:26–28).[167]

All the nations he had subdued (8:11). See sidebar on "The 'Empire' of David."

David became famous (8:13). The Hebrew reads literally "David made a name," which may recall Yahweh's promise to David in 7:9 that he would make David's "name great, like the names of the greatest men of the earth." Alternatively, "name" may connote a victory monument of some sort.[168] The effect, in either case, is much the same. The Old Assyrian king Shamshi-Adad I (1813–1781 B.C.), for example, boasts: "I established my great name and my steles in the land of Lebanon on the shore of the Great Sea."[169]

Valley of Salt (8:13). Though not positively identified, the Valley of Salt probably lay somewhere to the south or southwest of the Dead Sea (Salt Sea). Credit for striking down 18,000 Edomites in this valley is given to Abishai in 1 Chronicles 18:12 and, if the same encounter is in view in the superscription to Psalm 60, to Joab as well. That kings and their generals should respectively receive credit for victories is not without precedent (perhaps cf. 1 Sam. 13:3–4).

He put garrisons throughout Edom (8:14). It was common practice in the ancient Near East to establish garrisons in subject territories in order to assure communication and control, storage of supplies, monitoring of trade routes, collection of tribute or taxes, and rapid military response to any untoward activities. The placing of garrisons is mentioned frequently in ancient Near Eastern sources. For example, in a fragmentary inscription from the time of Shamshi-Adad I (see first comment on v. 13), the king describes his treatment of territories he had presumably conquered and "reorganized": "I installed my governors everywhere," and "I captured all the fortified cities of the land of Arbela. I established my garrisons everywhere."[170]

Some four centuries later, ʿAbdi-Ḫeba of Jerusalem pleads with his Egyptian overlord to station a garrison in Jerusalem: "May the king, my lord, know (that) no garrison of the king is with me.... And so may the king send 50 men as a garrison to protect the land. The entire land of the king has deser[ted]."[171]

Doing what was just and right for all his people (8:15). To modern ears, the phrase "what was just and right" suggests that which is fair and equitable, as expressed in the proper execution of justice. And, indeed, making correct judicial decisions was certainly part of King David's mandate. But as Weinfeld has demonstrated, at its core the phrase does not refer merely to "the proper execution of justice, but rather expresses, in a general sense, social justice and equity, which is bound up with kindness and mercy."[172] Similar phrases are used in the Hebrew prophets to refer not primarily (if at all) to "the correct execution of justice in court, but rather to the establishment of social justice, and the restoration of equilibrium to the society by aiding the needy: the stranger, widow and orphan."[173] Emphasis on social justice is attested also in ancient Near Eastern texts, as in the following passage from a Neo-Babylonian work:

> He did not neglect the justice of *kitti u mīšari* (truth and equity), judgment and decision, acceptable to Marduk the Great Lord, and established for the good of all men and the settlement of the land of Akkad, he wrote with counsel and wisdom. He enacted the laws of the city for good. He established the laws of the kingdom for all generations.[174]

Having demonstrated that a primary responsibility of kings, both in the Bible and in the wider ancient Near East, was the establishment of just societies, Weinfeld concludes in respect to the passage before us that it "refers to acts of liberation performed by David upon his ascent to the throne, and it reflects a practice known to us from Mesopotamia: the establishment of *mīšarum* upon coronation."[175] The Akkadian term *mīšarum* connotes "equity" in society, similar to the connotation of *mišpaṭ* ("justice") in the Old Testament.[176]

Over the army ... recorder ... priests ... secretary (8:16–17). See the similar, if fuller listing at 20:23–26. See sidebar on "Officials in David's Government."

Benaiah ... over the Kerethites and Pelethites (8:18). A man of outstanding military credentials (23:20–22), Benaiah son of Jehoiada was over the Kerethites and Pelethites, professional troops who served apparently as David's personal army. On the Cretan origin of the Kerethites and the linking of the Pelethites to the Philistines, see comments on 1 Samuel 30:14, 26. Benaiah was intensely loyal to David and later to Solomon (1 Kings 1:8, 36–37) and eventually, after carrying out Solomon's order to execute Joab, became commander-in-chief over Solomon's army (1 Kings 2:34–35; 4:4).

David's sons were royal advisers (8:18). The Hebrew text reads "priests," which is thought to be problematic in view of the biblical investiture of the tribe of Levi with the priesthood. As Armerding has argued, however, the Old Testament actually gives "evidence for several 'orders' of priesthood operative in early Israel, possibly connected with the status of the individual priest (Levite, royal figure, prophetic figure) and possibly relating to particular shrines (Gilgal, Shiloh, Gibeon, Nob, Jerusalem)."[177] David's (and perhaps his sons') was a royal priesthood, partaking of a priest-king tradition in Jerusalem, modeled after that of Mechizedek, who was both "king of Salem" and "priest of God Most High" (Gen. 14:18; cf. Ps. 110:4).

Many of the ancient versions do not call David's sons priests but, rather, "great men" or the like. Moreover, in the parallel Chronicles passage, David's sons are called "chief officials at the king's side" (1 Chron. 18:17). Taking such evidence into account, Wenham has suggested emending Hebrew "priests" (*kōhᵉnîm*) to "administrators (of the royal estates)" (*sōkenîm*), citing as support cognate official titles in Ugaritic and Neo-Assyrian.[178] The Chronicler's reading is not necessarily supportive of the change to "administrators," however, as "chief officials" could just as easily refer to priests,[179] and it is difficult to imagine that "the surprising designation of David's sons as priests" would have "arisen by corruption from an uncontroversial text."[180] In the end, given the multiplicity of priestly roles attested both in the Bible and in the ancient Near East (where royal and familial priests were not uncommon), the notion that David's sons served a (royal) priestly role is less problematic than is sometimes supposed.

David's Custody of Mephibosheth (9:1–13)

Anyone still left of the house of Saul to whom I can show kindness for Jonathan's sake? (9:1). Given the harsh treatment often meted out to former or potential rivals, David's actions are gracious. Note the cruel treatment that the much later Assyrian king Assurbanipal (669–633) gave to those who "had plotted against me": "I fed their corpses, cut into small pieces, to dogs, pigs, *zîbu* -birds, vultures, the birds of the sky and (also) to the fish of the ocean."[181]

Mercenary bodyguards
Z. Radovan/www.BibleLandPictures.com

Officials in David's Government

Each of these titles in 8:16–17 designates a high-ranking official in David's government. Israel's ancient Near Eastern neighbors attest to similar "cabinets" of high-ranking officials.[A-27] For instance, the Neo-Assyrian cabinet included a treasurer, palace herald (commander of the northeastern army?), chief cupbearer (commander of the northern army), chief eunuch (commander of the royal army), chief judge, grand vizier, and commander-in-chief.[A-28]

The fact that in the list of David's officers the chief military commander, Joab (see comment on 2:13), is named first is typical of ancient Near Eastern governments, where the military leader ranked second only to the king himself. Jehoshaphat holds the title of "recorder," an office mentioned here for the first time in the Old Testament. This title has led some to assume that this official's primary responsibilities must have included keeping the state records, but the Hebrew word may better (if inelegantly) be rendered "remembrancer," or herald.[A-29]

In a thorough study of state officials in the Israelite united monarchy, Mettinger concluded on the basis of Mesopotamian and especially Egyptian officials that the "recorder," like the Egyptian "herald," probably had two chief functions: "(a) the task of handling the communications between the king and the country, and (b) the care of the ceremonial at the royal audiences."[A-30] Thus, Jehoshaphat as "recorder" may be compared to both a modern press secretary and a chief of protocol. Jehoshaphat continues his service in this capacity during the administration of Solomon (1 Kings 4:3).

David's court also included two priests: Zadok, mentioned here for the first time in the Old Testament, and Abiathar (1 Sam. 22:20).[A-31] While Zadok and Abiathar both functioned as priests during David's reign, the latter was removed from office by Solomon (1 Kings 1:7–8), thus fulfilling the judgment pronounced on the house of Eli in 1 Samuel 2:31.

The name of David's "secretary," Seraiah, is spelled in several different ways elsewhere in the Old Testament (see 2 Sam. 20:25; 1 Chron. 18:16; possibly 1 Kings 4:3), which may suggest a non-Israelite origin—perhaps Egyptian, in which land the scribal and administrative traditions were well established. The "secretary" was among the highest ranking civil servants (cf. 2 Kings 12:10; 25:19), his duties likely including presiding over the secretariat, where "official documents were written" and where "the State records were kept."[A-32]

Relief from Persepolis shows dignitaries among the Medes and Persians that made up the Persian court.
Brian J. McMorrow

The Bible itself describes instances of rough justice (e.g., Judg. 1:6–7) and even the massacre of rival royal families (1 Kings 15:29). In view of such practices, David's sparing of Mephibosheth is indeed gracious. At the same time, bringing Mephibosheth into the royal court and to the king's table probably also serves David's own interests, as it places Mephibosheth under immediate surveillance (though the text gives no indication that self-interest is among David's motivations). From his own experience, David must recognize the potential dangers of allowing a rival into the royal court (note Ziba's comment in 16:3). Granted, Mephibosheth's crippled condition makes him an unlikely candidate for the throne, but he does have a young son named Mica (9:12).

Crippled in both feet (9:3). See comment on 4:4.

House of Makir son of Ammiel in Lo Debar (9:4). Lo Debar may tentatively be located in Gilead, ten miles north of Mahanaim (see comment on 2:8).[182] Makir son of Ammiel comes to David's aid in 17:27, and his associations suggest that he must have been a man of means, well able to play host to a descendant of Saul's first king. A different Makir (son of Manasseh) is mentioned in Joshua 17:1 as the ancestor of the Gileadites.

I will restore to you the land that belonged to your grandfather Saul (9:7). The practice of making land grants was the prerogative of the king in the ancient Near East, and the early monarchy of David is no exception.[183] See also comment on 19:42.

Dead dog like me (9:8). On this expression of self-deprecation, see comments on 1 Samuel 17:43; 24:14; 2 Samuel 3:8.

David's War with the Ammonite Coalition (10:1–19)

Show kindness to Hanun son of Nahash (10:2). The phrase "show kindness" suggests that a treaty or covenant relationship existed between David and Hanun's father, Nahash, even though it was the latter's aggression toward Israel that had in part contributed to Saul's rise to power (see 1 Sam. 11:1–11; 12:12). David's fugitive period, when he was on the run from Saul, would have been a logical time for him to enter into some kind of agreement with Nahash, and it probably was something akin to a "parity treaty" (between more or less equal partners), as distinguished from a "suzerain-vassal treaty" (between a greater and a lesser power).

Both kinds of treaties are well attested in the ancient Near East.[184] In a parity treaty between the Hittite king Ḫattušiliš III and the Egyptian pharaoh Ramesses II, the two kings agree to mutual nonagression, mutual defense, extradition of fugitives, and even assistance in cases of contested royal accession. All was designed to "establish good peace (and) good brotherhood be[tween us] forever."[185] That Hanun should dishonor David's emissaries is, in essence, to renounce the treaty of peace and wittingly or unwittingly to invite retaliation by David.

Shaved off half of each man's beard (10:4). "In cylinder seals; Assyrian bas-reliefs; ivory plaques from Samaria, Hazor, and Beth-zur; and drawings on pottery vessels from Ein Gedi, Ramat Rahel, and Kuntillet Ajrud, Israelite men are shown with full beards and long hair tied back with a linen band."[186] Beards were sometimes shaved off to express mourning (cf. Isa. 15:2; Jer. 41:5; 48:37), and it may be that Hanun is suspicious of David and decides to make a mockery of his stated intent "to express his sympathy to Hanun concerning his father" (2 Sam. 10:2).

Beards also were considered a sign of manliness. For example, in one of the Mari letters, the Assyrian king Shamshi-Adad challenges his son: "Are you not an adult? Is there no beard on your chin?"[187] Thus, to shave off half the beards of David's envoys was to rob them symbolically of their manhood. As if that were not enough, Hanun also "cut off their garments in the middle at the buttocks." McCarter remarks that the

Bearded Israelites in Assyrian relief of the siege of Lachish
Caryn Reeder, courtesy of the British Museum

combination of shaving the beard and exposing the buttocks "suggests symbolic castration."[188] In the ancient Near East, such acts of disdain, defiance, or disloyalty typically elicited strong responses from the affronted party or power, and David's response to Hanun's affront was to be expected.

Beth Rehob and Zobah ... Maacah ... Tob (10:6). Fearing David's retaliation, Hanun loses no time in hiring additional troops from his neighbors to the north. Such coalitions, whether based on payment or concern with a common enemy, were common in the ancient Near East and are frequently described in the Bible. Hanun seeks help from his closest neighbors to the north of Ammonite territory. On the location of Beth Rehob and Zobah in relation to Ammon and the heartland of David's kingdom, see comment on 8:3, 6 and accompanying maps. Maacah lay to the south of Aram-Zobah, in the Golan, northeast of the Sea of Galilee and south of Mount Hermon. Tob (usually identified with present-day eṭ-Ṭaiyibeh) lay some twelve miles southeast of the Sea of Galilee.

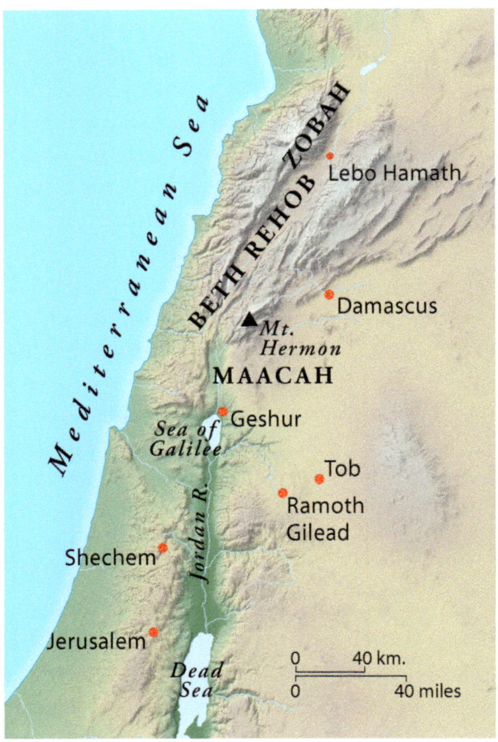

Aramean and Ammonite Coalition

Battle lines in front of him and behind him (10:9). As Herzog and Gichon point out, "any soldier with combat experience will agree that repulsing an enemy while being attacked in both front and rear is in itself no mean achievement."[189] How Joab finds himself caught between the Aramean and the Ammonite forces is a matter of conjecture. Yadin suggests that Joab makes a tactical mistake by marching directly to Rabbah (the probable Ammonite city of v. 8; modern Amman) via Jericho or Heshbon (see map of possible routes), rather than crossing the Jordan at Adam (Tell ed-Dâmijeh) and intercepting the Aramean forces in the region of Helam (a considerable distance north of Rabbah), as David apparently does in verse 17.[190]

Whether Joab arrives in his initial predicament by strategic error or simply because it cannot be avoided, his decision to divide his troops and fight on two fronts is, though risky, ultimately successful, at least to the point of a draw. No enemy casualties are mentioned in the text, however, only the enemy's flight, with the Ammonites escaping to the safety of their city, after which Joab returns to Jerusalem. It remains for David, in a second encounter, to soundly defeat the Arameans (vv. 15–19).

Hadadezer (10:16). See comment on 8:3. The Arameans, perhaps embarrassed by their hasty retreat, do not take long to regroup (10:15). Hadadezer, as one of the foremost Aramean leaders, musters reinforcements even from beyond the Euphrates and redeploys in the region of Helam. There they suffer a crushing defeat at the hands of David (vv. 17–18), eventuating in significant political realignments. Hadadezer's former vassals desert to make peace with David and become subject to him (v. 19).

Shifting political allegiances in accordance with the fortunes of war were commonplace in the ancient Near East. A clear example is provided by the ninth-century Assyrian king Ashurnasirpal II, who reports the results of a campaign to Carchemish and the Lebanon as follows: "I took over the chariot (-corps), the cavalry (and) the infantry of Carchemish. The kings of all (surrounding) countries came to me, embraced my feet and I took hostages from them and they marched (with me) towards the Lebanon (*Lab-na-na*) forming my vanguard."[191] David's relationships to the different tiers of his kingdom—heartland, conquests (as here), and subject allies—likely varied in scope and character (see sidebar on "The 'Empire' of David" at 8:1).

Helam (10:16). See comment on 10:9.

Made peace with the Israelites and became subject to them (10:19). See comment on 10:16.

So the Arameans were afraid to help the Ammonites anymore (10:19). This notice prepares the reader for the second assault on the Ammonite capital at Rabbah (modern Amman), recounted in chapter 11.

David, Bathsheba, and Uriah (11:1–27)

In the spring, at the time when kings go off to war (11:1). As straightforward as this notice seems in English translation, it is not without complications in the Hebrew text, which reads literally "return of the year" in place of "spring" and "messengers" instead of "kings"—that is, "at the return of the year, at the time of the messengers' going forth." This has led to the suggestion that the campaign described in this chapter is launched on the one-year anniversary of David's first sending of a delegation to Hanun, the new king of the Ammonites (10:2). The first delegation was treated shamefully by Hanun (see comment on 10:4), and the timing of the present delegation leaves no doubt of its retaliatory purpose.[192]

The more traditional reading (reflected in the NIV) is not without defense, however; for example, the Hebrew words "king" and "messenger" sound and are spelled much alike (differing only by one "silent" consonant), making confusion in transmission a possibility. Further, the Hebrew verb meaning "go forth" is often used for "going forth (to battle/war)." In any case, the spring of the year was a typical time for military campaigning in the ancient Near East; the winter rains have stopped and the labor-intensive harvest time has not yet arrived; thus, able-bodied men are available for military exploits.

Assyrian and Babylonian annals, which often mention the month in which a military campaign was launched, typically name the first month of the year (Nisanu) or the second (Aiaru), the new year beginning in the springtime.[193] Other events occurring in various months are, of course, mentioned, but the beginnings of military operations are typically linked to the spring months. A typical entry, from the annals of the Neo-Babylonian king Nabopolassar (625–605 B.C.), reads: "Sixteenth year: In the month of Aiaru, the king of Akkad called up his army and marched against Assyria."[194]

Besieged Rabbah (11:1). See comment on 10:9.

Clay figurine of a woman bathing found at Achzib; Iron Age I
Z. Radovan/www.BibleLandPictures.com

Got up from his bed and walked around on the roof (11:2). On the architecture of houses in this period, which typically had flat roofs, see comment on 1 Samuel 9:25.

He saw a woman bathing (11:2). As 11:4 indicates, Bathsheba's bathing was likely the purification rite prescribed in Leviticus 15:19–24 that followed menstruation. The reason for Bathsheba's bathing in a place where she could be seen is not explored by the narrator, whose only concern at this point is with the irresponsible actions of the king.

The daughter of Eliam and the wife of Uriah the Hittite (11:3). On the character and origin of the Hittites in Canaan, see comments on 1 Samuel 26:6; 2 Samuel 5:6. As with other people groups living among the Israelites, the Hittites may have served as mercenaries for David or as part of his personal troops, as did the Kerethites and Pelethites (see comments on 1 Sam. 27:2; 30:14). Uriah the Hittite is listed as the last of David's "mighty men" (2 Sam. 23:39).

Given the typically economic style of biblical narratives, the explicit naming of Bathsheba's father invites explanation. If he was the same Eliam as is mentioned in 23:34, "Eliam son of Ahithophel," then the fact the Ahithophel was Bathsheba's grandfather may help to explain Ahithophel's later betrayal of David in favor of Absalom's conspiracy (15:12; 16:15). Absalom was aggrieved over David's failure to execute justice (15:4, 6), and Ahithophel would certainly have nursed a similar grievance; note especially Ahithophel's counsel in 16:20–21 that Absalom should "lie with" his father's concubines, an action carried out on the roof of the palace where David first espied Bathsheba!

She had purified herself from her uncleanness (11:4). This notice eliminates any possibility that Bathsheba could have been pregnant by her husband, thus complicating David's attempt to cover up his misdeed.

Go down to your house and wash your feet (11:8). Whether the suggestion that "wash your feet" was a euphemism for sexual intercourse is true or not, Uriah certainly understood what David was getting at (v. 11). If sexual abstinence was a requirement for soldiers on active duty, as may be inferred from 1 Samuel 21:5 (cf. also Deut. 23:10), David may have been seeking to entrap Uriah in a ritual infraction and thereby to find legal grounds for eliminating him. In any case, David's hope was that Uriah would sleep with Bathsheba and thus cloud the paternity issue. Uriah's refusal to indulge himself while the armies of Israel were in the field must have been a stinging rebuke to David, whether Uriah intended it to be so or

Wall of what is believed by some archaeologists to be the palace of David in Jerusalem
Todd Bolen/www.BiblePlaces.com

not (we are left in the dark about what Uriah did or did not know of David's affair).

David wrote a letter to Joab (11:14). On literacy in Israel at the time of David, see comments on 1 Samuel 4:1; 10:25. While there is no other instance in the Bible of someone carrying a letter sealing his own doom, a parallel of sorts can be found in Homer's *Iliad* in Glaukos's description of his descent from the noble Bellerophontes (note also similarities to the account of Joseph and the wife of Potiphar in Gen. 39).[195]

Didn't a woman throw an upper millstone on him? (11:21). The allusion is to Judges 9:50–53. An upper millstone, not to be confused with the much larger upper stone of a wheel mill, probably weighed less than ten pounds.[196]

She mourned for him (11:26). For discussion of typical ancient Near Eastern and biblical mourning rites, see comment on 1 Samuel 4:12. The biblical text offers no indication of Bathsheba's feelings for Uriah, except to observe that she mourned for him for seven days, which may have been a customary period (cf. Gen. 50:10; 1 Sam. 31:13). National leaders were sometimes mourned for longer periods; Aaron and Moses were each mourned for thirty days (Num. 20:29; Deut. 34:8), and the Egyptians mourned for Jacob a full seventy days (Gen. 50:3). A chronicle from the reign of the Neo-Babylonian king Nabonidus (556–539 B.C.) states that when the wife of the king died, she was mourned "from the 27th day of Arahshamnu till the 3rd day of Nisanu"—over four months![197]

Nathan Rebukes David (12:1–14)

The LORD sent Nathan to David (12:1). While Nathan's parable does not speak of adultery and murder per se, Nathan's "rich man" does resemble David in two respects: first, he ignored the many sheep he had and took the one precious lamb of the poor man (a lamb that was like a "daughter" to him; Heb. *bat* ["daughter"] is the first syllable of the name Bathsheba); second, he followed his first offense with an act of audacious hypocrisy (i.e., his apparent show of hospitality in v. 4). Fundamentally, the rich man's crime involved an abuse of power, as did David's. In the ancient Near East, the king was to protect the socially weak; he was the executor of "justice in the land" at the behest of the gods who installed him. Hammurabi was not the only one who saw his primary task as guaranteeing "that the strong does no injustice to the weak."[198]

Millstone
Z. Radovan/www.BibleLandPictures.com

Like a daughter to him (12:3). See preceding comment.

He must pay for that lamb four times over (12:6). While David's emotional response is that the offender should die (v. 5), he restrains himself to remain within the law. Fourfold restitution for sheep theft is mandated in Exodus 22:1. While some commentators detect here a hint of David's subsequent loss of four sons—the first son of Bathsheba (vv. 14, 18), Amnon (13:28–29), Absalom (18:14–15), and Adonijah (1 Kings 2:24–25)—the LXX, perhaps in the interest of a further reminder of Bathsheba, reads "sevenfold" (instead of fourfold); the number "seven" (Heb. *šeba*ᶜ) corresponds to the second element in the name Bathsheba.

Man carrying small lamb
Erich Lessing/Art Resource, NY, National Museum, Aleppo, Syria

The Law Code of Hammurabi required thirtyfold restitution for theft of livestock from church or state and tenfold for theft from private citizen; should the offender be unable to make restitution, he was to die.[199]

I gave your master's house to you, and your master's wives into your arms (12:8). This statement (indeed all of ch. 12) should be read in the context of power—its use and abuse—and not as a comment on the (im)propriety of polygamy (on the latter issue, see comment on 1 Sam. 1:2). In the ancient Near East, the royal harem of a former monarch became the responsibility of a new king, if only to honor diplomatic relationships established through royal marriages. Indeed, "one way royal legitimacy was acquired was by the appropriation of the previous king's harem, both in Israel and in the rest of the ancient Near East."[200] In the present context, the point is that David has been given all that was Saul's and more, even "the house of Israel and Judah." And had that been too little, Yahweh would have given even more. How dare David, then, defraud a subordinate first of his wife and then of his life!

He will lie with your wives in broad daylight (12:11). This pronouncement is fulfilled in 16:21–22 by David's son Absalom. In addition to its gross immorality, such an act constituted a usurpation of David's power and throne (see comment on 3:7). As a loose analogy, one may compare the curse invoked in one of Esarhaddon's vassal treaties: "May Venus, the brightest among the stars, let your wives lie in the embrace of your enemy before your very eyes, may your sons not have authority over your house, may a foreign enemy divide your possessions."[201]

The son born to you will die (12:14). A prophecy predicting the death of a royal infant is found also in the Mari letters. Malamat offers a reconstruction of the fairly damaged Mari text and discusses its comparisons and contrasts with this episode in the life of David.[202] Beyond the basic similarities (e.g., the "concern for the public behavior of the king in time of misery and grief"), Nathan's oracle differs from its Mari counterpart by its "blatantly moral impetus"—the child's death is the result of David's adultery with Bathsheba and murder of her husband Uriah. As Malamat notes, "such an ethical motive and the idea of retribution usually set the Bible apart when compared with the prosaic, pragmatic reports known from Mari."[203]

The Child of David and Bathsheba Dies (12:15–25)

He fasted and went into his house and spent the nights lying on the ground (12:16). Having fasted *after* the deaths of Saul and Jonathan (see comment on 2 Sam. 1:12) and Abner (3:35), David fasts *prior to* the death of the child born of his illicit relationship with Bathsheba, but not after. Some suggest that the baby's death serves as a kind of atonement for David's sin of adultery, thus rendering "normal mourning customs ... inapplicable."[204] More to the point, however, is the statement with which verse 16 begins: "David pleaded with God for the child."

David knows (as others do not) that the child's life has been pronounced forfeit because of David's own sin (v. 14). His nights spent lying on the ground may well have been in the "house" of Yahweh (cf. v. 20) rather than his own house (the Heb. text does not specify, but reads only "he entered"; on Yahweh's "house," see comment on 1 Sam. 1:9). He also fasts (on fasting rites in general, see comments on 1 Sam. 7:6; 2 Sam. 1:12). The ancient Near East attests many prayers of petition to the various gods. A Neo-Babylonian prayer to the goddess Ishtar, for example, pleads: "Faithfully look upon me and hear my supplication.... Pity! For my afflicted house."[205]

Solomon ... Jedidiah (12:24–25). In the ancient Near East, naming meant more than assigning a label for purposes of identification. Rather, a name was to capture something of the essence of an individual. Thus, names were not usually decided in advance of birth but were usually triggered by something that happened or was said in connection with the birth (cf. the naming of Samuel [1 Sam. 1:20] and of Ichabod [4:21]).

The Sumerian mother goddess, for example, describes herself as the "good midwife of the gods" who says "only that which is wise at the time of birth."[206] The name "Solomon" sounds something like the Hebrew word for "peace" (cf. 1 Chron. 22:9) as well as the word "replacement" (i.e., for the first child of Bathsheba, which died). The name Jedidiah sounds like "beloved of Yah(weh)" and must have signaled hope for the future of the Davidic house, a hope in keeping with the remarkable promises made in 7:14–15.[207]

Ammonite deity wearing ceremonial crown

Z. Radovan/www.BibleLand Pictures.com

David Captures Rabbah (12:26–31)

Rabbah of the Ammonites (12:26). See comment on 10:9.

Royal citadel ... water supply (12:26–27). Joab's notice that both the royal citadel and water supply have been taken is sufficient to indicate that Rabbah cannot withstand Israelite pressure much longer. In the ancient Near East, particularly in the semiarid regions east and west of the Jordan, cities could not hold out under siege once their water supply was cut off. Conversely, elaborate water works were often constructed to secure access to springs and other water supplies.

He took the crown (12:30). This crown is quite different from Saul's lightweight crown, or diadem, that was handed over to David in 1:10. Not only is it described with a different Hebrew word, but its weight of almost seventy-five pounds would make it difficult to wear for any length of time, much less to wear into battle. The NIV retains the traditional reading "their king" (Heb. *malkām*), but it is far more likely (as in the NIV text note) that the crown sat atop a statue representing the Ammonites' god Milkom (Heb. *milkōm*), or Molech (according to the bastardization of the word in the Bible; on the vocalization of objectionable words to resonate with the word for "shame," see comment on 1 Sam. 7:4).

As for what is placed on David's head, either it is the crown itself, if only for a short period, or perhaps, as McCarter has suggested, the "precious stone" (singular in Heb.) that was set in the crown.[208] Ammonite statues showing individuals (gods or kings) wearing large crowns have survived to the present day.

Amnon and Tamar (13:1–22)

He raped her (13:14). Did Amnon's crime involve rape only, or did it also contravene prohibitions against incest? Tamar was Amnon's half-sister; both were children of King David but by different mothers. Incestuous relationships were condemned not just in Israel (e.g., Lev. 18:9, 11; 20:17; Deut. 27:22) but to a greater or lesser degree in the ancient Near East generally. See sidebar on "Brother-Sister Marriages in the Ancient World" for more on this issue.

Brother-Sister Marriages in the Ancient World

Although classical writers tended to "stress the prevalence of incest" among the ancient Egyptians, the fact is, as G. Pinch notes, that "except in the royal family, brother-sister marriages seem to have been very rare in Egypt before Roman times."[A-33] Among the Elamites of second-millennium Iran, royal incest appears to have been practiced, the son of a union between a king and his royal sister having greater legitimacy than a son born of a king and a woman who did not belong to his family; a son born of a union between the king and his daughter had higher legitimacy still.[A-34] In Hittite law, "incest was considered a serious offense, an execrable action ... and thus worthy of death."[A-35]

While some have argued that the prohibition of incest may not have yet been in force in David's day, this seems unlikely. The citation of Abraham's marriage to his half-sister Sarah (Gen. 20:12) proves nothing, as Abraham and Sarah preceded by some centuries the Mosaic legislation condemning consanguinous sexual relations. Nor can one deduce much from the present episode. In seeking to fend off Amnon's unwanted advance, Tamar asserts that if only Amnon would request to marry her, David the king "will not keep me from being married to you" (v. 13). But given the extremity of her situation, her assertion should not be taken at face value, as some commentators have done.

Gordon and Rendsburg, for example, assume that a marriage between Amnon and his half-sister "would have been permissible as the biblical text informs us."[A-36] This would make Amnon guilty of rape but not incest. Almost certainly, however, Amnon is guilty of both. His frustration "to the point of illness" over the impossibility of his "do[ing] anything to her" (v. 2), makes best sense against the backdrop of a ban on incest. Furthermore, as McCarter notes, "while our sources are very candid about, for example, foreign marriages made by the royal family in the time of the early monarchy, no sibling marriage is mentioned, and it seems probable that some kind of prohibition was in effect."[A-37]

A mourning woman puts dust on her head.
The Yorck Project/ Wikimedia Commons

Tamar put ashes on her head and tore the ornamented robe she was wearing (13:19). Robes signifying particular standing or offices figure prominently in 1–2 Samuel, as indeed throughout much of the ancient Near East (see comments on 1 Sam. 2:19; 18:3–4). The ornamented robe Tamar wore (v. 18) would likely have marked her as a virgin daughter of the king. Her tearing of this robe not only demonstrates her anguish, it also dramatically underscores her changed status. Putting dust or ashes on the head was a gesture of mourning and distress throughout the ancient Near East (see comment on 1 Sam. 4:12).

Absalom's Revenge (13:23–39)

Absalom's sheepshearers were at Baal Hazor (13:23). Baal Hazor is generally identified with Jebel ʿAṣûr, some two miles northwest of Ophrah (see comment on 1 Sam. 13:17) and almost fourteen miles north of Jerusalem.[209] Sheepshearing (see comment on 1 Sam. 25:4, 16) was an occasion of celebration, abundance, and generosity. Thus an invitation to join the shearing party would normally be most welcome. The fourteen-mile distance between Jerusalem and Absalom's sheepshearers is short enough to make an invitation to David and his sons plausible, but long enough to mask Absalom's true intent. Given the wrong that Amnon committed against Absalom's sister Tamar, David's granting of Absalom's request that Amnon, specifically, come to the shearing (vv. 26–27) is mystifying to say the least.

The king stood up, tore his clothes and lay down on the ground (13:31). On these actions as signs of deep distress and foreboding, see comments on 1 Samuel 4:12; 28:20; 2 Samuel 1:11. As David tears his clothes in anguished response to the violence commited by his son Absalom, so Esarhaddon, crown prince of Assyria, later rent his garments in anguished response to the violence of his brothers.[210]

Talmai son of Ammihud, the king of Geshur (13:37). Talmai was Absalom's maternal grandfather (cf. 3:3). Several places were named Geshur in the Old Testament (see comment on 1 Sam. 27:8). The Geshur in view here lay in Transjordan, in the southern part of the Golan Heights. Outside the Bible, Geshur may be mentioned in the Egyptian Execration texts and the Amarna letters.[211] Absalom's flight takes him more than fifty miles farther north and across the Jordan River, where he remains in exile for three years.

Joab Engineers Absalom's Return to Jerusalem (14:1–33)

Tekoa (14:2). Most famous as the birthplace of the eighth-century prophet Amos, Tekoa has been identified with Khirbet Teqûᶜ, a village situated some ten miles south of Jerusalem. By bringing a woman from outside Jerusalem, Joab probably hopes to improve the chances that she can fool David.

Wise woman (14:2). While the designation "wise woman" has not yet been discovered outside the Bible, women in the ancient Near East did sometimes fulfill priestly, prophetic, or other religious or civic functions. The Old Testament also cites women as fulfilling prophetic (though not priestly) and other roles. In the books of Samuel, two women are specifically called "wise"—the one here and another at 20:16, where a "wise woman" intervenes decisively to save the city of Abel. Abigail should probably be included as well, though she is not explicitly called a "wise woman" (see 1 Sam. 25).

The "wisdom" in view seems to connote skill in speech capable of persuading someone to follow a certain course of action (cf. the "wisdom" of Jonadab in 13:3 [NIV "very shrewd"]). That such wisdom was highly prized in the ancient Near East is illustrated, for example, in the so-called Protests of the Eloquent Peasant,[212] in which a wronged peasant is retained at court simply to regale

Geshur

Horus stands on the back of Seth, portrayed as a hippopotamus, in the visualization of the myth of the battle between Horus and Seth in the temple at Esna.
Angeline Law and Michael Szeto

the courtiers with his eloquent and persuasive speeches.[213]

Joab put the words in her mouth (14:3). By prompting the wise woman of Tekoa to raise issues of blood revenge (see comment on v. 11) and the survival of her family line on its ancestral property, Joab covertly forces David to render a verdict on the very issues he is facing, namely, his duty to avenge the blood of Amnon but his desire that Absalom not be cut off. The dynamic of the present episode recalls an earlier occasion in which David was drawn by a fictional story into indicting himself (2 Sam. 12). An analogue to the present scenario of disguise, deception, and self-indictment is found in the Egyptian Myth of Horus and Seth, in which Isis, the mother of Horus, disguises herself as a maiden and tricks Seth into pronouncing a verdict against himself and in favor of Horus.[214]

Get rid of the heir ... put out the only burning coal I have left (14:7). The paralleling of "heir" and "burning coal" is in keeping with the virtually universal use of the hearthfire to symbolize family life. Not only in the Bible does light/lamp symbolize life and hope (e.g., 2 Sam. 21:17; Job 18:5–6) but in the ancient Near East as well. Mesopotamian texts speak of family misfortune metaphorically as the oven or hearthfire being extinguished.[215] In Sumerian, the word "heir" may connote "one who keeps the oil (lamp) burning."[216]

Absalom's Conspiracy (15:1–12)

Chariot and horses and with fifty men to run ahead (15:1). For this "royal" behavior, see comment on 1 Samuel 8:11–17 (cf. also Adonijah in 1 Kings 1:5).

If only I were appointed judge (15:4). Absalom does not directly challenge his father's right to be king, but by questioning the administration of justice under David he effectively plants seeds of discontent. First and foremost among the responsibilities of the ancient Near Eastern king was the administration of justice (see comment on 8:15; cf. 5:12; 12:1–4; 1 Sam. 12:3). In the prologue to his law code, Hammurabi writes: "When Marduk commissioned me to guide the people aright, to direct the land, I established law and justice in the language of the land, thereby promoting the welfare of the people."[217] Similarly, Ur-Nammu, king of Ur, established "equity in the land" and "he banished malediction, violence and strife."[218]

In Israel, too, as Weinfeld succinctly puts it, "the establishment of a just society is the responsibility of the king."[219] The Ugaritic Kirta (Keret) Epic closes with a striking parallel example of a son challenging his royal father over the issue of justice:

> You do not judge the cause of the widow,
> you do not try the case of the importunate.
> You do not banish extortioners of the poor,
> you do not feed the orphan before your face
> (nor) the widow behind your back ... come
> down from the (throne of your) kingdom
> (that) I may be king, from (the seat of) your
> dominion (that) even I may sit (on it).[220]

Ahithophel the Gilonite (15:12). See comment on 11:3.

David's Flight (15:13–37)

Kerethites and Pelethites (15:18). See comment on 1 Samuel 30:14, 26.

Six hundred Gittites (15:18). These troops (mercenaries) from Gath were probably drawn to David during his stay in the territory of Achish, ruler of Gath (1 Sam. 27ff.).

Ittai the Gittite (15:19). The etymology of Ittai is unclear. One of the more intriguing suggestions, given Ittai's Philistine connections, likens the name to that of a governor of the Philistine city of Ashkelon, known from the Amarna letters. The governor, who lived some four centuries before David, was called Yidya or Idiya or, perhaps, Itiya or Witiya.[221] The loyalty of Ittai is striking and his introduction in the narrative at just this point is appropriate, as his status as a foreigner exiled from his home not only recalls the days of David's youth but mirrors David's current situation as well.[222]

Zadok ... Abiathar (15:24). See comment on 8:16–17.

Aren't you a seer? (15:27). David's words suggest a plausible excuse for Zadok to return, but they also cleverly suggest the helpful role he can play as a spy. On "seer," see comments on 1 Samuel 3:1; 9:9.

I will wait at the fords in the desert (15:28). As 17:16 indicates, the fords in question are at the Jordan River, almost twenty miles east of Jerusalem. David and his followers are undoubtedly exhausted after covering that distance, and overnighting on the west side of the Jordan serves the symbolic purpose of not abandoning the land entirely.

His head was covered and he was barefoot (15:30). Both are signs of sorrow and distress (cf. Est. 6:12; Isa. 20:2–4; Jer. 14:3–4; Mic. 1:8).

The summit, where people used to worship God (15:32). The identity and location of this place of worship has not been determined. One suggestion is the priestly town of Nob, which lay within a couple of miles of Jerusalem (see comment on 1 Sam. 21:1) and whose priests were massacred by Saul (22:19), thus perhaps the present notice that "people used to worship" there.

David's Encounter with Shimei (16:1–14)

David approached Bahurim ... Shimei son of Gera ... cursed (16:5). Shimei, as a kinsman of Saul, may hold David responsible for the deaths of Abner and Ish-Bosheth, and he probably resents David's permitting the execution of seven of Saul's descendants by the Gibeonites (see 21:1–14). Furthermore, as a resident of Bahurim, Shimei may have witnessed David's treatment of Michal, Saul's daughter, since it was at Bahurim that Paltiel, Michal's second husband, was ordered to cease following after his wife as she was being forcibly returned to David (3:16). The underlying grievance, of course, is that the kingdom once held by Saul, the Benjamite, has been forfeited to David.

Movements of David and Absalom

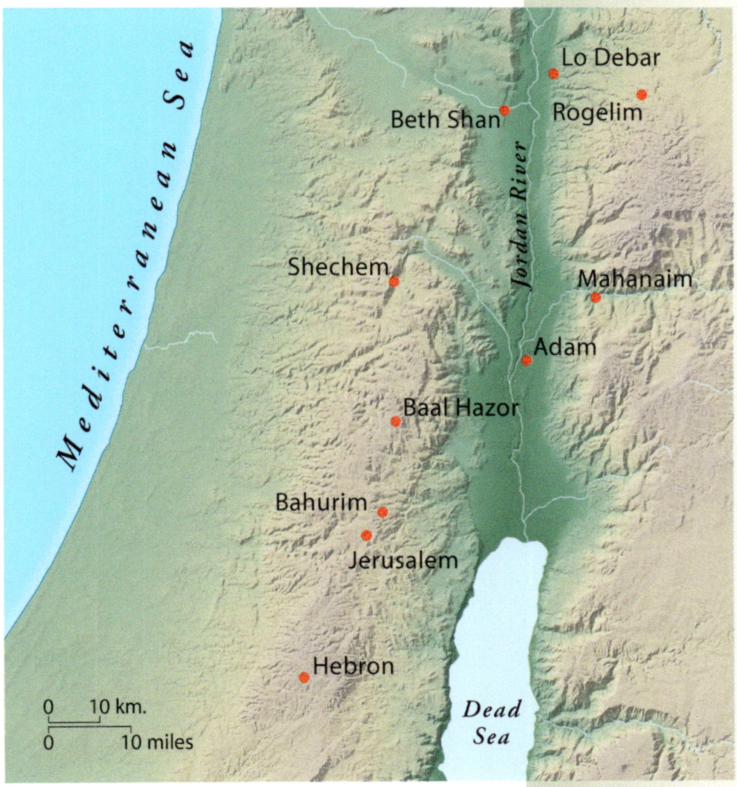

Absalom's Counselors: Hushai and Ahithophel (16:15–17:14)

Hushai the Arkite, David's friend (16:16). The word "friend" (*rēʿeh*) is not the usual Hebrew word for "friend" (*rēaʿ*), though it looks much like it, and it may actually represent a borrowing from the "Egyptian honoric *rḫ nsw*, 'acquaintance of the king.'" In other words, "friend of David" may have been an official court title held by Hushai in David's government, a sort of "privy counselor."[223]

This theory, argued earlier by de Vaux,[224] finds support from the fact that "Egyptian titles were used at David's court" and the fact that an Amarna letter from fourteenth-century Jerusalem seems to attest a similar title (*ru-ḫi šarri*).[225] In this light, Absalom's questions to Hushai in verse 17, twice using the normal Hebrew word for "friend," must be seen as involving an ironic wordplay something like this, "Is this how you show friendship to the one you serve as Friend?"

Lie with your father's concubines (16:21). In the ancient Near East a king's wives and concubines were regarded as indicative of his power and position (see comment on 3:7). Their acquisition often involved diplomacy or conquest. For an outsider to sleep with a member of the royal harem, therefore, was a direct affront to the monarch and tantamount to usurpation. The Assyrian king Sennacherib boasts of divesting King Hezekiah of his "daughters, concubines," and much else besides;[226] he did much the same to Merodach-Baladan of Babylon, entering his palace, taking charge of "the property and goods (laid up) therein," including "his wife, his harem," and so forth.[227] Ahithophel knows whereof he speaks when he says that Absalom's lying with his father's concubines will make him "a stench in your father's nostrils."

I would choose twelve thousand men and set out tonight (17:1). As discussed at 1 Samuel 4:10, the word "thousand" in Hebrew may in some contexts mean "unit" or even "clan." Thus, while 12,000 men is certainly a possible number, Ahithophel may not have been suggesting such a large force but, rather, a select force of crack troops (perhaps even one "unit" from each of the twelve tribes). The gist of his suggestion is that Absalom should exploit David's exhaustion and disorientation by a swift strike.

Ahithophel's military strategy is in fact good, as initially acknowledged by Absalom and the elders of Israel (v. 4) as well as by the biblical narrator himself (v. 14). But it was never tested, because Yahweh "had determined to frustrate the good advice of Ahithophel" (v. 14).

All Israel, from Dan to Beersheba (17:11). Hushai's counsel is the opposite of Ahithophel's. Not swift action but overwhelming force is the key. It is far better, he argues, for Absalom to gather "all Israel, from Dan to Beersheba" and to march into battle at the head of a force as "numerous as the

Qumran War Scroll
Z. Radovan/www.BibleLandPictures.com

sand on the seashore." Such a force can easily defeat David as certainly and effortlessly as "dew [that] settles on the ground" (v. 12).

Such a scenario may have appealed to Absalom's pride (cf. 14:26; 18:18). Though not found elsewhere in the Bible, the use of "dew" (or "light rain") as a military metaphor is attested in the War Scroll from Qumran: "The war hero is in our congregation; the army of his spirits, with our infantry and our cavalry. They are like clouds and dew to cover the earth, like torrential rain which pours justice on all that grows" (1QM 12:9–10a).[228]

All Israel will bring ropes to that city, and we will drag it down to the valley (17:13). The reference to "ropes" and to dragging the city down to the valley may imply the use of grappling hooks attached to ropes as a means of surmounting walls and destroying them. Reliefs from the ancient Near East depict various means of breaching and surmounting city walls, including the use of battering rams, siege towers, scaling ladders, and so forth. In addition, as Saggs explains, "sappers" sometimes "mined tunnels to bring about the collapse of sections of walls."[229] That the Hebrew root *ḥbl*, used by Hushai for "ropes," can also mean "destruction" and, in a verbal form, "to pull down," may have influenced the narrator's choice of words.

David's Escape (17:15–29)

Jonathan and Ahimaaz were staying at En Rogel (17:17). Jonathan and Ahimaaz are introduced as sons of the priests Abiathar and Zadok, respectively (15:27). All four (cf. 17:15) play a stragetic role in David's information gathering. En Rogel was a spring outside the walls of Jerusalem south of the Gihon Spring in the Kidron Valley. It has been identified with Bîr Ayyûb ("Job's Well"). Because springs and wells were visited many times a day by people porting water back into the city, they served as good spots for gathering information without attracting notice. But on this occasion, Jonathan and Ahimaaz are noticed, necessitating their flight to Bahurim, two miles northeast, where they hide in a well until danger passes (vv. 18–19).

Went to the house of a man in Bahurim (17:18). Bahurim was the site of Shimei's cursing (16:5). That Jonathan and Ahimaaz are able to find an ally there indicates that David is not without supporters even in this Saulide village.

Took a covering and spread it out over the opening of the well (17:19). Because of the semiarid climate of the land of Palestine, wells were both numerous and important. King and Stager report that the Philistine city of Ashkelon evidences more than a hundred wells "dating from the Philistine period to the present."[230] Wells were constructed by digging a vertical shaft down to the water table. The top opening of wells was typically five to six and a half feet in diameter, and the depth varied depending on the water table—one well discovered at Lachish was about 140 feet deep! To prevent collapse, the shafts of wells were often lined with field stones, and to prevent contamination of the water or danger to unwary people or animals, the opening was covered in some way (e.g., with a stone slab).[231] Flat covers could be disguised so as to prevent discovery of the well, as appears to have been done in the present episode.

He put his house in order and then hanged himself (17:23). Wise enough to recognize that Absalom's failure to follow

Lachish well
Dr. Tim Bulkeley, www.eBibleTools.com

his advice will lead to a victory and a return to power for David, Ahithophel understands that his life will end because of his treason. In taking his own life, he probably feels that he is only hastening the inevitable (after having put his house in order).

The Hebrew Bible does not contain any explicit evaluation of suicide, but of the six reported incidents, Abimelech and Saul are hardly to be read as heroic in their actions (see comment on 1 Sam. 31:4), Saul's armor-bearer is a lesser character who simply demonstrates loyalty to his deceased master, Samson gave his life not so much as an act of suicide but in order to rain down a crushing defeat on the Philistines, and the erstwhile Israelite king Zimri (like Ahithophel) understood that his failed power play left him with little hope of survival (1 Kings 16:18). Given the overall understanding that life is in the hands of a sovereign God who gives life and takes it away, suicide is hardly viewed as an honorable option.

In ancient Mesopotamian thought, suicide was apparently "not an act of defiance against the gods or even of vengeance on those who are thought to have wronged a person but a means of retrieving honor."[232] In ancient Egypt, "suicide was not an approved way to escape harsh realities and to begin a glorified existence in the afterlife," though in the New Kingdom, "suicide was an option allowed to the highest-ranking individuals who had been found guilty of capital crimes."[233]

David went to Mahanaim (17:24). On Mahanaim, see comment on 2 Samuel 2:8.

Absalom's Death (18:1–18)

Commanders of thousands and commanders of hundreds (18:1). These appear to be standard designations for military officers (cf. 1 Sam. 22:7).

A third under the command of Joab, a third under Joab's brother Abishai son of Zeruiah, and a third under Ittai the Gittite (18:2). On the three commanders, see comments on 1 Samuel 26:6; 2 Samuel 2:13; 15:19. With David having been convinced to remain behind (18:3–4), Joab was probably first among the three commanders.

Forest of Ephraim (18:6). That the forest in which the battle took place is called the Forest of Ephraim is puzzling at first glance. The tribe of Ephraim lived west of the Jordan, and yet the present context suggests that the battle likely took place near Mahanaim east of the Jordan—Absalom was pursuing David, not the reverse. Perhaps Judges 12:4, which refers to Gileadites as "renegades" or "fugitives" from Ephraim, suggests a solution. The presence of such Ephraimites east of the Jordan may account for the forest of Ephraim. Regarding the forest's specific location, Noth observed that "a well-wooded mountain country that had hardly been opened up at all" existed on both sides of the Jabbok River, where Mahanaim was located[234] (see comment on 2:8). This is a likely location for the forest of Ephraim.

The forest claimed more lives that day than the sword (18:8). Whether through actual casualties (the forest apparently posed various natural dangers; cf. vv. 9, 17), through temptation to desertion (which would have been facilitated by the thick cover), or through the advantages that savvy fighters can exploit in terrain where troop movements are impeded, the forest contributed to David's success. Outnumbered but well-trained troops often fare best in difficult terrain.[235]

Absalom's head got caught in the tree (18:9). Absalom's vanity regarding his hair (see 14:25–26) tempts the reader to see a fine irony in his head getting caught in a tree, although the text does not specifically mention his hair. It is possible that Absalom was suddenly caught up and suspended in midair when the disturbance of his passage released branches previously pinned in a flexed position by other branches. Whatever the case, to be hung on a tree signifies God's curse (cf. Deut. 21:23).

Ten shekels of silver and a warrior's belt (18:11). Ten shekels of silver (about four ounces) is no mean sum. In the period of the Judges, Micah offered a young Levite clothing, sustenance, and ten shekels a year to become his priest (Judg. 17:10).

Three javelins (18:14). The standard translations of verses 14–15 have raised questions: If three javelins were driven into Absalom's heart, how could it possibly be necessary for Joab's men subsequently to strike and kill him (v. 15)? McCarter suggests that a better understanding of the Hebrew text may be that Joab took three stout sticks in his hands and struck "against Abishalom's chest ... in order to dislodge him from the tree," after which Joab's men swarmed and killed him. The result was that no one person, least of all Joab, could be held directly responsible for Absalom's death.[236]

Joab sounded the trumpet (18:16). On Joab's use of the trumpet (*šôpār*) as a signaling device, see comment on 2:28. In a pretechnological age, communication was effected by sound, messengers, or visual signals. Regarding the latter, Mari texts attest the use of "fire signals."[237]

Piled up a large heap of rocks over him (18:17). This is a form of burial often reserved for criminals or defeated enemies (e.g., Josh. 7:26; 8:26).

A pillar ... in the King's Valley ... called Absalom's Monument to this day (18:18). This retrospective comment offers a fine irony in its current placement. Absalom, over whose corpse has just been "raised" a pile of stones (v. 17), had earlier in life "raised" a stone monument to himself, an act that recalls Saul's raising of a monument to himself (1 Sam. 15:12). Building on earlier work by Cross, T. J. Lewis cautiously suggests that "Absalom's monument may reflect a cult of the dead in ancient Israel," though he allows for other interpretations.[238]

The so-called "Tomb of Absalom" still found in the Kidron Valley dates from the Hellenistic period and should not be confused with the present passage. The location of the "King's Valley" is not known with certainty, but one viable possibility is the area south of the City of David, where the Kidron and Hinnom valleys meet.

Hellenistic monument known as Absalom's Tomb
Kevin A. Wong

David's Lament over Absalom (18:19–19:8)

Then Ahimaaz ran by way of the plain and outran the Cushite (18:23). As noted in the comment on 18:16, messengers were a chief means of communication in the ancient Near East, including battle situations. Messengers were of various sorts and delivered different kinds of messages. For instance, Mari attests regular messengers, letter carriers, fast couriers, express messengers, mounted messengers, and so forth.[239] Of particular interest are the *mubassirū* messengers, whose task, it seems, was to deliver the "good news of a military victory."[240]

In the present context, verse 27 suggests a correlation between the messenger chosen and the content of the message—whether good, bad, or mixed. Thus, Joab's disinclination to send Ahimaaz may have been prompted not simply by concern for Ahimaaz's safety, given David's likely reaction to the news, but also by a desire not to appear as himself taking

City Gates

Different types of gates are attested in ancient cities, some flanked by guard towers and some in which the towers became virtual small forts into which city leaders could retreat in times of danger. Many had several chambers or rooms as part of the gate complex, and many had both inner and outer gates. Often a sharp turn was required when moving from the outer to the inner gates, the purpose again being to prevent easy passage of attacking chariots or troops.

Important city gates in the time of David probably involved some combination of the above features—multiple chambers (four being the most common number in Canaan before the time of Solomon),[A-38] guard towers, inner and outer gates, and so forth. All of these features, along with a generally stepped approach way to the gate (which would hinder chariots), made gateways more defensible, while leaving them wide enough to accommodate commercial traffic and civic activity.[A-39]

Excavations at Tel Dan have uncovered structures that illustrate the outer and inner gates, with a (presumably canopied) seat/throne for the city ruler between them. Perhaps on such a throne "David was sitting between the inner and outer gates" (18:24).

Gate at Tel Dan with sharp turn
Todd Bolen/www.BiblePlaces.com

too much pleasure in Absalom's demise (cf. v. 22). In the end, Joab allows Ahimaaz to run, but only after releasing an earlier messenger. Ahimaaz, however, takes a faster route by way of the plain—as distinct from a perhaps shorter but more treacherous route through the forest—and arrives first.[241]

The inner and outer gates (18:24). Because city gates served a dual function in the ancient Near East, military and civic, their design reflected a compromise between these two competing aims. For civic and commercial purposes, the gates needed to be open and accessible, but for military purposes, they had to be narrow, difficult to navigate by chariots or large numbers of troops, and defensible. See sidebar on "City Gates."

The watchman went up to the roof of the gateway by the wall (18:24). The multistoried guard towers that flanked the gate served as lookout posts (see next comment).

The king ... went to the room over the gateway and wept (18:33). City gates had numerous rooms where commercial, civic, or military affairs could be conducted. David's retreat to one of the rooms afforded him a place where he could weep in relative privacy. His withdrawal from his position sitting in the gate to one of the rooms of the gate tower reflects the fact that he is "shaken" by news of Absalom's death, as his anguished fivefold repetition of "my son" and threefold repetition of "Absalom" aptly capture.

Reconstruction of city gate showing windows above
Alva Steffler/Susanna Vagt

You love those who hate you and hate those who love you (19:6). As Moran noted many years ago, "love" language is used in the ancient Near East and in the Bible to connote political loyalty.[242] This is clear in the Amarna letters. In one, Akizzi writes: "My lord, just as I love the king, my lord, so too the king of [. . .]; all of these kings are my lord's servants."[243] An even closer parallel to Joab's words is found in the following complaint by ʿAbdi-Ḫeba of Jerusalem: "Why do you love the ʿApiru but hate the mayors?"[244]

The king got up and took his seat in the gateway (19:8). This action signals David's resumption of his kingly duties, as gateways were frequently the place where official duties were performed. The Ugaritic ʾAqhatu Legend describes the ruler Danʾel taking a seat at the city gate, in the company of the leaders, and judging cases of widows and orphans.[245] The nature of David's duties here includes the encouragement of his victorious troops (v. 7) and perhaps the beginning of a process of reconciliation with those who sided with Absalom (cf. vv. 9–14).

David's Return to Jerusalem (19:9–43)

Gilgal (19:15). For location and significance, see comment on 1 Samuel 10:7–8.

Should anyone be put to death in Israel today? (19:22). In the ancient Near East,

Partially reconstructed ruler's seat at the gate of Dan
Jack Hazut

victors sometimes inflicted terrible punishment on the vanquished (see comment on 9:1). But in many instances, especially where the political situation remained delicate, they showed clemency toward those who sought to harm them. The Hittite kings Telepinu (seventeenth century) and Ḫattušiliš III (thirteenth century), for example, left behind records of such clemency: "They did me harm, yet I will not do them harm"; "Why should they die? Let them rather hide their faces."

Preference for imprisonment of rivals rather than execution appears to have been motivated by the political need to win over as many former supporters as possible.[246] Even where accession was not challenged, a new king might, at his accession and periodically thereafter, choose to proclaim a general amnesty, particularly relating to debts owed.[247]

I order you and Ziba to divide the fields (19:29). A Hittite text recounts a case in which an individual guilty of "unprovoked attacks on Ḫattušiliš" is required by the crown to relinquish half of his estate for damages.[248] Having earlier awarded all of Mephibosheth's property to his servant Ziba, David here adjusts this to a fifty-fifty split. This compromise arrangement suggests either that David is uncertain of the veracity of Mephibosheth's version of events or is simply unwilling to call Ziba to account, lest he jeopardize support from that quarter.

Grasping an opponent by the beard for execution
Francesca Smith-Archiapatti, courtesy of the British Museum

Have we eaten any of the king's provisions? (19:42). In the ancient Near East, those who were afforded the privilege of eating at the king's table were expected to respond with loyalty to their royal benefactor. In Mari, for instance, many tablets recording daily provisions for the king's table have been recovered.[249] The Judahites' protest to the northern tribes is that their loyalty to David has not been bought by privileges extended and enjoyed but by kinship: "We did this because the king is closely related to us."

Sheba's Revolt (20:1–26)

Troublemaker ... Sheba son of Bicri (20:1). If Bright is correct in linking "Bicri" to "Becorath" of the genealogy of Saul (1 Sam. 9:1),[250] then Sheba may have been not only a Benjamite but a relative of Saul. This may have contributed to his apparent eagerness to precipitate a general withdrawal of support from David.

The ten concubines ... [David] provided for them (20:3). This refers to the concubines left in Jerusalem in 15:16 to care for the palace during David's flight from Absalom; they were violated by Absalom in 16:22 (see comment on 16:21). Unable or unwilling to reinstate them in his harem, David provides for them as if they were widows. In ancient Near Eastern legal codes, provisions were often made for the care of unmarried kinswomen or widows.[251] One of Hammurabi's laws states that a wife who becomes unfit to perform her wifely duty may be replaced, but her husband "shall continue to support her as long as she lives."[252]

Joab took Amasa by the beard with his right hand to kiss him (20:9). In the ancient Near East a kiss connoted many things, such as obeisance, reconciliation, friendship, and affection. In 1–2 Samuel, Saul's anointing is accompanied by a kiss of honor by Samuel (1 Sam. 10:1; cf. Barzillai's kiss of David in

2 Sam. 19:39), Jonathan and David kiss one another in affection and sorrow (see comment on 1 Sam. 20:41), and David uses a kiss to effect a (partial?) reconciliation with Absalom (2 Sam. 14:33), only to have Absalom subsequently steal the peoples' affection and loyalty with a kiss (15:5–6).

In this episode, Joab's kiss feigns honor or reconciliation but facilitates treachery. The purpose of the unusually detailed description of his grasping the beard with his right hand is to enable the reader to visualize how Amasa is caught off guard.

Abel Beth Maacah (20:14). Worthy of attention from the Aramean king Ben-Hadad (1 Kings 15:20) and the Assyrian king Tiglath-pileser (2 Kings 15:29), Abel Beth Maacah has been tentatively identified with Tell Abil el-Qamh, located some twelve miles north of Lake Hulah and four miles west of Dan. On the kingdom of Maacah, see comment on 10:6. Abel Beth Maacah also appears to be listed among Pharaoh Thutmose III's Asiatic conquests.[253]

Siege ramp ... they were battering the wall (20:15). See comment on 17:13.

Wise woman (20:16). See comment on 14:2.

A city that is a mother in Israel (20:19). This curious expression suggests several possible interpretations. In Hebrew it reads literally "a city and a mother in Israel." One possibility is that the "wise woman" (v. 16) is referring not only to her city but also to herself, a mother in Israel (cf. Deborah's self-description as "a mother in Israel" in Judg. 5:7).

A second interpretation takes the phrase as a hendiadys (a single concept expressed with two words), reads it in the light of the general Hebrew perception of cities and regions as, figuratively speaking, the mothers of their inhabitants, and understands it to mean "a mother city," that is, a major city (cf. the Heb. phrase "a city and its daughters" [i.e., towns or villages]).

A third possible interpretation, and perhaps the most likely, relates the Hebrew term "mother" to cognates from Old Babylonian (Mari), Ugaritic, Phoenician, and the like that mean something like "mother unit" or "clan." The wise women's charge in the present passage, then, is: "You are trying to destroy a city and family [i.e., clan] in Israel."[254]

Joab was over Israel's entire army; Benaiah ... (20:23–26). Despite David's attempt to diminish Joab's power (19:13), Joab has managed to murder (20:8) his way back to the position of commander over "the entire army." Thus Joab again heads the list of David's chief officials, as he did in the shorter register of officers in 8:16–18 (see sidebar there on "Officials in David's Government"). Additions to the present list include Adoniram, who is in charge of "forced labor," Zadok and Abiathar the priests, and Ira the Jairite as "David's priest" (perhaps replacing his sons; see comment on 8:18).

The addition of an officer over the "forced labor," probably comprising war captives and

Siege ramp and battering ram from relief of the assault on Lachish by Sennacherib
Z. Radovan/www.BibleLand Pictures.com

non-Israelite Canaanites (cf. Josh. 16:10; Judg. 1:28), is suggestive of David's growing power and desire to develop the infrastructure of the kingdom: roads, fortresses, civic administrative buildings, and so forth. The title of officer "over the forced labor" is used in the Bible only in the administrations of David, Solomon, and Rehoboam; outside the Bible it is attested also in a seventh-century Hebrew seal.[255]

The ancient Near East attests "an abundance of titles for officers of all types, from minister and governor down to the lowliest overseer," though it is often difficult "to define with exactitude the corresponding administrative jurisdictions."[256] The reign of Nebuchadnezzar II has a lengthy roster of court officials.[257] The placement of David's list of court officials at the end of 2 Samuel 20 is logical. First, just as the section recounting the full establishment of David's kingdom ended with a summary of his officers (8:16–18), so the section recounting his reestablishment of control after the rebellions of Absalom and Sheba ends with such a summary; second, the "official summary" draws the narrative to a fitting close before the epilogue (chs. 21–24) that follows.

David Avenges the Gibeonites (21:1–14)

During the reign of David, there was a famine for three successive years (21:1). The four-chapter "epilogue" that completes the books of Samuel is introduced with an account of prolonged national catastrophe, specifically, a famine. It ends with a similar account, a story of plague (ch. 24). The first period of national distress was caused by Saul's misdeeds, the second by David's. In the ancient Near East generally, the king was regarded as representing the people, and his behavior could bring blessing or curse on those under his rule.

The three-year famine is placed generally "during the reign of David," and it most likely occurred earlier rather than later in his reign. Shimei's outraged reference in 16:8 to "all the blood you shed in the household of Saul" may allude to the actions David takes in the present chapter to end the famine. Famines were common occurrences in Canaan and the ancient Near East, and they were typically viewed as manifestations of divine displeasure. The first step, then, in seeking to avert further disaster was to "seek the face" of (i.e., seek an audience with) the deity, just as David "sought the face" of Yahweh (v. 1).

As has often been noted,[258] the plague prayers of the fourteenth-century Hittite king Muršili II[259] offer a number of comparisons to the present episode. In both, the cause of divine displeasure lies not with the current king but with a predecessor: "It is on account of Saul and his blood-stained house" (v.1) / "the offense ... was committed in the days of my father."[260] In both, the specific offense has to do with a breach of covenant: Saul put Gibeonites to death in breach of the covenant Israel made with them in Joshua 9, and Muršili II's predecessor broke an "oath of the gods" sworn with respect to the Egyptians.[261] In both, the treaty violation led to national catastrophe. The ancient Near East is replete with other instances of sacral desecration bringing national catastrophe and requiring sacral remedy.[262]

Saul in his zeal for Israel and Judah had tried to annihilate them (21:2). Political pragmatism, not religious zeal, appears to have motivated Saul's decimation of the Gibeonites. Not only was there an ancestral connection for Saul with Gibeon (see 1 Chron. 8:29–33), but the Gibeonites' strategic position within the centrally located tribe of Benjamin also posed a serious danger to the political unity of north and south, especially if the Gibeonites were to form an alliance with the Philistines to their west.[263]

Let seven of his male descendants be given to us to be killed and exposed (21:6). The number seven signifies "completeness," suggesting full restitution—not the number of Gibeonites slain by Saul, which was probably much higher. While some uncertainty

Impalement as punishment at Lachish
Caryn Reeder, courtesy of the British Museum

surrounds the correct understanding of the term "exposed,"[264] the bodies of the seven executed sons of Saul were in fact exposed to the elements (v. 10). The withholding of proper burial and the exposure of the bodies of the slain is a practice attested elsewhere in the ancient Near East in contexts of treaty violations.[265]

She did not let the birds of the air touch them (21:10). As in the ancient Near East generally, in Israel also it was considered a disgrace when the bodies of the slain were allowed to become carrion for birds and beasts, with no one to frighten them away (e.g., Deut. 28:26; 1 Sam. 17:44, 46). Threatened exposure of corpses to the elements was a frequent feature of curse formulations, as the following excerpt from a vassal treaty of Esarhaddon illustrates: "May Ninurta, leader of the gods, fell you with his fierce arrow, and fill the plain with your corpses, give your flesh to eagles and vultures to feed upon."[266]

It was precisely to drive away the "birds of the air" that Rizpah sets a vigil by the bodies of her sons "from the beginning of the harvest till the rain poured." The harvest in question is the barley harvest (v. 9), which begins in April. Thus, the "rain" should presumably be understood as an unseasonal downpour that ends the famine rather than the beginning of "winter rains," which will not commence until late October.

Exploits of David's Mighty Men against the Philistines (21:15–22)

Descendants of Rapha (21:16). "Rapha" has occasioned much discussion.[267] While certainty is not possible, it is probably best understood not as the name of a deity in Gath but as a collective noun to be associated with the Rephaites—pre-Israelite inhabitants of Canaan (Gen. 14:5; 15:20; Deut. 2:20; Josh. 17:15). The Rephaites were noted for their gigantic proportions (see comment on 1 Sam. 17:4).[268] Among the Rephaites were sometimes counted such peoples as the Emites, Zamzummites, and Anakites (Deut. 2:10–11, 20–21), all peoples distinguished

Birds devouring carcasses of the slain at Til-Tuba
Werner Forman Archive/The British Museum

Defeated soldiers captured in net
Jill Walton, courtesy of the Louvre

for their strength and stature. According to Joshua 11:21–22, the Anakites were driven from the hill country of Israel and Judah by Joshua but were able to survive in Gaza, Gath, and Ashdod—thus in the general area in view in the present context.

Lamp of Israel (21:17). On the metaphorical use of "lamp," see comments on 1 Samuel 3:3; 2 Samuel 14:7. Kings in the ancient Near East were often associated with light, in the sense of that which brings hope, justice, and well-being. In the prologue to his Code, Hammurabi speaks of his rising "like the sun ... to light up the land" and refers to himself as "the powerful king, the sun of Babylon, who causes light to go forth over the lands of Sumer and Akkad."[269] In one of the Amarna letters, the writer, after addressing the king as "my lord, my god, my Sun," goes on, "I looked this way, and I looked that way, and there was no light. Then I looked towards the king, my lord, and there was light."[270] For more on the righteous king as "like the light of morning at sunrise," see comment on 23:4.

Elhanan son of Jaare-Oregim the Bethlehemite killed Goliath the Gittite (21:19). The apparent contradiction between 1 Samuel 17 and this verse on who was responsible for Goliath's demise is a major *crux interpretum* in Samuel. See sidebar on "Who Killed Goliath?"

Six fingers ... six toes (21:20). Polydactylism (extra digits on hands or feet) was, like other physical abnormalities, a subject of considerable interest in antiquity.[271] In Mesopotamia, priests and diviners were consulted regarding the significance of physical abnormalities. A seventh-century Assyrian text runs through various possible cases of polydactylism and interprets them. "If a woman gives birth, and [the child] has six fingers on the right hand—poverty will seize the house of the man. If ... on the left hand—[the mother] is endowed with prosperity; [the man's] adversary will die." The list continues, describing all the possible configurations, and concludes: "If a woman gives birth, and [the child] has six fingers [and toes] on each of its right and left hands and right and left feet—the land will live undisturbed."[272]

The prevalence of this genetic abnormality, particularly common in inbred societies, is masked in the modern Western world by cosmetic surgical intervention at birth.

David Sings of His Deliverance (22:1–51)

God is my rock ... the horn of my salvation (22:3). For discussion of the metaphors "rock" and "horn," which connote refuge and strength, see comments on 1 Samuel 2:1 and 2, respectively.

The waves of death ... the torrents of destruction (22:5). Water imagery in the Old Testament can mean "both life and death, blessing and affliction, order and chaos."[273] In the ancient Near Eastern mindset, the power of water was such that only God or the gods could control it. Uncontrolled, it brought death and destruction. In the present context, David's being overwhelmed by "waves" and "torrents" leads to a cry for help (v. 7), which God, who alone is capable of rescue, answers with an awesome display of power (vv. 8–20). In

▸ Who Killed Goliath?

Various solutions have been attempted for the apparent contradiction between 1 Samuel 17 and 2 Samuel 21:19 on the killer of Goliath:

- "Elhanan" was David's personal name and "David" a throne name.
- An act originally accomplished by Elhanan was subsequently transferred to the more famous David.
- There was more than one individual named Goliath.

The parallel reading in 1 Chronicles 20:5 suggests a different solution, which asserts that Elhanan killed "Lahmi the brother of Goliath." While many commentators assume this reading is nothing more than an obvious attempt by the Chronicler to harmonize conflicting traditions, several points in favor of its superiority over the Samuel parallel can be made:

- There is clear evidence that the Samuel text, in some respects at least, is corrupt (e.g., "Oregim" appears to be an inadvertent duplication of the same word, translated "weaver's," at the end of 21:19).
- In Hebrew "Bethlehemite" and "Lahmi" (in combination with the Heb. sign of the direct object) look and sound much alike and could be confused by a copyist.
- The only other Elhanan in 1–2 Samuel is "Elhanan son of Dodo from *Bethlehem*" (23:24), making it conceivable that a scribe writing "Elhanan" could have misread the rare "Lahmi" (Heb. *ʾt lḥmy*) as the more expected "Bethlehemite" (Heb. *byt lḥmy*).
- The consequent loss of "Lahmi" as the one slain by Elhanan would have necessitated another victim, perhaps prompting the misreading of "the brother of Goliath" (Heb. *ʾḥy glyt*) to the similar "Goliath" (Heb. *ʾt glyt*).

In sum, if the Chronicler has preserved the superior reading (as many older commentators maintained), the problem is resolved: David killed Goliath, and Elhanan killed a brother of Goliath.[A-40]

Reconstruction of Egyptian relief from Medinet Habu shows a dead Philistine.
Kim Walton, courtesy of the Yigal Alon Museum

Hebrew, the concept of distress is expressed in terms of being in a narrow or tightly confined space, and it is from just such a "tight spot" that Yahweh brings David "into a spacious place" (v. 20).

The cords of the grave ... the snares of death (22:6). Cords and snares were used to capture and hold their victims. Adding to the water imagery of verse 5, David uses imagery of entrapment by death and the grave (Sheol) to express the extremity of his situation, had Yahweh not rescued him. The Old Testament concept of existence in Sheol is not described in any detail, but it seems to have assumed a shadowy existence in which, while the fate of the righteous was certainly preferable to that of the wicked, there was nothing approaching the New Testament understanding of heaven.

Ancient Near Eastern understandings of the grave were in some senses comparable. An Akkadian myth, for example, recounts the descent of the goddess Ishtar to the netherworld, in which the inhabitants were "bereft of light," feeding on "dust" and "clay," "clothed like birds, with wings for garments," and bolted in by a gatekeeper. This netherworld was the "Land of No Return."[274] David, with the "cords of the grave coiled" around him, was on the brink of the land of no return, had Yahweh not heard his cry and rescued him.

Cord imagery is used elsewhere in the Old Testament, usually of negative entanglements—e.g., "cords of affliction" (Job 36:8); "cords of death" (Ps. 18:4; 116:3); "cords of his sin" (Prov. 5:22); "cords of deceit" (Isa. 5:18)—but not invariably: "I led them with cords of human kindness, with ties of love" (Hos. 11:4).

The earth trembled and quaked.... He parted the heavens and came down (22:8–10). A Ugaritic passage describing a triumphant campaign by Baal, the storm god, employs similar imagery: He "opened a rift in the clouds. Baal sounded his holy voice, Baal repeated it from his lips; he uttered his holy voice and the earth quaked."[275]

The LORD thundered from heaven; the voice of the Most High resounded (22:14). On the imagery of "thunder" as the divine "voice," both in the ancient Near East and the Bible, see comment on 1 Samuel 2:10. There the focus was on Yahweh's "thundering" in judgment against evildoers. In the present context, Yahweh "thunders from heaven" in defense of David, who in his distress has called to Yahweh, and his "voice" has been heard.[276]

David Celebrates His Dynasty (23:1–7)

Light of morning at sunrise ... brightness after rain that brings the grass from the earth (23:4). The benefits of righteous rule, possible for the king who "fears God," are enlightenment, refreshment, and fruitfulness (cf. Ps. 72). In the ancient Near East, kings were often described as lamps, lights, or even the sun, giving light to the land (see comment on 2 Sam. 21:17). The fourteenth-century Hittite king Suppiluliumas, for example, introduces himself this way in a treaty: "I, the Sun Suppiluliumas, the great king, the king of the Hatti land, the valiant, the favorite of the Storm-god, went to war."[277] In an early second millennium Egyptian hymn to the god Amon-Re, the "goodly ruler" is described as "the lord of rays, who makes brilliance, to whom the gods give thanksgiving, who extends his arms to him whom he loves, (but) his enemy is consumed by a flame."[278]

David's Mighty Men (23:8–39)

These are the names of David's mighty men (23:8). The section is packed with information and has been the subject of considerable discussion

King's guards
Edward Silver, University of Chicago, courtesy of the Vorderasiatisches Museum

and debate among historians of the Davidic monarchy (see detailed discussions by Gordon, McCarter, and others).[279] A few brief comments will suffice here, focusing on the significance of the titles "the Three" and "the Thirty," and on the listing's principle(s) of arrangement.

Both titles seem to connote elite troops, distinguished from David's regular army. As the descriptions of some of the exploits of the Three suggest, these were probably high-ranking retainers who were closest to David (note, e.g., the statement regarding Eleazar in v. 9: "As one of the three mighty men, he was with David when they taunted the Philistines"). Following the presentation of exemplary exploits by the Three, two other champions are listed, Abishai and Benaiah, both as famous as the Three but not counted among them.

Next come the Thirty. Regarding the arrangement of the list of the Thirty, some have argued that it is structured geographically, beginning in Judah and expanding outward. As McCarter argues, however, the data do not conform to this scheme precisely, and more likely the arrangement is according to rank. In the section as a whole, the Three rank highest, next come Abishai and Benaiah, and then the Thirty, so perhaps the list of the Thirty is also in descending order of rank. Naturally, a loose pattern of geographical expansion is evident as well: "We would expect soldiers from towns close to Bethlehem to rank high in seniority and influence. Those from more remote areas stand farther down the list. Non-Israelites naturally fall at the end of the hierarchy."[280]

The LORD brought about a great victory that day (23:10). Such statements reaffirm the Divine Warrior theme and underscore the view that whatever heroic qualities human agents may bring to the task, the battle ultimately is in Yahweh's hands (see comment on 1 Sam. 14:6; cf. 14:15, 23; 19:5; 2 Sam. 8:6, 14).

Field full of lentils (23:11). The inclusion of this unusual detail may suggest the common tactic of debilitating foes by destroying their crops (cf. Judg. 6:3–6, 11).

David at the cave of Adullam … Philistines … in the Valley of Rephaim (23:13). See comments on 1 Samuel 22:1 and 2 Samuel 5:18, respectively. Adullam was twelve or thirteen miles west of Bethlehem, which itself was in the vicinity of the Valley of Rephaim and garrisoned by the Philistines.

Benaiah son of Jehoiada … in charge of his bodyguard (23:20–23). On Benaiah, see comment on 8:18. David's bodyguard presumably included the Kerethites and Pelethites (cf. 1 Sam. 30:14). David himself was at one time captain of Saul's bodyguard (1 Sam. 22:14).

Down into a pit on a snowy day and killed a lion (23:20). On lions in Palestine during the biblical period, see comment on 1 Samuel 17:37. The lion hunt is a regular motif in royal reliefs, the ferocity of the "king of beasts" serving to prove the mettle

Heroes are often portrayed fighting lions
Caryn Reeder, courtesy of the British Museum

of the one able to conquer him. In a legend extolling his hunting prowess, the fifteenth-century Pharaoh Thutmose III is credited with killing "seven lions by shooting in the completion of a moment."[281] In the present account, the added detail that it was "on a snowy day," with the slippery footing that this suggests, further dramatizes Benaiah's valorous feat.

Eliam son of Ahithophel (23:34). See comment on 11:3.

Beerothite (23:37). See comment on 4:3.

David Averts a Plague (24:1–25)

Take a census (24:1). Census-taking (of a limited sort, focused on current needs) was a regular feature of the ancient Near East. Evidence from as early as the third millennium in Mesopotamia and on into the first millennium exists.[282] From mid-second millennium Alalakh and Ugarit, for instance, we have "numerous registers of male individuals according to their village of origin and to their social grouping."[283]

Unlike modern censuses designed to study long-term trends, ancient censuses were directed to specific, contemporary needs. As Gordon observes, a census was taken for the purpose of assessing taxes, allocating land, determining "the strength of the national militia," and so forth.[284] Given these purposes, we may imagine the local populations did not always welcome the arrival of census takers, and this may have given rise to popular associations of censuses with misfortune or even divine displeasure.[285]

In the Old Testament, taking a census is not regarded as wrong per se (cf. Num. 1:1–2; 4:1–2; 26:1–4), although Exodus 30:11–12 does raise the possibility of a plague accompanying it. If merely taking a census was not wrong, then in the case before us the fact that David's census triggers a plague may have something to do with David's motive. The text provides no explicit commentary on motive, but David's order that the "fighting men" be numbered may suggest a desire to take pride or find security in the extent of his kingdom, or perhaps even to extend his borders beyond those granted him by Yahweh.[286]

Nine months and twenty days (24:8). Given that the distances involved in the itinerary described could have been covered in a matter of weeks, the vast majority of the time must have been spent in the census-taking itself. On average travel speeds, see comment on 1 Samuel 11:4.

Joab reported the number (24:9). On large numbers and population estimates, see comment on 1 Samuel 4:10.

Famine ... enemies ... plague (24:13). Death by starvation, by the sword, or by illness—this triad of woes constitutes the chief threats to life in the ancient Near East and figures prominently in descriptions of the consequences of covenant-breaking (Lev. 26:23–26; Deut. 28:21–26; etc.).

An altar to the LORD on the threshing floor of Araunah the Jebusite (24:18). On the Jebusites as inhabitants of Jerusalem prior to and during David's reign and on the possibility that "Araunah" is a title rather than a proper name, see comments on 5:6 and the sidebar "Jerusalem in Literary Sources and Archaeology." In the agrarian societies of the ancient Near East, large, flat outcroppings of bedrock, frequently "elevated to catch the breeze needed for winnowing," were often used as threshing floors.[287] Their prominence and spaciousness lent to their use as public gathering places.

The harvest activity conducted at threshing floors was often accompanied by religious celebration; thus, they were sometimes vested with cultic significance. In this light, it is plausible that the threshing floor of Araunah may have had some cultic associations prior to its purchase by David. It is at this very site that the temple of Yahweh is one day built (2 Chron. 3:1).

Threshing sledges (24:22). Threshing sledges were typically constructed of wooden planks bound together, into which were embedded "teeth" of flint, basalt, and

Threshing floor with sledge
Todd Bolen/www.BiblePlaces.com

the like. The sledge was dragged by oxen or donkeys across the stalks of grain deposited on the threshing floor, in order to loosen the kernels from the stalks and chaff. Winnowing (tossing the threshed grain into the air) allowed the chaff to be carried away by the breeze and the heavier kernels of grain to be retained.

BIBLIOGRAPHY

See also Annotated Bibliography of 1 Samuel for other commentaries and studies.

Commentaries

McCarter, P. Kyle. *II Samuel: A New Translation with Introduction and Commentary*. AB. Garden City, N.Y.: Doubleday, 1984. As with the *I Samuel* volume, McCarter's commentary is expansive in scope, particularly strong in text-critical matters, but attentive also to ancient Near Eastern background issues.

Special Studies

Athas, George. *The Tel Dan Inscription: A Reappraisal and a New Interpretation*. JSOTSup 360 / Copenhagen International Seminar 12. Sheffield: Sheffield Academic Press, 2003. The first book-length treatment of the three fragments of the so-called "House of David Inscription" discovered at Tel Dan in the early 1990s. In addition to surveying earlier studies of this inscription, Athas advances a novel theory of how the fragments should (not) be joined.

Ishida, Tomoo. *The Royal Dynasties in Ancient Israel: A Study on the Formation and Development of Royal-Dynastic Ideology*. Berlin: de Gruyter, 1977. An important exploration of the rise of kingship and especially the dynastic principle in Israel, against the backdrop of similar developments in Egypt, Mesopotamia, Anatolia, and Syria-Palestine.

Mettinger, Tryggve N. D. *King and Messiah: The Civil and Sacral Legitimation of Israelite Kings*. CB 8. Lund: Gleerup, 1976. Particularly strong on the ancient Near Eastern background to rites (such as anointing) relating to sacral kingship.

_____. *Solomonic State Officials: A Study of the Civil Government Officials of the Israelite Monarchy*. ConBOT 5. Lund: Gleerup, 1971. Effectively contextualizes biblical references to court officials on the basis of lists of state officials in Egypt, Mesopotamia, and so forth.

Main Text Notes

1. P. J. King and L. E. Stager, *Life in Biblical Israel*, ed. D. A. Knight (Library of Ancient Israel; Louisville: Westminster John Knox, 2001), 225–26.
2. A royal diadem, or tiara, may be mentioned in a Sumerian myth about the flood, in which, following the lowering of "kingship" from heaven, the "exalted [*tiara*] (and) the throne of the kingship" are also lowered (*ANET*, 43c).
3. R. J. Way, "נֵזֶר," *NIDOTTE*, 3:74–76.
4. D. R. Edwards, "Dress and Ornamentation," *ABD*, 2:232–38 (on 234).
5. See E. F. de Ward, "Mourning Customs in 1, 2 Samuel," *JJS* 23 (1972): 8–10.
6. *ANET*, 289c.
7. J. Muddiman, "Fast, Fasting," *ABD*, 2:773.
8. J. A. Scurlock, "Death and the Afterlife in Ancient Mesopotamian Thought," *CANE*, 1886.
9. Muddiman, "Fast, Fasting," 2:774.
10. See W. W. Hallo, "Lamentations and Prayers in Sumer and Akkad," *CANE*, 1871–81. Hallo discusses individual elegies on page 1875. For examples, see COS, 1.118:419–20; 1.119:420–21.
11. *The Epic of Gilgamesh: A New Translation*, trans. Andrew George (London: Penguin, 1999), 64–65. Cf. *ANET*, 87d. In a later recounting of his loss, Gilgamesh describes his unwillingness to accept the death of his friend "whom I still love so very much." "For days and nights did I weep over him, / And would not let them bury him, / As if my friend might rise at my cries /—for seven days and seven nights—/ Until a maggot dropped from his nose." The translation is found on p. 2329 in W. L. Moran, "The Gilgamesh Epic: A Masterpiece from Ancient Mesopotamia," *CANE*, 2327–36, which see for a succinct summary of the epic. For a different translation, see *ANET*, 89–90.
12. See the summary of theories in P. K. McCarter, *II Samuel* (AB; Garden City, N.Y.: Doubleday, 1984), 56–57.
13. On all this and more, see D. L. Christensen, "Jashar, Book of," *ABD*, 3:646–47.
14. On these and other matters, see the summary essay by Ashkelon's excavation director L. E. Stager ("Ashkelon," *NEAEHL*, 103–112). A briefer treatment is provided by D. Schloen, "Ashkelon," *OEANE*, 1:220–23. Both of these essays summarize the history and findings of archaeological investigation of the site. For authoritative, popular treatments of the ongoing excavations, see *BAR*, esp. the 1991 and 1996 volumes.
15. So Stager, "Ashkelon," *NEAEHL*, 104.
16. See, in order, EA 325; cf. 320–323, 326; EA 324; cf. 325; EA 287; EA 370. For translations, notes, and bibliography on all these, see W. L. Moran, *The Amarna Letters* (Baltimore: Johns Hopkins Univ. Press, 1992), 327–30, 350–54, 367.
17. R. P. Gordon, *1 & 2 Samuel* (Grand Rapids: Zondervan, 1988), 211.
18. *ANET*, 153.
19. See H. W. Wolff, "The Understanding of History in the Old Testament Prophets," in *Israel's Past in Present Research: Essays on Ancient Israelite Historiography*, ed. V. P. Long (Sources for Biblical and Theological Study 7; Winona Lake, Ind.: Eisenbrauns, 1999), 535–51, esp. 536–39.
20. See, e.g., Y. Yadin, *The Art of Warfare in Biblical Lands in Light of Archaeological Study* (New York: McGraw-Hill, 1963), 83–84.
21. See A. R. Millard, "Saul's Shield Not Anointed with Oil," *BASOR* 230 (1978): 70; cf. Gordon, *1 & 2 Samuel*, 212.
22. As is noted by H. A. Hoffner Jr. ("Incest, Sodomy, and Bestiality in the Ancient Near East," in *Orient and Occident: Essays Presented to Cyrus H. Gordon on the Occasion of His Sixty-fifth Birthday*, ed. H. A. Hoffner Jr. [Neukirchen-Vluyn: Neukirchener Verlag, 1973], 81–90), "there are few laws regarding homosexuality in Mesopotamian legal corpora" (82), though Middle Assyrian law does apparently punish such behavior severely: "If a seignior lay with his neighbor, when they have prosecuted him (and) convicted him, they shall lie with him (and) turn him into a eunuch" (*ANET*, 181 §20). Hittite law apparently does not explicitly outlaw homosexuality but focuses more on offenses involving incest (Hoffner, "Incest," 85 and *passim*). In ancient Israel, homosexual practice was viewed along with bestiality as a "dishonorable and unnatural passion" (ibid., 90).
23. Adapted from a longer selection in A. Taggar-Cohen, "Political Loyalty in the Biblical Account of 1 Samuel XX–XXII in the Light of Hittite Texts," *VT* 55 (2005): 256; italics are Taggar-Cohen's and highlight significant terms; I have omitted transliterated Hittite words that Taggar-Cohen includes in parentheses by some of these terms. For the full text in translation, see H. A. Hoffner, COS, 2.18:100–106 (cited above is a portion of §13).
24. For a listing of relevant literature, see Taggar-Cohen, "Political Loyalty," 258, n.24. Cf. also W. L. Moran, "The Ancient Near Eastern Background of the Love of God in Deuteronomy," *CBQ* 25 (1963): 77–87.
25. So Gordon, *1 & 2 Samuel*, 213. An alternate (biblical) theory links the name to Arba, an important man among the Anakim (Josh. 14:15; 15:13–14).
26. A. Ofer, "Hebron," *NEAEHL*, 607, which see for description of each.
27. Cf. *IVPBBC-OT*, 323–24.
28. D. V. Edelman, "Mahanaim," *ABD*, 4:473.
29. *ANET*, 243.
30. Gordon, *1 & 2 Samuel*, 214, which see for specific identifications and for comment on the vexed question of who the "Ashuri" were (Asherites?

Geshurites?); cf. also McCarter, *II Samuel*, 82–83, 87–88.

31. *IVPBBC-OT*, 324. Cf. perhaps the manner in which the vizier (and later pharaoh) Ay directed the young Egyptian pharaoh Tutankhamun, who reigned for only nine years, dying at age nineteen; for details see N. Grimal, *A History of Ancient Egypt*, trans. Ian Shaw (Cambridge, Mass.: Blackwell, 1993), 241–44.
32. On the excavation of el-Jib, see J. B. Pritchard, *Gibeon, Where the Sun Stood Still: The Discovery of a Biblical City* (Princeton, N.J.: Princeton Univ. Press, 1962), esp. p. 73 for photographs and drawings of Gibeonite jar handles. For further discussion of the archaeology of the site and debates surrounding it, see I. Provan, V. P. Long, and T. Longman III, *A Biblical History of Israel* (Louisville: Westminster John Knox, 2003); and more thoroughly, J. B. Pritchard, "Gibeon," *NEAEHL*, 511–14.
33. Pritchard, *Gibeon*, 156. For text, see *ANET*, 247.
34. *ANET*, 235.
35. For descriptions of the three water systems at Gibeon, see D. P. Cole, "How Water Tunnels Worked," *BAR* 6/2 (1980): 8–29 (on 22); M. D. Coogan, "10 Great Finds," *BAR* 21/3 (1995): 26–47 (on 43).
36. On this speculation, see Cole, "How Water Tunnels Worked," caption to photograph of large cylinder.
37. McCarter, *II Samuel*, 95; Gordon, *1 & 2 Samuel*, 215. For the early stages in the development of this understanding, see F. C. Fensham, "The Battle between the Men of Joab and Abner as a Possible Ordeal by Battle?" *VT* 20 (1970): 356–57, and the literature there listed.
38. Gordon, *1 & 2 Samuel*, 16; McCarter, *II Samuel*, 93; R. F. Youngblood, "1 and 2 Samuel," *EBC*, 825.
39. On the history of the Aramaeans of Tell Halaf (Gozan, Bit-Bakhiani), see Paul E. Dion, "Aramaean Tribes and Nations of First-Millennium Western Asia," *CANE*, 1281–94. For further photographs of the Tell Halaf reliefs, see C. Herzog and M. Gichon, *Battles of the Bible*, 2nd ed. (New York: Random, 1997), 136–40; and esp. Yadin, *Art of Warfare*, 360–65.
40. So NEB, cited by Gordon, *1 & 2 Samuel*, 216.
41. See, e.g., Yadin, *The Art of Warfare*, 352; J. Spanuth, *Die Philister, das unbekannte Volk: Lehrmeister und Widersacher der Israeliten* (Osnabrück: Otto Zeller, 1980), 50.
42. McCarter, *II Samuel*, 97.
43. D. Ilan, "Tombs," *OEANE*, 5:218–21 (on 218).
44. For a basic description, see, e.g., V. H. Matthews, *Manners and Customs of the Bible* (Peabody, Mass.: Hendrickson, 1988), 128–30. For a thorough treament, see E. Bloch-Smith, *Judahite Burial Practices and Beliefs about the Dead* (JSOTSup 123; Sheffield: Sheffield Academic Press, 1992), who describes eight different kinds of burials performed in Judah: simple, cist, jar, anthropoid coffin, bathtub coffin, cave and bench tomb burial, and cremation (summary on 133–51). For an attempt to draw out the sociological implications of burial practices, see A. Faust, "'Mortuary Practices, Society and Ideology': The Lack of Iron Age I Burials in the Highlands Context," *IEJ* 54 (2004): 174–90.
45. It is perhaps noteworthy that the daughter of Saul bears no child; so the house of Saul is not even strengthened in an indirect way.
46. For discussion of the social position of royal wives and concubines in both the ancient Near East and the Bible, see H. J. Marsman, *Women in Ugarit and Israel: Their Social and Religious Position in the Context of the Ancient Near East* (SOTS 69; Leiden: Brill, 2003), 371–81. Cf. also J. D. Levenson and B. Halpern, "The Political Import of David's Marriages," *JBL* 99 (1980): 507–18; S. A. Meier, "Diplomacy and International Marriages," in *Amarna Diplomacy: The Beginnings of International Relations*, ed. R. Cohen and R. Westbrook (Baltimore: Johns Hopkins Univ. Press, 2000), 165–73; A. R. Schulman, "Diplomatic Marriage in the Egyptian View," *JNES* 38 (1979): 177–93; M. Tsevat, "Marriage and Monarchical Legitimacy in Ugarit and Israel," *JSS* 3 (1958): 227–43.
47. On the possibility of elevating a concubine to the status of wife, according to Middle Assyrian law for example, see K. R. Nemet-Nejat, *Daily Life in Ancient Mesopotamia* (Peabody, Mass.: Hendrickson, 2002), 136. Cf. also J. N. Postgate, *Early Mesopotamia: Society and Economy at the Dawn of History* (London: Routledge, 1992), 149, on concubines of "intermediate status" at Mari.
48. Nemet-Nejat, *Daily Life*, 132.
49. For specific examples of and details regarding royal harems in the ancient Near East and in the Bible, see Marsman, *Women in Ugarit and Israel*, 371–81; cf. R. de Vaux, *Ancient Israel*, 2 vols. (New York: McGraw-Hill, 1961), 1:115–17.
50. Cf. R. Bergen, *1, 2 Samuel* (NAC; Nashville: Broadman & Holman, 1996), 307–8.
51. Complicating matters further are textual uncertainties which, depending on how they are resolved, could yield a reading as in the NIV or, alternatively, the reading "Am I a chief of Caleb, which belongs to Judah?" See McCarter, *II Samuel*, 106.
52. See McCarter, *II Samuel*, 113, which see for further possibilities; cf. also D. Winton Thomas, "*Kelebh* 'Dog': Its Origin and Some Usages of It in the Old Testament," *VT* 10 (1960): 410–27.
53. Cf. Bergen, *1, 2 Samuel*, 308, n.16.
54. M. T. Roth, ed., *Law Collections from Mesopotamia and Asia Minor*, 2nd ed. (SBLWAW; Atlanta: Scholars, 1997), 63 §§29–30. Cf. *ANET*, 162 §§29–30.
55. Roth, *Law Collections*, §134; cf. *ANET*, 171 §§133–35.
56. Roth, *Law Collections*, §136; cf. *ANET*, 171 §136.
57. Roth, *Law Collections*, §A36; cf. *ANET*, 183 §36.
58. The prohibition in Deut. 24:1–4 against remarrying a wife whom one has divorced and who has

married another does not apply to David's situation; he has not divorced Michal, and his absence is involuntary.

59. As J. Kessler ("Sexuality and Politics: The Motif of the Displaced Husband in the Books of Samuel," *CBQ* 62 [2000]: 414, n.27) observes, David's "stated reason" for demanding Michal's return "does not relate to his love for her but to his payment of her bride price, at great personal risk. Royal prerogative is clearly implied in David's demand."
60. Despite the fact that 2 Sam. 1–8 is largely positive toward David, the narrator "is beginning to move the audience toward a critical appraisal of David's actions" (Kessler, "Sexuality and Politics," 418).
61. S. R. Driver, *Notes on the Hebrew Text and the Topography of the Books of Samuel*, 2nd ed. (Oxford: Clarendon, 1960), 250; cf. Gordon, *1 & 2 Samuel*, 220.
62. McCarter, *II Samuel*, 117.
63. J. Milgrom, *Leviticus 1–16* (AB; New York: Doubleday, 1991), 820.
64. Cited in ibid.; see also his other examples. Cf. *ANET*, 179–80 §§50–60.
65. S. W. Holloway, "Distaff, Crutch or Chain Gang: The Curse of the House of Joab in 2 Samuel III 29," *VT* 37 (1987): 370–75 (on 370). Holloway offers a brief but well-supported discussion of the three main attempts to deal with this crux in 3:29.
66. Holloway, "Distaff," 370.
67. Ibid.
68. Holloway, "Distaff," 373.
69. Negev and Gibson, *Archaeological Encyclopedia*, 204.
70. See H. W. F. Saggs, *Civilization before Greece and Rome* (New Haven, Conn.: Yale Univ. Press, 1991), 240–66. For the Edwin Smith Papyrus cited, see 250–53.
71. Ibid., 260–61. For examples of less fanciful prognoses respecting spinal cord trauma, see J. Scurlock and B. R. Anderson, *Diagnoses in Assyrian and Babylonian Medicine: Ancient Sources, Translations, and Modern Medicine* (Urbana, Ill.: Univ. of Illinois Press, 2005), 309–10.
72. McCarter, *II Samuel*, 123, 125–26.
73. So H. Reviv, *The Elders in Ancient Israel: A Study of a Biblical Institution*, trans. L. Plitmann (Jerusalem: Magnes, 1989), 187.
74. Ibid., 187.
75. See H. Avalos, "Legal and Social Institutions in Canaan and Ancient Israel," *CANE*, 615–31, esp. 622–23.
76. For a concise description of ancient Israelite social structure based on family and kinship, see King and Stager, *Life in Biblical Israel*, 36–39.
77. J. D. Schloen, *House of the Father as Fact and Symbol: Patrimonialism in Ugarit and the ANE*, ed. L. E. Stager and M. D. Coogan (Studies in the Archaeology and History of the Levant; Winona Lake, Ind.: Eisenbrauns, 2001), 159.
78. Mazar, "Jerusalem," 699. For a listing of other possibilities, see S. A. Reed, "Jebus," *ABD*, 3:652–53. On the vexed question of the relationship between Anatolian and Canaanite "Hittites," see comment on 1 Sam. 26:6.
79. Whether Jerusalem and the city of Jebus are to be strictly equated has been questioned, e.g., by J. M. Miller ("Jebus and Jerusalem: A Case of Mistaken Identity," *ZDPV* 90 [1974]: 115–27), but even should Jebus and Jerusalem prove to be separate sites, it would remain the case that Jerusalem was under Jebusite control prior to the capture of the city by David.
80. On some of these, see Gordon, *1 & 2 Samuel*, 226.
81. Cahill, "Jerusalem in David and Solomon's Time," 26. For yet another creative theory that involves a radical retranslation of 2 Sam. 5:6–8, see S. Frolov and V. Orel, "David in Jerusalem," *ZAW* 11 (1999): 609–15.
82. See *HALOT*, sub צִיּוֹן.
83. Indeed, the context might even suggest a natural, as opposed to engineered, feature, as D. Gill has recently argued with respect to Warren's shaft ("How They Met: Geology Solves Long-Standing Mystery of Hezekiah's Tunnelers," *BAR* 20/4 [1994]: 20–33, 64).
84. On the various theories, see T. Kleven, "The Use of *ṢNR* in Ugaritic and 2 Samuel V 8: Hebrew Usage and Comparative Philology," *VT* 44 (1994): 195–204; cf. also his more popular treatment, with chart, in "Up the Waterspout: How David's General Joab Got inside Jerusalem," *BAR* 20/4 (1994): 34–35. Cf. also the succinct summary by McCarter (*II Samuel*, 139–40), who opts for "throat" in the sense that David wished no Jebusites to be mutilated (lamed or blinded) but to receive a fatal blow to the throat.
85. Kleven, "The Use of *ṢNR* in Ugaritic and 2 Samuel V 8," 200; idem, "Up the Waterspout," 35.
86. Cf. Y. Shiloh, *Underground Water Systems in Eretz-Israel in the Iron Age*, ed. Leo G. Perdue, Lawrence E. Toombs, and Gary L. Johnson (Archaeology and Biblical Interpretation; Atlanta: John Knox, 1987), 219–20.
87. R. Reich and E. Shukron, "The History of the Giḥon Spring in Jerusalem," *Levant* 36 (2004): 211–23.
88. Ibid., 216. For reference to other Middle Bronze II water systems at, e.g., Gezer, Tell Gerisa, Megiddo, see 213.
89. Ibid., 216.
90. McCarter, *II Samuel*, 140–41.
91. See *IVPBBC-OT*, 328, for further details and examples.
92. See M. Weinfeld, *Social Justice in Ancient Israel and in the Ancient Near East*, 2nd ed. (Minneapolis: Fortress, 2000), 101; see ibid., 97–131 for full discussion of the privileged status of temple cities, including Jerusalem.
93. Negev and Gibson, *Archaeological Encyclopedia*, 519–21.
94. For these and numerous other refereces, see H. J. Katzenstein, "Tyre," *ABD*, 6:686–87.
95. *ANET*, 283a.
96. *COS*, 2.55:181.

97. Cf. A. S. Gilber, "Flora and Fauna," *CANE*, 156.
98. *ANET*, 275a.
99. Cf. Gordon, *1 & 2 Samuel*, 229.
100. See Bergen, *1, 2 Samuel*, 325, n.35.
101. Mazar, "Did I Find King David's Palace?"
102. On both literary and military considerations, see G. Edelstein, "Rephaim, Valley of," *ABD*, 5:676–77. For a more detailed discussion of the location and course of David's two Philistine battles, see M. Garsiel, "David's Warfare against the Philistines in the Vicinity of Jerusalem (2 Sam 5,17–25; 1 Chron 14,8–16)," in *Studies in Historical Geography and Biblical Historiography*, ed. G. Galil and M. Weinfeld (Leiden: Brill, 2000).
103. For the former, see McCarter, *II Samuel*, 154; for the latter, see *IVPBBC-OT*, 329. For a discussion of attempts at more precise identification of Baal Perazim, see Garsiel ("David's Warfare," 159–60), who suggests identifying the site with Mount Abu Tor (Givat Hananya).
104. On both texts, see P. D. Miller and J. J. M. Roberts Jr., *The Hand of the Lord: A Reassessment of the "Ark Narrative" of 1 Samuel* (Baltimore: Johns Hopkins Univ. Press, 1977), 93, nn. 80–81.
105. See McCarter, *II Samuel*, 155–56 for discussion.
106. See A. Malamat, "How Inferior Israelite Forces Conquered Fortified Canaanite Cities," *BAR* 8/2 (1982): 24–35.
107. For a reconstruction of the likely course of the route, see *IVPBBC-OT*, 330.
108. See, e.g., A. F. Campbell, *The Ark Narrative (1 Sam. 4–6; 2 Sam. 6): A Form-Critical and Traditio-Historical Study* (SBLDS 16; Missoula, Mont.: Scholars, 1975), 179–91; Miller and Roberts, *The Hand of the Lord*, 9–17; McCarter, *II Samuel*, 178–82.
109. McCarter, *II Samuel*, 181.
110. *ANET*, 560; see McCarter, *II Samuel*, 181, for further discussion.
111. See McCarter, *II Samuel*, 169. For fuller description of ancient sistra, see J. Braun, *Music in Ancient Israel/Palestine: Archaeological, Written, and Comparative Sources*, trans. D. W. Stott (Grand Rapids: Eerdmans, 2002), 88–90.
112. See R. H. O'Connell, "מְנַעַנְעִים," *NIDOTTE*, 2:991–92, and literature listed there.
113. B. Bayer, "The Finds That Could Not Be," *BAR* 8/1 (1982): 20–33.
114. Miller and Roberts, *Hand of the Lord*, 15; cf. also ibid., 96, n.57.
115. *ARAB*, II:988–89. On the apparent discrepancy in the above-cited material—were sacrifices offered every double mile or every double hour?—see von Soden, *Akkadisches Handwörterbuch*, 130, "*bī / ēru* IV," among the definitions for which are included both "Doppelstunde" (double hour) and "Meile" (mile).
116. McCarter, *II Samuel*, 171. For fuller discussion of the significance of the ritual procession in relation to David and the new royal city, see P. K. McCarter, "The Ritual Dedication of the City of David in 2 Samuel 6," in *The Word of the Lord Shall Go Forth*, ed. C. L. Meyers and M. O'Connor (Winona Lake, Ind.: Eisenbrauns, 1983), 273–78.
117. See D. P. Wright, "Music and Dance in 2 Samuel 6," *JBL* 121 (2002): 216–24.
118. See S. de Martino, "Music, Dance, and Procession in Hittite Anatolia," *CANE*, 2666. For summary treatments of music and dance in various parts of the ancient Near East, see also R. Anderson, "Music and Dance in Pharaonic Egypt," *CANE*, 2555–68; A. D. Kilmer, "Music and Dance in Ancient Western Asia," *CANE*, 2601–13. An interesting instance of the king and queen processing in concert with "whirling" dancers, though themselves apparently not dancing, is found in the Hittite Festival of the Warrior-God (*ANET*, 358–61).
119. *NEA* 66 (2003): 96–132 presents a series of well-illustrated studies of dancing in various parts of the ancient Near East: D. Collon, "Dance in Ancient Mesopotamia" (96–102); U. Gabbay, "Dance in Textual Sources from Ancient Mesopotamia" (103–4); A. Mazar, "Ritual Dancing in the Iron Age" (126–32); P. Spencer, "Dance in Ancient Egypt" (111–21); J. N. Tubb, "Phoenician Dance" (122–25).
120. Gabbay, "Dance in Textual Sources," 103.
121. Ibid., 103 (trans. adapted from S. Parpola, *Letters from Assyrian and Babylonian Scholars* [SAA 10; Helsinki: Helsinki Univ. Press, 1993], 178).
122. On the different kinds of horns used in ancient Israel, see O. Keel, *Symbolism of the Biblical World* (New York: Seabury, 1978), 340–43. For full discussion, see Wright, "Music and Dance," 203–16.
123. For specifics regarding the kinds of foods mentioned here, see McCarter, *II Samuel*, 173; *IVPBBC-OT*, 332.
124. So J. W. Flanagan, "Social Transformation and Ritual in 2 Samuel 6," in *The Word of the Lord Shall Go Forth: Essays in Honor of D. N. Freedman in Celebration of His 60th Birthday*, ed. C. L. Meyers and M. O'Connor (Winona Lake, Ind.: Eisenbrauns, 1983), 361–72 (on 368). For the text in view, see K. Müller, *Das assyrische Ritual, Teil 1: Texte zum assyrischen Königsritual* (MVAG 41/3; Leipzig: J. C. Hinrichs, 1937), 8–9, i.29 (VAT 9583 [Ass. 6342] = *KAR* 216).
125. Cf. F. A. M. Wiggermann, "Theologies, Priests, and Worship in Ancient Mesopotamia," *CANE*, 1861.
126. *ARAB*, II:436–39.
127. *ARAB*, II:436.
128. For useful overviews of the roles of prophets as intermediaries in ancient Near Eastern (court) life, see J. C. Vanderkam, "Prophecy and Apocalyptic in the Ancient Near East," *CANE*, 2083–94; S. I. Johnston, ed., *Religions in the Ancient World* (Cambridge, Mass.: Belknap Press of the Harvard Univ. Press, 2004), 37–83.
129. *ANET*, 268.
130. See, e.g., V. A. Hurowitz, *I Have Built You an Exalted House* (JSOTSup 115; Sheffield: Sheffield Academic Press, 1992), esp. 135–67.
131. Ibid., 165.
132. Cf. Gordon, *1 & 2 Samuel*, 236.

133. See Kitchen, *Ancient Orient*, 110–11.
134. For proponents and opponents of the theory, see A. Malamat, *Mari and the Bible*, ed. B. Halpern and M. H. E. Weippert (SHCANE 12; Leiden: Brill, 1998), 117–18.
135. Malamat, *Mari and the Bible*, 106–21. The text in question (i.e., A.1121 + A.2731) is available also in M. Nissinen, *Prophets and Prophecy in the Ancient Near East* (SBLWAW 12; Atlanta: Scholars, 2003), 17 (#1), and in J. J. M. Roberts, *The Bible and the Ancient Near East: Collected Essays* (Winona Lake, Ind.: Eisenbrauns, 2002), 173–77 (#4).
136. S. Ackerman, in Johnston, ed., *Religions*, 551.
137. Ibid.
138. Outside the Bible, Barhadad king of Aram is attested in a votive stele to the god Melqart (*ANET*, 655).
139. A particularly startling example is found in the so-called Stele of the Vultures, in which the god "Ningirsu implanted the semen for [the king] Eanatum in the womb ... [his birth is presumably related in a broken space] ... rejoiced over Eanatum" (Postgate, *Early Mesopotamia*, 269).
140. See, e.g., Moran, *Amarna Letters*, 125 (EA 54) and 326 (EA 286).
141. Moran, "Near Eastern Background," 78.
142. For full text in translation, see H. A. Hoffner, "The Treaty of Tudḫaliya IV with Kurunta of Tarḫuntašša on the Bronze Tablet Found in Ḫattuša," *COS*, 2.18:100–106.
143. *COS*, 2.18:103–4 §20; cf. also McCarter, *II Samuel*, 208.
144. On the character of promissory covenants, or grants, and for further ancient Near Eastern examples, see the seminal essay by M. Weinfeld, "The Covenant of Grant in the Old Testament and in the Ancient Near East," *JAOS* 90 (1970): 184–203.
145. Gordon, *1 & 2 Samuel*, 241.
146. F. M. Cross, "A Philistine Ostracon from Ashkelon," *BAR* 22/1 (1996): 64–65. For more on late Philistine writing, see J. Naveh, "Writing and Scripts in Seventh-Century BCE Philistia: The New Evidence of Tell Jemmeh," *IEJ* 35 (1985): 8–21.
147. For fuller discussion, see, e.g., McCarter, *II Samuel*, 243, 247; Bergen, *1, 2 Samuel*, 346–47.
148. On this particular method, cf. Mic. 2:5.
149. See Bergen, *1, 2 Samuel*, 347.
150. On the treatment of "human spoil" in Mesopotamia, see Postgate, *Early Mesopotamia*, 254–58.
151. "The Annals of Thutmose III," trans. J. K. Hoffmeier (*COS*, 2:2.2A:12).
152. On all these, see A. R. Millard, "Tribute," *IBD*, 3:1595–97.
153. *ANET*, 278–79.
154. For an argument that the Tel Dan stele may allude to the events of 2 Sam. 8:3–12 and 10:6–19, and thus to Hadadezer I, see S. A. Levine, "The Last Battle of Hadadezer," *JBL* 124 (2005): 341–47.
155. On the kingdom of Zobah, see Kitchen, "Controlling Role," 100–101.
156. On the textual issue, see Gordon, *1 & 2 Samuel*, 243.
157. For arguments favoring the former view, see McCarter, *II Samuel*, 247–48; for the latter view, see Malamat, "Aspects of the Foreign Policies of David and Solomon," 3.
158. Cf., e.g., Yadin, *Art of Warfare*, 285.
159. Cf. Negev and Gibson, *Archaeological Encyclopedia*, 44–45. For a fuller treatment and references to sources, see A. R. Millard, "Arameans," *ABD*, 1:345–50.
160. See Millard, "Arameans," 1:348.
161. See Negev and Gibson, *Archaeological Encyclopedia*, 130.
162. See *HALOT*, sub שָׁלֶט.
163. For site identifications and literary attestations in ancient Near Eastern sources, see McCarter, *II Samuel*, 250.
164. McCarter, *II Samuel*, 250.
165. Cf. Malamat, "Aspects of the Foreign Policies of David and Solomon," 6–7.
166. D. Elgavish, "The Division of the Spoils of War in the Bible and in the Ancient Near East," *ZABR* 8 (2002): 257.
167. For fuller discussion and additional biblical and ancient Near Eastern examples of dedication of spoils to the deity, see ibid., 257–60.
168. On the latter theory, see McCarter, *II Samuel*, 251.
169. *ARI*, 1.128:20–21.
170. Ibid., 1.158:26.
171. *EA* 298. See Moran, *Amarna Letters*, 333; cf. also *COS*, 3.92B; *ANET*, 489.
172. Weinfeld, *Social Justice*, 36.
173. Ibid., 43, citing Zech. 7:9–10.
174. W. G. Lambert, "Nebuchadnezzar King of Justice," *Iraq* 27 (1965): 1–2 (lines 22–27); quoted by Weinfeld, *Social Justice*, 42–43.
175. Ibid., 47.
176. Cf. ibid., 45–46.
177. C. E. Armerding, "Were David's Sons Really Priests?" in *Current Issues in Biblical and Patristic Interpretation: Studies in Honor of Merrill C. Tenney Presented by His Former Students*, ed. G. F. Hawthorne (Grand Rapids: Eerdmans, 1975), 75–86 (on 85).
178. G. J. Wenham, "Were David's Sons Priests?" *ZAW* 87 (1975): 79–82.
179. Gordon, *1 & 2 Samuel*, 247.
180. McCarter, *II Samuel*, 255.
181. *ANET*, 288d.
182. For more precise attempts at site identification, see *IVPBBC-OT*, 336; McCarter, *II Samuel*, 256.
183. Z. Ben-Barak, "Meribaal and the System of Land Grants in Ancient Israel," *Bib* 62 (1981): 73–91.
184. For concise overview, see M. L. Barré, "Treaties in the ANE," *ABD*, 6:653–56.
185. *ANET*, 201–3.
186. M. I. Gruber, "Private Life in Canaan and Ancient Israel," *CANE*, 633–48 (on 643).
187. *ARM*, 1.73.43–44: "tu [n'est pas] un homme, il n'y a pas de barbe à ton menton!" English translation is from P. Villard, "Shamshi-Adad and Sons: The Rise and Fall of an Upper Mesopotamian Empire," *CANE*, 881.
188. McCarter, *II Samuel*, 270–71.

189. Gihon and Herzog, *Battles of the Bible*, 107.
190. Y. Yadin, "Some Aspects of the Strategy of Ahab and David," *Bib* 36 (1955): 332–51 (on 347–50, referenced by McCarter, *II Samuel*, 272–73). On the uncertain location of (the region of) Helam, see McCarter, *II Samuel*, 273. In a general discussion of David's military approach, Yadin suggests that David may have established "a second, advanced, strategic base in the Valley of Succoth, east of the Jordan, near the city of Adamah" [= Adam]. The purpose of this strategic base would be to "support onslaughts upon objectives at very distant ranges," as in the present encounters with the Arameans (Yadin, *Art of Warfare*, 270–71).
191. *ANET*, 275d.
192. On this general approach, see Bergen, *1, 2 Samuel*, 363–64; McCarter, *II Samuel*, 284–85.
193. On the Mesopotamian calendar, see J. C. Vanderkam, "Calendars (Ancient Israelite and Early Jewish)," *ABD*, 1:816.
194. *ANET*, 305b; cf. 277b, 303d, 304c; for the month Nisanu, *ANET*, 292c, 302d, 303c. Campaigns launched in the spring sometimes continued for many months.
195. See *Iliad* 6.156, 160–65, 168–70 (*The Iliad of Homer* [Chicago: Univ. of Chicago, 1951], 157).
196. For an amusing account of an empirical experiment involving upper millstones, walls, women, and a watermelon, see D. D. Herr and M. P. Boyd, "A Watermelon Named Abimelech," *BAR* 28/1 (2002): 34–37, 62.
197. *ANET*, 306d.
198. W. von Soden, *The Ancient Orient: An Introduction to the Study of the Ancient Near East*, trans. Donald G. Schley (Grand Rapids: Eerdmans, 1994 [German orig. 1985]), 66.
199. *ANET*, 166 §8; but see also ibid., n. 45, on the internal inconsistency of the code.
200. T. Ishida, "Adonijah the Son of Haggith and His Supporters: An Inquiry into Problems about History and Historiography," in *The Future of Biblical Studies: The Hebrew Bible*, ed. R. E. Friedman and H. G. M. Williamson (Atlanta: Scholars, 1987), 165–87. For further discussion, see Marsman, *Women in Ugarit and Israel*.
201. *ANET*, 538 §42.
202. See Malamat, *Mari and the Bible*, 122–24. The text in view, as Malamat (122) notes, was "initially published in *ARM* X 106 and newly collated in *ARM* XXVI 1 no.222." Transliteration and translation of this text are available in Roberts, *Bible and the Ancient Near East*, 236–39. Translation is also available in Heimpel, *Letters*, 263 (26.222).
203. Malamat, *Mari and the Bible*, 124.
204. Hertzberg, cited by J. Muddiman, "Fast, Fasting," *ABD*, 2:774.
205. *ANET*, 384cd.
206. Cited by D. Stuart, "Names, Proper," *ISBE*, 3:485.
207. Further on these two names, see M. Garsiel, *Biblical Names: A Literary Study of Midrashic Derivations and Puns*, trans. Phyllis Hackett (Ramat Gan, Israel: Bar-Ilan University, 1991), 189–92, 204–7.
208. McCarter, *II Samuel*, 311.
209. On the possibility that "Ephraim" in the NIV should be read "Ophrah," see McCarter, *II Samuel*, 333.
210. *ANET*, 289c.
211. EA 43 and EA 256 respectively; see Z. U. Ma'oz, "Geshur," *ABD*, 2:996.
212. *ANET*, 407–10.
213. *ANET*, 408–9, lines 75–84.
214. See summary in *ANET*, 15c.
215. Cf. K. van der Toorn, *Family Religion in Babylonia, Syria, and Israel: Continuity and Change in the Forms of Religious Life*, ed. B. Halpern and M. H. E. Weippert (SHANE; Leiden: Brill, 1996), 130.
216. T. H. Gaster, *Myth, Legend, and Custom in the Old Testament* (New York: Harper and Row, 1969), 479–80.
217. *ANET*, 165d.
218. *ANET*, 523c.
219. Weinfeld, *Social Justice*, 45–56.
220. *CML*[2], "Keret," 16.vi.46–54; cf. *COS*, 1.102:342; *ANET*, 149ab.
221. See EA 320–26, 370; Youngblood, "1 and 2 Samuel," 994; for alternative possibilities, see McCarter, *II Samuel*, 370; M. Delcor, "Les Kéréthim et les Cretois," *VT* 28 (1978): 409–22.
222. Cf. N. Na'aman, "Ittai the Gittite," *BN* 94 (1998): 22–25; Na'aman's assertion that "Ittai is, no doubt, a literary figure devised by the author" is mystifying.
223. McCarter, *II Samuel*, 372.
224. De Vaux, *Ancient Israel*, 1:122–23; cf. also now *HALOT*, ad loc.
225. See EA 288:11. So McCarter, *II Samuel*, 372, which see for discussion and literature.
226. *ANET*, 288.
227. *ARAB*, I:130–31 §260.
228. Translation of F. G. Martínez, *The Dead Sea Scrolls Translated: The Qumran Texts in English*, trans. W. G. E. Watson, 2nd ed. (Grand Rapids: Eerdmans, 1996), 106. Cf. McCarter, *II Samuel*, 387.
229. H. W. F. Saggs, *The Might That Was Assyria* (London: Sidgwick & Jackson, 1984), 260.
230. King and Stager, *Life in Biblical Israel*, 124.
231. For further discussion of wells, see ibid., 123–26.
232. Scurlock, "Death and the Afterlife in Ancient Mesopotamian Thought," *CANE*, 1890.
233. L. H. Lesko, "Death and Afterlife in Ancient Egyptian Thought," *CANE*, 1766.
234. M. Noth, *The History of Israel*, 2nd ed. (London: SCM, 1983), 60–61, 201.
235. On the topic generally, see Malamat, "How Inferior Israelite Forces Conquered Fortified Canaanite Cities," 24–35.
236. McCarter, *II Samuel*, 406–7.
237. *ANET*, 482b, 483a.
238. T. J. Lewis, *Cults of the Dead in Ancient Israel and Ugarit*, ed. F. M. Cross (HSM 39; Atlanta: Scholars, 1989), 120–22.
239. R. W. Fisher, "The *Mubassirū* Messengers at Mari," in *Mari in Retrospect*, ed. G. D. Young

(Winona Lake, Ind.: Eisenbrauns, 1992), 113–20.

240. Ibid., 116; cf. 119.
241. H. O. Thompson ("Ephraim, Forest of," *ABD*, 2:557) speculates that the Cushite "ran due N through the forest and over the hills, while the latter [Ahimaaz] ran by way of the Jordan valley ('the plain,' v 23)."
242. Moran, "Ancient Near Eastern Background," 77–87.
243. Moran, *Amarna Letters*, 125 (EA 54.40–44).
244. Ibid., 326 (EA 286).
245. *COS*, 1.103:346; *ANET*, 151a.
246. On all this, see H. A. Hoffner Jr., "Propoganda and Political Justification in Hittite Historiography," in *Unity and Diversity: Essays in the History, Literature, and Religion of the Ancient Near East*, ed. H. Goedicke and J. J. M. Roberts (Baltimore: Johns Hopkins Univ. Press, 1975), 49–62 (esp. 54–55).
247. See, e.g., the edict of the Old Babylonian king Ammisadupa, *ANET*, 526–28.
248. Hoffner, "Propaganda," 55.
249. See A. Malamat, *Mari and the Early Israelite Experience* (Oxford: Oxford Univ. Press, 1989), 20–22.
250. John Bright, *A History of Israel*, 4th ed. (Louisville: Westminster John Knox, 2000), 210; see also Malamat, *Mari and the Bible*, 235.
251. See, e.g., the Code of Hammurabi §178 (*ANET*, 174).
252. *ANET*, 172 §148.
253. Y. Aharoni, *Land of the Bible* (Philadelphia: Westminster, 1979), 162.
254. See Malamat, *Mari and the Early Israelite Experience*, 41–43.
255. N. Avigad, "The Chief of the Corvée," *IEJ* 30 (1980): 170–73.
256. Von Soden, *Ancient Orient*, 70; see 69–71 for succinct discussion.
257. *ANET*, 307d–308.
258. See the seminal essay by A. Malamat, "Doctrines of Causality in Hittite and Biblical Historiography: A Parallel," *VT* 5 (1955): 1–12; more recently K. C. Hanson, "When the King Crosses the Line: Royal Deviance and Restitution in Levantine Ideologies," *BTB* 26 (1996): 11–25.
259. *ANET*, 394–96.
260. Ibid., 395c.
261. Ibid., 395a.
262. See, e.g., *ANET*, 311b (Nabonidus); *COS*, 1:468–70 (Weidner Chronicle).
263. For discussion, see Malamat, "Doctrines of Causality," 10–11.
264. See McCarter, *II Samuel*, 442.
265. F. C. Fensham, "The Treaty between Israel and the Gibeonites," *BA* 27 (1964): 96–100.
266. *ANET*, 538c.
267. Cf. McCarter, *II Samuel*, 449–50.
268. On the topic generally, see M. Smith, "Rephaim," *ABD*, 5:674–76; cf. also R. S. Hess, "Nephilim," *ABD*, 4:1072–73.
269. *ANET*, 164b, 165d.
270. EA 292; see Moran, *Amarna Letters*, 335; *ANET*, 489d.
271. For an interesting survey of the topic, see R. D. Barnett, "Six Fingers and Toes: Polydactylism in the Ancient World," *BAR* 16/3 (1990): 46–51.
272. E. Leichty, *The Omen Series Ṣumma Izbu* (TCS 6; Locust Valley, N.Y.: Augustin, 1970), 59; cited by Barnett, "Six Fingers," 49. On omen collections generally, see W. Farber, "Witchcraft, Magic, and Divination in Ancient Mesopotamia," *CANE*, 1907. For an example Mesopotamian omen text, see *COS*, 1.20:423–26.
273. *DBI*, 929.
274. *ANET*, 107.
275. So J. J. Niehaus, *God at Sinai* (Grand Rapids: Zondervan, 1995), 106; cf. *CML*[2], "The Palace of Baal," 4.vii.28–31.
276. Ps. 77:18 uses similar imagery in a celebration of God's deliverance of his people through the waters at the time of the Exodus.
277. *ANET*, 318.
278. Ibid., 365d.
279. Gordon, *1 & 2 Samuel*, 311–16; McCarter, *II Samuel*, 499–501.
280. McCarter, *II Samuel*, 501.
281. *ANET*, 243d. Cf. also the thorough study by M. B. Dick, "The Neo-Assyrian Royal Lion Hunt and Yahweh's Answer to Job," *JBL* 125 (2006): 243–70.
282. See F. M. Fales, "Census," *ABD*, 1:882–83.
283. Ibid., 882. See further, McCarter, *II Samuel*, 512–14.
284. Gordon, *1 & 2 Samuel*, 316.
285. Cf. *IVPBBC-OT*, 353.
286. See R. Dillard, "David's Census: Perspectives on 2 Samuel 24 and 1 Chronicles 21," in *Through Christ's Word: A Festschrift for Dr. Philip E. Hughes*, ed. W. R. Godfrey and J. L. Boyd (Phillipsburg, N.J.: Presbyterian & Reformed, 1985), 94–107.
287. King and Stager, *Life in Biblical Israel*, 89.

Sidebar and Chart Notes

A-1. D. A. Dorsey, *The Roads and Highways of Ancient Israel* (ASOR Library of Biblical and Near Eastern Archaeology; Baltimore: Johns Hopkins Univ. Press, 1991), 121 and map on 118; cf. P. W. Ferris Jr., "Hebron (Place)," *ABD*, 3:107.

A-2. Cf. P. C. Hammond, "Hebron," *OEANE*, 3:13.

A-3. For a summary of excavation results by Hammond, see ibid., 3:13–14, and by Ofer, see "Hebron," 606–9. A further excavation was conducted on the northern side of the mound by E. Eisenberg in 1999; for results, see A. Negev and S. Gibson, eds., *Archaeological Encyclopedia of the Holy Land*, rev. ed. (New York/London: Continuum, 2003), 224.

A-4. Ofer, "Hebron," 609. For a recent discussion of the archaeology of Hebron, see J. R. Chadwick, "Discovering Hebron: The City of the Patriarchs Slowly Yields Its Secrets," *BAR* 31/5 (2005): 25–33, 70–71. Chadwick (33) contests Ofer's judgment that Hebron was sparsely occupied in the Late Bronze period.

A-5. H. A. Hoffner Jr., "A Hittite Analogue to the David and Goliath Contest of Champions," *CBQ* 30 (1968): 220–25 (on 221). We might think of the way the phrase "now the game begins" is sometimes used in serious circumstances where the struggle involves anything but a game.

A-6. R. de Vaux, "Single Combat in the Old Testament," in *The Bible and the Ancient Near East* (London: Darton, Longman & Todd, 1972; orig. 1959), 122–35 (on 130). De Vaux cites 1 Sam. 21:3–5; 25:5ff.; 26:22; 2 Sam. 16:2; 1 Kings 20:14–19.

A-7. J. G. Westenholz, *Legends of the Kings of Akkade* (Mesopotamian Civilizations; Winona Lake, Ind.: Eisenbrauns, 1997). On "playing" in the sense of "fighting," see *CAD*, 10:17 (*mēlulû* b).

A-8. For a succinct survey of Jerusalem's excavation history, see Negev and Gibson, *Archaeological Encyclopedia*, 260.

A-9. For a taste of the debate, see N. Na'aman, "Cow Town or Royal Capital? Evidence for Iron Age Jerusalem," *BAR* 23/4 (1997): 43–47, 67; M. Steiner, "David's Jerusalem, It's Not There: Archaeology Proves a Negative," *BAR* 24/4 (1998): 26–33, 62–63; J. Cahill, "David's Jerusalem, It Is There: The Archaeological Evidence Proves It," *BAR* 24/4 (1998): 34–41, 63.

A-10. See, e.g., *ANET*, 329.

A-11. E.g., EA 287, 289, 290 and more (Moran, *Amarna Letters*; a selection of letters is also available in *ANET*, 483–90).

A-12. E.g., Sennacherib's siege of Jerusalem (*ANET*, 287–88).

A-13. For a contrary view, see H. J. Franken and M. L. Steiner, "Urusalim and Jebus," *ZAW* 104 (1992): 110–11.

A-14. The gist of the opposing positions is briefly presented in Provan, Long, and Longman, *A Biblical History of Israel*, 228–30, which see for additional literature. For thorough, up-to-date treatments of the main issues, see A. G. Vaughn and A. E. Killebrew, eds., *Jerusalem in Bible and Archaeology: The First Temple Period* (Atlanta: Society of Biblical Literature, 2003). A series of popular treatments of the subject by major authorities can be found in the pages of *BAR*, one of the most recent being J. Cahill, "Jerusalem in David and Solomon's Time," *BAR* 30/6 (2004): 20–31, 62–63. For authoritative general articles on the archaeology of Jerusalem, see D. Bahat, "Jerusalem," *OEANE*, 3:224–38; B. Mazar et al., "Jerusalem," *EAEHL*, 698–757, esp. 698–704.

A-15. See Dorsey, *Roads and Highways*, maps 6, 7, 13, 15 and relevant route descriptions.

A-16. B. Halpern, *David's Secret Demons: Messiah, Murderer, Traitor, King* (Grand Rapids: Eerdmans, 2001), 428.

A-17. Bahat, "Jerusalem," 226.

A-18. E. Mazar, "Excavate King David's Palace!" *BAR* 23/1 (1997): 50–57, 74; idem, "Did I Find King David's Palace?" *BAR* 32/1 (2006): 16–27, 70.

A-19. Beckman, *Hittite Diplomatic Texts*, 109 [No. 18B]; note that the Tudḫaliya IV treaty, ibid., 119 [No. 18C §20], contains almost identical wording.

A-20. *ANET*, 563c.

A-21. "The Great Hymn to the Aten," trans. M. Lichtheim (*COS*, 1.28:46). For a more paraphrastic, literary rendering of the hymn, see J. L. Foster, "*The Hymn to Aten:* Akhenaten Worships the Sole God," *CANE*, 1751–61.

A-22. Saggs, *Civilization*, 289.

A-23. See K. A. Kitchen, "The Controlling Role of External Evidence in Assessing the Historical Status of the Israelite United Monarchy," in *Windows into Old Testament History: Evidence, Argument, and the Crisis of "Biblical Israel,"* ed. V. P. Long, G. J. Wenham, and D. W. Baker (Grand Rapids: Eerdmans, 2002), 111–30. The following is adapted from Provan, Long, and Longman, *A Biblical History of Israel*, 230–32, which see for fuller discussion.

A-24. The reference to the Edomites anticipates 8:13–14; the reference to the Ammonites may anticipate chs. 10–12; the reference to the Amalekites recalls 1:1.

A-25. Cf. Kitchen, "Controlling Role," 125. On the general notion of a multitiered kingdom, cf. E. H. Merrill, *Kingdom of Priests: A History of Old Testament Israel* (Grand Rapids: Baker, 1987), 300–302; and the earlier, thorough study by A. Malamat, "Aspects of the Foreign Policies of David and Solomon," *JNES* 11 (1963): 1–17.

A-26. For descriptions of all these, with accompanying maps, see Kitchen, "Controlling Role," 116–23.

A-27. See, e.g., S. Parpola, "The Assyrian Cabinet," in *Vom Alten Orient zum Alten Testament: Festschrift für Wolfram Freiheim von Soden zum 85. Geburtstag am 19. Juni 1993*, ed. M. Dietrich and O. Lorenz (AOAT 240; Neukirchen-Vluyn: Neukirchener, 1995), 379–401.

A-28. R. Mattila, *The King's Magnates: A Study of the Highest Officials of the Neo-Assyrian Empire* (SAAS 11; Helsinki: Univ. of Helsinki Press, 2000), see esp. summary on 161–68.

A-29. So McCarter, *II Samuel*, 255.

A-30. T. N. D. Mettinger, *Solomonic State Officials: A Study of the Civil Government Officials of the Israelite Monarchy* (ConBOT 5; Lund: Gleerup, 1971), 61.

A-31. NIV's "Ahimelech son of Abiathar" follows the Hebrew text, but the latter has likely suffered corruption, as the father/son relationship is usually the reverse. F. M. Cross has helped explain how the corruption may have occurred; for summary see McCarter, *II Samuel*, 253–54.

A-32. As argued by Mettinger, *Solomonic State Officials*, 36.

A-33. G. Pinch, "Private Life in Ancient Egypt," *CANE*, 363–81 (on 371–72).

A-34. See F. Vallat, "Susa and Susiana in Second-Millennium Iran," *CANE*, 1023–1033 (on 1029).

A-35. F. Imparati, "Private Life among the Hittites," *CANE*, 571–86 (on 576).

A-36. C. H. Gordon and G. A. Rendsburg, *The Bible and the Ancient Near East* (New York: Norton, 1997), 199.

A-37. McCarter, *II Samuel*, 324.

A-38. Cf. G. Barkay, "The Iron Age II–III," in *The Archaeology of Ancient Israel*, ed. Amnon Ben-Tor (New Haven, Conn.: Yale Univ. Press, 1992), 308.

A-39. For further details, see Z. Herzob, "Fortifications: An Overview," *OEANE*, 2:319–21; King and Stager, *Life in Biblical Israel*, 234–36.

A-40. For further discussion and literature, see Provan, Long, and Longman, *A Biblical History of Israel*, 224–25.

Picture Index

This is an index to all of the pictures used in the five volumes of *Zondervan Illustrated Bible Background Commentary—Old Testament*. This index does not list the page number for the appropriate entry in each volume; rather, it lists the approximate location of each picture by Bible book and chapter. Each entry should be easy to locate within a page or two of where the comments on each Bible chapter begin.

Altars and High Places

Arad Altar, Josh. 8; 2 Kings 5; 2 Chron. 3
Beersheba Altar, Ex. 29; Jer. 17; Amos 3
Bethsaida High Place, Isa. 15; Amos 7
Boat Shrine, Ps. 132
Cultic Site in Golan, Josh. 4
Dan High Place, Deut. 12; Josh. 22; Ps. 78; Amos 8
Hazor Altar, Judg. 6w
Hazor High Place, Ezek. 6
Hittite Altar, Ex. 32
Horn of Altar, Judg. 2
Incense Altar (model), Ex. 30
Megiddo Altar, 1 Kings 1
Megiddo Circular Stone Altar, Deut. 27; Hos. 12
Megiddo Incense Altar, Lev. 4; Judg. 2
Mt. Ebal Altar, Deut. 11; Josh. 8; 1 Kings 3
Shrine of Tutankhamun, 2 Chron. 3
Taanach Cult Stand, 1 Chron. 13; Ezek. 8; Hos. 1
Taanach Incense Altar, 1 Kings 11
Votive Altar (Astarte), 1 Kings 11

Amulets

Ketef Hinnom, 1 Chron. 16; Neh. 13
Lamashtu, Job 2; Ezek. 14
Phylacteries (modern), Deut. 6; Prov. 3

Ancient Maps

Babylonian Map of the World, Ps. 24; Ezek. 38; Zeph. 2
Egyptian Map, Job 28
Madaba Map, Gen. 13; 14; Josh. 4
Map of Canals, Prov. 21
Map of the City of Umma, Ezek. 4

Animals

Animals, Gen. Introduction; Num. 18; Deut. 4; 5; 1 Kings 20; Isa. 56; Job 1; Ps. 82; Ps. 147
Baboon, Prov. Introduction; Eccl. 3
Bird Hunting, Num. 11; Ezek. 13
Boar, Ps. 80
Bull, Ex. 21; 29; 32; Lev. 1; Num. 25; 33; 1 Sam. 1; 2; 1 Kings 12; 2 Kings 10; Job 36; 39; Ps. 106; Zech. 9
Bull Slaughtering, Ps. 51
Calf, Ex. 23; Judg. 17; 1 Kings 12; 2 Chron. 11; Hos. 1; 8
Camel, Gen. 24; Judg. 5; 1 Sam. 30; 1 Chron. 1; 2 Chron. 21; Isa. 21; 60
Cattle, Ex. 22
Cattle Sacrifice, Ps. 50
Cow, Deut. 22; Isa. 55; Amos 4
Cows Following Calf, 1 Sam. 6
Crocodile, Job 40; Ps. 58; Ezek. 29
Deer, Ps. 42
Dog, Lev. 17; Deut. 23; Ps. 140
Donkey, Gen. 12; Num. 22; 1 Sam. 9; Zech. 9
Duck, Job 31
Eagle, Deut. 32; 2 Kings 2; Job 30
Falcon, Deut. 32
Fish, Jonah 1
Fishing, Isa. 19
Flocks, Num. 31; 1 Sam. 25
Goats, Gen. 32
Hippopotamus, Job 40; Ezek. 29
Horse, 2 Kings 23; Est. 1; 6; Ps. 80; Isa. 1; 22; Mic. 1; Zech. 14
Hunting, Gen. 10; 1 Sam. 17; 2 Sam. 23; 1 Chron. 11; Job 18; 29; Ps. 22; 45; Jer. 22; 27; Nah. 2

Ibex, 1 Sam. 24
Jackal, Judg. 15; Job 30; Jer. 8
Lamb, Ex. 12; 2 Sam. 12
Leopard, Jer. 13
Lion, Gen. 6; Judg. 2; 14; 1 Kings 12; 2 Kings 17; Ezra 7; Ps. 15; Isa. 11; Jer. 2; Ezek. 22; Dan. 6; Amos 3; Zeph. 3
Lion Attack, 1 Kings 13; Isa. 31; Jer. 16; Ezek. 19
Lion Attacking Bull, Isa. 5
Lion Hunting, Gen. 10; 1 Sam. 17; 2 Sam. 23; 1 Chron. 11; Ps. 45; Jer. 22; 27; Nah. 2
Lion Scepter, Gen. 49
Lions after Hunt, 2 Kings 21
Locusts, Ex. 10; Isa. 33; Joel 1
Lord of Animals, Gen. 2
Mollusk, Ex. 25
Monkeys, Jer. 24
Murex Snail, Isa. 1; Ezek. 26
Ostrich, Job 39; Mic. 1
Ostrich Eggs, Lam. 4
Ox Butchering, Gen. 9
Oxen, 2 Kings 6
Pig Remains, Deut. 14; Neh. 10; Isa. 66
Quail, Ex. 16
Ram, Gen. 22; 30; 2 Chron. 32
Sheep, Gen. 12; 30; 1 Sam. 16; Isa. 32; Amos 1; Mic. 2
Snail, Gen. 49
Snake, Serpent, Gen. 3; Ex. 4; Num. 21; 2 Kings 18; Ps. 58; 140; Eccl. 10; Isa.22; 30; 37; Jer. 7; Jon. 2
Vulture, Ex. 19; Job 15; Ezek. 17; Mic. 1

Anointing

Anointing of Pharaoh, 1 Sam. 2; 10; 1 Kings 1; 1 Chron. 11; Isa. 45
Anointing Vessel, Lev. 8; 1 Sam. 10; 16

Banquet

Ashurbanipal Banquet, Est. 5; Ps. 23
Banquet, 1 Sam. 25; Isa. 5; Obad.; Job 21; Ps. 110
Beer Drinking, Prov. 20
Standard of Ur, Gen. Introduction; 1 Kings 10; 2 Chron. 1; Job 1

Boundary Stones

Astral Symbols, Deut. 4
Babylonian Land Grant (Nabu-apla-iddina), Gen. 13; Josh. Introduction; 1 Sam 22
Chaos Creature, Gen. 1; Ps. 75
Eanna-shum-iddina, Prov. 23
Gezer, Ruth 2
Marduk, Isa. 46
Marduk Temple, Deut. 19
Marduk-zakir-shumi, 2 Chron. 24
Melishihu, Dan. 8
Meli-shipak, Num. 28; Ps. 84; Isa. 13
Merodach-baladan, 2 Kings 20; Isa. 39
Michaux Stone, Job 24
Nabu-apla-iddina, 1 Sam. 22
Nature Gods, Isa. 43
Senusret III's Boundary Marker, Isa. 19
Setting Up Boundary Stone, Hos. 5
Shamash, Judg. 13
Sippar, 2 Kings 9
Unfinished Kudurru, Job 9; Ps. 104; Jonah 2

Bowing/Lifted Hands

Ashkelon relief (Merneptah), Lev. 9; Judg. Introduction; 2 Sam. 1; 2 Kings 3
Bowing backwards, Lev. 9
Bowing before Ruler, 1 Sam. 16; Est. 3
Bowing Captives, Deut. 20
Bowing in Lachish, 2 Sam. 10; Neh. 8; Ps. 95; Isa. 66
Bowing Servant, Isa. 60
Elamite Captive Bowing, Ps. 2
Hands Raised, Isa. 1; Job 11
Hazor Stone, 1 Kings 8
Kneeling Man, Jer. 7
Kneeling Pharaoh, 2 Chron. 6
Lady Taperet, Ps. 28
Praying Priest, 1 Kings 8; Ps. 44
Shalmaneser III's Black Obelisk, 1 Sam. 24
Worshiper Seal, Amos 5

Burial

Abraham's Tomb, Gen. 25
Absalom's Tomb, 2 Sam. 18
Achaemenid Tombs, Ezra 4

Ahiram's Sarcophagus, Gen. 37; 2 Kings 19; Jer. 4
Aspathines' Tomb, 1 Chron. 18
Burial Cairn, Josh. 7
Cyrus' Tomb, Neh. 2; Dan. 6
David's Tomb, Neh. 3
Embalming, Gen. 50
Eshmunazor II Sarcophagus, 1 Sam. 5
Funerary Stela, Josh. 6
Giza Pyramids, Ex. Introduction
Infant, Gen. 22
Ketef Hinnom, Lev. 21; Ruth 1
Kidron Valley Tombs, 1 Kings 2
Rachel's Tomb, Gen. 35
Roman Sarcophagus, Jonah 4
Sennedjem's Tomb, Isa. 19
Shaft Tomb, Gen. 23
St. Etienne's Tombs, 2 Sam. 2; 2 Kings 13
Terracotta Soul House, Job 4
Tomb of the Kings, Judg. 16
Tophet at Carthage, Deut. 12
Tumulus, 2 Chron. 16; Jer. 34
Xerxes' Tomb, Est. Introduction

Chaos Creature

Apophis, Gen. 3
Boundary Marker, Gen. 1; Ps. 75
Illuyankas, Job 7
Narmer Palette, Num. 23
Slaying of Chaos Creature, Job 7
Two Dogs, Lev. 17
Unfinished Kudurru, Job 9; Jonah 2

City Gate

Balawat Gates, Judg. 16; Isa. 45
Beersheba Gate, Judg. 19
Bench, Arad, Ruth 4; Prov. 8
Bench, Beersheba, Gen. 19; 1 Chron. 11
Bench, Dan, Josh. 20
Bethsaida, Deut. 17; 1 Kings 14
Dan Gate, Num.22; Josh. 20; Judg. 8; 18; Ruth 1; 2 Sam 18; 19; 1 Kings 20; 1 Chron. 26; Jer. 1; Amos 5
Gate Socket, Judg. 16
Gezer Gate, 1 Kings 9
Hazor Gate, 1 Kings 9
Ishtar Gate Drawing, Dan. 4
Ishtar Gate Model, Jer. 50
Megiddo Gate, 2 Sam. 3; 1 Kings 9
Megiddo Gate Drawing, 2 Sam. 18
Megiddo Gate Model, 2 Chron. 35
Nineveh Gate, Jonah 3
Shechem Gate, Josh. 20
Ugarit Gate, Nah. 3

Coins

Antiochus Epiphanes Coin, Dan. 8; 11
Coins, Ex. 30
Daric, Ezra 2
Persian Daric, 1 Chron. 29
Tetradrachma of Lysimachus, Dan. 8

Composite Creatures

Anzu, Deut. 31; Ps. 139; Ezek. 3; Dan. 7
Calah Bull, 2 Kings 8
Cherub, Ex. 25; 1 Kings 6; 7; Ezek. 10; 41
Cherub Throne, 1 Sam. 4; 1 Kings 10; 2 Kings 19; Ps. 99; Isa. 6; 20
Composite Creatures (drawing), Ezek. 1
Composite Creatures Pectoral, Ezek. 1
Eagle Headed Spirit, Ezek. 17
Fish Men, Job 15; Ps. 38
Genie, Gen. 3; 1 Sam. 2; Ezek. 28; Zech. 5
Goat-Fish, Ps. 106
Lamashtu, Ezek. 14
Lion/Hippopotamus/Crocodile Monster, Ezek. 32
Seraph; Winged Serpents, Isa. 6
Seven Headed Beast, Ps. 74; Isa. 11; Amos 9
Snake Dragon, Ps. 104
Sphinx, Gen. 3; Ex. 6; 17; 1 Kings 11; 2 Chron. 3; Ps. 36; Eccl. 1; Isa. 37; Jer. 36; Amos 3
Taanach Cult Stand, 1 Chron. 13; Ezek. 8; Hos. 1
Winged Bull, Num. 3; Isa. 37
Winged Caprid, Dan. 8
Winged Lion, Ps. 18; Dan. 7

Deities

Adad, Num. 25
Ahriman, Zech. Introduction
Ahuramazda, Ezra Introduction; Isa. 45; Ezek. 10; Zech. Introduction; Mal. 4

Amun, Gen. 1; 2 Chron. 32; Isa. 57; Jer. 13; Ezek. 39
Amun-Re, Genesis Introduction; Ex. 10; Job 6; Jer. 46
Anubis, Prov. 16; Hag. 2
Apis, Ex. 9
Apophis, Genesis Introduction; Ex. 7
Asherah, Judg. 2; 1 Sam. 1; Lam. 1; Hos. 4
Ashur, Judg. 4; Job 38; Ps. 7; 18
Astraea, Dan. 2
Aten, Deut. 6; 2 Chron. 9; Ps. 86; Isa. 35
Atum, Gen. 1
Baal, Judg. 2; 6; 1 Sam. 1; 7; 1 Kings 16; 2 Kings 1; Prov. 15; Isa. 43; Jer. 2; Dan. 2; Hos. 2
Chemosh, Judg. 11; Jer. 48
Dagon, 1 Sam. 5
Divine Council, Job 1
Ea, Joel 3; Ps. 139
Egyptian Cosmology, Gen. Introduction; Gen. 1
El, Gen. 14; Judg. 8; 1 Kings Introduction; 1 Chron. 20; Ps. 96; Jer. 2; Dan. 7
Enki, Gen. 2; Ex. 34; Job 26; Ezek. 28; 47
Ennead, Ex. 10
Etana, 2 Kings 2
Four-Faced God, Ezek. 1
Geb, Genesis Introduction; Job 22; Isa. 42
Gula, Deut. 23
Hadad, 1 Kings 12; Job 36
Hapy, Ex. 8
Hathor, Ex. 9; Est. 3; Song 4; Isa. 57
Heket, Ex. 8
Hemen, Isa. 30
Horus, 2 Sam. 14; Job 3; Ps. 36; 58; 104; 110; Isa. 49
Inanna, Jonah 3
Ishtar, Est. 2; Prov. 9; Isa. 6; Jer. 7; 44; Ezek. 16; Joel 3
Ishtar of Arbela, Isa. 11
Isis, Ruth 2; Job 3; Isa. 49; 57
Khnum, Gen. 2; Job 10; Isa. 43
Lama, Gen. 12
Lamashtu, Ex. 22; Ps. 113
Maʿat, Genesis Introduction; Deut. 1; 5; Ps. 89; Prov. 3; Isa. 40
Marduk, Gen. 1; Isa. 46
Meretsteger, Ps. 140
Min, Isa. 65
Mut, Hab. 2
Nabu, 1 Chron. 17
Nanaya, Num. 28; Ps. 84
Nanna, Ezek. 40
Nekhbet, Lam. 4
Nergal, Gen. 49; Ex. 12; Ezek. 11
Ninurta, Isa. 42
Nut, Genesis Introduction; Job 22; Ps. 8; 72; Isa. 24; 42; Ezek. 31
Osiris, Genesis Introduction; Ruth 2; Isa. 1; 24; Ps. 72
Pazazu, Deut. 32; Ps. 91
Ptah, Ezek. 30
Qadesh, Deut. 7; 2 Kings 18
Qaws, Deut. 6; Obad.
Qedesh, Job 6
Ra, Ex. 7; Ps. 28
Re-Horakhty, Deut. 1; Job 11; Isa. 1
Resheph, Deut. 6; Job 6
Sebek-Re, Ex. 20
Sekhmet, Isa. 53
Seshat, Zech. 2
Seth, Genesis Introduction; 2 Sam. 14
Shamash, Gen. 1; Ex. 18; Lev. 19; Judg. 13; 1 Sam. 8; Job 31; Ps. 29; 72; Isa. 1; 8; 66; Joel 1; 3; Mal. 4
Sharruma, 2 Chron. 1; Ps. 84; Isa. 41
Shu, Genesis Introduction; Job 22; Ps. 8
Sin, Num. 28; Job 31
Snake Goddess, Eccl. 10
Storm God, Ex. 9; 25; Judg. 4; 1 Sam. 2; Isa. 29
Tanit, Judg. 11
Thoth, Genesis Introduction; Deut. 1; Prov. Introduction; 16; Eccl. 3
Tiamat, Gen. 1
Utu, Job 26
Wadjet, Ex. 7
Warrior God (Assyrian), Ex. 25
Zeus, Dan. 11

Divination

Divination Letter, 1 Kings 14
Diviner Drawing, Dan. 2
Dream Book (Egypt), Gen. 40
Dream omen tablet (Sippar), Dan. 1
Extispicy tablet, 2 Kings 16

Izbu Omens, Dan. 7
Liver Model, Lev. 19; Judg. 1; 2 Kings 16; 1 Chron. 14; Isa. 2; Ezek. 21
Lunar Eclipse Tablet, Jer. 10
Reading Entrails, 1 Chron. 14; Jer. 31
Omens from Sheep's Stomach, Dan. 1
Sheep Intestines, Judg. 6

Drawings

Ahuramazda Drawing, Mal. 4
Chariot of Fire, 2 Kings 2
Cosmos, Job 9; Ps. 104; Isa. 40
Dagon Defeated, 1 Sam. 5
Diviner, Lev. 19; Dan. 2
Egyptian Cosmology, Gen. 1
Egyptian Gods, Gen. Introduction
Ezekiel's Vision, Ezek. 1
House, Deut. 6
Ishtar Gate Drawing, Dan. 4
Jerusalem, 1 Kings 7
Khorsabad, Eccl. 2
Lachish Siege, Ezek. 26
Lampstand, Zech. 4
Leviathan, Job 41
Maltaya Divine Council, Job 1
Megiddo Gate, 2 Sam. 18
Priest's Clothes, Ex. 29
Siege of Jerusalem, Jer. 21
Solomon's Temple, Jer. 27
Temple of Dagan, Judg. 16
Ziggurat, Gen. 11

Excavations

"Stables" Hazor, Deut. 17
"Stables" Megiddo, 1 Kings 4; 2 Chron. 1; Mic. 5
Gibeah Palace, 1 Sam. 10
Samaria Palace (Omri/Ahab), 1 Kings 20; 2 Chron. 18; Mic. 1
Zimri-Lim's Palace, 2 Kings 3

Excavations, Jerusalem

Gihon Towers, 1 Kings 1
House of Ahiel, Neh. 11
House of Bullae, 2 Chron. 36
Rock Quarry, Isa. 51
Stepped Stone/Millo, 1 Kings 7; 1 Chron. 11; Neh. 2; Mic. 4
David's Palace, 2 Sam. 11; 1 Chron. 14
Broad Wall, 2 Kings 18; Neh. 3; Lam. 2; Zeph. 1
Wall of Nehemiah, Neh. 6

Flowing Water

Ashurbanipal's Garden, Gen. 2; Zech. 14
Ea Seal, Joel 3
Enki, Gen. 1; Gen. 2; Job 26; Ezek. 28; 47
Gudea, Ps. 87
Inanna Temple, Gen. 2; Ezek. 47
Mari Fresco, Gen. 2; Ezek. 47
Mari Goddess, Ezek. 47
Nabu temple guardian, 1 Chron. 9
Shamash Plaque, Gen. 1
Stone water basin from temple of Assur, Gen. 4; Job 15
Water by Shrine, Ps. 46

Food and Food Production

Bakery, Lev. 2; Judg. 16; Hos. 7
Beer Jug, Judg. 14
Beer Making, Num. 6
Bread, Gen. 18; 1 Sam. 21; 2 Chron. 2
Bread Making, Gen. 40; Isa. 47
Churn, Job 10; Isa. 7
Cooking Meat, Mic. 3
Fig Gathering, Jer. 24
Fruit Bearing, Num. 13
Gleaning, Ruth 2
Grain, Ex. 21; Jer. 31
Grain Harvesting, Ruth 2; Isa. 17
Grain Mill, Ex. 11
Grain Offering, Lev. 2
Grain Piles, Ruth 3
Grain Threshing, 1 Sam. 23; Mic. 4
Grain Treading, Deut. 25
Grapes, Jer. 31
Iron Plow, Joel 3
Millstone, Deut. 24; Judg. 9; 2 Sam. 11
Oil Press, Josh. 24; Job 24; Hos. 2; 12
Olives, Jer. 31
Oven, Gen. 15
Pomegranates, 2 Chron. 3
Produce, Num. 11; Hos. 2
Threshing Floor, Ruth 3; 2 Sam. 24; 2 Chron. 3
Threshing Sledge, Ruth 3; 2 Sam. 24; Amos 1

Wheat, Judg. 15
Winnowing Grain, Ruth 2; Isa. 41; Jer. 15

Horns

Horned Alexander, Dan. 8
Horned Gods and Helmets, Ex. 34; Deut. 5; 20; 1 Sam. 2; Ps. 18; Isa. 14; Dan. 7; Obad.; Zech. 1

House

Four Room House, Deut. 6; Josh. Introduction; Josh. 7; Judg. 11; 19

Idols and Figurines

Baal, Judg. 2; 6; 1 Sam. 1; Ps. 135; Prov. 15; Jer. 2; Dan. 2
Canaanite Deity, Josh. 23; Isa. 44
Cult Figurine, Job 10
El, Gen. 14; Judg. 8; I Kings Introduction; Ps. 96
Fertility Figure, Gen. 11; Judg. 13; 1 Sam. 1
Idol Making, Ex. 20; Isa. 40; Jer. 10
Lama, Gen. 12
Molds for Goddess Images, Judg. 17; Jer. 44
Pillar Figurine, 1 Kings 16; Hos. 4
Qatna Idol, Isa. 2
Sebek-Re, Ex. 20
Sumerian Votive Statues, Lev. 27
Syrian God, Amos 2
Teraphim, Gen. 31

Ivory

Anointing Horn, 1 Sam. 16
Asherah, Judg. 2; Lam. 1
Cain and Abel, Gen. 4
Calf, Ex. 23
Cherubim, 1 Kings 7
Hazael, 1 Kings 19
Ishtar ("Mona Lisa"), Jer. 44
Lion Attack, 1 Kings 13
Lion Box, Amos 3
Megiddo Ivory, 1 Sam. 4; 1 Kings 10; Isa. 20; Ps. 99
Pomegranate, 1 Kings 7
Samaria Ivory, Ezek. 10
Sphinx, Amos 3
Warrior, Ps. 45
Woman, 1 Kings 22
Woman at the Window, Judg. 5; 1 Kings 6; 2 Kings 9

Jewelry

Ankle Bracelets, Isa. 3
Armband, Neh. 5
Bracelet, Gen. 24
Earring, Judg. 8
Finery, Isa. 3
Hathor Ring, Est. 3
Jewelry, Mic. 6
Necklace of Flies, Gen. 9
Ring, Jer. 22; Dan. 6; Hag. 2
Rings of Silver, Gen. 33
Silver, Isa. 1

Kings and Queens

Adad-nirari III, Jonah 3
Ahkenaten, Ex. 20; Num. 30; 2 Sam. 7; Song 1; Isa. 35
Alexander the Great, Dan. 8; 11
Amenhotep I, Ex. Introduction; Ps. 23
Antiochus Epiphanes IV, Dan. 8; 11
Apries, Jer. 36; 44
Ashurbanipal, 1 Sam. 8; 30; 2 Kings 21; Est. 5; Ps. 23; Isa. 28; 52; Zech. 3
Ashur-bel-kala, Gen. 9
Ashurnasirpal II, Judg. 4; 1 Sam. 9; 2 Chron. 33; Ps. 7; 45; Isa. 1; Ezek. 23
Bar-Rakib, 2 Kings 14
Bel-harran-bel-usur, 2 Sam. 5
Chephren, Deut. 32
Darius, Hag. 1; Zech. 1
Esarhaddon, 2 Kings 19; 2 Chron. 15; Isa. 37; Ezek. 11
Eshmunazor II, 1 Sam. 5
Etana, Deut. 32; Job 30
Gudea, Gen. 2; 1 Chron. 28; Ps. 87; 132; Zech. introduction
Hadadezer, 1 Kings 11
Hammurabi, Gen. Introduction; 10; 1 Sam. 8; Job 31; Ps. 19; 72; Isa. 1; 10
Hatshepsut, 1 Kings 2; Ps. 144; Jer. 13; Zech. 2
Hazael, 1 Kings 19
Horemheb, Deut. 1; Ps. 110
Idrimi, 1 Sam. 22

Jehu, 2 Kings 9
Khumban-khaltash III, 2 Chron. 33
Marduk-zakir-shumi, 2 Chron. 24
Meli-shipak II, Num. 28; Ps. 84; Isa. 13
Merneptah, Ex. 12
Merodach Baladan, 2 Kings 20; Isa. 39
Nabu-apla-iddina, Gen. 13
Napirasu, Est. 5
Naram Sin, Gen. 37; Deut. 20; Isa. 14
Necho, Jer. Introduction
Ombo, 1 Sam. 2
Osorkon, Deut. 17; Isa. 36
Ptolemy I, Dan. 11
Ptolemy VI, Dan. 11
Ramesses II, Ex. 1; 6; 9; 37; Josh. Introduction; Ps. 2; 82; Isa. 42; Ezek. 34; Hos. 1
Sargon II, 1 Sam. Introduction; 1 Kings Introduction; Isa. 6; 20; Joel 1
Sennacherib, 2 Kings 17; Ps. 51; Isa. 36; 47; Lam. 5; Jonah 3
Senusret III, Gen. 41
Sesostris, Num. 17
Seti I, Ex. 5; 13; Ps. 104
Shabako, Isa. 19
Shalmaneser III, 2 Kings 8; 9; 2 Chron. 21; Isa. 6
Shamshi-Adad V, Jonah Introduction
Taharqa, 2 Kings 19; 2 Chron. 32; Isa. 30; 37
Teumman, 2 Kings 8
Thutmose III, Ex. Introduction; Josh. 10
Tiglath-pileser III, 2 Kings 15; 1 Chron. 5; 2 Chron. 28; Isa. 1; 7; Jer. 23; Hos. Introduction; Jonah Introduction
Tudhaliya IV, 2 Chron. 1; Ps. 84; Isa.41
Tukulti-Ninurta I, Isa. 46
Tutankhamun, 2 Chron. 9; Song Introduction
Ur-Nammu, Ezek. 40
Ur-Nanshe, Ex. 40; Hag. 1
Xerxes, Est. 4
Yerah Azar, 2 Chron. 27; Jer. 49
Zimri-Lim, Gen. 2; Ezek. 47

Lamp

Lamp, Job 18; Ps. 119; Jer. 25; Zech. 4
Lampstand, Zech. 4
Menorah, Ex. 25; Num. 8

Laws

Eshunna Laws, Ex. 22; 2 Sam. 2
Hammurabi's Code, Deut. 5; 2 Kings 4; 8; Ps. 19; 72; Prov. 28; Isa. 1; Ezek. 34
Hittite Laws, Gen. 38
Lipit-Ishtar Law Code, Deut. 10; 2 Chron. 10
Middle Assyrian Laws, Ex. 22; Ruth 1; Hos. 2
Ur-Nammu Laws, Ex. 20; Lev. Introduction; Prov. 5
Uru-inimgina/ Urukagina Reforms, Lev. 19; Ezek. 22

Maps

Abram's Travels, Area of, Gen. 11
Ancient Mesopotamia, Gen. 10
Ancient Near East in the Iron Age, 1 Sam. Introduction
Ancient Near East in the Seventh Century, Zeph. Introduction
Ancient Trade Routes, 2 Chron. 9
Aram Naharaim, Gen. 24
Aramean Invasion, 1 Kings 15
Ararat, Location of, Gen. 8
Ark's Travels, Area of, 1 Chron. 13
Army Routes from Genesis 14, Gen. 14
Arnon to Jabbok Region, Judg. 11
Assyrian and Neo-Babylonian Empires, Jer. Introduction
Assyrian Control in the Ninth and Eighth Centuries BC, Jonah Introduction
Assyrian Invasion, Itinerary for, Isa. 10
Benjamin and Dan, Regions, Josh. 18
Benjamin's Modest Size, 1 Sam. 9
Bethlehem, Judah and Ancient Routes, 1 Sam. 16
Calneh, Hamath and Gath, Amos 6
Canaan, Gen. 12; Deut. 1
Canaan in the Iron Age, Judg. 3
Canaan, Late Bronze Age, Ex. 6
Canaan, Territorial Boundaries of the Land, Num. 34
Central Campaign, Region, Josh. 8
Cities of Refuge, Josh. 20
Cities of the Plain, Gen. 13
Cities of Zechariah 9, Zech. 9
Cities Subject to Assyria, Isa. 10

Coalition against David, 2 Sam. 10
Cushites, Philistines and Arameans, Amos 9
Dab'a, Tell ed-, Region, Gen. 45
Danite Scouts, Judg. 18
David and Absalom, Movements of, 2 Sam. 15
David and the Ammonites, 1 Chron. 19
David, Ishbosheth and the Philistines, 2 Sam. 2
David's "Mini-Empire", 2 Sam. 8
David's Exile, Region, 1 Sam. 22
David's Flight, 1 Sam. 23
David's Jerusalem, 2 Sam. 5
David's Pursuit of the Philistines, 2 Sam. 5
David's Raids, 1 Sam. 27
David's Revenge on the Amalekites, 1 Sam. 30
Divided Kingdom, 2 Chron. 10
Division of the Kingdom, 1 Kings 12
Dothan Region, Gen. 37
Edom, Obad. Introduction
Edom, Seir and Arabia, Isa. 21
Egypt around 600 BC, Ezek. 29
Egypt in the Late Bronze Age, Ex. 1
Elijah and Elisha, 2 Kings 2
Elisha's Area of Activity, 2 Kings 4
Empires at the End of the Seventh Century, Lam. Introduction
Ephraim and Manasseh, Territories, Josh. 16
Exodus, Possible Routes, Ex. 12
Four "Successor Kingdoms", Dan. 8
Four Corners of the World, Isa. 11
Geography of the Ancient Near East, Gen. Introduction
Geshur, 2 Sam. 13
Gibeah, Bezek and Jabesh Gilead, 1 Sam. 11
Gibeon, Region, Josh. 9
Gideon's Battles, Judg. 6
Gilead, Judg. 10
Hatti Land, Judg. 1
Hazael's Campaign, 2 Kings 12
International Boundaries in the Sixth Century, Jer. 51
Iron Age Hill Country Sites, Josh. Introduction
Israel and Moab, Ruth 1
Israel in the Eighth Century BC, 2 Kings 16
Israel under David and Solomon, 1 Kings Introduction
Israel, Expansion of, Obad.
Israel, Land of, Judg. 1
Israelite Itinerary in the Wilderness, Num. 33
Jeremiah's Cup of Wrath, Areas Experiencing, Jer. 25
Jeroboam II and Uzziah, Kingdoms of, 2 Chron. 26
Jeroboam's Expansion, 2 Kings 14
Jerusalem at the Time of Nehemiah, Neh. 11
Jerusalem Water Systems, 2 Sam. 5
Journey from Beersheba to Bethel, Gen. 28
Judah and Jerusalem, Isa. Introduction
Judah, Edom and Moab, 2 Kings 3
Judah, Territory, Josh. 15
King's Highway, Num. 20
Kings of the East, Regions, Gen. 14
Lebanon and the Coastal Regions, Josh. 13
Levant and the Settlement, Josh. 13
Levant in the Early Sixth Century, Jer. 35
Levant in the Second Millennium, Josh. 1
Levitical Cities, Josh. 21
Levitical Cities and Cities of Refuge, Num. 35
Libnah, 2 Kings 8
List of Lands That Remain, Josh. 13
Locations and Movements of People and Groups, Judg. 4
Major Highway Systems of Syria-Palestine, Deut. 2
Major Parties and Cities in the Syro-Ephraimite War, Hos. 5
Manassite Territories, 1 Chron. 7
Midian, Ex. 2
Mitanni and Hittite Kingdoms, Josh. 3
Moab, Judg. 11; Isa. 15
Moabites and Ammonites, Gen. 19
Mount Sinai, Possible Locations, Ex. 19
Nations in Amos, Amos 1
Nations Targeted in Isaiah's Prophecies, Isa. 13
Near East in the Ninth Century BC, 2 Kings 7
Necho's Advance, 2 Kings 23
Neo-Assyrian Campaigns in Israel and Judah, 2 Chron. 28
Neo-Babyolonian Empire, Dan. Introduction

Northern Campaign, Region, Josh. 11
Northern Kingdom of Israel under Assyrian Rule, Isa. 9
Northern Tribes, Regions, Josh. 19
Persian Advance on Babylon, Dan. 5
Persian Empire, Dan. 6
Persian Empire in the Time of Darius I, Zech. 1
Persian Empire, Satrapies, Hag. 1
Persian Empire: India to Cush, Est. 1
Persian Provinces, Ezra 5
Philistia, Shephelah and Samson's Travels, Judg. 14
Philistine Area and Region of Moriah, Gen. 22
Philistine Raiding Parties, 1 Sam. 13
Philistine Territory, 1 Sam. 4
Philistines and Israelites, 1 Sam. 17
Places in Joshua 12, Josh. 12
Pool of Gibeon, Battle at, 2 Sam. 2
Province of Yehud, Ezra 2
Psalm 60, Cities and Regions in, Psa. 60
Ptolemy I and Seleucus I, Realms, Dan. 11
Rainfall in Israel, Deut. 1
Re(e)d Sea,Possible Locations, Ex. 13
Rehoboam, Cities Fortified by, 2 Chron. 11
Rivers of Eden, Gen. 2
Samaria and the Coastal Highway, 2 Kings 1
Samaria, Region, Josh. 17
Samuel's Circuit, 1 Sam. 7
Saul's Last Stand, 1 Sam. 28
Shalmaneser III, Area of the Invasion of, 2 Kings 9
Shephelah, Mic. 1
Shephelah, Border Towns, 1 Sam. 23
Sinai Peninsula and the Book of Numbers, Num. Introduction
Solomon's Districts, 1 Kings 4
Solomon's Kingdom, 2 Chron. 7
Sorek Valley, Judg. 13
Southern Campaign, Region, Josh. 10
Sumer, Gen. 11
Syro–Ephraimite War, Parties in the, Isa. 7
Table of Nations, Gen. 10
Territories in Ezekiel 38, Ezek. 38
Tiglath-pileser III, Area Absorbed by, 2 Kings 15
Tribal Activities, Areas of, Judg. 1
Ziklag, Possible Sites, 1 Sam. 27

Metal

Gold Mining Map, Job 28
Gold Production, Job 28
Gold Weighing, Lev. 19
Metal Shop, Prov. 17
Metalworkers, Prov. 11; Isa. 40
Silver, Isa. 1; Jer. 32; Mic. 6
Silver Refining, Ps. 12; Isa. 48; Mal. 3
Silver Rings, Gen. 33; Prov. 2

Mourning

Dust on Head, 2 Sam. 13; Est. 4; Job 2
Mourners, 2 Sam. 1; Isa. 15; Lam. 1; Ezek. 24
Mourning Procession, Deut. 26
Mourning Women, Deut. 5; Jer. 2; 9; Lam. Introduction
Sackcloth, Gen. 37; Jer 4

Music

Cymbals, 1 Chron. 15; Ps. 150
Flute, Judg. 5; 1 Kings 1; Dan. 3
Harp, Gen. 4; Ex. 34; 1 Chron. 15; Lam. Introduction; Dan. 3; Amos 6
Harpist, 1 Chron. 25; Ps. 49; 96; 137; 150; Eccl. 9
Lute Player, 1 Sam. 16; Ps. 96
Musical Notation, Ps. Introduction; 150
Musicians, 1 Sam. 4; 10; 2 Sam. 6; 1 Kings 10; Neh. 12; Job 21; Ps. 99; Eccl. 1; Isa. 5; 20; 30; 40
Shofar, Josh. 6; Judg. 3; 7
Tambourine, Ex. 15; Judg. 11; 1 Chron. 15; Jer. 31
Trumpet, Num. 10; 1 Chron. 15; Ps. 98; Dan. 3

Net

Animals and Enemies, Hab. 1
Bird Hunting, Num. 11; Ps. 124; Ezek. 13
Fishing, Isa. 19
Hunting, Job 18
Hunting Nets, Ps. 140
Prisoners in Net, 2 Sam. 22; Job 19; Isa. 8; Ezek. 17

Offerings

Anthropoidic Terracotta Cult Stand, Mal. 1
Balawat, 1 Chron. 14
Bread, Lev. 24
Bull, Ex. 29; Lev. 1; Num. 6; 1 Sam. 1; 13; Ps. 50; 51
Cult Stand, 2 Chron. 4; Isa. 17
Cult Stand, Ashdod, 1 Sam 10
Cult Stand, Pella, 2 Kings 13
Cult Stand, Snake, Jer. 7
Cult Stand, Taanach, Ex. 25; 1 Chron. 13; Ezek. 8; Hos. 1
Egyptian Priest, Lev. 16
Food Offering, Lev. 3; Isa. 1; Hag. 2; Mal. 1
Goat, Judg. 13
Grain Offering, Lev. 2; Josh. 5
Incense, Isa. 1
Incense censer, Num. 16
Incense Offering, Lev. 10; Num. 16; 2 Kings 3; 2 Chron. 2
Iuny Stele, 2 Chron. 2
King Making Offering, 1 Sam. 13
Libation, 1 Sam. 7; Ps. 20
Libation after Lion Hunt, 2 Kings 21
Libation Stele, Isa. 57
Libation Vessel, 1 Kings 18; Ezra 1
Offering for Osiris, Num. 18
Offering Table, 1 Sam. 28
Offering to the Dead, Isa. 57
Osorkon, Deut. 17
Sebek-Re, Ex. 20
Shovel, 1 Kings 7
Snake Vase, Isa. 27
Stands, Movable, 1 Kings 7; 2 Chron. 4
Thigh Offering, Num. 6
Votive Dog, Deut. 23
Votive Figure, Ps. 23
Votive Rodent, 1 Sam. 6
Votives, Num. 30
War Camp Sacrifice, 1 Sam. 7
Wave Offering, Num. 18; 2 Chron. 6; Isa. 30

Pedestal

Animals, Deut. 5; Job 1; Ps. 82
Bull, Num. 25; 1 Sam. 2; 1 Kings 12; Job 36; Zech. 9
Calf, 2 Chron. 11
Crocodiles, Ps. 58
Eagle, Deut. 32
Lion, Deut. 7; Isa. 11
Winged Sphinx, Gen. 3; Exod. 25; Isa. 6; Ps. 18

Plants

Acacia Tree, Ex. 27; Deut. 10
Almond Tree, Jer. 1
Balm, Jer. 8
Broom Tree, 1 Kings 19
Calamus, Isa. 43
Cedars, 1 Kings 5; Ps. 29; Ezek. 17; 26; 27
Fig Tree, Mic. 4
Flax, Josh. 2; Isa. 19
Hyssop, Ex. 12; Lev. 14; Ps. 51
Lotus, Song 5
Lulav, Ezra 3
Mandrake, Gen. 30
Myrtle, Est. 2
Olive Tree, Gen. 8; Jer. 11; Josh. 24
Palm Tree, 1 Chron. 9; 2 Chron. 3; Ps. 92; Song 7
Papyrus, Job 8
Tamarisk Tree, 1 Sam. 22
Thorn Bush, Judg. 9
Tree Stump, Isa. 11
Wheat, Judg. 15

Pottery

Potter, Jer. 18
Potter Model, Jer. 18
Pottery, Ex. 15; 29; Josh. Introduction; Judg. 7; 14; 1 Sam. 16; 26; 1 Kings 17; Isa. 7; Jer. 19; Jer. 32
Pottery Kiln, Gen. 15

Reconstructions

Bakery, Lev. 2; Judg. 16; Isa. 28; Hos. 7
Breastplate of High Priest, Ex. 28
Brewery, Isa. 28
Dan Gate, Judg. 8
Four Room House, Josh. Introduction
Incense Altar, Ex. 30
Ishtar Gate Model, Jer. 50
Jerusalem Model, 2 Kings 11
Livestock Counting, Num. 18; Judg. 3
Megiddo Gate Model, 2 Chron. 35

Menorah, Num. 8
Nineveh Model, Jonah 3
Nineveh Walls, Nah. Introduction
Phoenician Ship Model, 2 Chron. 8
Susa Model, Est. 1
Tabernacle, Ex. 27; Num. 1
Ur, Gen. 11
Weaver's Workshop, Judg. 16; Isa. 19
Ziggurat Model, Dan. 1

Reliefs, Anatolian

Boghaz-Koy Altar, Ex. 32
Chariot Trampling, Ps. 66
Illuyankas, Job 7
Hittite God protecting King, 2 Chron. 1; Ps. 84; Isa. 41
Hittite Storm God, Ex. 9; Isa. 29
Maltaya Procession of Gods, Deut. 5
Musical Procession, 2 Sam. 6
Shofar, Judg. 7; Ps. 98; Dan. 3

Reliefs/Paintings, Egyptian

Abu Simbel, 1 Kings 20; 2 Chron. 18; Ps. 47; 82; Jer. 5
Abydos King List, Ex. Introduction
Akhenaten, Ex. 20; Song 1
Amenemhet, Eccl. 4
Amenhotep I, Ps. 23
Amenhotep III, Job 19
Amun, Gen. 1
Amun-Re, Ex. 10; Jer. 46
Ankh for Pharaoh, Ps. 72
Ankhmahor Tomb, Gen. 17; Ex. 20; Josh. 5; Ps. 12
Anointing of Pharaoh, 1 Sam. 2; 10; 1 Kings 1; 1 Chron. 11; Isa. 45
Anubis, Hag. 2
Apis, Ex. 9
Apophis, Gen. 3
Aten, Deut. 6
Beer Drinking, Prov. 20
Beer Making, Num. 6
Beni Hassan, Gen. 12; 37; Deut. 22; 1 Sam. 16
Bird Hunting, Ps. 124; Ezek. 13
Birthing Stool, Ex. 1
Boundary Stone, Hos. 5
Breath of Life, Lam. 4
Bull, Lev. 1; 1 Sam. 1
Bull Palette, Ex. 21
Butehamun Sarcophagus, Isa. 42
Cattle Sacrifice, Ps. 50
Chariot, 2 Chron. 1
Clapping Hands, Ps. 47
Cow, Deut. 22
Cows Following Calf, 1 Sam. 6
Cutting Down Trees, Deut. 20
Dancing, 1 Chron. 15; Ps. 149
Decimation of Army, 1 Sam. 14
Defeated Enemies, Gen. 10
Deir el Bahri, Ps. 74; Isa. 2; 62
Deity Conferring Authority, Num. 27
Dendera, Isa. 66
Donkeys, 1 Sam. 9
Ear Tablet, Gen. 35; Isa. 6; Ps. 116
Edfu, Ex. 25; Ezek. 18; Hab. 1
Edfu Birth House, Isa. 49
Egyptian Produce, Num. 11
Enemies as Footstool, Ps. 110
Ennead, Ex. 10
Esna, 2 Sam. 14; Isa. 45
Faience Tiles, Num. 13
Fig Gathering, Jer. 24
Fighting Men, Deut. 25
Food Offering, Lev. 3
Fruit Bearing, Num. 13
Gleaning, Ruth 2
Gods Giving Life, 2 Sam. 7
Gold Production, Job 28
Grain Harvesting, Isa. 17
Grain Treading, Deut. 25
Gua, Job 33
Hapy, Ex. 8
Harpist, 1 Chron. 25
Hathor, Ex. 9
Hathor, Isis, and Amun, Isa. 57
Hatshepsut, Num. 16; 2 Sam. 7; Ps. 20; 132; Zech. 2
Hesire, Ps. 45
Horemheb Stele, Deut. 1
Horemheb Tomb, Lev. 9
Idol Making, Isa. 40
Incense Burner, Lev. 10
Inherka Tomb, Ex. 6
Investiture of Vizier Paser, Gen. 41
Ity Tomb, Gen. 9; Ex. 29
Iuny Stele, Lev. 24

Karnak, 2 Sam. 1; 1 Kings 1; 14; 1 Chron. Introduction; 2 Chron. 12; Ps. 2; 18; Isa. 9; Jer. 13
Khnum, Gen. 2; Job 10
Kom Ombo, Lev. 23; 1 Sam. 2; 1 Chron. 11; Isa. 62
Lady Taperet, Ps. 28
Lamb, Ex. 12
Libation Stele, Isa. 57
Luxor, Gen. 2; 1 Sam. 7; 13; 1 Kings 3; Isa. 5; 28
Maʿat, Deut. 5; Isa. 40
Maya Tomb, Jer. 10
Medinet Habu, Ex. 15; 19; 37; Josh. 3; Judg. 3; 8; 1 Sam. 4; 6; 17; 2 Sam. 2; Job 12; Ps. 84
Memphis, Lam. 1
Menna Tomb, Ex. 2; Ruth 2; 3; 1 Sam. 23; Prov. 29; Song 3; Jer. 15; Mic. 4
Mereruka Mastaba, Isa. 19
Mereruka Tomb, Ex. 10; Prov. 17; Isa. 48; Mal. 3
Merneptah, Judg. Introduction; 2 Kings 3
Meryre Tomb, Deut. 27
Min, Isa. 65
Mourning Procession, Deut. 26
Mourning Woman, 2 Sam. 13; Est. 4; Job 2; Jer. 2
Musicians, Isa. 5
Nakht Tomb, Gen. 9; Judg. 6; Ruth 2; Eccl. 1; Isa. 10; Jer. 25
Narmer Palette, Ex. 17
Nebamun Tomb, Ex. 22; Job 8; 21
Nefertari Tomb, Deut. 4; Ezek. 23
Nefertiabt Stele, Lev. 2
Nekhbet, Lam. 4
Nespawershepi Coffin, Ex. 7; Job 22; Ps. 72; Prov. 16; Isa. 24
Nikaure, Ruth 1
Nubian Warriors, Jer. 46
Nursing Tree, Isa. 57
Nut and Shu, Ps. 8
Offering for Osiris, Num. 18
Offering to the Dead, Isa. 57
Ounsu Tomb, Ex. 21
Panekhmen Tomb, Lev. 19; Prov. 11
Papyrus Boat, Isa. 18
Perfumer's Workshop, Ps. 133
Petosiris Tomb, Num. 6
Pharaoh before Gods, 1 Sam. 24
Pharaoh Crowned by Gods, Deut. 17
Pharaoh on Chariot, Ex. 14
Pharaoh Selected by Gods, Josh. 1
Pharaoh Smiting, Num. 24; Deut. 2; Neh. 13; Ezek. 30
Ptahhotep, Hos. 14
Qenamun Tomb, Gen. 40
Quail, Ex. 16
Queen of Punt, 2 Chron. 9
Ramesses II, Ex. 9; 26; 2 Sam. 8; 2 Chron. 11; Ps. 2; Isa. 42; Ezek. 8
Ramesses III, Josh. 12
Ramesses VI Tomb, Isa. 26; Job 7; Ps. 147
Ramose Tomb, Ps. 86; Isa. 15; Jer. 9
Re-Horakhty, Job 11
Rekhmere Tomb, Ex. 1
Saqqara, Ex. 15; Num. 11; Deut. 7; Judg. 11; 1 Kings 10; 2 Kings 6; 1 Chron. 15; Job 9; 40; Prov. 3; Isa. 55; Jer. 31; Lam. Introduction; Ezek. 29; Jonah 1
Sebekhotep Tomb, 1 Sam. 16; Jer. 13
Sebek-Re, Ex. 20
Sennedjem Tomb, Gen. 50; Ps. 1; Prov. 1; Isa. 19; 38
Sesostris, Num. 17; Isa. 9
Seti I, Gen. 15; 36; Ex. 13; Ps. 104
Seti I and Ramesses II, Ex. 7
Sickle Sword, Josh. 8
Sidelocks, Lev. 19
Snake Heads, Gen. 3
Snake Standing, Ex. 7
Syrian Prisoner, Judg. 5
Taharqa, 2 Kings 19
Tassels, Num. 15
Telloh, Lev. 16
Thigh Offering, Num. 6
Thutmose III, Num. 33; Josh. 10; Ezek. 37
Trampling of Shasu, Judg. 5
Tutankhamun, Judg. 1; Song Introduction
Unas Tomb, Job 19; Ezek. 5
Userhet Tomb, Jer. 13; Ezek. 5; Hos. 2
Votive Offering, Num. 30
Wadjet, Ex. 7
War Standard, Num. 1
Wave Offering, Num. 18
Wine Offering, 2 Chron. 6
Winged Sun, Num. 9
Women Mourning, Deut. 5

Reliefs, Mesopotamian

Ahuramazda and Ahriman, Zech. Introduction
Archer, Ps. 11
Ashurbanipal, Gen. 2; 1 Sam. 8; 30; 2 Kings 15; 21; 1 Chron. 1; 2 Chron. 21; Est. 5; Job 18; Ps. 23; Isa. 21; 30; Jer. 4; 46; 51; Ezek. 12; Nah. 3; Zech. 14
Ashur-bel-kala, Gen. 9
Ashurnasirpal II, Judg. 3; 4; 1 Kings 18; 20; 1 Chron. 14; Ps. 7; 45; Prov. 3; Isa. 1; 52; Ezek. 29; Amos 3
Assyrian Scribes, Hab. 2
Assyrian Slave Labor, 2 Chron. 2
Balawat, Deut. 20; 21; Judg. 1; 5; 1 Sam. 13; 31; 2 Sam. 4; 1 Chron. 10; 14; 2 Chron. 21; 24; Isa. 2; 23; 45; Jer. 29; Lam. 1; Ezek. 22; 26; Amos 2; Mic. 1; Nah. 1
Bowing Before Ruler, Est. 3
Captured Flocks, Num. 31
Cedar Transport, 2 Sam. 7; 1 Kings 6; 2 Chron. 2
Chariot, 1 Kings 1; 1 Chron. 18
Cupbearer, Neh. 1
Cutting Trees, Isa. 1
Darius, Jer. 2; Dan. 7
Ebla, Ps. 110
Egyptian Fortress, Jer. 46
Elamite King, 2 Kings 8; 2 Chron. 33
Elamite Prisoners, 1 Sam. 17; Ps. 2
Esarhaddon, 2 Chron. 15
Eunuch, Deut. 23; Est. 1; Isa. 39
Garden, Ps. 1
Genie, 1 Sam. 2; Ezek. 17; 28; Zech. 5
Hard Labor, 2 Sam. 3
Harpist, Ps. 137; Eccl. 9
Heads, 1 Sam. 17; 2 Kings 10; Ps. 23; Jer. 34; Nah. 3
Hero and Lion, Gen. 6
Hunting, Job 29
Hunting Tools, Ps. 140
Inanna Temple, Gen. 2
Lachish, Num. 25; 1 Sam. 7; 2 Sam. 10; 20; 21; 1 Kings 16; 2 Kings 6; 18; 1 Chron. 28; 2 Chron. 28; 32; Ezra 9; Neh. 8; Est. 2; Ps. 95; 107; Isa. Introduction; 13; 22; 23; 36; 47; 66; Jer. 6; 8; 38; Nah. 2; Hab. 1
Lion Hunting, 1 Sam. 15; 17; 2 Sam. 23; 1 Chron. 11; Jer. 22; 27; Nah. 2
Mourners, Ezek. 24
Nimrud, Isa. 18; 40; 42; 51; 59; Dan. 6; Zech. 5
Nineveh, Isa. 7
Persepolis, Neh. 2; 12; Job 32; Isa. 5; 13; Zech. 1
Persian Immortals, Est. 9; Jer. 49
Plundering, 2 Chron. 36
Prisoners, 1 Kings 20; Ezra 9; Jer. 13; 39; Lam. Introduction
Reading Entrails, 1 Chron. 14; Jer. 31
Sacred Tree, Ex. 25
Sargon II, 1 Sam. Introduction; 2; Ps. 25; Isa. 6; 20; 36; Joel 1
Scribes, Ezek. 2
Sennacherib, Isa. 36; 47; Jer. 34; Lam. 5; Ezek. 27; Jonah 3
Servants, Deut. 22
Shalmaneser III, Judg. 3; 1 Sam. 24; 2 Sam. 8; 2 Kings 9; Ps. 68; Isa. 31; 60; Lam. 5; Ezek. 16
Shamash, Isa. 66
Shamash Plaque, Gen. 1
Siege, Jer. 21; Ezek. 4
Spinner, Prov. 31
Spoil, Obad.
Stone Basin Reliefs, Gen. 4; Job 15
Susa, 1 Chron. 9; Ezek. 39
Swimming, 1 Chron. 12
Tell Halaf, Gen. 24; Josh. 6; 1 Sam. 17; Isa. 6, Job 41
Tiglath-pileser III, Deut. 1; Josh. 8; 1 Sam. 5; 1 Kings 20; 2 Chron. 25; Job 1; Ps. 48; Isa. 7; 46; Hos. 10
Til Barsip, Isa. 11; Ezek. 23
Til-Tuba, 1 Sam. 4; 22; 2 Sam. 21; Ps. 79; Ezek. 32
Ugallu, Ezek. 13
Ur-Nanshe, Ex. 40
Uruk, Gen. 10
Vulture, Jer. 48; Ezek. 17
Vulture with Intestines, 1 Kings 14
Warrior on Cherub, Ex. 25
Water by Shrine, Ps. 46
Water Supply Cut Off, Jer. 8
Xerxes, Est. 4

Sacred Tree

Cherub and Tree, Gen. 3; 1 Kings 7; Ezek. 41
God as Tree, Dan. 4
Nursing Tree, Isa. 57; Ezek. 31
Sacred Tree, Ex. 25; 1 Sam. 10; 1 Kings 8; 2 Chron. 11; 14; Prov. 3; Isa. 1; Jer. 17; Ezek. 17; 28; Mic. 1; Zech. 5
Stylized Tree (Asherah Pole?), Deut. 7; 2 Chron. 14; Jer. 17

Scribes

Assyrian Scribes, 1 Chron. 34; Jer. 17; 36; Ezek. 2; Dan. 1; Hab. 2
Baboon and Scribe, Prov. Introduction
Egyptian Scribes, 1 Chron. 2; Ezra 7; Est. 8; Prov. Introduction; Jer. 13; 30; 36; 45
Scribal Kit, Isa. 8
Writing Board, Ezek. 37

Seals and Seal Impressions

Adaniyahu, 1 Kings 18
Ahuramazda, Ezek. 10
Amos, Amos 1
Anzu, Ps. 139
Astral Symbols, Deut. 5; Chron. 11; Job 9; 38; Amos 5; Zeph. 12
Baalis, Jer. 40
Banquet, Isa. 5; Obad.
Baruch, Jer. 32
Bashmu, Gen. 3
Divine Council, Ps. 82
Ea, Joel 3
Elhanan, Job 14
Enki, Gen. 2; Ex. 34; Job 26; Ezek. 28; 47
Etana, 2 Kings 2; Job 30
Gedaliah, Jer. 40
Genies and Sacred Tree, Gen. 3
Gilgamesh & Bull of Heaven, Gen. 2
Gilgamesh & Huwawa, Jonah Introduction
Glowing Deity, Isa. 2; Hab. 3
Grain Offering, Josh. 5
Hezekiah, 2 Chron. 32; Isa. 6; 10
Hoshayahu, Hos. Introduction
Ishtar, Isa. 6
Jaazaniah, Neh. 5
Jezebel, 1 Kings 16
Lachish Scarabs, Gen. 38
LMLK Seal, 2 Kings 18
Lord of Animals, Gen. 2
Lord of the Ostriches, Job 39
Marduk over Tiamat, Gen. 1
Muršili II, Lev. 26
Mushezib-Ninurta, 1 Sam. 10
Nergal, Ex. 12
Palm Tree, Judg. 4
Pedayah, 1 Chron. 3
Presentation to Deity, Ps. 42
Sacred Tree, Mic. 1
Shema Servant of Jeroboam, Judg. 2; 1 Kings 12
Shepherd, Isa. 40
Shining God, Ex. 40
Sin, Job 31
Storm Deity on Griffin, Ex. 25
Yishmael, Ps. 42
Yohoahaz, Zeph. 1
Ziggurat, Gen. 11

Sea Peoples

Ekron Inscription, 1 Kings 2
Medinet Habu, Ex. 15; Judg. 3; 1 Sam. 4; 6; 17; 2 Sam. 21
Philistine Beer Jug, Judg. 14
Philistine Cult Stand, 1 Sam. 10
Philistine Jug, 1 Sam. 16
Philistine Ship, Jonah 1
Philistine Temple, Judg. 16; 1 Sam. 5

Ships

Balawat, Judg. 5; Isa. 23; Ezek. 26; Amos 2
Egyptian Ship, Gen. 6; 1 Kings 10
Floating Cedars, 2 Sam. 5; 1 Kings 6; 2 Chron. 2
Medinet Habu, 2 Sam. 21
Papyrus Boat, Isa. 18; Job 9
Philistine Ship, Jonah 1
Phoenician Ship, 2 Chron. 8; Isa. 33; Ezek. 27
Ramesses VI Tomb, Ps. 147
Sailors, Jonah 1
Sacred Barque, Ex. 7; 25; Ps. 2; 19; 132
Trading Ship, Isa. 2; 5

Sites

Abusir, Eccl. 11
Acco, Dan. 11
Adam, Judg. 12; Hos. 6

Adullam, 1 Chron. 11
Ai (et-Tell), Josh. 7
Aijalon, Judg. 1
Aijalon Valley, 1 Sam. 14
Akrabim, Josh. 15
Amman, Plain North of, Num. 21
Anathoth, Jer. 1
Aphek, 1 Sam. 4; 1 Kings 20
Arad, Deut. 3; 1 Sam. 10; 1 Chron. 18; 2 Chron. 3; Prov. 8; Isa. 32
Araq el-Emir, Neh. 2
Ararat, Gen. 8
Arnon, Deut. 2
Arnon, Nahal, 1 Kings 17
Aroer, Jer. 48
Ashdod, 1 Sam. 5; Zech. 9
Ashdod Yam, Neh. 4
Ashkelon, Judg. 1; 14; Jer. 47
Azekah, Josh. 10; Jer. 34
Baal Meon, Ezek. 25
Bab-edh Dhra (Sodom?), Gen. 19
Babylon, 2 Kings 17; Isa. 13
Banias, Ps. 42; Dan. 11
Bashan, Josh. 12; Jer. 50
Beersheba, Gen. 22; Deut. 13; Josh. 2; 7; Judg. 19; 1 Sam. 8; 1 Kings 19; 2 Chron. 26; Neh. 11
Beitin (Bethel), Gen. 12; Josh. 8
Benjamin, 1 Kings Introduction
Besor, Nahal, 1 Sam. 30
Bet Netofa Valley, Josh. 18
Beth Horon, Josh. 10; 1 Chron. 7; 14; 2 Chron. 8
Beth Shean, 1 Sam. 31; 1 Chron. 10
Beth Shemesh, Judg. 1; 14; 1 Sam. 6; 2 Kings 14; 2 Chron. 25
Bethel (see Beitin), Judg. 1; Hos. 4
Bethlehem, 1 Sam. 16; Ruth 1; Mic. 5
Bethsaida, Deut. 17; 1 Kings 14
Bezek Region, 1 Sam. 11
Bornat, Tell (Libnah), Josh. 10
Bozrah, Judg. 5; Isa. 34; Jer. 49
Caesarea, Dan. 9
Carmel, 1 Sam. 25
Chinnereth, Josh. 11
Daba', Tell ed-, Gen. 47
Dan, Num. 22; Deut. 12; 2 Sam. 18; 1 Kings 6; 12; 20; 1 Chron. 26; Ps. 78; Isa. 2; Jer. 4; Amos 5; 8
Debir, Josh. 10
Deir ʿAlla (Succoth), Gen. 33; Judg. 8
Delta and Nile Valley, Ex. 1
Dothan, Gen. 37; 2 Kings 6
Ebla, 1 Kings 6
Edom, Job 1
Ein Hatzeva, Mal. 1
Ein Musa, Ex. 15
Ekron, Josh. 13
Elah Valley, 1 Sam. 17; 2 Kings 18
Elath, Amos 1
Elephantine, Ezra 10; Jer. 43; Ezek. 30
En Gedi, 1 Sam. 23; Jer. 17
En Rogel, 1 Kings 1
Endor, 1 Sam. 28
Ephraim, Judg. 17
Eshtaol, Judg. 13
Et-Tell (Ai), Josh. 7
Euphrates, Jer. 2
Ezion Geber, 1 Kings 9
Gath, 1 Sam. 5; Mic. 1
Gaza, Judg. 16
Geba, 1 Sam. 10
Gerar, Gen. 20; 2 Chron. 14
Geshur, 1 Chron. 5
Gezer, Josh. 10; 1 Kings 9
Gibeah, Judg. 19; 1 Sam. 10
Gibeon, Josh. 9; 2 Sam. 2; 1 Kings 3; 1 Chron. 16; 2 Chron. 1; Jer. 41; 48
Gilead, Gen. 31; Num. 32; Jer. 22
Haran, Gen. 11
Harod Spring, Judg. 7
Harod Valley, 1 Sam. 29
Hattin, Horns of, Josh. 11
Hazor, Deut. 17; Josh. 11; Judg. 4; 1 Kings 9; Ezek. 20; Dan. 9
Hebron, Gen. 25; Num. 13; Josh. 14; 2 Sam. 2; 1 Chron. 3
Heshbon, Num. 32; Judg. 11; Song 7
Hinnom Valley, 2 Chron. 28; Jer. 7
Huleh Valley, Judg. 18
Jabbok River, Gen. 32; Deut. 2; 1 Kings 12
Jabesh-Gilead, Judg. 21; 1 Sam. 11; 1 Chron. 10
Jalul, Tell el-, Deut. 2
Jarmuth, Josh. 10
Jericho, Deut. 34; Josh. 2; 4; 6; Judg. 3; 2 Kings 2
Jericho Road, 2 Kings 25; Jer. 52

Jerusalem, 2 Sam. 5; 1 Kings 7; 1 Chron. 15; 21; Ps. 48; Lam. 4
Jezreel, 1 Kings 21; 2 Chron. 22; Hos. 1
Jezreel Valley, Josh. 19; 2 Kings 23; Jer. 46
Jokneam, Josh. 12
Joppa, Jonah 1
Jordan near Jericho, Judg. 3
Jordan River, Josh. 3; 1 Kings 12; 2 Kings 2; Jer. 12
Judean Hills, Jer. 5
Kadesh-Barnea, Num. 13; Deut. 1
Karnak, Ps. 84
Keilah, 1 Sam. 23
Kerak (Kir Hareseth), 2 Kings 3
Kidron Valley, 2 Kings 23; Jer. 26
Kir Hareseth (el-Kerak), 2 Kings 3
Kiriath-jearim, Josh. 9; 1 Sam. 6; 1 Chron. 13
Kishon River, Judg. 4
Lachish, 1 Kings 14; 2 Chron. 32; Neh. 2; Jer. 33; 34; Mic. 1
Lebanon Mountains, Ezek. 17
Libnah, (Tell Bornat), Josh. 10
Luxor, Prov. 9
Mahanaim, Gen. 32; 2 Sam. 2
Malhatah, Tel, Num. 21
Mamre, Gen. 13
Maresha, 1 Chron. 4; Jer. 38
Mari, 2 Kings 3
Masada, 1 Sam. 22; Jer. 6
Masos, Tell, Num. 14; 1 Sam. 15
Megiddo, Josh. 12; 1 Kings 4; 9; 2 Kings 9; 23; 2 Chron. 1; 35; Mic. 5
Michmash, 1 Sam. 13
Miryam, Tell, Josh. 7
Mizpah, Judg. 20; 1 Sam. 7; 2 Chron. 16; Jer. 25; 40
Moab Plains, Ruth 1
Moresheth Gath, Mic. 1
Mt. Carmel, 1 Kings 18; Isa. 35
Mt. Ebal, Deut. 27; Josh. 8; Judg. 9; 1 Kings 3
Mt. Gerizim, Deut. 27; Judg. 9
Mt. Gilboa, 1 Sam. 31; 1 Chron. 10
Mt. Hermon, Deut. 3; Judg. 3; Ps. 29; Song 4; Jer. 18
Mt. Moreh, Judg. 7; 1 Sam. 28
Mt. Nebo, Deut. 32
Mt. Olives, Zech. 14
Mt. Tabor, Judg. 4
Mt. Zion, Jer. 31
Nebi Samwil, 1 Kings 3; 1 Chron. 16
Negev, Gen. 12; 1 Sam. 26; Jer. 17
Nile River, Ex. 1; Isa. 19
Nineveh, Jonah 3; Nah. Introduction
Ophrah, Judg. 8
Paran Wilderness, Num. 10
Penuel, Deut. 2; Judg. 8; 1 Kings 12
Perath (Ein Parat), Jer. 13
Persepolis, Est. Introduction; 1; 2
Pisgah, Deut. 3
Pithom (Tell el-Retabeh), Ex. 1
Punon, 2 Chron. 4
Rabbah, 1 Chron. 20
Ramah, 1 Sam. 1
Ramoth Gilead, 1 Kings 22
Rephaim Valley, Josh. 15; Isa. 17
Retabeh, Tell el- (Pithom), Ex. 1
Rogem Hiri, Josh. 7
Sa'idiyeh, Tell es-, (Zarethan), Josh. 3
Samaria, 1 Kings 16; 20; 2 Chron. 18; Isa. 58; Mic. 1
Sela, Isa. 16; 42; Obad.; Mal. 1
Sharon Plain, Isa. 33
Shechem, Gen. 12; Deut. 27; Josh. 20; 24; Judg. 9; 2 Chron. 10
Shiloh, Josh. 18; Judg. 18; 1 Sam. 1; 1 Kings 14; Jer. 7
Shunem, 1 Sam. 28
Sidon Area, Judg. 3
Sinai, Ex. 3; 17; 19; Deut. 4; Isa. 33; Mal. 4
Sinai Wilderness, Lev. Introduction
Sodom(?), Bab-edh Dhra, Gen. 19
Sorek Valley, Judg. 13
Succoth (Deir 'Alla), Gen. 33; Judg. 8
Susa, Est. 2; 5
Taanach, Josh. 12
Tadmor, 2 Chron. 8; Hos. 2
Tafileh, Deut. 1
Taiyibeh, Tell et-, Mic. 1
Tekoa, Amos 1
Timnah, Num. 31; Deut. 8; Judg. 1; 14; 1 Chron. 16
Tirzah, 1 Kings 14; Hos. Introduction
Tishbe, 1 Kings 17

Tyre, Isa. 23; Amos 1
Ugarit, Deut. 12; Nah. 3
Ur, Gen. 11; 2 Chron. 2
Valley of Kings, Ex. 5
Wadi es-Sir, Num. 25; Judg. 11
Wadi Qilt, Hos. 2
Wadi Rum, Jer. 49
Wadi Swenit, 1 Sam. 14
Wadi Tumilat, Ex. 12
Yarmuk Valley, Josh. 13
Yurza, Ezek. 25
Zaphon, Judg. 12
Zarethan (Tell es-Sa'idiyeh), Josh. 3
Zered, Num. 20; Deut. 2
Ziklag, 1 Sam. 27
Zin Wilderness, Num. 13
Zin, Nahal, Gen. 21
Ziph Wilderness, 1 Sam. 23
Ziz, Ascent of, 2 Chron. 20
Zorah, Judg. 13

Standard

Deir el-Bahri, Ps. 74; Isa. 62
Narmer Palette, Ex. 17
Snake Standard, Num. 21
Standard of Mari, Amos 5
Standard of Ur, Gen. Introduction; Lev. 1; Josh. 3; 1 Kings 10; 2 Chron. 1; Job 1; Ps. 96
War Standards, Num. 1

Standing Stones

Arad, 2 Kings 3
Bethsaida, 1 Kings 14; Isa. 15; Amos 7
Dan, Deut. 12; Josh. 22; 1 Kings 22; Ps. 78; Amos 8
Gezer, Gen. 28; Lev. 26; 2 Kings 12
Hazor, 1 Kings 8; 2 Kings 18; Ezek. 16; Mic. 5
Shechem, Gen. 12; Josh. 24; Judg. 9; 2 Chron. 10
Susa Model, Jer. 17

Stela

Adad-Nirari III, 2 Kings 10; Jonah 3
Amenhotep III Stele, Ex. 17
Amun Stele, Ezek. 39
Baal, Judg. 3; 1 Sam. 7; 1 Kings 16; 2 Kings 1; Isa. 43; Hos. 2
Balua Stele, Judg. 3
Bel-harran-bel-usur Stele, 2 Sam. 5
Bull, Num. 33
Chemosh, Judg. 11; Jer. 48
Dan, Tel Stele (House of David), 2 Kings 9; Isa. 7; Amos 1
Dream Stele of Thutmose IV, Ex. 6; Eccl. 1
Ear Tablet, Gen. 35; Isa. 6; Ps. 116
Elamite Victory Stele, Ezek. 39
Esarhaddon Stele, 2 Kings 19; Isa. 37; Ezek. 11
Gebel Barkal Stele, Judg. 5
Hadad Inscription, Lev. 24
Hammurabi, Deut. 5; 1 Sam. 8; 2 Kings 4; Ps. 19; 72; Prov. 28; Isa. 1; 10
Horemheb Stele, Deut. 1
Horus Stele, Ps. 58
Iuny Stele, 2 Chron. 2
Kamose Stele, Deut. 17
Kurkh Stele of Shalmaneser III, 2 Kings 1
Lady Taperet, Ps. 28
Libation Stele, Isa. 57
Merneptah Stele, Ex. 12; Josh. 10; Judg. 5
Mesha Stele (Moabite Stone), 1 Sam. 15; 2 Kings 1; Jer. 48; Nah. 1
Naram-Sin, Deut. 20; Isa. 14; Ps. 18
Nefertiabt Grain Offering, Lev. 2
Osorkon, Deut. 17
Qadesh Stele, Deut. 7; Job 6
Remi Stele, Lev. 21; 2 Sam. 4
Sargon Victory Stele, Ps. 25
Sennacherib Stele, 2 Kings 17
Senusret III's Boundary Marker, Isa. 19
Seti I, Ex. 5; Judg. 3
Shabako Stele, Isa. 19
Shamash-res-usur, Judg. 10
Sheshonq Stele, 2 Chron. 12
Si'gabbar Funerary Stele, Isa. 53
Sin zir Ibni Stele, Josh. 6
Tanit Stele, Judg. 11
Udjahorresnet Stele, Neh. 5
Ugarit Land Stele, Gen. 31
Ur-nammu Stele, Ezek. 40
Vulture Stele, Job 15; Ps. 5; Ezek. 17
Yehimilik (Yehawmilk) Stele, I Kings 7
Ziggurat Stele, Gen. 11

Temples and Sanctuaries

Ain Dara Temple, 1 Kings 6; Ps. 77; Ezek. 40; 43; Mic. 1
Arad, Josh. 8; 2 Kings 5; 3; 2 Chron. 3
Baal Shamin Temple (Tadmor), Hos. 2
Bethshean Temple, 1 Sam. 31
Bethshean Temple (Dagan), Judg. 16
Cosmos, Gen. 1
Dan, Deut. 12; 1 Kings 6; 1 Kings 12; Ps. 26; Amos 8
Ebla Temple, 1 Kings 6
Edfu, Ezek. 18
Ein Hatzeva Shrine, Mal. 1
Herodium Synagogue, Neh. 9
Hibis Temple of Amun, Ezra 6
Inanna Temple, Gen. 2; Ezek. 47
Karnak Temple, Josh. 21
Laver, Ps. 26
Shechem Temple, Judg. 9; 2 Chron. 10
Solomon's Temple Drawing, Jer. 27
Tel Miqne (Reconstruction), 1 Sam. 5
Tel Qasile, Judg. 16; 1 Sam. 5
Timnah, Ex. 26; 1 Chron. 16
Water by Shrine, Ps. 46
Ziggurat of Ur, Gen. 11; Gen. 28; 2 Chron. 2
Ziggurat Model, Dan. 1

Texts (Anatolia)

Arnuwandas Prayer, Ps. 44
Bronze Treaty Tablet (Tudhaliya IV and Karunta), Josh. 13
Deeds of Anitta, Judg. 9
Hattusili Apology, 1 Sam. 17
Hittite Laws, Gen. 38
Hittite/Egyptian Treaty, Josh. 1; 1 Chron. 19
Laqipum and Hatala Marriage Contract, Gen 16
Letter from Ramsses II to Hattusili III, Judg. 14
Muršili II, (seal on Ugaritic tablet), Lev. 26
Muršili II, Plague Prayer, Josh. 7
Shuppiluliuma Vassal treaty with Hakkuana, Josh. 24
Soldier's Oath, 2 Chron. 13
Substitute King, Isa. 53
Ullikummi Song, Job 3

Texts (Egyptian)

Amarna Letter, Gen. 33; Ex. 17; Josh. 10; Judg. 8; 1 Sam. 4; 25; 2 Chron. 2
Amenemhet, Wisdom, Prov. Introduction
Amenemope, Instruction of, Lev. 19; Prov. 22
Amenhotep III Stela, Ex. 17
Amennakht, Instruction, Prov. Introduction
Amon-Re, Hymn, Amos 4
Aten Hymn, Ps. 104
Book of the Dead, Gen. 6; Ex. 8; Deut. 5; 1 Sam. 2; Job 3; 30; 31; Ps. 31; Isa. 5; 14; Ezek. 32; Amos 8
Cairo Calendar, Ex. 12; Job 3
Chester Beatty Papyrus, Song 1
Dispute between a Man and His Soul, Ps. 31
Divination Letter, 1 Kings 14
Dream Book, Gen. 40
Dream Stele of Thutmose IV, Ex. 6; Eccl. 1
Ear Tablet, Gen. 35; Ps. 55
Ebers Papyrus Medical Text, Ex. 4
Elephantine Papyri, Ezra 6; Jer. 31; Mal. 3
Eloquent Peasant, Mic. 7
Execration Figurine, Ps. 2; Isa. 1
Execration Text, Gen. 14; Ex. 15; Judg. 1; Jer. 46
Famine Inscription, Gen. 41
Gebel Barkal Stela, Judg. 5
Harris Magical Papyrus, Ex. 3
Hittite/Egyptian Treaty, Deut. 4; 1 Chron. 19
Horemheb Stele, Deut. 1
Ipuwer, Admonition of, Prov. 30; Isa. 19
Kom Ombo Festival List, Lev. 23
London Medical Papyrus, Ex. 4
Love Song (Chester Beatty), Song 1
Magician and Crocodile, Ex. 7
Medical Incantations, Isa. 48
Memphite Theology, Gen. 1; Ps. 33; Isa. 42
Merneptah Stele, Ex. 12; Josh. 10; Judg. 5
Osiris, Hymn, Ps. 95
Osorkon I Inscription, Isa. 36
Papyrus Anastasi, Ex. 1 ; Josh. 18
Papyrus Leiden, Gen. 1
Prisse Papyrus, Prov. 11
Proto-Sinaitic Inscription, Gen. 21; Ex. 17
Qadesh Victory, Ps. 18
Ramsses II Letter to Hattusili III, Judg. 14

Senusret III's Boundary Marker, Isa. 19
Seti I Stele, Ex. 5; Judg. 3
Shabako Stone, Memphite Theology, Gen. 1; Ps. 33; Isa. 42
Sheshonq Inscription, 1 Kings 11; 2 Chron. 12
Sinuhe, Gen. Introduction; Isa. 19
Tale of Two Brothers, Gen. 39
Thutmose III's Annals, Josh. 10; 1 Chron. Introduction
Wayward Son, Prov. 31
Westcar Papyrus, Ex. 7; 14

Texts (Levant)

Abecedary from Tel Zayit, Judg. 8
Amarna Letter, Gen. 33; Ex. 17; Josh. 10; Judg. 8; 1 Sam. 4; 25; 2 Chron. 2
Ammonite Citadel Inscription, 1 Sam. 11
Aqhat Epic, Gen. 17; Judg. 13; 2 Kings 5
Arad Ostraca, Jer. 7; 37; Ezek. 1
Azatiwada Inscription, Zec. 3
Baal Epic, Deut. 14; 1 Kings 16; 2 Kings 1; Job 18; Ps. 29; Isa. 27; Hag. 2
Bar-Rakib, 2 Kings 14; Dan. 2
Birth of the Gracious Gods, Job 38
Chemosh Inscription, 1 Kings 11
Damascus Document, Ezra 10
Dan Inscription (Zoilos), Judg. 18
Dead Sea Scroll, 2 Sam. 17; Ezra 10; Neh. 8; Isa. Introduction; Ezek. 2
Deir ʿAlla Inscription, Num. 22; Josh. 8; Ezek. 7; Mic. 6
Divorce Decree, Deut. 24
Ekron Inscription, 1 Sam. 5; 1 Kings 2
Emar Inscription, 2 Kings 4
Esther Scroll, Est. 9
Gezer Calendar, Deut. 8; Ruth 1; Amos 7
Hadad Inscription, Lev. 24
Idrimi, 1 Sam. 22
Ivory Pomegranate, 1 Kings 7
Ketef Hinnom Silver Scrolls, Num. 6; 1 Chron. 16; Neh. 13
Khirbet el-Qom Inscription, 2 Kings 13
Kilamuwa Inscription, 2 Kings 8; Isa. 7
Kuntillet ʿAjrud, Ex. 3; 34; Judg. 3; Hos. 1
Lachish Bulla, 2 Kings 25
Lachish Ewer, Hos. 4
Lachish Ostraca, 2 Kings 24; Jer. 1; 29; 34; Ezek. 33
LMLK Handles, 1 Sam. 23; 2 Kings 18
Marzeah Text, Ezek. 8
Mesha Stele (Moabite Stone), 1 Sam. 15; 2 Kings 1; Jer. 48; Nah. 1
Nash Papyrus, Deut. 6
Ophir Ostracon (Qasile), 2 Chron. 8; Job 22
Osorkon I Inscription, Isa. 36
Proto-Canaanite Inscription, Deut. 1; 5
Proto-Sinaitic Inscription, Gen. 21; Ex. 17
Qasile Ostracon, 2 Chron. 8; Job 22
Qumran War Scroll, 2 Sam. 17
Royal Steward Inscription (Shebna), 2 King 10; Isa. 22
Samaria Ostraca, Josh. 17; Hos. 2; Mic. 1
Shebna Inscription, 2 King 10; Isa. 22
Si'gabbar Funerary Stele, Isa. 53
Siloam Tunnel Inscription, 2 Kings 20; Isa. 36
Silver Scrolls, Ketef Hinnom, Num. 6; 1 Chron. 16; Neh. 13
Sundial Inscription, 2 Kings 20
Tel Dan Stele (House of David), 2 Sam. 8; 2 Kings 9; Isa. 7; Amos 1
Tell Fekheriye, Gen. 1
Tell Siran Inscription, 1 Sam. 11
Three Shekel Ostracon, Neh. 10
Trumpet Inscription, Neh. 13
Ugaritic List of Gods, Jer. 2
Ugaritic List of Temple Officers, Ezra 2
Uzziah Reburial, Isa. 6
Widow's Plea, 2 Kings 4
Yabneh-Yam Ostracon, Deut. 24; Neh. 5; Amos 2
Yehimilik Stele, 1 Kings 7
Zakkur Inscription, 1 Sam. 3; 1 Kings 22; 2 Kings 5; Ps. 21

Texts (Mesopotamia)

Adad-nirari Inscription, 2 Kings 18
Akitu Tablet, Lev. 16; Joel 2
Almanac, Babylonian, Deut. 5
Ashurbanipal's Court Scholars, Prov. 25
Assyrian Prophecy, Jonah 3
Atrahasis Epic, Gen. 1; Deut. 12; Ezek. 5
Babylonian Chronicle, 2 Kings 24; Jer. Introduction; Ezek. 33; Nah. 1
Babylonian Land Grant (Nabu-apla-iddina), Gen. 13; Josh. Introduction

Balag Lament, Lam. Introduction
Behistun Inscription, Ezra 4
Calah Bull Inscription, 2 Kings 8
Cuneiform Tablet with Envelope, Isa. 8
Curse of Agade, 1 Chron. 17; Lam. 5; Nah. 1
Cyrus Cylinder, Ezra 1; Isa. 44; Dan. Introduction; Hab. 1
Cyrus Tomb Inscription, Ezra Introduction
Descent of Inanna, 2 Chron. 23; Joel 1
Descent of Ishtar, Ps. 49
Dream Omens, Dan. Introduction
Dumuzi and Enkimdu, Gen. 4
East India House Inscription, 1 Kings 8; Dan. 4
Enki and Ninmah, 1 Kings 18; Ps. 103
Enmerkar and the Lord of Aratta, Gen. 11
Enuma Elish, Gen. 1; Ps. 89; Dan. 7
Esarhaddon Prism, Ezek. 10
Esarhaddon Restoration of Babylon, 2 Kings 19; Ezek. 11
Esarhaddon and his Mother, Restoration of Babylon, 2 Chron. 15
Esarhaddon Stele, 2 Kings 19; Isa. 37
Esarhaddon Vassal Treaty, Deut. 28
Eshunna Laws, Ex. 22; 2 Sam. 2
Etana, Gen. 5
Extispicy Tablet, 2 Kings 16
Foundation Tablets, Neh. 6; Zech. 4
Gilgamesh Epic, Gen. 6; 41; Judg. 7; 2 Sam. 1; 1 Kings 12; Eccl. Introduction; Ezek. 18
Gudea Cylinders, Gen. 2; 2 Sam. 7; 1 Kings 6; 1 Chron. 17; Jer. 23; Hag. 2
Gudea Map, 1 Chron. 28; Ps. 132; Zech. Introduction
Hammurabi's Geneaology, Gen. 10; 1 Chron. 1
Hammurabi's Laws, Deut. 5; 2 Kings 4; 8; Ps. 19; 72; Prov. 28; Isa. 1; 10; Ezek. 34
Iddin-Dagan, Hymn, 2 Chron. 5
Ishtar Hymn, Ps. Introduction
Izbu Omens, Dan. 7
Jehoiachin Ration Tablets, 2 Kings 25; Dan. 1
King List, Antediluvian, Deut. 17; Ps. 90
King List, Assyrian, 1 Chron. 1
King List, Larsa, 1 Kings Introduction
King List, Sumerian, Gen. 5
Kurkh Stele of Shalmaneser III, 2 Kings 1
Lagash/Larsa Calendar, Deut. 16
Lamentation for Ur, 2 Kings 25; Ps. 74; Lam. Introduction
Land Grant (Nabu-apla-iddina), Gen. 13; Josh. Introduction
Land Sale, Ex. 32
Lexical List, 1 Kings 4; 2 Chron. 1
Lipit-Ishtar Law Code, Deut. 10; 2 Chron. 10
Lot of Yahali, Est. 3
Love Song, Song 1
Ludlul bel Nemeqi, Job Introduction
Lunar Eclipse Tablet, Jer. 10
Man and His God, Job Introduction
Map of Canals, Prov. 21
Map of the City of Umma, Ezek. 4
Map of the World, Ps. 24; Ezek. 38; Zeph. 2
Medical Text, Gen. 12; Ps. 38
Middle Assyrian Laws, Ex. 22; Ruth 1; Hos. 2
Musical Notation, Ps. Introduction; 150
Nabonidus Chronicle, Jer. 50
Nabonidus Inscription, 1 Kings Introduction; 1 Chron. Introduction; 2 Chron. 1; Jer. 1; Dan. 5
Nabonidus Sippar Cylinder, Zech. Introduction
Nabonidus Stele, Obad. Introduction
Nabopolassar Brick, Jer. 20
Nebo-sarsekim Tablet, Jer. 39
Nebuchadnezzar Cylinder, Dan. 1
Nebuchadnezzar East India House Inscription, 1 Kings 8; Dan. 4
Nippur Debt Note, Neh. 5
Nungal Hymn, Isa. 42
Nur Adad Ground Plan, Isa. 49
Nuzi Texts, Gen. 25
Omens from Sheep's Stomach, Dan. 1
Oracle Request, 1 Kings 17
Praise of Pickax, Gen. 1
Sacred Marriage, Ezek. 16; Song 1
Sargon Birth Legend, Ex. 2; Ezek. 16
Sargon II, 1 Kings Introduction; 2 Kings 17; Isa. 20
Satrapies of the Persian Empire List, Est. 1
Sennacherib Stele, 2 Kings 17; Ps. 51

Sennacherib's Prism, Josh. 12; 2 Kings 18; 2 Chron. 32; Isa. 36
Shalmaneser III's Foundation Tablet, Neh. 6
Shulgi Hymn, Ps. 110
Shurpu Text, Isa. 6; Mal. 3
Shuruppak Instruction, Ex. 20; Prov. Introduction
Sin-shar-ishkun's Letter, 2 Chron. 35
Sumerian God List, 1 Chron. 1
Sumerian Proverbs, Prov. Introduction
Sumerian Schooldays, Prov. 13
Synchronistic History, 2 Kings 1
Tammuz Text, Ezek. 8
Teima Inscription, Ezra Introduction
Temple of Ningishzida Measurements, Ezek. 40
Tiglath-pileser I Annals, Judg. 1; 1 Kings 14
Tiglath-pileser III Annals, 2 Kings 15; Ezek. 3
Tobias Inscription, Neh. 2
Tukulti-Ninurta II Annals, Deut. 10; 2 Kings 1
Ur-Nammu Hymn, Zech. 10
Ur-Nammu Laws, Ex. 20; Lev. Introduction; Prov. 5
Ur-Nanshe Temple Plaque, Ex. 40; Hag. 1
Uru-inimgina/ Urukagina Reforms, Lev. 19; Ezek. 22
Venus Tablet, Isa. 14
Xerxes Daiva Text, Neh. 1
Zimri-Lim Ice House, Prov. 25
Ziusudra (Sumerian Flood Story), Gen. 6

Tools

Awl, Gen. 4
Axe Head, Deut. 19; 2 Kings 6
Cubit Rod, Ezek. 40
Farm Tools, Isa. 2
Fork, 1 Sam. 2
Iron Plow, Joel 3
Mallet, Judg. 4
Mortal and Pestle, Est. 2
Olive Press, Josh. 24; Job 24; Hos. 2; 12
Ox Goad, Judg. 3
Peg, Judg. 4
Plumb Line, Amos 7
Razor, Judg. 13; Isa. 7
Rope, Eccl. 4
Shovels, 1 Kings 7
Sickle Blades, Ruth 2
Stake, Judg. 4
Threshing Sledge, Ruth 3; 2 Sam. 24; Amos 1

Viticulture and Brewing

Beer Making, Num. 6
Brewery Model, Isa. 28
Vineyard, Gen. 9; Judg. 21; Amos 9
Wine Cellars, Jer. 48
Winepress, Num. 6; Judg. 6; 2 Kings 6; Isa. 5; Jer. 25; Lam. 1
Wineskin, Job 32; Jer. 13

Warfare

Army of Pharaoh, 2 Chron. 11
Balawat, Deut. 21; Judg. 1; 1 Sam. 31; 2 Sam. 4; 1 Chron. 10; 2 Chron. 24; Ps. 144; Ezek. 22
Camel Warfare, 1 Sam. 30; 1 Chron. 1; 2 Chron. 21; Isa. 21
Capture of Ashkelon, 2 Sam. 1
Corpses in the River, 1 Sam. 18
Corpses impaled, Num. 25; Deut. 21; Josh. 8; 2 Sam. 21; Est. 2; Isa. 1; Jer. 8
Decimation of Army (Karnak), 1 Sam. 14
Flaying, Ezra 9; Isa. 13
Hand to Hand Combat, 2 Sam. 2
Heads Hung, 1 Sam. 31; 1 Chron. 10; Ps. 23
Lachish, 2 Kings 18; Isa. 23
Medinet Habu, Ex. 15; 2 Sam. 21
Mutilation, Judg. 1; 2 Sam 4; 1 Chron. 10; Ezek. 22
Naram Sin Stela, Deut. 20
Nubian Army, 2 Chron. 25
Papyrus Boat, Job 9
Sappers, 1 Kings 20; Ps. 144; Lam. 2
Siege, Lam. 2
Tiglath-pileser III, Josh. 8
Til-Tuba, 1 Sam. 4; 22; 2 Sam. 21; 2 Kings 8; Ps. 79

Warfare: Archers and Slingers

Archer, Josh. 8; Ps. 11
Ashurbanipal, 2 Kings 21; Ps. 7; Nah. 3; Amos 3
Bow Case, 1 Chron. 18
Chariot, 1 Chron. 18; 2 Chron. 1

Chariot Trampling Enemy, Judg. 1
Immortals, Jer. 49
Lachish Relief, 2 Kings 18; Isa. 23; 36; Jer. 6; Hab. 1
Lachish Siege Drawing, Ezek. 26
Lion Hunting, Gen. 10
Pharaoh, Ex. 14
Slinger, 1 Sam. 17; Job 41
Slingstones, Judg. 20

Warfare: Body Parts

Cutting off Head, 1 Sam. 31; 2 Sam. 20
Hands, Judg. 8
Head, 1 Sam. 17; 31; 2 Kings 10; 1 Chron. 10; Ps. 23; Jer. 34; Nah. 3
Phalli, 1 Sam. 18

Warfare: Cavalry

Cavalry, Jer. 46
Lion Hunting, Nah. 2
Scythian Horseman, Zeph. Introduction
Til-Tuba, Ezek. 32

Warfare: Chariot

Ashurbanipal, 1 Sam. 8; Isa. 52; Zech. 14
Ashurnasirpal II, Judg. 4; 1 Kings 18; 1 Chron. 14; Ps. 7; 45
Balawat, Deut. 21; Judg. 1; 5; 1 Sam. 13; 1 Chron. 10; Isa. 2; 23; Ezek. 22; 26; Amos 2
Chariot, 1 Kings 1; 1 Chron. 18; 2 Chron. 1
Chariot of Tutankhamun, 2 Chron. 1
Chariot Trampling Enemy, Judg. 1
Gods in a Chariot, Hab. 3
Lachish, 1 Chron. 28
Lion Hunting, Jer. 27; Nah. 2
Megiddo Ivory, 1 Sam. 4; 1 Kings 10; Ps. 99; Isa. 20
Pharaoh, Ex. 14
Sargon II, 1 Kings Introduction; Isa. 20
Seti I, Ex. 13
Standard of Ur, 2 Chron. 1
Tiglath-pileser III, Isa. 7
Til-Tuba, Ezek. 32
Trampling of Shasu, Judg. 5
Tutankhamun in Chariot, Song 1

Warfare: Enemies under Feet

Abu Simbel, Ps. 47
Darius, Ezra 6
Enemies as Footstool, Ps. 110
Decapitated Enemies Trampled, Nah. 3
Netjerikhet, 1 Kings 5; Ps. 83
Nimrud, Isa. 51
Ramesses III, Josh. 12
Sandals, Lam. 3

Warfare: Exiles and Prisoners

Abu Simbel, 1 Kings 20; Jer. 5
Ashtaroth, Ezra 9
Ashurbanipal, 2 Kings 15; Ezek. 12; Nah. 3
Balawat, Deut. 21; Judg. 1; 1 Chron. 10; Jer. 29; Lam. 1; Ezek. 22; Amos 2; Mic. 1; Nah. 1
Elamite Prisoners, 1 Sam. 17; Ps. 2
Esarhaddon Stele, 2 Kings 19; Isa. 37; Ezek. 11
Exiles, Ps. 147
Khumban-khaltash III, 2 Chron. 33
Lachish, Num. 25; 2 Sam. 21; 2 Kings 6; 18; 2 Chron. 28; Ezra 7; Neh. 8; Est. 2; Ps. 95; 107; Isa. Introduction; 13; 36; 47; Jer. 8; 38; Hab. 1
Lachish Siege Drawing, Ezek. 26
Medinet Habu, Job 12
Megiddo Ivory, 1 Sam. 4; 1 Kings 10; Ps. 99; Isa. 20
Nineveh, Isa. 7
Prisoner with Hook, 2 Kings 19; Isa. 37; Ezek. 11; 19; Amos 4
Prisoners, Num. 13; 2 Chron. 36; Jer. 13; 39; Lam. 5
Prisoners in Net, 2 Sam. 22; Job 19; Isa. 8; Ezek. 17; Hab. 1
Prisoners on Sandals, Lam. 3
Ramesses II, 2 Sam. 8
Sargon II, Ps. 25
Sea People, Ex. 15; Judg. 3; 1 Sam. 4; 6; 17; 2 Sam. 21
Shasu, Gen. 36
Syrian Prisoner, Judg. 5
Thutmose III, Num. 33
Tiglath-pileser III, Josh. 8; 1 Kings 20

Warfare: Mighty Arm

Karnak, Isa. 9
Narmer Palette, Isa. 9
Pharaoh, Ex. 6; Num. 24; Deut. 2; Josh. 8; Neh. 13; Ps. 2; Ezek. 30
Ramesses II, Ezek. 8
Ramesses III, Josh. 12; Judg. 6
Thutmose III, Josh. 10

Warfare: Plunder and Tribute

Assyrians Plundering, 2 Chron. 36
Balawat, Judg. 5
Captured Animals, Num. 31; Job 1
Gods, 1 Sam. 5; 2 Chron. 25; Isa. 46; Hos. 10
Sebekhotep Tomb, 1 Sam. 16
Shalmaneser III, Judg. 3; 2 Sam. 8; Ps. 68; Isa. 60; Ezek. 16
Spoil, 1 Sam. 30; Ezek. 2; 29; Obad.; Hab. 2
Weighing Tribute, Isa. 40

Warfare: Shields

Lachish, Nah. 2
Shields, 2 Sam. 23; Ps. 3; 5; Jer. 46
Soldiers, 2 Sam. 1
Til-Tuba, 1 Sam. 4
Warship, Ezek. 27

Warfare: Siege Engines

Ashurnasirpal, Amos 3
Battering Ram, Deut. 20
Lachish, 2 Sam. 20; 2 Kings 18; Isa. 23; 36; Jer. 6; Hab. 1
Lachish Siege Drawing, Ezek. 26
Siege Engines, 2 Kings 6; Ezek. 4
Tiglath-pileser III, Josh. 8

Warfare: Trampling

Ashurnasirpal II, Ps. 7
Balawat, 1 Sam. 13
Chariot Trampling Enemy, Judg. 1; Ps. 66
Naram-Sin, Deut. 20; Isa. 14; Ps. 18
Pharaoh on Chariot, Ex. 14
Soldiers Trampling, Nah. 3
Trampling of Shasu, Judg. 5
Tutankhamun, Song 1

Warfare: Vulture

Battlefield and Birds, 2 Sam. 21; Ps. 79; Isa. 18; Ezek. 39
Battlefield Palette, Jer. 16
Chariot Trampling Enemy, Judg. 1
Vulture Accompanying, Jer. 48
Vulture Stele, Job 15; Ps. 5; Ezek. 17
Vulture with Intestines, 1 Kings 14

Warfare: Weapons and Armor

Armor, 1 Sam. 17; 1 Kings 22; Isa. 59
Arrowhead, Ps. 127
Axe, 2 Kings 6; Ezek. 21
Bow, 2 Sam. 8
Dagger, Judg. 3
Flint Knife, Gen. 22; 1 Sam. 14; Isa. 56
Sickle Sword, Josh. 8
Slingstones, Judg. 20
Spear, 1 Sam. 26; 2 Sam. 1
Spear Butt, 2 Sam. 2
Spear Heads, 1 Sam. 26; Isa. 2.
Sword, Ps. 45; Ezek. 21

Water Systems

Cistern, Arad, Gen. 37
Cistern, Beersheba, Jer. 2
Gihon Spring, 2 Sam. 5
Hezekiah's Tunnel, 2 Kings 20; 2 Chron. 32; Isa. 22
Pool of Bethesda, Neh. 3
Pool of Gibeon, 2 Sam. 2; Jer. 28
Pool of Heshbon, Song 7
Pool of Shiloh, Isa. 22
Siloam Channel, Isa. 8
Warren's Shaft, 2 Sam. 5

Winged Sun

Egyptian, Num. 9; Ps. 84; 86; 139
Persian (Ahuramazda), Ezra Introduction; Isa. 45; Ezek. 10; Mal. 4
Neo-Assyrian (Ashur or Shamash), Gen. 3; Judg. 4; 1 Sam. 10; 1 Chron. 14; Ps. 7; 18; Prov. 3; Isa. 1; 8; 52; Mal. 4

ZONDERVAN®